GEORGE WASHINGTON
Painted on bed ticking at Valley Forge, by C. W. Peale
(Now at the State Normal School, West Chester, Pa.)

Frontispiece

GEORGE WASHINGTON
The Rebel & The Patriot
1762-1777

RUPERT HUGHES

1927

NEW YORK

WILLIAM MORROW & COMPANY

PRINTED IN THE U. S. A. BY
QUINN & BODEN COMPANY, INC.
RAHWAY, N. J.

"War is in itself an economic and social fact of overwhelming importance, and though its place in history may well be lessened, it can never be relegated to insignificance. . . . Though in miniature, here is fighting, here are heroes, here are personal encounter, terror, wounds, and death. In the tapestry the background has receded; and economics and politics, the statesman and the writer, are forgotten in the question of What Happened. . . .

"For there come, in every era, times when the men of action shoulder aside the men of thought, and take the conduct of affairs into their own hands. Then the very substance of history changes . . . When once again they leave the scene of history, the men of action have utterly changed the economic and the political landscape. And while they hold the stage they manufacture history according to the ancient manner, by strength and by arms."

ALLEN FRENCH,
*The Day of Concord and
Lexington*, pp. viii, 271.

"What is in itself an economic and social fact of over-whelming importance, and though it holds no place in history, may well be insisted, it can never be relegated to insignificance. ... Though in miniature, here is fighting, here are heroes, there are personal encounters, terror, wounds, and death. In the tragedy the background has receded; and economics and politics, the spectator and the writer, are forgotten in the question of What Happened? ...

"Yet there come, in every era, times when the men of action shoulder aside the men of thought, and take the conduct of affairs into their own hands. This is the very substance of historic chances. ... When once again they leave the scene of history, the men of action have merely changed the economic and the political landscape. And while they hold the stage they manufacture history according to the ancient manner, by straight and by arms."

Allen French,
The Day of Concord and Lexington, pp. vii, viii.

CONTENTS

CONTENTS

ILLUSTRATIONS

I

HIS BELATED GLORY

IF George Washington had died in his thirtieth year as he expected to, he would have died the death. And there would have been no great stir over the matter. Even his recently married wife, Martha, did not go with him to the obscure mineral springs where, as he wrote, "I once thought the grim king would certainly master my utmost efforts, and that I must sink, in spite of a noble struggle."

He might, indeed, have lived on to his forty-third year and then vanished without gaining mention in a single schoolbook. His name would have been lost in the twilight sleep of those encyclopædic histories where minor heroes and the mute inglorious great are innumerably entombed.

In monographs by candidates for a doctorate it would be perhaps stated that Governor Dinwiddie of Virginia sent a certain Major Washington (1732-1761) to the French near Lake Erie, warning them off the English King's territory, and that he had returned safely with a polite reply warning the English off the French territory. Later, Major Washington, having been sent out to recapture an English fort from the French, had not waited for war to be declared, but had fired into a band of French scouts claiming to be ambassadors to the English, and had killed a young man named Jumonville; that the French under the dead man's brother had trapped Washington in a little stockade called Fort Necessity and after a nine hours' siege had made him surrender and had secured his signature to a capitulation twice confessing the "assassination" of Jumonville.

(For all footnote references, see Appendix I, pp. 609-650.)

Nobody would have taken the trouble probably to find out that Washington did not understand French and denied both the assassination and the confession.

When Braddock's army attempted to recapture Fort Du Quesne, Washington's name might have been found among the records, but it would have been noted that he had no commission and merely carried messages for Braddock. The fable would never have been invented that he saved the remnants of the army.

State histories of Virginia would have referred briefly to the fact that he was put at the head of the colony's troops and, after a rather futile effort to check the French and Indians, and much abuse from the pamphleteers for the cowardice and debauchery of his troops, resigned again.

His killing of Jumonville might or might not have been blamed for the starting of the Seven Years' War, but little heed would have been paid to his reappearance under arms with General Forbes, his vain efforts to persuade Forbes to take the old Braddock Road, the rebukes he received for his insubordination and his selfish motives, or the fact that he commanded the pioneers and was with the troops that occupied the abandoned Fort Du Quesne, when its name was changed to Fort Pitt.

His resignation, his marriage to the rich widow of Daniel Parke Custis, and disappearance from all public life except a most obscure activity as a member of the House of Burgesses would probably not have been recorded even in a monograph, any more than the resignations of other officers and the committee memberships of other Virginians were mentioned.

In the preliminaries of the American revolution he played no important part and his selection as a compromise commander-in-chief, a "dark horse," for political reasons, amazed him as much as it surprised all the colonies.

From then on he developed into one of the greatest, noblest, and most influential souls in human chronicle. But if he had died, say, on June 14, 1775 (three days before the Battle of Bunker Hill, five weeks after Ticonderoga was taken, and two months after the battles of Concord and Lexington), he would have been even less remembered by an ungrateful republic than are hundreds of others who had done as much or more for the cause of freedom.

One proof of this is to be found in Nathaniel Ames' *Almanacks,* published annually at Boston from 1726 to 1775. The issue for 1756 mentions Washington twice, saying that he was "set upon by the French and Indians the 3d Day of *July* 1754, entirely defeated, and his Cannon all lost." [1] He is given no credit, and not even spoken of at all in various references to Braddock's "shameful sad disaster."

He makes his next and final appearance in the issue for 1763—"*Price* Half a Dollar *per Dozen,* & Six Coppers *single.*" Here he is included in the beginning of a long string of doggerel couplets called "A Brief Chronology of Remarkable Events, relating chiefly to the present War:

SINCE first the Sparks of this dire War begun, In this new World, which into Europe run. } 1749

Since the perfidious *French* in hostile Ranks The *English* drove from smooth *Ohio's* Banks. } 1751

Since *Washington* enter'd the List of Fame, And by a Journey to Lake *Erie* came. } October, 1753

Since he defeats a *French* detached Band, Under the brave *Junonville's* Command. } May 24, 1754

Since *Contrecœur* took hold of *English* Claim, His Fortress builds and calls it Fort *DuQuesne.* } June 13, 1754

Since *Beau-se-jour* yielded to *British* Fame, And *Cumberland* adorns its present Name.— } June 20, 1754

Since Fortune turn'd to *Washington* adverse, ⎱ *July* 3, 1754
Who makes good Terms with a superior Force. ⎰

Since *Braddock* slain and all his Soldiers fail, ⎱ *July* 9, 1755"
In a defeat near fam'd Monongahale.— ⎰

It goes on for ninety-six lines more, cataloguing British heroes, but making no further allusion to Washington. His fame stops in 1754 when "Fortune turn'd adverse." Ames' *Almanack* never referred to Washington again. Even in 1775 he was an almost forgotten man who had flared up twenty years before and retired into genteel oblivion, save for taking part in some of the numberless land-grabbing speculative bubbles that were set afloat after the French had been ousted from the West.

Those who knew Virginia could probably have said that the handsome young officer (whom some of the old people had seen when he rode up to Boston in 1756 and paid a brief visit to New York) was entertaining lavishly, and devoting himself to making friends and money, growing middle-aged gracefully and peacefully with no interest whatsoever in any of the wars that kept the borders anxious and red.

What would have happened to the American Republic if Washington had died at forty-three? It would be useless to try to imagine. In some ways it would be terrifying. For none of the other figures displayed quite the purity, selflessness, valor and resolution that made him forever after the standard by which all patriotisms are measured.

But certain it is that if he had lived only till forty-two, he would have cut no figure in such history as the public so inaccurately remembers. The weavers of myths would have chosen somebody else to obscure. The national capital would have worn some other name; and the demagogues, the genealogical societies and the others seeking their own ends, would have selected a different victim for their self-glorifying tributes, their gaudy rhetoric and their platitudinous fables.

However, Washington did not die until he had reached sublime heights of achievement and of abstention. He lived until, not by any means alone but more than any other man, he created out of chaos a nation to be patriotic to, and then lavished upon it the most spotless patriotism. The results of his devotion have bulked large in the world we know, and have been endlessly described. Great as they were, they have been exaggerated to a caricature, while little heed has been paid to the sort of man he was, and the minuter details of his evolution from a baffled soldier and a bewildered farmer into one of the masterpieces of human nature.

How slow and unforeseen his evolution was, and how much it depended upon changes in his environment, are manifest when he is compared with some of the other great generals of history. The credit for the successful siege of Boston hardly belongs to Washington since it was a success before he took command. The first of his pitifully few military victories took place when he was within two months of his forty-fifth birthday, the surprise at Trenton of an outpost of 1,500 revel-weary Hessians whom he routed with 2,300 Americans.

At sixteen, Alexander the Great had crushed the hill-tribes; at seventeen had led a charge that broke the finest troops in Greece. At nineteen, he succeeded to the throne; at twenty-one, he crossed the Danube and scattered the Getæ, whirled and annihilated the Thebans; at twenty-two, he was in Asia shattering the Persians; at twenty-four, in Egypt, at thirty in India. Three years later he was dead after a drunken carouse.

But Alexander inherited from his great father the finest

army in the world, made ready for the conquest of the world.

As a mere boy Hannibal proved his courage in battle, and at twenty-six was the commander-in-chief of all the Carthaginian armies. At thirty he was in Italy driving the best Roman armies before him, and was kept from taking the city only by lack of engines and reinforcements from Carthage.

He was the son of a great general.

At seventeen, Scipio Africanus (whom a recent biographer [2] calls "A Greater than Napoleon") commanded a troop of horse in a battle with Hannibal, saved the life of his father, and refused "the Roman V. C." At nineteen he was a staff officer; he took part in the devastating defeats Hannibal inflicted on the Romans, fearlessly put down a mutiny, and did many noble deeds. At twenty-seven, he was sent to Spain to retrieve the sunken fortunes of the Romans and revenge the death of his father and uncle in battle. He won speedily a victory as ingenious as it was complete. At twenty-nine, his 45,000 foot and 3,000 horse crushed Hasdrubal's 70,000 with brilliant strategy and drove the Carthaginians out of Spain.

At thirty-one, he had outwitted the jealous and hostile Roman Senate, and carried the war into Africa. At thirty-five he had conquered Rome's deadliest enemy, Carthage, and her greatest general, Hannibal. Then he anticipated Washington by nearly two thousand years in retiring to his farm and refusing a crown that was really pressed upon him, and not merely suggested in a letter by an obscure invalid, as Washington's was.

Still, Scipio also had a magnificent army to wield, and he was the son of a great general.

At twenty-one, Julius Cæsar won what corresponded to

the Victoria Cross of Rome for saving a soldier's life in battle; but he spent his life in politics and infamous dissipations until he was past forty, when he began his great Gallic wars. At forty-seven, he was in England, at fifty-eight, he was slain by his own friends, who feared his royal ambitions.

He also made use of the finest troops in the world, the all-conquering Roman legions.

At seventeen, Charles XII of Sweden, with 400 horsemen routed 6,000 Russian cavalry, and annihilated an army at Narva. At twenty he entered Warsaw and captured Cracow. At twenty-six he crossed the Vistula on the ice and crushed the Russians. In a winter so cold that wine congealed, wood would not burn, and birds froze and fell dead on the wing, he saw his army destroyed. He was a refugee in Turkey at twenty-seven. At thirty-two he returned to a ruined country, and at thirty-six was killed in battle.

He, too, inherited from two great soldiers, his grandfather, and his father, the finest army Sweden ever had.

At fourteen, James Wolfe took part in the Cartagena disaster along with Washington's half-brother, Lawrence. At fifteen, he fought on the Rhine and was so valorous that he was made a lieutenant. At seventeen, he was a captain and fought at Culloden and in Flanders where he was praised. At twenty-two, he was a major—of the rank that Washington at the same age received as a gift, without experience.

At thirty-one, Wolfe was a brigadier-general distinguishing himself at Louisbourg, during the war in which Washington was a colonel under Forbes. Both wrecked their health. Washington retired to a farm. Wolfe, in spite of his illness, went back and captured Quebec, dying in the hour of a victory that saw the death of his opposing general, Montcalm, who had entered the French army at nine, and

became a captain at nineteen, a colonel at thirty-one, a brigadier at thirty-five, and at forty-seven commander of all the
troops of France in Canada.

But then, Wolfe also was the son of a general, and he
despised the undisciplined Americans whom George Washington, the son of a farmer, had to weld into an army,
making his frail weapon as he went along.

At twenty-four, Napoleon, a fugitive from Corsica, found
himself in command of the French republican troops at
Toulon, where he behaved with such bravery and skill that
he was made a general of brigade. At twenty-five, he was
in disgrace and under arrest. At twenty-six, he whiffed away
the mob in Paris. At twenty-seven, he was at the head of
one of the most efficient armies in history, and was conquering Italy. At twenty-eight, he was managing the destinies
of Europe. At twenty-nine, he had invaded Egypt. At
thirty, he was head of the Consulate, and already the ruler
of France, soon to be its Emperor and eventually to wreck
his adopted country under his own insatiable ambitions. At
forty-five, he was a prisoner on Elba; at fifty-two, he was
dead.

Compared with such men as these, Washington at forty-
three had accomplished nothing at all.

In his seven offers of a resignation before he was thirty,
and in his frenzied complaints of the hardships put upon
him, there is no hint of the indomitable resolution and
almost angelic patience he afterward displayed.

There was no hint even of that unparalleled magnanimity
that kept him clean of all selfish ambition, led him to fight
without pay, refuse all reward, and retire to his farm at the
war's end until he was recalled as the one soul able to reunite
the quarreling colonies in a bond of peace.

Because of the white glory of his later patriotism and the
unequalled results of his influence, the homeliest of his

activities and all the phases of his development become not only fascinating but vitally important.

To disguise or falsify the qualities and the processes through which this man became so splendid and so useful to all the world is not merely impudent dishonesty; it is arrant folly.

It is the most tragic of farces that so many Americans should insist both that Washington could not tell a lie, and that his chroniclers may not tell the truth.

II

MENUS PLAISIRS OF A COUNTRY GENTLEMAN

TO imagine Washington dead at thirty is not mere fantasy. It was reality to him, and, though he was little given to brooding and felt as little concern for death as any man, it might have irked him to realize that if he died then, he would join the innumerable caravan of good men who have done well what their hands found to do, but found nothing at hand distinguished enough to compel remembrance by posterity.

It was not the first time that he had expected to die.

From November, 1757, to March, 1758, he was so far gone that he foresaw his "approaching decay." He nearly died before he met his destined wife, Mrs. Custis. In December, 1758, he was again so ill that he hardly expected to live to be present at his own wedding.

Few men noted for their physical prowess have suffered so many illnesses as Washington. In the first place, one might say of him what Robert Benchley [1] said of one of his characters, that he was "well known for his ability to catch cold." Washington was flat-chested and constantly threatened with the consumption that carried off his half-brother, Lawrence, and countless hosts of colonists. His face was pitted all his life by the marks of early smallpox. He had a scar on his cheek from an ulcerated tooth. Malarial fevers and agues rattled his bones often. He was frequently disabled in his military campaigns. When Braddock marched, Washington fell so ill that he was left behind, was brought up supine in a supply-wagon the day before the battle, and rode into it with a pillow in his saddle. Later in life, he

10

was to lie in one position for six weeks, suffering tortures from an anthrax, or malignant carbuncle. He was to grow somewhat deaf and somewhat blind, as well as toothless.

But he was most frequently afflicted with dysentery, that bane of the soldier's existence, and the scourge of civilians then and now.

In his day it decimated and disabled armies, and was vividly described by its then name, "the bloody flux."

Along with that disgusting and disheartening torment went high fever, griping pain, nausea, painful micturition, profound melancholy and extreme prostration.

Washington's home was both a tavern of hospitality and a hospital. Some one was always in dire distress. The slaves were constantly coming down with the smallpox and other plagues. His bride, Martha, had the measles after her marriage. Martha's daughter, "Patcy," was the constant subject of epileptic attacks or "fitts," in spite of every effort to cure her by "aether," "nostrums," an iron ring, or trips to the Warm Springs.

Doctor's bills play a prominent part in Washington's account books, and he kept a physician on salary for his slaves. He frequently called in his pastor, who was also a physician, Rev. Charles Green of Pohick church, near Mount Vernon.

There exists an unpublished letter of his as early as 1757, saying:

"REVEREND SIR

"Necessity—(and that I hope will apologize for the trouble I must give you—) obliges me to ask the favour of a visit—that I may have an oppertunity of consulting you on a disorder which I have lingerd under for three Months past— It is painful to me to write— Mr. Carlyle will say the rest—I shall only add, that I am with very great esteem

"Yr. most Obed! Hble Servt

"Go WASHINGTON" [2]

His "disorder" was this same bloody flux, and, as his friend, Captain Stewart,[3] described it, it included "Stitches & violent Pleuretick Pains," yet nothing but death itself, it seems, could have prevented his courteous soul from stringing out that elaborate preface to his signature.

He had a recurrence of the bloody flux in 1761, and, when Mr. Green failed to cure him, he decided to try a health resort in the mountains which he had visited on his first surveying expedition as a boy of sixteen. He mentioned it in his earliest journal: "We this day call'd to see y. Fam'd Warm Springs."

They were thus described by Thomas Jefferson:[4] "On Patowmac River, in Berkely county, above the North mountain, are medicinal springs . . . the waters weakly mineralized, and scarcely warm. They are more visited, because . . . always safe from the Indians."

They are now known as Berkeley Springs, and lie in what has been called West Virginia since 1862. In Washington's time the name Warm Springs was changed to Bath, "in deference to the English resort," says a French traveller, Captain Bayard,[5] who describes the town as having, in 1791, "two public buildings—the theatre and the bathhouse. The first is a log edifice, and the second a framed barrack, partitioned into eight cells, in each of which there are steps arranged for the convenience of the bathers. The spring is hard by. The water is dispensed in a goblet by the man in charge. The water is clear, lukewarm, and insipid but very efficacious. I have seen many come to Bath fearfully rheumatic, who had to be carried to the spring at first, and in three weeks were able to walk with a crutch."

On the occasion of Washington's second visit there, there was no theatre and the visitors had to provide their own shelter.

The Warm Springs were about ninety miles from Mount

Vernon as the crow flies, but poor Washington made no such travel. He went in a carriage or on horseback with his baggage in a wagon, and, except for an attendant slave, he went alone. Martha had to stay at Mount Vernon with her always ailing children.

He hired "a Fairfax man returning home . . . to carry some letters to Mrs. Washington," but she doubtless destroyed them when, after his death, she burned all his letters to her except two.

We have, however, among the few bits left of his correspondence in this period, a letter he sent in the same parcel with his messages to Martha. It was addressed to his pastor, Mr. Green, and describes his visit to the Warm Springs at length:

"Our journey as you may imagine was not of the most agreeable sort, through such weather and such roads as we had to encounter; these last for 20 or 25 miles from hence are almost impassible for carriages, not so much from the mountainous country, (but this in fact is very rugged,) as from trees that have fallen across the road and rendered the way intolerable.

"We found of both sexes about 200 people at this place, full of all manner of diseases and complaints; some of which are much benefited, while others find no relief from the waters.—Two or three doctors are here, but whether attending as physicians or to drink of the waters I know not. . . .

"Lodgings can be had on no terms but building for them; and I am of opinion that numbers get more hurt by their manner of lying, than the waters can do them good. Had we not succeeded in getting a tent and marquee from Winchester we should have been in a most miserable situation here.

"In regard to myself I must beg leave to say, that I was much overcome with the fatigue of the ride and weather together. However, I think my fevers are a good deal abated, although my pains grow rather worse, and my sleep equally disturbed. What effect the waters may have upon me I can't say at present, but I expect nothing from the air—this certainly must be unwholesome. . . .

"I have made out a very long, and a very dirty letter, but hurry must apologize for the latter, and I hope your fondness will excuse the former. Please to make my compliments acceptable to Mrs. Green and Miss Bolan and be assured Revd. Sir that with a true respect I remain &c.

"P.S. If I could be upon any certainty of your coming, or could only get 4 days previous notice of your arrival, I would get a house built such as are here erected, very indifferent indeed they are tho', for your reception." [6]

How long he remained in that bleak place is not known, but two months later he wrote from Mount Vernon to a London agent, Richard Washington, that he was well. In this letter he confesses utter ignorance of the progress of the Seven Years' War, and indifference as to the border troubles that once drove him frantic; but he goes into great detail as to the matter of the fashion and fit of his clothes:

"Since my last, of the 14th July, I have in appearance been very near my last gasp. The indisposition then spoken of increased upon me, and I fell into a very low and dangerous state. I once thought the grim king would certainly master my utmost efforts, and that I must sink, in spite of a noble struggle; but, thank God, I have now got the better of the disorder, and shall soon be restored, I hope, to perfect health again."

He makes shrewd and somewhat cynical observations on the Virginia troops, which he had commanded too long to trust overmuch:

"I dont know, that I can muster up one tittle of news to communicate. In short, the occurrences of this part of the world are at present scarce worth reciting; for, as we live in a state of peaceful tranquillity ourselves, so we are at very little trouble to inquire after the operations against the Cherokees, who are the only people that disturb the repose of this great continent, and who, I believe, would gladly accommodate differences upon almost any terms; not, I conceive, from any apprehensions they are under, on account of our arms, but because they want the supplies, which we and we only can furnish them with. . . .

"On the other side is an invoice of clothes, which I beg the favor of you to purchase for me, and to send them by the first ship bound to this river. As they are designed for wearing-apparel for myself, I have committed the choice of them to your fancy, having the best opinion of your taste. I want neither lace nor embroidery. Plain clothes, with a gold or silver button, (if worn in genteel dress,) are all I desire. I have hitherto had my clothes made by one Charles Lawrence, in Old Fish Street. But whether it be the fault of the tailor, or the measure sent, I can't say, but, certain it is, my clothes have never fitted me well. I therefore leave the choice of the workman to your care likewise. I enclose a measure, and, for a further insight, I dont think it amiss to add, that my stature is six feet; otherwise rather slender than corpulent." [7]

This tailor, Lawrence, in spite of his failure to fit him, continued to receive Washington's patronage, for, a year and a half later, he wrote on April 26, 1763, and gave a detailed self-portrait:

"Be pleased to send me a genteel suit of Cloaths made of superfine broad Cloth handsomely chosen—I shoud have Inclosed you my Measure, but in a general way they are so badly taken here that I am convinced it woud be of very little Service   I woud have you therefore take measure of a Gentleman who Wares rich made Cloaths of the following size.—to wit.—6 feet high and proportionably made—if any thing rather slender than thick for a person of that highth with pretty long arms and thighs.—You will take care to make the Breeches longer than those you sent me last, and I would have you keep the measure of the Cloaths you now make, by you; and if any alteration is required in my next it shall be pointed out.—Mr Cary will pay your Bill & I am
Sir   Yr Very Hble Servt.   G. WASHINGTON

"NOTE. for yr furthr governmt & knowledge of my size I have
          sent ye Inclosed.—& you must observe that from the
          Coat end.—
               To No1 & No3 is the size over ye Breast & Hips
               No2. over the Belly. &
               No4. rd ye Arm—& from ye Breeches end—
          To Noa. is for waistband.
               b thick of the Thigh
               c upper button hole

d kneeband—&

e for length of Breeches—therefore if you take measure of a Person ab^t 6 feet high of this bigness I think y^u can^t go amiss—you must take notice y^t ye Inclosed is ye exact size with^t any allow^e for Seams &c.

G. WASHINGTON" [8]

Strangely enough, Washington persisted in announcing that he was only six feet tall, yet his dead body measured "6 feet 3½ inches. exact" according to the testimony of his secretary, Lear,[9] who was present when Doctor Dick measured it.

Either the figures are in hopeless confusion, or he must have grown an inch after he passed his prime, for George Mercer, an intimate friend of his, stated in 1760 that he was then "six feet two inches in his stockings." David Ackerson, of Alexandria, said that in 1776 he "seemed six feet and a half" but his "exact height was six feet two inches in his boots." [10] G. W. P. Custis [11] said he was six feet two inches.

In 1760 Washington had aroused a certain interest in England as the commander of the Virginia troops, and somebody there wrote for a description of him. Captain George Mercer sent the best substitute he could find for the photography that was not to be invented for nearly a century.

He was Washington's aide-de-camp, and accompanied him on the festive ride to New York and Boston in 1758. He knew, therefore, whereof he spoke when he painted this picture of his friend:

"Although distrusting my ability to give an adequate account of the personal appearance of Col. George Washington, late Commander of the Virginia Provincial troops, I shall, as you request, attempt the portraiture. He may be described as being as straight as an Indian, measuring six feet two inches in his stockings, and weighing 175 pounds

when he took his seat in the House of Burgesses in 1759.
His frame is padded with well-developed muscles, indicating great strength.   His bones and joints are large, as are
his feet and hands.

"He is wide shouldered, but has not a deep or round
chest; is neat waisted, but is broad across the hips, and has
rather long legs and arms.   His head is well shaped though
not large, but is gracefully poised on a superb neck.   A large
and straight rather than a prominent nose; blue-gray pene-
trating eyes, which are widely separated and overhung by a
heavy brow.   His face is long rather than broad, with high
round cheek bones, and terminates in a good firm chin.   He
has a clear though rather a colorless pale skin, which burns
with the sun.   A pleasing, benevolent, though a commanding countenance, dark brown hair, which he wears in a cue.

"His mouth is large and generally firmly closed, but
which from time to time discloses some defective teeth.   His
features are regular and placid, with all the muscles of his
face under perfect control, though flexible and expressive of
deep feeling when moved by emotions.   In conversation he
looks you full in the face, is deliberate, deferential and engaging.   His voice is agreeable rather than strong.   His de-
meanor at all times composed and dignified.   His movements and gestures are graceful, his walk majestic, and he is
a splendid horseman." [12]

Whatever the quirk of mind it was that made Washington always understate his size, there are at least three people
whom it is not safe to deceive, one's doctor, lawyer, and
tailor.

To the poor tailor in London, those withheld three inches
were of as vital importance as the three-thousand miles distance of his client.   And there was no opportunity for even
a single try-on.

But it was the custom of the Virginia planters to order

their luxuries and some of their necessities six months ahead, and trust to luck to receive them. They were at the mercy of the London merchants in the matter of price and quality, and Washington often complained of both.

On the other hand, the London merchants had to carry long accounts, and take their money out of the profits (if any) remaining from the tobacco consignments sent over from Virginia with no regularity as to condition, quantity, or date.

If the London merchants exacted too high a commission for sales and too high a price for the goods sent back, many of the Virginians revenged themselves by showing no haste in settling or diminishing their debts. They were themselves at the mercy of the weather, their crops and the fortunes of the ships.

Washington himself wrote many letters protesting his inability to pay what he owed. In the same month, perhaps by the same ship that took the letter to his tailor, he wrote to his old fellow-soldier, Captain Stewart, that letter in which he apologized for being able to advance only £300 of the £400 Stewart had asked for as a loan, enclosing a copy of a dunning letter from a London creditor, Robert Cary, and mentioning still another merchant who "have also a ballance against me." [13]

There is a delightful Damon and Pythias devotion in this reluctance to pay a merchant a debt when the money would comfort a friend, but Washington realized that Mr. Cary would not look at it in this light.

Washington was not the only Virginian who was buying splendors abroad while letting his debts run on. The province was full of gentlemen who were doing the same thing with even more extravagance and even less certainty of paying in the long run.

As a consequence, the colony, though it was growing rap-

John Parke ("Jacky") Custis

Martha ("Patsy") Custis, at 16

idly in wealth and population, was also drifting deeper and deeper into debt to England, and the relations were growing as cordial as those of Antonio and Shylock.

During the Seven Years' War, the Americans were enjoying a war-time boom, with little thought of a day of reckoning. Washington was trying to live up to the standard expected of the consort of Martha, the richest woman in Virginia. He strove to make a stately mansion out of Mount Vernon, and, immediately on his marriage, had ordered numberless things from London including busts of his heroes, Alexander the Great, Julius Cæsar, Charles XII of Sweden and the King of Prussia, two wild beasts, and sundry small ornaments for the chimneypiece.

The London art dealer, William Cheere,[14] answered:

"There is no Busts of Alexander ye Great, (none at all of Charles 12th of Sweden,) Julius Cæsar, King of Prussia, Prince Eugene, nor Duke of Marlborough."

He sent instead, groups of Æneas carrying his father out of Troy, Bacchus and Flora, festoons of grapes and vine leaves, and "Two Lyons after the antique Lyons in Italy, finished neat and bronzed with copper. . . .

"These is the best ornaments I could possibly make for the chimney piece. And of all the wild beasts as coud be made, there is none better than the Lyons. The manner of placing them on ye chimney piece should be thus:

A groupe of — Vase — Æneas — Vase — Groupe of
     Flora   Bacchus."

While Washington was meeting disappointments as a patron of foreign art, he was having his ups and downs with the tobacco he raised to export in payment for his artistic and other importations.

His London agent, Cary, actually complained of short weight in Washington's shipments, and Washington answered in self-defence with language showing what a scholar and experimentalist he was in tobacco-culture:

"I perceive you bring the shortness of some of the bundles of tobacco shipped in the *Bland* to account for the lowness of the price. That some of the tobacco was small, I shall not undertake to dispute; but at the same time I must observe, that it was clean and neatly handled, which I apprehended would have rendered the other objection of very little weight. As to stemming my tobacco, in the manner you recommend, I would readily do it, if the returns would be equivalent to the trouble, and loss of the stem; and of this I shall be a tolerable judge, as I am at no small pains this year to try the quality with the advantages and disadvantages of different kinds of tobaccos, and shall at the same time find out the difference between a hogshead of leaf and a hogshead of stemmed tobacco. By comparing then the loss of the one with the extra price of the other, I shall be able to determine which is the best to pursue, and follow that method which promises the most certain advantages. . . ." [15]

Tobacco was a difficult and a fickle mistress and threatened constant ruin to her devotees:

"We have had one of the most severe droughts in these parts that ever was known, and without a speedy interposition of Providence (in sending us moderate and refreshing Rains to modify and soften the Earth,) we shall not make one ounce of tobacco this year. Our plants in spite of all our efforts to the contrary, are just destroyed, and our grain is absolutely perishing. How it may be in other parts of the country I can not positively say, yet I have heard much complaining." [16]

News from London was slow and frequently bad. He tried various agents, each worse than the other. When his neighbor and friend, Colonel George William Fairfax, sailed for England with his wife Sally, who had been Washington's best beloved of women, Washington sent along with them a letter to Richard Washington, complaining:

"I must confess that my disappointment in the sales of my tobacco per Cozzens was a very sensible one . . . mine being all sweet scented and neatly managed, left me no room to suspect coming in at the tail of the market." [17]

Wounds came even from friends. The Fairfaxes had been so close to him as lifelong neighbors that he was deeply hurt when Colonel George forgot to write home, though Sally evidently was not so remiss. Washington protested to Richard Washington:

"Colo. Fairfax very much surprizes his friends in Virginia by not writing to any of them. Just upon his arrival at London he favored a few with a short letter advertising them of that agreeable circumstance and I have heard of no other letter that has come from him since, altho' I have seen some from the ladies, the superscription of which has been in his handwriting." [18]

The purpose of that Fairfax voyage was peculiar. Colonel Fairfax had gone abroad to convince his relations that he was not a negro! This must have interested Sally also, as she could not have enjoyed the accusation of marrying one and incidentally spoiling her chances to become Lady Fairfax.

Her husband's English cousins wanted to be sure that they were not admitting black blood into their blue. He had been born in the Bahamas, and the story had spread to England that his mother was a dusky beauty.

The story was ridiculous, but in view of the great estates involved it seemed advisable to deny it in person. We learn this from Sally Fairfax herself,[19] and though she does not mention the year, it is highly probable that the present voyage was the one undertaken to quench the gossip.

While abroad the Fairfaxes left the management of their possessions to their closest neighbor, George Washington, whose wide shoulders were a convenient shelf for everybody's troubles. When they returned from England and arrived in lower Virginia, Washington greeted them with this:

"I am sorry to be the messenger of the news, but it is incumbent upon me to inform you of the death of the mare, you committed to my care. How she died, I am able to give you but a very unsatisfactory account. For on the 3rd inst., I set out for Frederick and left her to all appearance as well as a creature could be, Mr. Green and I observing a day or two before, how fat and frolicksome she seemed. And on my return in 8 days time, I got the news of her death. She discovered no visible signs of ailment, as I am told, in the morning of the 7th, when let out of the stable; but before night was swelled to a monstrous size and died in a few hours.

"Bishop (my old servant) opened her, but could perceive no hurt bruise or other apparent cause of so sudden a death which inclines me to think it was occasioned by eating blasted corn, a piece of which I had in ground I wanted to clean and never could fence my chariot Horses of it. The rest consequently followed, and this I am persuaded puffed her up in the manner related."

The domestic affairs of his animals always seemed to amuse him and he grows wittier on such subjects than on any other:

"She had no foal in her, which assures me that she never would breed, as I am convinced, she had a competent share of Ariel's performances; not content with which, she was often catched in amorous mood with a young horse of mine, notwithstanding my utmost endeavors to keep them under. You will feel the loss of this accident more sensibly but can not be more concerned at the account than I was, for I had pleased myself with the thoughts of delivering her to you in fine order, when you returned to below.

"We received the news of your return with a great deal of pleasure and if there is any thing previous to it in which I can be serviceable, I hope you will command me. You did me singular services in a like case, and why won't you give me an oppertunity of making a grateful return. Mrs. Washington writes to Mrs. Fairfax under this cover, to whom and Miss Fairfax please to offer my best wishes." [20]

Washington's soul was busied now only with such things as the death of a mare, the laziness of his slaves, or the shiftlessness of a carpenter. Indolence always stirred his deepest emotions, and he could be driven to frenzy by such dolts as John Askew, a joiner to whom he paid £25 a year, and who annoyed him for eleven years. To Colonel Fairfax he poured out this choleric epistle, a vivid character-study incidentally of both author and subject:

"I shall beg leave to say a little now in regard to Jno. Askew. That he went to work at your House, was not only with my knowledge but by my express desire, and had he stayd there 'til this time it would have been perfectly agreeable to me; but as you know when he left your work, so I can assure you that he never came to mine until Wednesday or Thursday last.

"I then asked him if he did not think himself one of the most worthless and ungrateful fellows that ever lived for his treatment of me—for you must know Sir that so small a job as making the Front Gate in my yard was left him to do when I went to Williamsburg abt the 10th of May last, and was found undone at my return, altho I urged him in the strongest manner I could to get it finished for this very prevalent Reason namely, that I might inclose my Chariot Horses in a Pasture round my House secured by a Post & Rail fence and by that means prevent them from breaking into a field where I had about 10 acres of Peas, that is now by his Idleness and there letting in my sheep, entirely rooted out.

"This as I before said he neglected, and I was from that time untill a day or two before Mr. Carlyle asked for him to go to Belvoir, ere I could get him to work again; so that you may partly judge from this of the provocation he has given me, but you will be more convinced of it when I tell you that the Ballce. he owes me is for Tools Imported for him, and money actually lent to keep him from starving, and from a Gaol, from whence (at least the Sheriff's custody) I have once or twice redeemed him—and lent him money to cloath & by necessaries for his Family.

"This is the real truth of the case, and it is so far from any wanting to keep him (longer than he will finish the Gate, and repays 7 days work due to my Carpenters, and how about) that I never desire to see his face again, if he can fall upon any method of paying me what he owes me in money." [21]

Such were the things that held Washington's soul close to the ground while all the nations were wrung with gigantic conflict, and hundreds of men were flashing into supposed immortality and thousands perishing in nameless misery.

Who could have imagined that this late-rising sun would one day drown them all in his light?

III

HE IGNORES THE WARS

LIKE a boy who flings a careless match into a powder magazine and runs far off after the first few detonations, George Washington started the world-rocking World War, but did not stay to finish it.

Voltaire, Parkman, and others say that when, during a state of formal peace between England and France and their colonies, Washington's men shot down young Jumonville, who carried the credentials of an ambassador as well as the instructions of a spy, he touched the fuse to the stored explosives collected on both sides.

Peace did not officially end until 1757, two years after Braddock's Defeat, but Washington retired to his farm at the close of his first campaign with Forbes in 1758. Though he was then only twenty-six, nothing could draw him into battle again for seventeen years. There were opportunities enough and almost unbroken, not only for the five remaining years of the great war, but throughout the following decade.

Americans were fighting everywhere and winning ridicule, defeat, death, victory and fame everywhere. These things did not interest Washington. The borders of Virginia were constantly under attack, but he was not even tempted apparently to go to the rescue of his own province.

In 1759 the Cherokees came to clash with the Governor of South Carolina, who violated the laws of war and refused to release two hostages. The Indians were enraged and killed a number of Americans. The Americans retorted by butchering the hostages. The Cherokees took a fierce revenge and butchered settlers.

The British sent Colonel Montgomery to crush them, but Washington commented, "Let him be wary. He has a crafty, subtle enemy to deal with, that may give him most trouble when he least expects it." [1]

Montgomery, indeed, fell into an ambush and was heavily defeated, but later dealt the Cherokees a severe blow and returned to Albany for the attack on Canada. His successor, Major Hanson, was compelled to surrender Fort Loudoun to the Indians, with a garrison of two hundred, many of whom were slain. This was not the Fort Loudoun reluctantly built by Washington at Winchester, but Fort Loudon on the Holston, thirty miles southwest of the present site of Knoxville, Tennessee.[2] The irony of it was that Governor Dinwiddie had spent £7,000 in 1756 "to assist the Cherokees in build^g a Fort to defend y^r Women and Children from the Insults of the French w^n they go to War in assist'^{g} y^r Bro^s, the English." [3]

Three years later the Cherokees proceeded to besiege an English garrison in the fort, and Virginia sent a relief force under Washington's old second in command, Colonel William Byrd of Westover, who had been coupled with Washington when General Forbes rebuked those two gentlemen for mercenary motives in advocating the old Braddock Road.[4] He made such slow progress that he grew disheartened and gave up the command to Washington's former lieutenant-colonel, Adam Stephen, who made no better progress.

Then the British sent down Lieutenant-Colonel Grant.

This was the very officer who had served with Washington under Forbes in 1758, and had insisted on making a dash against Fort Du Quesne. He had taken along with his own kilted Highlanders, a major, eight officers and 168 of

Washington's men. The French and Indians had inflicted on him another Braddock's Defeat, thrown the Scotch and the Virginians into a complete panic, and slaughtered a quarter of them.

Washington had raged at Grant in a letter to Sally Fairfax.[5] But Grant had returned from the dead as an exchanged prisoner, and had better luck fighting the unaided Cherokees.

For once Washington sympathized with the Indians, and wrote to Robert Cary:

"We have little or no news stirring. Our assembly is at present convened to grant supplies for carrying on the war against the Cherokee Indians, should they choose to continue it; but this I am persuaded they are by no means inclined to do, nor are they prepared for it, as they have been soliciting peace for some time past. I wish the powers of Europe were as well disposed to an accommodation as these poor wretches are. A stop would soon be put to the effusion of human blood, and peace and plenty would resume their empire again, to the joy and content, (I believe,) of most ranks and degrees of people." [6]

Grant overpowered the Cherokees and peace was signed November 19, 1760. Later, when Pontiac's War threatened to crumple the whole Western border and played havoc with forts and settlements, Washington remained a simple country gentleman, though Dr. Koontz [7] says that the Indians were kept from overrunning Virginia by the line of forts that Washington had built when he was commander-in-chief of the Virginia troops. But he had almost come to mutiny in his reluctance to build them, and their defence was left to Colonel Adam Stephen and Major Andrew Lewis, while the Swiss Colonel Bouquet must relieve Fort Pitt from siege by winning the ferocious battle of Bushy Run, with a force of 500, only a third of Braddock's, and against nearly three times as many Indians.

An example of Washington's aloofness from the border

wars and his intense interest in his own agricultural distresses
is shown in an unpublished letter now in the Pierpont Morgan Library. It was written July 5, 1763, to Martha's
brother-in-law, Colonel Bassett:

"Dear Sir, So good an oppertunity as Turner Crump on a visit
to his Father (affords) I coud not omit of asking how you do; for
I have nothing to require, and as little to communicate in this
Epistle, as it cannot be News to inform you, that the Peace of the
Frontier Inhabitants seems to have met with almost as rude a shock
from the late Indian Insults, as it did from any of their Barbarities
in the course of the War, altho' no great mischeif has been done
(to the People of this Colony not any) I mean as to their Butchery,
for I heard of only nine Persons killed on this side the Alliganies,
and those were of Pennsylvania near Fort Bedford or Rays Town,
but it is melancholy to behold the Terror that has seized them,
and the fatal consequences that must follow, in the loss of their
Harvest and Crops; the whole Back Country being in Forts or
flying— I came from Frederick only last Week, and had an
oppertunity of well knowing the confusion that prevailed in the
County above.

"Our Wheat in this part of the Country is in a great measure
destroyed by the Rust & other defect in the ear; and our Crops of
Indian Corn & Tobacco in a manner lost in Weeds & Grass, occasioned by continual & excessive rains, that has not only forced
these out in very uncommon abundance, but prevented all sorts of
tillage where our Lands lay flat.—I brought down your Colt, & a
little run in my pasture will give him a good Coat of flesh, at present he is in low case to what cause owing I cannot tell, as he has
never been broke.—If Capt Boyes is arrived please to advise me of
it, for we are at a loss to acct for the delays of the London Ships.—
You will be so good as to present my love to Mrs Bassett & the
little ones, and accept of the best wishes yourself of

"Dear sir   Yr Most Affecte & Obed.

"G. Washington."

Still later, when Cornstalk fought his tremendous battle
on the Great Kanawha, in the very heart of the lands Washington claimed as his own from an early grant of Dinwiddie's, Washington kept at home and let Major (now

Colonel, later General) Andrew Lewis save his property for him.[8]

While the vast turmoil of the Seven Years' War rolled around the globe, Washington knew of it only from the gazettes.

The British captured Gorée, Guadelupe, Ticonderoga, and Niagara. Wolfe and Montcalm perished on the Heights of Abraham. Hawke smashed the French fleet in Quiberon Bay. Montreal fell. In India, Clive took Chandernagor, and Coote took Pondicherry. The wealth of Bengal, Bahar, and the Carnatic fell to the British. On the Continent, the English money of the Hanoverian King helped the Prussians and their Frederick the Great to cripple France and her allies.

All this while, Washington cultivated his farm and his new wife, hunted foxes, fished, and tried to conquer tobacco.

Learning of the fall of Quebec and Ticonderoga, he rejoiced that "the French are so well drubbed, and seem so much humbled in America." [9] But he did none of the drubbing.

He noted, "We are in pain here for the king of Prussia, and wish Hanover safe." As for his old desire to visit the unseen land he called "home," he wrote prophetically— "My indulging myself in a trip to England depends upon so many contingencies, which, in all probability, may never occur, that I dare not even think of such a gratification. Nothing, however, is more ardently desired. But Mrs. Washington and myself would both think ourselves very happy in the oppertunity of showing you the Virginia hospitality, which is the most agreeable entertainment we can give, or a stranger expect to find, in an infant, woody country, like ours."

Now and then Washington wrote blindly about the war and its rumors:

"We have received the account of Belle Isle's reduction, and hear of another expedition fleet destined for some service, of which we are ignorant. But that, which most engrosses our attention at this time, is the congress at Augsburg, as I believe nothing is more sincerely desired in this part of the world, than an honorable peace." [10]

"We catch the reports of peace with gaping mouths." [11]

"Upon the important conquest of the Havanna I heartily congratulate you." [12]

The Americans who had taken part in this expedition were under command of General Phinehas Lyman, who would later be a competitor of Washington's in wholesale real estate.

He had high hopes that a treaty would bring prosperity to Virginia:

"We are much rejoiced at the prospect of Peace which 'tis hoped will be of long continuance, and introductory of mutual advantages to the merchant and planter, as the trade to this Colony will flow in a more easy and regular channel than it has done for a considerable time past." [13]

News was of such slow travel in that day that this last letter was written April 26, 1763, though the formal Treaty of Paris had been already signed on February tenth.

There was a vast readjustment of boundaries and the entire continent of North America as far west as the Mississippi river was turned over to the British, save for the town and island of New Orleans. Canada, as well as Louisiana, was taken away from the French, and Florida from the Spanish. Certain Englishmen opposed the taking over of Canada; they were ignored.

Though France did not suffer by any means in the exchanges of territory her pride was gone, and her fleet annihilated.[14]

The French minister of foreign affairs, Choiseul, tried to solace his countrymen in their humiliation by saying that

England would one day regret the possession of Canada since it removed from the colonists the threat of French invasion, which had been their sole reason for remaining loyal to England, on whose army and navy they relied to keep the French in check.

In his *Mémoire* to the King he said:

"It remains for me to speak to Your Majesty of the maritime powers. England is the declared enemy of your power and of your state, and she will be so always. Many ages must elapse before a durable peace can be established with this state, which looks forward to the supremacy in the four quarters of the globe. Only the revolution which will occur some day in America, though we shall probably not see it, will put England back to that state of weakness in which Europe will have no more to fear of her." [15]

He was quoted as saying to the English envoy that the colonies "would not fail to shake off their dependence the moment Canada should be ceded."

This struck nearly everybody as laughable. Benjamin Franklin, remembering how vainly he had striven to link the colonies together in his Albany Plan of Union, ridiculed Choiseul's theory by the very well-taken argument:

"If they could not agree to unite for their defence against the French and Indians . . . can it reasonably be supposed there is any danger of their uniting against their own nation . . . which 'tis well known they all love much more than they love one another? . . . An union amongst them for such a purpose is not merely improbable, it is impossible." [16]

And in Boston James Otis, addressing a town-meeting with grandiloquent rejoicing in the conquest of the "heathen" and the glorious solidity of the British realm, added the pious prayer, "What God in his providence has united, let no man dare attempt to pull asunder." [17]

Yet James Otis was the first and the leading spirit in the prompt attempt of the colonies to secure a divorce from their beloved England, and Benjamin Franklin in a dozen years was turning Choiseul's ridiculous notions into true prophecy, as the darling of the French and the abomination of the English, making his home in Paris and wheedling France into a new war with England.

Washington was often something of a prophet himself, and when he wrote to his friend, Robert Stewart, expressing his delight in the Treaty of Paris, he mingled with it expressions of the anxiety over sudden developments that threatened financial war:

"Signing of the definitive treaty seems to be the only piece of news, which prevails here at present, and diffuses general joy. Our Assembly is suddenly called, in consequence of a memorial of the British merchants to the Board of Trade, representing the evil consequences of our paper emissions and their Lordships' report and orders thereupon, which, I suppose, will set the whole country in flames. This stir of the merchants seems to be ill-timed, and cannot be attended with any good effects, bad, I fear it will. However, on the 19th instant the Assembly meets; and till then I will suspend my further opinion of the matter." [18]

The merchants of England had long since gained control of the English parliament, and the merchants of England believed that the colonies existed merely for their benefit. They did not at all approve of the colonial fondness for issuing large quantities of paper money for the convenience of their own merchants, planters, and innumerable smugglers.

The merchants of England, having seen France crushed at their own expense, studied solemnly the load of debts that weighed them down, and resolved to push some of the burden onto the shoulders of the prosperous colonists. And this pleased neither the American merchants of the North nor the planters of the South, who dealt largely with Scotch merchants established in America.

Washington foresaw a commercial war, but even his keenly practical foresight was not troubled by any fantastic nightmare that it would put him back in his old uniform of buff and blue with the colonies united at last for war—not against France but England, and led by an arch-traitor to the King who would be, of all the men on earth, himself.

How could he have suspected that he himself, by his martial activities, would bring France and England and Spain to war again, just as he had done when he fired on Jumonville in 1754? Had not the treaty of 1763 been a document guaranteed to end war forever? So its preamble solemnly declared:

"There shall be a Christian, universal, and perpetual peace, as well by sea, as by land, and a sincere and constant friendship shall be re-established between their Britannic, Most Christian, Catholic and Most Faithful Majesties."

This was one of the numberless Leagues of Nations, and it failed about midway of the Hundred Years' War, which ended in 1815 with Napoleon's crash.

IV

HIGH LIFE AT WILLIAMSBURG AND
FREDERICKSBURG

THOUGH Washington attended the sessions of the Virginia House of Burgesses conscientiously, and as conscientiously collected his expenses and what he called "my Burgess wages," his activities for the first fifteen years were so unimportant that almost our only knowledge of his being there at all is taken from his own carefully kept diaries and ledgers, and from the lists of members in the Virginia *Almanack* and elsewhere.

Even such a monograph as Dr. Leake's "The Virginia Committee System and the American Revolution," mentions his name but once, and then only in a reference to the report of his mission to the French in 1754, when he had not yet encountered the first of his two defeats as a candidate.[1]

Rejected as a candidate by his home county, he had managed to win an election in Frederick County in 1758, but his only recorded assignment seems to have been on a committee to draught a law forbidding hogs to run at large in Winchester.[2]

It was not until 1765 that he stood for Fairfax, receiving 208 votes to his colleague's 148.

He took his political duties apparently as lightly as the average modern member of the lower house of a state legislature. He said nothing in the Assembly and spent most of his evenings playing cards, or attending the theatre.

His wages as Burgess were ten shillings a day, and he charged mileage in the form of "Travelling days" at ten

34

shillings each, as well as ferry charges each way. And there were ferriages enough.

We can follow him in his diary through one long hard journey from Mount Vernon to Williamsburg taken in April through rainy weather and over numerous streams swollen with what he called "freshes." Though this journey was not on Assembly business, it gives a lively picture of a rural state senator on the way to his capital. On this occasion he had to cross the Potomac by ferry into Maryland and recross it by another ferry into Virginia to avoid the swamps and submerged roads he usually took by way of Fredericksburg.[3]

As in the Revolutionary War, Washington kept a strict account of his expenses and a careful record in his ledgers.

In 1764 he collected ten pounds ten "of the Treasurer, for pay as a Commissioner, app[d] to settle the Militia acct."

He always charged the colony at least ten days' travel pay, and included his ferry-fees. But then his elections cost him something. Though it was against the law to buy wine for voters, the lawmakers were allowed some discretion at critical times.

At Williamsburg Washington found himself in a town of small size but fine quality. The college of William and Mary was there, from which Washington had received his appointment as Fairfax county surveyor in 1749, the capitol, the royal Governor's "palace," beautiful Bruton Church, and many homes whose fine architecture is still impressive.

The Rev. Andrew Burnaby[4] (who visited, admired, and corresponded with Washington) visited Williamsburg in 1759, saw it through English eyes and found the capitol and the college "far from being magnificent," the governor's house "one of the best on the continent, . . . only tolerably good." Even the jail and the church were "extremely in-

different," and the unpaved streets dusty. The only remarkable thing was the absence of mosquitoes. The women
were "rather handsome . . . seldom accomplished . . . im-
moderately fond of dancing . . . it is usual to dance jiggs."

For America, however, the town was impressive, though a
place of only a thousand inhabitants.

Washington revelled especially in its theatre. There had
been dramatics of a sort there ever since the capital was
removed thither from Jamestown in 1699, to remain until
1779, when it was moved to Richmond. As early as 1702
the college students had recited a "pastoral colloquy" for the
royal governor. In 1716 a theatre was built and actors and
actresses imported from England—a thing forbidden by the
founders who said that the colony had "three great enemies
. . . even the Divel, Papists, and Players." In the Daily
Prayer of 1602 was a petition against temptation from all
three.

Charles Stagg and his wife, Mary, were the first stars and,
after her husband's death, Mary Stagg carried on the business, also holding dancing "assemblies," in which she was
rivalled by the daughter of Count de Graffenreidt. The
admission was half a pistole, about $1.90.

At a time when, in New England, the theatre was ac-
cursed, William and Mary College encouraged its students
to produce such plays as "Cato," given in 1736, and even
such audacious comedies as "The Recruiting Officer" and
"The Beaux' Stratagem." The students were aided by "the
gentlemen and ladies of this country."

The vivacity of the Williamsburg atmosphere is shown in
a humorous advertisement published in the Virginia *Gazette*
for 1736:

"ADVERTISEMENT.—Whereas a Gentleman Who towards
the latter end of the Summer usually wore a Blue Camlet coat
lined with Red and trimmed with Silver, a silver laced hat and

a Turpee wig, has often been observed by his Amoret, to look very languishingly at her, the said Amoret, and particularly one night during the last session at Assembly, at the Theatre, the said Gentleman ogled her in such a manner as shewed him to be very far gone, the said Amoret desires the Gentleman to take the first handsome opportunity that offers to explain himself on that subject.—N.B. She believes that he has very pretty teeth."

Dr. Tyler [5] says, "This public notice was doubtless a great joke directed against the town dude, whoever he was."

Under Governor Dinwiddie the theatre prospered. The professor of moral philosophy at William and Mary once played a drunken peasant, and the young ladies of the town witnessed comedies that would startle Broadway of the Twentieth Century, and bring the police patrol wagons to the stage door for the players.

On one occasion a Cherokee "emperor and empress" saw a play, and, during a stage fight, the empress ordered one of her attendants "to prevent the actors from killing each other."

The Rev. Samuel Davies abused Virginia because "Plays and Romances were more read than the history of the blessed Jesus." The organist at Bruton Church, by the way, played the music for the theatre.

In 1768 the Virginia Company of Comedians gave a season of two months, and Sarah Hallam, a ravishingly beautiful actress, established herself as such a favorite that she made the town her permanent home and later founded a fashionable boarding school for young ladies, and taught dancing.

There was no more devoted attendant at this theatre than Washington, and he could not have missed many performances, judging from his diaries and ledgers.

In Ledger A are constantly such entries as in 1760:

"By Play Tickets at Sundry Times £7. 11. 3."

He encouraged his stepchildren to go to the theatre as to the races, and insisted upon their being good dancers.

Another favorite resort of his was the Raleigh Tavern, known also as Hay's or Southall's. It was built probably in 1735. Washington played cards there often, as at other taverns and private houses in Williamsburg, always apparently for money.

The Apollo room at the tavern was a noble banquet hall with a great fireplace over which was a Latin motto meaning:

"Hilarity is the offspring of wisdom and a good life."

In his Burgess years at Williamsburg, Washington seems to have accepted this as excellent counsel. The Apollo room was used for dancing, and Washington loved dancing even better than the theatre. Banquets were held there, too, and he loved a formal feast. Doctor Tyler says of the Apollo, "This ancient room saw, at one time or another, all that was brilliant and graceful in the Virginia society of the eighteenth century."

The room saw also the beginnings of the Revolution, and Washington and others gathered there as eagerly to plot defiance of the parliament as to revel with the belles, or toss off the innumerable toasts of a banquet.

In Williamsburg there was a Masonic lodge, at which Washington visited often enough to be nominated for the office of grand master in 1777. But he declined to accept it, as he was very busy to the northeast at that time.

The town had other interests also for Washington. His wife had come from there, and the region was filled with her people. Her estate was under his management, and he had rents to collect from residents in the town houses and from tenants on the farms.

He rode out to buy slaves, to hunt, to fish, to dance, to eat, to ponder agricultural problems.

The extraordinary festivity of his life at the capital is evidenced by the frequency of the dry entries in his diary, where he makes no mention of legislative incidents, but piles up the social record:

May "2. Went to Williamsburg with Colo. Bassett, Colo. Lewis and Mr. Dick. Dind with Mrs. Dawson, and went to the Play.

"3. Dined with the Speaker.

"4. Dined with Mrs. Dawson, and Suppd at Charlton's.

"5. Dined at Mrs. Campbell's.

"6. Rid to the Plantations near Williamsburg and dined at Mr. Valentine's.

"7 Came up to Colo. Bassett's to Dinner.

"8. Went to Church and returnd to Dinner.

"9. Went a Fox hunting and catched a Fox after 35 Minutes chace; returnd to Dinner and found the Attorney, his lady and daughter there.

"10. Rid to the Brick House and returnd to Dinner; after which went a dragging for Sturgeon.

"11. Dined at the Glebe with Mr. Davis.

"12. Went to New Kent Court with Colo. Bassett.

"13. Went after Sturgeon and a Gunning.

"14. Went to my Plantation in King William by Water and dredgd for Sturgeon, and catchd one."

Nov. "1. In Williamsburg Dined at the Speaker's, with many Gentlemen.

"2. In Ditto. Dined at the Attorney Genl's with Lord Botetourt (ye Govr.) and many other Gentlemen.

"3. In Ditto. Dined at Mrs. Dawson's.

"4. In Ditto. Dined with several Gentlemen at Ayscough's. Colo. Byrd's Lottery began drawing.

"5. Dined at Mrs. Campbell's, where I had spent all my Evenings since I came to Town."

Sometimes he went to Williamsburg alone; sometimes he took Martha and her children Jacky and Patsy Custis along. Then there were house parties at the homes along the way, and in Williamsburg purchases of music books and instruments, dresses, trinkets, consultations with doctors and dentists, but, above all, dinners and dances.

Perhaps because of the crowded condition, Washington apparently lodged at one boarding house, and Martha and the children at another.

Into the compact village of Williamsburg there was crowded an amazing amount of dissipation, especially when the members of the Assembly and their families filled all the taverns and boarding houses, and visited with the dozen great gentlemen who had their residences there.

Prize-fights were frequent, with a particular affection for "gouging," the object of which was the extraction of at least one of the opponent's eyeballs.

President J. A. C. Chandler, who has reawakened William and Mary College to a new and greater life and prosperity, states:

"Cards and dice were also popular amusements, indulgence in which sometimes amounted to a widespread craze. More than once the Grand Assembly felt that the widespread custom demanded official recognition and regulation. Debts for gambling could not be collected by any process of law, and keepers of taverns and public houses were forbidden, under severe penalty, to allow gambling in public places." [6]

Washington enjoyed cock-fighting as he enjoyed practically all forms of sport. But he was more devoted to horse-racing, as breeder, racer, and better.

The sessions of the Assembly were enlivened by brilliant sessions at the race-tracks with interludes, between the events, of cudgelling matches, foot-races, singing tourneys, and beauty contests with silk stockings as the prizes.

"Provisions were made for starters, judges and the usual regulations as to weights, handicaps of one sort and another. The course at Williamsburg was for the mile, two-mile, three-mile and even four-mile heats, it being plainly evident that the Virginian was seeking not simply the quality of speed, but the combined qualities of speed and durability in their racing stock." [7]

Democracy had not begun to rear its hateful head in Virginia, and even Thomas Jefferson (who was a student at William and Mary, danced at every opportunity, especially with his "Belinda" in the Apollo room, and enjoyed the other amusements of the aristocracy) would have made no protest against the punishment inflicted on a tailor who dared to aspire to horse-racing. He was heavily fined for that; but for the minor offence of fixing the race received a minor punishment. The court itself gives the record:

"James Bullock, a tailor, having made a race for his mare to run with a horse belonging to Matthew Slater, for two thousand pounds of tobacco and caske, it being contrary to law for a laborer to make a race, being a sport only for gentlemen, is fined for the same one hundred pounds of tobacco and caske, . . . whereas Mr. Matthew Slater and James Bullock, by conditions under the hand and seal of the said Slater, that his horse should run out of the way so that Bullock's mare might win, which is an apparent cheat, is ordered to be put in the stocks and there sit for one hour." [8]

An English physician, John F. D. Smyth,[9] who settled in Williamsburg in 1769 and later wrote a book about his travels, was struck by the Virginians' passion for racing, and their skill in it:

"Very capital horses are started here, such as would make no despicable figure at Newmarket; nor is their speed, bottom or blood inferior to their appearance . . . Their stock is from old Cade, old Crab, old Partner, Regulus, Babraham, Bosphorus, Devonshire Childers, the Cullen Arabian, the Cumberland Arabian, &c., in England; and a horse from Arabia named the Bellsize, which was imported into America and is now in existence."

The quarter-racing of Southern Virginia and North Carolina struck Smyth as being a strange institution. Many early travellers devote a page or two to these matches between two horses to run one-quarter of a mile straight out. Smyth observes: "They have a breed that performed it with astonishing velocity, beating every other, for that distance with great ease; but they have no bottom. However, I am confident that there is not a horse in England, nor perhaps the whole world, that can excel them in rapid speed; and these likewise make excellent saddle horses for the road. The Virginians, of all ranks and denominations, are excessively fond of horses, and especially those of the race breed. . . . Nobody walks on foot the smallest distance, except when hunting; indeed, a man will frequently go five miles to catch a horse, to ride only one mile afterwards."

It is noteworthy that he makes a joke on Virginian hostility to pedestrianism that has been revived for the modern cowboys. He tells another, showing that America was already beginning, not only to form its own language, but to forget old-country words—among them the use of "meat" to mean any solid food:

"I arrived at Stewart's Ordinary to breakfast, which was toasted Indian hoecake and very excellent cyder. Being always particularly careful of my horses, and they having fared very indifferently the night before, I ordered the hostler to give them plenty of meat." The hostler, understanding meat to mean meat, put bacon before these Petersburg horses. A crowd assembled, and this new balanced ration became a great joke.

Washington was, of course, active in organizing the races at Williamsburg.

On his way to and from Williamsburg he usually tarried a while at Fredericksburg, where his mother and his sister, Betty, lived.

He was very fond of Fredericksburg, and well he might be, for it is still a strangely lovable town, demurely peaceful in spite of the great people who have dwelt there and the tremendous battles that have drenched its gentle slopes with blood. It was there and then that John Paul lived when he added Jones to his name.

The Rappahannock saunters through the realm that Washington called "the place of my growing infancy," and one can see where he threw the Spanish dollar across its banks, the Cherry Tree Farm, where he confessed his inability to tell a lie, the little home his mother occupied from 1775 to her dying day, the stately mansion where his sister, Betty Lewis, lived, and the tavern where he spent so many hours of moderate gambling.

His mother's little story-and-a-half house, though now cut off by modern buildings, was at first connected by a long box-bordered walk with Kenmore, the home of Fielding Lewis. Washington was doubly bound to Fielding Lewis, whose first wife was Washington's aunt, and whose second wife was his sister. Betty Lewis kept in close touch with her mother, with whom she seems to have been on far tenderer relations than George ever was.

"Sister Lewis," as Washington usually calls her, bore her husband six children, some of whom later stood close to Washington in battle. Like so many others in the colonies, they also borrowed money from him.

With Fielding Lewis, a prosperous merchant and a burgess (therefore a vestryman), Washington had much in common. They went in together on various businesses, and in 1760 Washington paid Lewis £5, "on account of Iron Work Scheme," which was a plan to erect a foundry at "The Bloomery" where, as he wrote in his Diary, "The Convenience of Water is great . . . I saw none of the Ore, but all People agree that there is an inexhaustable fund of that that

is rich. But wood seems an obstacle." [10] The scheme came
to naught.

But iron foundries never succeeded well in Virginia. The
mother country kept passing laws to make all forms of manufacture impossible to the colonists. They could not even
make beaver hats in a world of beavers.

Still, Fielding Lewis came to be a great gun-maker for
the Revolution, and succeeded in shattering his health and
his fortune for his ungrateful country. After borrowing
thousands of pounds to lend to Virginia, he was unable to
pay his taxes and was sold out.[11] At this time, however, he
was rich and happy. His home was, and is, a paragon of
grace.[12] Washington loved it, designed a very ingenious
ornament for its mantelpiece, and later set Hessian prisoners to work upon its exceedingly graceful ornate white
ceilings.

Perhaps Washington and Fielding Lewis were in sympathy concerning Mary Washington, whom George found
a difficult mother, though he was a devoted son. In an address to "the Worshipful the Mayor and Commonalty of
the Corporation of Fredericksburg" he thanked them for the
"honorable mention which is made of my revered mother,
by whose maternal hand (early deprived of a Father) I
was led to manhood."

In Fredericksburg one hears the most exciting things
about Mary Washington. They are handed down by oral
tradition alone and are impossible to confirm—or disprove.

While Mrs. Pryor [13] and others defend her, as her son is
defended, from the imputation of any human frailties whatever, the legend of her fierce temper is still vivid in Fredericksburg, and the story is told that she was so angered
once by the disobedience of a slave lad who drove her carriage that she seized the whip from his hands and gave him

a furious lashing with it before all the bystanders, cursing him richly the while.

This demonstration took place, if at all, in front of an apothecary shop, the oldest in America, kept by Dr. Hugh Mercer, a Scot by birth, who turned out to be a brilliant general, and as valiant a soldier as ever apothecary was. His statue with drawn sword now decorates one of the city squares. In his earlier years he kept a singularly graceful drug store, which still stands in Fredericksburg.

Mary Washington is said to have been an earnest pipe-smoker, in which she would have differed radically from her son, George, as she did on so many points. George grew sick at the least puff of tobacco, though he had many snuff-boxes. And he grew to hate the plant as a crop since it exhausted the none too rich soil of Virginia, and failed to bring him the profits he hoped for in spite of all his devotion to it.

Whether his mother smoked or not, or drank or not, is no great matter except that she was the mother of George. The wife of the Puritan Governor Winthrop wrote to her husband in 1627: "My good mother commends hir love to you all and thankes you for hir tobacko." [14]

Countless other women in that tobacco-worshipping land smoked in those days, as now; and the anecdotes of Mary's flares of temper are no more cruel to her than some of the grandiloquent icy speeches put into her mouth by equally uncertain legend.

A pathetic, but typically querulous letter of hers was probably the cause of Betty's moving her off her farm to the town house. It was written to her son, John Augustine:

"DEAR JOHNNE,—I am glad to hear you and all the family is well, and should be glad if I could write you the same. I am a going fast, and it, the time, is hard. I am borrowing a little

Cornn—no Cornn in the Cornn house. I never lived soe poore in my life. Was it not for Mr. French and your sister Lewis I should be almost starved, but I am like an old almanack quite out of date. Give my love to Mrs. Washington—all the family. I am dear Johnne your loving and affectionate Mother.

"P.S. I should be glad to see you as I dont expect to hold out long." [15]

Mary's name appears incessantly in Washington's account books and diaries. He took good care of her business for her, visited her with filial regularity, and paid her profound respect, saying at the last: "I attribute all of my success in life to the moral, intellectual, and physical education which I received from my mother." [16]

But if she was as terrifying as all the traditions indicate, it is not to be wondered at that her son spent so much of his time at the Rising Sun Tavern kept by George Weedon, who also became a general in the Revolution, and whose inn still stands in the all-preserving amber of Fredericksburg.

The legends abide that Washington fought many a long night-battle with the local card-sharks at Weedon's, and admitted that they were "too smart for him." But he never gave up trying to bring his winnings up to his losses, and never succeeded.

The ledgers he kept show, in his own handwriting, how constantly he played and just how he stood when they blew out the candles and went home.

After he had tasted the idolatry that came to him in his later years, he withdrew himself from the mob, rather in self-defence than in self-worship, but at Fredericksburg he was always among old friends, and remained the boy and the young man.

General Maury,[17] a distinguished Fredericksburg soldier, perpetuates one of the more genial traditions that came to him direct from a friend of Washington's:

"His arrival was the occasion of great conviviality and

GEORGE MASON
(From Hesselius' portrait in the Virginia State Library)

rejoicing. Dinner-parties and card-parties were then in order, and we find, in that wonderful record of his daily receipts and expenditures, that on one of these occasions he won thirty guineas at loo. Probably it was after this night that he threw the historic dollar across the river, the only instance of extravagance ever charged against him. A dinner party was usually given to him on his arrival at the old Indian Queen Tavern, where, tradition tells us, drink was deep and play was high.

"It is generally believed that Washington did not laugh or enjoy a joke. I have often heard Judge Francis Taliaferro Brooke, for many years Chief Justice of Virginia, say this was not true. Washington often dined at Smithfield, the home of the Brooke family. It is now known in the histories of the battle of Fredericksburg as the 'Pratt House.'

"Judge Brooke used to tell of a dinner given to Washington at the Indian Queen Tavern, at which he was present. A British officer sang a comic song,—a very improper song, but as funny as it was improper,—at which Washington laughed till the tears ran down his cheeks, and called upon the singer to repeat it."

Washington had been initiated into the Lodge at Fredericksburg when he was only twenty, and he was an enthusiastic member all his life, belonging also to the Alexandria lodge. At the Fredericksburg lodge is an extraordinarily fine portrait which he had painted for its walls. He doubtless took his turn at the two venerable demijohns, "one called 'Jachen,' full of Jamaica rum, and the other called, 'Boaz,' full of Holland gin, with an old-fashioned loaf of sugar, kept in the ante-room for the refreshment of the brethren." [18]

More prosaic but more certain it is that Washington was once brought before a justice of the peace and fined for trading horses on Sunday.

Also, he and George William Fairfax, and half a dozen others were fined for not reporting their taxable wheeled vehicles according to law.[19]

The Rev. Dr. Goodwyn [20] thinks that the prosecution was mere "spite work," but it is comforting to Sabbath-breakers and tax-dodgers to have so illustrious a patron saint.

During the anti-Masonic agitation of the 1830's, it was violently denied that the Father of his Country could ever have stooped to the degrading rites of a secret organization, but like so many other statements of his aloofness from human concerns, the documents destroy the myth.[21]

V

HE KEEPS HIS BOOKS

SO well concealed is the Washington of this period that one is delighted to find in the account books he kept a rich store of humanity of which there is no other record.

Even the men who knew him well were so overawed by his final achievements and the reverence he inspired in those who were not jealous of him that they simply ignored his activities as a private citizen. His friend, Justice Marshall, in his famous five-volume biography—in which he did not get Washington born until the second volume—devotes to the first twenty-six years of his hero's life only the first fifty-two pages of his second volume. Chapter I ends at 1758. Chapter II begins in 1775 with this brief enough summary of seventeen years:

"The attention of Colonel Washington, for several years after his marriage, was principally directed to the management of his estate. He continued a most respectable member of the legislature of his country, in which he took an early and decided part against the claims of supremacy asserted by the British Parliament."

Having given fifty-two pages to Washington's first twenty-six years, he gave fifty-one words to the next seventeen!

Parson Weems, though horrified by Marshall's omission of all anecdotes (especially as the Parson was expected to sell Marshall's work, being more book-agent than evangelist) is no more satisfactory concerning these years.

His seventh chapter ends with the marriage to Martha,

of whom he says, "gratitude to that bright saint, now in heaven, who was my noblest benefactress, while I preached in her parish, compels me to say, that her VIRTUES and CHARITIES were of that extensive and sublime sort, as fully to entitle her *hic jacet* to the following noble epitaph, a little altered, from one of the British poets.

> "UNDERNEATH this marble hearse,
> Lies the subject of all verse.
> Custis' widow—great George's wife—
> Death! ere thou robb'st another life,
> Virtuous, fair, and good as SHE,
> Christ shall launch a dart at thee."

This fantastic whimsicality makes his biography hardly less delicious and hardly more veracious than Sterne's "Tristram Shandy." Having put Martha's epitaph right on top of her epithalamium, Weems parodies Ben Jonson's ancient verses on "Lady Pembroke" as ruthlessly as he fastened old anecdotes on Washington's life.

His eighth chapter begins with a long account of a bad dream that came to Washington's mother and foretold the beginning of the Revolution. Though a trifle out of place in time and importance, it is so exquisitely Weemsish that it is worth quoting in its entirety in order that a generation that knows not its Weems may realize upon what Washingtoniana our earlier generations were fed for nearly a hundred years:

WHEN a man begins to make a noise in the world, his relatives, (the Father, *sometimes*, but, always that tenderer parent, the *Mother*) are sure to recollect certain *mighty odd dreams*, which they had of him *when he was a child*. What rare dreams, for example, had the mothers of "Macedonia's madman, and the Swede," while pregnant with those butchers of the human race! Mrs. Washington also had her dream, which an excellent old Lady of Fredericksburg assured me she had often heard her relate with great satisfaction; and, for the last time, but a few weeks before her death.

"I DREAMT," said the Mother of Washington, "that I was sitting in the piazza of a large new house, into which we had but lately moved. George, at that time about five years old, was in the garden with his corn-stalk plough, busily running little furrows in the sand, in imitation of Negro Dick, a fine black boy, with whose ploughing George was so delighted that it was sometimes difficult to get him to his dinner. And so as I was sitting in the piazza at my work, I suddenly heard in my dream a kind of roaring noise on the *eastern* side of the house. On running out to see what was the matter, I beheld a dreadful sheet of fire bursting from the roof. The sight struck me with a horror which took away my strength, and threw me, almost senseless, to the ground. My husband and the servants, as I saw in my dream, soon came up; but, like myself, were so terrified at the sight, that they could make no attempt to extinguish the flames. In this most distressing state, the image of my little son came, I thought, to my mind more dear and tender than ever: and turning towards the garden where he was engaged with his little corn-stalk plough, I screamed out twice with all my might, *George! George!*—In a moment, as I thought, he threw down his mimic plough, and ran to me saying, *'High! Ma! what makes you call so angry! 'an't I a good boy—don't I always run to you soon as I hear you call?'* I could make no reply, but just threw up my arms towards the flame. He looked up and saw the house all on fire: but instead of bursting out a crying, as might have been expected from a child, he instantly *brightened* up, and seemed ready to fly to extinguish it. But first looking at me with great tenderness, he said, *'Oh, Ma! don't be afraid: God Almighty will help us, and we shall soon put it out.'*—His looks and words revived our spirits in so wonderful a manner, that we all instantly set about to assist him. A ladder was presently brought, on which, as I saw in my dream, he ran up with the nimbleness of a squirrel; and the servants supplied him with water, which he threw on the fire from an *American gourd*. But that growing weaker, the flame appeared to gain ground, breaking forth and roaring most dreadfully, which so frightened the servants, that many of them, like persons in despair, began to leave him. But he, still undaunted, continued to ply it with water, animating the servants at the same time, both by his word and actions. For a long time the contest appeared very doubtful: but at length a venerable old man, with a tall cap and an iron rod in his hand, like a lightning rod, reached out to him a curious little trough, like a *wooden shoe!* On receiving this, he redoubled his exertions, and soon extinguished the fire. Our joy on the occasion was unbounded. But he, on the contrary, showing no more of transport now than of terror before, looked rather sad at sight of the great harm that had been done. Then I saw in my dream that after some time spent as in deep thought, he called out with much joy, *'Well, Ma! now if you and the family will but consent, we can make a far better roof than this ever was; a roof of such a quality, that if well kept together,* it will last for ever; but if you take it apart, you will make the house ten thousand times worse than it was before.' "

THIS, though certainly a very curious dream, needs no Daniel to interpret it; especially if we take Mrs. Washington's *new house,* for the young Colony Government—the fire on its east side, for North's civil war—the gourd which Washington first employed, for the American 3 and 6 months inlistments—the old man with his cap and iron rod, for Doctor Franklin—the *shoe-like* vessel which he reached to Washington, for the Sabot or wooden-shoed nation, the French, whom Franklin courted a long time for America—and the new roof proposed by Washington, for a staunch honest Republic—that *"equal government,"* which, by guarding alike the welfare of all, ought by all to be so heartily beloved as to *endure for ever.*

But this is absolutely all that Weems tells of Washington's life between his wedding and his rebellion.

His next biographer, Sparks, spends half of one short chapter on Washington's activities between his marriage and his selection to command the Continental troops.

Such was the entire spirit and content of the Washington who was described to America for a century. It established him as an impersonal creature who did great things only.

Of late there has been an impatience to seek out the face behind the white mask, and the actual man is still in process of reconstruction from the fossil remains of him. Of these the ledgers are not the least valuable. From them one learns many facts not otherwise to be discovered concerning even his obscure political life.

There are only two of these ledgers, A and B. A carries him from 1750 to 1774. C, long believed lost in a fire at Alexandria with other precious documents, was found in 1927 by Eugene E. Prussing among the collections of Lloyd W. Smith.[1]

In these ledgers one happens on items of captivating homeliness. They would have small importance in any other man's biography, but are almost melodramatic when brought forward from the gloom of the Washington legend.

On May 4, 1758, is a hint of his dependence on Sally Fairfax:

"By Cash sent Mrs. Fairfax to Pay Miss Dent for making some Shirts for me,   £3: 12/"

On June 5:

"By do [i. e. Cash] paid for Liquor & in Recruitg   6/6"

There are constant entries of charities, which immortalize some gracious gesture of this generous man, often in the words: "By gave a Beggar," so much or so much.

"Oct. 17 1759   By a Begger   2/6
Mar 29 1760   By a Beggar   5
Apr 29 1760   By Cash given at the Charity Sermon   £1:9:10
May 18 1760   By a Begging woman   £1:1/3
June 22 1760   By Cash gave for the Sufferers
                    at Boston by Fire   12s."

Such entries are innumerable.

Since he spent so much time at the home of the Fairfaxes, he evidently tipped their servants as he tipped the servants he encountered on his ride to Boston. So we read:

"June 5 1758   By Mrs. Custis's Servants   12s.
Jan   7, 1766   By Colo Fairfax's Servants   22s. 6d.
Dec 26, 1766   By Colo. Fairfax's Servants   £1. 5. 0."

There are pleasant glimpses of him cheerfully going
his ways:

"May	29,	1760	By lost on the Race	3s.
"	"	"	Tickets for Ball	25s.
May	30,	"	By Treating the Ladies	4s.
June	10	"	By 6 packs Cards	7s. 6d.
			Lost at Ditto	7s. 6d.
Oct	8	"	By cards (loss)	30s.
			Coach hire	1s. 3d.
			Cards (loss)	10s.
			By Barber	2s. 6d.

In 1762 he enters a handsome total of disbursements to
the poor, and to his rivals across the table:

"Charity to Sundry^s at Differ^t times   £37: 9s 3d
Cards &c   £17 — —"

In the next year he writes down:

"April	20.	By my Mother	£15 — —
April	26	By Charity	12/ 6
May	3	Coffee	1s 3d
May	25	By Raffling for Glasses	20s
		Do. for Buckles	6s
Oct	25	By 2 Musick Books	15s
Nov	8	Cash for cards	£ 5
Dec	22	By my Mother	£19 — —"

In 1764 life still flows on, though it begins with heavy
losses—twenty-five dollars in one sitting, and five dollars
in another:

"Jan^y	5	By Cards	£5 — —
		By Cards	20s. —
Feb^y	13	By Cash for Cards	5s. —
	23	By Charity	10s.
Ap^l	25	By Raffling	30s
May	1	By Charity	20s

May 24	By Card Money	£5 — —
June 19	By Miss Wades . . making Shift for	
	Patcy Custis	16s
Oct 6	By Chesnuts	2s 6d.
Oct 16	By Dancing Master—Mackey for Child^n	£1. 0 0
Nov 1	By Childrens Books for J(acky) P. C.	5 shilling".

He records several Prizes in the York Lottery totalling
£16. 0. 0.

From 1767 one may cull:

	"May 6	By Cards (loss)	7s.
		Gave Mrs. Washington	24s.
	May 20	By Exp^s in seeing Slight of hand	
		performed	£1. 7s. 6d.
	June 7	To Ditto (cash) Won at Cards	7s 6d
	July 20	By Mrs. Washington in small money	4s. 0.
	Aug 26	By old Acct. for entertaining Horses	7s 6d
	Sept.	By Cards at different times	£2. 14. —
	Oct 9	To Do. won at a horse Race	3s 6.
	Sept 16	By Putting a Crystal in Mrs. P.	
		Custis's Watch	2s. 6d.
	Oct 9	By Mrs. Cleveland for her trouble	
		of keeping 9 H^e [horses] while	
		we were at the Springs in Aug^t	16s. 0.
	Nov 8	By Raffling for Necklace &ca	£1. 0. 0.
	Dec. 14	By Patcy Custis for Pocket money	12s. 0
	Dec 19	By Cash gave my Mother	£10. 0. 0
1768	May 5	By Club at Charltons	5s.
		Play Tickets	12s. 6.
	May 7	By Mrs. Dawson chances in	
		Raffling for her Coach—for	
		Colo. Lewis & myself	£2. 0. 0.
	Oct 25	By Cards (loss)	11s. 6d
	Nov 4	By Cards	£1. 5s. —
	Nov 5	By Cards	20s"

And so it goes on indefinitely not overlooking such bits as
1770, Feb. 5. "By a dog. (Spaniel) 1. 16. 0. Feb. 19. By

mend^g Coffee Pot 1s 6d." He lost £1. 4 "in raffling for Encyclopadia Britannica, which I did not win."

On Sept. 23, 1771, he enters his losses at cards at different times as £13. 4/3. He does not forget "By a hair Bag 5 shillings & hair Powder 3 shillings. By Oysters, 12 shillings."

His expenditures for liquors of all sorts make a majestic total. They include large and small payments ranging on up from the emergency purchase on March 5, 1767 of "1 Quart Whiskey 1s. 3d." to the buying of a "pipes" of wine. A pipe ranged from 110 gallons in the case of Madeira to 138 gallons in the case of port. A "butt" of wine was a somewhat similar measure often confounded with "pipe," but likewise varying in content according to the contents. In 1765 he paid out:

"Feb.   By Mr. Searle for a Pipe of Madeira   £29.   3s. –
  "   By Maynes of Lisbon for Wine   12.   7s. –
        By Mr. Searles Excha to A. Bacon
        for Pipe M: Wine   28. 12"

The next year he paid "for a But of Madeira Wine £37: 14s. 1."

On September 3, 1767, he paid Henry Hinton
                "for 1 Hhd Rum   £17. 2. 10"
In 1768 "for a Butt of Mª Wine   £37:6: 11"

Yet a statement was published in the newspapers during 1927 that two firechiefs, examining Mount Vernon to see how safe it was, reported that there was no wine cellar. This was used widely for a solemn rebuke to those who dared to hint that Washington ever bought liquor. He kept his immense stores, of course, in a separate building.

So much has been made of Washington's passion for exact accounting and the perfection of his bookkeeping that it is encouraging to fallible admirers to find that he was human in this respect also. He could and did make mistakes.

At the end of every year he totaled up on one page all the sums taken in, whether from tobacco, Burgess wages, house or farm rentals, and other sources of income, not neglecting an occasional winning at cards—for he was not even perfect as a gambler: he sometimes won.

On the opposite page he summed up the outgo of all sorts, and then struck a balance. It is delightful to find that his books never came out right. Some of his explanations are lovably ingenuous.

In 1764 he must indite this confession:

"By mistake in Count of the English Silvʳ last
    year   £15. 5. 10½"

In finishing his books for 1769 he must acknowledge a smart lapse of memory concerning his sister's husband:

"Dec 30   By Cash Paid Colo. Fieldˢ Lewis in May
           last & neglected to be charged before   £52. 16. 1½
           By Cash lost, stolen or paid away without
           charging   143. 15. 2"

This means that he had missed his calculation by nearly two hundred pounds.

A somber note is found in the dealings in slaves, their purchase, sale, and clothing, the care of their health and the help given them in bringing into the world the valuable merchandise of their offspring. Washington hated slavery for two reasons, the cruel indignity of it, and the inferiority of the labor it provided. But he kept slaves to his dying day.

Since slaves were slaves and had no rights, they had no right to run away. But they did and had to be brought back by anybody that met them. We find that the versatile Rev. Mr. Green, who was preacher and physician, could also pick up a penny for apprehending fugitive negroes:

"1761, March.   The Revd Mr Green.
         By paid for taking up one of my Runaway Negroes   £2."

There are many entries of this sort and the fee for taking up a fugitive was apparently fixed at two pounds.

It is harrowingly quaint to read in his cash book these four entries in succession:

"By Cards (loss)	15 shillings.
By 1 new whole Duty of Man	4s 6d.
By Charity	£1. 0. 0.
By Taking up Negroe Tom	2. 0. 0."

1764. Jan 23   Negroes bought at Publick Sale and for
         wch my Bond was taken payable 12th June next

Robin	£ 65
Charles	74
Terry	65
	——
	£204
Ben	£ 72
Lewis	36. 10
Sarah	20
	——
	£128. 10

The next page shows that three of these were bought for his friend, "J^n Robinson Esqr Speaker" of the Assembly, to whom he sold Charles and Terry for what they cost him, though he made a hundred percent profit on Lewis:

Lewis	£ 76
Charles	74
Terry	65
	——
	£215

In his separate accounts with individuals there is one with John Prescot, who shod the negroes and indentured servants:

1763,	Sept	14	By making Negroe Shoes viz	20 pr
		24	By Do Do	19
	Oct	4	By Do Do	23
		15	By Do Do	18

80 pr a 1/3 .. £5 – –

There were the doctors to be paid and Washington kept a physician on salary. There were epidemics of smallpox and other diseases, accidents, lightning strokes, and all manner of ills. Emergencies were met by special calls as on November 8, 1763, "By Negroe Doct^r 10 shillings."

The breeding of slaves was in the beginnings of what it became later, one of the chief industries of Virginia. The services of a midwife were in frequent demand. She was usually the wife of Bishop, the old soldier whom the dying Braddock had turned over to Washington.

It is interesting to note that Washington increased his wages from time to time. Bishop was acquired in 1755. In 1762, under the page given over to him, is the entry, "By 1 Years Wages, £10." Two years later he has been raised to £15. In 1770 he is paid £25.

His wife added to the family wealth by hurrying to the aid of negro women in travail, at half a pound per visit. Washington writes on Bishop's page in 1776:

			"By your Wife's bringing Betty to Bed—	10s.
1767	July	8	By Thos Bishops wife bring^g Kate to Bed	10s
	July	31	By Susanne Bishop deliv^g Sue	10s
1769			By Susanna Bishop deliv^g Muddy hole	
			Kate and Catherine	10s each."

Muddy Hole was the name of one of the plantations.

In 1770 Mrs. Bishop is credited with the following on her husband's page:

> "By yr Wifes bringing Lame Alce to Bed   10s
> By your Wifes delivering Negro Moll   10
> By your Wifes delivg Betty at ye Ferry   10
> By your Wifes delivering House Alce   10"

It is pitiful to observe that these poor bondwomen did not even have last names. They were labelled like cattle by their pastures or some deformity, "Muddy Hole Kate, Lame Alice, House Alice" (who worked in the house).

Few of them had husbands and Haworth [2] has written that Washington apparently never cared whether they had or not. He was a citizen of his time and his environment.

Paul Haworth says, "If our Farmer took any special pains to develop the mental and moral nature of 'My People,' as he usually called his slaves, I have found no record of it. Nor is there any evidence that their sexual relations were other than promiscuous—if they so desired. Marriage had no legal basis among the slaves. . . . A friendly Polish poet who visited Mount Vernon in 1798 was shocked by the poor quarters and rough food provided for them."

Washington's doctor bills are no inconsiderable item. On one page he lumps them together as follows for the year 1761, adding the account of his beloved and ill-fated step-daughter, "Patcy":

"1761	Mar	5	Jas Craik pr Acct	£ 8. 11. 10
	May	1	Laurie a years Wgs	15 — —
	Aug		Doctr Hamilton fr Advce	2. 3. —
	Ditto		Ditto for Prescription	2. 3.
Do	Octr		Ditto for 3 Visits & ca	2. 16.
	Novr	14	Doctor Hay visits and attendance	15. — —
	Do	17	Dr Small (?) Ditto Ditto	20 — —

£65. 13. 10

Ditto for Patcy Custis

              to Dr. Hamilton   £10 — —

              to Doct^r Hay   3

              Doct^r Small 2 V^{ts}   6

                                                  ————

                                                  £19"

It will be seen how hard a year he had when his physicians'
fees were over 80 pounds.

His dealings with his neighbors, George William Fairfax and his wife, Sally, contain odd domestic touches: "To
6 best Dutch Blankets lent" and on the opposite page "By 6
best Dutch Blankets returned."

"By 1 Barrel of Pickled Porke   3. 5. 0.

By 1 Barrel—or small Cask of Porter   3. 5. 3

By 1 Dozen White Earthen Chamber Pots   15. 0."

The ledger contains, of course, formidable entries of all
sorts of dealings in merchandise, tobacco, land, equipment,
borrowings and lendings.

The accounts of his management of the estates of each of
the Custis children are minutely handled. His business
dealings with his mother are as rigidly recorded.

Ledger B carries Washington on beyond and contains
much the same record of everything big and little from buying land to tossing shillings to beggars, from losing more
than he won at cards to dealings in slaves, tobacco, rum, land
and hope.

All the entries are made carefully in the large script of
his huge but exquisite pen.

VI

HIS DAILY AUTOBIOGRAPHY

"I HAVE never said anything or written anything that I cared to recall, nor ever done anything that I regretted."

So Washington once said to King Louis Philippe, then an exile in this country. Or so King Louis Philippe told his son, the Duc d'Aumale. Or so the Duc told Chauncey M. Depew; who told Norman Hapgood,[1] who tells it in his life of Washington.

Few verbal quotations from Washington's lips have come down in so straight and so responsible a line. And, true or not, this one has the support of Washington's own life and writings, which are frank and voluminous past all belief, past all counting and all calculating.

If justification were needed for discovering and disclosing as much as possible about the life and character of so great a man, Washington himself has given it in the care he took to record and to preserve his thoughts and deeds.

Many of his writings were burned—some intentionally, by others; a warehouse in Alexandria where masses of documents were stored caught fire; during the Civil War invaluable manuscripts of unimaginable importance were lost in the endeavor to save them or in the ravages of war; and the first possessors of his autographs gave them away wantonly as souvenirs, going so far as to rip his diaries apart and distribute pages and sections of them here and there, with the result that there are wide gaps in the series.

Even after these disasters, there remains a mass of his

autographs greater perhaps than exists from the hand of any other figure in history.[2]

Yet, by a perversion of fate, it was possible until recently even for historians of such research as McMaster [3] to plead that Washington was unknown as a man.

Yet all the while the only reason why he has not been as well known as any other public character has been that so many people have not wanted to know him, or let him be known.

From the first, there has been a high-minded conspiracy to suppress the facts about him on the plea that he should be kept mysterious and left in the clouds to supply a national need for somebody to revere.

The value of a reverence buttressed by ignorance is open to question. One might go farther and say that there is no sane or scientific reason for the desire to revere any human being.

Washington, alive, was as much embarrassed and terrified by the adulation he received from certain elements as he was infuriated by the contempt and ridicule he received from others. If his great eagerness to provide materials for a true history of himself had been respected, he would have been revealed always as what he was, in no sense a deity, but a remarkably various and eager-living man to whom nothing human was alien, and who, through opportunity and willingness to work for what he thought ideal, helped to accomplish some of the most important and far-reaching of human achievements.

He could distort or conceal the truth when it served a money-making or a military purpose, but, to a remarkable degree, he was without hypocrisy, fanaticism, or ethereal ideals.

Beyond almost all other historical characters he was capable of saying:

"I have never said anything or written anything that I cared to recall, nor ever done anything that I regretted."

And this was because he loved the world and the things of the world, the manure as well as the flowers, the breeding of animals and crops, the gamble of horse-race and card game, as well as the conquest of the wilderness and the clash of armies; the vivacity of beautiful women dancing and well-dressed men paying courtesy to one another, as well as he loved freedom and prosperity and etiquette among nations.

So he wrote down with great care just what the weather was, counted the seeds he planted and what came of them, told who came to dinner and exactly what happened to just what fox he chased, what work his slaves did, and what they neglected, just how much everything cost, how much he lost and how much he won.

He did not pretend to be a better marksman than he was, or a better farmer or a better citizen.

He wrote down when he went to church and who came to dinner after, but he never mentioned the topic of the sermon, or its influence on making him repent his sins. If he ever prayed, he never said so. One searches his diaries in vain for those soul-searchings and grovellings and condemnations of secret sins that fill so many other journals.

He says nothing of either repenting or sinning, and the mystery of that silence is amply explained by his alleged statement to Louis Phillipe, which, in other words, might be translated:

"I have never repented any sins because I have committed no sins."

That is magnificent candor. It would amount to unbearable self-glorification but for his evident opinion that he simply did what was natural to him among his neighbors in the times and conditions he was born to; and that that was no sin.

He loved to ride his goose-quill across the paper as indefatigably as he rode his horse across the hills. When the non-importation agreements were made, he saw to it that paper was not included in the boycott, for what could he have done without paper?

Nearly every day, even in his illnesses, he sharpened the tip of a goose feather and followed it for hours. There is a largeness about his writing even when his space was confined.

He differed in this from Thomas Jefferson, who whittled his quill so fine and wrote so minutely that a microscope is necessary now to decipher many of his pages. But profuse as he was with his ink, he never built up the pyramid of writings that Washington left.

No man except himself, living or dead, ever read all of Washington's writings, extant or lost. Nobody living has ever even counted them, and the estimate of their number ranges from 26,000 to 40,000 [4]—a difference of 14,000 manuscripts, in itself an astounding heritage.

Nobody knows how many more are in private hands or lying unknown in old bundles, old trunks, or unvisited attics. They keep turning up in the most surprising places with the most upsetting results.

It was not until 1877 that his letters to Sally Fairfax came to light when her effects were sent from England, where she had died long ago.[5] They had been written a century and a score of years before and disclosed, seventy-eight years after his death, that he had made a passionate declaration of hopeless and forbidden love to his best friend's wife after he had plighted his troth with the woman who became his own wife.

They altered the whole conception of the almost petrified

Washington so amazingly that they were promptly smothered and a violent attempt made to forget them.

What further letters may appear with what further confusion cannot be foretold. It is known that many letters are held in seclusion by their owners, and it is reiterated that some have been burned on the pretext of saving Washington's reputation.

When Mr. William L. Clements [6] bought the papers of the English general, Clinton, a number of intercepted letters of Washington's were found.

Hardly a month passes that some new document is not turned up. In the spring of 1927 three of his letters appeared in Richmond, having been found in a Virginia garret. They are written in his own unmistakable hand on paper bearing his own water-mark. Two of them are authenticated by the duplicates in his own copy-book; the third carries on the correspondence, which concerned a "thrashing machine" in which he was interested because he hoped it would prove slave-proof.

The soul back of them is also Washington's, because of the farmer mind revealed, the great courtesy to a stranger, his anxiety lest the inventor think his motives improper, and the graciousness with which Washington wishes him success.

Yet so numerous are Washington manuscripts that when these three perfect specimens were offered to a collector, he refused to pay a thousand dollars for them, though he had just paid fifty thousand dollars for one brief letter from Button Gwinett, that signer of the Declaration of Independence who had been inspired to die shortly after affixing his signature, thus reaching an almost unique immortality among collectors.

It is a tribute to Washington's fame that his almost infinite autographs should have any commercial value whatever.

None of them are so revelatory of his character and yet so unsatisfactory as his Diaries, because, disclosing so much, they suggest so much more that it seems almost impossible he should have stopped where he did.

They are the iconoclasm for his own image, and the recent publication of as many of them as could be recovered has done more than anything else to bring Washington back to the earth he once walked with feet of clay.

Every night after a hard day of riding about his plantations in all weathers, and dining with copious toasts to all the guests (and there were nearly always guests), or playing cards, the tall man bent over a table between two candles and wrote in tiny little books the records of his activities.

First he sharpened his quill and wrote with great care. "Where & how—my time is—Spent." His log-book was a brief and hasty chronicle with a singular lack of comment on personalities, or events. Of the famous and picturesque personages he met, he gave never a line of description. After some of the greatest days in his own history, and the world's, he neglected to mention anything except where he had dined.

Of introspection he betrayed never a hint. A more emotionless diary was probably never written. His only warmth was shown in the pages over which he wrote at the top, "Acc^t of the Weather—in Feb^y" or whatever the month might be. Here it singularly pleased him to be minute, enthusiastic and as near to poetic as he ever came. Except for the sufferings of his soldiers, his highest eloquence was reserved for the weather.

Yet in February, 1767, he wonders if the weather, of which he has kept such faithful record, has any rules after all:

Where & how—my time is—Spent

Septr. 11th. Reach'd my Mothers to
Dinner after Baiting at Peytons

12. Rid above the Plant at the Wt.
House & then went to the Quarter and rid all over that &
return'd to Dinner Coll. Lewis &
my Brors. Charles being there
—his their Qr. in nears weins Sa-
to Fredg.

13. Return'd to my Mothers to
Breakfast and Survey'd the
Fields before Dinner & return'd
to Town afterwards.—

14: Rid with Coll. Lewis to his Mill
before Dinner—after it went
over to my Mothers & stay'd all
Night.—

15 Set of home—Din'd in Dam-
fries and got up by Sun set

16. Rid by the Ferry Plantation
to the Mill—dyed washington &
return'd from Dr. Cracks this Evening

17. Rid to the Mill—from thence to
Dog Run and Muddy hole before
Dinner.—After Dinner Rid into
the Neck.—

18. Went up to Court.—Din'd at
arrells and Lodg'd at Mr. Rt. hosts

19. Went to Court again—Din'd at
arrells & come home in the after
noon—found young Mr. Warmely
here

20. Went with Mr. Warmley to Bela
on a Mornge. Visit & return'd to Din-

Where & how — my time is — Spent

21. Set out with Mr. Wormeley for the Annapolis Races: — Din'd at Mr. Will. Digges's & Lodg'd at Mr. Ignat'. Digges. —

22. Din'd at Mr. Sam Galloway's & Lodged with Mr. Boucher in Annap.

23. Dined with Mr. Loyd Dulany & spent the Evening at the Coffee H.

24. Dined with the Govr. and went to the Play & Ball afterwards.

25. Dined at Doct. Steuards and went to the Play and Ball afterwards.

26. Dined at Mr. Ridouts and went to the Play after it. —

27. Dined at Mr. Carrolls and went to the Ball. —

28. Dined at Mr. Bouchers and went from thence to the Play and afterwards to the Coffee H.

29. Dined with Maj'r. Jenifer and Supp'd at Dan'l. Dulany Esq'rs.

30. Left Annapolis, & Din'd and Supp'd with Mr. Sam'l Galloway.

WASHINGTON'S DIARY.

"Feb. 26 Brisk wind from the Southward. Clear, warm and pleasant. According to Colo. West ye greatest part of the next Moon should be as this day i,e, the same kind of weather that happens upon thursday before the change will continue through ye course of the next Moon, at least the first and 2d quarter of it. quere—is not this an old woman's story."

In July, 1763. one encounters nothing more picturesque than:

"19-20   Cut'g Hay at Hell hole.
21-22   Mak'g Do. Rainy.
23   People doing Jobs."

That was about all there was to record in those years. The war was over. England had hardly begun to bestir herself about those activities which were to stir the colonists to astounding impatiences and unheard-of pretensions. Virginians were simply "People doing Jobs."

All that the word "Washington" now means to the world was at this time hardly so much as begun, not conceived, least of all by him. As a man he was full-grown and hearty and getting rich, but as a patriot he was hardly yet even an embryo in the womb of time.

While his own diaries contain many passages of startling frankness and abound in blunt words not now considered printable, the little books in which they are written could not be sent through the mails at all, even with the prestige of Washington's glory back of them. The publisher who would reproduce one of them in full would doubtless be arrested.

This is a typical instance of the folly of prudery, and a fine test of hypocrisy. Washington is sacred, yet what was good enough for Washington may not even be mentioned nowadays. The books that were distributed everywhere in colonial America and were read by all our revered forefathers and their children are considered unfit for the eyes of this generation, which is at the same time much abused for its laxity.

Many of Franklin's utterances are too high for the modern nostril. The almanacs used by Washington abound in passages that would cause many of his worshippers to shriek with horror.

The booklets were printed in the little town of Williamsburg, and sold in such vast numbers that they undoubtedly fell into the hands of everybody. The broad jokes doubtless set the families to guffawing, and must have been popular or they would not have been so commonplace.

Washington had a love of laughter and could roar as heartily as the next one. Chief Justice Marshall describes him going into paroxysms over the appearance of two men in misfit garments, and it is said that he once rolled on the ground in an agony of laughter.

One can well imagine him, therefore, as he seated himself in his room to make his careful chronicle of the day's weather and his fox-hunts, and house-guests, pausing to read some of the spicy remarks sprinkled among the weather forecasts.

Out of the little volumes that Washington decorated with his only autobiography, a few passages may be taken from their nestling places in print alongside his steel-plate script.

Here is one for the month of March, 1771:

"Now the spring approaches, which will make the blood be stirring: but if thou canst not live honestly, take a wife of thy own, for there is never anything got by wenching, but duels, ———, and ———. And mistresses, like green pease, at first coming, are only had by the rich, but afterwards they come to everybody; and being once common, like butchers meat in dog days, in a little time they stink abominably . . .

"A young maid must make a puppy of her sweetheart now and then or love will be too serious."

For August the cynicism continues:

"Some simple people may be inveigled to venture at the fatal game *for better for worse;* but let them have a care, for a woman and a wet eel have both slippery tails."

Running down the margins of the October calendar is this:

"He that weds an old hag that had three men before,
Has one hell on earth, and another in store."

For the same month there is an unprintable warning to maidens, and this sad reflection:

"How many are overcome by the temptations of the petticoat!"

At the back of each almanac, a long astronomical treatise, then a list of "Family Receipts for the Palsy, the Piles, the Epilepsy, the Bloody Flux, the Whooping Cough, the Rotten Quinsy, and to provoke the Menses, a deobstruent electuary."

For those days when water was so perilous, a device is given:

"To quench thirst, where drink is improper.

"Pour vinegar into the palms of the hands, and snuff it up the nostrils, and wash the mouth with the same."

Then follow half a dozen pages of short stories, most of them mildly indecent. Among the tamer ones are these:

"A Lady said she had discovered that there were three sexes, and being desired to inform the company how she made it out, said, there are the men, the women, and the fribbles."

The word "fribble" was slang for something like flapper or her male friend. It is allied to "frivol" and was much in vogue during the latter part of the eighteenth century.

Did Washington smile as he read the story of Henry IV

of France and his rebuke to the Abbot who reproached him for his love of other women beside the Queen?

According to the Almanac, the Abbot loved roast partridges inordinately: so the King had him imprisoned and fed him nothing but partridges. The Abbot protested. The King answered:

"You told me that was the diet you loved above anything in the world. It is true, I do so, says the Abbot, but to be always fed with partridge, that makes me loath it, and desire other diet. Very well, replied the King, it is just so with me, my Lord, I love my Queen above all women in the world; but, my Lord, always the Queen, always the Queen—"

Even religion was not spared in these rough-spoken pages, and one might wonder what Washington thought of this:

"The Armenians practice frequent fasting, as the most effectual means of obtaining paradise; upon which Schach Abbas said they were the only besiegers in the world who thought to carry a place by starving themselves."

In the following year, and all the years, the tone still mocks all solemnities:

"He that hath a Wagtail to his Wife, to trust her to walk abroad with a Friend on the Holidays is all one as to trust his Home in the Throat of a Lion. . . . He that loseth such a Wife, and Sixpence, hath some Loss by the Money."

"Some clergymen spend one Hour of the Week in a Pulpit and the rest in a Tavern, and so undo a good Sermon by an ill Example."

Printed at the back of the Virginia Almanack for 1771, Washington found in the "List of Members of His Majesty's Council and Representatives," these names: "from Fairfax, George Washington & John West."

But the next year the list was omitted.

If the modern reader were as much of a "fribble" as the editors of those Almanacs, he might pose these riddles:

The reverend forefathers and foremothers of the Republic were raised upon reading matter far more cynical and far more ribald than anything permissible or accessible to their degenerate and notoriously loose descendants. Is the abuse of our generation a slander, or does coarse literary fare make for purity of mind? If the children who were reared on obscenity grew up strong enough to fight for a new freedom and build a republic in a wilderness, is it wise to feed the children of our time on sterilized, censored, and predigested fare? In other words, is whole-wheat bread more nourishing than over-refined soda biscuits?

Among the most tantalizing features of Washington's Diaries are the unexplained initials, numbers, dots and vertical lines scored against certain dates and names.

Mr. Woodward,[7] in his biography, called attention to these "cryptic symbols," which "in the year 1771 Washington began to make . . . evidently entries in cipher."

He quoted Mr. John C. Fitzpatrick's letter to him assuming them to be "merely farm memoranda of some kind or another . . . of relatively slight importance, as by comparison of these symbols with the diary entries for the days on which they are marked, nothing is noted which would give us the faintest clue for the reason of the markings. They could, of course, have been a record of card games, but for the fact that oftentimes the entries are on days that Washington was not at Mount Vernon. It is a puzzle, but I take it to be so insignificant a one that there is no need of getting excited about it, especially as it can never be deciphered."

Mr. Woodward protested that he was "not the least bit excited about it," but could not agree that the symbols were either insignificant or agricultural. He remarked that

Washington was voluminous in his writings about farm operations, and invariably recorded his card games in his account books.

He declared that "the symbols, if ever solved, will reveal important information . . . men and women use symbols in their diaries only for the purpose of recording secrets of an important and highly personal nature."

In *Scribner's Magazine* for April, 1926, Mr. Fitzpatrick discussed the subject further:

"In some of the later diaries, after Washington's retirement from the presidency, there is an untranslatable record on the margins of the printed almanac page in which the diary was entered. It consists of dots and sometimes tally strokes and minute circles, followed by the names of various female slaves, or vice versa.

"This, because it cannot now be explained, has been viewed with suspicion; but the appearance and grouping of these marks strongly suggests some plantation-work record, while the number of them, in any given period, make it physically impossible to sustain an immoral inference."

The letter "A" appears frequently opposite various dates. This letter, at least, Mr. Fitzpatrick assumes to be the name of the carpenter, John Askew, who gave Washington much trouble.

Instances of puzzling initials are to be found in the diary for 1771, where the following letters are set against the dates indicated:

"Feb. 20 . . S, March 26 A, April 12 a, April 25 a, May 16 M, June 4 A, June 9 A, June 19 A, June 23 A, June 29 A, July 20 A."

Just because his heroism and the results of his life are so awe-inspiring, there is, for certain readers at least, a kind of refreshment in catching him recording his petty moods and his matter-of-fact concerns with a bluntness that almost seems to beseech us not to deny him the privileges of having his unheroic hours.

No farmer could be plainer. In the words of Eugene E. Prussing [8] he was "the busiest and biggest man in Virginia just before the Revolution. He took off his coat when need be and pitched hay with his negro slaves, or helped to repair the broken-down carriage of a wayfarer.

"He mixed manure with his own hands, planted gardens to please his wife, and swam regularly in the Potomac because plumbing was unknown."

In January, 1768, he began an astonishing record of his variety of activities and interests, hunting, surveying, fishing, playing cards, going to church, entertaining guests, incessantly visiting Sally Fairfax and her husband at Belvoir or being visited by them at Mount Vernon.

All the colonies were flaming with resistance to the parliament. Women were combining as "Daughters of Liberty." The Virginia Assembly was astir with ominous excitement, but Washington tells only where he ate, and that he went to the theatre and to church, followed the hounds, or attended to his multifarious businesses.

"6. Doeg Run People finishd grubbing ye Swamp they were in and proceeded to another adjacent.

"12. Threshing Wheat at all Plantations. Ground being too hard froze to Grub to any advantage.

"16. Finishd my Smith's Shop—that is the Carpenters work of it.

"18. Carpenters went to Saw Plank at Doeg Run for finishing the Barn there.

"18. Will put new girders into my Mill where they had Sunk.

"26. Laid of a Road from Mt. Vernon to the Lain by Mr. Manley's.

"March 3d. Deliver'd a Load of 508 Bushels of Muddy hole Wheat to Mr. Kirk's ship and my Schooner returnd

"April 12. White fish began to Run, catching 60 or 70 at a Haul with some Her[rin]g.

"June 5. The Maryland hound Bitch lady took Forrester and was also servd by Captn, and refusd the Dogs on the 11th.

"22. Musick was also in heat and servd promiscuously by all the Dogs, intending to drown her Puppys.

"25. Went to Alexandria and bought a Bricklayer from Mr. Piper and returnd to Dinner. In the afternoon Mr. R. Alexander came.

"August 24. Imbarkd on board my Schooner for Nomony. Lay of Captn. Laidler's.

"Sept. 8. Went to a Ball in Alexandria.

"9. Proceeded to the Meeting of our vestry at the New Church and lodgd at Captn. Edwd. Payne's.

"20. Colo. Burwell, &ca. went away to Belvoir; and (I with) Mrs. Washington and ye two childn. went up to Alexandria to see the Inconstant, or Way to Win him Acted.

"21. Stayd in Town all day and saw the Tragedy of Douglas Playd."

The concluding entry is:

"13th. Killd Hogs."

England was boiling with the expulsion and re-expulsion of John Wilkes from the House of Commons, and his re-election and re-reelection, and fourth election in spite of a conviction for libel. The Junius Letters were the mystery of the day. James Otis, the father of the Revolution, went insane. The colonies were reeling toward the end of all loyalty. Washington "Killd Hogs."

Incessantly the diary runs on the even tenor of its way. In January, 1769, as so often:

"2. Went to Colo. Fairfax's with the Family and stayd all Night.

"6. The two Colo. Fairfax's and Mrs. Fairfax and Dr. Rumney dind here and spent the Evening.

"12. Went out in the Morng. with the Hounds in order to meet Colo. Fairfax, but did not. In Hell hole started a fox and after an hours chase run him into a hole and left him. In ye afternoon went to Alex. to ye Monthly Ball.

"16. Went a ducking in the forenoon—otherwise at home all day. In the afternoon Mr. B. Fairfax came here.

"10. A very spewing frost among Wheat, particularly in ye little field at Doeg Run. Note the consequence of this.

"22. The hound bitch Musick got out of her confinement and was lind by Pilot.

"26. She was lined by Mr. Fairfax's Hound Rockwood.

"Feb. 3. Went a Gunning up the Creek. Killd 7 Ducks.

"16. At home all day, Joshua Evans, who came here last Night, put an Iron Ring upon Patcy (for Fits) and went away after Breakfast.

"18. Went a hunting with Doctr. Rumney. Started a fox, or rather 2 or 3, and catchd none. Dogs mostly got after Deer and never joind."

And thus he goes on and on, registering only the least momentous happenings of a period when nearly every day marked an epoch in the advance of his people and himself. The conclusion is hardly to be escaped that one of the reasons he did not write history was that he did not know it was being made, and least of all that he would soon be summoned to make it and himself immortal.

VII

HE FIGHTS THE SOIL

IN agriculture, as in the military and political and other fields, Washington had the strange luck to build out of a few brilliant strokes and a majority of defeats a lofty fame as a triumphant success.

Indomitable earnestness and his persistent recovery from persistent defeat make in themselves a kind of glory.

He has been the subject of unbounded praise as a farmer, as "the Farmer," yet his own secretary, Lear, said that he could not have made his farm pay expenses but for his sales of land. But he loved to farm and cherished an undying illusion of success. He wrote of Mount Vernon:

"No estate in United America is more pleasantly situated than this. It lies in a high, dry, and healthy country, 300 miles by water from the sea . . . on one of the finest rivers in the world. Its margin is washed by more than ten miles of tide water; from the beds of which and the innumerable coves, inlets, and small marshes, with which it abounds, an inexhaustible fund of rich mud may be drawn as a manure. . . . The soil of the tract . . . is a good loam. This river . . . is well supplied with various kinds of fish at all seasons of the year . . . the whole shore, in short, is one entire fishery." [1]

In this Paul Haworth bluntly contradicts him:

"Only ignorance of what good land really is, or an owner's blind pride in his own estate, can justify the phrase 'a good loam' . . . To an observer brought up on a farm of the rich Middle West, Mount Vernon, except for a few scattered fields, seems extremely poor land. For farming

79

purposes most of it would be high at thirty dollars an acre. Much of it is so broken by steep hills and deep ravines as scarcely to be tillable at all." [2]

He points out that while Washington had a lot of land, little of it was better than mediocre; much of it was uncleared, and the best of it was "hopelessly distant from a market." It was so scattered that he could not look after it in person, must rent, trust to a manager, or let it lie idle. Even Mount Vernon was really far from a good market, with cost of transportation forbiddingly high. Finally his labor was expensive and not very productive, even though he fed the slaves pork and corn and herring.

As for Washington's boast that his farm was healthy, Professor Haworth "must take exception . . . the tidal marshes breed a variety of mosquito capable of biting through armor plate and of infecting the devil himself with malaria . . . a large part of the population, both white and black, suffered every August and September from chills and fever. The master himself was not exempt."

Tobacco was his mainstay and he "made" over 34,000 pounds of it in 1759; the next year 65,000; in 1763, 89,000, and never again so much. Two years later the crop fell to hardly more than half of the 1765 output. In 1773 he produced only 5,000 pounds, and after that hardly enough to consider.

His tobacco, for all his toil and care, was of inferior grade and did not bring the best prices, for which he naturally blamed his agents.

He began to feel himself a slave to tobacco and to his slaves, and wished to emancipate himself from his slaves and from the weed before he developed his wish to free himself from England.

He tried corn later, but could not exceed fifteen bushels per acre against the hundred that farmers in good corn regions now expect. He went on raising it to feed to his slaves and his swine.

As a by-product he used his Indian-corn and rye for distilling whiskey. Finally he had to buy corn from outside. Eventually he devoted himself to cattle and hay.

It was not for lack of earnestness that Washington failed. He bought all the books he could import, made notes and experiments. He subscribed to *Young's Annals* for which William Pitt wrote on storing turnips and deep plowing, and George III also under a pen name. It was this same Young that Washington corresponded with earnestly in later years.

That tireless pen of his, which plodded so doggedly after so much dull ink, did not recoil from making lengthy abstracts of the agricultural works of Tull, Duhamel, Horne, and Young.

His eagerness to conquer the soil was pathetic. Agriculture as a science was almost as well throttled by prejudice and tradition as the other sciences, which were just beginning to wake from ages of stupor and try the effects of experiment, observation, and the collection of facts.

Washington was a scientist at heart in so far as honest observation and indefatigable experiment are concerned.

Some of his most acute problems would puzzle no country boy today, says Haworth.[3] But somebody had to learn.

He spent much thought upon scatological problems and his diary is adorned with such bucolic passages as this: (April 14, 1760)

"Mix'd my Composts in a box with ten Apartments in the following manner, viz: in No 1 is three pecks of the Earth brought from below the Hill out of the 46 Acre Field without any mixture. . . . 4. Has a Peck of Horse Dung: 5 Has mud taken out of the Creek; 6, Has Cow Dung; 7. Marle from the Gullys on the Hill side, wch. seemd to be purer than the other; 8. Sheep Dung;

9. Black Mould taken out of the Pocoson on the Creek side; 10. Clay got just below the Garden." [4]

In each division he planted 3 grains each of wheat, oats and barley, "and of equal depth (done by a machine made for the purpose.)" Two or three hours later "I waterd them all equally alike."

This is far from the marble Washington of legend, this dirty farmer jumbling such stuff together in a cloth and combining a mixture as loathsome as the medicines of an ancient physician.

On the following May day, he observed the results and solemnly set them down with the meekness of a modern scientist:

"The Ground was so hard bakd by the drying winds when I came home that it was difficult to say which Nos. lookd most thriving. However in

No. 1 there was nothing come up;
      2 . . . . 2 Oats . . . . 1 barley;
      3 . . . . 1 Oat . . . . 2 barley;
      4 . . . . 1 Oat;
      5 . . . . 1 Wheat 2 Oats;
      6 . . . . 1 Do.   3 Do. . . . . 1 Do.
      7 . . . . 1 Do.   2 Do. . . . . 2 Do.
      8 . . . . 1 Do.   1 Do.
      9 . . . . 2 Do.   3 Do. . . . . 2 Do.
     10 . . . . 1 Do.

"The two Grains in No. 8 were I think rather the strongest, but upon the whole No. 9 was the best."

Counting those few seed was as nothing to one of the tasks he set himself later, when he computed the number of various seeds in a pound, and how much of each would be needed per acre. He "ascertained" that there were 71,000 seeds of red clover in a pound; 298,000 timothy seeds, and 13,410, ooo in a bushel; 2,300 black-eyed peas, and 8,925 barley.[5]

As Haworth says, "The spectacle . . . is ridiculous or sublime, according to the viewpoint!" [6]

He neglected nothing. Like Thomas Jefferson, he invented a plow "and found She answerd very well." He imported a plow, bought a stump-puller, investigated threshing-machines, and a horse-power dredge to lift river mud as a fertilizer.

He ran three mills and turned streams aside for their benefit. He was proud of his three grades of flour, and boasted that none better was made. He writes such commercial letters as this:

"Inclosd you have Invoice of 26 Barrl of Biscuit stuff . . . Please to let me know what you think my best Superfine Flour would sell at in Norfolk." [7]

He was a magnificent horseman, a devoted horsebreeder, and a breaker of horses. From the time when, as a boy, he killed a colt by breaking its heart first he was a superb rider, to his latest years when he was somewhat crippled from a horse that bolted and threw him before he was in the saddle.

He was fond of stallions, and made some money renting them out, his name often appearing in advertisements of such services. He guaranteed foal. At one time he had as many as 130 horses on his farms.

When the ordinary horses were worn out, he had his farmer dispose of them "as you judge best for my interest." His favorite horses he kept till they died of old age.

He claimed to be the first American to raise mules.

He raised also hogs, chickens, turkeys, swans, ducks, geese, pheasants, always experimenting with methods of breeding them, feeding them, and even killing them to the best advantage.

His interest in fruits and flowers, trees and vegetables, was keen. He took the same interest in landscape-gardening that he did in interior decorating, though his ideas of art were chiefly displayed in a love of splendor and a desire to be in style.

Of course he raised sheep, and did better with them than most of his neighbors. He had 600 of them at one time. He had only fair success with cattle and reached the usual goal of gentlemen farmers, for he wrote:

"It is almost beyond belief, that from 101 Cows actually reported on a late enumeration of the Cattle, that I am obliged to buy butter for the use of my family."

His slaves were an eternal annoyance to him because of their natural lack of interest in their work. He was accused, and credited, with being very harsh with them, feeding them little and overworking them, but in a contract made with an overseer, Nelson Kelly, he included not only pledges to "beat the apples into cyder" and "count his ground for both Corn and Tobacco with the greatest care and exactness" but also to "take all necessary and proper care of the negroes committed to his management, treating them with humanity and tenderness when sick, and preventing them when well, from running about and visiting without his consent." [8]

Still, his slaves were constantly running away, and he had to pay for their recapture. One of them was so ugly that Washington sent him to the West Indies to be sold for a hogshead of rum and some sweetmeats.

His white servants also ran away and cost him money for advertisements.

Bad weather and the freakishness of his crops spared him no more than less favored sons of heaven. His diaries and letters are full of bad news, and ruination taking place before his eyes, as in the following all too typical entry in his Diary for 1768:

"June 1st. Upon looking over my Wheat I found all those places which had been injurd by the March frosts extreamly thin, low and backward, having branched but little, and looking puny. Indeed, in many places the Ground was entirely naked; and where it was not, there was but too much cause to apprehend that the Wheat would be choked with Weeds. . . .

"It was also remarkable that the Red straw Wheat had a great number of Smutty or blasted heads in the same manner it had last year, when they did put out."

And incessantly there came also from his tenants and managers on distant farms of his or his wards', evil tidings such as Job received serially. The following is one of many:

"Sir: The last time I Rote to you I acquainted you with the misfortain of our Crops Being drounded & overdone with the wet and now it is ass Bad the other way we have had no Rain Sence to do any Service to the Corn or tobacco & it Burns up for being over done with the wet before it Cannot stand the drouth now the Corn Cannot Shoot out nor fill the tobacco the Roots of it was So mutch Sobd and overdone with the Rain before that the drouth Burns it up at the Bottom & fires at Sutch a rate that I Can Scarsly tel what to do with it and more particular on the Leavel Stiff Land wheare the foundation would not let the water Sink from it for Sum time it is not Quite so bad on the light or hilley Land. if providence pleases to Send us a good Rain in a little time I hope it will make a great alteration in our Crops for the Better.

"Sir the young negro fellow will Shag who formerly lived at old Quarter and ass he was allways Runaway I moved him down heir to Settle theis places and thought he might be better but he Runaway Sum time in June went to Yorke and past for a free man By the name of will Jones but at last was taken up and put in prison. . . ." [9]

But enough of such woes. The final comment on Washington's success as a farmer is that in later years he tried to rent all his lands, retaining (as he wrote to Arthur Young) only "the mansion house farm for my own residence, occupation and amusement in agriculture." [10]

It is all too evident that the soil gave him more occupation than amusement. The profit was minus.

For one thing, the soil was new, the native crops were new, and the European mind had to adapt itself slowly and expensively to the new world.

Practically every plant and domestic animal now common to America was introduced before the Revolution in spite of the trying conditions imposed by land that could be got for almost nothing and labor that could hardly be got at all. In Virginia workmen were so scarce that they had to be stolen from Africa, and kidnapped, deported, or purchased from England.

"The result was," as J. Franklin Jameson notes, "that, in the times just preceding the Revolution, colonial agriculture was in a poor condition. The fields had been worn out by hasty methods, and better methods were not learned because, with all the experimenting that had gone on, the results of experience were not diffused among farmers, for lack of agricultural societies and periodicals. . . . In particular, the domestic animals of America were, on account of the inferiority of the native American grasses, much smaller and poorer than those of Europe." [11]

If Washington failed, it was because the task was too great for him. He realized then what is little realized now, how backward America was in agriculture, in knowledge and in willingness. He did his utmost to teach himself and others. He consulted all the books he could find, and read the earth with tireless eyes.

In Virginia, however, the land was of such a friable nature that heavy rains eroded it and carried the topsoil off into the rivers. The plowman had to abandon it until the new growth of broom-sedge and pine restored a little of its fertility. Professor A. O. Craven,[12] in a recent book, has added "soil exhaustion" to the many contributing causes, as perhaps the chief cause of farm deterioration in early Virginia; hence a vital cause of the political discontent.

Add to this loss of soil and the choice of tobacco as its chief product, the restrictions placed upon that product by the home-government, and one will see why Moncure D. Conway [13] said:

"A true history of tobacco would be the history of English and American liberty."

The trials of the Virginia farmer are vividly condensed by Daniel Grinnan in reviewing Professor Craven's book:

"He had to struggle to earn his bread. England, his only permitted market for his tobacco, his single crop, was 3,000 miles away across a stormy sea, and when the tobacco, after the sweat and toil of raising and curing it had been endured, and the expense of putting it on a ship in the river had been paid, it then was plucked by so many harpies, that there was but little left to the credit of the planter; and this small balance went into the purchase of English articles at swollen prices that were shipped to him at heavy cost across the same wild sea.

"The proud Virginian was really regarded as a helot that was useful only for the crop he raised. It is difficult to enumerate the charges that the tobacco had to bear: there were charges for freight, insurance, drayage, English tariff taxes for coming in and for going out, charges for handling, warehouse charges, inspection charges, factor's charges and some others. Being across a wide ocean the planter had to accept any statement that his factor chose to render, and being always in debt to the factor there was an interest charge: and for the purchase of the articles that were shipped to Virginia there was another factor's charge and the prices paid for articles as shown by the factor's statement had to be accepted as correct solely on faith. In addition, the price of tobacco fluctuated and was often so low that the planter received only a pittance and sometimes received nothing but a debit entry. He was cut off from trade of all kinds with other countries than England, and the value of tobacco stored in England that could not be sold nor exported to the Continent was soon consumed by warehouse charges." [14]

From all these vexations and tribulations Washington, a helot like the others, suffered the more from the fact that he was one of the largest holders of land in Virginia. He could only free his farm from ruin by freeing Virginia and the other colonies from the English capitalists. The gentleman loyalist was gradually forced to become an agrarian radical.

There was more than mercantile desperation in the letter he wrote to his London brokers protesting against the mishandling of his prosperity:

"Upon the whole, the repeated disappointments which I meat with has reduced me to a delemma which I am not very well reconcild to." [15]

VIII

BUSY MOUNT VERNON

JUDGING from the devotion Washington lavished on Martha's children and grandchildren, he would have made as tender a father as ever lived.

In the presence of these youngsters he seemed to unbend in a way that he could not in the presence of men. Women and children placed him at his ease, but with the generality of men he tended to hold himself aloof, and inspired in them either a sense of awe or of resentment against apparent pomposity.

We know now that pomposity, like bluster, is a manifestation of timidity, and all the early accounts of Washington emphasize his diffidence and his taciturnity.

But young people drew him out of his shell.

There is much pathos in the fate of Martha's children. At Williamsburg, in old Bruton churchyard, one can see the ornate tomb above the remains of the first two. The daughter, called Frances Parke Custis, died at the age of three, Daniel Parke Custis at the age of four, in the same year with his father.

The widowed Martha, with a remaining boy of five and a girl of three, and a great estate to care for, turned to Washington and put their destiny in his hands. He did not default in this trust, or any other. The children were lucky in having him for a stepfather even though they were luckless otherwise.

A precious memory of Washington's conduct toward children is preserved in the story of Mrs. John M. Bowers, who recalled that as a child of six she had been taken to see

Washington, and that he had dandled her on his knee and sung to her about:

> "The old, old man and the old, old woman
> Who lived in the vinegar bottle together." [1]

He was especially fond of little Martha (born in 1757), whom he called by the same pet name he used for the elder Martha, "Patsy," which he almost always spelled "Patcy." Her mother refers to her in one of her letters as "My little patt." [2]

The boy, John Parke, was generally called "Jacky," and written down as "Jacky," "J. P. C.," "J. C." or "Mr. [for Master] Custis."

Washington made a valiant attempt to build the characters of the children and to keep them not only happy but luxurious. They were rich in their own right, but he tried to enrich life for them, and he squandered on them what wisdom he had.

It has been noted that in all the reams of advice he wrote to his wards, he never once mentioned the value of religion or church-going. Which was in itself a merciful kindness. He left that to their mother, who was very pious, and piously profane, judging from her letters, where "God" constantly occurs as a word of emphasis.

When Washington took his bride and her babes to Mount Vernon, the house had but four rooms on each of its two floors and most of the outbuildings were yet to be added. [3]

Washington usually rose at four o'clock, often building his own fire, for a little early bookkeeping before his breakfast of hoe cakes, honey and tea at seven-thirty.

Martha probably rose, shivering, at the same hour and, with her great bunch of keys jangling, went about unlocking doors and supplies to the slaves who were noted for their thievishness, especially of liquor.

No matter what the weather, Washington was rarely kept from riding about the plantations. If the snow were too deep for his horse, he left it and plunged ahead on his own long legs. At times he wore an umbrella fastened to his saddlebow. He averaged fifteen miles a day on his horse, and often more, for he sometimes rode to the hounds all day from three to five days a week.

In the early afternoon, unless a fox or a deer decoyed him too far, he came in and washed up for dinner, which was served at two or three.

John Hunter [4] described him as coming off the farm in a plain blue coat, white cassimere waistcoat, black knee-breeches and boots. He retired and returned in a clean shirt, a plain dark coat, white waistcoat, and white silk stockings, with his hair neatly powdered.

Since Virginia plantations were then largely self-sustaining, the wife was in a sense the head of a large manufacturing establishment. She superintended plants of all sorts with negro labor requiring extra supervision.

It is amazing to read what a variety and quantity of products Martha turned out. In one year she had woven 815 yards of linen, 365 yards of woolen, 144 yards of linsey, 40 yards of cotton, a total of 1,364 yards. She turned out patterned stuff, too, striped and plaided woolens, striped cotton, cotton filled with wool, cotton striped with silk, dimity, broadcloth, diaper, fustian, bed-ticking, herring-box, and shalloon.

She ran a large dairy, and a smoke-house, and catered to a home that was like a small hotel, purveying entertainment for man and beast at all hours.

There was never any telling how many guests would drop in for dinner and, if the mood struck them, remain over-night or perhaps for many nights.

Martha, like her husband, was a severe taskmaster for her

servants, but she kept a happy home for him, for her children, and the visitors. She even took music lessons from her daughter's teacher.

She took good care of herself and kept herself neat and comely. In those days when bathtubs had not been invented to fill an unfelt want, perfume was relied upon to do the work expected of soap in later, and in earlier, days.

The Roman fops and belles, spending a large portion of their lives in the baths, believed in Martial's epigram, "Even better than smelling good, is not smelling at all."

But, as Londoners then carried a bag or ball of perfume, a pomander, to shield the nose, so Virginians trusted to highly scented garments. Even the hairpowder was odorous.

There still exists a little volume of recipes in Martha's own handwriting.[5] It has been partly gnawed by flames, but it shows her interest in maintaining a sweet savor everywhere.

One of them describes how to make "A Perfume to Stand in a Roome":

"Take two or three quarts of roses buds or ye leaves of damask roses & put them in a pot with bay salt, 3 or 4 grayns of musk & as much of ambergreece, 20 or 30 drops of oyle of rodium, a little benjamin & storeax, beat together in a cheyney pot or any other yt is handsome & keep it allways close covered, but when you have a mind to have yr roome sweet you must take of ye cover."

Another tells how "To Make Sweet Water to Perfum Cloaths in ye foulding after they are Washed." Another how to perfume "ordinary hayer powder"; this included instructions to put into it:

"4 grayns of musk & a shillingsworth of amber & a groatsworth of oyle of ovpinum which oyle you must put in ye powder & set it into an oven after bread is drawne, & when you take it out of ye oven againe put into it ye muske and amber & then keep it close in a box."

She had a recipe "To keep ye Hayre Clean and Improve It." And this was the substitute for the toothbrush and paste of today: "To Keep Teeth Clean & White and To Fasten Them.

"Take cuttle fishbone and make it into a very fine powder & rub ye teeth therewith, then wash them after with white wine & plantan water & 3 or 4 drops of spirrit of vittorell mixt with them and rub them well with a cloth, & it will preserf ye teeth from putrefaction & keep them fast, white & clean & preserf from ye toothach iff it be used every day."

As a face cleanser she had a lotion difficult enough to prepare:

"Take a quarter of a pound of French barley & boyle it in allmoste a gallon of spring water: shift it in three waters till it be clear; when ye latter water hath boyled ye 4th part away, clear it from ye barley in a dish & let it stand till it be cold, then put into ye water a quarter of a pound of bitter almonds, blanched and beaten very small, & ye juice of 2 or 3 leamons then strayne it and bottle it & put into ye bottles some leamon pill & when it hath stood a week you may use it shaking it every day. This water is good to clear ye skin & to take away inflamations of ye face by washing of it night & morning."

Silk stockings were as hard to preserve then as now. Martha put hers "through three lathers . . . lett them dry on the wrong sides" and ironed "theym smooth on ye wrong side."

Washington's fame as a beau is well known. He was such a devotee of the dance that, even when Martha's interest waned, as her figure waxed, he was always ready to organize an Assembly Ball, ride a great distance to attend a dance and keep it up all night.

He saw to it that his stepchildren should not lack for

instruction, and a master was a necessity in his curriculum. Jacky's teacher, Rev. Jonathan Boucher, once complained that Jacky was neglecting his dancing lessons, and should not miss any more.[6]

In a letter written to Mr. Boucher, April 24, 1769, Washington devotes serious thought to the matter of the "science" of dancing and its instructors:

"In respect to the Dancing Gentry, I am glad to find you have such a choice of them, and that Newman has got the start of his rival Spooner, because I have heard him well spoken of as a teacher in that Science. The others misfortunes might recommend him to the notice & charity of the well disposed, but if his accomplishments in that way are inferior to the others it ought by no means to entitle him to the preference—you will be so good therefore sir to enter Mas[tr] Custis with M[r] Newman for a year or otherwise as he may form his school."

Mrs. Pryor[7] states that the saintly blind preacher, James Waddell, had his daughters taught to dance, and, when his Presbyterian flock protested, answered:

"No parent has a right to make his children unfit for polite society."

It was the custom for a number of families to engage a teacher and give a series of house parties in turn with all the dancing-pupils (Washington called them "Scholars") as guests and the dancing teacher one of them.

Washington frequently mentions such visitations, and Mount Vernon must have been a lively place with half-a-dozen girls and their beaux piling in for a few days of wild romping under the name of scholarship. He often stood and peeked at them through a half-opened door, but he retired if he found that his presence checked their hilarity. They learned jigs and hugging dances as well as prim minuets, and the lessons were followed by kissing games.[8] It is not to be wondered at that Jacky was pleading to be allowed to marry one of the little belles by the time he was seventeen.

The Washington household, with its card tables crowded, dancing routs, drinking feasts, oyster parties, and excursions to horse-races, balls, and play-houses, was just such a home as is now denounced as the origin of all vice.

It was denounced then, too, and in the same terms that were used by the Puritans in ancient Assyria, Greece, Rome, old England, new England. They are used today and will be used while the world lasts.

The gist of numberless such complaints in the days when Washington was the most indulgent of stepfathers is condensed by William Nelson:

"The departure of the women of the day (1760, say) from the 'good old customs' of their paragons of grandmothers (paragons usually belong to a past and gone generation) is sadly bewailed by dolorous and long-winded correspondents in the newspapers. The ladies, especially the young, are wholly given over to frivolity and the extremes of fashion. Their gowns lack the simplicity of an earlier day. Their chief pursuits are parties, dancing, and other trifling amusements. They evince a lack of appreciation of the solid acquirements, the grave and sensible attractions of the opposite sex—meaning, obviously, of the aforesaid correspondents. They are fonder of pleasure than of sober, housewifely duties and cares. How can young men afford to take such light-headed and light-hearted young women to wife?" [9]

Patsy Custis was an adorable child, but plainly doomed. She had inherited her father's tubercular predisposition, and suffered besides from a form of epilepsy, as did many others of that time.

The Rev. Mr. Boucher tells of a girl in Fredericksburg, "the first fortune in that part of the country, being in a ballroom at Fredericksburg, at which I also was, miffed, as was thought, by some other lady's being asked to dance before her, fell down in a fit in the public room. And on this occasion it came out that she had been all her life subject to fits." [10]

Mr. Boucher had already asked for this young woman's hand, but on being told by Dr. Hugh Mercer of her affliction, declined to accept her. Or so he says in that quaint book of his.

One young woman who had dreamed that she was to marry him, almost fainted when she saw him and exclaimed,

"Good God, yonder is the man I dreamed of that I was to marry!"

In those days ladies, young and old, seem to have been as fond of gasping, "Good God!" as French women of tossing in a "Mon Dieu!" Washington himself is often quoted as using the expression, and he frequently wrote it into his letters.

Boucher became the tutor of Jacky, whom he calls "the son-in-law of the since so celebrated General Washington." Washington also called his stepson his "son-in-law."

Boucher was one of those who had little reverence for Washington, and his book is full of sneers at him, at his parents, his brother Lawrence, at Washington's lack of education, at the "ridicule" he incurred by the publication of his elsewhere so much praised journal of his journey to the frontier in 1754, and even at his conduct at Braddock's Field where "he acquitted himself much in the same manner as in my judgment he has since done, i.e., decently, but never greatly."

He goes on:

"I did know Mr. Washington well; and tho' occasions may call forth traits of character that never would have been discovered in the more sequestered scenes of life, I cannot conceive how he could, otherwise than through the interested representations of party, have ever been spoken of as a great man. He is shy, silent, stern, slow and cautious, but has no quickness of parts, extraordinary penetration, nor an elevated style of thinking. In his moral character he is regular, temperate, strictly just and honest (excepting that as a Virginian, he has lately found out that there is no moral turpitude in not paying what he confesses he owes to a British creditor) and, as I always thought, religious: having heretofore been pretty constant, and even exemplary, in his attendance on public worship in the Church of England. But he seems to have nothing generous or affectionate in his nature." [11]

Boucher, who thought better of himself than of anyone else, states that when he withdrew to Maryland, two of his pupils "insisted on accompanying me, Mr. Custis, General Washington's son-in-law, and Mr. Carr." Later young Calvert of Baltimore joined the class, and Jacky fell madly in love with his sister.

While teaching these boys and preaching his sermons, Boucher carried on the courtship of a Miss Nelly Addison, whom he married eventually after writing to her uncle a very long appeal for her hand, in which he made every imaginable indecent play upon the pretty conceit that the young woman was a plantation and he a sturdy plowman.

Boucher managed to get into no end of trouble with the people by his Tory views, and preached for a time with two loaded pistols on either side of the Bible. He and Washington exchanged many letters, his final epistle before his departure for England being full of insult.

In strong contrast with the nervous irritability of the clergyman is the calm tone of Washington, tremendously eager that his stepson should gain a good education and keep a clean soul.

It was in 1768 when Jacky's first tutor, Mr. Magowan,
had left for England, that Washington first appealed to
Boucher to be his successor. He wrote of Jacky:

"He is a boy of good genius, about 14 years of age, untainted
in his morals and of innocent manners. Two years and upwards
he has been reading of Virgil and was (at the time Mr. Magowan
left him) entered upon the Greek testament.

"I presume, he has grown not a little rusty in both having had
no benefit of his tutor since Christmas, notwithstanding he left the
country in March only. If he comes, he will have a boy (well
acquainted with house business, which may be made as useful as
possible in your family to keep him out of idleness) and two horses
to furnish him with the means of getting to Church and elsewhere,
as you may permit; for he will be put entirely and absolutely under
your tuition and direction to manage as you think proper in all
respects. . . .

"I do not think it necessary to enquire into and will cheerfully
pay ten or twelve pounds a year, extraordinary, to engage your
peculiar care of, and a watchful eye to him, as he is a promising
boy, the last of his family and will possess a very large fortune.
Add to this my anxiety to make him fit for more useful purposes
than horse racer." [12]

Boucher hastened to accept the flattering commission, but
explained that he was moving to Annapolis. He wrote unc-
tuously:

"Ever since I have heard of Mast^r Custis, I have wish'd
to call Him one of my little Flock." [13]

Boucher always writes of Jacky Custis as "He" or "Him,"
as if he were indeed the sacred personage whose initials he
wore.

He bewailed the fact that he has never succeeded in raising one scholar because the moment the boys reach the age
of real study "they either marry, or are remov'd from
School." He was prophetic in Jacky's case.

But Jacky was sent to him and all went well except for
"a Pain in his Stomach, which I at first took for the Cholic,

but since think it more likely that it might be owing to Worms."

He wrote again of Jacky's "peculiar Innocence & Sanctity of Manners . . . teeming wth all ye softer Virtues," and expressed his ideals of education as "not only to form wise but good Men, not only to cultivate ye Understanding, but to expand ye Heart, to meliorate ye Temper, & *fix ye gen'rous Purpose in ye glowing Breast.*"

When Washington learned that Boucher had quietly sent Jacky to Baltimore to be "Innoculated with the Small Pox," he was delighted, but he was so eager to prevent Martha from worrying over the boy that he kept the news from her, and asked Boucher to write to him under cover to Lund Washington and in a disguised handwriting lest Martha take alarm:

"Her anxiety & uneasiness is so great, that I am sure she coud not rest satisfied without knowing the contents of any Letter of your writing to his Family . . . she having often wishd that Jack woud take & go through the disorder without her knowing of it, that she might escape those Tortures which suspense wd throw her into, little as the cause might be for them.—When he is returned to Annapolis, you will be so good as to write me a Line by Post to Williamsburg which shall be the first intimation of this affair I purpose to give if I can keep it concealed so long." [14]

Here Washington is shown commanding and conniving at deception of a most lovable sort.

Furthermore the amiable conspiracy and tender duplicity show the depth of Washington's affection for Martha, as do innumerable other little words and actions.

When Boucher broached a plan for giving Jacky the advantage of travel and study abroad, Washington demurred. He believed in the idea, but said that, as a guardian, his conduct was so carefully scrutinized by the Court that what he calls "a faupas" would incur the severest censure. Furthermore, Jacky could not afford it; though his estate was "what is called a good estate, it is not a profitable one . . . tho' he has a number of slaves, slaves in such cases only add to the Expence. About 60, and from that to 80 Hogsheads of Tobacco, is as much as he generally makes of a year." And finally his mother would not be able to endure his absence, especially since Patsy's life hangs by so scant a thread. Or, as Washington puts it compassionately:

"The unhappy situation of her daughter has in some degree fixed her eyes upon him as her only hope." [15]

In 1770 Jacky came home for a visit, and Washington sent him back with an uneasy note that "His mind is a good deal released from Study, & more than ever turnd to Dogs Horses and Guns; indeed upon Dress and equipage."

He feared now that Jacky might lose his innocence of manners and go "rambling about of Nights in Company with those, who do not care how debauched and viceous his Conduct may be . . . I have his welbeing much at Heart."

On December 18, 1770, Boucher wrote of Jacky:

"I must confess to You I never did in my Life know a Youth so exceedingly indolent, or so surprisingly voluptuous: one w^d suppose Nature had intended Him for some Asiatic Prince." [16]

He had become interested in actresses at the theatre. "It was about the time of the Players being here." Among them was Sarah Hallam, who was setting the poets afire, and the critics as well.[17] Jacky also fancied Miss Galloway, the sister of a wild student, whose father was an Annapolis wine-merchant. "Jack has a Propensity to the Sex. . . . I took such Steps as I judged most likely to wean Him in Time." [18]

After his Christmas holidays, Washington wrote, January 2, 1771, that the boy had promised to apply "close to his Studies" but "Time slips of a pace." Washington confessed

C. W. Peale's Portrait of Washington in 1779
(By permission of the Huntington Library)

that he had deceived Jacky about a trip to England, though he saw no immediate prospect of it.

"I cannot discover that he is much farther in Latten than when he left Mr. Magowan, knows little Arithmetick, and is quite ignorant of the Greek Language." [19]

He explained his philosophy of education and his desire that Jacky should be well grounded in his studies:

"Not that I think his becoming a mere scholar is a desirable education for a gentleman, but I conceive a knowledge of books is the basis upon which other knowledge is to be built."

In September, 1771, Washington visited Annapolis, and took Jacky with him, apparently into the betting-ring, for he charges in his Ledger, "By John Parke Custis at ye Annapolis Races £8." [20] He dined with the Governor and lodged with Mr. Boucher, and went to the theatre four times, and to balls three times, twice after the theatre.

In 1772 he excused Jack's delay in returning to Boucher by saying that he paused "to take the Benefit of a Ball at Alexandria." In September Washington went up to Annapolis with Martha and Patsy and Jacky to visit Mr. Boucher. On Saturday night he won £1. 15 playing cards at Rev. Mr. Boucher's. The next day he went "to Church with Govr. Eden in his Phaeton."

In October he went back to Annapolis, leaving and returning illegally on a Sunday. Monday, Wednesday, Thursday and Friday he went to the theatre, Tuesday to a ball. He lost at the races £1. 6. 0., but proudly enters in Ledger B that he won £13. 7 at cards.

In 1773, with all the political clouds gathering about his head, Washington was horrified to encounter in Jacky a mad determination to marry Eleanor Calvert, sister of a fellow-pupil, and daughter of Benedict Calvert.

Martha, feeling that her daughter would not be long with her, was in despair. Washington wrote a long letter to the girl's father. Nothing could be more tactful, or kindlier:

"Dear Sir, I am now set down to write to you on a subject of importance, and of no small embarrassment to me. My son-in-law and ward, Mr. Custis, has, as I have been informed, paid his addresses to your second daughter, and, having made some progress in her affections, has solicited her in marriage. How far a union of this sort may be agreeable to you, you best can tell; but I should think myself wanting in candor, were I not to confess, that Miss Nellie's amiable qualities are acknowledged on all hands, and that an alliance with your family will be pleasing to his.

"This acknowledgment being made, you must permit me to add, Sir, that at this, or in any short time, his youth, inexperience, and unripened education, are, and will be, insuperable obstacles, in my opinion, to the completion of the marriage. . . .

"If the affection, which they have avowed for each other, is fixed upon a solid basis, it will receive no diminution in the course of two or three years, in which time he may prosecute his studies, and thereby render himself more deserving of the lady and useful to society. If, unfortunately, as they are both young, there should be an abatement of affection on either side, or both, it had better precede than follow marriage.

"Delivering my sentiments thus freely will not, I hope, lead you into a belief, that I am desirous of breaking off the match. To postpone it is all I have in view; for I shall recommend to the young gentleman, with the warmth that becomes a man of honor, (notwithstanding he did not vouchsafe to consult either his mother or me on the occasion,) to consider himself as much engaged to your daughter, as if the indissoluble knot were tied; and, as the surest means of effecting this, to apply himself closely to his studies, (and in this advice I flatter myself you will join me,) by which he will, in a great measure, avoid those little flirtations with other young ladies, that may, by dividing the attention, contribute not a little to divide the affection.

"It may be expected of me, perhaps, to say something of property; but, to descend to particulars, at this time, must seem rather premature. In general, therefore, I shall inform you, that Mr. Custis's estate consists of about fifteen thousand acres of land, a good part of it adjoining the city of Williamsburg, and none of it forty miles from that place; several lots in the said city; between two and three hundred negroes; and about eight or ten thousand pounds upon bond, and in the hands of his merchants. This estate he now holds independent of his mother's dower, which will be an addition to it at her death; and, upon the whole, it is such an estate as you will readily acknowledge ought to entitle him to a handsome portion with a wife. But as I should never require a child of my own to make a sacrifice of himself to interest, so neither do I think it incumbent on me to recommend it as a guardian." [21]

Mr. Calvert replied with equal grace, confessing that his daughter would bring Jacky no money, but a fine character.

A portrait of Eleanor Calvert at this time is described by her son: "It represents a young lady of a romantic and slight figure in a riding costume, with a boy's hat and open jacket. She seems scarcely fifteen, with bright and hopeful countenance. Such was her temperament, we are told, through all the toils of life." [22] The portrait usually published as hers is really a portrait of Mrs. Siddons!

Jacky was finally persuaded to promise that he would give up all thoughts of marriage for two years, and devote himself to his studies. In order to enlarge his ambitions, and doubtless to put him at a safe distance from the irresistible siren in Baltimore, it was decided to send him to study in New York at what was then called King's College, though the name was soon to be changed to Columbia, and the word "King" erased from all American titles and pasted over in the prayerbooks.

His stepchildren were by no means the only ones to share in Washington's fatherliness. He took the whole world for his family and was forever playing the Samaritan to his relations, his neighbors, and even to strangers. Nobody's trouble seemed too great or too small for him to add to his own.

It was said that Alexander the Great liked to receive petitions and grant them lavishly, but never gave to those who did not ask. Washington could rarely resist an appeal, and he went often out of his way to volunteer benefits to those too meek or too proud to ask for them.

There was, for example, the letter he wrote, in 1769, apparently out of a clear sky, to his old friend, William Ramsay, the founder of Alexandria, Virginia:

"Having once or twice of late heard you speak highly in praise of the Jersey College, as if you had a desire of sending your son William there (who, I am told, is a youth fond of study and instruction, and disposed to a sedentary studious life, in following of which he may not only promote his own happiness, but the future welfare of others), I should be glad, if you have no other objection to it than what may arise from the expense, if you would send him there as soon as it is convenient, and depend on me for twenty-five pounds this currency a year for his support, so long as it may be necessary for the completion of his education. If I live to see the accomplishment of this term, the sum here stipulated shall be annually paid; and if I die in the mean while, this letter shall be obligatory upon my heirs, or executors, to do it according to the true intent and meaning hereof. No other return is expected, or wished, for this offer, than that you will accept it with the same freedom and good will, with which it is made, and that you may not even consider it in the light of an obligation, or mention it as such; for, be assured, that from me it will never be known." [23]

So kind, indeed, was Washington's heart that, at a time when he was almost frantic with his many worries, he could write the following letter to his old friend, John West, who, feeling himself about to die, asked Washington to assume the burden of the guardianship of his only son:

"Your letter of the 8th, which is just handed to me, could not have given you more pain in writing, than it has given me in reading, because I never deny or even hesitate in granting any request, that is made to me, especially by persons I esteem, and in matters of moment, without feeling inexpressible uneasiness. I do not wonder at your solicitude on account of your only son. The nurturing and bringing him up in a proper course is, no doubt, an object of great concern to you, as well as importance to him; but two things are essentially necessary in the man to whom this charge is committed, a capacity of judging with propriety of measures proper to be taken in the government of a youth, and leisure sufficient to attend to the execution of these measures. . . . I can solemnly declare to you, that, for a year or two past, there has been scarce a moment, that I could properly call my own.

"What with my own business, my present ward's, my mother's, which is wholly in my hands, Colonel Colvill's, Mrs. Savage's, Colonel Fairfax's, Colonel Mercer's, and the little assistance I have undertaken to give in the management of my brother Augustine's concerns (for I have absolutely refused to qualify as an executor), together with the share I take in public affairs, I have been kept constantly engaged in writing letters, settling accounts, and negotiating one piece of business or another; by which means I have really been deprived of every kind of enjoyment, and had almost fully resolved to engage in no fresh matter, till I had entirely wound up the old.

"Thus much, Sir, candor, indeed the principle of common honesty, obliged me to relate to you, as it is not my wish to deceive any person by promising what I do not think it in my power to perform with that punctuality and rectitude, which I conceive the nature of the trust will require. I do not, however, give a flat refusal to your request. I rather wish you to be fully informed of my situation, that you may think with me, or as I do, that, if it should please the Almighty to take you to himself as soon as you apprehend (but I hope without just cause), your son may be placed in better hands than mine. If you think otherwise, I will do the best I can, merely as a guardian.

"You will act very prudently in having your will revised by some person skilled in the law, as a testator's intentions are often defeated by different interpretations of statutes, which require the whole business of a man's life to be perfectly conversant with them. I shall not, after what I have here said, add any thing more than my wishes, which are sincerely offered, for your recovery, and that you may live to see the accomplishment of your son's education." [24]

Like magnanimity he revealed in endless instances.   For
the sake of his friends and his wards he became almost a
genius of kindliness with an infinite capacity for taking pains
in behalf of others.

IX

HIS STRUGGLE FOR WEALTH

GET-RICH-QUICK handbooks were as much in favor in Washington's day as in this. Then, as now, neither the authors nor the readers seem to have profited by the mystic lore.

As soon as Washington married Martha he wrote to London for "a Small piece in Octavo—called a New System of Agriculture, or a Speedy Way to grow Rich." [1] Either there is a contradiction in terms or the system is still so new as to be undiscovered.

The fact that Washington had captured one of the richest women in America did not make him indolent, but rather quickened his energies.

Martha brought him an estate of about 15,000 acres, town lots and houses, 150 negroes, and a hundred thousand dollars in cash and securities. These belonged to her and, through her, to her second husband, and to her son and daughter by her first marriage in equal shares. By law he became administrator and he immensely increased the value of his tract.

The guardianship of the children's shares also fell to him, and he doubled the value of their property in the seventeen years of his administration. The difficulties of his task can be imagined if it is remembered that there was not one bank in all the thirteen colonies until 1782, and only three in 1789. [2]

Jack Custis inherited fifteen thousand acres of land, cultivated and uncultivated, in various Virginia counties. Their management involved tremendous labor for Wash-

ington, for they were farmed by slaves under the supervision of overseers, or leased to tenants who paid their rental
in shares of the crop. The crops themselves had to be
watched, harvested, sent to warehouses, shipped to England
and the West Indies, and the money received for them collected in an intricate manner with a lack of nearly all the
facilities afforded by modern banking. Strict accounts of all
these details had to be kept, and Washington spent numberless hours at his desk, posting his books, verifying his vouchers, and keeping all straight.

The fidelity and the vigor of his administration is shown
in the fact that when Jacky Custis reached his majority he
found himself the richest young man in Virginia.

It is one of the sharpest sarcasms with which fate rewarded
Washington's toil and honesty, that a large part of the
Custis fortune and his own was lost through the almost ludicrous depreciation of the currency put forth by the young
nation which he made such sacrifices to create and defend.[3]

While he had more than enough to do in conserving the
Custis estates, he had his own personal fortune to build. He
kept the wheels turning at his father's mill, and he ran a
wholesale fishery and many other businesses.

His honesty was so automatic that, while he exacted the
least penny due himself, he also exacted from himself the
least penny due to another.

He was a money-lender who could never quite succeed
in being a Shylock. He never exacted a pound of flesh or
blood-money, or usury. He was rather the typically generous financier, lending to everyone who comes begging and
thereafter becoming a beggar himself, pleading for some
return of the money laid out and humiliating himself to
explain that he would not ask for it if he were not in desperate straits himself.

When he was cheated, or thought himself cheated, he

could rage and he could go to law. He often sued and at times he was sued.

Though he is constantly spoken of as a rich man, the richest in America, he seems never to have known a year in which he had a comfortable reserve of cash. His marriage to Martha put him in deeper instead of lifting him out of debt. He had to borrow money of a comparative stranger in order to go to the capital as President, and to his dying day he was worried about his small margin of cash.

He endured abject humiliations from creditors who insulted him because he was such "slow pay."

On August 10, 1764, he wrote to Robert Cary & Co., explaining what "caused me to fall so much in arrears to you . . . mischances, rather than misconduct, hath been the causes of it. For it was a misfortune that seasons and chance should prevent my making even tolerable crops . . . for three years successively; and it was a misfortune likewise, when they were made, that I should get little or nothing for them. It may also be looked upon as unlucky at least, that the debts which I thought I had collected and actually did remit to you, should be paid in bills void of credit." [4]

He was indignant and hurt at having received an apparently peremptory demand for money, and he added: "It is but an irksome thing to a free mind to be any ways hampered in debt."

A year later he wrote to protest against the bad returns from his tobacco shipments:

"The sales are pitifully low . . . worse than many of my acquaintance upon the Potomac have got in the outports." [5] He threatened to change his agents unless they did better.

One of his chief reasons for being in debt was the unreliability of those who were in debt to him. His relations with Captain John Posey fill some of his most excited letters.

Posey—whose name he spelled "Possey" for years—
was sometimes useful to him in enlarging his estate at
Mount Vernon, in whose growth Captain Posey's estate was
also swallowed up eventually.

For example, Washington spent four years trying to buy
from two orphans 210 acres adjoining his plantation whose
name (called after the tribe of Doeg Indians) he spelt variously as Dogue Run, Doeg Run, Doge Run, and Morris's.
At last he secured it in 1764 by using Captain Posey as his
undercover agent.[6]

This Captain Posey took up so much of Washington's time
and temper, and his son innocently involved Washington in
so persistent a scandal, that a chapter is devoted to the
Poseys in the Appendix.

He enjoyed a good wrangle over real estate, and could
hold up his end of an argument.

In business as in battle he was alert for the deception of
his adversary. He constantly tells of his stratagems in his
own letters and diaries.

Remove from Washington's life his careers as a soldier
and a statesman, and there remains little to distinguish him
from the average successful business man of his day and
ours.

He made good investments and bad. He lent and he
borrowed. He had his moods of anger and stinginess. He
had his moods of patience and liberality.

And like many another capitalist, he could play and play
hard. As the financier of today makes a religion of his
eighteen holes of golf and lingers often at the nineteenth
hole, so Washington, who knew not golf, hunted incessantly
and used to linger over the liquor and chatter at the nineteenth hole. He gave thousands of hours to sport.

As the capitalist of today must have his costly limousine,

so Washington always looked to it that his carriages should be of the finest quality.

In June, 1768, he wrote to Robert Cary & Co. of London:

"My old chariot having run its race, and gone through as many stages as I could conveniently make it travel, is now rendered incapable of any further service. The intent of this letter, therefore, is to desire you will bespeak me a new one, time enough to come out with the goods (I shall hereafter write for) by Captn. Johnston, or some other ship.

"As these are kind of articles that last with care against number of years, I would willingly have the chariot you may now send me made in the newest taste, handsome, genteel and light; yet not slight, and consequently unserviceable; to be made of the best seasoned wood, and by a celebrated workman. The last importation which I have seen, besides the customary steel springs, have others that play in a brass barrel and contribute at one and the same time to the ease and ornament of the carriage. One of this kind, therefore, would be my choice; and green being a color little apt, as I apprehend, to fade, and grateful to the eye, I would give it the preference, unless any other color more in vogue and equally lasting is entitled to precedency.

"In that case I would be governed by fashion. A light gilding on the mouldings (that is, round the panels) and any other ornaments, that may not have a heavy and tawdry look (together with my arms agreeable to the impression here sent) might be added, by way of decoration. A lining of a handsome, lively colored leather of good quality I should also prefer, such as green, blue, or &c., as may best suit the color of the outside." [7]

In September the chariot was shipped to him at a cost of £133. Two years later he complained that he had been cheated, "the wood so exceedingly grien that the panels slipped out of the mouldings before it was two months in use—Split from one end to the other." [8]

He was fond of lotteries and raffled for glasses, buckles,

necklaces, for a coach. But, of course, lotteries were not illegal then. They were in especial favor for churches and colleges. Eight churches in Virginia were built with lottery money. William and Mary College, Harvard, and Yale, and Faneuil Hall, "the cradle of liberty," were aided by lotteries. But in 1769 the Virginia Assembly decreed that no lotteries should be drawn without special authority.[9]

On June 20, 1770, Washington invested £41 in a lottery, probably without travelling to secure legislative sanction.

If he could return today he would be dazed at the changes that have come over the world. He would be glad to find the slaves freed, and not at all surprised to find that few of their descendants have acquired social equality or prominence.

He would be astounded to find universal suffrage with no property qualification. He would be glad to see that religious qualifications have been thrown into the discard.

He would find a number of his most delightful recreations under the ban; first, the manufacture, sale, purchase, possession, and taking of liquors, in all of which he was active. What he would think of the law it is not possible to know. He would find that the vast majority of the sort of people he called his friends were freely indulging in the purchase, possession, manufacture and distribution of liquor in spite of the law. He would dine at few homes where drinks were not served as an extra obligation because of their very prohibition. Since he was in his day the greatest rebel of them all and won his immortality by defying the law, it is not certain that he would join the Anti-Saloon League as eagerly as he joined the anti-British associations.

He would find horse-racing forbidden in many states, and betting on them forbidden in more. He would find that playing cards for money is forbidden by many states and strongly condemned by various creeds. He would even find many laws against the tobacco to which he devoted so much of his time.

Since the members of the two largest Protestant churches are committed by their creeds to solemn pledges of abstention from liquor, horse races, theatres, dances, and many other amusements, it is only natural that their members should consider it immoral to publish the fact that the most revered of all Americans devoted himself to these forbidden activities.

Whether Washington would have obeyed the growing multitude of ordinances infringing on personal conduct is a riddle. He was human in this, that when he was an official in power he had his soldiers flogged for gambling and profanity and, as President, he was eloquent about respect for the sacredness of the law.

But as a private citizen he gambled and swore, and he joined organizations committed not only to the breaking of many laws but to their organized defiance. He threatened to raise troops at his own expense to join Boston in defeating the laws of the empire and the military police force sent to enforce them. In due course of time he actually took up arms against the authorities, and became an outlaw, and often a fugitive liable to be hanged if captured.

While Washington was adding to his land-holdings near and far, he kept groping about in every direction to find some quicker way of getting rich than by relying on lazy negroes and fickle tobacco.

Among his earliest ventures was the redemption of the Dismal Swamp, one of those vexatious eyesores that are always tempting ambitious men to rebuke nature and turn them to profit if not to grace.

The Irish poet, John Boyle O'Reilly,[10] explored the

swamp and found it "an agony of perverted nature." He
called the lake within it, "the very eye of material anguish."
Yet he admitted that "the swamp itself is probably the
healthiest spot in America." This was because of its delicious juniper water.

That was not the opinion of the earliest visitors to it. Ex-
cursionists and others who frequent it or hurry through it
now find it a paradise of game, including bear, deer and fox,
and a hell of mosquitoes and serpents, the former of which
swarm about every boat in such numbers as to "take off
your head," while snakes are apt to drop in from the crowded
branches. O'Reilly says that "the flying game of the continent centers in this region."

Colonel William Byrd of Westover, who surveyed the
Swamp in 1728—four years before Washington was born—
was one of the commissioners appointed by Virginia to
settle the boundary between that colony and North Carolina, and the task inspired him to a long-neglected work,
with the unpromising title, "The History of the Dividing
Line." It contains some of the most captivating English
ever written in this country and is just coming into its right-
ful fame.

The dividing line chanced to pass through the Dismal
Swamp, and Colonel Byrd was one of the first to be teased
with the dream of correcting the vast mistake.

He wrote a proposal to drain the region. Then settlers
were to be encouraged, also "let 10 seasoned negroes be
purchased, of both sexes, that their breed may supply the
loss." These were to clear and trench the ground and
raise corn, make shingles and set up tight casks. Cattle were
to be provided, and fresh negroes brought in as fast as room
could be made for them. The breeding of the negroes was
to be looked to carefully. Boys and girls were to be sent
in, and wives for the grown slaves. "Besides the advantages

of propagation, there is another benefit in provideing wives
for the men: it will keep them at home, and prevent their
rambling abroad anights, from which arise many great in-
conveniences. By this practice they learn to be dishonest,
take cold, and lose their rest, whereby they are less fit to
do their work the following days. Besides, when they have
wives in other familys, they are frequently poisoned by the
jealousy of their rivals, who think they have a much better
right to the affections of their fellow servants, than any
stranger. By this many lose their lives."

The project fell through, but it was taken up again thirty-
five years later when it attracted the attention of Washington.

He and five others organized themselves as "The Adventurers for draining the Dismal Swamp," and put up money
for a rough survey, which Washington made in the three
days beginning May 25, 1763, and described on October
15th after a second brief visit to it. This is an unusually
long entry in his diary, where he wrote it in pencil on the
front and back pages, copying it in ink in the 1764 diary.[11]

He lacked the charming touch of Colonel Byrd, and his
account is as dull as ditchwater with no flavoring of juniper.
It was not intended for literature, however, but for a surveyor's "memmorandom," as he called it, with notes of interest to a farmer concerning soil and timber.

He rode in half a mile deep, "without any sort of difficulty, the horse not sinking over the fetlocks." He found
a number of farmers in the swamp, and some "prodigeous
fine land, but subject to wets and unhealthiness."

The Dismal proved to be a swamp on a hill, and the
waters flow down out of it, not into it.

In November, six hundred pounds was voted by the Adventurers to carry out the plan of drainage, and the Assembly was appealed to for licence to proceed.

In January, 1764, a bill prepared by Richard Henry Lee and Lemuel Reddick was passed and approved by the Council and the Governor, authorizing the Adventurers to have "free passage, and make such canals or causeways, through the lands of any person whatsoever adjacent to the said Dismal Swamp."

Washington and John Robinson furnished slaves, and set them to work. In December £480 more was subscribed; in June, 1765, there was another assessment, of £300; and in May, 1766, one of £300.

Land was purchased to the extent of forty thousand acres, and in 1768 Washington paid £300 for such purchase.

For the present, however, the project was allowed to lapse, though a quantity of shingles was produced. Washington took up the adventure again in later years and never lost his interest in it.

Many other matters tempted him. At Occoquan creek, twelve miles from Mount Vernon, there were a ferry, an iron works, and a sawmill to which his schooner plied. In July, 1766, he says, "My Schooner also came up with 10,031 feet of Plank from Occoquan Saw Mills." [12]

These mills were run by a Scotsman, John Semple, who had brought to America a knowledge of the financing of public utilities. He called on Washington several times in 1770 with "Proposals for clearing the Potomac." [13] The work was to be done by a stock company, the profits to be secured from authorized tolls.

Such projects had not been tried in Virginia, but Washington liked the idea well enough to introduce a bill in the Assembly in 1770 licensing the scheme. He did not have influence enough to push it through, but he succeeded two years later. An agent was sent to England to sell stock, but at that time there were reasons enough to discourage the British from investing heavily in American promises, and the scheme collapsed. Eleven years later Washington still remembered it, revived his dream of making the river navigable, and made the "Patowmack Company" one of the chief businesses of his life.

But this was also unsuccessful, though he told Elkanah Watson in after years that it would pay twenty percent on its stock,[14] and died believing in its value so sincerely that he left his shares to endow a university.

The ambition was a noble one, but the shares were wiped out soon after his death, and the university was never even begun.

Still, he was not the only brilliant financier who left in his strong box shares of stocks that were mere wallpaper. And, in spite of all his disappointments and losing investments, he had by his fortieth year gathered in real estate to the amount of

5,518 acres in Fairfax County		
2,498	" "	Frederick "
1,250	" "	King George "
240	" "	Hampshire
275	" "	Loudoun
2,682	" "	Loudoun Fauquier

12,463

Besides these, he had a claim on thousands of Western acres.

He was paying taxes on 87 slaves in 1770, and four years later on 135.

Haworth [15] quotes his receipts from his farm as £1,839 in 1759; about £2,535 in 1760; in 1772, £3,213, and from August, 1775 to August, 1776, £2,119.

As a marketer of fish he seems to have had fair success.

In April, 1769, he caught 60 or 70 whitefish at a haul. In April, 1769, he "catchd abt. 300 at one hawl." In May,

1772, he sold over 11,000 fish, mainly herring.   In July, 1772, he sold 30 barrels of shad for £40.

It has been said that the man who is not wise, wealthy, or famous at forty will never be any of them.   Yet Washington at forty had shown no evidences of unusual wisdom; what little attention he had attracted could hardly be called fame, and even that was waning.   He could be called wealthy only by an elastic use of the word.

X

WAS HE "THE FATHER OF THE WEST"?

"VIRGINIA" in Washington's early life meant by no means the state that we know today, nor the state as it was before it lost West Virginia, and what it called "the county of Kentucky." It meant as much as was meant by "Louisiana," which has also shrunk to infinitesimal proportions of its original significance.

Virginia, in Washington's ears, meant half a continent—half of a continent whose limits were only imagined, but imagined with magnificent fancy.

To be a Virginian was to be a part owner of this realm and its cloudy opportunities. It was well understood that other colonies had similar claims and that the boundary lines were a matter of bitter dispute, all the bitterer for being concerned with uncertainties.

Being by nature a warm patriot and having only Virginia to squander his patriotism on, Washington looked upon England as the fatherland, and the other colonies as lying, cheating, lazy, greedy neighbors, hardly children of the same parent. And they regarded Virginia with the same brotherly love shared by Cain and Abel, Jacob and Esau.

Washington from his early youth had his ambitions turned westward. As the heir of his half-brother, Lawrence, and as a soldier on his own account, he had a claim on lands in the Ohio Valley, and he was determined to make them good. His first ill-starred military expedition had been inspired by the hope of driving the French and Indians off the territory of 500,000 acres granted by the King to the Ohio Company.

119

The Ohio Company had promised 200,000 of those acres to be divided among the troops that should free them from the enemy's clutches. Washington, as Colonel, was entitled to 5,000 acres, the captains to 3,000, subalterns to 200, and private soldiers to 50 acres apiece.

Now he wanted his pay. Collecting it was another thing, but he set his heart on it and would not give up.

Nothing is more unwarranted than the ascription to him of unique importance in the opening of the West. Nothing is more unjust to other Americans.

Yet of late years it has come to be the fashion of authors and orators to call him such names as "the Father of the West," "the prophet of the West," "the original expansionist." [1]

This is hardly less flattering than it would be to call Peter Stuyvesant the Discoverer of America or Abraham Lincoln the Original Emancipationist.

Benjamin Franklin's claim to the Fatherhood of the West has complete priority over Washington's. There was never any personal rivalry or hostility between the two men, and in time great mutual respect, but for one thing Franklin was born twenty-six years before Washington, and had settled himself in Philadelphia as a publisher three years before Washington was born. He founded the Philadelphia Library about the time Washington was begotten, and "Poor Richard's Almanac" and Washington came into the world in the same year.

By the time Washington was twenty Franklin had accomplished the first of the two great achievements the French credited him with, when they said that "he ripped the lightning from the skies and the scepter from the tyrants."

His distinguished son, William, was born out of wedlock three years before Washington was born in it; and five years before Washington made his famous journey to Lake Erie in 1753 (under the guidance of Christopher Gist, who knew the wilderness well) William Franklin had explored the same country with Conrad Weiser as his guide, and written an account of it on which his father reported to England in 1758.[2]

Fifty years before Washington's birth, American traders had been buying furs from the Indians in the Ohio Valley.[3] The fact that hundreds of traders had established themselves there before Franklin was born does much to upset his claim as well as Washington's to any great innovation.

Of course, the word "Father," in such a sense, is the baldest and most ancient rhetorical trickery, but if the West must have a father, and a distinguished one, Benjamin Franklin's claim should be heard among others.

Professor Alvord, in his classic work, "The Mississippi Valley in British Politics," calls Franklin the "protagonist" of the Philadelphia enterprises, and notes that his ideas were "seconded by the most famous colonial map-maker of the day, Lewis Evans." [4]

While the Ohio Company was sending out troops to take from the Indians the lands the English King had given them, the Pennsylvanians were arranging for a large purchase of Indian territory. In the same year, 1754, Franklin, at the Albany conference, had not only proposed the establishment of two colonies beyond the Ohio, but had proposed a union of the thirteen colonies—a project so ridiculous that the colonies laughed at it. Virginia did not even send delegates. It was in 1754, too, that Franklin published in his newspaper a cartoon representing the colonies as portions of a snake in fragments labelled "Join, or Die." It was much used after 1765.[5]

Franklin had spoken of "the great country back of the

Appalachian Mountains" as bound to become "perhaps in less than another century, a populous and powerful dominion." [6]

So far-sighted was Franklin that as early as 1767 he was writing to his son, "A settlement should be made in the Illinois country . . . raising a strength there which on occasions of a future war might easily be poured down the Mississippi upon the lower country and into the Bay of Mexico to be used against Cuba, the French Islands, or Mexico itself." [7]

The final proof that Franklin was a greater figure than Washington in the opening of the West is the fact that Franklin's Walpole, or Vandalia Company, finally swallowed up Washington's Ohio Company entire in a great merger called the Grand Ohio Company.

Furthermore, while Washington was a farmer in Fairfax county, and an obscure Assemblyman, Franklin was America's chief representative in England, learning the diplomacy that brought France into alliance with the colonies and saved the Revolution. Franklin was consorting with the biggest figures in England and doing his utmost to secure British capital as a backing for American energy, and to make peace among the fiercely contending agents of the rival American syndicates.

Franklin had great influence, too, in shaping the ideals of Lord Shelburne, the English Secretary of State, who was himself one of the many fathers of the West.

Of Shelburne, Alvord says, "Like a prophet he had caught a vision of the inexorable march of the white men across the American continent." [8]

Shelburne had an Englishman's contempt for the wrangles of the colonies, and what he called "all the nonsense of Charters" and the "talk of extending as far as the sun sets." [9] He had also a horror of the cruelty and dishonesty of the colonists toward the Indians, and hoped to protect the red men from their murderous greed. Nevertheless, he had his dream of the expansion of white civilization into the West, and worked toward that end.

If a Washington is to be the Father of the West, why not Lawrence Washington, George's brilliant half-brother, who had been the chief founder of the Ohio Company at a time when George was only sixteen years old? He even went so far as to advocate religious tolerance in order to encourage settlers.[10]

But oblivion has been most cruel of all to the great George Croghan, who has perhaps the best right to the title, Father of the West. He had crossed the Ohio river, and gone on to the borders of Lake Erie, and had established a great trading system by 1744, before Washington was twelve years old. He was long associated with Franklin, and now and then with the Virginians, in the most elaborate plans for taking care of the westward mania. And there was a mania, a stampede, for land out there before Washington had even started on his alleged fatherhood.

Immediately after the peace of 1763, the chorus of "Westward Ho!" was choked off by Pontiac's War, which almost annihilated the western dream,—"nine forts were surprised and captured, two thousand English soldiers, traders, and settlers captured or killed, often with the foulest barbarity, some thousands of English settlers driven to beggary, and traders and troops plundered of goods valued at nearly £100,000." [11]

While Croghan was in England Pontiac's armies were crushed, but he was still a menace, and in 1765 Croghan was sent to quiet the fierce warrior. On his way down the Ohio, he was attacked by roving Indians and escaped death only, as he said, because "a thick skull is of service on some occasions." He reached Vincennes, pushed on out into

Illinois, met Pontiac and accompanied him to Detroit where he made a treaty of peace—"a brilliant diplomatic achievement which satisfied the most sanguine expectations." [12]

He went by canoe to Niagara, then on to Ontario, meeting Indians and making peace. When he finally returned, the Illinois country was "permanently opened to Anglo-Saxon civilization."

The Philadelphians took up the new field with enthusiasm, a Quaker group rivalling a Jewish group, and Croghan working with both and with the bankers in London.

As early as 1766 there was such a rush for the West, with its immense resources in fur, timber, water-power, mines and farms, that Croghan wrote to Sir William Johnson:

"One half of England is Now Land mad and Every body there has thire Eys fixt on this Cuntry."

In this year, of 1766, four years before Washington finally made his first journey beyond Fort Pitt, there was already a shipbuilding establishment at Pittsburg which had built 65 batteaux. Three hundred boatmen were plying the Ohio, and in one year goods to the value of £50,000 were sent West.

The ubiquitous Benjamin Franklin acted as insurance agent.

Croghan left Fort Pitt in 1766 with 17 batteaux and reached Fort de Chartres (where the Kaskaskia River empties into the Mississippi below Saint Louis). There he held a council with a thousand Indians and sent delegates across the river into Missouri and Arkansas. Then he went on down the Mississippi to New Orleans and came back to New York by sea.

These are only a few of Croghan's superb achievements as a business man, diplomat and explorer. They preceded Washington's lesser journeys and services as far as Croghan's land accumulations exceeded Washington's.

"George Croghan," says Volwiler, "was the leading exponent of the expansion of the Anglo-Saxon race into the Ohio region during the generation before 1775. He was preeminent as an Indian trader, an Indian agent, a land speculator, and a projector of inland colonies. . . . Croghan was one of the first Englishmen to grasp a clear vision of the future greatness of the forest-clad kingdom beyond the Appalachians. This vision came to dominate all of his later activities and it exerted great influence upon other colonial leaders and upon imperial officials. . . . These interests exerted an important influence upon constitutional development during the period from 1775 to 1789. From one point of view, the history of the United States until the twentieth century is the story of a long struggle for the possession of a continent. In this struggle, George Croghan was one of the leaders of the vanguard of that mighty host which made the great march across the continent and carved an empire out of an uncharted wilderness." [13]

Sir William Johnson is another once gigantic name tending to drift into twilight. He came to America in 1738, was made a Mohawk sachem in 1743, then superintendent of Indian affairs with the Six Nations.

Braddock commissioned him a Major-General, and he won success while Braddock failed. He commanded the expedition to Fort George in which Dieskau was captured. He was made a baronet and given sole charge of Indian affairs in the north. He captured Fort Niagara in 1759, and received a tract of 100,000 acres of land. He kept the Iroquois from joining Pontiac, and lived like an emperor.

In 1754 he endorsed Benjamin Franklin's plan of colonization. Franklin went to England and secured permission for a great purchase of land from the Indians. Johnson was instructed to make it. Over 3,000 Indians were assembled by Croghan and Johnson at Fort Stanwix in 1768, and twenty boatloads of presents, valued at £10,000, were turned over to them in return for an imperial realm.

Incidentally, Johnson, the Wharton brothers, Trent and William Franklin made secret deals for private grants of enormous extent, conflicting in many ways with Virginian claims.

But then all the claims conflicted and overlapped, and there followed a riot of claim-jumping, chicanery, brutality, trickery, bribery of legislation and officials such as has rarely been surpassed even in the ugly annals of land booms.

Still, the Indians were pacified for the time being, and the pioneers came over the broken levees in a flood. The Penns opened their land office on April 3, 1769, and on the first day received nearly 3,000 applications. In the first four months they sold a million acres.

In Virginia six million acres in what is now West Virginia were disposed of. An effort to clear up the chaos of land companies is made in Appendix III.

It was not until 1770 that Washington joined the rush in person, though he had had feelers out for some years. Great as his claims sound when mentioned alone in thousands of acres, they grow faint when compared with the millions handled by other fathers of the West. They were furthermore belated.

It is hard to believe, but indisputably true, that all this turmoil of westward ambition, and much more than can be hinted here, had taken place in spite of the fact that as soon as England had made peace with France and taken Canada from her in 1763, the war-worn empire had thought to quiet the fierce Indian allies of the French by a prompt royal proclamation issued in 1763 guaranteeing the Indians the quiet possession of the Ohio and nearly all the rest of the territory they claimed.

An ulterior purpose was to keep the colonists from out-growing English control and spreading too far inland to be reached by the navy. They must be held "in due subordination to, and dependence upon, the mother country," said the Lords of Trade.[14]

The colonists had been encouraged to years of war and had spent money and lives to drive the French out of the West and break the wall built up by papist troops and Indian allies.

When the war ended in 1763, the wall went down, and the colonists girded up their loins and cinched up their horses for a grand trek into the world so long denied them by an ancient enemy.

Imagine their amazement when the English Ministry not only said to them: "You must help pay our debts by paying taxes out of the money you made from smuggling supplies to the French while we fought them," but actually threw up a new wall of parchment to replace the French and Indian wall of bullet and tomahawk.

Imagine their incredulity when the English King decreed that all that territory was sacred to the dear Indians who must not be annoyed by squatters! "that no Governor or commander-in-chief of our other colonies or plantations in America do presume for the present, and until our further pleasure be known, to grant warrants of survey or pass patents for any lands beyond the heads or sources of any rivers, etc. etc." [15]

The only thing to do was to take it as a joke. To rebel against their sacred monarch was at that time inconceivable, beyond the point of going ahead with their previous plans quietly and sending agents to England to bribe the powers to submission by arguments or money, or both.

All the land-hungry people in all the colonies had proceeded to do just that, and London had been a battleground of American agents and money-loving peers. The corruption of English official life at that time was beyond belief. The King bribed and was bribed. The peers and commoners bribed, and parliament was an auction room.

While the merry war of agents went on in London, the Americans had carried on an equally merry, if less luxurious, war of bribing officials and claiming each other's claims.

Washington was right in the van. We have it in his own words that he did not take the King's proclamation seriously and laid his plans secretly while showing open deference to his Majesty's least whim.

In these years of his life, he was above all things a relentless partner in land-grabbing corporations, an insatiable speculator. He was gigantically a "plunger in land titles . . . a typical representative of these Virginia speculators." This is the expression used of him by so sober an historian as Alvord, who goes on to say:

"When Colonel Byrd of Virginia made out a good argument for the rights of the colonial officers and soldiers to land under the proclamation of 1763, which was always interpreted in England as limited to members of the regular army, Washington regarded the possibility of establishing such claims as a good gamble and instructed his brother to sound the officers he should meet as to the chance of purchasing their rights." [16]

He notes also how darkly politics was mixed with all this speculation. Many of the members of the Virginia Council were gambling heavily, and petitioning for grants of 100,000 acres apiece, among them John Robinson and Richard Corbin, two of the few men who seemed to have called Washington, "George."

Washington was himself a member of the House of Burgesses, and there was such a scramble among them all for land grants that Washington wrote to his brother:

"There appeared by a list laid before the House of Burgesses by order of the governor to be between 6 and 7,000,000 acres actually granted and petitioned for; and most of the grants made in such general and indeterminate terms, that if confirmed no man can lay off a foot of land to be sure of keeping it till they are served." [17]

In these days when so many things are frowned on that were accounted honorable in those days, if a member of the Senate, or of a State Legislature, should take so energetic a part in the acquisition of vast masses of public land, there would be an earthquake of scandal and impeachment.

Washington, however, followed the codes of his day, and as yet he had had no opportunity to show his readiness to make supreme and unique sacrifices of money and luxury for the sake of an ideal.

XI

HE HUNTS BUFFALO IN OHIO

THE fascination the Western wilderness had for Washington gave him no rest. It woke his hunger, his guile, and his loftiest vision.

Not content with his shares in the big corporations, he cast about for personal acquisitions.

There was a Captain William Crawford who had been an officer in his regiment under General Forbes and had settled in Pennsylvania. To him Washington wrote in 1767 that he had heard that claims might now be made for lands, and commissioned him to "look me out a tract of about fifteen hundred, two thousand, or more acres . . . ordinary or even middling land would never answer my purpose. . . . No: a tract to please me must be rich."

He asked Crawford to make haste as there would be an undoubted rush. He feared that Pennsylvania laws might not admit so large a quantity of land to be entered at once.

"If so, this may possibly be evaded by making several entries to the same amount. . . . But this I can only drop as a hint."

His canniness may be emphasized by italicizing a few phrases.

He proposed to join Crawford "in attempting to secure some of the most valuable lands in the King's part, which I think may be accomplished after a while, *notwithstanding the proclamation,* that restrains it at present, and prohibits the settling of them at all; for I can never look upon that proclamation in any other light (*but this I say between ourselves*), than as *a temporary expedient to quiet the minds of Indians.* . . .

"I would recommend, it to you to *keep this whole matter a secret*, or trust it only with those, in whom you can confide, and who can assist you in bringing it to bear by their discoveries of land. And this advice proceeds from several very good reasons, and, in the first place, because I *might be censured for the opinion I have given in respect to the King's proclamation*, and then, if the scheme I am now proposing to you was known, it *might give the alarm to others*, and, by putting them upon a plan of the same nature, (before we could lay a proper foundation for success ourselves,) set the different interests a clashing, and, probably, in the end, overturn the whole.

"All which may be avoided *by a silent management*, and the (operation) *snugly* carried on by you *under the guise of hunting other game*, which you may, I presume, effectually do, at the same time you are in pursuit of land, which when fully discovered, advise me of it, and if there appears but a bare possibility of succeeding any time hence, I will *have the lands immediately surveyed, to keep others off*, and leave the rest to time and my own assiduity to accomplish." [1]

He wrote similarly to Colonel John Armstrong, who was in the land office, and for whose special favors in facilitating his claims he offered reimbursement.

Crawford answered encouragingly. He knew the country well, a good part of it had been taken up but "when I cam down there was som un settle^d yeat very good which I think would Please you. . . . I have pitch^d upon a fine peace of Land on a Camp called Shirtees Creek." He referred to Chartier's Creek which was "fit for water works."

As for the land forbidden by the King's proclamation, it was also forbidden by the Indians—"by the Endies ho I understand says the shall not Run any farther till they are paid for the Land."

Still, he says, "I shall heartily imbrass your Offer" and promises to "set out in scharch," secretly "under a hunting sceem. . . . You may depend upon my Keeping the hole a profond secret." That is as far as he can satisfy him "as to the particqualars" and he hopes to be excused for "any Eror that I may have comited." [2]

Colonel Armstrong also answered in a friendly vein, saying that the land could only be taken up after it had been purchased of the Six Nation Indians, with whom various people were dealing. He promised to see Governor Penn and "take the Liberty of feeling his Hon^rs Pulse."

He admitted that the rules concerning claims "has been much eluded especially of late when the Artifice of borrowing Names" was used, which "occasion^d some noise among the populace." [3]

The boundary was then being surveyed between Pennsylvania and Maryland by Mason and Dixon, whose vague line made their names immortal.

Washington sent Crawford £20 and in January, 1769, received from him a letter saying that since he found "the Survayor was Runing Land out for such as was Redy to pay him, Emedatly I got him to Run out your Land . . . taking all the good Land and Leveing all that was sory."

Impatient of distance and distrustful of agents, Washington resolved to make the journey to the 200,000 acres of the soldiers' grant. In August, 1770, he went to Fredericksburg for a conference and "Met the Officers of the first Virga. Troops at Captn. Weeden's where we dined and did not finish till abt. Sun set." Here it was agreed that he should act as their representative in pushing their claims on the Ohio.

He wrote about this tour more fully and more fervidly than he seems to have written about anything else except his second tour in 1784, of which he wrote even more.[4] His story is in each case over fifteen thousand words long.

He set out October 5th, 1770, with his physician and devotee, Doctor Craik, his negro boys, Billy and Giles, also a lead horse and baggage. On the tenth he bought two new horses and sent Giles back home "with those I rid up." His "Portmanteau horse faild in his Stomach."

On the way he had a talk with old Colonel Thomas Cresap, whose place he had visited as a sixteen-year-old lad in 1748. Cresap lived to be a hundred and five, and was one of the many pioneers who had settled in the wilderness and given their names to the map years before Washington dreamed of it.

He passed unhappy old battlefields but no reminiscences decorate his pages. He does not even mention his surrender at Fort Necessity, nor the fact that he was to get Crawford to buy the spot for him at a cost of 30 pistoles (about $108). Later he said it could be "reclaimd at an easy comparitive expence and is a very good stand for a Tavern." [5]

He visited the plantation of Thomas Gist, son of his old guide, Christopher Gist, who had led him on his first important mission to the French. He liked the country, "the Ld. appeard charming; that which lay level being as rich and black as any thing coud possibly be." He noted "the beautiful white Oaks that grows thereon."

He pushed on to Crawford's plantation, where he saw a coal mine. He had now reached the site of the present town of Connelsville, Pennsylvania. Here he viewed some claims that Crawford had taken up for him near the river, "some as fine Land as ever I saw, . . . well waterd, and has a valuable Mill Seat." Crawford had also taken up land for Washington's brothers, Samuel and John, and for Lund Washington while he was at it. It was not so rich as George's.

In order to secure this land for himself he had to get a military title to it, since he was saving his own military title for another 5,000 acres. So he very ingeniously persuaded his impecunious old neighbor, Captain John Posey, to claim

it, and sell it to him for eleven guineas. Which made the
3,000 acres cost him two cents per acre.[6]

Pushing on to Fort Pitt, he found there two companies of
Royal Irish, and dined with the officers, and with Colonel
Croghan. Croghan and he had quarreled in 1754 when
Washington seized some of Croghan's trade horses on his
retreat to Fort Necessity, causing Croghan a loss of more
than £5,000. But Croghan was no longer the contemptible
Indian trader that Washington had despised; he was now
a Turkish sultan of the wilderness.

He had already managed to circumvent the royal proclamation of 1763 and had purchased 100,000 acres, under
cover of thirty-nine alleged associates.[7] By 1770 he had
acquired over 250,000 acres, excellently selected, and eventually merged in the Grand Ohio Company, of which he
was a member.

At Fort Pitt on October 18th, 1770, Washington and
Croghan buried the hatchet and became allies for a time.
Washington dined with "Colo. Croghan the next day at his
Seat abt. 4 miles up the Alligany."

There a flattering reception was in store for him, for
Croghan invited a group of Indian chiefs to greet him.
They had not forgotten him in seventeen years, and the
White Mingo gave him a string of wampum and a speech
"to the following effect":

"That as I was a Person who some of them remember to have
seen when I was sent on an Embassy to the French, and most of
them had heard of; they were come to bid me welcome . . .

"To this I answerd (after thanking them for their friendly
welcome) that all the Injuries and affronts that had passd on either
side was now totally forgotten, and that I was sure nothing was
more wishd and desird by the People of Virginia than to live in the
strictest friendship with them."

After dinner he returned to the village already known as
Pittsburgh, and Colonel Croghan, having engaged an Indian

guide and an interpreter, went along with Washington, Crawford, Doctor Craik, and five others, when they "imbarked in a large Canoe." Another canoe filled with Indians attended them and they paddled to Logs Town, where Croghan left them.

They pushed on, and hid "a Barrl. of Bisquet in an Island to lighten our Canoe." They ran into snow, and "ugly Rifts, and Shoals," "Killd five wild Turkeys," had "the disagreeable news of two Traders being killd . . . which causd us to hesitate whether we shoud proceed or not."

But they went on, passed through part of Ohio, camped in what is now West Virginia, saw "Deer watering, . . . some of which we Killd." It snowed every day for over a week, but they drifted on past the mouth of the "Muskingham" river which had "a gentle currant."

On Sunday, the 28th, they encountered an Indian hunting party under Chief Kiashuta, "an old acquaintance, he being one of the Indians that went with me to the French in 1753. He expressd a satisfaction in seeing me . . . giving us a Quarter of a very fine Buffalo."

Washington was too considerate of others to make long speeches, and he did not relish hearing them:

"The tedious ceremony which the Indians observe in their Councellings and speeches, detaind us till 9 Oclock."

After "a Night of Rain," they moved on. On November 2nd they went ashore, "incampd and went a Hunting; Killd 5 Buffaloes and wounded some others, three deer etca. This Country abounds in Buffalo."

It lay near the present site of Gallipolis, more than a hundred miles due east of Cincinnati.

Here, at the mouth of the Great Kanawha river where it empties into the Ohio, he made a rough survey of the 200,000-acre grant which he called:

"The Soldiers Ld. . . . This is a good Neck of Land the Soil being generally good; and in places very rich. Their is a large proportion of Meadow Ground."

On November 3rd they set out for home. Washington cared less for Indian friendship than for Indian enmity. He notes dismally that "by the Kindness and Idle ceremony of the Indians, I was detaind at Kiashutas Camp all the remaing. part of this day."

From here on for several days the leaves of the diary are so eaten away by mice as to give a free-verse effect to his description,

> "little stream, imperceptable
> the view in our passage
> now pouring in her mite,
> River raising very fast
> grows so muddy as to ren
> water irksome to drink."

They had an anxious time fighting the flood but finally reached Mingo Town in Jefferson County, Ohio:

"And here then will end our Water Voyage along a River."

He describes the Indians and their "poor and perishing life" and says that they

"view the Settlement of the People upon this River with an uneasy and jealous Eye, and do not scruple to say that they must be compensated for their Right. . . .

"On the other hand, the People from Virginia and elsewhere, are exploring and Marking all the Lands that are valuable . . . along down the Ohio as low as the little Kanhawa . . . how difficult it may be to contend with these People afterwards is easy to be judgd. . . . A few Settlements in the midst of some of the large Bottoms, woud render it impractable to get any large qty. of Land Together."

He hired two Indians to take his canoe to Fort Pitt for "6 Dollars and a Quart Tinn Can." They rode on horses to Fort Pitt, reaching there November 21st. He invited the officers to dinner with him, and it cost him £26. 1. 10. He paid the Indians and the Interpreter and traded some of his horses.

He then "set of on my return home. . . . The Snow upon the Alligany Mountains was near knee deep. . . . The Old Town Gut was so high as to Wet us in crossing it."

He reached home December 1st after a tour of "Nine Weeks and one day." His Diary once more is a brief mention of dinners, hunts, and kennel gossip.

Mightily impressed by Croghan's magnificence at Croghan Hall and his 200,000-acre estate near Pittsburgh, Washington wrote to him, asking him to have Crawford appointed surveyor. He tried also to buy Croghan's two shares in the Grand Ohio Company, but did not succeed.[8]

Washington wrote him again and ordered his agent to locate and survey 10,000 acres as close to the colony of Vandalia as possible. Croghan was a man to be cultivated at that time and for some years after, for his claims put him in the class of Lord Fairfax and Sir William Johnson.

But he had laid out too much money and "practiced a system of finance very much like that which was used to build railroads in the West after the Civil War; he 'bonded' his great ideas when he could and mortgaged any property which represented them, in order to secure capital for further 'development.' " [9]

He borrowed lavishly in New York, Albany, Philadelphia, began to sell his holdings, and based everything on the granting of the Vandalia charter with its twenty million acres.

In the meanwhile, Crawford kept an anxious eye on Croghan, whose claims were cut up by Pennsylvania and Virginia speculators.

In desperation Croghan tried to sell Washington various tracts, offering him one whole township of 27,500 acres for cash. But Washington was too cautious now to plunge so heavily, even if he had had the money. He wrote Croghan that he would try to organize a syndicate, but he never did.

Conditions resembled bonanza times in the gold rushes eighty years later. As Crawford wrote to Washington:

"There will be [no] Posability of taking up such a Quantity as you want near Fort pitt as there is such numbers of People out now Looking for Land and one takeing Each others Land from him as soon as a mans back is turnd an other is on his Land the man that is strong and able to make Others Afraid of him Seems to have the best Chance as tims go now. . . . I do not find I can get you the Quantity of Land . . . without I cold stay all Summer and be on the spot as People Crowd out in such numbers the Like never was seen." [10]

Lord Botetourt died in October and was succeeded as governor of Virginia by Lord Dunmore, who warned Croghan that he would grant patents to Crawford and Washington for their surveys, under Virginian authority, which authority the Pennsylvanians denied. To fix this dubious claim, Crawford hired settlers to build log cabins and clear an acre of ground each. Croghan's brother engaged others to do the same in his behalf.

A homestead war followed, which Crawford described in a letter to Washington:

"they took your Land and say the will Keep it, I cold Drive them away but they will com back Emedetly as soon as my back is turnd, They man I put on the Land they have drove away and Built a house so Close to his dore he cannot get into the house at the dore . . . there is no getting them of without by Force of Arms." [11]

There was war also in London, where all depended on the decision as to the Vandalia grant. The feeling in England

had swung against such tremendous gifts to grasping speculators, a feeling that would be well approved in these days.

A new imperial land policy was announced by which
small tracts from a hundred to a thousand acres each would
be sold to individual bidders. This plan was fought by the
best legal ability in England.

Croghan was so frenzied at the impending ruin, that, having borrowed $4,000, he offered a million acres in payment
for it.[12]

Something had happened in England. The Philadelphia
philosopher, Franklin, and the Philadelphia merchant, Samuel Wharton, had fought the Vandalia grant and the Grand
Ohio Company merger through all opposition, forcing even
Lord Hillsborough to resign in defeat.

But a reaction set in. General Gage, hero of Braddock's
Field and not to prove so heroic in Boston, had been sent
to America to report on the western problems. "From a
radical expansionist he had become a most conservative anti-
expansionist." [13]

He was accused of opposing the Vandalia scheme. The
Virginian opposition in London was blamed. But a greater
reason prevailed. The town of Boston had a tea party.
Thomas Wharton wrote from Philadelphia to his brother,
Samuel:

"I most ardently wish thou may be in possession of the
grant, before the arrival of the full accounts respecting the
conduct of the Americans touching the tea."

But he was not. The arrival of the news threw the British ministry into such a rage against all Americans that the
Grand Ohio Company bubble burst forthwith.

Thus it was from Boston that Washington had the answer
to his prayers against the Vandalians. He did not realize his
debt, but his heart swung from the West to the East, and he
tossed aside his dreams of wealth by speculation.

He devoted his soul to the salvation of his people, and saved it thereby in the sacrifice.

But Croghan wavered, was never quite rebel, never quite Tory, and died in poverty before the Revolutionary War was over, while Washington went on and on, enlarging in greatness.

This, however, is no justification for stealing from Croghan his merited fame and labelling Washington the Father of the West, as well as of the Constitution, his Country, and nearly everything else worth fathering.

While he fought, the wrangle between the Virginians and the Pennsylvanians over the West raved on. It was carried through the Revolution, invaded Congress, delayed the union of the colonies, and was kept up in the early days of the young republic.

Washington took up the fray again after the war was over, and devoted his augmented powers to western problems; but that was far in the future, and it is necessary to revert to the days of 1771, when he did not even suspect a rebellion, and was still pleading with the English authorities to do him and his soldiers justice for their services.

XII

HE FIGHTS FOR HIS SOLDIERS' LANDS

IN peace as in war, Washington found it more than hard enough to persuade the soldiers for whom he was fighting to keep in line behind him. He could not even collect an assessment of charges attending the surveys, for which each subaltern officer was supposed to pay £10, the rest in proportion.[1]

He complained of the backwardness and lukewarmness of the authorities, the difficulty of getting cooperation from the scattered claimants, so that "a few are obliged to wade through every difficulty, or relinquish every hope."

So he wrote November 7, 1771, to his friend, George Mercer, who had been in London all this while defending the interests of the Ohio Company. Washington had entered the claims of Mercer, as well as of Stobo and Van Braam, the old soldiers whom he had not seen since 1754 when he had turned them over to the French as hostages at the surrender of Fort Necessity. The hostages had never been redeemed and had had to escape for themselves after years of French captivity.

Washington asked Mercer to try to buy up their claims for him "provided they will take a trifle for them." [2] But his soldiers were not all willing to accept his trifles, and when they did their poverty and not their will consented.

In his letter to Mercer, Washington complained further because the English Board of Trade was so scrupulous. He made exactly the plea offered always for huge corporations, land-schemes, railroad ventures, trusts; great risks should promise great profit, or they will not be taken:

"It is a fact well known, and every age evinces it, that no country ever was or ever will be settled without some indulgence. What inducements have men to explore uninhabited wilds, but the prospect of getting good lands? Would any man waste his time, expose his fortune, nay, life, in such search, if he was to share the good and the bad with those that come after him? Surely not." [3]

A new arrangement was at last made by which each field officer would receive 15,000 acres instead of 5,000; each captain, 9,000; each subaltern, 6,000, and each private soldier, 400.

But Washington found many of the soldiers unwilling to pay their share of the costs, and he had an insulting letter from Major George Muse, who had been one of his military teachers, but had been accused of cowardice at the Fort Necessity battle. To him Washington wrote with unusual fire:

"SIR, Your impertinent letter was delivered to me yesterday. As I am not accustomed to receive such from any man, nor would have taken the same language from you personally, without letting you feel some marks of my resentment, I would advise you to be cautious in writing me a second of the same tenor. But for your stupidity and sottishness you might have known, by attending to the public gazette, that you had your full quantity of ten thousand acres of land allowed you, that is, nine thousand and seventy-three acres in the great tract, and the remainder in the small tract.

"But suppose you had really fallen short, do you think your superlative merit entitles you to greater indulgence than others? Or, if it did, that I was to make it good to you, when it was at the option of the Governor and Council to allow but five hundred acres in the whole, if they had been so inclined? If either of these should happen to be your opinion, I am very well convinced, that you will be singular in it; and all my concern is, that I ever engaged in behalf of so ungrateful a fellow as you are. But you may still be in need of my assistance, as I can inform you, that your affairs, in respect to these lands, do not stand upon so solid a basis as you may imagine, and this you may take by way of hint." [4]

On November 5, 1772, he wrote to Lord Dunmore and the Council the glad tidings that the whole 200,000 acres

LORD DUNMORE
(From the Virginia State Library)

had finally been obtained, and most of the certificates deposited.

But many soldiers were still not heard from and, in spite of all his efforts, there were complaints that he and Doctor Craik had taken advantage of the others. He defended himself hotly.

Incidentally, while waiting for the soldiers' grants, he had obtained some land in West Florida by buying up the claims of Captain John Posey and the Rev. Dr. Thruston, who were connected with Lyman's "Military Adventurers." [5]

He wrote to the Governor of Florida to pick the best. He was even casting about for purchases "on the Mississippi, the Mobile, or elsewhere [which] promise *in futuro* to become most valuable." He asked his old political manager, James Wood, who was travelling in Florida, if he found "good lands easy to be obtained, and not difficult to keep under the established rules of government, that you would increase my quantity to fifteen, twenty, or twenty-five thousand acres."

In the fall of 1773, Washington published large advertisements in various newspapers offering to subdivide his 20,000 acres "between the mouths of the two Kanhawas . . . into any sized tenements that may be desired, and lease them upon moderate terms, allowing a reasonable number of years rent free" provided certain tilling and planting were done. He praised his lands: "None can exceed them in luxuriance of soil, nor convenience of situation . . . many of which (by the bountiful hand of nature) are, in their present state, almost fit for the scythe. From every part of these lands, water carriage is now to be had to Fort Pitt . . . vessels of convenient burthen, may and do pass continually." [6]

This last statement is Washington's own unconscious denial of the posthumous claims that he was the Father of the West. The first lands he offered were on a stream already thronged with traffic. And he was not yet sure of his title to those.

There was already, in 1773, fear that his lands might be taken over by the Vandalia government, but he assured the purchasers that they would have the advantage of being near "the seat of government, which more than probable will be fixed at the mouth of the Great Kanhawa."

The only seats of government near there now are Point Pleasant, West Virginia, with a population of about two thousand, and Gallipolis, Ohio, with something over five.

In September, 1773, Washington wrote excitedly to Crawford that Dunmore might transfer the patents for the soldiers' lands to a district lying below the Scioto. He wanted ten thousand acres surveyed at once, "five thousand of which I am entitled to in my own right, the other five thousand by purchase from a captain and a lieutenant." He urged Crawford to pick out "the most valuable land you can," but not to run into any counter-claims of Pennsylvania officers who were also receiving grants.

"Old David Wilper, who was an officer in our regiment . . . tells me, that they have already discovered salt springs in that country. . . . I wish I could establish one of my surveys there; I would immediately turn it to an extensive public benefit, as well as private advantage."

If Crawford should find other salt springs by aid of the Indians:

"I would join you in taking them up in the name or names of some persons, who have a right under the proclamation, and whose rights we can be sure of buying, as it seems there is no other method of having lands granted; but this should be done with a good deal of circumspection and caution, till patents are obtained."

The next day he wrote to Michael Cresap, saying he had learned that a Doctor Brisco had squatted on a choice piece of land that Washington had especially selected when he was out on the Ohio River. He had warned Brisco off only to learn that Cresap had supplanted him. He now begged Cresap to go quietly to save a lawsuit, and offered to pay him for any improvements he might have made. Cresap, who was a fearless Indian fighter, declined to yield, and Washington had much trouble with him and other squatters.

In October he had to write to Col. Armstrong that Lord Dunmore had denied promising any grants on the Scioto. He wrote to Dunmore imploring him to settle the papers before emigrants settled on the lands.

Despairing of the Governor, he appealed to the Virginia Council and from that body, by some exercise of pull or persuasion, secured an order granting the lands he had first hoped for. This is made evident in a letter included in neither the Ford nor the Sparks' collections, and quoted only by the hostile pen of an Englishman, the Rev. Bennet Allen, an Oxford M. A., who published a sketch of Washington in the *London Morning Post* for June 7, 1779.[7]

Allen also wrote sketches of Franklin, Henry, Daniel Dulany and others. Dulany's brother, then in London, challenged the anonymous author to a duel and the clergyman not only disclosed his identity, but met the American and killed him in Hyde Park.

For this he was fined one shilling and given six months' imprisonment in Newgate. Which at that time was a high price to pay for killing an American.

Allen, who claimed to know Washington, described him thus:

"Ambitious, with the fairest professions of moderation, and avaritious under the most specious appearance of disinterestedness— particularly eager in engrossing large tracts of land, though he has no family, but by a widow lady of fortune he married, who bore children by a former husband. He has not perhaps less than two

hundred thousand acres surveyed for him on the Ohio, first purchasing officers rights for a trifle, and then procuring an order of
the council of Virginia to extend the proclamation of 1763 to the
Provincials employed in the last war."

To justify this charge Allen quotes a letter (probably to
George Mercer, since it speaks of his brother), saying:

"The following extract of a letter from Colonel George Washington to his agent, dated December 27, 1773, will explain a
transaction but little known in England. 'I have just obtained an
order of council to grant lands under the King's proclamation of
October, 1763, to the officers and soldiers, by which a lieutenant is
entitled to 2,000 acres, but that the Governor would not grant his
warrants of survey to any that did not personally apply for them.
Numbers, however, are obtaining these warrants, and locating them
with the surveyors of Augusta, Botetourt, and Fincastle, by whom
and their deputies, all these surveys are to be made.

" 'Till I see your brother I am at a loss to locate my own lands
under the proclamation of 1763, and am sensible that every day's
delay may prove hurtful, as I suppose every officer and soldier
within the three provinces, either is or will be upon the move to
locate their lands, by which means all the valuable spots will be
engrossed.

" 'G. W.

" 'P.S.—No land will be granted to any but officers and
soldiers.' "

The Rev. Mr. Allen goes on to say:

"It is evident Washington egregiously outwitted the Governor
of Virginia; his request was singularly modest, to include the
Provincial officers and soldiers in the grant, for whom the King's
proclamation could not design these lands, for this obvious reason,
that the object of the war was answered by securing them in possession of their own lands—and to exclude the British officers and
soldiers, for whose reward they were assigned, and to whose distressed families they might hereafter have proved a seasonable
refuge, by insisting upon their personal application in Virginia.
Many friends of Government likewise on the spot were excluded
by the grants being only made to the military—and the possession

of these lands, as it will afford a safe asylum to the American leaders, if unsuccessful, so it will enlarge their territory to a boundless extent, if they establish independency."

How he really secured the grants at last is not known, though the Beards say: "The land office in Virginia was a sink of corruption . . . and everywhere the disposal of patronage was viewed as a branch of colonial trade." [8]

Whatever Washington's motives and methods, he felt the call of the West and having, as he thought, finally secured a legal right to the lands, he devoted himself to replacing the savages who loafed upon it, with farmers and safe people who would fence the wilderness and plant it with corn. He saw cities there.

He thought for a time of importing a number of Germans from the Palatine for that purpose. He had heard that a ship had refused "an offered freight of these Germans at forty shillings sterling." He considered a plan to bring in also people from Ireland or Scotland.[9]

He was warned by Robert Adam that the Palatines "are in general much prejudiced against coming into Virginia or Maryland, as in either they are not allowed the same liberty of conscience in enjoying their own religion. This naturally inclines them more to Pennsylvania."

Washington, remembering perhaps his dead brother, Lawrence's understanding of the excellent real estate value of religious tolerance, hastened to give assurance "that I see no prospect of these people being restrained in the smallest degree, either in their civil or religious principles; which I take notice of, because these are privileges, which mankind are solicitous to enjoy, and upon which emigrants must be anxious to be informed."

In his anxiety to secure Palatines he appealed to a German who had been a captain in his regiment in 1754. This man, David Woelper (whose name Washington characteristically misspelled as "Wilper" or "Wilpert") answered with a quaint letter, first offering to sell his own military land titles:

"If your Honnour Choose to buy my Claim, of the 2000 acers, for which I got my warrant, in the kings proclamaision, 1763. you are will come to it, If you can get the warrant altherd, to a Nother County, where you pleas,

"Sir, as you have Some Intainsion, to Impord Some of my Countery man, To Sattlen your Land, and to Resolve your Quistion, which you has macke, to your Servant, To which I will give you, my Humble answer, to the best of my knowledge, and Informaision,"

He described at length the conditions on which the Palatines would sell themselves for ship-money, explained that a "freight," "Is a man or a woman," and described the lodgings they required on board:

"They are Logged in Bed Stals, macke of boards, 6-feet Long and 2 feet waith, This Bed Stals, are so Regulatted, acorting, to the vessel, Some Bed Stals are made for 2. 3. 4. 5. 6 Fraight, to hold, and Lay in it, and To keep Theries Nessisary by them, The other paggach, muss be but Down, in the hold,—" [10]

Woelper did not, however, procure the Palatines, and Washington had to content himself with a purchase made for him abroad of "four men convicts, four indented servants for three years and a man and his wife for four years." His agent paid £110 for them, and said that more could be had. The price was high but they were "country convicts" and "likely people."

The importation of contract labor is another practice of Washington's day that is now illegal.

Washington advertised again in May, 1774, that he had sent out carpenters to build houses and clear and enclose lands, and he offered "leases for lives, renewable forever." [11] So many British families were persuaded to "venture their future in the Ohio Valley" that the British feared the depopulation of England.[12]

Once more Washington's plans were thrown into confusion. A war broke out in the very heart of his western plantations. Yet he was no more tempted to take part in it than he had been in the Cherokee Wars that had flared during the Seven Years' War. He had put up the sword for good.

This war was named after his slippery friend, Lord Dunmore, whom Curwen called "the unimportant, insignificant, fribbling governor of Virginia." [13]

Lord Dunmore had a gift for making trouble, and after being transferred from New York to Virginia, had speedily succeeded in disgusting all his new subjects. But then no governor could have been true to his King and pleased them.

On a trip he made to the Ohio, Dunmore is believed to have had his own land-hunger wakened to such a degree that he planned to secure some of the loose millions himself. He was even accused of foreseeing the war with England, stirring the Indians up to combine against Virginia, and endeavoring to start a civil war between Virginia and Pennsylvania.[14]

This charge may have been due to after-bitterness against him, but in any case, upon his visit to Fort Pitt, he decided to renew the old Virginian claims to the whole region. He seized Fort Pitt and called out the Virginian militia "to hold it as a gate to the over-river country." [15]

This naturally aroused the Pennsylvanians to rage, and the Penns disputed his claim with vigor. At the same moment a white hunting party from the Kanawha settlement was attacked by the still restless Cherokees, and the settlers under that Michael Cresap whom Washington was still vainly ordering off his lands, ambushed and butchered some Shawnees, or Shawanese. Incidentally a pack of drunken whites massacred the family of the great Mingo Chieftain,

John Logan, who had always been friendly to the pioneers.

Naturally, Logan blamed Cresap and declared war. The Mingoes were joined by the Shawnees, Delawares, and far distant tribes. They drove off Col. (or Major) Angus Macdonald, whom Virginia had sent out to make the surveys of the soldiers' lands, but Macdonald came back with a body of militia and built a fort near the present site of Wheeling.

Though people in England had been shocked by the Virginian faithlessness to their treaties with the Cherokees,[16] Lord Dunmore took personal command and gathered as aides George Rogers Clark, Michael Cresap, and the unspeakable fiend, Simon Girty. Then he advanced down the Ohio with a navy of a hundred canoes.

Dunmore knew that a new British law called the Quebec Act had turned the whole West over to Canada, but he kept his knowledge secret and used Virginia troops to crush the Indians. Lewis' backwoodsmen made up "one of the finest armies of frontiersmen ever assembled."[17] They fought for what they supposed to be Virginia—a land extending to the Pacific Ocean, and filled with heathen of no rights at all.

Lewis fought a bloody battle with the Indians at Point Pleasant, near the mouth of the Kanawha, and won it from the great chief, Cornstalk. According to Theodore Roosevelt, "It was the most closely contested of any battle ever fought with the northwestern Indians; and it was the only victory gained over a large body of them by a force but slightly superior in numbers. It kept the Indians of the Northwest quiet for the first two years of the Revolutionary struggle; and meantime rendered possible the settlement of Kentucky, and therefore the winning of the West."[18]

It was too bad that Washington could not have been present and seen Virginians whip Indians at last.

After the battle the exultant Virginian troops under Lewis marched on to destroy another army, but were ordered back to Virginia by Dunmore, who was engaged in making a treaty with the Indians.

Chief Logan refused to accept Dunmore's invitation and addressed his messenger in that immortal, and perhaps genuine, masterpiece of eloquence known as "Logan's Speech."

The tactless Dunmore, having offended the victorious Lewis and his men by ordering them away from the scene of the treaty council, returned to Virginia like a triumphing Cæsar. But the Virginians at that time had delegates, including George Washington, at a continental congress in Philadelphia, to discuss the browbeating of Boston, and the very resolutions of November 5, 1774, congratulating Dunmore and avowing loyalty to the King, mentioned the willingness of Virginians to strive "for the defence of American liberty."

Dunmore was soon involved in war with the Virginians and tried to bring down upon them the very Indians he had pacified. But that was hidden in the stormy tomorrows.

For the present, the Indians had buried the hatchet "in the center of the earth"—a very accessible place for storing it—and in January, 1775, Washington sent out another group of workmen to work on his lands and plant corn, "Water-Mellon seed—Cucumbers—& every Kind of Seed," with negroes and white servants. He instructed his agent:

"If you should find any of the white servants obstinate, and determined not to behave well, I hereby give you full power and authority to sell and dispose of them to the best advantage. I have given Stevens a description of each, that in case any should attempt to runaway, they may be advertised, and every pains taken to recover them that can be consistently. . . .

"After you have got a place inclosed, try and buy me all the buffalo calves you can get, and make them as gentle as possible. I would not stick at any reasonable price for them, especially the cow calves, but I should like at least two bull calves for fear of accidents, as I am very anxious to raise a breed of them." [19]

He laid out so much money that he had to write to John Washington: "So far am I from having £200 to lend, that, involved as I am with one expence and another particularly on a very heavy charge of Seating my Lands over the Alligany Mountains in order to comply with the conditions of the Grant. I would gladly borrow that Sum myself for a few months, so exceeding difficult do I find it, under the present scarcity of cash to collect enough to answer this emergency & at the same time comply with my other engagements." [20]

With no inkling of the great fact that his career was to lie to the northeast instead of the west, Washington laid all his plans to go back to the Ohio not later than May, 1775.

Suddenly a thunderbolt broke from the blue. He learned that the grants under the proclamation of 1754, surveyed under an order of 1769, and certified by Lord Dunmore in 1773, had been, in April, 1775, declared null and void, leaving him and his soldiers high and dry and their lands nowhere.

He wrote a long letter to Lord Dunmore describing the dismay of all the soldiers at this final blow to their ancient hopes. He rehearsed Dinwiddie's reasons for promising the lands as an addition to their "very small daily pay" and the cruelties of the wilderness. He reminded Dunmore of "the experience your Lordship has lately had of a warfare in that country," and "the hardship and difficulty which the first troops had in exploring a trackless way over those great ridges of mountains . . . and making roads for the armies which afterwards followed, and in which they joined."

After all the expense incurred and the definite order to survey the tract, the new order was incredible. "I hardly know yet how to persuade myself into a belief of the reallity of it." [21]

It turned out that Dunmore was merely investigating

the qualifications of the surveyors, and the grants were not disturbed. But there was so much red tape and complication that some of the claimants never did get anything, though Washington by buying and exchanging secured entire tracts for himself. Promptly he abandoned his soldiers' claims, and washed his hands of the matter, having accumulated titles to no less than 32,373 acres,[22] with a water-front of sixteen miles on the Ohio and of forty miles on the Great Kanawha.[23]

Then things happened that postponed Washington's second trip to his beloved Kanawha for nine years, during which he became the most famous man of his day.

In the meanwhile, amidst all this land-jobbing, and at a time when he wailed, "I have never been a day well . . . nor a day without company" [24] there were family matters that he somehow found time to handle: Jacky Custis' love affair, and Patsy Custis' fight for life.

XIII

HIS SECOND VISIT TO NEW YORK

ALL this time it has been necessary to keep Jacky Custis waiting, for Washington, no less determined to secure his western lands than to prevent Jacky from marrying Eleanor Calvert before he had gone to college, planned to take him in person to New York.

It had been seventeen years since Washington visited the "Matrapolis." He had stopped there twice on his ride to and from Boston. He had become deeply interested in the heiress to enormous estates, Mary Philipse, and there are fragmentary evidences that he sought her hand. There is even a story that he rode back to New York from the border wars in midwinter to throw himself at her feet, only to be rejected in favor of Captain Roger Morris.

Whatever the truth of that legend may be, Washington came back in 1773 no longer the heart-free, superbly dressed martinet, but forty-one years old, solidly married, a farmer who had not commanded a soldier for fifteen years. His errand was the venerable and paternal task of putting a boy in college.

It was good of him to give so much of his time to the education of this youth who had a Washington for preceptor, but, with all the good will in the world, had neither the ability nor the luck to profit by it.

Washington's reward was hidden in the future now, but this ride undoubtedly had a great influence on his career.

Having planned to accompany Lord Dunmore on what he called an "excursion," through the western lands, he deferred that journey until he had disposed of his stepson. He wrote to Dunmore explaining his absence and his date of return, and added:

"The design of my journey to New York is to take my son-in-law, Mr. Custis, to King's College. If your Lordship, therefore, has any letters or commands, either to that place or Philadelphia, I shall think myself honored in being the bearer of them, as well as benefited by means of the introduction." [1]

By this courteous proffer he secured for himself the quality almost of an ambassador from colony to colony. He was royally welcomed, entertained as a personage of state, and acquired the acquaintance of the most eminent people in all the capitals and towns he passed through.

His purposes were social, for his own amusement; the results were military and historical.

The consequence was that his magnificent presence, his unsurpassed ability for making a profound impression, his polish, graciousness, and knowledge of affairs were exhibited to numbers of persons whose influence was great.

Incidentally, there must have been much remembering of old stories of his bravery, reviving him in the public's mind as a dauntless soldier at a time when there was soon to be a call for soldiers.

There is no reason to believe that Washington thought this all out, or conspired to attract attention. He was merely taking his boy to school.

Yet if he had been the cleverest of schemers he would have followed a plan of retiring from public gaze, and of waiting to be sent for, since there is always a reluctance to accept those who thrust themselves forward, and an eagerness to drag forward those who modestly fall back.

Kindliness, not policy, led Washington toward his hidden goal. He laid aside his big duties at home simply in order to keep a homesick, lovesick stepson of nineteen from falling into danger or despondency. His only conspiracy was against the impetuosity of Jacky Custis, who was so madly infatuated with an infatuated girl that he could not wait to be educated or to reach his majority.

He and Jacky set out in May, 1773, and spent the night of May 10 at the home of the Calverts, where the girl doubtless exercised her fascinations with dire results for Washington's hopes.

On the eleventh they were at Annapolis, and lodged with the Governor of Maryland. On the 15th they rode into Wilmington. The next day they were at Philadelphia. Washington dined three times with Governor Penn, went to the races and to a ball, and spent two evenings at the Jockey Club. Ledger B says he won £2. 5 at the races.

After eight days of gaiety in the metropolis of the new world, they rode out with Lord Stirling, dined at Trenton with Governor Franklin of New Jersey—Benjamin Franklin's illegitimate son who turned Tory. They slept at Trenton, breakfasted at Princeton, and lodged with Lord Stirling at Basking Ridge. Washington usually spells Stirling with an "e."

He reached New York on the evening of the 26th, and Jacky was installed in the college. Washington sent to President Cooper, "a set of bills for one hundred pounds sterling . . . to answer Mr. Custis's expenses at college . . . but hope, if . . . you should find him inclined to run into any kind of extravagance, you will be so good, by your friendly admonition as to check its progress." [2]

He arranged for credit with the merchants that Jacky might buy needed clothes, and invited Doctor Cooper to visit him in Virginia.

The trip cost £50. 14. 3. including the "fixing" of Jacky at the college.

Washington rewarded himself for his long land-voyage by lingering in New York four days.

He went to the theatre May 28th and to Hull's Tavern afterward. He records the fact that the tickets cost him eight shillings, but omits to mention that the play was "Hamlet" and the after-farce "Cross-Purposes," written by an actor who had married the daughter of an earl. Washington does not even mention that the *Ophelia* was the fascinating Sarah Hallam, whom he had seen in Williamsburg, and who finally resided there. Odell [3] thinks that she was "doubtless an almost unique Ophelia, with her tragic gifts and her singing voice."

There is no evidence that he met his former inamorata, Mary Philipse, or her husband, Capt. Roger Morris, who had been one of Braddock's aides with him. But he did meet another fellow of that campaign. The first night he went to an entertainment given by the citizens of New York to General Gage, a popular English officer who had visited the colonies in 1765 as a lieutenant-colonel with Braddock's troops.

He had commanded the advance party in that catastrophe, and had been wounded in the battle. It was Gage, not Washington, who took command in the panic and gathering eighty men about him bravely held the ford against the Indians and French and drove them back.

Washington and he had been friends, and they met again now in New York to talk over old times at a dinner. Gage had been concerned in western land affairs, and was returning to England with no suspicion that in a few years he would be in America again to put down a revolution, or that his dinner companion, the ex-soldier and farmer, would soon be the commander-in-chief of a rebel army engaged in driving him away from Boston.

On May 31st, Washington set out on his return. He

records no meetings with Governors, but he did dine again with the Calverts in Baltimore and on the 8th of June "reach'd home to dinner, about 2 o'clock."

Three shattering blows were preparing for him. He was about to lose both Jacky and his sister from the household, and the Fairfaxes from his neighborhood.

XIV

THREE BEREAVEMENTS

AMONG the untranslated cryptic symbols that Washington made on the margins of his almanac-diary in the year 1769, were a number which, Mr. Fitzpatrick [1] is sure, refer to the increasing frequency and violence of the epileptic attacks that were seizing the pretty body of Patsy Custis, and shaking it to pieces.

She had failed rapidly, and one of her many physicians advised a visit to the spa at Frederick, the same Warm Springs that Washington had gone to in 1761 to retrieve his own health.

Martha and Patsy and George made the pilgrimage, setting out July 31, 1769, and reaching there August 6th. The place was a gay summer resort now, and the diary lists dinner after dinner. Ancient Lord Fairfax was there, and two Colonels Fairfax. Robert and George William. Sally is not mentioned.

One reads:

"13. We dined with Lord Fairfax.
"17. We drank Tea with My Lord.
"18. My Lord, the two Colo. Fx's and others drank Tea here."

The catalog of festivals is interrupted by one sudden solemn note:

"23rd. Dined alone—Patcy unwell."

On September 9th, Washington seems to have left Martha and Patsy there and "set out on my Return home about 8 Oclock but broke the Chariot and made it 11 before we got a Mile."

He had to hasten back because there was an election. He reached Mount Vernon two days before it, and on the 14th was returned without opposition.

While at the Warm Springs, Washington neglected the care neither of Patsy nor his Ledger A, for he enters:

"Miss Custis—to—George Washington—D^r.

To the Expences of a Journey to the Fred^k Springs in Augt 1769.—Undertaken solely on her Acc^t to try (by the advice of her Physician) the effect of the Waters on her Complaint—viz.—

July.　To a Cot............................... 15 –
　　　　To Travelling Expen^s up.............. £20. 18. 9."

Among other things he charged her for a "Dinner &c^a at Snicker's, 7 shillings," and for other dinners and lodgings; for "Repair^g Houses & Build^g an Arb^r" 15 shillings, for "Roots, Green's & Fruit, £1. 18. 7½." "For Paid the Bathkeeper" £1. 10.—"Oats & Pasturage for ye Hors^s £8. 4. 1."

Then he deducted "25 pCt to reduce it to Virginia currency." He charged her for expenses down, and for servants' expenses there.[2]

The journey to the springs or the resilience of youth helped Patsy to weather two more winters.

In April, 1771, Washington and Martha made a journey to Williamsburg to put her under special care. His Ledger shows that he paid the Williamsburg physician and druggist, "Mr. Jno. Carter for 4 bottles of Fit Drops £1. 5. 0." He bought other drugs there, including four ounces of "aether," which was sometimes prescribed.

He transacted some personal business, but did not neglect to go to the theatre three times. He also "Drank a Bowl or two of Punch at Mrs. Campbell's."

In October he took Patsy and Martha with him to Williamsburg again, dining with his mother and spending the

25th "at my Mother's all day having lost my Horses. Spent ye Eveng at Weedon's"—the tavern. He spent £1. 1. 0 for "sundry play tickets at Williamsburg." He went to the theatre five times, and saw "the Fireworks" once.

On his return he consulted Dr. John Johnston of Maryland about Patsy, and paid him £14 for his vain advice.

In March, 1772, he took Patsy and Martha again to Williamsburg through wicked weather. He went to the theatre seven times, a concert, and a ball. He lost £4. 10 at cards and spent "By a pair of Drawer's," 5 shillings.

He paid a dentist £4 for himself, as his teeth were beginning already to give him the trouble that robbed him of all of them in 1789.

He took Patsy to a Dr. W. Pasteur, who charged her another £14 for useless treatment.

In May, 1772, he sat for his first authentic portrait. The painter was Charles Willson Peale, a Marylander, who had practiced the arts of saddlery, coach-making and watch-making before he decided to try portraiture. He was sent to London by generous gentlemen of Annapolis, studied with Benjamin West for a year and returned in 1770 to Maryland.[3]

Two years later he was called to Mount Vernon where he painted the famous portrait of Washington as a Colonel (used as a frontispiece to Volume I of this work). He remained at Mount Vernon for several weeks and painted miniatures of the whole family. He painted fourteen portraits of Washington from life, and his pictures have a strong resemblance to one another, though little to the portraits by other painters.

Washington afterwards spent an appalling amount of his life frozen for portraiture, but his first sitting made him solemn and sleepy. He described his sensations as a model in a letter to Dr. Boucher:

"Inclination having yielded to Importunity, I am now contrary to all expectation under the hands of Mr. Peale; but in so grave— so sullen a mood—and now and then under the influence of Morpheus, when some critical strokes are making, that I fancy the skill of this Gentleman's Pencil, will be put to it, in describing to the World what manner of man I am." [4]

He paid Peale £18. 4. 0. for "Draw^g my Pict^e." and £39 for three miniatures of himself for Mrs. Washington, Jacky and Patsy.

In July he took Patsy over to Alexandria, once "to see Mr. Adam's new Store," and once to a Ball. There was another Ball in August, and Martha spent £12. 12. 6 getting gowns made and altered, and Patsy spent 15 shillings.

Patsy was strong enough to make the wearing trip to Williamsburg again in November. He bought her a "Musick Book" for 6s 6d. and paid £1 for "2 Bottles Norris's Drops for Miss Custis." Evidently he tried to cheer her up, for he enters in Ledger B, "By Cost of seeing Wax work, 7s 6d. By Puppit Shew, 11s. 6 d."

In the harsh March of 1773 she went again.

Just before Washington rode up to New York with Jacky in April, he learned that Martha's sister, the wife of Colonel Bassett, had lost a daughter, and wrote a letter of warm condolence:

"The interruption of the post for several weeks, prevented our receiving the melancholy account of your loss until within these few days. That we sympathize in the misfortune, and lament the decree which has deprived you of so dutiful a child, and the world of so promising a young lady, stands in no need, I hope, of argument to prove; but the ways of Providence being inscrutable, and the justice of it not to be scanned by the shallow eye of humanity, nor to be counteracted by the utmost efforts of human power or wisdom, resignation, and as far as the strength of our reason and religion can carry us, a cheerful acquiescence to the Divine Will, is what we are to aim; and I am persuaded that your own good sense will arm you with fortitude to withstand the stroke, great as it is, and enable you to console Mrs. Bassett, whose loss and feelings are much to be pitied." [5]

He soon had an opportunity to test his own philosophy. The Diary for June says abruptly:

"19. At home all day. About five oclock poor Patcy Custis Died Suddenly.
"20. Colo. Fairfax and Lady, as also Mr. Massey dined here, Patcy Custis being buried. The first went away, Mr. Massey stayd."

Mr. Massey was the clergyman of whom Ledger B says:

"June 20. By Cash pd. the Revd. Massey Readg. ye. Service over Miss Custis £2. 6. 3."

The day after the sixteen-year-old girl died, Washington wrote to Colonel Bassett. In this unusually fervent, and somewhat incoherent, outpouring, Washington again shows his deep affection for Martha in his prayer that her mother, Mrs. Dandridge, would come and live with her thereafter to comfort her:

"It is an easier matter to conceive, than to describe the distress of this Family; especially that of the unhappy Parent of our Dear Patcy Custis, when I inform you that yesterday removed the Sweet Innocent Girl Entered into a more happy & peaceful abode than any she has met with in the afflicted Path she hitherto has trod.
"She rose from Dinner about four o'clock in better health and spirits than she appeared to have been in for some time; soon after which she was seized with one of her usual Fits, & expired in it, in less than two minutes without uttering a word, a groan, or scarce a sigh.—This sudden, and unexpected blow, I scarce need add has almost reduced my poor Wife to the lowest ebb of Misery; which is encreas'd by the absence of her son, (whom I have just fixed at the College in New York from whence I returned the 8th inst) and want of the balmy consolation of her Relations; which leads me more than ever to wish she could see them, and that I was Master of Arguments powerful enough to prevail upon Mrs. Dan-

dridge to make this place her entire & absolute home. I should think as she lives a lonesome life (Betsey being married) it might suit her well, & be agreeable, both to herself & my Wife, to me most assuredly it would.

"I do not purpose to add more at present, the end of my writing being only to inform you of this unhappy change.—" [6]

The story is told that when Washington learned of Patsy's death, he ran to her bedside and fell to his knees, sobbing aloud and praying that she might be spared.

Patsy's estate, amounting to about sixty-six thousand dollars, was divided equally between her mother and her brother.

From New York the heart-broken Jacky wrote on July 5th:

"Things My dear Mother were going on in this agreable Manner, till last Thursday, the day I receiv'd Pappa's melancholy Letter, giveing an account of my dear & only Sister's Death. I myself met the Post, & brought the sad Epistle to Doctor Cooper; who I beg'd to open his Letter immediately, the Direction I did not know, but the Seal I knew too well to be deceiv'd, my confusion & uneasiness on this occasion is better conceiv'd than expresst. Her case is more to be envied than pitied, for if we mortals can distinguish between those who are deserveing of Grace & who are not, I am confident she enjoys that Bliss prepar'd only for the Good & virtuous. let these considerations, My dear Mother have their due weight with you, & comfort yourself with reflecting that she now enjoys in substance what we in this world enjoy in imagination, & that there is no real Happiness on this side of the Grave." [7]

Washington had planned another journey to the Ohio country, this time with Lord Dunmore, but he postponed it to comfort Martha.

Another blow was to follow.

On July 8th, Colonel Fairfax and his wife, Sally, came "to take leave of us." The next day "Mrs. Washington and self went to Belvoir to see them take Shipping."

Thus Sally Fairfax went out of Washington's life forever. He had loved her frantically. Their parting at just this time must have added to his loneliness, now that Patsy was gone from his home. She took with her in her trunks those two rash love letters he had written to her fifteen years before.

Belvoir, the beautiful estate which he had visited as a boy, and which had been a second home to him, was empty hereafter of the two friends who had been closest to him. Dinners and visits and hunts and all manner of intimacy had held the two houses together.

It made him forlorn all his life to look at the deserted estate, whose guardianship was now added to his large collection. Colonel Fairfax had been called to England by a new inheritance of property, and the expectation of becoming Lord Fairfax. But he did not live long enough to secure the title. Sally, however, outlived both him and Washington.

Jacky's sweetheart, Nelly Calvert, tried to take the place of Patsy in the lonely home, for she was constantly there.

In September, Washington "Went to a Barbicue of my own giving," then to the Annapolis Races, and plays. He lost £3. 6 "By Cards & Racing" and tipped servants £1. 15. 3. In October Jacky came home, unable to endure separation from Nelly Calvert. His two years at King's College lasted only a month or two; but President Cooper and one of the teachers sent after him letters of highest respect and affection.[8]

Jacky now persuaded Washington and Martha to go down to Williamsburg to look over his property and release him partially from Washington's guardianship. Nelly Calvert went along.

Jacky and George did a good deal of hunting together, until, on February 3rd, Jacky was married to Nelly at her father's home. As Washington put it, he "could not be contented till he had got a Yoke fellow in Miss Nelly Calvert." [9]

Martha was too deep in mourning for her daughter to attend the wedding of her son. But she cherished no bitterness against the gracious Nelly Calvert for taking her last child from her. She sent to the wedding, by her husband, this dear effort of her aching heart:

"My Dear Nelly:

"God took from Me a Daughter when June Roses were blooming—He has now given me another daughter, about her Age when Winter Winds are blowing, to warm my Heart again. I am as Happy as One so Afflicted and so Blest can be. Pray receive my Benediction and a Wish that You may long live the Loving Wife of my happy Son, and a Loving Daughter of
"Your Affectionate Mother,
"M. Washington." [10]

The young couple made their home at Abingdon on Jacky's estate, not far from Mount Vernon.

The groom was only nineteen, but it was well that he made haste to marry, for he managed to provide his mother and Washington with four grandchildren before he died in his youth.

He lived again for Washington in the son he named George Washington Custis. And strange to say, long years after, in 1797, George Washington was to write again to a tutor, imploring him to overcome a boy's "indolence in everything that did not tend to his amusements."

The step-grandson, like Jacky, protested his fond intentions:

"Good God, how just your letter! . . . That I have abused such goodness is shocking!" [11]

To prove his earnestness, this young Custis wrote that the students at Princeton were going to give a ball at the tavern.

But he added nobly: "I shall not attend, as I do not consider it consistent with propriety."

And then the then ex-president of the new United States was to protest:

"If it has been usual for the students of Nassau college to go to the balls . . . I see no reason why you should have avoided it, as no innocent amusement or reasonable expenditure will ever be withheld from you." [12]

Loving children as he did, it was a thousand pities that he had to depend upon his wife's first husband and their children to provide them for him.

XV

THE DRIFT TOWARD REVOLUTION

ON a bright day in May (the exact date is not given by Doctor Sparks,[1] who tells the story) a solitary horseman might have been seen wending his way across the gentle landscape of northeastern Virginia.

He was six feet, three and a half inches high, and a centaur could hardly have been more at ease as man and horse galloped about the fields. The rider took a peculiar joy in his broad acres, in the crops he studied with a scientific curiosity and a calculating mind, and in the sky, whose moods he recorded with a Boswell's care.

Led by Pilot, the Master Dog, a pack of hounds, named Musick, Chaunter, Singer, Sweetlips, Truelove, Chloe, Tipler, Drunkard, Busy, Duchess, Countess, Lady, and the like, laughed and sniffed about the horse's hoofs. Suddenly Pilot sounded his hoarse bugle and struck out for the nearest woods, his nose tracing a wavering line along a scented trail. The rest of the pack scampered after him, noses down, tails aloft. They were off on what the rider called a "self-hunt." It might mean a fox or a bitch-fox; a doe or a stag. The farmer whirled his horse to join the race.

But his eye was caught by a flutter of wild wings above one of the many coves scalloping the water line of his domain. He reined his horse in with a turn of his enormous hand, and walked him slowly toward the gleaming ripples of the Potomac.

He saw sprigtail duck and teal restlessly leaping into the air and dropping back. He wished he had brought his gun. He saw something else—a furtive visitor from across the water pushing a canoe stealthily into the reeds.

The huntsman's warm heart froze. He was as generous a man as ever was, liberal to the poor and lavish to the rich. If the foreigner had asked for a duck he could have had a dozen. But for a poacher he had no tolerance.

This fellow had been warned off once, twice, forgiven and told not to repeat the theft. Here he was again.

Washington felt that rare but monstrous wrath of his gathering within him. The poacher raised his fowling piece, fired. A duck fell in a whir of color.

Down the steep slope, straight into the water and right through the bushes, Washington rode, with a shout of rage. The poacher, seeing a horse dashing the water from his breast and splintering the reeds aside, raised his gun and cried:

"Stop or I shoot!"

The rider, who found a certain charm in the whistling of bullets, spurred straight on, checked his horse at the boat's edge, bent over, seized the prow of the canoe, and willed his horse back to land, drawing the boat with him. Then he caught the terrified invader by the scruff of the neck, lifted him, and dragged him ashore.

Dismounting, he cuffed and beat and kicked the helpless, howling wretch until he vowed he would never poach again on the Mount Vernon preserves. Then Washington, hearkening the faint music of the hounds, mounted his horse, lifted him into a run, and surged up the hill, taking walls and ditches as they came.

That incident might serve as an allegory of his share in the Revolution.

A more gracious, a more loyal, subject could not be found in His Majesty's realm. The King was welcome to his honest quitrents and taxes, and to all the hospitality of the wilderness. But when he began to poach on Washington's rights as an Englishman, even His Majesty must be warned off, once, twice, forgiven, and appealed to. But after that, no!

His Majesty might come overseas with his army and navy and brandish his weapons, but Washington would ride straight at him, and would rather die than fail to drive him back across the water for good and all.

Washington from the first observed the formalities and graces even towards his enemies. He never fought a duel, but he conducted his controversies with all the stilted elegance of the code.

He had an immense pride behind his shy and retiring manner, yet he could make himself understood, and, from the first, resented every affront to his dignity. He had confidence in himself and inspired it in others. The twenty-two-year-old gentleman without military experience of any sort, whom Governor Dinwiddie commissioned a Major and put at the head of the Virginia troops in the first advance against the French, could promptly ask for promotion to a lieutenant-colonelcy. When he got it, he could immediately threaten to throw up his commission because his pay was only half that of a lieutenant-colonel with a royal commission.

He could storm against the Assembly because of the nakedness of his unpaid troops, and, when his critics grew harsh, answer them in kind and again threaten to resign.

The man who rode all the way to Boston to secure authority for the squelching of a Maryland Captain with a royal commission, was not lacking in assertiveness of his own or American dignity.

Washington felt himself the social equal of anybody on earth, and did his utmost to build up a fortune sufficient to prove his equality and enable him to give foreigners as polite entertainment as they could find at home.

He was so busy at money-getting and so afraid of himself as a speechmaker that, while he attended the House of Burgesses regularly, he took little part in its growing activities. He held up his end, and that was all. His name is not even mentioned among the early architects of American dignity. George Mason, Peyton Randolph, R. H. Lee, Patrick Henry, Pendleton—those were the names that filled the day.

Since Washington was all but invisible politically during the preliminaries of the Revolution, and since the theories as to its origins are so many and in such conflict, those who care to read a sketch of them must look in Appendix IV, for anything beyond the following hasty review of the salient events subsequent to the year 1763, when the English finished the Seven Years' War, and woke to the ambition for overpowering empire, mercantile and military.

The English merchants first attacked the rights of the colonies to print their own money, and sent a protest to the Board of Trade. But the colonies could not conduct their business on the amount of "hard money" available.

As Washington wrote to his friend, Robert Stewart, on May 2, 1763, in a letter previously quoted, the joy over the definite peace with France was followed by alarm over the British attitude:

"Our Assembly is suddenly called, in consequence of a memorial of the British merchants to the Board of Trade, representing the evil consequences of our paper emissions and their Lordships' report and orders thereupon, which, I suppose, will set the whole country in flames. This stir of the merchants seems to be ill-timed, and cannot be attended with any good effects, bad, I fear it will." [2]

The Board of Trade did indeed, as Washington wrote later, "rebuke us in the most ample manner for our paper emissions." [3]

The wealth of the colonies made them shining marks for English taxation and envy, and it also made them proud and dangerous. They had all the love of taxes that rich men have, and the same readiness to evade them.

The English were proud, and rich and flushed with the victorious peace of 1763. They had a triumphant navy chafing for something to do. Let it put down American smuggling and collect the customs. Let the army settle in America and earn its board and keep.

William Pitt was tied up in sick agonies from the gout. He was friendly to the colonies, but perhaps has won more affection in America than he deserves. He made the building of the slave trade one of his chief objects,[4] though it was already odious to the colonies, especially to Virginia. He had himself proposed a stamp tax during the Seven Years' War.[5] In due time, he would bitterly oppose the idea of American independence in 1776, though, in 1766, he had cried: "The Americans are the sons, not the bastards of England!" [6]

Perhaps he would have been friendlier to the end, and wiser, if he had had better health and less worship for a title.

Add, then, to the causes of the Revolution, Pitt's gout.

His brother-in-law, Grenville, was at the head of the British government in 1763. He put through the House of Commons a resolution calling upon the colonies to pay for the troops that were assigned to guard them.

He passed "the Sugar Bill," a revival of the Molasses Act of 1733, which had imposed heavy duties and had of course been ignored or evaded. Molasses was necessary to the Northern colonies. They made rum of it. Rum had not only its own price, but it was legal tender in the New England slave trade.

In 1763 Massachusetts had imported 15,000 hogsheads of French and Spanish molasses to make into rum, and the embargo meant ruin. G. E. Howard [7] says of rum:

"It lies at the bottom of the revolutionary contest."

James Truslow Adams lays the blame for the passage of the Sugar Act on the selfish English colonists in the West Indies to whom he gives a rôle of "prime importance . . . in complicating and embittering the relations between old and New England." [8]

Grenville also put a duty on Madeira and other wines that Washington was not alone in loving. The Virginians complained especially that "the tax upon Madeira Wine will be very inconvenient to us." [9]

The smuggling of wine from Madeira and the Azores, on which there was a duty of seven pounds per ton, had been so extensive that Schlesinger [10] adds to John Adams' remark concerning the power of molasses, the claim:

"Wine was another essential ingredient of American independence."

They make a strange company for the inspiration of a revolution:

Molasses, Sugar, Rum, Wine, Tobacco, and Tea.

Beer (the historian not the beverage) estimates that the income from the new acts would add only £20,000 to the revenue; yet the colonies roared prompt protests. [11]

Grenville finally had an act passed for collecting taxes by the device of requiring government stamps to be put on all legal documents, books, almanacs, playing cards, dice. He did not include business papers and receipts, which are now stamp-taxed in England, and have been on occasion in America. The revenue expected from this was from £60,000 to £70,000, but he tried to soothe the colonies by stipulating that it should all be spent for the protection of the colonies. However, he denied a jury trial to offenders, knowing from experience that American juries practically always acquitted Americans accused by English officials of smuggling or anything else.

Lecky [12] deemed the Stamp Act, "one of the most momentous pieces of legislation in the history of mankind," and Professor Woodburn, who calls the year 1763 "a turning point not only in the history of America but in the history of the world," quotes Lord Broughham's statement that the American Revolution was "the most important in the history of the human species."

We are among the superlative superlatives now, and the American colonists seemed to realize it. They had no doubt that they were creating an epic.

The Stamp Act had awakened little interest in England, and had been passed by an almost empty House. The English were dazed at the instant earthquake in the colonies.

The Stamp Act awoke the Americans to an astonishing amount of resentment. They called it a "tax" and appealed to the old British Constitutional maxim, "No taxation without representation."

This amazed the English, for their citizens were in no sense represented in Parliament, some great cities having no representatives at all. Liverpool, Leeds and Manchester had not one representative, while some tiny hamlets had two. Certain individuals of title had several representatives. The Duke of Norfolk had eleven! [13] Not one Englishman in fifty possessed a vote. [14] In all Scotland there were only 3,000 voters.

The English could not understand what the colonists were talking about. The English had their popular liberties still to win, while representation in the colonial assemblies, aside from the religious and property qualifications, meant much what it does now.

In Virginia, where twenty-seven out of the forty-one most influential burgesses had been educated in Great Britain or at William and Mary College, [15] Richard Bland, who had been educated in both places, took the lead in preparing

scholarly arguments against British autocracy. Bland was
the man who wrote a defence of Washington's troops in
1758 when "Centinel No X" called them cowards and
"dastardly debauchees." [16]

But the Virginian who set America aflame was Patrick
Henry, just elected, and already famous for his ferocious
attack two years before on the Anglican clergymen (who had
refused to accept their salaries in tobacco at the ratio set by
the burgesses, and had secured the King's veto to the act
of the Virginians).

Henry now rose in the Assembly and offered a set of
resolutions so fiercely asserting colonial rights and so flatly
declaring any tax laid except by the Virginia Assembly
"illegal unconstitutional, and unjust," that Bland, Peyton
Randolph, George Wythe, and others protested against the
extravagance of his backwoods eloquence.

Henry shouted part of that oration which every school
boy knows, about Tarquin having his Brutus, Charles his
Cromwell, and let George III beware lest—but he did not
say the famous line, "If that be treason make the most of
it."

As with so many other noble utterances, tradition was the
inventor of this, and it must go by the board in view of the
report recently discovered in the National Archives at
Paris.[17]

Nevertheless his speech shocked the more aristocratic and
tactful members. Peyton Randolph, the Attorney General,
cried, "By God, I would have given 500 guineas for a single
vote." [18]

But wild enthusiasm was kindled among the humbler
people, and Henry's fame ran through the colonies. And
Henry's resolutions known as "The Virginia Resolves" were
published everywhere. They raised a frenzy of enthusiasm
for resistance. Secret societies called "Sons of Liberty" mul-

tiplied, and agreements were made to consume no British goods.

By the time the stamps arrived from England and the officers appointed to sell them were ready to open shop there was rioting everywhere. Every stamp distributor was driven to resign, and a Boston mob wrecked the house of Lieutenant-Governor Hutchinson, who was also chief justice, and had aided the prosecutors of the smugglers by deciding in favor of the "writs of assistance," authorizing their prosecution.

Washington's bosom friend, Colonel George Mercer, was appointed chief distributor of stamps for Virginia, but he bowed to the storm, appointed his brother James to be his deputy, and sailed to England in his long and futile effort to save the Ohio Company from disintegration.[19] R. H. Lee thought of taking the post of collector but was frightened off.[20]

Washington's opinion of the Stamp Act is contained in a calm letter to Martha's uncle in London. He had feared to write before, he said, since, "I rather apprehended that some disgust at the news of your niece's marriage with me— why I could not tell—might have been the cause of your silence upon that event."[21]

James Otis of Massachusetts had already made fiery speeches against the royal invasions of American liberty, warning England against the tyranny that "cost one king of England his head, and another his throne."[22] John Adams[23] said:

"American independence was then and there born."

A Congress of the assemblies of the colonies was invited to meet in New York October 7, 1765. Since the delegates were chosen by the assemblies and the governors of Virginia, North Carolina and Georgia refused to call the assemblies, those colonies sent no delegates. But Virginia's sympathy was strong.

This "Stamp Act Congress" issued a Declaration of Rights, protesting allegiance to the crown, but denying the right of anybody to tax the colonies save their own legislatures, and insisting that the trial by jury was "an inherent and invaluable right of every British subject in these colonies."

For nearly a hundred years the British had tried to get the colonies to meet together and combine measures against the French. Suddenly they met and combined against the English. Franklin's old cartoon, "Join, or Die!", was revived with a new menace.

In the meanwhile, Grenville had been dismissed by the King for reasons of his own, and the Marquis of Rockingham had taken his place. Pitt made two speeches congratulating the colonies on their resistance, and Benjamin Franklin, still in England, advised the withdrawal of the Stamp Act. The English merchants also feared to lose trade if their American customers were offended.

The Stamp Act was repealed in 1766, but with an accompanying bill called the Declaratory Act, which announced that Parliament still had the right to tax the colonists whenever it pleased.

The repeal caused as much joy in England as in America; bells were rung, coffee-houses illuminated, bonfires heaped up.[24]

Washington, writing to Robert Cary in London, expressed his relief.[25] He wrote to the Hanburys wishing that the commercial system of the colonies might be

"put upon a more enlarged and extensive footing, than it is; because I am well satisfied, that it would ultimately redound to the advantage of the mother country, so long as the colonies pursue trade and agriculture, and would be an effectual let to manufacturing among them. The money, therefore which they raise, would center in Great Britain, as certainly as the needle will settle to the poles." [26]

But such farsightedness was beyond the muddled British ministry.

Pitt was made the Earl of Chatham and took over the reins of government, though the Duke of Grafton was the official head. Pitt (or, as he was henceforth called, Chatham) was too ill to rule, and Charles Townshend as minister of finance "began to undo all of Chatham's work." He secured the passage of various acts known by his name and intended to draw revenue from America "without offence."

Townshend set a duty on lead, certain kinds of glass and paper, and on tea, expecting to raise £40,000 thereby. He proposed that England pay the salaries of her royal officers, thus depriving the Americans of their chief hold over them. He strengthened the old Navigation Acts, which, says Van Tyne,[27] "had been endured, chiefly because they were not obeyed."

Then Townshend died, leaving Grafton to reap the whirlwind. He tried to recall the acts, but was not heeded, and George III took the reins.

The American response was furious. John Dickinson's serial "Letters from a Farmer" had immense influence in stirring the country. Washington records in his Ledger A the purchase of a copy. Dickinson's motto was, "We are only as much dependent on Great Britain as one perfectly free people can be on another."

Suddenly the hard times of 1767 sharpened the American wrath, throttled prosperity, stifled trade, and threw great numbers into bankruptcy. And, as every American politician has known, hard times mean woe for the official whose term coincides with them. The reasons for the crash in the colonies included the facts that they received no more money from England for supplying troops; the colonies to which they had smuggled were now British, and Danish rum undersold American.

Hard pressed as the American merchants were now, they joined in non-importation agreements and made every effort to stimulate domestic manufactures. The movement had its beginning in the North, but Virginia took it up and sent an important circular letter to the other colonies calling them to join in a petition to the King.

Conditions in Virginia caused the non-importation agreements to run a different course from that in the North. As Schlesinger says:

"The marketing of the staples of the South was largely in the hands of English and Scotch merchants and factors, whose business had been very little affected by the parliamentary duties of 1766 and 1767. The planters constituted the chief discontented class, because of their losing struggle to pay the debts they owed to their mercantile creditors. Animated by a desire to curtail living expenses and to strike at their creditors, the planters assumed the initiative in promoting non-importation associations, while the southern trading class stood aloof or were actively hostile." [28]

Now George Washington, the silent and the timid planter, was stirred to action. He took up his tireless pen, and hinted that there might be need for the sword.

XVI

WASHINGTON ORGANIZES A BOYCOTT

FOR the first time Washington took the initiative in Virginian politics. Receiving from the North a copy of the non-importation agreement circulating there, he sent it over on April 5, 1769, to his neighbor, George Mason, with a long and vigorous letter breathing such wrath that he even broached the subject of insurrection, though, by a quaint feeling of delicacy, he spelled the terrible word, "arms," with a dash as if it were something sacred or indecent:

"At a time, when our lordly masters in Great Britain will be satisfied with nothing less than the deprivation of American freedom, it seems highly necessary that something should be done to avert the stroke, and maintain the liberty, which we have derived from our ancestors. But the manner of doing it, to answer the purpose effectually, is the point in question.

"That no man should scruple, or hesitate a moment, to use a—ms in defence of so valuable a blessing, on which all the good and evil of life depends, is clearly my opinion. Yet a—ms, I would beg leave to add, should be the last resource, the *dernier resort*. Addresses to the throne, and remonstrances to Parliament, we have already, it is said, proved the inefficacy of. How far, then, their attention to our rights and privileges is to be awakened or alarmed, by starving their trade and manufactures, remains to be tried . . .

"That there will be difficulties attending the execution of it every where, from clashing interests, and selfish, designing men, (ever attentive to their own gain, and watchful of every turn, that can assist their lucrative views, in preference to every other consideration) cannot be denied; but in the tobacco colonies, where the trade is so diffused, and in a manner wholly conducted by factors for their principals at home, these difficulties are certainly enhanced, but I think not insurmountably increased, . . .

"The more I consider a scheme of this sort, the more ardently I wish success to it . . .

"But how, and in what manner to begin the work, . . . is a thing I am somewhat in doubt upon, and should be glad to know your opinion of." [1]

To this Mason replied on the same day:

"I entirely agree with you, that no regular plan of the sort proposed can be entered into here, before the meeting of the General Court at least, if not of the Assembly. . . . Our all is at stake, and the little conveniences and comforts of life, when set in competition with our liberty, ought to be rejected, not with reluctance, but with pleasure." [2]

This was a big moment in Washington's life, and yet his reticent Diary does not even mention the hours he must have spent writing the letter, or the stir he received from Mason's answer. He records only the fact that he did some surveying on the original Mount Vernon grants of 1674, which were still called "the Spencer and Washington Patent."

On the 30th he "set of for Williamsburg." On the 3rd of May, he reached the capital and, according to his Ledger, the first thing he did was to take part in a subscription to arrange some horse races!

"By Anthony Hay for 3 purses (that is Supscripn. to 3 Wmsburg Purse Races) £3." [3]

Anthony Hay kept the Raleigh Tavern, which Washington frequently calls "Hay's," and many historians mistakenly call "a private house." [4]

Even more surprising than beginning these fateful days with horse-races is the fact that Washington describes what Fitzpatrick [5] calls "one of the momentous days in Virginia history" in the following words and no more:

"17. Dined at the Treasurer's, and was upon a Committee at Hay's till 10 oclock."

Yet this was the dramatic occasion when the Burgesses meekly resolved upon an address to the King, "the father of his people," pleading that they had the exclusive right to tax Virginians, regretting certain recent acts of the ministry, and protesting against the horrible plan to transport colonists overseas for trial on any ground.

The Governor was then Lord Botetourt, a scapegrace and dishonored bankrupt sent over to save his face and recoup his fortunes, though Howard [6] calls him "sensible, industrious, and in the main just."

He took alarm at the impudence of the Burgesses in denying the full authority of Parliament and going over its head to the King, and he promptly dissolved the Assembly.

Thereupon the members (including a newcomer named Thomas Jefferson) went over to Hay's Raleigh Tavern, elected Peyton Randolph chairman, and heard George Washington introduce a non-importation agreement drawn up, probably, by George Mason, who was not then a Burgess. It was passed with the exception of a clause which would also have forbidden the exportation of tobacco.

The members organized at once the Virginia Non-Importation Association, and pledged themselves to secure the signatures of everybody of consequence in the province, or learn the reason why.

Nobody was more zealous than Washington in collecting autographs, appended to the solemn pledge not to use goods on which duty was charged, import any of a long list of enumerated luxuries, and not to buy slaves imported after November first.

The list included, "Spirits, Wines, Cyder, Beer, Pease, Beef, Sugar, Pickles, Hoes, Axes, Clocks, Upholstery, Millinery, Silks, Callico, Hats, Shoes and Boots."

Despite this ferocious onslaught on the prosperity of the Mother Country, the Burgesses drank the usual toasts to the King, the Queen, the Governor, to "the Farmer" (John Dickinson), "To a Speedy and Lasting Union between Great Britain and her Colonies," and to "The Constitutional British Liberty in America."

Two evenings later the Burgesses went to the Governor's palace and celebrated the Queen's Birth Night. The next day Washington returned home. By June 18th he was able to write that the association in Fairfax and the two adjoining counties was "compleat, or near it. How it goes in other places I know not, but hope to hear of the universality of it." [7]

The Virginia merchants, however, fought shy of the pledge, and in the North, where the American merchants had found the radical elements and the mob element useful, they began to dread the alliance and make vain attempts to break free.

Throughout the country there was the most eager effort to bend England's spirit by way of her purse. But in all quarters there was opposition on the part of the loyalists, and tyranny on the part of the signers, who did not always keep their pledge. A Scotch journalist in Boston, John Mein, fought the agreement, and accused even John Hancock of violating it. Hancock flatly denied the charge, and there was harsh treatment of those who were caught smuggling in goods, for smuggling was a crime now that it violated American instead of British regulations.

In Mein's paper appeared protests of a sort that were to be made increasingly throughout this period and throughout the Revolution. A writer signing himself "Martyr" demanded:

"Shall we still pretend to talk of LIBERTY, PROPERTY and RIGHTS without a blush? Have we not . . . established courts of inquisition in the colonies unparalleled in any age or nation? . . . Was there ever an instance of men, free men, being summoned by illegal and mock authority to answer for actions as offences, which are warranted by the laws of the land, the laws of nations and the law of God?"

Another boycotted merchant exclaimed:

"I had rather be a slave under one master, for if I know who he is, I may perhaps be able to please him, than a slave to an hundred or more who I don't know where to find nor what they will expect from me." [8]

A cynical wit burlesqued the non-importation agreement with rich irony by pointing out that it was dangerous now to marry lest children be "imported" into the world. He advised against the risk and promised that nothing would mortify the British like "our fixed determination to depopulate the country." So he proposed to have all the women put in storage under guard of a committee. He volunteered to be its chairman. And he exclaimed: "If any man should refuse to deliver up his wife or daughter upon such an interesting occasion, he must be deemed AN ENEMY TO HIS COUNTRY."

But neither appeals for freedom nor sarcasm could quell the boycotters. There were numberless assaults and when one badgered wretch fired into a mob and killed a child, the boy was hailed as the "little hero and first martyr to the noble cause."

The "Boston Massacre" was a similar martyrdom.

While all the country was turbulent, Boston was a maelstrom of conflicting emotions and violences. The respectable merchants saw the radicals, whom they had awakened and armed, going to lengths they could not stomach. The oldest families of the purest strains were at war with one another.

Those who did not shed blood or draw it broke windows or heads, or combined the sluggish tar with the downy feather on the persons of conservatives. Others showed their enthusiasm by self-denials. They would not drink tea, wear imported mourning, or foreign fabrics of any sort. It was estimated that on funerals "according to the new mode" at least £10,000 would be saved a year.

The Yale students agreed unanimously to drink no foreign liquors. Harvard students graduated in homespun. The girls of Providence agreed not to listen to lovers who did not hate the Stamp Act. Women started to spinning, weaving. In South Carolina the standing order for members of the Assembly to wear wigs and stockings was changed to permit caps and pantaloons. In Maryland an imported tombstone was smashed.

The effect of the non-importation agreement was staggering in the northern colonies, where British receipts from exports fell from £2,157,218 in 1768 to £1,336,122 in 1769.[9]

But in the South, where there was little opposition to the Stamp Act, the imports actually increased, because the merchants were largely British and could not be watched. The planters themselves were not able to watch one another much better, and even the initiator of the agreement in Virginia, George Washington (says Van Tyne [10]), "was lax when it came to literal obedience," and Schlesinger [11] points out that on July 25, 1769, he ordered a bill of goods from London including "household luxuries and personal fineries that were equally under the ban with the dutied articles."

His intentions, however, seem to have been faithful, for he wrote to a London merchant:

"If there are any articles contained in either of the respective invoices (paper only excepted) which are taxed by act of Parliament for the purpose of raising revenue in America, it is my express desire and request, that they may not be sent, as I have very heartily entered into an association. . . . I am fully determined to adhere religiously to it, and may perhaps have wrote for some things unwittingly which may be under these circumstances." [12]

A year later, with another order, he repeated the warning, and his determination not to receive "any Articles contrary to our Non-Importation Agreement to which I have Subscribd, & shall Religiously adhere to, if it was, as I coud wish it to be, ten times as strict."

When Lord Botetourt dissolved the Assembly in May, 1769, this meant that there must be a new election. Washington stood again and at the election on September 14, "was chosen, together with Colo. West, without a Pole, their being no opposition." [13]

The Association of non-importation worked so badly that a new one was projected, and in May, 1770, when Washington went down to Williamsburg, it was modified.

Still there was "dissatisfaction & murmuring" and he was plainly shocked by the lack of "Public Virtue" in the people. He left the Assembly five days before it ended, and exerted himself to get as many signatures as possible.

Yet when he found a British frigate anchored off Mount Vernon he entertained the officers with a cordiality unimpaired by the boycott he was carrying on.

A meeting of the Association was called at Williamsburg in December, but so few attended that it was adjourned till the next summer, by which time the whole non-importation business had almost completely collapsed all about the country. In July the agreement was cancelled for all articles except tea, paper, glass and paints, on which a duty was charged.[14]

The worst of the elaborate boycott was that it failed to harm England, since the outbreak of the Russo-Turkish War in 1768 brought an immense demand for British goods.

Then floods in Europe made American corn so necessary that American merchants caught up with their debts to England.

Prosperity came back and put down the spirit of rebellion. Tea-drinking began again, nine tenths of it smuggled.[15]

The discontented element led by Sam Adams found its occupation gone. A general lethargy lulled the nation. The great brain of James Otis had gone wool-gathering; for, in a coffee-house brawl in 1769, he received a sword-cut on the skull, and went slowly insane. He was now a half-witted spectator of the Revolution he had done so much to set on foot. (A month after it ended, he was struck dead by lightning, as he had once asked to be.)

In May, 1771, there was another session of the Assembly, and Washington attended it, but tells of nothing more important than that he went to the Play three times. He was down again in July, and this was so lifeless a session that he did not even mention it in his Diary.

But he wrote a long letter July 20, 1771, to Robert Cary, quarreling over a matter of window-glass which had been sent cut to the wrong measure. He complained that Cary's latest letter "appears to me to contain an implication of my having deviated from the truth."

He argued the matter out indignantly and further protested that imported goods cost him more than the price at the local stores, "which is a mystery not easy to be accounted for." [16]

For a year or two Washington was again a peaceful farmer, fretting over Patsy Custis' illness, Jacky Custis' indolence, arranging for a new manager for his "Mother's Quarter in Rappahannock" and an overseer "at the place my Mother lives at," and continuing the struggle for the western lands.

At this time Washington was at the peak of his religious enthusiasm. It was never a high peak, but he took a great interest in his duties as a vestryman. That must not be

taken to mean too much concerning his piety, for Thomas
Jefferson was also a vestryman, and, as will be seen, recom-
mended a day of fast in spite of his non-Christian views.
He also contributed more liberally to church building than
Washington ever did, and he was much concerned with
Jesus, whom Washington never once mentioned by name
in his countless writings. A Virginian had to be a vestryman
to be a Burgess.

Washington's lifelong respect for Providence did not,
however, include an awe of the church authorities any more
than his reverence for the King included an awe of the ministry. When either class interfered with the freedom of
his soul or his country, he could rebel. In time he flouted
the sacred majesty of the King, and became unwittingly the
destroying angel of the Episcopal Church in America, which
could not be revived for nearly half a century.

Among the causes of the Revolution most nearly permitted to slip into oblivion is the religious phase. It was
tremendously important at the time, and added the peculiar
fanaticism and cruelty of all wars of creed to the inevitable
evils of wars for property and freedom.

Chamberlain [17] says that the attempt to set up the Anglican
episcopal system in the colonies must be counted among the
chief causes of their separation from the parent state.

John Adams asked long afterward: Who "will believe
that the apprehension of Episcopacy . . . contributed as
much as any other cause, to arouse the attention, not only of
the inquiring mind, but of the common people, and urged
them to close thinking on the constitutional authority of
parliament over the colonies? This nevertheless was a fact
as certain as any in the history of North America. The objection was not merely to the office of a bishop, though even
that was dreaded, but to the authority of parliament, on
which it must be founded"; for "if parliament can erect

dioceses and appoint bishops, they may introduce the whole hierarchy, establish tithes, forbid marriages and funerals, establish religions, forbid dissenters." [18]

A fuller presentation of the religious causes of the Revolution is deferred to Appendix IV.

There was a further result of the war of what a later loyalist called "altar against altar." [19] The controversy over the bishops came at an unfortunate time, for it drove many an otherwise patriotic churchman into the loyalist ranks. Washington lost many of his best friends in this way.

Washington certainly was an Episcopalian, officially, and it is one of the peculiarities of the Revolution that, in a conflict which was often called a Presbyterian War, the New England Puritans should have called upon an Episcopalian to lead them.

XVII

"THE INTOLERABLE ACTS"

THE great day of March 12, 1773, when the Virginia Assembly led the way to the unifying of the colonies by a system of secret Committees of Correspondence, finds Washington more reticent than usual, if possible.

He was present in Williamsburg with Martha and Patsy at the time, and he wrote many letters concerning his western lands. But he never mentions the Committee of Correspondence, and he was not placed upon it, though Fitzpatrick says, "In the rosters of these committeemen of 1773 are to be found the names of nearly every Revolutionary patriot most familiar to us." [1]

Samuel Adams originated the idea and placed it before a Boston town meeting he had called. Three hundred citizens accepted it unanimously. He read a paper reviewing all the wrongs the Americans had suffered, or might expect to suffer. It warned the colonies of the danger of an English bishop; it discussed the ministry's kind offer to relieve the colonists of the burden of the salaries of governors and judges, and exposed it as a trick to remove from Americans all control over those officials. Adams' plan advocated the establishment of a standing committee "to state the Rights of the Colonists and of this Province in particular . . . to communicate and publish the same to the several Towns in this Province and to the World as the sense of this Town . . . Also requesting of each Town a free Communication of their Sentiments." [2]

In seventy-eight other towns radicals gathered and ap-

pointed local committees. Governor Hutchinson had previously said that the town meetings had for some time been
controlled by "the lowest class of the people under the
influence of a few of a higher class, but of intemperate and
furious dispositions and of desperate fortunes. Men of
property and of the best character have deserted these meetings, where they are sure to be affronted." [3]

This is the very portrait of a group of radicals, and it
fits all periods as perfectly as Governor Hutchinson's contempt fits the eternal mood of the ever-recurring conservative. Both groups are as visible today as then, but it remains to be seen if posterity will come to revere the radicals
of this era and despise the conservatives as fervently as our
generation reveres the radicals of 1775 and loathes the
Tories.

When the news of the Massachusetts town committees
reached Virginia, the Assembly was inspired to enlarge
Adams' local idea into an intercolonial exchange of information, warning and advice. From this evolved a whole system of revolutionary government that took over gradually
the power of Great Britain, as it was disavowed. Somebody had to handle it, for there was anarchy indeed.[4]

The Virginia Assembly instructed the Virginia Committee
"to obtain the most early and authentic intelligence of all
such acts and resolutions of the British parliament . . . as
may relate to or affect the British colonies in America," and
to carry on a correspondence concerning them with the other
colonies.

The "radicals of the Virginia House of Burgesses," as
Schlesinger [5] calls them, seized the opportunity, and the
committee was made up almost altogether of "radical
planters."

It seems strange to us today to hear the word "radical"
applied to the forefathers, sanctified as they are by tradition

and ossified by the same conservative spirit of today that resented all innovation in theirs.

But the word is now used by the most solid of modern historians in treating of this period and its time-sanctified leaders. Thus Van Tyne says:

"Radicals everywhere in the colony were now given an organization hitherto unknown, and over against the governmental machine, fairly in the control of British officials, stood a revolutionary organization full of sinister potentialities. . . . It represented the radical faction and was its agent to resist the will of the British Ministry." [6]

The word "radical" has an ugly meaning only to those whose convictions or powers the radicals plan to eradicate. The founders of American liberty gave the term sufficient honor for all time. A radical is literally and spiritually a person who believes in uprooting something, and the Sons of Liberty, who are now called its forefathers, were certainly bent on digging out the last rotten stump of imbedded tyranny.

The pity of it is that so many of the descendants of the Sons of Liberty have successively assumed the exact positions of the Tories and conservatives of those days and waxed as fierce with their criticisms of later revolutionists as were Governor Hutchinson and other Americans, who called Adams "the Grand Incendiary," and his committee "the foulest, subtlest and most venomous serpent that ever issued from the eggs of sedition." [7]

From such appalling slander Washington managed mysteriously to escape. He was occasionally called harsh names, but never such harsh names by the British or the Tories as by those in his own ranks who disagreed with him. There was something then as now in his justice, his dignity and his self-sacrificing indifference to notoriety or fame that softened the wrath even of those whom he fought.

Samuel Adams, however, who was, says Howard, [8] "perhaps the first American to foresee independence," and who was as radical in words as Washington came to be in deeds, had a genius for drawing the lightnings of hatred and abuse. Like James Otis, who was struck dead by actual lightning, he is only a vague name to his posterity, though he wrought and conspired and inspired with maniac concentration against the enemy to the East while Washington's eyes were on the West and its agricultural possibilities.

Governor Hutchinson denounced Adams and his Boston group as "deacons, atheists, and black-hearted fellows." Samuel Adams, son of a brewer who was a deacon in the Congregational Church, was actually a religious fanatic. "Atheist" was then as now a word for anybody with whom one violently disagrees.

When England sent orders to seize and send abroad for trial the hundred or more men who had captured and burned the British customs-boat, *Gaspée,* the alarm spread. Everybody knew who the incendiaries were, but nobody informed on them. They were never seized or sent.

This panic was dying away when Samuel Adams found an unexpected and unintentional confederate in Frederick North, known to his contemporaries and to fame by his courtesy title of "Lord North," though he did not earn it until his father's death just two years before his own.

Oddly enough, Lord North was born only two months later than George Washington. Washington was commissioned an officer at twenty-two, and North entered Parliament at the same age. He succeeded the Duke of Grafton as first Lord of the treasury in 1770, and thus became the head of the ministry, though he would never call himself prime minister. He has had to bear the odium of America for what he tried to do, and the odium of England for failing to do it; but he was as far as possible from being the black devil or the insensate idiot of tradition.

He was a fussy, sweet-tempered snob to whom his King

was as sacred really as most of his subjects merely said he was. He permitted George III (who was half the time as crazy as James Otis) to coerce him into many things against which his wisdom rebelled. Still, he would rather be premier than right.

Just as "Adams' demagogic devices" began to pall on the colonies, to whom he seemed to have called "Wolf!" once too often, Lord North came to his rescue, while meaning only to rescue the East India Company.

To the English of that day India was a far more promising and important hope of revenue than America. It was what a diamond mine is to a hardscrabble farm. But in spite of its orgies of cruelty, corruption and exploitation, the great East India Company fell upon hard times. Among its products was tea, and in 1773 it found itself with a surplus of no less than seventeen million pounds. The happy idea came to the English to unload that mass upon the American colonies, at half price, to give up selling it at auction, and license the Company to export it and market it in America under its own agents.

Dealing in legal or "dutied Tea" was a prosperous business for the merchants, and smuggling it in was one of the chief industries of the mariners. Also a large number of American middlemen grew rich buying tea at London auctions and selling it to American retailers.

The new tea act secured for the East India Company a monopoly of the American market, and wiped out the middlemen, mariners and merchants with one fell stroke. The tea plus its duty was offered at half price and undersold the smuggled tea. The general public profited, yet everybody was outraged.

The colonists were great lovers of tea, none more than Washington. Even the Indians had learned to like it, and the colonies could have drunk up the surplus in short order.

But now the drink was included in the cyclone of wrath, and denounced as a moral and physical poison. It was believed that England was planning the destruction of the whole colonial fabric of trade. The merchants, whom Samuel Adams and his followers had alienated by their anarchy, rushed back to him. Mobs raged and sacked, and delicate spinsters put away their cups of Bohea.

The backsliders who had returned to their tea-sipping renewed the pledge, and the East India Company's wares were a drug on the market. The ministry, facing a loss of £400,-000 annual revenue from the corporation as well as its ruinous collapse, determined to force the tea down the American gullets. Parson Weems is our sole authority for the following anecdote:

"Lord Fairfax happened to be at Mount Vernon when Washington received advice from a friend in London that the tea-ships were about to sail. . . . *'Well, my lord,'* said he, *'and so the ships, with the gun-powder tea, are, it seems, on their way to America!'*

" *'Well, but colonel, why do you call* gunpowder tea?'

" *'Why, I am afraid, my lord,'* replied Washington, *'it will prove inflammable, and produce an explosion that will shake both countries.'*

"The event corresponded with Washington's prediction." [9]

When the ships reached the big ports, their cargoes were seized and stored or shipped back to England by the rebellious Americans, who now made tea the test of treason to the country.

In Boston, the loyalist element refused to heed the demands of Samuel Adams and his town-meeting men. On the evening of December 16, 1773, a mob of pretended Indians boarded the ships, and threw 342 chests, worth £15,000, into the bay—in Weems' words, "furiously emptying their fragrant cargoes into the flashing deep."

The Indian disguise had long been a favorite one for

those who felt a need of anonymity in their violences, and there were prominent citizens among the painted Mohawks.

"The Boston Tea Party" is one of the incidents of which every schoolboy knows. Once glorified as a fearless defiance of tyranny, it is now regretted as a wanton destruction of private property.

It was called "an Act of violent Injustice on our part," even by Benjamin Franklin, then in London (where he had been accused of being a thief, a scoundrel, and a blackguard for giving Hutchinson's private letters publicity). He wrote to the Massachusetts committee of correspondence protesting against "such Extremity as, in a Dispute about Publick Rights, to destroy private Property," [10] and suggested compensation to the company—which, of course, was never made.

Others saw "liberty degenerating into anarchy" and property losing all security. The merchants again fell back in dismay from their allies, the radicals and the rabble.

Gouverneur Morris wrote of the radicals: "Believe me, Sir, freedom and religion are only watch words. . . . These fellows become the Jack Cades of the day, . . . the heads of mobility grow dangerous to the gentry and how to keep them down is the question. . . . It is the interest of all men, therefore, to seek for reunion with the parent state." [11]

Once more Sam Adams had overplayed his hand. Once more Lord North dealt the trumps back to him. In England even the friends of America were shocked, and punishment was demanded. So Lord North proposed the Boston Port Bill, which removed the customhouses from the city, and sent warships to close the harbor to all traffic until full reparation should be made to the East India Company.

A few members of parliament like Burke and Barré opposed so drastic a measure, but a Mr. Van cried that "Boston ought to be knocked about their ears and destroyed, *delenda est Carthago!*" [12] General Burgoyne pleaded for mild measures and was as furiously abused in Parliament as he later was in America.

The Port Bill was passed, and to it other bills were added, breaking the charter and taking from the Boston towns-people the right to meet, to appoint jurors, councillors, judges or sheriffs, and authorizing the royal governor to send rebellious persons to England for trial. Besides this, the Quartering Act ordered the townspeople to provide quarters for British troops.

As if these were not enough, the Ministry brought out and passed the old Quebec Act to make up the "Five Intolerable Acts." This last was a noble gesture of tolerance for the 80,000 French Canadian Catholics taken into the Empire at the surrender of Canada in 1763, and furnished them with belated protection from rapacious Englishmen who had taken advantage of the fact that they were Catholics and had no rights under English law. This "grossest and absurdest and cruellest tyranny that a conquering nation ever practiced over a conquered territory," according to the English Attorney General, had been an oversight that was now honorably rectified.

The Quebec Act gave the French Canadians tolerance in the free exercise of their religion.

To the Puritans this was simply infuriating. They had always burned the Pope in effigy with the Devil on Guy Fawkes' day, and Samuel Adams, who was politician enough to know that the best way to subdue the intelligence and justice of the mob is to arouse its religious passions, raised the terrifying cry of "Popery!"

Many of the otherwise sanest Americans answered the call and were as frenzied against the Canadians as they were friendly later when their help as allies was a thing to be besought.

Washington was one of the strongest denouncers of insult to Catholicism after the war broke out, and later stopped his soldiers from burning the Pope on Guy Fawkes' Day; but imagine his consternation when he learned that the Quebec Act carried, for its final supreme addition of insult to injury, a provision giving to the province of Quebec all that vast region between the Ohio and the Mississippi.

The English thus with one overwhelming insanity locked the easternmost seaport and closed the whole West.

The avalanche of bad news reached Boston and America just a week before General Gage arrived to take military command. Gage had an American wife, and had fought with Washington and dined with him, but he carried out his orders, and in Boston harbor nothing stirred save British warships and troopships.

The presence of an army of repression naturally and rightly incensed the Bostonians, but they took out their spite on the poor officers, who were compelled to obey their orders, and upon the luckless soldiers, who had nothing whatever to say about where they went or what they had to do.[13]

Few things are more disgraceful in American history than the treatment the British troops received in Boston. Not so much because hoodlums and riffraff committed the vilest and most cowardly excesses—they always do in every community—in England mobs were even more vicious; but because respectable Americans, historians and orators have defended them, and made a sacred incident of a riot in which eight badgered soldiers caught at bay fired on seventy-five ropewalkers and killed five.

Paul Revere made an engraving and called the event, "The Bloody Massacre." Bancroft described it as an unprovoked and murderous assault on peaceful citizens by a debased soldiery. The incident was sanctified until 1887, when a proposal by the Massachusetts Legislature to erect a monument to the victims was met by a vote of the Historical Society that it "heard with regret" of the intention; it would have been, says Van Tyne,[14] "to put the martyr's crown on the brow of vulgar ruffians." The Boston "Massacre" may now be safely and honestly dismissed as a regrettable incident, not one to be upheld before school children as an example to emulate.

The only redeeming feature of the event is that certain Americans, John Adams and Josiah Quincy, had the decency and bravery to act as lawyers for the British troops and the jury had the honesty to acquit all the soldiers except two, who were, says Howard,[15] "lightly punished for manslaughter"—"lightly" meaning a branding on the hand.

But blood is blood, however it is drawn and from whomsoever, and it was inevitable that British troops in an American city should be made as unwelcome as possible.

Blood began to spurt in all quarters of the colonies. The British schooner *Gaspée*, active in rounding up smugglers, was burned, and its commander shot in the groin. In North Carolina the Regulators, infuriated by the extortions of the officials, started a little rebellion that Governor Tryon crushed ruthlessly. It was in no sense a move for independence, but it added to the fury.[16]

Boston faced starvation as well as paralysis, and all the colonies felt their hearts touched with a sympathy that added a brotherhood to their blind wrath and dismay. Provisions poured in by land from everywhere. Lord North had done what Franklin had failed to do in 1754, and nobody else had even begun to accomplish: he made the colonies forget their ancient mutual hatreds and unite in a brief but ardent mutual love. George Washington headed a subscription list passed round in Fairfax county with a subscription of £50 for Boston.

The ambrosial Parson Weems cried out:

"How adorable the goodness of God for ordering that the ministerial attack on our liberties, should fall on the *populous* and high-toned, New-Englanders! The heroic spirit with which they repelled it, should, to eternity, endear them to their *southern brethren.*" [17]

"Eternity" was a slight exaggeration that ended with a bang in 1861.

Another English churchman of the same district as Parson Weems was of another mind.

Jacky Custis' tutor, the Rev. Jonathan Boucher,[18] refused to preach a sermon for the suffering people of Boston. He refused to join any of the associations. He refused, he tells us himself, to drink to a toast:

"Damnation to General Gage, the troops under his command, and all who wish well to them."

Hearing another toast proposed:

"May the Americans all hang together in accord and concord," he cried:

"In any cord, so it be but a strong cord."

He believed that all the revolutionary sentiment arose from "private resentment." He says:

"I have heard Governor Franklin, the son of the arch-traitor of that name, repeatedly declare he knew his father was stimulated to do what he did (and who did more?) by the indignities which he fancied were put upon him."

Boucher tried to save Washington from the horror of treason. They "long and fruitlessly debated."

He does not accuse Washington of personal motives, but if ever private resentment could enrage a man, Washington had reason for it when the Quebec Act threw into the hands of French Canadians all those western lands which made up his one dream of wealth, power, grandeur—the land for whose conquest he had made his first march as a soldier, and to whose acquisition he had devoted a score of years since.

XVIII

THE SLOW AWAKENING OF WASHINGTON

THOUGH the memorable Assembly of 1774 convened on May 5, Washington did not reach Williamsburg until the 16th.

On the way down, luck was with him. He stopped a night at Fredericksburg, and, according to his Diary, dined with his sister "and spent the Evening at Weeden's." According to Ledger B., he won a pound at cards that night at the tavern.

On the night of his arrival at the capital he played cards at Mrs. Campbell's and lost 15 shillings. On the 18th he lost £2. 10 there, but, on the same day, won back £1. 13 at the Raleigh Tavern, which J. B. Southall had recently bought from Anthony Hay.

On the 23rd he won £1. 10 at the home of the Attorney General, John Randolph, whom he was later to suspect of forging letters to be used against him.

The Assembly discussed fresh outbreaks of the border Indians and old boundary troubles with Pennsylvania, but the main topic was the Boston Port Bill, which had caused "infinite astonishment and equal resentment." [1] There was a demand for a new and more cogent boycott against England.

While Washington was playing cards and losing money, Thomas Jefferson, then a young new member, was busy at serious affairs. He tells how he and some of his friends took the lead away from "the old members, Mr. Henry, R. H. Lee, Fr. L. Lee," and determined to swing the House into an "unequivocal stand in the line with Massachusetts." [2]

"We were under conviction," he says, "of the necessity of arousing our people from the lethargy into which they had fallen, as to passing events; and thought that the appointment of a day of general fasting and prayer would be most likely to call up and alarm their attention. No example of such a solemnity had existed since the days of our distresses in the war of '55, since which a new generation had grown up. With the help, therefore of Rushworth, whom we rummaged over for the revolutionary precedents and forms of the Puritans of that day, preserved by him, we cooked up a resolution somewhat modernizing their phrases, for appointing the 1st day of June, on which the port-bill was to commence, for a day of fasting, humiliation, and prayer, to implore Heaven to avert from us the evils of civil war, to inspire us with firmness in support of our rights, and to turn the hearts of the King and Parliament to moderation and justice. To give greater emphasis to our proposition, we agreed to wait the next morning on Mr. Nicholas, whose grave and religious character was more in unison with the tone of our resolution, and to solicit him to move it. We accordingly went to him in the morning. He moved it the same day; the 1st of June was proposed; and it passed without opposition."

It is striking that Jefferson, the so-called "atheist," should have been the one to "cook up" a day of prayer and fasting, and it shows that political manipulation of religious emotions is not the invention of our own day. Edmund Randolph afterward said, "Such is the constitution of things that an act of public devotion . . . is registered in the cabinet of the politician as an allowable trick of political warfare." [3]

So James Otis had said for the North when he "lamented bitterly that the profession of a saintly piety was in New England the best means of obtaining political power."

Governor Dunmore was so incensed at the fast-day plan and took it as such an insult to the King, that on the 25th he dissolved the Assembly to choke off further resolutions. This meant that all were dismissed from office and must even seek reelection before they could meet again.[4]

Yet Washington's concern in the matter was so slight that, according to his Diary, he dined with the autocratic Governor on the 25th, and on the next morning he "rid out with the Govr. to his Farm and Breakfasted with him there."

Washington seems not to have attended the meeting of eighty-nine dismissed members at the Raleigh Tavern, where rebellion began to rear its head and an association was formed to carry out R. H. Lee's resolution of non-importation, and a summons was drawn up calling for a continental congress.

The next night, Friday, Washington, and doubtless most of the rest, "went to the Ball given by the House of Burgesses to Lady Dunmore." It cost him £1 and he must have worn his uniform for he bought a new "Sword Knott" for 4 shillings 6 d., and some hair powder, and visited the barber.

The quarrel with England had by no means reached the point where card games or balls need be interrupted. On Sunday, the 29th, Washington was pious; he "went to Church in the fore and afternoon. Dined at Mrs. Dawson's and spent the Eveng. at my Lodgings."

Though it was Sunday, couriers rode in from northern colonies with committee letters urging a union of the southern colonies. Most of the Burgesses had gone home, but on Monday the twenty-five remaining members, among them Washington, were called together by Peyton Randolph.

They unanimously agreed on an enlargement of the boycott and a call for a convention of the burgesses on August first. The Williamsburg citizens met and "cheerfully acceded."

At the meeting in Raleigh Tavern, Thomas Jefferson and Patrick Henry proposed to stop all payments of debts to the British. R. H. Lee and George Mason favored the step.

While the Americans were accusing the English of tyranny, the English were accusing the Americans of thievery. They ridiculed the prayers and fastings as hypocritical, and scouted the American claim that their poverty, due to British oppression, accounted for their inability to pay their debts, and pointed to the luxurious living of Americans, and particularly to the heavy purses offered at the Philadelphia horse-races,—where Washington was a devoted visitor and better.

Washington had stated it as a principle of honor, in 1769, and again in 1774 that Virginians must pay their debts, no matter how difficult the task might be. But this was not done until years later when American currency had so depreciated that payment of the debts amounted to a mockery —a repudiation. The same depreciation almost wiped out the estate of Washington's wife.

Thomas Jefferson [5] estimated that the Virginians owed the British merchants "certainly two million pounds sterling" in 1775. Jefferson himself owed approximately ten thousand pounds. Patrick Henry, Edmund Pendleton, the Lees, the Balls, and others owed vast sums, which they eventually cancelled with depreciated currency.[6]

It is small wonder that British creditors felt that the resounding cries of "liberty or death" were mere rhetoric, and the real passion was for liberty from debt.

It is a much-neglected fact that the practical bankruptcy of Virginia abroad and at home could not but have had its influence in the war-spirit. When men are frantic with the hopeless effort to clear themselves of mortgages, they feel that war itself cannot be worse.

Washington's descriptions of the collapse of Virginia fortunes has been quoted. In the words of Professor Harrell, in his book on "Loyalism in Virginia":

"With their plantations, slaves, and sometimes household furniture hypothecated, the planters were in an almost inextricable position in 1775; it seemed that nothing less than virtual repudiation could relieve them." [7]

On Tuesday, the first of June, Washington noted: "Went to Church and fasted all day."

George Mason wrote home: "Please to tell my dear little family . . . that I desire my three eldest sons and my two oldest daughters may attend church in mourning, if they have it, as I believe they have." [8]

Thomas Jefferson said that "the effect of the day, through the whole Colony, was like a shock of Electricity, arousing every man, and placing him erect and solidly on his feet."

Edmund Randolph wrote, in his unpublished history of Virginia: "The fast was obeyed throughout Virginia with such rigor and scruples, as to interdict the tasting of food between the rising and setting sun. With the remembrance of the king, horror was associated; in churches, as well as in the circles of social conversation, he seemed to stalk like the Arch-enemy of mankind." [9]

Randolph, who was then twenty-two, threw his heart into the cause of liberty, though his father, John Randolph, kept his oath of allegiance to the King and later sailed for England. Peyton Randolph, his brother, became eminent in the patriotic cause. Edmund reached a high post long afterward, then had a quarrel with Washington and published a pamphlet in self-defence that led Washington to beat the table till the ladies and the teacups jumped as he raged, "By the eternal God, he is the damnedest liar on the face of the Earth."

Yet this same Edmund Randolph, composing a history in his old age, wrote of Washington this eulogy:

"At the beginning of the year 1774 . . . some others were more prominent. It could not have been then truly foretold that even those germs of his solid worth which afterwards overspread our land with illustrious fruit, would elevate him very far above many of the friends of the revolution . . . His youth had developed no flattering symptom of what the world calls genius; but he had been conspicuous for firmness, for a judgment which discriminated the materials gathered by others of a quicker and more fertile invention, and for a prudence which no frivolousness had ever chequered. He possessed a fund of qualities which had no specific direction to any particular calling, but were instruments for any crisis. By nature, by his attention to agriculture, an exposure of himself in the chase, and his occupation of a surveyor of land, he was remarkably robust and athletic. . . . His economy, without which virtue itself is always in hazard, afforded nutriment to his character." [10]

After the Burgesses had dispersed, Washington lingered about Williamsburg with Martha, visiting and dining. On June 10th there were fireworks, probably in celebration of the anniversary of the burning of the *Gaspée* a year before.

Washington dined at the Governor's on the 16th amiably enough, and went to "Anderson's" to play cards, losing a pound even. He had won there nine shillings and sixpence June 6th. The next night at the Raleigh he had won a pound, ten shillings. On the 10th at the Raleigh he lost five pounds, fifteen shillings—a bad night for one "whose economy was the nourishment of his virtue." On the thirteenth, however, he won most of it back at Anderson's, where he cleaned up five pounds, five shillings. On the 15th he atoned for his levity by attending the "Society for promoting useful Kn."—where he subscribed £1 to knowledge.

Altogether on this epochal visit to the Assembly, he had

won £11. 7. 6 and lost £9, which was somewhat better than his average.

It was a vast improvement over his disastrous season at Williamsburg in March, 1772, when he won £17. 17. 6 in five games and lost in twelve games no less than £39. 11. 3.

He apparently played cards no more in 1774, for in his Ledger B., where he devotes two great pages to a study of his card business, he stops here, having begun the record January 2, 1772, with a loss of £6. 2, his first winning of £2. 3. 6 being on February 28. He mentions no gambling accounts after this Williamsburg trip of 1774, but does slip in a winning of £7 at Philadelphia in October, in order to sweeten the bitter a little.

Then he totals his losses as £78. 5. 9, and his winnings at £72. 2. 6, and closes the double entry with:

"1775 Jan. 1 By Balc̊ against Play from Jan 1772
to this date £6. 3. 3"

Which was not bad for sixty-three games, of which he lost 36 and won 27. At his own home he won only five times with an intake of £15. 17, and lost thirteen times with an output of £16. 16. 6.

It is picturesque to find him playing so hard during the most epic legislative sessions, and it is evident that he did not share John Adams' contempt for card-playing, of which he said:

" 'It gratifies none of the senses, neither sight, hearing, taste, smelling, nor feeling. It can entertain the mind only by hushing its clamours, cards, backgammon, etc., are genteel antidotes to reflection, to thinking—that cruel tyrant within us. They choke the desire for knowledge,' he added. In his early and intellectually priggish days, he confided to his diary his amazement that men could play cards, drink punch and wine, smoke tobacco and swear 'while a hundred of the best books lie on the shelves, desks, and chairs in the same room.' " [11]

Cards & other Play ... Dr

1772					
Feby.	28	To Cash lost at Fredericksburg	3	2	3	6
Mar.	2	To Ditto lost in Williamsburg	3		8	9
	13	To Ditto lost in Ditto	3	1	0	0
	16	To Ditto — Ditto	3	3	10	—
	17	To Ditto — Ditto	4		15	—
	21	To Ditto — Ditto	4		5	—
		To Ditto — Ditto	4	6	10	
	24	To Ditto — Ditto	4	1	17	6
	28	To Ditto — Ditto	4	6	5	
April	1	To Ditto — Ditto	4	6	10	
	2	To Ditto — Ditto	4	5		
	6	To Ditto — Ditto	4	6	5	
	7	To Ditto — Ditto	4	1	5	
	12	To Ditto — in Fredericksburg	5		7	6
June	2	To Ditto — in Frederick	50	1	0	0
	15	To Ditto — at Home	50		8	9
July	2	To Ditto — at Ditto	55		8	9
	15	To Ditto — at Do	55	1	10	
	27	To Ditto — at Do	55	1	10	
Augt	20	To Ditto — in Alexandria	55		5	—
Septr	16	To Ditto — in Fredericksburg	60	1	5	
	30	To Ditto — at Home	60	2	0	
Novr	13	To Ditto — in Williamsburg	61	1	0	0
Decr	12	To Ditto — at Home	62		12	6
1773.		To Ditto — at Ditto	63	8	9	
Mar	13	To Ditto — at Ditto	82	3	10	—
	27	To Ditto — at Ditto	88	1	10	—
April	24	To Ditto — at Home	88		7	6
Augt	31	To Ditto — Ditto	91	3	4	
Octr	1	To Ditto — at Annapolis	93	3	16	—
		To Ditto — in Williamsburg	96	3	1	—
Decr	31	To Ditto — at Home	98		16	3
1774		To Ditto — Do	105		10	-
May	16	To Ditto — Williamsburg	110		15	—
	18	To Ditto — Ditto	112	2	10	—
June	10	To Ditto — Ditto	112	5	15	—
			£78	5	9

WASHINGTON'S OWN ACCOUNT OF HIS

(From Ledger B

Contra - Cr.

1772						
Jan 7	2	By Cash won at home	3	6	2	
Mar 4		By Ditto in Williamsburg	3		5	
6		By Ditto in Ditto	3		7	6
23		By Ditto ... Ditto	4	2	0	0
30		By Ditto ... Ditto	4	9	10	
April 3		By Ditto ... Ditto	4	5	15	
June 30		By Ditto ... at Home	55	4	17	6
Sept 5		By Ditto ... at Mr Boucher's	60	1	15	
Oct 7		By Ditto ... In annapolis	60	13	7	
Nov 3		By Ditto ... In Williamsburg	61	1	5	
Dec 21		By Ditto ... at Home	63	1	18	
1773 Jan 5		By Ditto ... at Ditto	82	1	10	
9		By Ditto	82		14	
April 17		By Ditto	88	1	5	
24		By Ditto	88	1	4	0
May —		By Ditto ... won at Phila	90	2	5	0
Sept 13		By Ditto	93		7	6
1774		By Ditto	105	1	8	0
Feb 28		By Ditto ... at home		2	10	0
May 13		By Ditto ... at Fredericksburg	160	1	0	0
18		By Ditto ... Williamsburg	110	1	13	0
23		By Ditto ... Ditto	112	1	10	0
June 6		By Ditto ... Ditto	112		9	6
7		By Ditto ... Ditto	112	1	10	0
13		By Ditto ... Ditto	112	5	5	0
16		By Ditto ... Ditto	115	1	0	0
October —		By Ditto ... won at Phila	125	7	0	0
				72	2	6
1775 Jan 1		By Bal against Play from Jan 7 1772 to this date		6	3	3
				£78	5	9

LOSSES AND WINNINGS AT CARDS.
1772-1774.)

Washington seems to have cared little for books except on agriculture; but he played for small stakes that he could well afford, and his investments in cards and horses are as nothing compared to those of such men as Charles James Fox, the friend of America, the heroic statesman who made 50 guinea bets on almost anything, and whose extravagances piled up a debt of £140,000 by the time he was twenty-four.

Washington's gambling was what he called his dancing, an "agreeable and innocent amusement." Only a hopeless prig could blame him for it, wish to conceal it, or be scandalized at the mention of it.

It may be interesting in evidence of his activity as a sportsman, that his diaries from January, 1768, to March, 1774, a period of about six years, show that he went fox-hunting 155 times, got nothing 85 times, and killed 71 foxes and one "Rakoon." Fox must have been plentiful about Mount Vernon.

In the same period he went gunning 31 times with no results; hunted duck 9 times with a total bag of 26; hunted deer 6 times and killed 3; hunted pheasants once without result.

Aside from his business of fishing, he went fishing five times for sport.

He went to the theatre 37 times, to race-meets 6 times, to 29 balls, 5 concerts, and 2 "barbicues."

By adding all these festive occasions to the evenings spent at cards, a picture is gained of jovial revelry and love of companionship, and a wise eagerness for happiness.

In days when the Constitution is upheld as something that no true patriot could violate, it is strange to find Washington upholding violations and eventually the wreckage of the only Constitution he then had before him. Like other alleged desecrators, he defended himself by accusing his accusers. And he defended himself on July 4th!

Bryan Fairfax, the religious and eccentric brother of George William Fairfax, could neither approve the oppressions of the British government nor the insubordination of the radicals. He refused, indeed, to run for election as a delegate to the House of Burgesses. He quoted what was said in England, that America was "encroaching," denying the authority of Parliament though it had never been disputed till the Stamp Act.

And Fairfax added the familiar counsel of obedience:

"Whatever we may wish to be the case, it becomes good subjects to submit to the Constitution of their country." [12]

In a later letter he repeats his plea:

"Altho' I wish it as much as any one that we were legally exempted from it, yet I hold it clearly that we ought to abide by our Constitution."

In answer to his arguments, Washington wrote two letters setting forth his views.

On July 4th, 1774, he says that there is no hope of "a humble and dutiful petition to the throne." It is "as clear as the sun in its meridian brightness, that there is a regular, systematic plan formed to fix the right and practice of taxation upon us." [13]

He feels strongly that the debts owing to Great Britain must be paid. "Whilst we are accusing others of injustice, we should be just ourselves. . . . Nothing but the last extremity" could justify the non-payment of the debt. "Whether this is now come, is the question."

In his second letter he attacks again the right of Parliament to tax the colonies. He sees General Gage's conduct as "more becoming a Turkish bashaw. . . . Shall we, after this, whine and cry for relief, when we have already tried it in vain? . . . I think the Parliament of Great Britain hath no more right to put their hands into my pocket, without my consent, than I have to put my hands into yours for money. . . . The voice of mankind is with me."

On the fifth of July he went to a meeting at Alexandria where he was appointed on a committee with George Mason and others to draw up resolutions concerning the situation. These were presented on July 18th. There were twenty-four of them written by George Mason probably, and they are known as the Fairfax or Alexandria resolves.

These Fairfax Resolves are in themselves justification enough for the Revolution. They are so well-reasoned, so eloquent, so superbly written that they give George Mason a place among the masters who poured forth the noble literature of that time. They are given in the Notes [14] and will repay perusal. Since Mason was not a Burgess, Washington was instructed to present them to the Virginia Convention.

On July 14th an election had been held, since the dissolving of the House of Burgesses required it. Washington was elected and "Staid all Night to a Ball."

A young English traveller who happened to be present at the election states that "the Candidates gave the populace a Hogshead of Toddy," which was against the law, but according to the custom. He noted that tea was not served, "This Herb is in disgrace amongst them at present." [15]

He miscalls the other successful candidate, Major Broadwater, "Major Bedwater."

Creswell had called for "a load of Flour from Col. Washington's mill," which he found "a very complete one." It made "as good flour as ever I saw." Washington always made the same boast.

Creswell's diary includes this picturesque summing up of Washington's character with some surprising comments:

"He married a Mrs. Custis, a widow lady, with whom he had a very good fortune. By her entreaties he left the Army, in which he never gained any great esteem by his own country Officers or men. By all accounts it was his frugality that lost him the good-will of his Officers, and the strict discipline he always observed, the love of his men. Indeed, any kind of order or subordination illy agrees with his countrymen, in general.

"After he quitted the Army, he was made a member of the Virginia House of Burgesses, in which he was much respected for his good private character, but always looked upon as too bashful and timid for an orator. He lived as a Country Gentleman, much noted for his hospitality, great knowledge in agriculture, and industry in carrying his various manufactories of Linen and Woollen to greater perfection than any man in the Colony . . .

"His education is not very great nor his parts shining, his disposition is rather heavy than volatile, much given to silence. In short, he is but a poor speaker and but shines in the epistolary way. His person is tall and genteel, age betwixt forty and fifty, his behaviour and deportment is easy, genteel, and obliging, with a certain something about him which pleases everyone who has anything to do with him. . . .

"His friends and acquaintances reckon him a just man, exceedingly honest, but not very generous. Perhaps they may give him this character, because he manages his Estate with industry and economy, very seldom enters into those foolish, giddy and expensive frolics natural to a Virginian.

"He keeps an excellent table and a stranger, let him be of what Country or nation, he will always meet with a most hospitable reception at it. His entertainments were always conducted with the most regularity and in the genteelest manner of any I ever was at on the Continent (and I have been at several of them, . . .). Temperance he always observed, was always cool-headed and exceedingly cautious himself, but took great pleasure in seeing his friends entertained in the way most agreeable to themselves. His lady is of a hospitable disposition, always good-humoured and cheerful, and seems to be actuated by the same motives with himself, but she is rather of a more lively disposition. They are to all appearances a happy pair. . . .

"It is said (and I believe with great truth) that he never had an intimate, particular bosom friend, or an open professed enemy in his life. . . . His private character is amiable, he is much beloved and respected by all his acquaintances."

There is something startling, yet hardly to be gainsaid, in
young Creswell's remarkable phrase:

"He never had an intimate, particular bosom friend; or
an open professed enemy in his life."

Late in July, 1774, Washington "set of" for Williamsburg to the convention of August first, the opening of which
he attended. Jefferson, too ill to be present, sent down an
essay, called "A Summary View of the Rights of British
America," which frightened the members, though they did
organize a new non-importation Association of the most
drastic sort, boycotting slaves, tea, and nearly all other
merchandise except medicines, and agreeing to buy nothing
whatsoever of the East India Company so long as it insisted
on payment for the Boston Tea Party. Also it was agreed
not to export tobacco or anything else, and to try to raise
better sheep so that woolen factories might be encouraged.
Washington had bad luck with his.

The most important act, however, was the election of
seven delegates to the first Continental Congress at Philadelphia. Washington was one of those chosen, the others
being Peyton Randolph, Richard Henry Lee, Patrick
Henry, Edmund Pendleton, Richard Bland, and Benjamin
Harrison.

A subscription was taken up to defray the expenses of the
delegates, and Washington put himself down for the tidy
sum of £90. 13. 9 as his proportion. His name was always
on subscription lists.

His selection as a delegate must have been partly due to
his sudden appearance among the orators. Brooding over
the wrongs of Boston and the insolence of the English
who were throttling the American town to death, he rose to
his feet and made that brief but tremendous utterance which
one Lynch, a South Carolina delegate who dropped in at the
House of Burgesses, described to John Adams, and Adams [16]
transmitted to posterity in its only record:

"He told us that Colonel Washington made the most eloquent speech at the Virginia Convention that ever was made. Says he,

" 'I will raise one thousand men, subsist them at my own expense, and march myself at their head for the relief of Boston.' "

A better speech could not be made.

XIX

THE ASSEMBLYMAN BECOMES A CONGRESSMAN

THIS amazing flare of fire from the most silent of the Assemblymen had been smoldering long. Some years later a man wrote to him, saying that he had never forgotten "your declaration when I last had the pleasure of being at your house in 1768, that you were ready to take your musket upon your shoulder whenever your country called you." [1]

In making this declaration of open rebellion, he suddenly risked everything he had striven so hard to build. He put his neck in the halter and became one of the men whom General Burgoyne later referred to as "those whose lives by the law of the land are destined to the cord."

But there was something magnificent about his defiance. It was the rich man's superb gesture, scattering freely the gold that justified itself in its splendor:

"I will raise one thousand men, subsist them at my own expense, and march, myself at their head, for the relief of Boston."

His offer was not accepted at the moment, but his words must have skirled along the colonies. They were better than, "Give me Liberty or give me Death!" They promised money and power and command.

They put Washington at once to the fore as a great soldier, and his wealth disguised the poverty of his experience. He became for Virginia once more commander-in-chief by acclamation.

The thought of war seems to have been kindled everywhere at once. In every Virginia county a company was organized, with a hoped-for total of six thousand men. The eagerness to get into a uniform was so great that one writer said, "Men who served as commanding officers last war and have large fortunes, have offered themselves as private men." [2]

But Washington moved on calmly about his affairs. On his way home, he spent a night in Fredericksburg and saw his mother, for he wrote in his Ledger B., "By Cash paid my Mother £20." He did not put down the name of a witness as he had done two years before when he made such curious entries under his account with her as:

"1772 Sept 16   To Cash paid you in presence of my brother Charles   £30

1773 Dec   To Ditto paid you in presence of my sister Lewis   £30"

At the farm everything went on as before. The slaves were fruitful, and Bishop's wife still earned fees. In Ledger B. under his name are these entries:

"By your Wife's delivering Doll at the Ferry—& House Betty   1. 0. 0

By your wife for delivering Kate, Hannah, & Ione at 10s each   1. 10. 0

By your Wife laying House Alice   10."

He went to an auction of Colonel Fairfax's furniture at Belvoir. It must have been doleful seeing the mansion of his happiest hours, long unvisited by Sally Fairfax, now emptied of her relics. He bought a few things including a Wilton carpet, which he sold to Dr. Craik for £8. 10. 0. He paid £4 to "Colo. Thos. Ludwell for a Card Table wch. he bot. at Colo. Fairfax's Sale & let me have." A card table would be useful at Mount Vernon.

He did a graceful, tender thing for the Fairfax memory in having the family "cypher" carved on their empty pew, while he was having his carved on his own.

He knew that the Fairfaxes would probably never return, for they had asked him to sell Belvoir. But there were too many estates for sale in Virginia, and the house burned down before it could find a purchaser.

On August 30th, Patrick Henry and Colonel Pendleton, delegates to the First Continental Congress, gathered at Mount Vernon "and stayd all Night."

Pendleton afterward wrote to a friend that "Mrs. Washington talked like a Spartan to her son on his going to battle. 'I hope you will all stand firm,' she said, 'I know George will.'" [3]

After dinner the next afternoon they rode away for Philadelphia, reaching there four afternoons later. Having subscribed £90. 13. 9 out of his own pocket towards the fund for paying the delegates' expenses, Washington now received back £100 "on acct. of my Exps. to Phila.—born by the Country."

The congress met at the New Tavern, then walked to Carpenters Hall, a "respectable looking building . . . originally constructed for the hall of meeting for the Society of House Carpenters." [4] It was later used as the first Bank in the subsequent United States.

All the colonies except Georgia were represented, the delegates having been chosen by the committees of correspondence, not, of course, by the people, much less, of course, by the conservatives, who naturally (and truthfully) declared that the Congress represented nobody but the radicals. [5] Yet there were men among them who afterwards turned Tory.

The Bolshevik, Sam Adams, who made his first excursion outside Massachusetts, was so shabby that anonymous friends sent him a complete new outfit from hat to boots. [6] John Adams wailed to his Diary, "We have not men fit for the times. We are deficient in genius, in education, in travel, in fortune, in everything." It was characteristic even of these times that cynical men should doubt the greatness of their contemporaries. Adams looked down upon a group that has since been praised as one of the noblest ever assembled.

Mr. Lynch of South Carolina nominated Peyton Randolph for President, thus making him in a sense "the first American President." [7]

Fabulous anecdotes now begin to multiply about Washington's head. Here is one:

"General Washington, then a member from Virginia, was observed to be the only member to *kneel*, when Bishop White first offered his prayer to the Throne of Grace—as if *he* was thus early impressed with a sense of *his and their dependence* on 'the God of battles.' " [8]

There are two objections to this. Bishop White did not officiate, but Mr. Duché did. And Bishop White over his own signature wrote in answer to repeated anxious queries as to Washington's alleged habit of kneeling in prayer: "I owe it to truth to declare, that I never saw him in the said attitude." [9]

The Congress was hardly seated, and the oath of secrecy taken, when it began to wrangle over the matter of voting. The large colonies wanted more than the small. The turmoil was stilled by Patrick Henry, who looked like a shabby village parson and spoke like an angel. He pleaded that there should be no more distinctions between colonies, and cried:

"I am not a Virginian but an American."

It was agreed that each colony should have one vote no matter what its size.

John Adams furnishes us with almost our only record of the occasion except the reminiscences of the secretary. Samuel Adams, disclosing unusual diplomacy, proposed on the second day that there should be a prayer, and an Episcopalian should deliver it. The chaplain was Rev. Jacob Duché, who managed to get himself and Washington into an ugly tangle later, when Duché turned Tory and tried to swing Washington with him.

Adams helped put through the radical Suffolk Resolves denying any obligation to obey any of the recent acts of Parliament, and hinting at armed resistance, though denying any thought of independence.

Joseph Galloway, who went loyalist later, offered a plan of union with Great Britain and a colonial parliament subject to the imperial parliament's veto. It came within two votes of passing.

A Declaration of Rights and Grievances was agreed upon, and an Association of non-importation, non-exportation, and non-consumption, with committees to enforce it by inflicting as the only punishment, "infamy." This Association, says Doctor Howard, is "the only thing resembling at all a written constitution which the people had until the Articles of Confederation were finally ratified nearly seven years later." [10]

A petition to the King, an invitation to Quebec to join a congress set for the following year, and other appeals were drawn up.

In the appeal to the King they reviled Catholicism, in the appeal to Canada they did not mention it. This made their enemies laugh. [11]

Washington contributed to the Congress perfect silence. John Adams, writing forty-four years later concerning the belief of Richard Henry Lee and others that England would surely yield, recall her troops and withdraw her acts, paid a tribute to Washington's cold common sense in prophecy; and common sense is the one element most essential to prophecy and the most rare in it:

"Washington only was in doubt. He never spoke in

public. In private he joined with those who advocated a non-exportation, as well as a non-importation agreement. With both he thought we should prevail; without either he thought it doubtful. Henry was clear in one opinion, Richard Henry Lee in an opposite opinion, and Washington doubted between the two. Henry however appeared in the end to be exactly in the right." [12]

Contemporary verses by Dr. Solomon Drowne,[13] show that Washington wore his beloved uniform and sword to the meetings:

> "With manly gait
> His faithful steel suspended by his side,
> Passed W'-shi-gt-n along, Virginia's Hero."

"This Col. Washington," he added, "is a man noted as well for his good sense, as his Bravery. I heard, he said, he wished to God the Liberties of America were to be determined by a single Combat between himself and G(eorg)e."

This last does not sound like him, but his commanding height and his almost irresistible magnetism were beginning to exert their amazing sway.

Patrick Henry was more impressed by Washington's quiet conversation than by the fervid oratory of the others. When asked whom he considered the greatest man in Congress, he answered:

"Rutledge, if you speak of eloquence, is by far the greatest orator, but Col. Washington, who has no pretensions to eloquence, is a man of more solid judgment and information than any man on that floor." [14]

So much for the heavy business of the Congress. The social end of it was doubtless equally to Washington's liking. While, of course, his Diary makes no allusions to the immortal measures of Congress, it tells of his dining with a different personage nearly every afternoon, many of his most cordial friends turning Tory later. He went riding,

visited a Quaker meeting in the forenoon of a Sabbath, and
Duché's church in the afternoon, inspected a hospital, "dined
at the Tavern with the Virga. Gentn, etca"; next day "spent
the afternn. with the Boston Gentn," dined at the Governor's
Club and with the Pennsylvania Assembly, and went to a
Ball afterwards, then to another Episcopal church. On the
third Sunday "to the Presbyterian Meeting in the forenoon
and Romish Church in the afternoon," and dined at a
tavern; "drank Tea with Mrs. Roberdeau," daughter of a
New York clergyman. He seems to have done everything
but play cards and go to a theatre or a horse race; but then,
the Congress voted for consecration to solemn things and
banned extravagance, dissipation, cock-fighting, horse-racing,
in spite of its own gorgeous revelry.

Washington was in his element, and made no such complaint as was wrung from John Adams: "A most sinful feast
again . . . curds and creams, jellies, sweetmeats of various
sorts, twenty sorts of tarts, fools, trifles, floating islands, and
whipped sillabubs . . . turtle and every other thing, flum-
mery. . . . Wines most excellent and admirable. I drank
Madeira at a great rate." [15]

The most brilliant affair was the "Entertainment given by
the City to the Members of the Congress." They gathered
at the City Tavern, marched to the State House and were
received by "the Clergy, such genteel strangers as happened
to be in town, . . . making in the whole, near 500." [16]
There were thirty-six toasts accompanied by music and great
guns, and they included tributes to the King, the Queen, the
Prince of Wales, and to "The Perpetual Union of the Colonies," which meant also, of course, a perpetual union with
England.

It may have been on this occasion that Washington
shocked the aristocrats by dancing with the daughter of a
mechanic.[17]

During the Congress false rumors of the bombardment of Boston shook the members.

The Congress ended October 27th, and its acts were ratified widely by the committees of correspondence that created it. The public began an orgy of self-denial in British goods, and a ghastly festival of persecution for those who did not sympathize until, as Channing says, "The story of tarrings and featherings, riotings and burnings becomes monotonous." [18]

The radicals were in the saddle.

While in Philadelphia, Washington bought a sword chain, a pocket-book for Martha, and gave a pound apiece to the doorkeepers of Congress. He bought for his mother a cloak and a riding chair. But he charged her for the cloak and for the freight on the carriage as his Ledger B shows:

"1774. Oct 24. To Ditto pd Phl Marchinton of
　　　　　　 Phila for a Cloak lind with silk
　　　　　　 Shag　　　　　　　　　£10. 2. 1
　　　　　 To Freight of your Chair round
　　　　　　 from Philadelphia　　　　 £1. 4. 0"

But then that was his way. He loved Colonel Fairfax, but when he advertised his estate for sale he put down "Charge Colo. Fairfax with ye advertisg. 6s 5d."

During his stay at the Congress he received a letter from Captain Robert Mackenzie, a native Virginian, one of his captains in the French war, but now a British lieutenant under Gage in Boston. To him the despotism was all on the part of the colonists. He spoke of "their tyrannical Oppression over one another, of their fixed Aim at total Independance . . . their scandalous and ungenerous Attacks upon the best Characters in the Province, obliging them to save their Lives by Flight." He added that Gage had been compelled to fortify his troops in the town.[19]

Washington wrote him affectionately and invited him to Mount Vernon, but begged to be permitted:

"With the freedom of a friend . . . to express my sorrow, that fortune should place you in a service, that must fix curses to the latest posterity upon the contrivers, and, if success (which, by the by, is impossible) accompanies it, execrations upon all those, who have been instrumental in the execution.

"I do not mean by this to insinuate, that an officer is not to discharge his duty, even when chance, not choice, has placed him in a disagreeable situation."

He disagreed with Mackenzie's opinion of Boston, insisted that it was "the new-fangled counsellors" who lent "their aid to overturn the constitution," and assured him that though Mackenzie had been led to believe:

"That the people of Massachusetts are rebellious, setting up for *Independency, and what not,* give me leave, my good friend, to tell you, that you are abused, grossly abused. . . . I think I can announce it as a fact, that *it is not the wish or interest of that government, or any other upon this continent, separately or collectively, to set up for independence;* but this you may at the same time rely on, that none of them will ever submit to the loss of those valuable rights and privileges, which are essential to the happiness of every free state, and without which, life, liberty, and property are rendered totally insecure. . . .

"More blood will be spilled on this occasion, if the ministry are determined to push matters to extremity, than history has ever yet furnished instances of in the annals of North America, and such a vital wound will be given to the peace of this great country, as time itself cannot cure, or eradicate the remembrance of.

"But I have done. I was involuntarily led into a short discussion of this subject by your remarks on the conduct of the Boston people, and your opinion of their wishes to set up *for independency. I am well satisfied, that no such thing is desired by any thinking man in all North America.*" [20]

The italics have been interpolated to point up the wide difference between Washington's views at this time and later.

Mackenzie was wounded at Bunker Hill, fighting for the British, while his fellow Virginian was ridiculing what he called "Independency and what not."

The Congress had given Washington an opportunity to convince himself of the quality of the Massachusetts men and to acquaint himself with their principles. He defended them with the same ardor that had led him to offer to lead a thousand men to their rescue.

The soldiers were falling in already. The country was interested only in war. Washington went to Alexandria to a meeting of his Potomac Company, but "None met." Next day he was visited by officers who had organized the Prince William County Independent Company, and they asked him to be their field officer. He consented, having already accepted a similar command with the Fairfax County Independent Company. By Christmas time the Northern Neck had raised a thousand volunteers, and William Black wrote of them to Boston that they were "as fine fellows and good woodsmen as any on our continent, who have put themselves under the command of Col. George Washington, a brave and experienced officer, whom it is said has undertaken the command of them, and that they are soon to march for your place." [21]

The name "Washington" was somehow a rallying cry, and various county companies asked to serve under him. It was evident that he would once more become Commander-in-Chief for Virginia.

In Ledger B appears the ominous note:

"1775, Jany 2. By Cash for a yard of Cockade Ribb^n. £1."

Of the quality of Virginia troops, Richard Henry Lee wrote to Arthur Lee in London, in February, 1775:

"This one County of Fincastle can furnish 1000 Rifle Men that for their number make most formidable light Infantry in the

World. The six frontier Counties can produce 6000 of these Men who from their amazing hardihood, their method of living so long in the woods without carrying provisions with them, the exceeding quickness with which they can march to distant parts, and above all, the dexterity to which they have arrived in the use of the Rifle Gun. Their is not one of these Men who wish a distance less than 200 yards or a larger object than an Orange—Every shot is fatal." [22]

Governor Dunmore, who was on the frontier quelling restless Indians, wrote anxiously to the Earl of Dartmouth that every county was arming men sworn to obey the local Committee, that the courts were closed, that the justices of the peace were all committeemen, that lawyers refused to attend. [23]

He saw one reigning motive, the desire "to avoid paying the debts in which many of the principal people here are much involved." Yet he predicted that the non-consumption agreements would fail, the times of "anarchy" would pass, and "the lower class of people too will discover that they have been duped by the richer sort, who for their part elude the whole effects of the association, by which their poor neighbors perish."

On the next to the last day of December, 1774, Mount Vernon was visited by General Charles Lee, an English soldier of fortune with whom Washington was to have a famous clash on Monmouth Field.

Lee was then, and perhaps always, ardently in favor of the colonies and against the British Government. He had impressed Richard Henry Lee so deeply that he wrote to Samuel Adams:

"I take pleasure in introducing to your acquaintance General Lee, a most true and worthy friend to the rights of human nature in general, and a warm, spirited Foe to American oppression. This Gentlemans principles do him honor, and I am sure his acquaintance will give you much pleasure." [24]

Washington was enough impressed with him to lend him £15 when Lee moved on after a six day visit. He got it back from the estate many years later.

In spite of the Quebec Act, Washington continued to send people out to work on his lands on the Ohio, though the act had definitely destroyed the claims of Virginia, Pennsylvania, the Ohio Company, and the others to that region.

On January 16th Washington went to Alexandria to review the Fairfax company and drill it, and to help organize a Committee of Safety. On the 17th he was "Under Arms this day also, and in Committee in the Eveng."

Judge Jones, the Tory historian, accuses Washington of being very severe with the loyalists:

"He . . . was appointed Chairman of the Committee of the county in which he resided, and enforced the resolutions and recommendations of Congress with a high hand. Some who refused obedience to the Committee, he ordered punished, and others he imprisoned. He even levied taxes upon the inhabitants, and ordered them collected and paid, by dint of his own power, threatening such as should disobey his illegal and arbitrary mandates with being advertised in the public papers as 'enemies to America and the rights of mankind.' A punishment of this kind, if not death, was certain banishment, the destruction of property, and the ruin of families, of wives, and of innocent children." [25]

He was growing in national stature visibly. But he was still a farmer, hunting foxes. Again he went to a meeting of the Potomac Company Trustees. Again—"None met." He "bot. a parcel of Servants." He visited his sick slaves.

On February 18 he "went up to Alexandria to meet and exercise the Independant Company." He advanced for ammunition for the county £350. 16. 6 in Pennsylvania Currency, which he charged in Virginia currency as £140. 6. 6. He paid for "8 Quarter Casks of Powd^r 27£ Pennsa. equal to £21. 12. 0." He received from the Prince William County Independent Company "for Colours & Drums," £10. 8. 7.

In March "I set my People off for the Ohio." On the 15th he "set of" for Richmond to attend the second Virginia Convention, which ratified the acts of the Congress, pushed through a bill for arming and ruling a force of militia "composed of gentlemen and yeomen" as "the natural strength and security of a free government."

It was rather sarcastically resolved that such a militia "would forever render it unnecessary for the mother country to keep among us, for the purpose of our defence, any standing army of mercenary forces . . . and would obviate the pretext of taxing us for their support."

Such ardent men as Bland, Harrison, and Pendleton, who had gone to the Congress, fought with all their power against the arming of the colony, but Patrick Henry and Thomas Jefferson swept them away.

From Richmond Washington wrote to his brother, John Augustine, who had caught the fever and was engaged in the "laudable pursuit" of training a company. Washington had been asked to review the Richmond company and accepted his brother's invitation to review his: "and shall very cheerfully accept the honor of commanding it, if occasion require it to be drawn out, as it is my full intention to devote my life and fortune in the cause we are engaged in, if needful. I remain, dear Sir, your most affectionate brother." [26]

Though Virginia was full of experienced officers who had been in arms and won victories, and Washington had been out of the service for sixteen years, the command seemed to come back to him by the popular will, and the new troops all begged him to command them. It was an astounding evidence of public confidence.

During the Convention, which ended on the 27th, Washington was put on a committee for the encouragement of arts and manufactures, and on the committee for organizing the militia. He and the other delegates to the First Continental Congress were relected to the Second.

He wrote to George Mercer in London that the people were "resolved, altho' they wish for nothing, more ardently, than a happy & lasting reconciliation with the parent State, not to purchase it at the expence of their liberty." [27]

He advertised for two runaway white servants:

"Fairfax County, April 23, 1775.

"FORTY DOLLARS REWARD. Ran away from the subscriber, on the 19th instant, at night, two servant men, viz. THOMAS SPEARS, a joiner, born in *Bristol,* about 20 years of age, 5 feet 6 inches and a half high; slender made. He has light grey or blueish colored eyes, a little pock marked, and freckled, with sandy colored hair, cut short; his voice is coarse, and somewhat drawling. He took with him a coat, waistcoat, and breeches, of light brown duffil, with black horn buttons, a light colored cloth waistcoat, old leather breeches, check and oznabrig shirts, a pair of new milled yarn stockings, a pair of old ribbed ditto, new oznabrig trowsers, and a felt hat, not much the worse for wear. WILLIAM WEBSTER, a brickmaker, born in *Scotland,* and talks pretty broad. He is about 5 feet 6 inches high, and well made, rather turned of 30, with light brown hair, and roundish face. He had an olive colored coat, pretty much worn, with black horn buttons, duffil waistcoat and breeches (same as *Spears's*) oznabrig trousers, and check and oznabrig shirts. They went off in a small yawl, with turpentine sides and bottom, the inside painted with a mixture of tar and red lead. Masters of vessels are cautioned against receiving of them; and the above reward is offered to any person who will deliver them at my dwelling-house in this country, or TWENTY DOLLARS for each from

"GEORGE WASHINGTON." [28]

With all this ferment, the black slaves also grew restless and an insurrection was feared. The Virginians might find their troops of liberty useful for crushing it.

It was part of human nature then as now to cry for liberty and withhold it. There was nothing unnatural in owning slaves while demanding freedom. The Virginians were also clamoring against England's outrage of "taxation without representation" while they mocked the same protest from the back counties.

In the meanwhile the news from the North was growing hotter and hotter. On April 19th General Gage's troops went out and met the embattled farmers at Lexington and Concord and came back on the run, their tongues covered with dust. The farmers gathered in droves and held the British fast in Boston.

The Second Continental Congress gathered at Philadelphia, May 10, 1775, with war no longer a dreadful possibility, but a reality.

On his way up, Washington was invited to review the troops at Baltimore. He wore his uniform, of course. He was never seen without it now.

At the Second Congress, Washington was put on a committee to prepare a plan for protecting New York, and another for securing ammunition, making a budget, and compiling regulations for the army.

He bought 40 muskets for one of the Virginia companies, and paid £150 for them; also £30 for "Cartooch Boxes &ca." He paid 7s 6d to have his holsters covered, and 5 shillings for a "Cirsingle."

He paid £1. 12 for "5 Books—Military."

He received from George William Fairfax in London a long letter dated March 2nd, 1775, about his business affairs and Washington's tobacco, and the furniture at Belvoir:

"Unless we can gett near the Value of that in the Chinch Room, I should like to have it sent Over if Possible . . . and that entire in the Blue, or Dressing Room, I must beg your acceptance of."

He asks Washington to look up "a peice of paper in a little Trunk," and reminds him that "Mr Dalton was in the House, the morning you & Lady, was so good as to come and see Us the day we Embarked, You possibilly may remember."

Fairfax was active in England on a committee working for America. He spelled the "Ministry" and the "Crown" with a dash in awe or discretion, but he was drawing up "a Petition to the C—n in favour of America," and he adds much that shows how unpopular the oppression of America was in England:

"What can, or dare I say, about the unhappy difference between this Country and America. That you are condemned by the M—y, and their dependents, and much Aplauded by ever welwisher to the Antient and Constitutional Right of Englishmen, whether on this, or the other side of the Atlantic; of which there are a great Majority in this County. You'l hear probabelly before this reatches you, what Steps have been taken, how supported, and defended, and at last how inconsistantly they have Acted in the great World, various are the Conjectures about the much talked of Motion, and sudden change, some thinks it proceeds from unfavourable Accounts from the Continent of Europe, some that they are frightened at the Expence, and others that it was only intend to Intimidate, and cause a disension in the Colonys, But I rather think that they find they have gone far enough, that the Americans are not so easily Duped, and that a War cross the Atlantic will be the most expences one they have had, and the difficulty of raising the Supplys to support so unnatural a one.

"It is pretty certain that the M—r [Minister, Lord North] has lost ground, that many of his Friends, did desert him upon the late Question, and such a jealousy has arose, that its thought, a change in the M—y must soon take Place.—God grant, that it may be for the better, worse I think it cannot be, consequently we all hope for an Amendment, yett I fear it never will happen while the Premier, has so many lucrative Places in his disposal, and People grow more and more Extravigant, However this We can, and I believe very justly say, that Law is on our side, for all the Law Lords that do not fill some high Office, and many great disinterested Gentⁿ in the Commons, are in support of America, and by examining the List, you may find that many of the Worthies are sent from this part of the Kingdom.

"It is reported in London, that you are Training the People of Virginia to the Use of Arms, I hope you do not find those of your own County the most defficient, or that they misbecome their new uniform. They are going to have a General Review of all the Militia here, but for what I know not, as it's not Customary, time only will shew the Event of all things, and God grant you, your Privilages and a happy and speedy Reconciliation upon Constitutional Principles, is the daily Prayer of Dear Sir

"Your Affect: and Most Obliged humble
"Serv:
"G: W: FAIRFAX" [29]

By the time Washington was able to answer this, May 31st, 1775, great things had happened at the battle of Lexington:

"Between the ministerial troops (for we do not, nor can we yet prevail upon ourselves to call them the King's troops), and the provincials of that government . . . if the retreat had not been as precipitate as it was, and God knows it could not well have been more so, the ministerial troops must have surrendered, or been totally cut off. . . . Unhappy it is, though, to reflect, that a brother's sword has been sheathed in a brother's breast, and that the once happy and peaceful plains of America are either to be drenched with blood or inhabited by slaves. Sad alternative! But can a virtuous man hesitate in his choice?

"I am with sincere regard, and affectionate compliments to Mrs. Fairfax, dear Sir, your Etc."

On June 15th he was unanimously chosen Commander-in-Chief of all the forces raised, or to be raised, by the colonies. Going back to his rooms with that immortal honor on him, he wrote in his Diary:

"15. Dined at Burnes' in the Field. Spent the Eveng. on a Committee."

Simply that and nothing more.

Yet the inexperienced Washington, ignorant of victory or

large war, had been chosen out of all the distinguished soldiers whom the colonies had acclaimed, to command them all in their first united action.

Why?

XX

THE MYSTERY OF HIS SELECTION

"HIS exertions, sacrifices, and general merits in the cause of his country, had been incomparably greater than those of Colonel Washington."

So John Adams wrote of John Hancock, who had succeeded Peyton Randolph as president of the Second Continental Congress, when Randolph was called back to Virginia.

"But the delicacy of his health, and his entire want of experience in actual service, though an excellent militia officer, were decisive objections to him in my mind." [1]

They were in Adams' mind, not Hancock's. He expected to be offered the command, even if he decided to decline it. In America, political leaders have not often been unwilling to accept military powers as well as titles. They suspect themselves of genius and their doubts of their experience are no greater than those of the fearless man who said that he did not know whether or not he could play the violin; since he had never tried to.

The New Englanders, having begun the Revolution and having chased the British army into Boston and locked it up, felt that, while they were willing to accept aid from the colonies, the leadership should remain where it was. They already had General Artemas Ward in command, and he had friends. So had Generals Heath, Putnam, and others.

But even they were all writing to Adams that they could not hold their men together without the help of Congress. Yet Adams could not divert Congress from its many businesses; one party was fighting with another for a petition to

MAJOR-GENERAL CHARLES LEE
(By B. Rushbrooke)

the King, and against all independent action; another against all united action since the King would not receive a joint petition from his several colonies.   The North and the South were already in cleavage, and the Southerners were stirred by "a jealousy against a New-England army under the command of a New-England general."

Adams was finally convinced that the South would not budge unless it could furnish a Southern general.   "The intention was very visible to me that Colonel Washington was their object, and . . . that we could carry nothing without conceding to it.

"Another embarrassment, which was never publicly known, and which was carefully concealed by those who knew it, the Massachusetts and other New-England delegates were divided."

On the other hand the Southerners could not agree among themselves.   "I found more than one very cool about the appointment of Washington, and particularly Mr. Pendleton was very clear and full against it."

The Virginian politicians had their own ambitions.   They were nearly all "colonels," the word meaning hardly more than "Esquire."

The opposition of the Virginians to Washington was to be expected on the principle that a prophet is most without honor in his own country.   Besides, Virginia had a favorite son, Colonel William Byrd of Westover, who succeeded Washington as commander-in-chief of the colony's troops and had been an active soldier while Washington farmed and speculated in Western lands.   And there was Col. Andrew Lewis, who had won the great battle of Point Pleasant and freed Kentucky from menace.   It was said that Washington urged Lewis in preference to himself; but Lewis had recently lost popularity owing to the intemperate language of some of his troops.[2]

Richard Henry Lee, though friendly to Washington, was never convinced of his superior ability, and later took part in the Conway Cabal against him. This was not from hostility in his case any more than in Pendleton's, but just from human inability to see grandeur in a neighbor.

Throughout his life, indeed, Washington found some of his coldest critics among the people from his home country. But that has always been the case, and it is among the bitterest lees in the cup of fame.

Washington bore the doubts of his friends as bravely as his other burdens and with the same absence of any feeling that their homage was his by divine right. He never claimed anything for himself save the respect due him as a man and a courteous man, though he exacted the last tributes of deference to any office he held,—but for the office's sake, not his own.

Since he wrote Martha that she knew well how he tried to avoid being chosen as Commander, it is certain that he was active in the discussions, but did nothing to win the office except to be there and to be himself.

A formidable contender for the post, and one who did everything in his power to win it, was General Charles Lee, a puzzling and picturesque figure. Because of his rivalry with Washington, his clashes with him and the posthumous discovery of an apparently treasonable plan, he has been elected to play secondary Judas to Benedict Arnold. There is all the more reason to deal fairly with him, since our heroes can dispense with justice, but our villains need every protection from the villainies of popular condemnation.

Lee was an Englishman, about a year older than Washington, and "born in the army." His father was a colonel in the English service, and Lee is said to have received a commission at the age of eleven. He knew Latin, Greek, and four European languages. At the age of twenty he was commissioned a lieutenant in his father's regiment in Ireland, and came to America with it in 1754, the same year in which Washington began his military career. Lee was at Braddock's defeat with Washington, though nothing is known of his behavior on that occasion, and he never boasted of it.

The next year he "purchas'd a company for nine hundred pounds." [3] He was with William Johnson among the Indians and was adopted into a tribe under the descriptive title of Ounewaterika—"Boiling Water"—an element in which he managed to keep himself most of his life.

After having two ribs broken by a musket shot in battle, and enjoying other picturesque adventures, Lee went to Europe, fought in Portugal brilliantly well, was taken to Poland by the last of the Polish Kings and made a major general. His literary skill as a satirist was very great, and when he returned to America he won distinction in the war of pamphlets.

Hopeless of promotion in the English army, where he was still only a major on half pay, he devoted himself to the cause of American independence, and, in order to overcome any scruples the Americans might have against a foreigner without property, he bought a plantation in Virginia—characteristically borrowing the money to pay for it. [4] He also took pains to be present in Philadelphia at the first Continental Congress.

He won the admiration of R. H. Lee, who was of no kinship with him, and, through Lee, met Samuel Adams. He won the high favor of the New Englanders, who would probably have voted for him as commander-in-chief if it had not been for the necessity of placating and stimulating the South.

His cutting satire and irreverence for everything and everybody offended many people, but there is no reason for doubting his devotion to the American cause at this time, though subsequent events give a look almost of prophetic insight to the comment the Reverend Ezra Stiles [5] wrote in his diary after meeting him:

"Whether he is a Pimp of the Ministry or a sincere Friend to public Liberty, is to me uncertain."

For the present, however, he had convinced both himself and many of the colonists that his experience and ability fitted him to the supreme command.

Whether to choose him or Washington had been a matter of debate in New England for some time, and of much discussion in Philadelphia.

Washington ceased to write a diary on June 19th, 1775, and did not resume it for six years.

On May 30th, 1775, he had written that he "Dined at Mr. Mease's, and after setting a while with the Boston Gentlemen, returnd to my own Room."

His last entry on June 19th, referring to Colonel Joseph Reed, who became his military secretary, states that he "Dined at Colo. Ried's. Spent the Evening at Mr Lynch's."

Thomas Lynch and his son were both delegates from South Carolina, and the father was the man who had told John Adams about hearing Washington offer to equip and lead a thousand men to the relief of Boston. John Adams was one of the "Boston Gentlemen" with whom Washington had "set a while."

These two things have perhaps not been hitherto put together, but they may explain partly why John Adams, representing beleaguered Boston and seeking to bring to her aid all of the colonies, should have been impressed by Washington's cry of challenge and his financial resources and courage. Adams was canny enough, too, to realize that by offering to Washington the supreme command, he could bind the South to the North, the planters to the merchants.

Samuel Adams had at the first Congress proposed that a Church of England man should say a prayer, and the luckless Mr. Duché was chosen. He became the chaplain also of the second Congress, though not so appointed until July 8, 1776.[6]

Now John Adams wanted to name a Church of England vestryman from Virginia to lead the Continental Army. In doing this thing, he must mortally offend his colleague, John Hancock, who was one of Massachusetts' rich men, and had counted on the post.

Altogether, the problem of selecting a commander-in-chief was a matter for anxious thought. Against the trained skill of experienced British generals leading regular troops, must be pitted somebody who was not only a strategist but capable of organizing a rabble into an army.

On May 29th, John Adams had written to his wife:

"Colonel Washington appears at Congress in his uniform, and, by his great experience and abilities in military matters, is of much service to us." [7]

That uniform of Washington's was a deciding factor, according to Adams' great grandson, Charles Francis Adams, one of our keenest military historians—he was a brevet brigadier general of the Civil War—and one of Washington's frankest critics. He said of Washington's strange custom of sitting in the Congress as a soldier:

"He was not at that time acting in any military capacity. Neither does it appear what was the uniform he wore; probably that of a colonel of Virginia militia. Certainly the attendance of any member of a deliberative body, dressed in uniform, would be regarded as startling at this day. It had always been construed by Mr. Adams as Washington's way of announcing that his mind was made up, and that he was ready to take his place in the ranks in any capacity to which his country should call him. He was no maker of speeches, and this act was more significant than many speeches. It was no solicitation for place after the manner of an office-seeker; for nobody would suspect him of it; but it was the highest aspiration of patriotism, offering to meet danger in any situation which such services as he could render might avail to defend his country.

"Viewed in this light, then, it would seem as if, when answering the much agitated question, 'Who nominated Washington to the chief command?' it might be affirmed that he most unconsciously nominated himself." [8]

That six feet three in buff and blue, combined with Washington's golden silence, doubtless cast a spell over Congress, though Washington's own words indicate that he had no desire to be chosen.

Adams must have discussed his qualifications for the command before he came to Philadelphia as well as the qualifications of the British General, Charles Lee; for on May 7th, James Warren had written to Adams that he dared not propose putting "your friends Washington and L— at the head of the army." [9]

Lee had had none too much experience, but he was trained from childhood in the British army, while Washington at twenty-two had never drilled a soldier. He had since seen few battles, and none at all for seventeen years. But he was rich.

In those days when wealth was not the suspicious handicap that democracy has since made it, there was a feeling that no commander could command the respect either of his own soldiers or his enemy unless he had social prestige and wealth.

The New York Congress felt so strongly in this matter that, in instructing its delegates at Philadelphia concerning the various requisites of a chieftain, it emphasized this point:

"On a General in *America*, fortune also should bestow her gifts, that he may rather communicate lustre to his dignities than receive it, and that his country in his property, his kindred, and connexions, may have sure pledges that he will faithfully perform the duties of his high office, and readily lay down his power when the general weal shall require it." [10]

Compared to Washington, no other American officer had so much wealth, such social distinction and such manifest freedom from personal ambition. He was famous for his bravery, and his calm. His head was remarkably level, and above all he was a Burgess from that vital colony of Virginia, where his influence was evident since so many of the rapidly forming military companies had paid him honor.

But the real solution of the mystery of his choice must be shifted to the mystery of his overwhelming magnetism. He was not a man of education, high intellect, or military brilliance, yet his personal magnetism amounted to genius—if indeed genius is ever anything else but personal magnetism expressing itself in one form or another. He was no orator, sculptor, dramatist or poet, but he was a genius in his power to compel homage by merely being.

It is impossible otherwise to account for the emotions both of reverence and affectionate awe that he had inspired in strangers from his earliest youth. What had he done as yet to make an astute New England politician like Elbridge Gerry—whose name was later immortalized in the word "gerrymander"—refer to him as "the beloved Colonel Washington"?

"I should heartily rejoice to see this way the beloved Colonel Washington: and do not doubt the New England generals would acquiesce in showing to our sister Colony, Virginia, the respect which she has before experienced from the continent in making him *generalissimo*. This is a matter in which Dr. Warren agrees with me." [11]

But this letter of June 4, 1775, as C. F. Adams points out, could not have reached John Adams in Philadelphia until after Washington's selection.

Adams' autobiography is the only account we have of the benevolent intrigue, and it is racy:

"Full of anxieties concerning these confusions, and apprehending daily that we should hear very distressing news from Boston, I walked with Mr. Samuel Adams in the statehouse-yard for a little exercise and fresh air before the hour of Congress, and there represented to him the various dangers that surrounded us. He agreed to them all, but said, 'What shall we do?' I answered him that he knew I had taken great pains to get our colleagues to agree upon some plan, that we might be unanimous; but he knew that they would pledge themselves to nothing; but I was determined to take a step which should compel them and all the other members of Congress to declare themselves for or against something. 'I am determined this morning to make a direct motion that Congress should adopt the army before Boston, and appoint Colonel Washington commander of it.' Mr. Adams seemed to think very seriously of it, but said nothing.

"Accordingly, when Congress had assembled, I rose in my place, and in as short a speech as the subject would admit, represented the state of the colonies, the uncertainty in the minds of the people, their great expectation and anxiety, the distresses of the army, the danger of its dissolution, the difficulty of collecting another; and the probability that the British army would take advantage of our delays, march out of Boston, and spread desolation as far as they could go.

"I concluded with a motion, in form, that Congress would adopt the army at Cambridge, and appoint a general; that though this was not the proper time to nominate a general, yet, as I had reason to believe this was a point of the greatest difficulty, I had no hesitation to declare that I had but one gentleman in my mind for that important command, and that was a gentleman from Virginia, who was among us, and very well known to all of us; a gentleman whose skill and experience as an officer, whose independent fortune, great talents, and excellent universal character would command the approbation of all America, and unite the cordial exertions of all the colonies better than any other person in the Union.

"Mr. Washington, who happened to sit near the door, as soon as he heard me allude to him, from his usual modesty, darted into the library room."

When Washington, on hearing Adams' veiled reference to him, fled from the room, it was partly, no doubt, from a sense of delicacy toward the men who must vote for or against him, but also surely because of the great surge of emotion that must have overswept him when the ineffable honor was proffered to him.

If the ruthless Julius Cæsar could be excused for having an epileptic attack when the crown of triumphant Rome was held out to him, Washington might be expected to be shattered a little by the offer of a sword to fight his King with.

Adams goes on:

"Mr. Hancock, who was our president, which gave me an opportunity to observe his countenance while I was speaking on the state of the colonies, the army at Cambridge, and the enemy, heard me with visible pleasure; but when I came to describe Washington for the commander, I never remarked a more sudden and striking change of countenance. Mortification and resentment were expressed as forcibly as his face could exhibit them. Mr. Samuel Adams seconded the motion, and that did not soften the president's physiognomy at all.

"The subject came under debate, and several gentlemen declared themselves against the appointment of Mr. Washington, not on account of any personal objection against him, but because the army were all from New England, had a general of their own, appeared to be satisfied with him, and had proved themselves able to imprison the British army in Boston, which was all they expected or desired at that time.

"Mr. Pendleton, of Virginia, Mr. Sherman of Connecticut, were very explicit in declaring this opinion. Mr. Cushing and several others more faintly expressed their opposition, and their fears of discontent in the army and in New England. Mr. Paine expressed a great opinion of General Ward, and a strong friendship for him, having been his classmate at college, or, at least, his contemporary; but gave no opinion on the question. The subject was postponed to a future day. In the meantime, plans were taken out of doors to obtain a unanimity, and the voices were generally so clearly in favor of Washington, that the dissenting members were persuaded to withdraw their opposition, and Mr. Washington was nominated, I believe by Mr. Thomas Johnson, of Maryland, unanimously elected, and the army adopted." [12]

Thomas Johnson was the uncle of Adams' mother, and Washington afterwards offered him important posts, but they were never accepted.

John Adams was, in a very real sense, Washington's creator. If afterwards he came to fear that he had played Frankenstein and manufactured a monster who might devour the republic; if he came to be revolted by the groveling idolatry the public felt for this general who somehow won almost no battles; if Adams dreaded that the adulation Washington received might, and must, waken royal dreams in that lofty head, this was only natural in one who had read so much history and had found few or no men in whom power failed to waken lust for more power. Saviors of liberty always destroyed it.

Never before, if ever since, did any soul of such flawless patriotism appear upon the dirty pages of history. Besides, Washington had, in a measure, to build the altar on which he laid the sacrifice of his complete devotion.

There was, indeed, always a note of fatherhood and trusteeship in his attitude. He regarded the country much as he regarded the unformed lad whom his dying colleague, John West, begged him to take into guardianship.

The same profound modesty that beautified his letter to an old friend, the same sincere "I am unworthy of the honor but I will do my best if you want me," is found in his speech accepting the nomination to the command of the almost invisible army of the republic just shaping out of chaos. Its shape was still uncertain, for he and almost all the congressmen, and almost all the Americans outside believed that the war was but a rebellion against the best of Kings, by whom they would all be received again as prodigals as soon as they had argued it out with him.

When Washington was summoned the next day to receive the most perilous and difficult of honors, his peculiar nobility in humility shines forth even in the cold minutes of the Congress:

"Friday, June 16, 1775.

"The Congress met according to adjournment.

"The President, from the chair, informed *George Washington*, Esquire, that he had the orders of the Congress to acquaint him that the Congress had, by a unanimous vote, made choice of him to be General and Commander-in-Chief, to take the supreme command of the Forces raised, and to be raised, in defence of *American* liberty, and desired his acceptance of it. To which Colonel *Washington*, standing in his place, answered:

" 'MR. PRESIDENT: Though I am truly sensible of the high honour done me, in this appointment, yet I feel great distress, from a consciousness that my abilities and military experience may not be equal to the extensive and important trust. However, as the Congress desire it, I will enter upon the momentous duty, and exert every power I possess in their service, and for support of the glorious cause. I beg they will accept my most cordial thanks for this distinguished testimony of their approbation.

" 'But, lest some unlucky event should happen, unfavourable to my reputation, I beg it may be remembered, by every gentleman in the room, that I this day declare, with the utmost sincerity, I do not think myself equal to the command I am honoured with.

" 'As to pay, Sir, I beg leave to assure the Congress, that as no pecuniary consideration could have tempted me to accept this arduous employment, at the expense of my domestick ease and happiness, I do not wish to make any profit from it. I will keep an exact account of my expenses. Those, I doubt not, they will discharge, and that is all I desire.'

"Upon motion, *Resolved*, That a Committee of three be appointed to draught a Commission and Instructions for the General.

"The Committee to consist of the following persons, viz; Mr. *Lee*, Mr. *E. Rutledge*, and Mr. *J. Adams*." [13]

His commission came from a group that has an unfamiliar sound today: "the Delegates of the United Colonies of New-Hampshire, Massachusetts-Bay, Rhode-Island, Connecticut, New-York, New-Jersey, Pennsylvania, the Counties of New-Castle, Kent, and Sussex, on Delaware, Maryland, Virginia, North-Carolina, and South-Carolina, in Congress Assembled."

Congress pledged itself to "maintain and assist him, and adhere to him, the said George Washington, Esq., with their lives and fortunes."

"The Congress then proceeded to the choice of the Officers in the Army by ballot; when

"*Artemas Ward,* Esq., was chosen first Major-General.

"*Horatio Gates,* Esq., Adjutant-General.

"*Resolved,* That *Horatio Gates,* now chosen Adjutant-General, shall have the rank of a Brigadier-General.

"*Charles Lee,* Esq., was chosen second Major-General.

"*Resolved,* That this Congress will, on *Monday,* resolve itself into a Committee of the Whole, to take into consideration the state of *America.*

"Adjourned till *Monday* next, at nine o'clock."

The triumphant John Adams wrote to his wife:

"I can now inform you that the Congress have made choice of the modest and virtuous, the amiable, generous, and brave George Washington, Esquire, to be General of the American army, and that he is to repair, as soon as possible, to the camp before Boston. This appointment will have a great effect in cementing and securing the union of these colonies. The continent is really in earnest, in defending the country. They have voted ten companies of riflemen to be sent from Pennsylvania, Maryland, and Virginia, to join the army before Boston. These are an excellent species of light infantry. They use a peculiar kind of musket, called a rifle. It has circular or—groves within the barrel, and carries a ball with great exactness to great distances. They are the most accurate marksmen in the world.

"I begin to hope we shall not sit all summer. I hope the people of our province will treat the General with all that confidence and affection, that politeness and respect, which is due to one of the most important characters in the world. The liberties of America depend upon him, in a great degree."

Congress proceeded to appoint a day of approach to heaven for its aid, and Adams wrote home:

"My dear children, come here and kiss me. We have appointed a Continental fast. Millions will be upon their knees at once before their great Creator, imploring his forgiveness and blessing; his smiles on American councils and arms." [14]

The wording of the proclamation did not, however, please everybody, and the President of Yale College entered in his diary:

"I am sorry to see nothing of Christ in it. Under the Notion of an unexceptionable Thing adapted to all religious Sects, the Congress carried their politeness so far, as to repress their Belief of the Xtian Religion, & come too near being ashamed of Christ. This Proclam[a] might have been issued by a Congress of Deists." [15]

For the time being, Congress was more interested in money and soldiers than in dogma, and Adams wrote to Elbridge Gerry, anxiously telling of the agreement of Congress to issue bills of credit for the tremendous sum of two million dollars; the decision to support an army of fifteen thousand "at the expense of the Continent," the choice of officers, and his fear that the two English officers, Lee and Gates, might be unwelcome to Americans, though Washington, blind to his future wrangles with both of them, expressed an "earnest desire" to have them.

Adams dreaded lest the pay voted to the officers should be deemed extravagant. Generals Ward, Lee, Putnam and Schuyler were to get $166, or £75, a month—when they got it. Brigadier-Generals were rated at $125 a month; and so on down to captains at $20; lieutenants, $13⅓; privates, $6⅔ a month. And all were "to find their own Arms and Clothes," which was even harder to do than to find their pay.[16]

Adams hoped that New England would receive them with

"all the pride, pomp, and circumstance of glorious war displayed; no powder burned, however."

He knew that the colonial troops besieging Boston had practically no powder. Washington was to learn this later, and almost collapse with anxiety.

Adams ended his letter thus: "There is something charming to me in the conduct of Washington. A gentleman of one of the first fortunes upon the Continent, leaving his delicious retirement, his family and friends, sacrificing his ease, and hazarding all in the cause of his Country! His views are noble and disinterested. He declared when he accepted the mighty trust, that he would lay before us an exact account of his expenses, and not accept a shilling for pay." [17]

On the same day the disgruntled John Hancock wrote to Gerry, of Washington's appointment, "I shall sign his commission tomorrow. . . . He is a fine man." Later he wrote to Washington asking for a berth, and saying: "I am determined to act under you, if it be to take the firelock and join the ranks as a volunteer." Washington dodged the matter gracefully and Hancock did not take the firelock.

There was no cry of pride or exultance in any of the new commander's references to his appointment. Martha could not have been entirely surprised, for his announcement shows that he had kept her informed of the possibility of his selection; but it is hard to forgive her for sparing none of his letters from the flames except, by accident, this one and the little note he sent her in 1758. It is curious that both letters bid her farewell as he is going to the wars: the first was written to her when she became his betrothed, this one when she became his war-widow. The first has a certain pomposity that is lacking in the second, as if he had come to love her better after sixteen years of "domestic felicity":

"Philadelphia, 18 June, 1775.

"My Dearest,

"I am now set down to write to you on a subject, which fills me with inexpressible concern, and this concern is greatly aggravated and increased, when I reflect upon the uneasiness I know it will give you. It has been determined in Congress, that the whole army raised for the defence of the American cause shall be put under my care, and that it is necessary for me to proceed immediately to Boston to take upon me the command of it.

"You may believe me, my dear Patsy, when I assure you, in the most solemn manner, that, so far from seeking this appointment, I have used every endeavor in my power to avoid it, not only from unwillingness to part with you and the family, but from a consciousness of its being a trust too great for my capacity, and that I should enjoy more real happiness in one month with you at home, than I have the most distant prospect of finding abroad, if my stay were to be seven times seven years. But as it has been a kind of destiny, that has thrown me upon this service, I shall hope that my undertaking it is designed to answer some good purpose. You might, and I suppose did perceive, from the tenor of my letters, that I was apprehensive I could not avoid this appointment, as I did not pretend to intimate when I should return. That was the case. It was utterly out of my power to refuse this appointment, without exposing my character to such censures, as would have reflected dishonor upon myself, and given pain to my friends. This, I am sure, could not, and ought not, to be pleasing to you, and must have lessened me considerably in my own esteem. I shall rely, therefore, confidently on that Providence, which has heretofore preserved and been bountiful to me, not doubting but that I shall return safe to you in the fall. I shall feel no pain from the toil or the danger of the campaign; my unhappiness will flow from the uneasiness I know you will feel from being left alone. I therefore beg, that you will summon your whole fortitude, and pass your time as agreeably as possible. Nothing will give me so much sincere satisfaction as to hear this, and to hear it from your own pen. My earnest and ardent desire is, that you would pursue any plan that is most likely to produce content, and a tolerable degree of tranquillity; as it must add greatly to my uneasy feelings to hear, that you are dissatisfied or complaining at what I really could not avoid.

"As life is always uncertain, and common prudence dictates to every man the necessity of settling his temporal concerns, while it is in his power, and while the mind is calm and undisturbed, I have, since I came to this place (for I had not time to do it before I left home) got Colonel Pendleton to draft a will for me, by the directions I gave him, which will I now enclose. The provision made for you in case of my death will, I hope, be agreeable.

"I shall add nothing more, as I have several letters to write, but to desire that you will remember me to your friends, and to assure you that I am, with the most unfeigned regard, my dear Patsy, your affectionate, &c." [18]

The will he speaks of seems to be lost. He must have known that Pendleton opposed his nomination, but he admired Pendleton's legal acumen, and he was remarkably superior to personal spites.

With the usual infatuation of soldiers going to war, he expected to be home "in the fall," or at the latest during the winter. He did not see Mount Vernon for more than six years, and then only for two days. But his devoted wife spent a large part of the time with him.

His solicitude for her is shown in the letter he wrote the following day to his stepson:

"DEAR JACK . . . My great concern upon this occasion is, the thought of leaving your mother under the uneasiness which I fear this affair will throw her into; I therefore hope, expect, and indeed have no doubt, of your using every means in your power to keep up her spirits, by doing everything in your power to promote her quiet. I have, I must confess, very uneasy feelings on her account, . . .

"I am always pleased with yours and Nelly's abidance at Mount Vernon; . . . I think it absolutely necessary for the peace and satisfaction of your mother; a consideration which I have no doubt will have due weight with you both, and require no arguments to enforce." [19]

His modesty was not blind either to the political trades back of his selection, or the penalties of failure, for he wrote to Martha's brother-in-law, Colonel Bassett:

"I am now Imbarked on a tempestuous ocean, from whence
perhaps no friendly harbor is to be found. . . . It is an honor I by
no means aspired to. It is an honor I wished to avoid . . . but the
partiallity of the Congress, added to some political motives, left me
without a choice. May God grant, therefore, that my acceptance of
it, may be attended with some good to the common cause, & without injury (from want of knowledge) to my own reputation. . . .

"P.S. I must entreat you and Mrs. Bassett if possible to visit
at Mt. Vernon, as also my wife's other friends. I could wish you
to take her down, as I have no expectation of returning till winter
& feel great uneasiness at her lonesome situation. I have sent my
Chariot & Horses back." [20]

To his brother, John Augustine, he wrote in the same
spirit, and much the same words, again begging that Martha
be comforted.

Even to the officers of the Fairfax military companies, he
wrote in the same humble tone:

"GENTLEMEN: I am now about to bid adieu to the companies
under your respective commands, at least for a while. I have
launched into a wide and extensive field, too boundless for my
abilities, and far, very far, beyond my experience. I am called by
the unanimous voice of the Colonies to the command of the Continental Army—an honour I did not aspire to; an honour I was
solicitous to avoid, upon a full conviction of my inadequacy to the
importance of the service. The partiality of the Congress, however,
assisted by a political motive, rendered my reasons unavailing, and
I shall to-morrow set out for the camp near Boston." [21]

If he wrote to his mother, his letter has not been disclosed.
It is persistently told that she was always Tory in her sympathies; and well she may have been, for the very religion
she cherished included unfailing obedience to the English
King and to one's earthly parents. George broke with both.
The story is told that when she heard of the Revolution, she
exclaimed:

"Is there to be more fighting, more bloodshed? Surely
it will all end in the halter." [22]

That sounds like her. She had tried frantically to keep Washington from all of his other adventures, but tried in vain. On this occasion she could not reach her son to implore him to abstain from war. The story that Washington was afraid even to call on her with the news of war can hardly be true since he did not return to Virginia from the Second Congress. She did not love war, and she did not take pleasure in her son's habit of risking his neck.

And he was risking it now; for his wealth, his home, and his head were all subject to confiscation.

Nothing has won Washington more reverence than the fact that he insisted upon serving without pay, though Congress had voted £150 a month (about $333) for the commander-in-chief.

Charles Lee was well-to-do but improvident, and though he boasted that he made large financial sacrifices, he took the precaution to wring from Congress a promise to indemnify him for any losses.[23]

While Washington was one of the richest men, if not the richest man, in the colonies, his wealth was largely on paper, agricultural, therefore uncertain. He was always in debt and always short of money enough to meet his needs and his charities. The refusal of pay was a genuine sacrifice. His affairs and his farms suffered grievously by his absence, yet he would accept none of the land offered him as recompense when the Revolution was over. He kept his account with the nation with a scrupulous exactness that overlooked little or nothing.

At the end of the war he made a careful transcript of his vouchers, into a beautiful ledger headed:

"Dr . . . The United States . . . in account with—G: Washington Cr."

At the beginning of his bookkeeping there was no such thing as the "United States."

Giving so much as he did to his country, he felt justified in asking the little he demanded, not so much for George Washington as for the Commander-in-Chief of the United Colonies going out to meet the royal hosts. The first charge he makes is for a suitable chariot. As a respite from the fatigue of the saddle, he went to war in a phaëton! And he ran hardly less risk than the young man his carriage was named after. He puts down at the top of page one:

"1775 June. To the purchase of five Horses (two of which were had on credit from Mr Jas Mease) to equip me for my journey to the Army at Cambridge—and for the Service I was then going upon—having sent my Chariot & Horses back to Virga — —   £239

"22   To a light Phaeton bot of Doctr Renaudet —   55.
To double Harness for Ditto. bot from Mr Todd   7. 15
To Cash paid for Sadlery, a Letter Case, Maps, Glasses, &cc &ca &ca for the use of my Command—pr Memm book   29. 13. 6"

On the opposite page he entered:

"By Cash for a Gun and accoutrements   £3. 0. 0."

This he had sold to a committee for arming the militia.

He charged the government £7. 10s. 6d. for wine purchased in New York. He charged also for sealing wax, table linen, and writing paper. In September he charged £35. 6. 11 for Madeira wine and in October £28, and so on.

His dealings with spies begin with this entry: "To 333⅓ Dollars given to —— to enduce him to go into the Town of Boston; to establish a secret corrispondence for the purpose of conveying intelligence of the Enemys movements and designs." He adds a note, "The names of Persons who are employed within the Enemys lines, or who may fall within their power cannot be inserted."

He paid £7. 10 for a steward, his wife and daughter, and

a separate account was kept for his table which averaged $1,000 a month.[24]

The night before Washington left Philadelphia for Boston, he was lavishly banqueted at the City Tavern.

Those were days when feasts were feasts. Philadelphia has always been proud of her banquets and her Madeira. Washington was never more at home than when the Madeira was flowing free and the toasts were numberless.

But the days were not far off when food would be scarce and the tables lean; when his gaunt soldiers must quench their thirst with snowballs, and he himself would make the sacrifice that John Adams [25] described to his wife:

"General Washington sets a fine example. He has banished wine from his table, and entertains his friends with rum and water."

XXI

HE RIDES AGAIN TO BOSTON

IT was a little more than nineteen years since Washington had visited Boston to see the commander-in-chief of the British forces in America, Governor Shirley.

And now he was going over to visit his old friend, General Gage, the present commander-in-chief of the British forces in America.

Washington had no more idea of disloyalty to the King in this second journey than in the first. In 1756 he had gone to protest against the misbehavior of a royal officer who was interfering with the efficiency and dignity of a colonial officer going about the King's business. Now, in 1775, he was simply intent upon restoring to their places the King's misleading Ministers and the troops sent over by a parliament bent upon violating the Constitution in order to diminish the efficiency and dignity of the King's most loyal subjects overseas.[1]

A strain was rending the heartstrings of the people, and many of Washington's former guests at Mount Vernon, many of his colleagues in the House of Burgesses and at the Continental Congress would soon be resolving that, for all their devotion to the rights of Englishmen, they could not go the whole way with Washington.

He was riding away from many old friends and many old faiths. He was riding forward into decisions that he dreamed not of.

It was part of the cross he had to bear that so many of his comrades, so many ancient families, old-blooded Americans would come to hate him as a traitor to his King.[2]

255

For the moment, however, all was bugles and drums and high emprise. When Washington rode away from Philadelphia on June 23rd,—a Friday—he inspired the poor drudge, John Adams, with a sense of such woeful envy, that he wrote to his wife:

"I have this morning been out of town to accompany our generals, Washington, Lee, and Schuyler, a little way on their journey to the American camp before Boston. The three generals were all mounted on horse-back, accompanied by Major Mifflin, who is gone in the character of aid-de-camp. All the delegates from the Massachusetts, with their servants and carriages, attended; many others of the delegates from the Congress; a large troop of light horse in their uniforms; many officers of militia besides, in theirs, music playing, etc., etc. Such is the pride and pomp of war. I, poor creature, worn out with scribbling for my bread and my liberty, low in spirits and weak in health, must leave others to wear the laurels which I have sown; others to eat the bread which I have earned; a common case." [3]

The escort turned back after a five-mile parade, and Washington had not gone fifteen miles further when a hard-riding courier bringing despatches to Congress from the East reined in to give him the first verbal news of Bunker Hill. The battle had been fought on June 17th, and it took only six days to get the tidings to Philadelphia.

How grim a picture of the engagement the rider gave we do not know, but the New Englanders had exchanged about 115 killed, 350 wounded, 30 prisoners and the Hill for an admitted British loss of 226 killed and 828 wounded.

Washington is reported to have demanded eagerly:

"Did the militia fight?"

On being told that they did, he is said to have said:

"Then the liberties of the country are safe."

If he ever made such a premature Fourth-of-July oration, he must have regretted it when he reached Boston and saw what the militia was that guaranteed American freedom, and began the long series of courts-martial for cowardice that followed the battle.

He must have regretted it, too, when he crossed the Delaware again a year and a half later at the head of a beaten herd that he called "not men but sheep."

Some of the militia had indeed fought gloriously at Bunker Hill. They staggered and shattered the British regulars and England was thunderstruck when the reports arrived of the terrific blood-price exacted for the conquest of a little mound on a neck of land: more than one-quarter of the whole force engaged. The British lost on this day, in officers killed, one-eighth of their total loss in the whole seven years of war; and in officers wounded, one-sixth.[4] That day was as a year to them.

For one thing, the rebels were in trenches—which was wise and a particularly American way of fighting. They had dug in with a speed that was dumfounding to the British. They held their fire well, too, and delivered smashing volleys. They might have won the day but for one thing; their powder gave out.

On the other hand there was much cowardice, much scandal, much talk of courts-martial to dim the glory of the brave and the dead. The plans had gone wrong, orders had not been carried out, and General Ward did not even visit the field.[5] The patriots had carefully entrenched themselves at the tip of a peninsula where the enemy had nothing to do but take the obvious step of seizing the base of the spit of land and bagging the whole force under cover of his fleet-fire.

Only one thing could have been more insane than the strategy of the Americans, and that was the decision of the British General, Gage, to make a frontal attack. His subordinate, Clinton, showed him the manifest maneuver, but he refused to adopt it and sent his army across the bay

under General Howe. When the Americans broke and ran,
after covering Howe with the blood of his slaughtered
soldiers, and mortally wounding all but one of his staff,
Clinton implored Howe to pursue and capture the powderless rabble. But Howe seemed to have an absolutely hopeless inhibition against finishing well the battles he always
began well. So the Americans escaped.

Charles Francis Adams graphically pictures the battle and
Prescott's stupendous blunder in marching across Charlestown Neck to occupy Bunker Hill, leaving his rear unpro-
tected and easily assailable. Prescott then, of his own
initiative, pushed on beyond Bunker Hill and fortified the
lower Breed's Hill, "at which point he was helplessly in the
trap, unless his opponent, by coming at him in front, drove
him bodily out of the hole in which he had put himself.
His opponent did just that." The next day Prescott begged
General Ward in vain for fifteen hundred men, that he
might recapture Bunker Hill—"in other words, go back
into the trap from which the stupidity of his opponents had
forcibly driven him." [6]

Fourteen months later, Adams goes on, Washington,
"Ward's more famous successor got himself and his army
into a position on Long Island scarcely less false and difficult
than Prescott's at Bunker Hill. He, also, was then saved
from irretrievable disaster through sheer good luck, happily
combined with his opponent's incompetence."

Washington sharply criticized the mismanagement at
Bunker Hill as he gathered the details on his way to Boston.
He was yet to learn how dire was the poverty of the militia
both in spirit and in material.

The Americans as always had entered war without equipment or discipline. The liberties of the country were far
from safe.

Washington must have felt this the more keenly now that

he was selected to set the disjointed times right. On the
first day out from Philadelphia, he reached Trenton and
spent the night there. On the morrow he halted at New
Brunswick to consider which of the three roads he had best
take into New York. On the way General Lee borrowed
some more money, £6. 13. 6, which he repaid seven years
later, posthumously, from his estate.

Washington approached New York with anxiety, as the
loyalist element was in the majority, and there was danger
of attack or capture by the royal soldiers or sailors, who
understood his seditious motives. He waited, therefore,
while General Philip Schuyler sent a note ahead to the
President of the New York Congress, a more or less conservative set of radicals. Though it was a Sunday, Congress
hurriedly met and sent an escort to conduct by the most
"prudent" crossing the party of rebels on the way to the
rebellion.

It was an embarrassing coincidence that the royal governor, Tryon, returned from a leave of absence in England
on the very same day. As Tryon was naturally an out-and-
out loyalist and even the rebel Congress was still formally
loyal, the situation was delicate. But Washington would
not turn back. He rode up to Hoboken and crossed the
river in the early afternoon.

Nothing could be more picturesque or more illuminative
concerning the general confusion of the Americans and the
absolute ambiguity of their intentions than this noisy Sabbath in New York. Perhaps "amphibious" is a truer word
than "ambiguous" for Washington's party and the Tories as
well were desperately trying to be loyal both to their King
and to America. The Tories were as discontented with the
actions of Parliament as the radicals were, but the Tories
stopped at an open breach with their royal master and the
radicals did not as yet know how far they would go.

At the moment even Washington was amphibiously wavering between the solid earth of loyalty and the deep waters of rebellion.

A living picture of this 25th of June, 1775, is given by the Tory historian Thomas Jones, a justice of the supreme court of New York at the time. No critic of the British was ever more severe than he, but his disgust with the rebels was even greater. He thus describes the day when Washington crossed the Hudson to spend the night at the country home of Leonard Lispenard:

"Upon this occasion the volunteer companies raised for the express purpose of rebellion, the members of the Provincial Congress, those of the city committee, the parsons of the dissenting meeting-houses, with all the leaders and partisans of faction and rebellion . . . waited upon the beach to receive them upon their landing from the Jersey shore and conducted them up to Lispenard's, amidst the repeated shouts and huzzas of the seditious and rebellious multitude, where they dined, and towards evening were escorted to town, attended and conducted in the same tumultuous and ridiculous manner.

"This happened on a Sunday, and while William Walton, Esq., who was Colonel of one of the Governor's Company of Guards, was at church; Rudolphus Ritzema, before mentioned, who had the command of a rebel company of fusileers, under a false pretence got possession of the colours belonging to Col. Walton's Company, a present from General Tryon, then Governor of the province, and decorated with his arms, which he never afterwards had the honour, the honesty, or the good manners to restore to the proper owner. This was swindling to all intents and purposes, but in those days of anarchy and confusion perfectly justifiable among the ruling powers, as the swindler was a whig, a republican, and a rebel." [7]

The site of Lispenard's house, then far out in the country, is now far down in the city. It stood on a hill overlooking the Hudson River near the present Canal, Desbrosses and Hudson Streets.[8]

From this mansion after a mid-afternoon dinner, Washington was escorted down the present Greenwich Street to the Fields, now City Hall Park, and probably spent the night with General Schuyler's cousin, William Smith.

On the same evening, at nine o'clock, Governor Tryon landed at the Exchange and was welcomed by Judge Jones and the rest of the Supreme Court, the Clergymen of the Church of England, all the dignitaries. Judge Jones goes on:

"But strange to relate! yet strange as it is! it is nevertheless a fact, that those very people who attended the rebel Generals in the morning, and conducted them from place to place with repeated shouts of approbation, congratulated them on their respective appointments to such principal commands, in so virtuous an army, upon so important an occasion; wished them joy of their safe arrival in New York, prayed God to bless their 'great and glorious undertaking,' and to grant them success in all their measures in the management of 'so great and necessary a war,' a war undertaken (as they asserted) for the sole defence of the just rights and liberties of mankind. I must again say, strange to relate! these very men, who had been not five hours before pouring out their adulation and flattery, or more probably the real sentiments of their souls, to the three rebel Generals, now one and all joined in the Governor's train, and with the loudest acclamations, attended him to his lodgings, where, with the utmost seeming sincerity, they shook him by the hand, welcomed him back to the Colony—wished him joy of his safe arrival, hoped he might remain long in his Government, enjoy peace and quietness, and be a blessing to the inhabitants under his control. What a farce! What cursed hypocrisy! A scheme was at this very time laid by these very people to subvert the British Government in the Colonies, in Church and State, and to erect one of their own upon its ruins.

"A Provincial Convention, composed of some of these identical people, a thing unknown to the British Constitution, was then sitting in New York. Under their authority troops were then actually raising, in order to form an army to carry on an offensive war against his Majesty's Colony of Quebec, and the officers engaged in this service, were actually receiving commissions from the President of this illegal and unconstitutional body, signed by himself, countersigned by their secretary, by order of the Convention, and a seal of their own formation affixed. But what is still more strange, if anything can be more strange, this very set of people as a body, nay further, even pretending to be a constitutional body, the very next day waited upon the rebel chief, and presented him with an address in the name of all the inhabitants in the Colony, who they had the impudence to call their constituents, and congratulated him on his appointment to the chief command of the American army, wished him success in the great, arduous, and glorious undertaking."

In view of the subsequent sufferings of Judge Jones, his emotions may be understood.

On Monday morning, the Provincial Congress met, and adopted an address to Washington, stating that "the most loyal of his Majesty's Subjects" were "reduced to the unhappy Necessity of taking up Arms to defend their dearest Rights," and expressing a rather tactless and guarded confidence that "whenever this important Contest shall be decided by that fondest Wish of every American Soul, an Accommodation with our Mother Country, you will cheerfully resign the important Deposit committed into your Hands, and re-assume the Character of our worthiest Citizen."

Then Congress waited on Washington and he read them his answer, deploring "the unhappy Necessity of such an Appointment, as that with which I am now honored," and assuring them that "every Exertion of my worthy Colleagues and myself, will be equally extended to the Re-establishment of Peace and Harmony, between the Mother Country and these Colonies."

He answered not as an individual but for the group of officers and added one of those splendid phrases that occasionally spring forth from his usually lumbering style:

"When we assumed the Soldier, we did not lay aside the Citizen."

He closed, saying that he and his colleagues would "most sincerely rejoice with you in that happy Hour, when the Establishment of American Liberty, in the most firm and solid Foundations, shall enable us to return to our private Stations, in the Bosom of a free, peaceful and happy Country." [9]

He was mistaken about his future, and was destined to lay aside his dream of reconciling the King with his subjects, but he never gave up his plan to return to private life. He was no Cæsar, no proconsul or conquistador, making war in order to accumulate wealth; he was a farmer called away from his lands to end a breach of the peace.

While in New York he wrote to Congress the first of that almost daily series of letters which occupied so much of his time and wore out his mind and heart until the wonder is that he found strength or leisure for his military duties.

He was persuaded to open a letter on its way from Boston to Congress, and, after apologizing for the liberty, called attention to the appeal of the Bostonians for powder. He mentioned that New York had sent a thousand pounds to Boston three days before, "which has left this Place almost destitute of that necessary article, there being at this Time . . . not more than four Bbs of powder in the City of N York."

He left General Schuyler in command of the New York department, instructing him to "Keep a watchful eye upon Governor Tryon." He said that he would advise "forcible measures" if necessary were Congress not sitting, but, since it was, he urged General Schuyler to refer to that body.

Thus from the first, he established the never-forsaken policy of regarding the Congress as his complete master, and himself as only its executive.

This hampered him almost fatally as a military genius, and subjected him to torments, frustrations, humiliations innumerable. It laid him open to the severest criticism from his own people, and from posterity, as a general whose inactivity, indecisiveness, and want of splendid audacity rendered him inferior to numberless other great strategists. The French historian, Doniol,[10] says that he did not even want freedom from Congress—"*jugé . . . comme indécis, en réalité esclave de la volonté du Congrès.*"

But Washington was the greater citizen for this very defect as a soldier. He had the defects of his qualities and the qualities of his defects. He was never in any danger from that Cromwellian ambition, by which sin the angels fell. He could never rescue his country as Napoleon did and then ruin it for his own insane lusts of power; never impose himself on it as the other Cromwell did; never make a Stadtholdership a family heirloom as William of Orange did; never turn a republic into a personal empire as the Cæsars did.

Other governments have always had reason to fear their best generals lest in getting rid of King Log they bring on

King Stork. But the American republic, though it faced numberless dangers, incurred none from Washington's ambition. The example he set has been a priceless heritage, for, since his time, no American has ever dreamed, or at least none has ever disclosed the thought, of an attempt at such a seizure of power as every other nation has had to meet or dread from its most brilliant warriors.

The luster that Washington the general lacked, glows with an eternal fire in his patriotism.

On Tuesday, June 27, 1775, Washington, with Lee, left New York on the way to Cambridge. At New Haven on Wednesday, he reviewed a militia company of Yale College students on the Green. One of them was Noah Webster, who played the fife or the drum.

On Thursday, Washington left for Hartford. He rode in his phaëton to Windsor. On Friday, he was in Springfield where he was met by a committee of the congress of Massachusetts Bay. One member of this committee, Dr. Benjamin Church, a highly valued man in the early movements, won the pitiable honor of being perhaps the first of the long list of American traitors. He was later caught conveying information to the enemy, was tried, imprisoned, and finally vanished on a sea-voyage.

On Saturday, July 1, 1775, Washington left Springfield and lodged at Worcester. He arrived at Watertown Sunday morning, where he was greeted with an address preparing him for the disorganized army he might expect to find and was expected to regulate.

He was warned that the volunteers though "naturally brave and of good understanding," lacked experience even in "divers things most essential to the preservation of health, and even life," including "the absolute necessity of cleanliness in their dress and lodging, continual exercise and strict temperance."

He answered that "in exchanging the enjoyments of domestick life for the duties of my present honourable but arduous station, I only emulate the virtue and publick spirit of the whole Province of the Massachusetts-Bay, which, with a firmness and patriotism without example in modern history have sacrificed all the comforts of social and political life."

It was only natural, he said, that the troops should lack order, but he was sure that it would be made up for by "the activity and zeal of the officers and the docility and obedience of the men."

The bitter irony of this last he was soon to learn.

He asked for "the assistance of every good man and lover of his Country" and most earnestly implored "that Divine Being, in whose hands are all human events, to make you and your constituents as distinguished in publick and private happiness, as you have been by Ministerial oppression and private and publick distress."

When these formalities were concluded, a troop of light horse and a retinue of citizens escorted Washington across the remaining three miles to the headquarters selected for him in Cambridge, the Craigie mansion, later the home of Longfellow, who wrote his poems in the room, to the right of the front door, where Washington wrote his epic prose.

Though Washington must have been an impressive man as he rode through the staring throng of soldiers and civilians, the stories of his reception with loud cheers and thundering artillery seem to have been made up by later historians who believed in writing of the past as it should have been, not as it was.

No contemporary authority, not even a diarist, mentions a celebration of any sort. The Americans had been warned not to waste powder, and even the British guns were silent.

A Sabbath hush seems to have greeted the Virginian and the Englishman who had come to displace the local heroes, and Washington must have felt solemn enough even for a New England Sunday afternoon, as he passed through the village and the college buildings taken over as billets. He looked on a huddle of half-naked farmers and villagers with nothing uniform in garb or carriage, or armament, and saw beyond them the huts of board, stone, turf or brush and the sorry and insufficient tents which Washington described as "help'd out by a Collection of now useless sails from the Sea Port Towns." [11] In the distance he looked across the water to Boston, half-encircled by nearly ten miles of trenches and redoubts.

More to Washington's liking was the Sunday evening dinner General Ward gave him. There was much hilarity and Adjutant Gibbs was "hoisted, chair and all, upon the table, and gave the company a rollicking bachelor's song, calculated to make the immobile features of the chief relax. . . . Glasses clinked, stories were told, and the wine circulated." [12]

Washington might have felt himself back in Fredericksburg, and he liked a good "bachelor's song." Remembering the vigorous phrases then considered proper for pulpit and parlor, a "bachelor's song" must have been what one of the most popular ballads of that time called "hot stuff."

Washington had need of a good laugh or two before he settled down to his difficulties. For one thing, he had entered upon something like the tortured existence of a grand opera impresario. At times military men outshine *prime donne* in their excitement over precedence.

John Adams was writing to his wife at a later date after maddening experience of the squabbles that threatened to throttle liberty in her own home:

"I am wearied to death with the wrangles between military officers, high and low. They quarrel like cats and dogs. They worry one another like mastiffs, scrambling for rank and pay like apes for nuts. I believe there is no one principle which predominates in human nature so much, in every stage of life from the cradle to the grave, in males and females, old and young, black and white, rich and poor, high and low, as this passion for superiority. . . . But I never saw it operate with such keenness, ferocity, and fury as among military officers. They will go terrible lengths in their emulation, their envy, and revenge in consequence of it." [13]

Old General Artemas Ward swallowed his humiliation with grace and modestly wished that his commission as first of the Majors General "had been conferred upon a Person, better qualified to execute a Trust so important. . . . I always have been & am still ready to divote my Life, in attempting to deliver my native Country, from insupportable Slavery." But he wished that the appointments might not "have a Tendency to create Uneasiness among us." [14]

How vain the wish!

In Washington's first letter to Congress from camp, he mentioned "the great Dissatisfaction expressed on this Subject and the apparent Danger of throwing the Army into the utmost Disorder."

He was so alarmed, indeed, that he dared not give out the commissions handed to him by Congress for distribution "except General Puttnam's" which was delivered "before I was apprized of these Uneasinesses." He assured Congress, "I have not, nor could have any private Attachments; every Gentleman in Appointment was an intire Stranger to me but from Character."

Yet behold the exodus:

"General Spencer was so much disgusted at the preference given to General Puttnam that he left the Army without visiting me, or making known his Intentions in any respect. General Pomroy had also retired before my Arrival, occasioned (as is said) by some Disappointment from the Provincial Congress. General Thomas is much esteemed and earnestly desired to continue in the service; and as far as my Opportunities have enabled me to judge I must join in the general opinion that he is an able good Officer and his Resignation would be a publick Loss. The postponing him to Pomroy and Heath whom he has commanded would make his Continuance very difficult, and probably operate on his Mind, as the like Circumstance has done on that of Spencer." [15]

Charles Lee had been indignant enough at having Washington preferred to him, not to mention being second Major General to Artemas Ward, whom he called "an old churchwarden." In speaking of Congress he wrote, "I do not mean one or two of the cattle, but the whole Stable." [16] Yet even Lee was so distressed by the disgraceful jealousies that he wrote to the sulky General Thomas:

"You think yourself not justly dealt with in the appointments of the Continental Congress. I am quite of the same opinion, but is this a time Sir, when the liberties of your country, the fate of posterity, the rights of mankind are at stake, to indulge our resentments for any ill treatment we may have received as individuals? I have myself, Sir, full as great, perhaps greater reason to complain than yourself. I have passed through the highest ranks, in some of the most respectable services in Europe. According then to modern etiquette notions of a soldier's honor and delicacy, I ought to consider at least the preferment given to General Ward over me as the highest indignity, but I thought it my duty as a citizen and asserter of liberty, to waive every consideration. . . .

"For God Almighty's sake, for the sake of everything that is dear, and ought to be dear to you, for the sake of your country, of mankind, and let me add of your own reputation, discard such sentiments." [17]

Washington wrote a long letter himself of much the same appeal as Lee's but in a far more impersonal and lofty key and at length General Thomas came back to duty and soon received the post of first brigadier in place of Pomeroy, who had never acted under his commission.

Throughout the siege of Boston, throughout the whole war, Washington had to face not only wholesale desertions and furious mutinies among the private soldiers, but also the most exquisitely embarrassing feuds among his officers with threats of wholesale resignation. His prudence, fairness and devotion to the government were tested to the last degree.

But the British officers then and later were equally at odds. "The Generals in Boston are upon bad terms together," wrote Lee.[18] There were some famous controversies among the royal factions throughout the war and long after. Fortunately for Washington and the cause of freedom, everything that crippled his powers from within or from without was duplicated on the other side.

American historians have usually ignored the hardships of the British, but they were innumerable; else, the American military machine would have been destroyed even before it shook itself to pieces.

On the morning of Monday, July 3rd, 1775, General Ward, having had the twenty-one drummers and twenty-one fifers especially rehearsed, and having ordered the troops turned out early, surrendered to Washington the command of the army, which consisted entirely of men from four New England colonies.

At the same time he turned over all the sacred honors and privileges inalienable from a commanding general, the right to be abused, disobeyed and frustrated. General Ward had been called old, indecisive and devoid of initiative. From now on these epithets were reserved for Washington.[19]

Tradition tells that Washington majestically drew his sword under a great elm at Cambridge.[20] But tradition is the sole authority, for there are no contemporary documents describing the place or the event, though, quaintly enough, three diaries say of this day, "Nothing new," "Nothing remarkable," "Nothing extraordinary." [21]

If Washington had been keeping his diary he would probably have said even less.

Of Ward, Edward Everett Hale wrote in 1880: "If you should ask ten Boston men, 'Who was Artemas Ward?' nine would say he was an amusing showman." [22] Forty years later they would have forgotten also the comic circus manager, "Artemus Ward," created by the once celebrated humorist, Charles Farrar Browne. But Hale mentions one noble silence of General Ward's, who had a commanding general's right to whatever glory belongs to the battle of Bunker Hill. When, after the battle, Prescott begged for men and bayonets and powder to reënter the trap, Ward refused—"only too well pleased if he were left without attack. Ward knew, what he would not tell to any man even to save his reputation, that he had in store that day only sixty-nine hundred pounds of powder,—not half a pound for every soldier in his command."

To this dearth of powder Washington succeeded, and to the necessity of keeping secrets even at the cost of the criticism to which he also succeeded.

Artemas Ward should not be so well forgotten. Five years older than Washington, and a graduate of Harvard, he had taken part in the Ticonderoga campaign of 1758, in which Charles Lee was wounded. Ward was promoted from Major to Lieutenant Colonel in the field, and later to Colonel, but his health was wrecked and like Washington, he had not appeared in arms since that year. He was too ill to take part at Lexington or Concord, but risked his head as a traitor by accepting the command of the besiegers of Boston. Like Washington, he pleaded in vain for sufficient equipment and supplies. He was a man of extreme piety and made morning prayers an important part of the service.

It was he who shut the British up in Boston, and held them helpless there. He had to call to Virginia for help to drive them out. But so had Washington to call for help from overseas before he could win his war.

The Revolution was already in a strange state of stalemate. Both Americans and British were in an apparently impossible situation. The Americans had only to hang on, for they had a fruitful continent back of them. The British had a stormy ocean between them and help.

XXII

HIS PROBLEM AND HIS MATERIALS

PATRIOTISM hallows nearly all crimes in times of invasion and war, but permits every chivalry to wounded enemies and prisoners. When peace smiles, the fiercest warriors are expected to be the most prompt and the most generous in their treatment of their late foes, praising their achievements liberally and modestly deprecating one's own perfections. The ideal soldier, indeed, often finds his heart warming irresistibly toward the adversaries who fought him hardest.

But there has been a curse upon American historians until of late in their treatment of their opponents in the Civil War of 1776-1783. It has been, and still is in certain circles, made a test of patriotism to avoid common honesty, not to speak of generosity or modesty, in all phases of the treatment of it.

But one wonders what a purely neutral historian (say, a scholar from Mars) would make of the Revolutionary War.

Lacking all the sweet furies of partisanship and regarding only the indisputable facts taken from the authentic records, such an historian might take back to Mars what he would hardly dare publish on the western hemisphere of this planet, a statement somewhat to this effect:

The rulers of the British empire, while incidentally carrying on a war in India,[1] trying to keep Ireland down and frighten Europe off, and more or less successfully stifling a civil war at home, and much hampered thereby, were mad enough to believe that they could crush the independence of thirteen restless colonies separated from them by three thousand miles of ocean.

The American colonies had a seacoast over a thousand miles long, broken with innumerable bays, inlets, rivermouths, and land-locked harbors offering perfect refuge to the vessels of the colonists who were adepts at shipbuilding and seafaring. The land to be conquered was six hundred miles deep; it extended back into illimitable wilderness, and was not only poorly provided with roads, but was to a large extent covered with forests and broken with hills and mountains favorable to bush-fighting, in which the colonists excelled and the imperial troops were ignorant. As one Englishman said, conquering America would be like conquering a map.

The empire had a standing army aggregating on paper less than fifty thousand men, largely recruited by kidnapers called press-gangs, and far more hostile to their officers and government than to their kinsmen, the rebels. Twelve thousand of the British soldiers were engaged in crushing Ireland, ten thousand were in the West Indies, Africa, Asia and elsewhere, and eight thousand had been sent already to America, only to be immobilized in one port-town.[2]

To conquer the colonies permanently there would be required a vast multitude of troops of occupation, at least fifty thousand, as well as mobile armies of great size. The English had no commander-in-chief except their occasionally crazy King; and their next highest officer, Adjutant General Harvey, flatly said in 1775:

"Taking America as it at present stands, it is impossible to conquer it with our British Army."[3]

He wrote to Howe:

"Our army will be destroyed by damned driblets— America is an ugly job—a damned affair, indeed."

GENERAL SIR WILLIAM HOWE

(Drawn and engraved by Corbett, 1777)

A larger army was simply unobtainable. Even a bounty of £3 per man did not bring in Englishmen. Recruits could only be had by purchasing mercenary officers and slave troops from Hesse and other principalities dealing in human flesh.

The expense of this was likely to cause a revolt at home among the already overburdened taxpayers, a goodly proportion of whom sympathized so thoroughly with the rebels as to refuse to vote supplies against them, to cheer their victories and to defend them openly, even in parliament. Some of the officers broke their swords and resigned rather than fight Americans, and after the battle of Lexington certain Englishmen took up subscriptions and put on mourning—not for the slain English, but for the colonists.[4]

The enormous mass of supplies, artillery, clothing, munitions for the army overseas must be sent across the ocean in sailing vessels subject to such delays that it often took weeks to get them out of the English Channel into the open sea. One great shipment of much-needed beef was so completely shattered just outside the home-port that the Channel was strewn for days with the bloated carcases of numberless cattle. At times the cavalry horses and cattle had to be cast overboard to save them from dying slowly of hunger or thirst. Strikes and labor troubles among the dockworkers were frequent.

Furthermore, the soldiers themselves had to be shipped oversea and the losses from ship-fever and the plagues of the time were ghastly. A non-commissioned officer sent out to Howe's army wrote home:

"There was continued destruction in the foretop, the pox above-board, the plague between-decks, hell in the forecastle, the devil at the helm."[5]

Many of the officers and soldiers brought their wives and

children along on the transports and their sufferings were
heartbreaking; death was a commonplace and suicides not
infrequent.

Storms and calms and plagues were not the only perils of
the sea. The colonies speedily equipped privateers who
preyed upon the supply-ships more devastatingly than the
hurricanes, and, what was worse, turned over the British
uniforms and munitions to the colonists.

From the start, the ancient enemy, France, fully recovered from the late Seven Years' War, made ready to regain
her lost prestige and territory, and with the connivance of
Vergennes, the foreign minister, and the leadership of Beau-
marchais, the playwright, meanwhile encouraged the colonists with huge secret loans of money and supplies. Holland
and Spain, the other immemorial enemies, reared their heads
again and did all they dared to thwart the British.

The hopelessness of the Empire's conquest was seen in
the appalling result of the first attempt to crush just one of
the colonial centers. The harbor of Boston, a town of only
seventeen thousand people, had been easily seized, but the
fist of the mighty was caught in the trap of the weak.

And now, having failed to conquer the one town of
Boston, they had brought to her aid the united power of
all the thirteen colonies. From far-off Virginia came a
commander-in-chief to lead the armies mustering everywhere. At his side were two generals of British training,
Lee and Gates, turning against their mother-country as hundreds of others had done.

Soon the French and the Germans, Swedes and Poles
would be sending ambitious soldiers to the aid of the
colonies. By and by France and Spain would declare open
war, while other nations maintained a farcical neutrality.
Worst of all, the tyrant was forced to put his army and his
navy into the charge of the brothers Howe, both of whom

had openly declared in parliament their sympathy with the colonies and their refusal to fight against them, but had accepted the commissions, perhaps, because of their financial needs.

Surely a visitor from Mars would have said that never was a tyrant in more impotent condition than the British parliament; and the war was lost before it was begun.

Imagine his stupefaction then when he found the colonies so disabled by mutual jealousies, by individual autocracies, indolences, and poltrooneries that their armies dwindled steadily from the first brief uprising, with intervals of almost total disappearance; and their indifference to success was so great that, no matter how vital the problem offered to their suffrages, hardly a handful would even take the trouble to go to the polls.

In the important election of the radical Samuel Adams, at Boston, less than 10 percent of the voters voted, and his majority was 183 out of a total of only 448. In electing Revolutionary committeemen and delegates "not more than one third of the adult white males in America ever set the seal of their approval on the Revolution." [6] There is reason to believe that more Americans actually served as loyalists with the British army than in the revolutionary army.[7]

The British general, Henry Conway, protesting that the colonies could never be conquered, reckoned that with a population of between two and three million people, they could raise an army of one hundred and fifty thousand.[8] But at least a third of the population was ardently loyalist, and in many quarters, a much higher proportion.

Because of this, Fisher [9] cuts the estimate of the patriot population from 2,200,000 to 1,400,000, which should have given Washington an expectation of at least 50,000 men, the number Congress also counted on. Washington never once had a total force of half that number.

The American navy, so to speak, that is, the privateering service, was far more popular and it has been estimated that ninety thousand Americans were, first and last, engaged in the cruises. "New England shipping interests, it is said, were never more prosperous than in the last years of the war." [10]   But, of course, the privateers were mere raiders and could never attack the British navy.

Victory depended upon the army and the dismaying fact is certain that the military establishment reached its height in the first year of the struggle and dwindled away to a third of its original number, while the British gradually doubled their forces.

A great number of American men did indeed pass through the army for brief periods, but they came so slowly and went so fast that they were hardly registered before they were gone.

Accepting the population of the patriot people as 1,400,000, that would mean a fighting strength of 400,000. Yet the Revolutionary Army never surpassed a paper strength of 90,000, including the undisciplined militia. The field forces never reached 30,000 and the actual number of effectives ranged from 20,000 down to 14,000 and often far less. Fisher says, "between 5,000 and 10,000 men were all that could be raised and maintained continuously." [11]   He gives Washington as his authority.

When Knox became Secretary of War he reported in 1790, that in 1775 the total number of troops was 27,443, besides 10,180 militia in the Southern colonies. In 1776 the high spot was reached with 46,901 Continentals and 42,760 militia, a total of 89,661, more than twice the highest British strength.

Yet the Boer Republic in 1899 with a population of 300,000 kept an army of 40,000 in the field and fought for two and a half years against the empire. At that rate the forefathers of the American republic should have kept 180,000 men in the field.

During the Civil War, the Union States had about five and a half million men between the ages of eighteen and sixty, and kept only a million in the field at any one time. Yet that was nearly one-fifth of the possible. The Confederacy reached the point of one-third.

During the Revolutionary War, according to Jameson,[12] the proportion was never better than one-eighth and fell to one-sixteenth. His only term for it is "widespread apathy."

If the patriots had risen with that magnificent unanimity described in those fairy tales called schoolbooks, the British would have been swept into the sea in a few weeks.

Altogether, the showing is one that cannot be regarded with unmixed pride, except in the sublime heroes who persisted in the face of greater discouragements at home than from the enemy.

The worst of such armies as Washington had to command was their volatility. Desertion was incessant. On occasions, hundreds would march off the field at once, and on the eve of great battles, giving the dastardly excuse that their enlistments had expired. The spectacle was then to be seen of desperate officers trying to bribe a few to remain for extra pay. Such bribery was nobly refused as a rule.

As late as January 31, 1777, Washington was writing with bitter wit that, unless the people gave him help in returning deserters, "we shall be obliged to detach one half the army to bring back the other."

Recruiting was hopeless without bounties, and these ran sometimes as high as $750 to $1,000 a man.[13] At a time when the English soldiers were receiving eightpence a day the patriots demanded $150 for a term of five months, $1,500 for nine months. Many of the Americans enlisted under one officer, deserted, enlisted under another, deserted again and so on, receiving a bounty on each occasion and then often failing to serve. The thievery and brutality of some of them was unbelievable.

The officers were hardly better than the men. Eighteen generals abandoned the service, many from pique, some to escape arrest for taking double pay; one was broken for drunkenness. Washington said: "Many of the surgeons are very great rascals . . . often receiving bribes to certify indispositions," and drawing "medicines and stores in the most profuse and extravagant manner for private purposes."

No form of intrigue was beneath some of the officers, and many of them robbed their own troops of their pay.

Despite their partial confederation, the colonies kept alive their ancient jealousies. They would not pay their contributions. They were outraged at the thought of taxation. They retained at home a large part of their fighting forces to defend the local boundaries. They never turned over even the modest proportion of soldiers assigned to them. At a critical period in the struggle Washington said that "scarce any State in the Union" had furnished "an eighth part of its quota."

Against the assemblies of the several colonies, the Continental Congress fought a constant war. It had neither authority nor power to do anything, yet somehow accomplished, or coincided with, a few miracles. Congress was a fearful and wonderful thing that only its unmerited success and the amazing oak that grew from the almost unaided acorn could have justified.

In no sense could it be said to be representative of the American people it pretended to represent. The energy and audacity of a few driving radicals alone kept it from collapse.

The delegates had been elected in general by little groups of self-delegated powers, representing hardly anybody but themselves. Not a hundredth part of the people had voted in some districts. In one place it was charged that "two men met and one appointed the other delegate to Congress."

In North Carolina committees of only a dozen selected the delegates. In New York great majorities opposed the sending of any delegates at all.

The men thus illegally chosen had, furthermore, no commission to govern even from the little groups that selected them. And most of what decisions they tardily reached were carried by such close majorities that they meant almost nothing.

Abuse has always been leveled at all representative bodies since time began, but this Congress has had some injustice done to it. It has been the custom to accuse it of such fear of militarism that it purposely hampered Washington, especially by upholding the fatal policy of short-term enlistments. Both of these old charges are libels, according to Herbert Friedenwald,[14] who says that the time-worn arguments are false; that Congress had no fear of the soldiery and that it opposed brief enlistments. Its policies were wrecked by the unwillingness and disunion of the public.

While it must be admitted on behalf of Congress that it could not receive support for many of its greatest desires and was in the words of the Beards,[15] "little more than a glorified debating society speaking for thirteen independent states," yet it was guilty of nearly all the sins within the power of its weakness.

The quality of the membership degenerated, too, as the war went on, and new politicians replaced the original members. The story is told that Gouverneur Morris long afterwards said to John Jay:

"Jay, what a set of damned scoundrels we had in that Second Congress!"

And Jay, as he knocked the ashes from his pipe, replied: "Yes, we had!" [16]

Yet Washington, who must have realized this better than anyone else, never failed to treat the Congress with the deference a subject shows a monarch. He had, indeed, transferred his reverence from the third George to the Second Congress. He even requested the aid and personal presence of a committee from Congress. Sometimes he carried modesty to the point of a vice.

The Martian historian, coldly recording these facts, would probably chronicle the rest of the war as a chaos of blunders on both sides from which one man emerged with even more than his great share of glory.

If all this sounds like an indictment of the founders of the republic where panegyric is *de rigueur,* the blame must be laid upon the facts that continue to stink under the flowers. And the principal witness is Washington himself, whose testimony is not to be impeached, and whose achievement cannot be understood if the truth is suppressed.

No stronger language can be uttered against the evil phases of that time than Washington wrote down himself.

He must have been almost crushed when he realized what material he had in hand for making an army and leading it to triumph.

At best the technical problem was exceedingly difficult. In the name of the Continental Congress he must "adopt" the New England troops, and reorganize them entirely on a military basis as part of a national force.

Army men alone can realize the frightful difficulty of this even under the best circumstances. Washington had to do the thing in the face of the enemy, while strengthening the redoubts and other works. The enemy was the least of his difficulties, and never made even a sortie in force against any of the weak spots in the thinly held "Semicircle of eight or nine miles."

Washington could not even get the slovenly officers to make the returns of what men they had and how they were named. The feuds of pride that had led the generals to resign were almost handsome compared to the lack of pride among the lesser officers.

When he found a Connecticut captain of horse attached to his own person, shaving a private soldier on the parade near headquarters, the sight of an officer bustling barber-wise about the lathered jaw of a seated commoner almost gave him apoplexy. He severely reprimanded a lieutenant "for infamous conduct in degrading himself by voluntarily doing the duty of an Orderly Sergeant." [17] Many of the officers owed their elections to their men and toadied to them. Appallingly many of them also conspired with their men to cheat and steal.

Social distinctions were vital in Washington's mind, and to his dying day, democratic manifestations were abominable to him.

He bought poor whites and rented or sold them. They were not much inferior in his mind to negroes. He called them both "servants." Their pretensions to be as good as anybody revolted him.

If the officers condescended, the men presumed. There was an exact parallel to the Bolshevism of modern Russia. Many of the private soldiers refused to salute their officers, considering the mere gesticulation a confession of inferiority.

The soldiers quarreled with their officers in a fine democracy. Washington said the men "regarded their officers no more than broomsticks." The orderly books are filled with trials of privates, sergeants, wagoners, artificers and others who knocked down their officers, pulled them off their horses, and threatened to shoot them. Sometimes the men were acquitted because of "the extreme and unpardonable warmth" of the officers.[18]

Washington is said to have grown pardonably warm himself on one occasion:

"One morning, while Sullivan was closeted with Washington at headquarters, on some mission from the house, Col. Glover, of the Marblehead regiment, which was encamped in an enclosed pasture north of the Colleges, came in to announce that his men were in a state of mutiny. Washington instantly strode to his horse, kept always in readiness at the door, leaped into the saddle, and, followed by Mr. Sullivan and Col. Glover, rode at full gallop to the camp. His servant, Pompey, sent in advance to let down the bars, had just dismounted for the purpose, when Washington, coming up leaped over Pompey, bars and all, and darted into the midst of the mutineers. It was on the occasion of the well-known contest between the fishermen of Marblehead and the Virginia riflemen under Morgan; the latter of whom, in half-Indian equipments of fringed and ruffled hunting shirts, provoked the merriment of the northern troops. From words they proceeded to blows, and soon at least a thousand combatants, armed for the most part only with snow-balls, were engaged in conflict. 'The General threw the bridle of his horse into his servant's hands, and, rushing into the thickest of the fight, seized two tall, brawny riflemen by the throat, keeping them at arm's length, talking to, and shaking them.' " [19]

But he was always eager for justice. His severity was equally eager. He was an earnest advocate of flogging for almost every offense from disobedience and dishonesty, to playing cards.

The term "bloody backs," given to the British because of their bleeding shoulder blades, was soon applicable to Washington's Americans. He felt justified in ordering for a soldier 100 lashes, or even 300. On some occasions to the torture of the thongs was added the detail, "to be well washed with salt and water after he has received his last fifty." [20]

The Northern attitude toward negroes was already changing from that in the South, and Washington could hardly stomach the respect shown toward the black heroes. There were several negroes among the Northern minute-men.

Washington instructed his adjutant-general, Gates, to issue orders to enlist no more "deserters, strollers, or negroes," [21] but there were already so many of them in the ranks that an effort was made in Congress to order Washington to "discharge all the Negroes as well Slaves as Freemen in his Army." It was voted down.[22]

In 1778 there were 378 negroes in seven brigades of Washington's army. Later, Alexander Hamilton advocated raising battalions of negroes and planned "to give them their freedom with their muskets." [23]

The Southerners abhorred the idea, especially as Lord Dunmore, who was conducting another private war of his own, this time against the Virginians, was offering freedom to the negroes and trying unsuccessfully to raise a black insurrection.

In that Falstaffian host about Boston Washington found also a company of Indians. As early as April, 1775, the Provincial Congress of Massachusetts had approached the Iroquois with this warning:

"We have thought it our duty to tell you, our good Brothers, what our Fathers in *Great Britain* have done, and threaten to do with us . . . they have told us we shall have no more Guns, no Powder to use and kill our Wolves and other game, nor to send to you, for you to kill your victuals with, and to get Skins to trade with us to buy you Blankets, and what you want. How can you live without Powder and Guns? But we hope to supply you soon with both, of our own making.

"Brothers: They have made a law to establish the religion of the Pope in *Canada*, which lies so near you. We much fear some of your children may be induced, instead of worshiping the only true *God*, to pay his due to images made with their own hands . . . as we fear they will attempt to cut our throats, and if you should allow them to do that, there will nobody remain to keep them from you, we therefore earnestly desire you to whet your Hatchet, and be prepared with us to defend our liberties and lives." [24]

In view of what the colonists had done to the Indians by way of slaughter, slavery, and annihilation, and in view of the fact that one of the chief causes of the Revolution was the British effort to keep the colonists from taking away all the Indian lands, this was—well, say, a trifle sophisticated. In any case it was too complex to convince the simple-minded Indians, especially as the image-worshipers had been far gentler and more just with them than the colonists. They even represented the saints as wearing Indian costumes.

The Stockbridge Indians, however, had been so thoroughly Puritanized that a company of them joined the besiegers of Boston in April. Shortly before Washington arrived two Indians had killed four British soldiers with bow and arrow, and robbed their bodies. The British complained of this as "ungenerous." But the Indians continued to kill the sentinels. [25]

Washington, himself, advised Congress to employ Indians to prevent their going to the other side, "which would be a most fatal stroke." [26] He advised that Schuyler send Senecas against the British forts at Niagara and Detroit. John Adams said, "We need not be so delicate as to refuse the assistance of Indians." A treaty was made as soon as possible with the Eastern Indians who agreed to furnish a regiment of six hundred with white officers. Lafayette raised a troop of Indians. [27]

An American diarist [28] describes how he "sent out a party for some dead Indians. . . . Toward morning found them, and skinned two of them from their hips down for bootlegs; one pair for the Major, the other for myself."

It was good business at the time for the Americans to

howl protests against the British employment of Indians against Americans, and yet it showed a lamentable lack of good sportsmanship even for war.

The least noble of Benjamin Franklin's many frivolous deeds was surely the low trick he played when he forged a letter and pretended that it had been captured and that it accompanied a collection of nearly a thousand American scalps taken by Indian allies of the British and prepared for sending to England. The imaginary officer listed "eight packs of scalps, cured, dried, hooped and painted with all the Indian triumphal marks," with an "invoice" cataloguing 43 scalps of Congress soldiers, 98 of farmers killed in their houses, 97 of farmers killed in their field; 102 of farmers variously killed, 18 burned alive, one of "a rebel clergyman, his band being fixed to the hoop of his scalp; 88 scalps of women, hair long, braided in the Indian fashion, to show they were mothers"; 193 boys' scalps, 211 girls' scalps, 122 assorted scalps.

To these Franklin attached an invented Indian speech requesting that the scalps be sent "over the water to the Great King, that he may regard them and be refreshed." [29]

This joke of Franklin's may have been a good one, but the glee is a trifle ghoulish, especially as he came from a Puritan realm where it had been the habit of the settlers to pay handsomely for the scalps or even the skulls of Indian women and children as well as warriors. Balzac said that Franklin invented the lightning rod, the hoax, and the republic.

Franklin was a great and versatile genius and his scalp-story was quite as good as the 1916 accounts of Belgian women whose breasts were sliced off and the children whose hands were chopped off by the German uhlans, or the excellent doctored photograph showing a carload of corpses from the battlefield on their way to a fertilizer factory.

In the Revolutionary time the Indian was to the American what the "Hun" was to the anti-German propagandist. The difference is that it was only a few years after the World War when the propaganda weapons were recognized as empty shells, while the accusations against British atrocity in the use of Indians are still enshrined in the American museum of hate.

As a matter of fact, the English officers dreaded the American fondness for Indian allies, and Col. Bouquet had refused to heed Washington's prayers to use them on Forbes' expedition.

A hitherto unpublished letter of Washington's shows how little squeamish he was about scalps white or red. He wrote it in 1758:

"You yet seem to be unacquainted with the Villainy of the Raven Warrior and his Party. I shall therefore inform you, that he brought two White Men's Scalps from his Nation, and after making a small excursion from Fort Frederick in Maryland endeavourd to impose them upon us for some of the Enemy's, but being detected in the deception by the rest of the Warriors, & fearing the effects of their Resentment & being conscious of his own guilt thought proper to March of." [30]

His horror was not at the taking of the white scalps, but at the pretence that they were the enemy's.

Propaganda is as good a weapon in war as poison gas, but it does not belong in the pages of honorable history. To allege that it was infamous of Burgoyne to bring Indians into the war against Americans, who had always used them, is carrying hypocrisy a trifle beyond the line of decency.

Out of Indians, "Boys, Deserters and Negroes," cowards, thieves, good honest blockheads, farmers, sailors, tradesmen, and heroes, Washington was expected to form a conquering machine.

Within gunshot of Boston, he accomplished what he accomplished with the unwilling connivance of the British, who, from lack of energy and supplies, contented themselves with occasional bombardments, so casual that women and children gathered about the cannon to see the fun.

The cannon balls rarely did any damage, and the colonists chased them as they rolled, and pulled the flaming fuses out of the shells. On one occasion two men were killed trying to stop a projectile, but the soldiers were encouraged by the knowledge that everyone who took a British cannon ball to his captain received a gallon of rum.

In spite of the colonial need of powder, some of the soldiers shot at crows flying overhead, or fired off their arms in sheer hilarity till Washington threatened heavy penalties. Then they went outside the lines and wasted their powder on the atmosphere.

The camp resembled in many ways a county fair or a gigantic rural picnic, with an extraordinary amount of gambling going on—which Washington called "infamous"—a strange word coming from such a devotee.

Bad as the troops were, the paucity of their numbers was worse. Washington wrote to Congress that it fell "so far short of the Establishment and below all Expectation . . . I entertain some doubts whether the number required can be raised here." [81]

In this first letter his patience was angelic:

"This unhappy and devoted Province has been so long in a State of Anarchy, and the Yoke of ministerial Oppression has been laid so heavily on it that great Allowances are to be made . . . their Spirit has exceeded their Strength."

He ended with a wish for more immediate "Assistance and Direction" from Congress.

On the same day he wrote to his friend, Benjamin Harrison, a letter which is lost. It evidently bewailed his fatigues and troubles, judging from Harrison's reply, which in its turn was intercepted by the British.

It was published in the London *Advertiser*. In republishing it in the *Gentleman's Magazine,* some zealous hand seems to have added a famous and scandalous passage.

According to the revised version, Harrison described the attractions of a girl, "pretty little Kate the washerwoman's daughter" who came into the room where he was writing, and might have yielded to his blandishments if another woman had not happened in, "and but for the cursed antidote to love, Sukey, I had fitted her for my General against his return."

This whiff of persiflage is almost as blood-curdling as Franklin's witty handling of the thousand scalps, and it has delighted numberless people who hate to think of Washington as superhuman or, worse yet, sub-human.

The original manuscript of the letter is in the Public Record Office in London, but it does not contain this much-quoted passage at all. In the words of Mr. Fitzpatrick,[32] "the brazen forgery seems to have been a facetious attempt to spice up a sober-toned, political news-letter."

He thinks it is the foundation for an even more famous mythical letter, which everybody quotes and nobody can find. According to this legendary epistle, Washington invited Jefferson (or Lafayette—or almost anyone else) to visit him at Mount Vernon, and promised the guest as an extra inducement the society of a mulatto maiden variously and vividly described.

The will-o'-the-wisp itself has not been more tauntingly dangled before the seekers than this letter, nor more vainly clutched at. Lodge [33] and other biographers confess their unavailing efforts to trace it; but the more it eludes the eye, the more it flits from mouth to ear.

It belongs in that undying undercurrent of scandal that

flows beneath the ice of Washington's public fame, and there is no evidence whatever that it ever existed, except in the imagination of the same playful malice that invented Benjamin Harrison's reference to the tawny Kate, the washerwoman's daughter.

In Harrison's actual letter the Congressman hints slyly at the Virginian antipathy to the New Englanders, saying that Washington's distresses "are not more than I expected, knowing the people you have to deal with by the sample we have here." Washington was soon expressing his disgust in language of no restraint, laying about him with a kind of bewildered ferocity in an abuse of nearly everything, and with abundant cause.

XXIII

HIS STRUGGLE TO BUILD AN ARMY

"WE are in an exceedingly dangerous situation," Washington wrote to R. H. Lee on July 10, 1775. "We have but about sixteen thousand effective men in all this department, whereas, by the accounts which I received from even the first officers in command, I had no doubt of finding between eighteen and twenty thousand; out of these there are only fourteen thousand fit for duty. . . .

"The abuses in this army, I fear, are considerable, and the new modelling of it, in the face of an enemy, from whom we every hour expect an attack, is exceedingly difficult and dangerous. If things therefore should not turn out as the Congress would wish, I hope they will make proper allowances." [1]

The returns of strength which should have been ready in an hour, were put off and put off and were so imperfect that it took him eight days to find out what men he had. Three years later the army paper-work was still in such shape that some men were carried on the rolls after an absence of a year.

In his first letter to Congress Washington had begun that eternal cry of his about the nakedness of his men. He notes that they are "very deficient in necessary Cloathing." [2] Back in 1754, a letter to Governor Dinwiddie on taking command of his first troops had said the same thing: they were "destitute of Cloaths. There is many of them without Shoes, other's wants Stockings." [3] He would keep up the cry throughout the war.

The country he fathered has taken his counsel so much to heart as to the necessity for preparedness that when the nation mobilized for the World War in 1917 the sick soldiers froze in camps without blankets, and when the Rainbow Division reached France and wore out its shoes in the Vosges Mountains, the men left bloody footprints in the snow, until they could be shod with French shoes.

As an evidence of the inveterate American habit of giving soldiers the worst of everything that fits them for their task, it may be pertinent to quote from a letter sent to the author by a recent victim of the system:

"I don't know why there has been so little said on this, although I do know the press is lacking the courage to tell the story, for I am not alone in much that I know. I was not the only soldier who, in 1917 and 1918, during a very severe winter, wore cotton Khaki uniforms, and though less than 50 miles from home, had to write home twice for civilian shoes when my feet were on the ground, my shoes being mere uppers.

"The reason given was that all the supplies had been sent to France for the men there. But, arriving there in the early spring, lo! they were in British uniforms and shoes, and sleeping under blankets bought in Spain. So on, ad nauseam. My regiment used cannon made in 1875, which had lain, unused and useless in French coast fortifications for years; built for black powder, we fired H. E. in them. To the everlasting credit of the Creusot Works of Schneider & Cie., only one of them blew up, cleaning out two gun crews, more than we lost in the entire tour of duty from August to Nov. 11th from enemy fire."

Throughout the World War the Americans were largely supplied with foreign equipment.

Fortunately, however, that was a War to end War, and at the present writing a movement is on foot to "outlaw" War altogether. The lovers of eternal peace-by-acclamation are once more able to prevent the wasteful accumulation of supplies in anticipation of a war, which, we are once more well assured, will never come.

The plan of reorganization, or rather of organization, adopted by Washington was to form three Grand Divisions of two brigades each. He issued an order [4] to that effect, without waiting for the permission of Congress. He assigned Major General Ward to command the first division and established it as his right wing, with Generals Thomas and Spencer in command of the two brigades. The left wing was commanded by Major General Charles Lee with its two brigades under Generals Sullivan and Greene. The center he assigned to Major General Israel Putnam, the brigadiers to be designated later.

The difficulty lay in the complete lack of uniformity in the organizations. In Massachusetts a general had his own regiment as well as a brigade, in Connecticut he had both his own regiment and his own company. In Rhode Island a general had no regiment, but the field officers had companies. Worse yet, in Massachusetts some regiments had ten companies of 590 men and officers each, some had eleven companies with 649. Connecticut gave 1,000 men to a regiment.

New troops were expected and there were sharpshooter companies forming to use the new weapon, the rifle. Washington persisted in calling them "Riffle Companies."

The riddle was how to reduce all these units to the same size. To do this, "it would be necessary to dismiss a Number of Officers in Possession of Commissions, without any Fault of theirs." This was no time for throwing men out of the army.

With other bodies of troops from other provinces it would be necessary to add new officers. A great shifting of grades would be required. The engineer, Colonel Gridley, if his commission were renewed, would be senior to all the other officers including the majors general.

It is well known that soldiers grow surly when their familiar officers are changed, or they themselves are thrown in with strange organizations. As Washington wrote to Congress: "the Experiment is dangerous, as the Massachusetts Men under the Privilege of chusing their own Officers, do not conceive themselves bound if those Officers are disbanded." [5]

Here was a quandary, indeed, and he wrestled with it long and anxiously.

The mutual love of the colonies was such that they would almost have preferred a British officer to one from another colony. As late as November, Washington was still struggling with his puzzle. He wrote to Joseph Reed of "what sets heaviest on my mind, the new arrangement of officers. . . .

"Connecticut wants no Massachusetts man in their corps; Massachusetts thinks there is no necessity for a Rhode-Islander to be introduced amongst them; and New Hampshire says, it's very hard, that her valuable and experienced officers (who are willing to serve) should be discarded, because her own regiments, under the new establishment, cannot provide for them. . . . Something must be hit upon, as time is slipping off."

That he was in a state of nerves is shown by the postscript:

"P.S. I had just finished my letter when a blundering Lieutenant of the blundering Captain Coit, who had just blundered upon two vessels from Nova Scotia, came in with the account of it, and before I could rescue my letter, without knowing what he did, picked up a candle and sprinkled it with grease; but these are kind of blunders which one can readily excuse. The vessels contain hay, live-stock, poultry, &c., and are now safely moored in Plymouth harbour."

The one bright field of his horizon was the sea, whence the hustling tars of New England were snatching prizes laden with uniforms, provisions, what not? He devoted much time to creating a navy, and was, in a sense, Admiral as well as General.

His problems would have maddened a chief of staff in an inland capital, but Washington was sitting close to the British, whose numbers he naturally exaggerated and whose recent reinforcements led him to expect an onset at any moment at any point. In this appeal to Congress for help in solving his delicate problems of reorganization, he shows his vigilance:

"Having some Reason to suspect they were extending their Lines at Charles Town, I last Saturday Evening ordered some of the Riffle Men down to make a Discovery, or bring off a Prisoner. . . . They brought in Two Prisoners whose Acct confirmed by some other Circumstances removed my Suspicions in part."

Filled with young hope Congress offered such inducements to enlistment that the generals issued an address to allay the mumblings and desertions of the soldiers, telling them much good news and scolding them thus:

"The ease and affluence of your circumstances, as soldiers, might alone prompt you to remain. Never were soldiers whose duty has been so light, never were soldiers whose pay and provision has been so abundant and ample. In fact, your interest and comfort have been so carefully consulted, even to the lowest article, by the Continental Congress, that there is some reason to dread that the enemies to New-England's reputation may hereafter say, it was not principle that saved them, but that they were bribed into the preservation of their liberties." [6]

But the soldiers would neither be satisfied nor obedient. They continued to wander in and out, holding nothing so sacred as the day of the expiration of enlistment.

One of the first and most unpleasant duties of Washington at Cambridge was to authorize the trials before courts martial of the men and officers guilty, or accused, of cowardice at Bunker Hill.

In his Orderly Book, July 7, 1775, he stated:

"It is with inexpressible Concern that the General upon his first Arrival in the army, should find an Officer sentenced by a General Court Martial to be cashier'd for Cowardice—A Crime of all others, the most infamous in a Soldier, the most injurious to an Army, and the last to be forgiven; inasmuch as it may, and often does happen, that the Cowardice of a single Officer may prove the Distruction of the whole Army."

He promised all rewards and honors to the brave, and to any coward "the utmost martial severity; and no connections, Interest, or Intercessions on his behalf will avail to prevent the strict execution of Justice." [7]

He approved the sentence of Captain John Callender and cashiered him. Callender enlisted at once as a private and at the battle of Long Island proved himself so brave that Washington ordered the sentence erased from the orderly book and restored his commission.

The son of Colonel Gridley (the engineer who was later supplanted by Colonel Knox) was found guilty, but in view of his youth was permitted to hope for another commission, finally receiving one intended for Benjamin Thompson, afterwards famous as a scientist under his title, Count Rumford.

The other officers tried were acquitted; but Washington stated it as "an uncontradicted Fact, that the principal failure of Duty on that day was in the Officers, tho' many of them distinguished themselves." He gave a pair of pistols to one Joseph Ward when he heard of the young man's bravery. [8]

The martial court continued, however, to be one of the busiest of the army's activities. In August, Washington was writing how sorry he was for the frequency of the trials:

"Since my last, Capt. Parker of Massachusetts for Frauds both in Pay, and Provisions, and Capt. Gardiner of Rhode Island for Cowardice in running away from his Guard on an Alarm, have been broke." [9]

Next he discovered that great numbers of soldiers absented themselves to work on the farms of their officers or on their own plantations or for hire while drawing public pay. He called this "base and pernicious" and the men "infamous deserters and defrauders."

With no little diplomatic lack of frankness he tried to check the practice by issuing an order saying that he was "unwilling to believe" the "insinuations" that "any officer can be so lost to all sense of honor as to defraud the public in so scandalous a manner," and promised to pay "no further regard to the insinuation," but, if such a thing should ever occur, he would "show no favor to any officer guilty of such iniquitous practices." [10]

This is exactly the good old Scotch verdict: Not guilty, but don't do it again!

Other examples of his court-martial grist are a captain reprimanded for abusing his major; a captain found guilty of drawing more provisions than he was entitled to and unjustly confining and abusing his men; a captain letting people through the lines; an ensign absent without leave; a colonel belatedly found guilty of bad conduct at Bunker Hill.

On September 13th, 1775, thirty-three men were condemned for "disobedient and mutinous behavior," and a little later a sergeant was tried for disrespectful reference to "the Continental association, and drinking General Gage's health." He was put in a cart with a rope around his neck and drummed out of the army for life.

Washington's patience was wearing thin, and he wrote to the Provincial Congress of New York concerning the disgraceful venality of many Americans, some of whom were actually selling provisions to the British while Washington was trying to starve them out. He issued an order August 10th:

"It is a matter of exceeding great concern to the General to find, that at a time when the united efforts of America are exerting in defence of the common rights and liberties of mankind, that there should be in an army constituted for so noble a purpose, such repeated instances of officers, who lost to every sense of honor and virtue, are seeking by dirty and base means, the promotion of their own dishonest gain, to the eternal disgrace of themselves and dishonor of their country. Practices of this sort will never be overlooked, whenever an accusation is lodged; but the authors brought to the most exemplary punishment." [11]

As a Virginian who had left his home and all his interests to come to the rescue of Boston, Washington was infuriated to find the New Englanders so hungry for all the honors and profits that it was hard to assert the claims of any outside volunteers or assign them any places. Jealous of each other, the four New England "governments" were closely knit in the determination to prevent commissions from going to men of other colonies.

In his wrath at such lack of team play, Washington wrote to R. H. Lee an assault on New England so violent that it was censored for years. Sparks not only corrected its spelling to suit himself, but omitted three whole sections of over four hundred words without putting in even an asterisk. Ford prints the letter entire in his collection, with the author's own spelling.

Washington begins by saying that he has accepted Lee's recommendation of young Edmund Randolph and taken him into his "Family," as an aide in the room of Mifflin whom he appointed quartermaster general.

He now had a staff which he called, after the fashion of the time, his Family. Though Randolph's father was a confirmed Tory and was afterwards blamed for the forgery of letters imputed to Washington, the son was treated tenderly until a violent quarrel in later years wrung Washington to one of his hottest rages.

In his letter to Lee, Washington said that, while he accepted Randolph because of "a thorough perswasion of his Integrity," his final reason was that he stood "unconnected with either of these Governments; or with this that or t'other man; for between you and I there is more in this than you can easily immagine."

Then he lashed out against the New Englanders, whom he could not keep vigilant against the enemy:

"It is among the most difficult tasks I ever undertook in my life to induce these people to believe that there is, or can be, danger till the Bayonet is pushed at their Breasts; not that it proceeds from any uncommon prowess, but rather from an unaccountable kind of stupidity in the lower class of these people which, believe me, prevails but too generally among the officers of the Massachusets *part* of the Army who are *nearly* of the same Kidney with the Privates, and adds not a little to my difficulties; as there is no such thing as getting of officers of this stamp to exert themselves in carrying orders into execution—to curry favour with the men (by whom they were chosen, & on whose smile possibly they may think they may again rely) seems to be one of the principal objects of their attention."

He complains of the difficulty of giving a post to any outsider, and waxes savage:

"I have made a pretty good slam among such kind of officers as the Massachusets Government abound in since I came to this Camp having Broke one Colo. and two Captains for cowardly behavior in the action on Bunkers Hill,—two Captains for drawing more provisions and pay than they had men in the Company—and one for being absent from his Post when the Enemy appeared there and burnt a Housefull by it. Besides these, I have at this time— one Colo., one Major, one Captn., & two Subalterns under arrest for tryal. In short I spare none & yet fear it will not all do as these People seem to be too inattentive to every thing but their Interest. . . .

"There has been so many great, and capital errors, & abuses to rectify—so many examples to make—& so little Inclination in the officers of inferior Rank, to contribute their aid to accomplish this work, that my life has been nothing else since I came than one continued round of annoyance & fatigue; in short no pecuniary recompense could induce me to undergo what I have especially as I expect, by shewing so little countenance to irregularities & publick abuses [to] render myself very obnoxious to a greater Part of these People." [12]

It is well to keep such outbursts of Washington's out of general circulation; for if some of the patriotic societies and politicians ever heard of them, they would assuredly pass resolutions condemning Washington for defaming the dead and belittling their ancestors.

In the course of the letter, Washington answered a suggestion of Lee's that he should try to seize the entrance to Boston harbor and prevent the egress of the British troops or the ingress of supply ships.

The idea had occured to him from the first, but he was having a hard enough time keeping his indolent soldiers alert in what lines he had. To extend his lines to hold the suggested position, thirty miles away, was quite beyond his power because of the alarming lack of powder.

He realized that this put him in a very unfavorable light, but such was "the fate of all those who are obliged to act the part I do."

A week before he had written gratefully to one J. Palmer who had given him the same tantalizing advice.[13]

It was characteristic of him to thank a private citizen for giving him counsel, but it was cruel that he should have had to endure the sneers of his own people.

He was especially tormented by requests to send troops to protect the coast-towns from raids by the British. When the town of Falmouth (now Portland) in Maine was destroyed by a wanton bombardment, he dared not explain how perilous such a division of his weak force would have been, and had to indulge in talk of general military principles of concentration and his inability to consult individual towns or provinces as against the general interest.

It seemed to him, and it seems to the later inspector of the records, that at this time Washington was almost the only man in America who had a sense of national entity and national duty. The rest talked of liberty, and indignation at tyrants, but their interests were almost altogether individual, municipal, or provincial.

Few of the troops would accept the idea of a Continental army. They were afraid to subscribe to the Continental articles of war lest "it might subject them to a longer service." He wrote, "It is in vain to attempt to reason away the prejudices of a whole army." [14] He doubted his ability to form his new army out of the old.

There was acute dissatisfaction over the pay and many valuable officers planned to retire. The clothes were so insufficient that the men might "be deemed in a state of nakedness."

He tried to secure a uniform, but there was little hope of that. The men were generally in brown. There was some effort to imitate Washington's own uniform of buff and blue, but there was more blue than buff. He never did secure anything approaching uniformity except perhaps in raggedness often approaching indecency, not to mention pathetic lack of comfort.

There were numbers of red British uniforms in the ranks. Some of the tatterdemalions would desert to the British, secure a new costume, and desert back again. Later as the privateers captured ships carrying supplies to the British, whole companies would blossom out in scarlet to the confusion of the enemy, which they often turned to profit. Sometimes they dyed the red with startling results.

Washington again, as in 1758, strongly urged the hunting shirt of the Indians, the woodsmen, and his old Virginia regiment; but there were not enough of the "shirtmen" to make even that feature predominant.

An army without uniform is incorrigibly a mob, lacking comfort, convenience, precision, as well as the sense of union and the strange exultance that a uniform inspires. It was doubly hard to instill pride and obedience in the throngs that milled about in shabby motley while the enemy strutted in scarlet with gleaming buttons, pipe-clayed leather, lofty helmets, epaulettes, gold lace, and sashes of tasseled silk.

There was no way of telling soldiers from visitors or officers from men. Even Washington in his old buff and blue rode about unrecognized and unsaluted until he felt that something must be done at a cost of next to nothing.

To distinguish general officers from the rest, he issued an order July 14, 1775, announcing that "to prevent mistakes," the commander-in-chief would be distinguished by "a light blue Ribband wore across his breast between his Coat and Waistcoat," the major and brigadier generals by a pink ribbon, the aides-de-camp by a green.

A week or so later he ordered that "Field officers may have pink coloured Cockades in their Hatts; the Captaines yellow or buff—and the Subalterns green. . . . The Serjeants may be distinguished by an Epaulette, or stripe of red Cloth, sewed upon the right shoulder, the Corporals by one of green." [15]

His own ribbon cost less than four shillings, for in his account book, he entered on July 10th:

"By Ribbon to distinguish myself . . . . 3/4"

The greatest lack, however, was a spiritual uniform, a united soul.

In this same order he complained of the spears in use:

"The people employed to make spears, are desired by the General to make four dozen of them immediately, thirteen feet in length, and the wood part a good deal more substantial than those already made; those, particularly, in the *New-Hampshire* lines, are ridiculously short and light and can answer no sort of purpose; no more are therefore to be made on the same model."

A letter from Schuyler begged for "cutlasses, stinkpots, and hand grenades."

With so much profiteering going on Washington lacked funds. By September 21, 1775, he was confessing to Congress:

"The military chest is totally exhausted; the paymaster has not a single dollar in hand: the commissary-general assures me he has strained his credit . . . to the utmost. The quarter-master-general is precisely in the same situation; and the greater part of the troops are in a state not far from mutiny . . . if the evil is not immediately remedied, and more punctually observed in future, the army must absolutely break up." [16]

A month later he writes that from a third to a half of the officers plan to retire. He fears they will "communicate the infection" to the men.

With cold weather coming on, the need of wood grew dire. He wrote the General Court of Massachusetts concerning the supply:

"I little thought that we had scarce four hours', and that different Regiments were upon the point of cutting each others' throats for a few standing locusts near their encampments, to dress their victuals with. This, however, is the fact; and unless some expedient is adopted by your honourable body to draw more teams into the service, or the Quartermaster-General empowered to impress them, this Army, if there comes a spell of rain or cold weather must inevitably disperse; the consequence of which needs no animadversion of mine."

In the same month he writes to Congress:

"The trouble I have in the arrangement of the army is really inconceivable. Many of the officers sent in their names to serve, in expectation of promotion; others stood aloof to see what advantage they could make for themselves; while a number, who had declined, have again sent in their names to serve. . . . The difficulty with the soldiers is as great, indeed more so, if possible, than with the officers. They will not enlist, until they know their colonel, lieutenant-colonel, major, captain, &c.; so that it was necessary to fix the officers the first thing; . . .

"I have other distresses of a very alarming nature. The arms of our soldiery are so exceedingly bad, that I assure you, Sir, I cannot place a proper confidence in them. Our powder is wasting fast, notwithstanding the strictest care, economy, and attention are paid to it. The long series of wet weather, which we have had, renders the greater part of what has been served out to the men of no use."

A personal distress came to him in the desire of his personal secretary and aid, Joseph Reed, to be excused from further service. Washington humbly and affectionately pleaded with him to continue, writing later, "I miss you exceedingly."

He made complaint of the quality of his sailors, who were turning out as badly as his soldiers:

"Our rascally privateersmen go on at the old rate, mutinying if they cannot do as they please."

"The plague, trouble, and vexation I have had with the crews of all the armed vessels, are inexpressible. I do believe there is not on earth a more disorderly set. Every time they come into port, we hear of nothing but mutinous complaints." [17]

He continued to hold out his big, empty hands for funds. Congress had decided to take the easy step of printing money, but the bills had to be signed, and the signers were preoccupied. So he wrote to R. H. Lee.

"For God's sake hurry the signers of money, that our wants may be supplied." [18]

In a daze he wrote to Joseph Reed:

"What an astonishing thing it is, that those who are employed to sign the Continental bills should not be able, or inclined, to do it as fast as they are wanted. They will prove the destruction of the army, if they are not more attentive and diligent. Such a dearth of public spirit, and want of virtue, such stock-jobbing, and fertility in all the low arts to obtain advantages of one kind or another, in this great change of military arrangement, I never saw before, and pray God I may never be witness to again. . . .

"Pray impress this upon the members, and the necessity of forwarding the last sum voted, as one hundred thousand dollars will be but a flea-bite to our demands at this time." [19]

He was drifting into a despair about making up his army. He wrote to Congress:

"From what I can collect by my inquiries amongst the officers, it will be impossible to get the men to enlist for the continuance of the war, . . . I am very sorry to be necessitated to mention to you the egregious want of public spirit, which reigns here. Instead of pressing to be engaged in the cause of their country, which I vainly flattered myself would be the case, I find we are likely to be deserted, and in a most critical time. Those that have enlisted must have a furlough, which I have been obliged to grant to fifty at a time, from each regiment. The Connecticut troops, upon whom I reckoned, are as backward, indeed, if possible, more so than the people of this colony. Our situation is truly alarming; and of this General Howe is well apprized, it being the common topic of conversation, when the people left Boston last Friday. No doubt, when he is reinforced, he will avail himself of the information." [20]

To Reed he was franker still:

"Such a dirty, mercenary spirit pervades the whole, that I should not be at all surprised at any disaster that may happen. In short, after the last of this month our lines will be so weakened, that the minute-men and militia must be called in for their defence; these, being under no kind of government themselves, will destroy the little subordination I have been laboring to establish, and run me into one evil whilst I am endeavoring to avoid another; but the lesser must be chosen.

"Could I have foreseen what I have, and am likely to experience, no consideration upon earth should have induced me to accept this command. A regiment or any subordinate department would have been accompanied with ten times the satisfaction, and perhaps the honor." [21]

The Connecticut troops finally approached mutiny. Their time being up, Washington "requested and ordered" them to remain till they were relieved. Though he tried to stop them by force, "several got away with their arms and ammunition." [22]

Gen. Charles Lee described how, "in passing through the lines of other Regiments They were so horribly hissed, groan'd at and pelted that I believed they wish'd their Aunts, Grandmothers, and even sweethearts to whom the day before they were so much attached at the Devils own Palace—it is said They have been scurvily treated on the road and worse by the very connexions from whom They could not bear to be separated."

He ran on:

"What a tryal is a civil war or as I find that it is not quite decent at Philadelphia amongst your wise ones to term slaughtering of men, women & children and laying waste with fire and sword your sea coasts, a civil war—what a tryal are civil contentions? . . . My God, why does not your whole Province arouse themselves, kick the Assembly from the seat of representation which they so horribly disgrace and set 'em to work German Town stockings for the Army—an employment manly enough for 'em. Oh, in the language of Piercy, 'I cou'd brain 'em with their wives distaffs.' " [23]

The people at home did indeed send back some of the deserters, but Washington had to call in militia.

All this was especially humiliating in the presence of the British garrison. Yet Howe was having worse trouble with a devastating plague of smallpox, and Washington was told by a deserter that Howe, who had been getting rid of throngs of indigent Bostonians, "useless mouths," was going to send out a number of plague victims "with the design of

spreading the smallpox through this country and camp." [24]
Washington believed the story and took what precautions
he could.

He had reason also to believe that the other New England
troops were no more reliable than the Connecticut and were
ready to break away at any moment. He could take few
precautions against that.

He found the company that misery loves in a letter from
General Schuyler saying that his troops in New York were
as bad as Washington's, and he was planning to resign along
with General Montgomery, who was equally disgusted.
Washington wrote to Schuyler ardently on Christmas Eve:

"God knows, there is not a difficulty, that you both very justly
complain of, which I have not in an eminent degree experienced,
that I am not every day experiencing; but we must bear up against
them, and make the best of mankind as they are, since we cannot
have them as we wish. Let me, therefore, conjure you and Mr.
Montgomery to lay aside such thoughts,—thoughts injurious to
yourselves, and excessively so to your country, which calls aloud
for gentlemen of your abilities." [25]

Washington could long for peace and obscurity or the
thick of the fight, but he could not desert the cause. He
often felt, and had reason to feel, that the cause was sinking,
but he planned always to go down with the ship.

At times he grew so weary of criticism for inaction, so
fagged with the sickening detail of military bookkeeping and
bargaining, that he was frantic to attack. The dearth of
powder was the negative to everything. He never ceased
to plead for it, but it was not to be had except in driblets.
In August he had written to Congress:

"Our Situation in the Article of Powder is much more alarming
than I had the most distant Idea of."

On his arrival he had found in the returns:

"303½ Bbbl's. . . . But on ordering a new Supply of Cartridges yesterday, I was informed to my very great Astonishment that there was no more than 36 Bbbls of the Massachusetts Store, which with the Stock of Rhode Island, New Hampshire and Connecticut makes 9,937 lb—not more than 9 Rounds a Man." [26]

The mistake was due to the fact that the Committee of Supplies, "not being sufficiently acquainted with the Nature of a Return, or misapprehending my Request, sent in an Account of all the Ammunition, which . . . included not only what was on Hand, but what had been spent."

A most optimistic way of keeping accounts, but horrifying to Washington, who hastened to confer with the authorities upon measures of raising more. Secrecy was so important that the thought of the enemy finding it out was "terrible even in Idea."

He warned Congress that "the Existence of the Army, and the Salvation of the Country" required something both speedy and secret.

Nearly a month later he wrote R. H. Lee: "We have only 184 Barls of Powder in all (including the late supply from Philadelphia) wch is not sufficient to give 25 muskets cartridges to each man, and scarcely to serve the artillery in any brisk action one single day."

The British regulars carried 60 rounds each, and had no lack of reserve. Once Washington's men had gone into a battle with only 25 they would soon have been driven off as at Bunker Hill, and again have had nothing to rely on but their legs.

On one of these occasions when Washington found himself helpless to attack or defend for lack of powder, General Sullivan wrote of him as so crushed "that he did not utter a word for half an hour."

While other troops about the country were moving here and there and a great invasion of Canada by Arnold and

Montgomery was preparing, Washington grew so sick of his own impotence that he determined to attempt a desperate deed.

He resolved to put his powderless army aboard rowboats, carry them a mile or more across open water which he described as "surrounded in a manner by ships of war and floating batteries," and attack the British army, which he also admitted was "so strongly fortified, as to render it almost impossible to force their lines, . . . without great slaughter on our side, or cowardice on theirs." [27]

Such an attack was the passing frenzy of a fearless soldier maddened by idleness. He wanted to get at the British, crush them, and return to his home. He did not like New England as a summer resort and the winter promised even less charms. He doubted if the soldiers, who were so recklessly burning up everything available in their campfires of the chill evenings, would hold together at all when the snows came.

Washington actually called a council of war after sending a circular letter about among the generals advocating the attempt, and giving as his reasons the approaching cold, the lack of firewood and blankets, and the fear that Congress would find the army too expensive to continue:

"I hope the honorable Congress can need no assurance, that there is not a man in America, who more earnestly wishes such a termination of the campaign, as to make the army no longer necessary." [28]

His plan was a desperate inspiration for a man who wrote in the same letter, "The paymaster has not a single dollar in hand."

The attack might not have rendered "the army no longer necessary," but it would certainly have rendered it nonexistent.

For once, a council of war justified itself by following the usual habit of councils of war, and advising a postponement of action. The generals unanimously voted not to send against the British fortifications and battleships a rowboat army with little powder and less audacity.

What steadiness the troops had shown at Bunker Hill had been recognized as due to the fact that they stood in trenches and had their legs covered. What would they have done in open boats under fire from ships, floating batteries and other artillery? How could they have landed and pushed up toward the redoubts?

Five months later Washington himself said, after he heard of the shameful behavior of the troops he had sent to Canada:

"The account given of the behavior of the men under General Montgomery, is exactly consonant to the opinion I have formed of these people, and such as they will exhibit abundant proofs of, in similar cases whenever called upon. Place them behind a parapet, a breast-work, stone wall, or any thing that will afford them shelter, and, from their knowledge of a firelock, they will give a good account of their enemy; but I am as well convinced, as if I had seen it, that they will not march boldly up to a work, nor stand exposed in a plain." [29]

Fortunately for once, he yielded to the council of his officers, and escaped a crushing disaster and possibly death in a rowboat or on the shore.

He solaced his dismal heart with a vow that he would cross the water as soon as winter locked the bay, "thereby rendering any movement upon the ice as easy as if no water was there." [30]

It was inevitable under the conditions of the siege, that the British should know most of the things that Washington was trying so desperately to keep secret. How clear a picture they had of the camp, and what an incredible Pandemonium it was, can be seen in a document found among General Gage's papers. This is a letter from an American loyalist acting as a spy in Washington's lines. He uses "our" for the American side, and shows how hard Washington tried to keep his own army deceived as well as the British. He also gave the British full warning of Washington's contemplated rowboat attack:

"Never was a people lead on blindfold and so imposed on as this people have been with respect to Arms and Amunition: I am not alone in this matter I heard Mr. Hancock Say the very day he came from Congress that we had more Powder on the Road coming to the Camp, than we could Expend in one twelve months, this was believed by all coming from Hancock. The Army begin to inquire for themselves, about these matters, and are not satisfied to find themselves so deceived in a matter of so much importance. but our Chiefs say, it is absolutely necessary, nay Justifiable for such reports when all is at Stake, and the Courage of the Soldiers must be kept up high by some means or other. . . .

"Great disturbences in the Camp of late with Mutinying, many Soldiers are now Confined in Guard for Mutiny.

"A Quarrell happened between Col. Bruer and Col. Patterson, at length they got so high, that they ordered out both their Regiments to fire on Each other, but were Quelled by a third that was ordered to fire on them both in case they did not disperce which they did, but of all seens that ever happen'd not long since our people got a famous New large Standard, Got upon the Hill   Doctor Leanard made amost Solem prayer over the Standard   Gen[ll] Putnam pulled of his hat, gave the Signal for three Chears which was given, Cleargeman and all of us huzzard at once, than the Indeans gave the war hoop and to conclud, of went Cannon, Major, that was worth you seeing.

"They begin to try Colonels and Captains for bad behaviour at Bunkers Hill battle, . . . and could the Army in General have their will General Ward wou'd go for one, for he never so much as gave one Written order that day. If you will believe me Mr. Pidgeon the Commessary General then, now declairs that we had not one half lb: of powder left that night the bunker hill was taken and had you pursued, the Camp must have been broken up— this they Confess. . . .

"One hundred 50 flat bottom boats are ordered to be Compleated within 30 days they are building them as fast as they can at Water town and Cambrige I see them every day, this you may depend on. And I am not a little Surprised to find them so Engaged in making these boats, for I know the people in general think it impossible ever to go into Boston, you in it. . . . I heard General Sullivan say at a Court of inquiry where I was that had they only powder Sufficient they would keep up a Continual fire on the town, and force you and your ships to go off, but says he what can we do without it, and that it was a happy thing that General Gage was not made acquainted with our matters." [31]

In October a committee from Congress came for a visit: Doctor Benjamin Franklin, the Hon. Thomas Lynch, and Colonel Benjamin Harrison. Along came notables from other colonies and there were long conferences in which Washington was entrusted with the disposition of prizes taken by the privateers, and the inability of each colony to furnish the troops desired was explained. The committee was actually instructed to urge Washington to attack Boston before British reinforcements could arrive, and especially urged that if no attack were planned the army should be partly dismissed "and the pay of the men lessened to five dollars a month"! Again Washington called a council of war. Again the wise generals were unanimous that attack was improper and impracticable.[32]

The committee went back to Philadelphia, and Congress authorized Washington to attack Boston when and how he saw fit, and even to destroy it. But they did not give him anything to destroy it with.

He had a sharp correspondence with Gage concerning captured officers who were treated without regard for their rank or their wounds. Washington said that this had a "fatal tendency to widen that unhappy breach, which you, and those ministers under whom you act, have repeatedly declared you wished to see for ever closed."

He warned Gage that he would retaliate upon British prisoners "painful as it may be to me."

Gage replied tartly that the charge was a falsehood:

"Britons ever preeminent in mercy, have outgone common examples, and overlooked the criminal in the captive. Upon these principles your prisoners, whose lives by the law of the land are destined to the cord, have hitherto been treated with care and kindness, and more comfortably lodged than the King's troops in the hospitals; indiscriminately it is true, for I acknowledge no rank, that is not derived from the King."

He declared that Washington's captives taken by "the rebels" were "laboring, like negro slaves, to gain their daily subsistence, or reduced to the wretched alternative, to perish by famine or take arms against their King and country."

Out of old friendship, perhaps, Gage said:

"I would willingly hope, Sir, that the sentiments of liberality, which I always believed you to possess, will be exerted to correct these misdoings." He had the insolence to rebuke Washington's lofty allusion to liberty with a curt and very English: "Be temperate in political disquisition." He advised Washington of all people to "give free operation to truth."

He issued a warning that if "those under whose usurped authority you act . . . dare to call severity retaliation, to God, who knows all hearts, be the appeal for the dreadful consequences."

As for Washington's "insinuations in regard to ministers, I conceived that I had acted under the King." He expressed the King's wish to have the breach closed but denied that "those who long since projected the present crisis" had any such desire.[33]

Washington in rage ordered the prisoners he had on hand to be thrown into jail with disregard of all differences of rank. But in a few days he revoked the edict and called for "every indulgence and civility." [34]

To Gage, however, he wrote a rather excited and grandiloquent glorification of the rebels and the "sacred cause." He denied flatly that his prisoners had been treated except with "a tenderness due to fellow citizens and brethren." Referring to the Tories, he said that "even those execrable parricides, whose counsels and aid have deluged the country with blood, have been protected from the fury of a justly enraged people."

The next sentence in his letter was somewhat remarkable except for the standards of war. Though he had been, and was even now, moving heaven and earth to get and keep enough soldiers to man his lines, and furiously denouncing both soldiers and citizens on his own side, he felt compelled by the necessity of concealing his country's weakness from the enemy (who knew it as well as he did) to deny the charge that British soldiers were encouraged to desert, and utter this sublime mendacity:

"Far from compelling or permitting their assistance, I am embarrassed with the numbers, who crowd to our camp, animated with the purest principles of virtue and love to their country."

After becoming somewhat involved in a retort to Gage's advice about the truth, he closed with this majestic answer to Gage's refusal to recognize any authority except the King's:

"You affect, Sir, to despise all rank not derived from the same source with your own. I cannot conceive one more honorable, than that which flows from the uncorrupted choice of a brave and free people, the purest source and original fountain of all power. Far from making it a plea for cruelty, a mind of true magnanimity and enlarged ideas would comprehend and respect it.

"What may have been the ministerial views, which have precipitated the present crisis, Lexington, Concord, and Charlestown can best declare. May that God, to whom you then appealed, judge between America and you. Under his providence, those who influence the councils of America, and all the other inhabitants of the United Colonies, at the hazard of their lives, are determined to hand down to posterity those just and invaluable privileges, which they received from their ancestors.

"I shall now, Sir, close my correspondence with you, perhaps for ever. If your officers, our prisoners, receive a treatment from me different from that, which I wished to show them, they and you will remember the occasion of it. I am, Sir, your very humble servant."

This was the last exchange between Gage and Washington. He was still the haughty Virginian of 1754 who refused to recognize a royal commission as superior to a provincial; but he and Gage had traveled a long distance from the Monongahela banks where Gage gathered a few soldiers and turned back the Indians and French while the shattered wreck of Braddock's army reeled past, and Washington attended the dying general to the rear. They had traveled a long distance, too, from the friendly dinner they had taken together in New York when Washington fetched Jacky Custis up to King's College.

Gage was a sincere man, keeping his oath to the King, and his opinions of the provokers of the rebellion were hardly less flattering than Washington expressed.

In September Gage received orders calling him home and putting Howe in his place. From the first Gage had said that his mission could not be accomplished with the force at his disposal, and had reported that Boston should be evacuated as useless and New York occupied as a far better strategic post.[35]

The loyalists praised him highly and he expected to return to Boston, but on reaching England found that he was relieved of his command.

Strangely, one of the last acts of Gage was to appoint "Joshua Loring, Jr., Esq., to be sole vendue master and auctioneer, in and for the town of Boston." Loring was a Bostonian of an old family, and a member of what Rev. Henry Belcher calls "the noblesse of high Boston society."

Now Sir William Howe, says Belcher, "liked his glass, his lass, and his game of cards, as indeed did all British warriors at that time and American, too. Commissary Joshua Loring proceeded to push his fortunes on with success while his wife pursued hers. She was . . . fond of the cards . . . and would gamble away a hundred guineas or so with any pretty fellow in love with sport." [36]

During the next two years Mrs. Loring rarely left Howe's side, "while her husband," says Belcher, "accompanied his spouse as a kind of purser to the army with much opportunity for the pursuit of what the Americans call 'graft.'" It was commonly asserted that "the husband of Sir William's *maîtresse en titre*, shared his profits as commissary with her protector." The Hessian officers said "that if the General were paid by the job and not by the day, the business had been settled very speedily."

There are many volumes about the glorious services rendered to the cause of liberty by noble American women, but there has been no tribute paid to this most effective daughter of the Puritans. Yet, as Belcher goes on:

"In Boston, as Americans were fond of saying, this British Antony found his Cleopatra. In her company there is no question but that Howe wasted much of his time, his strength, his opportunities, and his fortune; his vacillations, his native inertness were accentuated by her baneful influence.

"'This illustrious courtesan,' says Judge Jones, 'lost Sir William Howe the honour, the laurels, and the glory of putting an end to one of the most obstinate rebellions that ever existed.'

"If this be so, this daughter of America was among the best and truest of patriots."

The Tories, at least, gave Mrs. Loring full credit for playing Delilah to Howe's Samson. Judge Jones had this to say of her and her husband, and their connection with the sufferings of 10,000 captive Americans in New York later:

"Joshua had a handsome wife. The General, Sir William Howe, was fond of her. Joshua made no objections. He fingered the cash, the General enjoyed madam. Everybody supposing the next campaign (should the rebels even risk another) would put a final period to the rebellion, Loring was determined to make the most of his commission, and by appropriating to his own use nearly two-thirds of the rations allowed to the prisoners, he actually starved to death about 300 of the poor wretches before an exchange took place, which was not till February, 1777. And hundreds that were alive at the time were so emaciated, and enfeebled, for the want of provisions, that numbers died upon the road on their way home, and many lived but a few days after reaching their habitations."

Mrs. Loring was a Miss Lloyd. Of her two sons, one became a clergyman and archdeacon of Calcutta, another was knighted and became vice-admiral in the British navy.

Mrs. Loring occupied a large place in the gossip, the balladry, bawdry and pamphletry of the time, and is too picturesque an American to be lost from the sparse gallery of royal favorites permitted to a republic.

Francis Hopkinson (to whom really belongs Betsy Ross's fabulous credit for designing the American flag) devoted this stanza to Howe's enchantress in the most popular and most famous poem of the period, The Battle of the Kegs:

> "Sir William, he, snug as a flea,
>   Lay all this time a snoring,
> Nor dream'd of harm as he lay warm,
>   In bed with Mrs. L—g." [37]

Washington had many clashes with Loring over prisoners, but his opinion of Mrs. Loring is not recorded. He was a close friend of Hopkinson's, however, and must have roared with laughter over the ballad of the Kegs.

Howe, who was an ingenious strategist, always whipped Washington in battle and always failed to follow up his victory. His eagerness to return to the arms of Mrs. Loring was blamed for this.

His enormous addiction to gambling was also to blame, and an English letter-writer who called him "the worst general that ever a British army was cursed with" lays at his door the ruin of hundreds of young officers at the gaming tables in America:

"Our officers were practising at the dice-box, or studying the chances of picquet, when they should have been storming towns, and crushing the spirit of rebellion; and the harlot's eye glistened with wanton pleasure at the general's table when the brightness of his sword should have reflected terror on the face of the rebels. Cleopatra's banquet was in continual representation, and the American Antony at the head of each feast." [38]

When a nation is at war it must adopt the strict regimen of an athlete. Diversions and luxuries that are harmless in peace are fatal in war, and personal vices assume national importance.

Washington doubtless had this in mind when he called gaming pernicious and punished it heavily during the Revolution, though he practiced it at other times.

While Howe was squandering his genius on a gambling mistress, Washington was sending to Virginia for the exceedingly domestic Martha to be his companion.

XXIV

AN INTERLUDE OF PERSONAL AFFAIRS

WHEN Washington left his wife at Mount Vernon on May fourth, 1775, he rode away as a civilian, yet wore his uniform because he loved it.

When he was drafted into the command of the armies he did not ask for time to go back and tell his household good-by or even to set his affairs in order. He simply moved on to Boston, sending Martha a love letter, and a promise to be back in the fall.

He turned his business affairs over to his kinsman, Lund Washington, a cousin twice removed, their great-grandfathers being brothers.

Lund was five years younger than George and took on the task for the few months of the war. And the war might indeed have been over in the fall if the patriots had risen as one man and fought with the divine courage of tradition. As it turned out, Lund's job lasted for six years. But for him, Washington's property might have gone to ruin.[1] In spite of Lund, he barely escaped a complete financial crash as a result of the utter failure of revolutionary financing.

Hardly had Washington gone to Philadelphia before history began to be made in Virginia, without his help. The political giants who had brought the colony to the fore in so many of the first struggles for liberty, continued to throw off not only the financial and political, but also the moral and religious, shackles imposed on them by the monarchy and the established church of England.

The history of the province cannot be followed here, but

GENERAL SIR HENRY CLINTON
(Engraved by A. H. Ritchie)

one of its chapters concerned Washington personally in that it threatened Martha's safety.

While Boston was calling Washington and the Virginia riflemen under Morgan to her aid against General Gage and the British ships, Lord Dunmore was trying to suppress the rising pride of the Virginians. First he refused to reconvene the Assembly, next he seized the store of ammunition kept in the round tower magazine still standing at Williamsburg and known as the Powder Horn. He took away sixteen of its twenty barrels of powder, April 20, 1775, the day after General Gage tried to destroy the stores at Lexington and Concord. When the Assembly asked for it back, Dunmore threatened to burn Williamsburg.

Thereupon Captain Patrick Henry girded on his sword and with a hundred and fifty men marched for Williamsburg. So many volunteers flocked to him that he had nearly five thousand men under arms.

The Governor armed Indian hostages and slaves and brought ashore sailors and marines from a British warship, on which he put his wife and children for safety. Then he backed down and paid £330 for the stolen powder; and Henry dismissed his army. Henry was now made colonel of the First Virginia Regiment, and what Washington had once been, commander-in-chief of the Virginia forces. Immediately a local civil war ensued.

In fact the Revolution was one gigantic civil war with little civil wars going on madly inside it everywhere, like the separate whorls of furious eddies within a maelstrom.

Eminent Virginians, many of them now drifting into loyalism, though hating Dunmore, once more condemned Henry as an upstart radical and trouble-maker. A new "Committee of Safety," made up of Pendleton, George Mason and others, would not let him take the field because of his lack of military experience. Some of his officers flouted him, and finally he was in effect degraded by the appointment of two brigadiers over him; for, when the Continental Congress "adopted" the Virginia troops as it had adopted those of Massachusetts, it offered to continue Henry as a colonel, but named Colonel Robert Howe of North Carolina, and Colonel Andrew Lewis brigadier generals.

Henry was as much hurt at not being made a brigadier as John Hancock had been at not receiving the offer of the entire command. He resigned.[2]

This pleased Washington, who had written to Joseph Reed:

"I think my countrymen made a capital mistake, when they took Henry out of the senate to place him in the field; and pity it is, that he does not see this, and remove every difficulty by a voluntary resignation."

In the meanwhile Lord Dunmore had gathered a fleet of British ships, and after being repulsed in an attempt to burn Hampton, captured Norfolk, offered freedom to all slaves and indentured servants, and tried to organize "Lord Dunmore's own Regiment of Indians" as well as "Lord Dunmore's Ethiopians."

Dunmore was acting exactly as a devoted servant of the King should have acted, but it is hardly to be expected that the burnt-out and harried Virginians should think so.[3]

Driven off by minute-men, among whom was Lieutenant John Marshall, he bombarded and burned Norfolk. Then he roamed at large and there was much fear that he might try to descend on Mount Vernon, burn it as a rebuke to Washington and kidnap Martha as a hostage. The men of Alexandria offered her a refuge there and the people of Loudoun county planned to send a guard to conduct her to Berkeley.

Washington sent Martha several letters on the matter, as we know by a reference of Lund's, but those letters are lost.

Most of Washington's letters to Lund are also lost; but one has recently turned up in which he says:

"I can hardly think that Lord Dunmore can act so low, & unmannerly a part, as to think of seizing Mrs. Washington by way of revenge upon me; howev^r as I suppose she is, before this time, gone over to Mr Calverts, & will soon after retu&, go down to New Kent, she will be out of his reach for 2 or 3 months to come, in which time matters may, & probably will, take such a turn as to render her removal either absolutely necessary, or quite useless—I am nevertheless exceedingly thankful to the Gentlemen of Alexandria for their friendly attention to this point & desire you will if there is any sort of reason to suspect a thing of this kind provide a kitchen for her in Alexandria, or some other place of safety elsewhere for her and my Papers." [4]

In this letter, which is published in none of the collections, Washington was still expecting that the war would be over by the winter; for he asks Lund to "quicken" the carpenters about the dining room chimney piece, "as I could wish to have that end of the House compleatly finished before I return.—I wish you had done the end of the New Kitchen next the Garden as also the old Kitchen with rusticated Boards. . . . What have you done with the well?—Is that walled up?"

He orders the carpenters discharged as he does not care to "pay men £100 a year to be Idle." He objects to the overseers keeping horses of their own "& for what purpose, unless it be to make fat Horses at my expence, I know not, as it is no saving of my own Horses. I do not like the custom, & wish you would break it—but do as you will, as I cannot pretend to interfere at this distance."

The outbreak of war had thrown the non-importation and non-exportation associations into confusion, and Scotch and many native Virginia merchants were not inclined to follow the new movements any further. Washington breaks out against them in this letter to Lund:

"The acc^t given of the behaviour of the Scotchmen at Port Tobacco & Piscataway surprised & vexed me.—Why did they Imbark in the cause?—What do they say for themselves?—What does other say of them?—Are they admitted into Company?—Or kicked out of it?—What does their Countrymen urge in the Justification of them?"

This was written August 20th, 1775, the date of his noble letter to General Gage with its hymn of praise for his united people, and the enforced pretence that he was "embarrassed with the numbers, who crowd to our camp, animated with the purest principles of virtue and love to their country."

We are all Januses, and have one face for foreigners and another for the family; but it is evidence of the painful dilemma of Washington, that he had to avow such reverence for his fellow-countrymen to a Briton, while, on the very same day, he had to relieve his soul, to his third cousin, of this most informal opinion of the New Englanders, in which he repeats what he wrote to R. H. Lee, but more nervously:

"The People of this government have obtained a character which they by no means deserved—their officers generally speaking are the most indifferent kind of People I ever saw. . . . in short they are by no means such Troops, in any respect, as you are led to believe of them from the acc^ts which are published, but I need not make myself enemies among them, by this declaration, although it is consistent with truth.—I dare say the men would fight very well (if properly officered) although they are exceeding dirty and nasty people. . . .

"What does Doct^r Craik say to the behaviour of his Countrymen, & Townspeople?—Remember me kindly to him, & tell him that I should be very glad to see him here if there was anything worth his acceptance; but the Massachusetts People suffer nothing to go by them that they can lay hands upon."

In this letter he discusses many other details and urges Lund to send Colonel George William Fairfax immediately the money that is due to him.

He had written a month before to Fairfax announcing his appointment to the command of the Continental army, giving him the exact losses on both sides at Bunker Hill, and enclosing him the second Address of Congress to the inhabitants of Great Britain, and a declaration setting forth the necessity of taking up arms.

The next day he wrote again:

"In my hurry, yesterday, I forgot the principal thing I had in view, when I sat down to write to you, and that was, to inform you of the indispensable necessity you must now be under of appointing another Attorney. The nature of the business I am now engaged in (which alone is full sufficient to engross the time and attention of any one Man) and the distance I am removed from your business, as well as my own, puts it absolutely out of my power to be of any further service to you in Virginia." [5]

He never wavered in his affections for both George and Sally Fairfax and when, later in the war, the enormous Fairfax properties were confiscated as Tory wealth, he wrote to his brother-in-law, Lewis, that it was "a cruel proceeding as the uniform tenor of his conduct has been friendly to the rights of this country—his going to England the result of necessity and before hostilities either commenced or were thought of, and his return with his family in a manner impracticable." [6]

Washington's own lands in the West were in grave danger of being lost to him by reason of the anarchy of the times and his absence at war. After all his difficulty in securing his patents three years before, his attempts to settle them had been thwarted. He summed up his unbroken series of troubles in an appeal for help to his friend, Thomas Everard, of Virginia:

"As I believe it will be three years next December since some of my Ohio lands (under the proclamation of 1754) were patented; and as they are not yet improved agreeably to the express letter of the law, it behoves me to have recourse, in time, to the common expedient of saving them by means of a friendly petition. My distance from Williamsburg, and my ignorance of the mode of doing this, lays me under the necessity of calling upon some friend for assistance. Will you, then, my good Sir, aid me in this work? I shall acknowledge it as a singular favor if you will, and, unless you discourage me, I shall rely on it." [7]

Valentine Crawford wrote to Washington describing the escape of five white servants of Washington's and the trouble his agent had recovering them. What happened afterward is an example of the manner in which white flesh was marketed in those days:

"He has sent three of them [the runaways] up by a man he had hired, with a letter to my brother William or myself, to sell them for you; but the man sold them himself somewhere about Wheeling, on his way up, and never brought them to us. He got £20 Pennsylvania currency for them, and gave one year's credit. . . . I think it would be advisable, if the men they are sold so low to are not good, to take them from them, and sell them again." [8]

Throughout the war Washington was tormented by the fear of losing these lands, and his inability to get anybody to act for him in their preservation. The Revolution was a luxury indeed to him.

He kept up a correspondence with Lund concerning his interests, writing him every week or two; but, by an odd whim of fate, his letters have almost all vanished while Lund's are preserved. He kept a copy of part of one of his letters "to remind me of my engagements and the exact purport of them." It beautifully reveals his generosity:

"Let the hospitality of the house, with respect to the poor, be kept up. Let no one go hungry away. If any of this kind of people should be in want of corn, supply their necessities, provided it does not encourage them in idleness; and I have no objection to your giving my money in charity, to the amount of forty or fifty pounds a year, when you think it well bestowed. What I mean by having no objection is, that it is my desire that it should be done. You are to consider, that neither myself nor wife is now in the way to do these good offices."

In view of the danger of his death, he set down his obligations to Lund, and added:

"The above is copied, not only to remind myself of my promises and requests, but others also, if any mischance happens to
"G. Washington." [9]

The loneliness of his crowded life at Cambridge turned his heart toward Martha. The fall had come, the winter was near. He was evidently to be indefinitely the prisoner as well as the jailer of the British, and he finally resolved to ask Martha to come to him.

She had often told Lund that she would go to his camp if he would permit her, and when he wrote to ask her she lost no time in complying. He was uneasy about Dunmore's "diabolical schemes" and he wrote to R. H. Lee, "If, my dear Sir, that man is not crushed before spring, he will become the most formidable enemy America has." [10]

Dunmore did, indeed, threaten Mount Vernon, but George Mason wrote to Washington:

"Dunmore has come and gone, and left us untouched except by some alarm. I sent my family many miles back in the country, and advised Mrs. Washington to do likewise, as a prudential movement. At first she said 'No; I will not desert my post;' but she finally did so with reluctance, rode only a few miles, and, plucky little woman as she is, stayed away only one night."

At length, but not from fear, she went down to New Kent County and visited her sister, Mrs. Bassett, taking along Jacky Custis and his wife.

There she received one of the letters she burned. Washington mentioned it in a letter to his brother.[11]

The "plucky little woman" was no more afraid of the

weather than of Dunmore, and she accepted the "invitation" with alacrity. Washington sent down for her his chariot with four horses, a black driver, and an outrider in white-and-scarlet livery. So Martha and Jacky and Nelly made a stir as they sped North in a royal progress of four-hundred-and-fifty miles to Philadelphia, the distance being Washington's own estimate.[12]

Washington wrote to Joseph Reed, then in Philadelphia, asking him to meet his wife and get her past the danger zone of New York.[13]

The impatient Martha beat this letter to Philadelphia by several days. It arrived the day she left. But she was not neglected, for the Pennsylvania *Gazette* of November 22, says:

"Yesterday the Lady of his Excellency General Washington arrived here, upon her way to New England. She was met at the Lower Ferry by the officers of the different battalions, the troop of light horse, and the light infantry of the 2d battalion, who escorted her into the city."

She was probably lodged at Joseph Reed's home.

Philadelphia was always strongly loyalist and the presence of the radical congressmen won no more converts to the cause than delegations of the sort usually do. As the wife of the rebel general, Martha was as welcome as Mrs. Trotzky would be to the Russian aristocracy if she passed through Paris. Only a few women callers darkened her door.

To offset this, a great ball was planned in her honor at the City Tavern for the night of the 24th. Then the long-faces remembered that Congress had passed a resolution against all amusements during the solemn times, and there were threats to wreck the tavern if the ball was not given up.

Christopher Marshall, a retired old druggist who had been expelled from the Quaker church for his Revolutionary

sympathies, bestirred himself to prevent a riot, and he tells
in his own diary how turbulent Philadelphia was:

"*24th.*—After dinner, as I had heard some threats thrown out,
that if the ball assembled this night, as it was proposed, they presumed that the New Tavern would cut but a poor figure to-morrow
morning, these fears of some commotion's being made that would
be very disagreeable at this melancholy time, in disturbing the peace
of the City, I concluded, if possible, to prevent, in order to which,
I went to Col. Hancock's lodgings, and finding he was not come
from Congress, and the time grew short, being three o'clock, I
walked up to the State House, in expectation of meeting him.

"That failing, I requested the door-keeper to call Samuel Adams,
which he accordingly did, and he came. I then informed him of
the account received of a ball, that was to be held this evening, and
where, and that Mrs. Washington and Col. Hancock's wife were
to be present, and as such meetings appeared to be contrary to the
Eighth Resolve of Congress, I therefore requested he would give
my respects to Col. Hancock, desire him to wait on Lady Washington to request her not to attend or go this evening. This he
promised.

"Thence I went and met the Committee at the Philosophical
Hall, which was large and respectable, being called together for
this only purpose to consider the propriety of this meeting or ball's
being held this evening in this city, at the New Tavern, where,
after due and mature consideration, it was then concluded, there
being but one dissenting voice, (Sharp Delany,) that there should
be no such meeting held, not only this evening, but in future,
while these troublesome times continued, and a Committee was
appointed, immediately to go to inform the directors of this meeting
not to proceed any further in this affair, and also to wait upon Lady
Washington, expressing this Committee's great regard and affection
to her, requesting her to accept of their grateful acknowledgment
and respect, due to her on account of her near connexion with our
worthy and brave General now exposed in the field of battle in
defence of our rights and liberties, and request and desire her not
to grace that company, to which, we are informed, she has an
invitation this evening, &c. &c. Came home near six.

"After I drank coffee, I went down to Samuel Adams's lodgings,
where was Col. Dyer. Spent some time pleasantly, until Col.

Harrison came to rebuke Samuel Adams for using his influence for the stopping of this entertainment, which he declared was legal, just and laudable. Many arguments were used by all present to convince him of the impropriety at this time, but all to no effect; so, as he came out of humour, he so returned, to appearance.

"*November 25th.*—At half past eleven, went to the Committee Room at the Coffee House; came away near two. At this time, Major Bayard, one of the four gentlemen appointed to wait on Lady Washington, reported that they had acted agreeably to directions, that the lady received them with great politeness, thanked the Committee for their kind care and regard in giving such timely notice, requesting her best compliments to be returned to them for their care and regard, and to assure them that their sentiments on this occasion, were perfectly agreeable unto her own." [14]

Strange, how riotous good people grow when their ordinances are disregarded. When fanatics threaten to wreck a building where activities they disapprove are carried on, it is called anarchy. When the Puritans threaten to wreck a hotel because a dance is to be held there, it is called law, order and morality.

Few things are more eloquent of the varying schools of revolutionary emotion than the fact that the wife of the radical rebel, Washington, was snubbed by the conservative wives of Philadelphia, and that when the people of a more amiable clique welcomed her with a festival, the dour moralists threatened to tear down the building to prevent it, and a large committee held a special meeting to consider it and voted it a dangerous ceremony. The only two people who emerge with real honor are Sharp Delany and Colonel Harrison, who fought the meddlers.

What Martha thought of all this tempest in a teapot is not recorded. What Washington must have thought of it when she told him, it is easy to imagine. He was a devotee of dancing and when he could, he completely ignored that Eighth Commandment of Congress against "vain amusements." Throughout the war he and his officers gave balls whenever and wherever they had the chance.

All his life he broke such laws as he thought to be the mere tyranny of bigotry in power.

The plump little woman who had never been out of Virginia was now "Lady Washington," the wife of his "Excellency," the General.

The question of titles had not yet been solved. If the Revolution had not broken out, the English would probably have instituted an American peerage. There was some talk of it. In time the American horror of titles would develop, but at this period when social distinctions were all important, their absence was felt as an inconvenience and Washington himself would later consent to be called "His High Mightiness" and only be saved from that horror by others.

Curiously, in 1775, the ambitious General Charles Lee made one of the few protests against resounding titles. On September 19th he wrote to Dr. Benjamin Rush:

"I condemn with you the barbarous, dangerous custom of loading the Servants of the People with the trappings of Court Titles. I cannot conceive who the Devil first devis'd the bauble of Excellency for their Commander in Chief, or the more ridiculous of His Honour for me— Upon my Soul They make me spew—even the tacking honorable to the Continental Congress creates a wambling in my stomack— What cou'd add dignity to the simple title of the Continental Congress of America, as long as they do their duty? And the instant They grow corrupt or slavish from timidity all the rumbling sounds of honorable, serene, mighty, sublime, or magnanimous, will only make their infamy more infamous." [15]

But "Lady Washington" stuck, and Martha enjoyed it. She must have reveled in the clanking, glittering cavalcade of soldiers who swept with her through the new landscapes of the North. She left Philadelphia under military escort that accompanied her five miles. At Elizabethtown another troop of light horse met her and rode as far as Newark, where the church bells greeted her. She escaped a possible loyalist trap at New York by crossing the Hudson at Dobb's Ferry, and reached Cambridge and her husband on the eleventh of December, having taken just two weeks to go from Philadelphia.

Washington had stationed one of his aides at an inn outside Cambridge to watch for her, but though he waited for several days, the weather-beaten carriage with the worn-out horses slipped past unheeded, and Martha arrived unwelcomed in the bleak sunset of a New England December.

For many reasons Washington must have made her welcome to his headquarters in the Craigie house.

Washington wrote to Reed expressing his "gratitude for the attentions shown to Mrs. Washington at Philadelphia. It cannot but be pleasing, although it did in some measure impede the progress of her journey on the road." [16]

That touch of loverly impatience is in keeping with his unfailing Virginian tact.

By Christmas day, he had ready a package of letters of thanks addressed to various persons who had been courteous to Martha, and sent them to Joseph Reed to have them delivered.

Martha settled into her new nest comfortably and made friends with the wives of the other officers, particularly with Lucy Flucker, now the wife of Colonel (later General) Henry Knox, a former bookseller in Boston. Lucy Knox was fat of body but not of brain, and Washington loved to dance with her. Mrs. Horatio Gates had come along with Martha from Philadelphia. Charles Lee called Mrs. Gates "that Dæmoness."

Martha was now forty-four years old—still eight months senior to her husband by the family Bible though he had aged centuries from the country squire she had seen riding away, seven months before, to a political convention.

She visited now a strange man, the commander-in-chief of all the colonies and all their armies, with a wall around the troops of his King. Yet he was more meek than before, for now his own people were dissatisfied with him and he was feeling that he had spoken the truth about his glory when, at Philadelphia, "with a tear glistening in his eye," he had told Patrick Henry, "This will be the commencement of the decline of my reputation."

Martha, too, had undergone amazing experiences, but the letter she wrote to her friend, Miss Ramsay, December 30th, 1775, shows that the wars made no change in her lovable little plump soul.

"Dear Miss I now set down to tell you that I arrived hear safe, and our party all well . . . we were so attended and the gentlemen so kind, that I am lade under obligations to them that I shall not for get soon I dont dout but you have seen the Figuer our arrivel made in the Philadelphia paper—and I left it in as great pomp as if I had been a very great some body

"Every person seems to be chearfull and happy hear,—some days we have a number of cannon and shells from Boston and Bunkers Hill, but it does not seem to surprise any one but me; I confess I shuder every time I hear the sound of a gun . . . I just took a look at pore Boston—& Charlstown—from prospect Hill charlestown has only a few chimneys standing in it, thare seems to be a number of very fine Buildings in Boston but god knows how long they will stand; they are pulling up all the warfs for fire wood— to me that never see any thing of war, the preperations, are very terable indeed, but I endevor to keep my fears to my self as well as I can.

"your Friends Mr Harrison & Henly are boath very well, and I think they are fatter than they were when they came to the Camp— and Capt Baylor is a lusty man to what he was when you see him The girls may rest sattisfied on Mr Harrisons account for he seems two fond of his Country to give his heart to any but one of his Virginia Friends, thare are but Two Young Laides in Cambridge, and a very great number of Gentlemen so you may gess how much is made of them—but neither of them is pritty I think,

"This is a beautyfull Country, and we had a very plasent journey through new england, and had the plasure to find the General very well we came within the month from home to the Camp." [17]

A quaint evidence of the value of rumor is the fact that slander followed even the devoted Martha, who had just ridden a thousand miles or so to be with her husband. A newspaper published this:

"Mr. Washington, we hear, is married to a very amiable lady, but it is said that Mrs. Washington, being a warm loyalist, has separated from her husband since the commencement of the present troubles, and lives, ve.y much respected, in the city of New York." [18]

She found Washington in a state of mind in which he needed her help. A letter from Joseph Reed had warned him that he was being criticized in Philadelphia. Some of his own criticisms must have leaked out. Also the Virginia riflemen had been boasting of their superiority to the New England militia.

Worse yet, he had neglected to invite some of the Massachusetts bigwigs to his dinner table. He was learning that politicians can be as hungry for social honors as women. He wrote to Reed, thanking him for calling his attention to the jealousies that had gone abroad:

"I have studiously avoided, in all letters intended for the public eye, I mean for that of the Congress,—every expression that could give pain or uneasiness;—and I shall observe the same rule with respect to private letters, further than appears absolutely necessary for the elucidation of facts. I cannot charge myself with incivility, or what, in my opinion, is tantamount, ceremonious civility, to the gentlemen of this Colony; but if such my conduct appears, I will endeavour at a reformation, as I can assure you, my dear Reed, that I wish to walk in such a line as will give most general satisfaction. You know that it was my wish at first to invite a certain number of the gentlemen of this Colony every day to dinner, but unintentionally, I believe by any body, we some how or other missed of it; if this has given rise to the jealousy, I cannot say that I am sorry for it; at the same time I add, that it was rather owing to inattention, or more properly too much attention to other matters, which caused me to neglect it." [19]

A superb phrase, that! for his gracious ideal of courtesy: "I cannot charge myself with incivility, or what, in my opinion, is tantamount, ceremonious civility."

Now he turned over to Martha the nuisance of the book-keeping of hospitality and the old Craigie house became another Mount Vernon, filled with a gay company of men and women.

About this time Washington began to be troubled about what people were saying of him. This was a confession of humanity as well as a recognition of the importance to the cause of popularity in the commander.

People had a way of bringing to him unpleasant things that other people said of him, and he may have learned that John Adams had expressed a general disapproval of his inactivity when he wrote to Mrs. Mercy Warren that he hoped Martha "might have ambition enough for her husband's glory to give occasion to the Lord to have mercy on the souls of Howe and Burgoyne." [20]

In his anxiety over the slow enlistment he could not but feel that the little support he was receiving was due to a lack of public approval. He appealed to Reed again and again to tell him how he stood with the people:

"Nothing would give me more real satisfaction than to know the sentiments which are entertained of me by the public, whether they be favourable or otherwise; . . . the man who wished to steer clear of shelves and rocks, must know where they lie. I know— but to declare it, unless to a friend, may be an argument of vanity—the integrity of my own heart. I know the unhappy predicament I stand in. I know that much is expected of me. I know that without men, without arms, without ammunition, without anything fit for the accommodation of a soldier, that little is to be done,—and, which is mortifying, I know that I cannot stand justified to the world, without exposing my own weakness, and injuring the cause by declaring my wants, which I am determined not to do, further than unavoidable necessity brings every man acquainted with them. If, under these disadvantages, I am able to keep above water (as it were) in the esteem of mankind, I shall feel myself happy; but if, from the unknown peculiarity of my circumstances, I suffer in the opinion of the world, I shall not think you take the freedom of a friend, if you conceal the reflections that may be cast upon my conduct. My own situation feels so irksome to me at times, that if I did not consult the public good more than my own tranquillity, I should long ere this have put every thing to the cast of a die." [21]

Sometimes deep melancholy shrouded him in such despair that he repented his whole mission and found no comfort except in the strange Being behind the cold stars over the night-stilled camp, that Providence which he believed in and dreaded, and in whose least mercies he saw an inscrutable wisdom though its kindliness was far less generous and frequent than his own:

"The reflection upon my situation, and that of this army, produces many an uneasy hour, when all around me are wrapped in sleep. Few people know the predicament we are in, on a thousand accounts—fewer still will believe, if any disaster happens to these lines, from what cause it flows.

"I have often thought how much happier I should have been, if, instead of accepting of a command under such circumstances, I had taken my musket upon my shoulder, and entered the ranks;—or if I could have justified the measure to posterity and my own conscience, had retired to the back country, and lived in a wigwam.

"If I shall be able to rise superior to these, and many other difficulties which might be enumerated, I shall most religiously believe that the finger of Providence is in it, to blind the eyes of our enemies." [22]

XXV

HIS TRY FOR CANADA

THE gnawing restlessness that preyed on Washington was due not only to the troubles with the mercenary militia and the council of officers who would not let him wreck himself on the British lines, but also to the contrast of the doldrums about Boston with the seething activity in other quarters.

On the sea, along the borders, in the assemblies, everybody else seemed to be doing something while he wrote letters. Only the most amazing power of character in repose could have kept for him the public respect.

Before he had been made Commander-in-Chief brilliant victories had been won. After he took the control, hardly anything good happened.

He loved fearless men like himself and he was particularly drawn toward Benedict Arnold—nine years his junior, born of an old and distinguished family in 1741, reared by a singularly pious mother, and always of a religious faith. Arnold had run away to war as a fifteen-year-old lad in 1756. He had been brought back by a mother who hated war as well as Mary Washington did.

He was already the captain of a well-drilled and well-uniformed company at New Haven when the news of the battle of Lexington fired him to march at once with his volunteers, including a number of Yale students. When the selectmen refused to give him the town supply of powder, he threatened to take it by force. Receiving it, he marched straight to Cambridge.

It has been overlooked as a rule that Arnold's company

was in a sense a sacred band solemnly pledged to an agreement containing these words:

"To all Christian people believing and relying on that God to whom our enemies have forced us to apply; and having taken up arms for the relief of our brethren and for the defense of their and our just rights; to prevent disorders, etc., each bound himself by all that is sacred to observe and keep this mutual covenant. . . .

"2nd. Drunkenness, gaming, profanity and every vice, should be avoided and discountenanced." [1]

At Cambridge, Arnold had visited the Committee of Safety and proposed to capture Fort Ticonderoga at the strategic junction of Lakes Champlain and George, where weak British garrisons guarded an invaluable wealth of artillery, small arms, ammunition, and military stores. He was admired and seconded by Dr. Joseph Warren, "the first great martyr of the Revolution," for whose impoverished children's education Arnold afterward provided. Like Washington, he believed in educating orphans.

Arnold hurried away with a Massachusetts commission as colonel, but, outside Ticonderoga, found Colonel Ethan Allen ahead of him with his Green Mountain Boys. After some wrangling, Arnold consented to yield the command, but insisted on fighting.

The patriots, as every American schoolboy thinks he knows, surprised the fort on the night of May 10th, 1775, and when the commander came to the front door in his undershirt, breeches, and bare feet, and asked what was the matter, Ethan Allen called on him to surrender "In the name of the Great Jehovah and the Continental Congress."

This was pretty good for Allen, since, though he was a notorious deist, Congress had not yet given anybody any authority to do anything. In fact Congress had just convened on that very day in far-off Philadelphia, and had done nothing but elect a president and a secretary, ask Mr. Duché to open the morrow's session with prayer, and adjourn.

Allen had eighty-three men and the British forty-eight, twenty of whom Allen had managed to get dead drunk for the occasion. At least the British say that he called on the commander in the afternoon, told a pathetic story and persuaded the trusting officer to lend him twenty soldiers to help him across the lake.[2]

There was no reason why Captain de la Place should have refused the kindly act, for war had not been declared. In any case, Allen mercifully filled the men with rum instead of bullets, and no blood was spilled.

Congress received the news on May 18th and promptly atoned for Allen's deed by ordering an inventory of the material captured in order that it might be returned to the mother country as soon as "the restoration of the former harmony between Great Britain and these Colonies, so ardently wished for by the latter, shall render it prudent and consistent with the over-ruling law of self-preservation." [3]

More than a hundred cannon and a wealth of ammunition fell to the firm of Allen and Arnold, who then swallowed up a corporal and eight men at Crown Point. Arnold, seizing the one British boat on Lake Champlain, sailed to St. Johns and took it without trouble.

"These acts of burglarious enterprise secured for Congress about 200 pieces of cannon, and placed Congress . . . in a very awkward position," says Belcher.[4] "In May, 1775, it was no part of their policy to approve of overt acts of war on the part of Patriots. The Congress was not a constitutional body. . . . There was a savour of brigandage in it not quite to the taste of the respectable gentlemen collected in Philadelphia. Hence the war declared itself."

Though Stedman [5] says that "the whole military force of Canada, at this period, did not exceed . . . eight hundred men," the British commander, Sir Guy Carleton, promptly recaptured St. Johns, and fortified it against an attack on Montreal, only twelve miles away. The British agent of the Iroquois Indians joined Carleton with five hundred warriors, and offered to recapture Ticonderoga also, but the Americans held it, except for a few weeks in 1777.

While Arnold usually managed to do more or less financial cheating during the war, he seemed to inspire the more moral elements to cheat him out of his glory. He almost rivaled Washington in the number of times he proffered his resignation, but his purpose was to fight and he was frequently spectacularly brave while revealing also fine tactical gifts. Fortescue calls him "a man of inborn genius for war." [6]

As a reward for his splendid achievements on Lake Champlain, Arnold was invited to return to Massachusetts and explain certain money matters. This was the first of a series of such requests. He always displayed a fine explanation and an abundance of indignation, but when a man is forever being investigated, there is likely to be something at the bottom of it. His soldiers loved him in any case. Arnold resigned and returned to Cambridge in July, 1775, finding Washington there.

On his way to Boston, Washington had planned an invasion of Canada by way of Lakes George and Champlain, and instructed Schuyler to make up an army and lead it north to the capture of Montreal.

The way now lay open to that conquest of Canada, which has always seemed so easy to Americans and has brought only disaster when attempted. Great expectations were also cherished of persuading Canada to join the colonies in resisting England. But the Quebec Act had persuaded the French that the British were better friends to Canada than the Americans, who made the Quebec Act one of the causes of the war. A number of Canadians did join the Conti-

nental armies, but the majority of the unfortunate ones who
publicly expressed their sympathy with the colonies suffered
for their rashness when the Canadian soul was finally revolted by the extreme cowardice and the extreme rapacity
of the American troops who invaded Canada and met defeat
after defeat.

Arnold called on Washington and proposed a simul-
taneous invasion by way of the Kennebec River with Quebec
as the object of a surprise attack. Schuyler, he said, would
hold Carleton at Montreal while Quebec, "the Gibraltar
of America" was left helpless, especially if Arnold could
get through the Maine woods and pounce without warning.
This woke the enthusiasm of Washington, and the Congressional Committee that visited Boston approved the plan.
Washington lent to Arnold his own Virginia riflemen under
Daniel Morgan, once a runaway wagoner at Braddock's field,
now the commander of the sharpshooters from home, whose
arrival at Cambridge had given Washington one of his few
bright moments.

The story goes that, seeing a band of dusty men march
into camp, Washington asked them whence they came, and
Morgan answered with words of music to Washington's ear:

"From the right bank of the Potomac."

Whereupon Washington flung himself from his horse and
wrung their hands as tears filled his eyes. Morgan had
marched his ninety-six men six hundred miles in twenty-one
days. These fine woodsmen he gave to Arnold. The nine-
teen-year-old Aaron Burr was there, too, another brave be-
ginner who finished badly in American history.

Washington gave Arnold eleven hundred men and they
soon vanished into a midnight of trackless wilderness.

Washington had his heart set on the addition of Canada
to the union of the colonies. Though he opposed a
projected attack on Nova Scotia as "a measure of conquest,

rather than defence," [7] and also a hopeless defiance of British sea-power, he knew that General Carleton had only eight hundred regulars in Canada and was experiencing the same difficulties with recruits and deserters that maddened the Americans.

It was the friendship of the Canadians he wanted, and he gave Arnold the most careful instructions not even to offend them—to retire indeed, if he found them hostile:

> "You are, by every means in your power, to endeavor to discover the real sentiments of the Canadians towards our cause, and particularly as to this expedition, bearing in mind, that if they are averse to it and will not coöperate, or at least willingly acquiesce, it must fail of success. In this case you are by no means to prosecute the attempt; the expense of the expedition, and the disappointment, are not to be put in competition with the dangerous consequences, which may ensue from irritating them against us, and detaching them from that neutrality, which they have adopted." [8]

He ordered Arnold to punish severely any person who offended a Canadian and to make "ample compensation to the party injured." The Indian allies must be kept from cruelty, lest they "irritate our fellow-subjects against us." He was still a loyal subject of the King:

> "Check every idea and crush in its earliest stage every attempt to plunder even those, who are known to be enemies to our cause. It will create dreadful apprehensions in our friends, and, when it is once begun, no one can tell where it will stop. I therefore again most expressly order, that it be discouraged and punished in every instance without distinction."

He advised Arnold that if he met General Schuyler, Schuyler was his superior: "I recommend most earnestly to avoid all contention about rank. In such a cause every post is honorable, in which a man can serve his country."

He emphasized the importance of repressing the New England tendency to scoff at the Catholics. On a long-past invasion of Canada by the New Englanders they had fired a cannon at a picture of the Virgin Mary.

Always impatient of religious intolerance, Washington's final instructions to Arnold were:

"As the contempt of the religion of a country by ridiculing any of its ceremonies, or affronting its ministers or votaries, has ever been deeply resented, you are to be particularly careful to restrain every officer and soldier from such imprudence and folly, and to punish every instance of it. On the other hand, as far as lies in your power, you are to protect and support the free exercise of the religion of the country, and the undisturbed enjoyment of the rights of conscience in religious matters, with your utmost influence and authority."

In a personal letter he said the same things less formally, and showed that his tolerance was due to no respect for Catholic "errors," but to a kindly condescension:

"Prudence, policy, and a true Christian spirit will lead us to look with compassion upon their errors without insulting them. While we are contending for our own liberty, we should be very cautious not to violate the rights of conscience in others, ever considering that God alone is the judge of the hearts of men, and to him only in this case they are answerable." [9]

He also had an address to the Canadians printed on handbills for distribution.

He waited with the most poignant anxiety for news, and was shocked when Colonel Enos returned with three hundred men, alleging a failure of provisions. Enos was courtmartialed and acquitted but never cleared of blame.

The story of Arnold's march is one of the most harrowing pages in history. Two hundred of his soldiers starved to death, two hundred were sent back sick, and he lost three hundred by the defection of Colonel Enos. There were women with the expedition whose courage shamed some of the men.

All America was aquiver with the glory of invading foreign soil. One British army was under siege in Boston, two American hosts were advancing on Montreal and Quebec.

Schuyler, after breaking his heart all summer at Ticonderoga, trying to collect troops and managing by his wealthy Dutch-aristocrat manner to offend nearly everybody, moved against St. Johns with a thousand men in September. Instead of marching around it to Montreal and exposing his line of communications, he sat down to besiege it.

He had longed to resign but Washington dissuaded him. Now he fell ill and his command devolved on General Richard Montgomery, an Irishman trained in the British Army.

Soon Montgomery was affixing his signature on the testimonial to the nobility of the Revolutionary troops; he wrote to his wife:

"I am so exceeding out of spirits and so chagrined with the behavior of the troops, that I most heartily repent having undertaken to lead them. . . . Such a set of pusillanimous wretches never were collected."

It seems to have been the unanimous opinion of the generals that the sons of liberty were also the sons of something else. It is distance that has lent them their enchantment and given them the majesty they wear on the Fourth of July.

In the meanwhile, Ethan Allen had almost captured Montreal as easily as he took Ticonderoga. He and a Major Brown had been sent into Canada to recruit troops, and had such success that Allen moved on Montreal with thirty Americans and eighty Canadians, counting on Brown to attack from another point. But Brown failed to appear and Carleton sent out 260 soldiers, Indians, and gentry and gobbled up Allen, who, after a harsh experience of Joshua Loring's mercy in New York, was sent in irons to England.

The New Yorkers later wished that he had been kept there, for when he was exchanged, he set up claims in Vermont against New York that started another side-issue civil war and took away from New York troops sadly needed by Washington.

However, Montgomery's thousand men managed after a two months' siege of St. Johns, to force the surrender of the five hundred British regulars and the hundred Canadian militia on Nov. 3, 1775. Montgomery then marched against Montreal where Carleton had three hundred men.

Montreal fell on the 13th, but General Carleton disguised himself as a trapper, got away in a boat and made for Quebec.

The secret of Arnold's march became known through the capture of one of his messengers, and when he broke out of the wilderness on Nov. 5th, he found Carleton in Quebec with nearly two thousand men.

Arnold's hopes of finding Canadian volunteers flocking to his standards were dashed to the ground, partly because some of the French priests refused absolution to the enemies of Great Britain—which robbed death of its last promise.

With only 650 men, emaciated and tattered, only 400 muskets and five rounds of ammunition, Arnold gazed across the St. Lawrence at Quebec and vowed to conquer it.

And he would probably have done it, too, if the worst luck in the world had not coincided with the infamous defection of Montgomery's troops, all but three hundred of whom refused to reënlist or overstay their dates of enlistment. His prayers availed nothing and the easy capture of Canada was turned into fearful disaster by the patriots whose loyalty was measured by the calendar.

Some of Montgomery's officers had upbraided him for being humane to the British prisoners. He was so offended that he resigned at once. They apologized and he resumed command, but three hundred of his men marched off in one body. General Schuyler wrote to Washington Nov. 22, 1775, that these men reached him too feeble to do military duty until he gave them their discharge, when they "instantly acquired health, and . . . undertook a march from here of two hundred miles with the greatest alacrity." [10] He commented:

"Nothing can surpass the impatience of the troops from the New England colonies to get to their firesides."

Montgomery joined Arnold before Quebec and the combined army of less than a thousand men challenged Carleton to come out and fight. He wisely preferred to let the winter fight the scarecrows for him. So the two wild generals resolved to storm the city, and chose a bitter night of blizzard for the surprise. Montgomery was killed and Arnold had his leg shattered. Morgan got lost in the crooked streets and was captured, weeping with rage. Four hundred and twenty-six men surrendered.

Fate was saving Arnold for another immortality, but as he lay blazing with fever and pain in his icy tent and thought of the cowardice of the home-seeking heroes there must have begun in his soul a festering contempt for the poltroons who would not follow him to battle but afterward followed him with investigations.

General Carleton suffered the wreck of the two American armies to lie out and freeze and plead for reinforcements while he kept his own uncertain troops warm for more important days, and thereby saved Canada to the Empire.

The anxious Washington received the news through General Schuyler:

"I wish I had no occasion to send my dear General this melancholy account. My amiable friend, the gallant Montgomery, is no more; the brave Arnold is wounded; and we have met with a severe check in an unsuccessful attempt on Quebec. May Heaven be graciously pleased that the misfortune may terminate here! I tremble for our people in Canada; and nothing, my dear Sir, seems left to prevent the most fatal consequences, but an immediate re-enforcement that is nowhere to be had but from you." [11]

From Arnold came a description of the defeat and the disgraceful conduct even of some of the men who had been brave enough to attempt the assault:

"Our loss and repulse struck an amazing panic into both officers and men, and, had the enemy improved their advantage, our affairs here must have been entirely ruined. It was not in my power to prevail on the officers to attempt saving our mortars, which had been placed in St. Roque's. Of course they fell into the hands of the enemy. Upwards of one hundred officers and soldiers instantly set off for Montreal, and it was with the greatest difficulty I could persuade the rest to make a stand. . . .

"Our finances are very low. However, I hope we shall be able to rub along. . . . I wait with great anxiety the arrival of a re-enforcement from below. I have wrote the Honorable Congress my opinion, that five thousand men will be necessary to insure us Quebec, . . . had not the General been basely deserted by his troops, we should doubtless have carried the town. . . .

"I hope soon to have the pleasure of seeing General Lee, or some experienced officer, here. I heartily wish you the protection and blessing of the Almighty." [12]

The irony of being asked for a whole army when he could not fill his own gaps, did not deter Washington from raising three regiments from Massachusetts, Connecticut and New Hampshire and sending them north in the stubborn hope of taking Quebec after all.

He apologized to Congress for presuming to arrange this reinforcement without consultation, humbly asking that his orders be countermanded if they did not please, and adding, "do me the justice to believe that my intentions were good, if my judgment has erred." [13]

So modest a man, and so truly a servant of the people! It is perhaps small wonder that they piled such heavy loads on a giant both willing and meek.

XXVI

HE CREATES AN ARMY AND CAPTURES BOSTON

"THE finger of Providence is in it, to blind the eyes of our enemies," wrote Washington to Reed in the cold January of 1776.[1]

But wherever else that interfering finger of Providence may have been, it was certainly not in the eyes of Sir William Howe, and there is really no mystery at all in his failure to attack Washington's thinly held trenches and redoubts.

What good would it have done?

It would have been, at best, a repetition of Bunker Hill, with a far more devastating loss, since Washington, in spite of his shortage of powder, had a great superiority in numbers and could be endlessly reinforced, while the British could not hope for any replacement at all of men killed or wounded, and would move farther and farther from their base, where their own supplies were dwindling rapidly.

If Howe defeated Washington easily and drove the Yankees off in wild panic, what then?

He could do nothing to make good his victory, for he had no horses to pull his supply train or his guns. He had not forgotten that Braddock had met with ruinous delays, and Forbes' expedition had been all but stopped short for lack of horses of any quality.

If he had his horses, where would he get forage for them? The inability to secure horses and forage was Howe's explanation of his indolence in pursuit, and a large element in the failure of the British throughout the war, preventing mobility in attack and often rendering pursuit impossible.[2]

Washington always had trouble enough securing horses

and forage, but he had other advantages the British could not share.

So Howe wisely refused to smash his small army on Washington's breastworks.

He kept up a pretence of cannonade and preparation for attack to fool the Americans and his own men, while he awaited orders from home and the opportunity to leave Boston as soon as he could secure sea-carriage.

He had to wait transports, not only for his men, but for the loyalists, whom he had not the heart to leave behind him.

As Burgoyne had put it (in his memorandum to Gage in August), leaving Boston included the evacuation of

"All the inhabitants who may claim the protection of Government, many of whom are gentlemen's families with a numerous train of women, children, and servants, together with all the merchandise, computed at the value of three hundred thousand pounds, and which it is conceived ought on no account be left to the enemy.

"All these persons and articles combined would make the fleet immense—not an armament but a colony afloat—and that too at an advanced season of the year (for so it must be before the preparations could be made, and still later if an answer to the plan must be awaited for from England), and not a single friendly port to take shelter in case of tempestuous weather; a return to Boston would be impracticable." [3]

It is so easy to ridicule the British officers from a distance across the horizon of their final defeat, that few American historians have done anything else.

It is the duty and the wisdom of the historian as of a general to put himself in his enemy's place. It takes very little investigation to realize the why of Gage's and Howe's failure to attack Washington, and the wherefore of their activities and inactivities. These were only a masquerade to kill time and disguise the expedition to New York.

In his desperation over the Canadian débâcle, Washington once more sought for release of his pent-up emotions through an attack on Boston. But again his council of war voted him down, and he would not overrule it—fortunately.

The powder situation had improved, and a privateer commanded by Captain Manly captured the big "Nancy" with 2,000 muskets, 30,000 round shot, and 100,000 flints—and fresh flints were most important. The British suffered much in their marksmanship from worn-out flints.

The "Nancy" also yielded a 13-inch brass mortar weighing 2,700 pounds, and it was welcomed with "universal joy." General Putnam, "Old Put," straddled it, "with a bottle of rum in his hand, standing parson to christen, while Godfather Mifflin gave it the name of Congress." [4] Putnam also called it the "sow." It exploded at the first fire.

Far better was the gift of Colonel Henry Knox. He had come to Washington, with a request for permission to fetch all the military stores captured at Ticonderoga and Crown Point and since impounded for return to England when the reconciliation was effected. Washington had granted him the authority. Now he plowed through the snows and returned with a magnificent caravan of ox-teams dragging over frozen lakes and through snowdrifts forty-two sledges laden with 14 mortars, 2 howitzers, and 39 cannon.

He had found more ice than he wanted, but to Washington, praying for it so that he might cross to Boston, none was vouchsafed.

Washington sent to Howe a letter of protest against the cruelty of Colonel Ethan Allen's subjection to "all the hardships inflicted upon common felons," and threatened a retaliation on the British General Prescott, who had fallen into American hands, and whom he blamed for inspiring Allen's ill treatment.

Washington expressed for Howe "the highest regard and reverence for your great personal qualities and attainments," but could not refrain from a dig at "the wicked ministry." [5]

He asked for an exchange of prisoners, but the King had forbidden such recognition of traitors whom he was saving for condign punishment, and Howe merely answered with an indignant reference to Washington's indelicacy and insult. Washington asked Congress what he should do with General Prescott to carry out his threat. He swapped General Prescott for one of his own captured generals several months later.

He urged that the pay of the chaplains should be increased. Morning and night services were held in camp, and incessant prayers went up for peace and reconciliation with the King. If the chaplains had been paid according to the success of their petitions—!

He issued order after order demanding cleanliness of the soldiers and their quarters, and asked why the well-paid patriot soldier could not manage to look as well as the underpaid British soldier.

"Why cannot we in appearance also be superior to them, when we fight for Life, Liberty, Property and our Country?"

To the sharp criticism the New Englanders received (then and before and since) from the Virginians and the New Yorkers, they found their own answers and counter criticisms in abundance.

The soldiers resented the floggings, and the officers said Washington and Lee and all the others had done no more than old Artemas Ward; they even said that Washington prolonged the siege to prolong his own importance! [6]

The first of January, 1776, found him feeling that he was getting somewhere. That date has been called "the birthday of the Continental Army." [7] It was a sickly child and hard to raise. Washington issued a general order, saying:

"This day giving commencement to the new army, which, in every point of view is entirely Continental; The general flatters himself, that a laudable Spirit of emulation, will now take place, and pervade the whole of it . . . it is subordination and Discipline (the life and soul of an Army) which next under providence is to make us formidable to our enemies, honourable in our selves, and respected in the world." [8]

In a letter to the President of Congress, he permitted himself a bit of refreshing and well-justified boastfulness:

"It is not in the pages of history, perhaps, to furnish a case like ours. To maintain a post within musketshot of the enemy, for six months together, without   , and at the same time to disband one army, and recruit another, within that distance of twenty-odd British regiments, is more, probably, than ever was attempted. But if we succeed as well in the last, as we have heretofore in the first, I shall think it the most fortunate event of my whole life." [9]

The word "powder" was omitted from the blank space lest the letter fall into the hands of the enemy, who knew well enough how little powder he had, but could not take advantage of the knowledge.

About this time came from overseas the anxiously awaited answer of the King to the petition sent him by Congress. Washington described it thus: "the throne, from which we had supplicated redress, breathes forth vengeance and indignation, and a firm determination to remain unalterable in its purposes, and to prosecute the system and plan of ruin formed by the ministry against us." [10]

To Joseph Reed he used lighter terms, calling it "his Majesty's most gracious speech, breathing sentiments of tenderness and compassion for his deluded American subjects." [11]

By a chance which he calls "farcical enough," on the very day the speech reached Boston he hoisted the new flag adopted by the colonies. It retained the King's colors or the union jack to indicate loyalty, but added thirteen stripes of alternate red and white to indicate the union of the colonies. Washington gaily informed Reed that the British in Boston, recognizing the union jack, took it as "a signal of submission." "By this time I presume they begin to think it strange, that we have not made a formal surrender of our lines."

From the moment he read the stubborn answer of George III, Washington's hopes of reconciliation with England died. Though he had hitherto flouted the very thought of independence, he was converted to it by the King's rebuff, and by Thomas Paine's pamphlet, *Common Sense,* which spread like wildfire through the country, converting tens of thousands who had been cold to the idea, and raising to a blaze the enthusiasm a few men like Samuel Adams and General Greene had long cherished.

As Washington wrote to Reed:

"A few more of such flaming arguments, as were exhibited at Falmouth and Norfolk, added to the sound doctrine and unanswerable reasoning contained in the pamphlet 'Common Sense,' will not leave numbers at a loss to decide upon the propriety of a separation." [12]

The almost hilarious tone of Washington's letter to Reed concerning the first flying of the union flag was quenched even as he wrote it by the knowledge that Admiral Shuldham had just reached Boston with further reinforcements, and by the continued reluctance of his own troops to remain in camp.

"The same desire of retiring into a chimney-corner seized the troops of New Hampshire, Rhode Island, and Massachusetts, (so soon as their time expired,) as had worked upon those of Connecticut. . . . Thus it is, that for more than two months past, I have scarcely immerged from one difficulty before I have plunged into another. How it will end, God in his great goodness will direct. I am thankful for his protection to this time. We are told that we shall soon get the army completed, but I have been told so many things which have never come to pass, that I distrust every thing." [13]

He noted now that the British in Boston were fitting out a fleet and embarking troops, which he supposed were intended to attack New York, so he yielded to the urgent advice of General Charles Lee to send him to Connecticut to pick up such volunteers as he could there and hasten to New York to fortify it and disarm the Tories.

Lee begged Washington not to wait for Congress to consent and he accepted the advice, ordering Lee incidentally to confiscate such "medicines, shirts, and blankets" belonging to the King's supplies as he might find at New York. [14] He explained his act to Congress and begged its approval. [15]

He reverted to despondency when he found that his new army was far weaker than he had imagined, and the militia still vanishing. Worse yet, in spite of all his orders, they carried their muskets off with them.

He wrote to Congress respectfully, but expressed his real anger to Joseph Reed:

"We are now without any money in our treasury, powder in our magazines, arms in our stores. We are without a brigadier (the want of which has been twenty times urged), engineers, expresses (though a committee has been appointed these two months to establish them), and by and by, when we shall be called upon to take the field, shall not have a tent to lie in. Apropos, what is doing with mine?

"These are evils, but small in comparison of those, which disturb my present repose. Our enlistments are at a stand; the fears I ever entertained are realized; . . .

"Our total number upon paper amounts to about ten thousand five hundred; but as a large portion of these are returned not joined, I never expect to receive them, as an ineffectual order has once issued to call them in. Another is now gone forth, peremptorily requiring all officers under pain of being cashiered, and recruits as being treated as deserters, to join their respective regiments by the 1st day of next month, that I may know my real strength; but if my fears are not imaginary, I shall have a dreadful account of the advanced month's pay. . . .

"With regard to arms I am yet worse off . . . so many have been carried off, partly by stealth, but chiefly as condemned, that we have not at this time one hundred guns in the stores, of all that have been taken in the prize-ship and from the soldiery, notwithstanding our regiments are not half complete." [16]

It was then that he wished he had never taken the command, and he broke out with an impatient snarl at the council of war:

"Could I have foreseen the difficulties, which have come upon us; could I have known, that such a backwardness would have been discovered in the old soldiers to the service, all the generals upon earth should not have convinced me of the propriety of delaying an attack upon Boston till this time."

He had seized a few points, gained a little ground, burned a few houses in the outskirts of Boston, but it was well for him that he did not make an assault.

While he fumed, the people distrusted his ability and fastened their hopes on General Charles Lee. The New Englanders were alarmed by his absence in New York, and Mrs. John Adams, who had been profoundly impressed by Washington on his first appearance, now seemed to overlook him entirely, for she wrote to her husband concerning Lee:

"How can you spare him from here? Can you make his place good? Can you supply it with a man equally qualified to save us?" [17]

A genuine grief to Washington was his final loss of Joseph Reed as his secretary. After downright prayers to him to return, he received word that Reed was elected on January 26th to the Pennsylvania Assembly and Washington dismally wrote, "I congratulate you upon your election, although I consider it as the *coup de grace* to my expectation of ever seeing you a resident in this camp again. I have only to regret the want of you, if that should be the case." [18]

Reed left in his heart a void later filled by Alexander Hamilton, who, like Reed, was impatient of the drudgery of the secretarial service and humiliated Washington by his resentment.

At last, in February, 1776, the ice that Washington had longed for formed, and he felt that he must make the assault in spite of the incompleted army, the "amazingly great" deficiency in firelocks and the "little or no powder," of which he had complained. He called a council of his officers and again they refused to sanction his plan. They were wise as the event proved, though the return of February 16th showed that the Continental army had a force of 8,797 men fit for duty, and 1,405 men on hand who could be assigned to regiments. More were coming in and he felt that he could handle the 5,000 men fit for duty in Boston, but powder was sadly wanting, and the fortifications in the town made it impregnable to attack by any such powderless rabble as Washington had on hand.

Very mournful, very meek, is his letter to Congress telling how he was held in leash by his officers:

"The result will appear in the enclosed council of war; and, being almost unanimous, I must suppose it to be right; although, from a thorough conviction of the necessity of attempting something against the ministerial troops before a reinforcement should arrive, and while we were favored with the ice, I was not only ready, but willing, and desirous of making the assault, under a firm hope, if the men would have stood by me, of a favorable issue, notwithstanding the enemy's advantage of ground, artillery &c.

"Perhaps the irksomeness of my situation may have given different ideas to me, from those which influenced the gentlemen whom I consulted, and might have inclined me to put more to the hazard, than was consistent with prudence. If it had, I am not sensible of it, as I endeavored to give it all the consideration, that a matter of such importance required. True it is, and I cannot help acknowledging it, that I have many disagreeable sensations on account of my situation; for, to have the eyes of the whole continent fixed with anxious expectation of hearing of some great event, and to be restrained in every military operation, for want of the necessary means of carrying it on, is not very pleasing, especially as the means, used to conceal my weakness from the enemy, conceals it also from our friends, and adds to their wonder.

"I do not utter this by way of complaint. I am sensible that all that the Congress could do, they have done; and I should feel most powerfully the weight of conscious ingratitude, were I not to acknowledge this." [19]

He bewailed that "a golden opportunity has been lost, perhaps to not be regained again, this year," but he admitted that he had only "24 rounds a man which are less by one half than the Regulars have." [20]

He was the more frantic to attack from the news that came out of Boston indicating that the British were preparing to take ship and sail away, either to New York or Virginia. He wrote Lee to be ready to receive them at New York.

The British had reason enough to want to escape from Boston. They were being destroyed by smallpox, by hunger and by cold. They burned all the church steeples to keep off the winter rigor. They gave farces and entertainments for charity, but their plight was irremediable and rendered all but insufferable by its futility.

As early as the autumn of 1775, a British officer had written home in great bitterness a letter published in the *London Evening Post* Oct. 7, 1775. He said that he had tried three times to throw up his commission without success, that twenty or thirty other officers were eager to do the same, and that the common soldiers swore they would not "sacrifice their lives in an attempt to butcher their friends and fellow subjects." He went on:

"Boston, the metropolis of North America (where we now are, and have been so long cooped up) may very justly be termed the grave of England, and the slaughter house of America. Nothing is to be heard in it but execrations and clamour; nothing is to be seen but distractions and melancholy, disease and death. The soldiery, and inhabitants likewise, I am sure have done sufficient penance here for the sins of their whole lives. The latter are all ruined; many that were worth 16 or 20 thousand pounds, have not a sixpence left; and if any one of them in the anguish of his heart, or the bitterness of his soul, dares mutter any thing like resentment for the loss of his fortune, a distressed family, or a murdered friend, he is immediately thrown into a loathsome prison.

"If we hear a gun fired upon the Neck, we are all under arms in a moment, and tremble least the Provincials should force their way into the town, and put us all to the sword for our cruelty at Lexington, and setting fire to the large, ancient and flourishing town of Charlestown . . .

"With regard to diet, we are obliged to live on salt beef and salt pork, much the greater part of which is as hard as wood, as lean as carrion, and as rusty as the devil. Could we have good beer, it would, in some measure, prevent their pernicious effects and alleviate the hardships we labour under; but that is impossible, our only beverage being new rum or spruce liquor, which soon throws us into the bloody flux, and runs us off our legs in a few days, and has made the remains of our famished army look like so many regiments of skeletons.

"Could you view our hospitals, and see how fast we drop off, your very heart would bleed within you. Thirty bodies are frequently thrown into a trench at a time, like those of so many dogs, no bell being suffered to toll upon the occasion. But the glorious expedition we are upon, is approved of by an all-wise, all-merciful Ministry; and therefore all must be right. Your news-writers, indeed, have had the modesty to assert, that we are in high spirits, and want for nothing; but unless we have a speedy supply of English flour, sheep, oxen, coals, potatoes, porter, cloaths, &c. we shall perish for want of them; . . . 'Tis well for our Generals that we have no where to run to; for could the men desert, I am of opinion that they would soon be left by themselves; but situated as we are, we must unavoidably live and die together." [21]

From Boston on January 15, 1776, a letter was written by "the lady of an officer" lately arrived from Cork:

"No manner of business is carried on here but the military; the five churches are turned into barracks, and the people who have commodious houses, obliged to give them up for the use of the soldiery; all kinds of provisions difficult to be had, and those of the worst kind sold as follows: Mutton 20d. per lb. beef 1s. 6d. butter 2s. and every thing else in proportion.

"In the midst of these horrors of war, we endeavour as much as possible to forget them. There is a very elegant play-house erected here, which we resort to frequently, and which is not without performers of merit. I was one of a number who crouded it the other night, to see a new piece, written by Gen. Burgoyne, called 'The Blockade of Boston'; but just before the curtain drew up, we were alarmed by some firing from the lines, which induced the whole audience to make a precipitate retreat. It turned out, however, a false alarm; but in this situation do we hourly live." [22]

It is generally forgotten that Burgoyne was a successful playwright. The money taken in at the plays was given to the families of soldiers.

On March 3, "an officer of distinction" wrote from Boston:

"England seems to have forgot us, and we endeavoured to forget ourselves. . . . Never troops in so disgraceful a situation, and that not in the least to their own fault, or owing to any want of skill or discretion in our commanders, but entirely owing to Great Britain being fast asleep. I pity General Howe from my soul." [23]

The magnificently abused British ministry was little happier at home. The criticism it endured from the opposing party was devastating. An immense effort was made to relieve the starving garrison in Boston: five thousand oxen were purchased, fourteen thousand sheep, herds of hogs, ten thousand butts of beer, coal and wood, £22,000 worth of vegetables, £500,000 worth of corn, flour and salted provisions, and much other store.

The cost of transport rose with the demand. Unforeseen delays held the ships in port for months, and when they ventured forth contrary winds kept them in the Channel until the storms could gather for their destruction and the ruination of their cargoes. Many sank, many were driven to far-off ports for shelter. Only a small portion of the supplies ever reached Boston. England was learning what it meant to fight across an ocean.

Many of the soldiers, freezing, famished, terrified and slaughtered by the plague, were driven to pillage and could not be entirely restrained, though Howe had them whipped to the extent at times of a thousand lashes. Even the almost milder fate of hanging failed to curb their desperation.

The wives and other camp women shared the hard lot of the men. The wife of one thieving private was sentenced to a hundred lashes on her bare back while she was led through the town at the tail of a cart. Boston had hardly seen such a sight since the half-naked Quaker women had been even worse handled for refusing to go to church.

Howe had had no word from England since October, and he was evidently making up his mind to abandon Boston without waiting for the full amount of shipping desired, when Washington took a step that precipitated the necessity for flight. Washington seized Dorchester Neck and the heights which commanded Boston and made it untenable under bombardment.

This has always been praised as a piece of splendid strategy, as indeed it was. The credit seems, however, to belong not to Washington, but to Artemas Ward, who has been starved out of American gratitude.

His original orders for the Bunker Hill battle appear to have included the assignment of a force to Prospect Hill to prevent the British from seizing Charlestown Neck, the one wise move they did not make after all.[24]

Before Washington arrived at Cambridge to take command, Ward, according to his biographer, Martyn, had three times planned to occupy the Dorchester hills. He never gave up his dream and kept urging it on Washington, who inspected them on February 11th (his birthday by the calendar then in use), and again on the 12th when he was frightened off by an alarm. On February 13th, a detachment of British horse crossed on the ice, raided the Neck and destroyed what houses were there and all the cover that might offer the Americans concealment.

Howe has been criticized for not occupying the place, but he did not expect an attack from the powderless Americans and he was eager only to get away.

Washington apparently was as indifferent to its importance as Howe, and it required the unanimous vote of his council of war to persuade him to agree to Ward's idea. Ward, in the meanwhile, had had his men busily and secretly cutting swamp brush, weaving fascines and gabions, and making a new device known as "chandeliers"—wooden frames in which fascines could be set, picketed down and covered with earth.[25]

Once Washington was persuaded, he grew very impatient. Greene and Sullivan drew up the plans for the occupation, which, like that of Bunker Hill, was to be carried out in one swift night's work. Washington prepared to attack Boston across the ice after all, in case the British made an assault on Dorchester Heights.

At sunset on March 4th, 1776, he ordered the fiercest cannonade that Boston had undergone, in order to divert attention from the attempt on the Heights.

The bombardment was largely bluff, in view of the small supply of powder, but the British replied with three for one and the earth was so shaken that, according to one American soldier, the wells were dried up [26]—he probably meant that their walls were broken and the water leaked out.

While this thunder was roaring from the Roxbury side, the march on Dorchester was led by Brigadier-General Thomas, whom Washington and Lee had shamed out of resigning and who had, nearly a year before, opposed Ward's plan to do just what he was doing on this night.[27]

A covering party of eight hundred men preceded the carts with the intrenching tools and a working party of twelve hundred men; then three hundred and sixty carts followed with the fascines, gabions and chandeliers and bundles of twisted, or "screwed," hay to serve as a screen.

The parade stealthily crossed the marsh and the Neck, dropping the wall of hay as it went. The various points to be seized and fortified were reached and under a bright moon the digging began. The men worked with an astonishing speed and were relieved by over 2,000 men after three o'clock. Artillery was lugged into place. Five companies of riflemen went into ambush down by the water's edge.

While Washington remained at his headquarters to receive reports, his right wing burrowed itself in and, as a last protection to the breastworks, laid along the fore-edge of the abattis of sharp timber, a row of barrels filled with stone and sand to roll down on the British if they tried to climb the steep.

This idea was attributed to General Heath [28] and the British historian, Stedman,[29] gave it credit for rendering the Heights absolutely unassailable. Heath gave the credit to a Boston merchant, William Davis.

Dawn disclosed the gnome-like magic to the British in Boston. They had to admit, as at Bunker Hill, that the Americans were astonishingly quick and clever at intrenchment and fortification.

Washington rode over to look upon the work and found it good. Putnam waited with a fleet of rowboats in the Charles River to attack the town the moment a sally should be made against Dorchester.

Now Washington prayed for an attack. As he wrote Congress, "They will be so galled and annoyed, that they must either give us battle or quit their present possessions." [30] For once he was able to praise the militia, whom he had called out for the big battle. Soldiers poured in with three days' provisions and their spirits were high.

Thousands were always ready to flock to a few days of battle; it was the long steady absence from their farms and families that broke their spirit.

Though Howe had given orders for his army to be ready to embark at 4 o'clock Sunday morning, on seeing the enemy so close at hand, he wanted to fight and Shuldham warned him that the ships would have to move out of the range of the American artillery unless dislodged. An effort was made to organize an attack under Lord Percy, and soldiers were packed on transports, but "a hurrycane," "as violent a storm as was ever known" arose and flung three of the vessels ashore.

The Americans on the bleak Heights suffered horribly in the lashing rain, but went on pushing their lines closer and closer to Boston. Many of them broke down with exposure and the "Fatiegues & Hardships that were underwent." [31]

The three days' emergency men went home, leaving the Continentals to the March weather and the shovel and pick.

Howe was tactician enough to know when he was checkmated, and he let it be known to the people of Boston that if General Washington would not molest him, he would get out as quietly as possible. The citizens let Washington know what Howe had implied, but he declined to take any official notice of it, though he did nothing to molest the British in their pell-mell departure.[32]

This was not at all generosity on his part, as he confessed in a vivacious letter to Joseph Reed:

"The Rumpus which everybody expected to see between the Ministerialists in Boston, and our troops, has detained the bearer till this time." [33]

He told of the British embarkation for attack and how their transports "were drove on shore by a violent storm." He thought that their later agitation was "with a view to move bag and baggage . . . but if we had powder, (and our mortars replaced . . .) I would . . . give them a dose they would not well like."

On March 13th, in order not to call Ward and Thomas from their posts, he rode over and held council with them. The council agreed to fortify Nook Hill and to send at once to New York five regiments and a rifle battalion to reinforce Lord Stirling, now commanding at New York in place of Charles Lee, who had been ordered to the South to defend Charleston, South Carolina, from Clinton's fleet.

Washington wrote to Congress of Howe:

"Notwithstanding the report from Boston, that Halifax is the place of their destination, I have no doubt but that they are going to the southward and, I apprehend, to New York." [34]

He and his council agreed that, once the British were out of Boston, there would be no need of an army to keep them from coming back, and that he and most of his force could "immediately repair to New York," to prevent a British lodgement in that important center.

He issued an order to his troops that, in spite of the apparent evacuation:

"Neither Officer, or Soldier, presume to go into Boston . . . as the enemy with a malicious assiduity, have spread the infection of the smallpox through all parts of the town, nothing but the utmost caution on our part, can prevent that fatal disease from spreading thro' the army, and country, to the infinite detriment of both, His Excellency expressly commands every officer, to pay the exactest obedience to this order.

"If upon the retreat of the Enemy any person whatsoever, is detected in pillaging, he may be assured the severest punishment will be his lot. The unhappy Inhabitants of that distress'd Town, have already suffer'd too heavily from the Iron hand of oppression! —Their Countrymen surely will not be base enough to add to their misfortune."

The evacuation took place on March 17th, which happened to be St. Patrick's Day and important to the great numbers of Irishmen in both armies. They were in nearly all armies, then, for their own distressful country was incapable of lifting her head, and the spirit of "the fighting race" had to be kept alive.

The 17th happened to be a Sunday also. Washington was fond of Sundays. He entered New York on one; Cambridge on one; and now Boston, for as the last British were rowed out to the packed transports, the first Americans marched in, with old Artemas Ward at the head of five hundred men. Putnam's men came over soon after in rowboats.

It was a great moment for Artemas Ward. The shame he had endured for his share in the Bunker Hill attack had a brief compensation. The town did not receive him, however, with flowers and song. Howe had ordered the inhabitants to keep within doors during the embarkation, and "the town presented a frightful solitude in the bosom of a numerous population." [35]

Ward resigned at once on account of age and ill health— saying, "To eat the Continental bread & not do the duty is what I am much averse to." Washington wrote of him rather contemptuously to Reed and to Charles Lee, because of his dread of "removing from the smoke of his own chimney." [36]

Though Ward reconsidered his resignation (at the plea of his men, who loved him) and served for several months, we may grant him his farewell to history in the words of his biographer, Martyn:

"But what if Washington had had his way, instead of Ward? A boat attack, or a musket assault across the ice, on a town 'almost impregnable—every avenue fortified.' Quebec on a larger scale! Suppose the Americans had lost, as at Quebec? Then—a broken army, accomplishing a miracle if it could even hold the enemy within the town. A great moral loss also, which might have obliterated the effect of Bunker Hill. Instead—the enemy driven out of the province, and the American forces, strength unimpaired, free to march to New York." [37]

Washington himself admitted the strength of the city in a letter to Reed:

"Their works all standing, . . . especially that at Bunker's Hill, we find amazingly strong; twenty thousand men could not have carried it against one thousand, had that work been well defended. The town of Boston was almost impregnable—every avenue fortified."

He must have been glad he was not permitted to destroy himself and his army in a doomed assault.

On the 19th of March, 1776, Washington could write to the President of Congress, for once, "with the greatest pleasure." He could even "beg leave to congratulate you, Sir, and the honorable Congress, on this happy event."

With that unfailing graciousness of his that never forgot the most considerate courtesies he included in this letter to John Hancock these words:

"The town, although it has suffered greatly, is not in so bad a state as I expected to find it; and I have a particular pleasure in being able to inform you, Sir, that your house has received no damage worth mentioning. Your furniture is in tolerable order, and the family pictures are all left entire and untouched. Captain Cazneau takes charge of the whole, until he shall receive further orders from you." [38]

Nor did he forget to select only soldiers who had had the smallpox to garrison the Heights against the return of the British fleet, which still rode at anchor. He ordered the rest of his force to stay out until "the Select Men report the Town to be cleansed from Infection," and he ordered every possible precaution taken to destroy the plague. Also, as always, he warned his soldiers not to annoy or plunder the inhabitants, and if insulted "to seek redress in a legal way, and no other."

He found at once that "jealousies and uneasinesses" were springing up again between the Massachusetts men and the others, and that the problem of the few remaining Tories was a delicate one.

Most of the loyalists had besought Howe to take them aboard his ships. Suddenly their security under the mighty ægis of Great Britain had been removed and they scurried about in panic. Howe could give them no room and he had hardly seamen enough for his own transports.

The loyalists, eleven hundred of them, managed to squeeze into such small vessels as could be procured in the harbor and manned by themselves. Among the self-exiles were eighteen Episcopal clergymen—all there were in town, indeed, except one poor Mr. Samuel Parker, an assistant at Trinity Church, who consented to remain behind to prevent the complete eradication of the Church of England. [39]

Nothing could be more pitiable than the situation of the Tories. They were as American as anybody, and far more truly American than thousands of the foreigners who filled the rebel armies. After all, they had at worst guessed wrong. They had simply refused to change their minds with the changing conditions. They had maintained the vows of allegiance that many other Americans kept taking and retracting.

It was fortunate that Tory counsels did not prevail, and it was inevitable that those who turned against England should hate and persecute them as dangerous enemies of the new liberty. But there is no reason for history to hate them or malign them.

Sympathy at least can be extended to the women and children who fled from all that was dear to them and piled into sloops, dories, any sort of craft that could carry them, and faced death in the ruthless gales of March.

To the surprise of all of them, their little bobbing vessels did not founder in the storms and when they reached Nova Scotia, they found not only a kindly people, but an early and unusual spring like a divine relenting.[40]

They were descendants of the Pilgrims and their second pilgrimage found in Canada a new Canaan. They and the thousands of refugees that followed created a race, known for years as the United Empire of Loyalists, that has never forgiven the United States for its persecutions.

America still rings with sympathy for the original Pilgrims driven from cruel England by the oppressor, but it forgets this other phase of the story. Lorenzo Sabine, whose patriotism and the patriotism of whose rebel forefathers is unquestionable, had this to say:

"Among the banished ones thus doomed to misery were persons whose hearts and hopes had been as true as Washington's own; for, in the divisions of families which everywhere occurred, and which formed one of the most distressing circumstances of the conflict, there were wives and daughters, who, although bound to Loyalists by the holiest ties, had given their sympathies to the right from the beginning; and who now, in the triumph of the cause which had

had their prayers, went meekly—as woman ever meets a sorrowful lot—into hopeless, interminable exile.

"I have stood at the graves of some of these wives and daughters, and have listened to the accounts of the living, in shame and anger. If, as Jefferson said, separation from England was 'contemplated with affliction by all;' if as John Adams testified, Whigs like himself 'would have given everything they possessed for a restoration to the state of things before the contest began, provided they could have had a sufficient security for its continuance;' and on the ground of policy alone,—how ill-judged the measures that caused the settlement of the hitherto neglected possessions of England in this hemisphere,—Nova Scotia.

"By causing the expatriation of many thousands of our countrymen, among whom were the well-educated, the ambitious, and the versed in politics, we became the founders of two agricultural and commercial Colonies; . . .

"Dearly enough have the people of the United States paid for the crime of the 'violent Whigs' of the Revolution; for, to the Loyalists who were driven away and to their descendants, we owe almost entirely the long and bitter controversy relative to our northeastern boundary, and the dispute about our right to the fisheries in the Colonial seas.

"The mischief all done,—thousands ruined and banished, new British colonies founded, animosities to continue for generations made certain,—the 'violent Whigs' of Massachusetts, New York, and Virginia, were satisfied." [41]

Washington had a blazing hatred for the Tories. On December 11, 1775, he had ordered a number of them into confinement in the tunnels of abandoned mines at Simsbury, Connecticut, incredibly horrible dungeons eighty feet underground, where the conditions made the Black Hole of Calcutta comparatively merciful and the British prison ships barges of comfort. [42]

There is a positive ferocity in Washington's reference to these poor Boston loyalists in a letter he wrote to his brother:

"One or two have done, what a great number ought to have done long ago, committed suicide. By all accounts, there never existed a more miserable set of beings, than these wretched creatures now are. Taught to believe, that the power of Great Britain was superior to all opposition, and, if not, that foreign aid was at hand, they were even higher and more insulting in their opposition than the regulars. When the order issued, therefore, for embarking the troops in Boston, no electric shock, no sudden explosion of thunder, in a word, not the last trump could have struck them with greater consternation. They were at their wits' end, and, conscious of their black ingratitude, they chose to commit themselves, in the manner I have above described, to the mercy of the waves at a tempestuous season, rather than meet their offended countrymen." [43]

His head did not cool on reflection, for on the next day he repeated his expressions almost exactly word for word to Joseph Reed, with, however, this addition:

"They would have humbled themselves in the dust, and kissed the rod that should be held out for chastisement. Unhappy wretches! Deluded mortals! Would it not be good policy to grant a generous amnesty, and conquer these people by a generous forgiveness?"

This is more characteristic of Washington in general, but his heart soon hardened itself again toward the Tories.

Washington believed at this time, and long afterward, that without Canada, the Revolution must fail. These fugitives from Boston and others who joined them added to the Canadian distrust of the United Colonies a new leaven of wrath that made the peaceful or the forceful conquest of Canada impossible.

Still, at this moment, Washington had earned the privilege of taunting his enemies a little, and of giving himself a bit of most unusual credit. In this same letter to his brother he permitted himself these words for the family comfort:

"I believe I may with great truth affirm, that no man perhaps since the first institution of armies ever commanded one under more difficult circumstances, than I have done. . . . I am happy, however, to find, and to hear from different quarters, that my reputation stands fair, that my conduct hitherto has given universal satisfaction. . . .

"It is a great stake we are playing for, and sure we are of winning, if the cards are well managed."

XXVII

HE MOVES ON NEW YORK——AND THE TORIES

AS the twenty-four-year-old Napoleon won his first fame by driving a British fleet and army out of Toulon in 1793, so the forty-four-year-old Washington made his name a world-word by forcing eleven thousand British soldiers and sailors and a throng of 170 sail out of Boston. In both cases, the royalists suffered heavily. Hood left his allies behind. Howe took his along.

But Washington's triumph was poisoned with anxiety, for the ships did not sail out to sea as he had expected. They lurked ominously in the lower waters.

He wrote to Ward (whom he replaced in command of the city by Putnam and, a few days later, by Greene) that he had "a strong violent presumption" and was "extremely apprehensive" that something was "meditating," and Howe had "some scheme in view & designs of taking advantage of the hurry, bustle and confusion among our troops which he may immagine his departure to have occasioned."[1]

He wrote to Governor Trumbull of Connecticut that in spite of favorable winds the fleet was perhaps unfit for sea:

"But for my own part, I cannot but suspect they are waiting for some opportunity to give us a stroke at a moment when they conceive us to be off our guard, in order to retrieve the honor they have lost, by their shamefull and scandelous retreat diminishing from that Lustre and renown which British armies were wont to boast and justly claimed as their right.—Suspecting them of such motives, I shall not detach any more of the Army than what is gone already; untill they have taken their departure and quitted the Coast."[2]

372

He wrote to Joseph Reed:

"The enemy have the best knack at puzzling people I ever met with in my life. . . . What they are doing, the Lord knows. . . . My opinion of the matter is, that they want to retrieve their disgrace before they go off, and I think a favorable opportunity presents itself to them. They have now got their whole force into one collected body, and no posts to guard. We have detached six regiments to New York, and have many points to look to, and, on Monday next, ten regiments of militia, which were brought in to serve till the first of April, will be disengaged.

"From former experience, we have found it as practicable to stop a torrent, as these people, when their time is up. If this should be the case now, what more favorable opening can the enemy wish for, to make a push upon our lines, nay, upon the back of our lines at Roxbury, as they can land two miles from them and pass behind? I am under more apprehension from them now than ever, and am taking every precaution I can to guard against the evil; but we have a kind of people to deal with, who will not fear danger till the bayonet is at their breast, and then they are susceptible enough of it." [3]

These were almost his exact words to R. H. Lee eight months before.

Two days after, on the 27th of March, he wrote to Congress that the British had vanished from the face of the waters so far as it could be read from Boston. Washington continued to believe that they were bound for New York, which was their logical point of attack, and whither he was eager to be making his way over highways that would make his footmen almost as tardy as the ships that marched against the wind.

It is almost impossible for latter-day minds to realize the nature of war in those days of bad roads or none, and seaways that fought the slow-sailing ships with every trick of wind and current.

When a fleet left a port, it was impossible for anybody

ashore or afloat to say where it would arrive, or when, if at all.

Contrary to Washington's shrewdest guesses, Howe was bound for Halifax. It took him only six days to reach there in amiable winds. He began at once to make ready to descend upon New York.

He had left to Washington, according to Stedman, "250 pieces of cannon . . . 4 mortars, 2,500 chaldrons of sea-coal, 25,000 bushels of wheat, 2,300 bushels of barley, 600 bushels of oats, 100 jars of oil, 150 horses . . . Sir William Howe might have carried with him the greatest part of the ammunition and all the provisions. . . . Besides these, there were other articles, those of bedding and clothing particularly, of which the enemy stood greatly in need." [4]

Better yet, in the absence of all means of communication, some of the belated supply-ships blundered into the harbor or fell into the hands of privateers, and fetched Washington a dazzling amount of belated Christmas gifts. The "Hope," for example, contributed 1,500 barrels of powder, besides carbines, bayonets, and all sorts of tools.

Lieutenant-Colonel Archibald Campbell came along later with 700 Highlanders, who were taken prisoner. Stedman says that Campbell was "treated in a savage and cruel manner" and quotes his letter two years later describing his dungeon "black with the grease and litter of successive criminals."

The British have all too many documents to prove that American mercy was as far from universal as British mercy was.

Naturally, Washington was covered with laurels. Congress ordered a gold medal struck in Paris; his head was on the obverse, and Boston on the reverse, with Washington on horseback in the foreground and a British fleet very much in the background. Around his head was this Latinity:

Georgio Washington supremo duci exercituum adsertori libertatis Comitia Americana.

Around Boston was this:

Hostibus primo fugatis Bostonium recuperatum. XVII Martii MDCCLXXVI.[5]

With an avalanche of Latin that must have dazed him, Harvard made him a Doctor of Laws.—*Georgium Washington, Doctorem utrius Juris.*

But "Doctor Washington" was a title that somehow never stuck.

A vote of thanks was conveyed to him from Congress and an address from the legislature of Massachusetts. To these he replied with the nobility characteristic of him.

While he was at Boston there began that endless array of his spurious portraits. Joseph Reed sent him a ferocious mezzotint made out of fancy by Alexander Campbell, who represented him sword in hand advancing to battle, and Washington commented ironically:

"Mr. Campbell, whom I never saw, to my knowledge, has made a very formidable figure of the Commander-in-chief, giving him a sufficient portion of terror in his countenance." [6]

Eleven days later he wrote to Reed that he might be "amused" by reading what he had come across "in searching over a parcel of papers the other day." It was "a letter and poem addressed to me by Mrs. or Miss Phillis Wheatley. . . . . At first, with a view of doing justice to her great poetical genius, I had a great mind to publish the poem; but not knowing whether it might not be considered rather as a mark of my own vanity, than as a compliment to her, I laid it aside, till I came across it again in the manner just mention." [7]

Phyllis Wheatley was born in Africa and brought to Boston in a slave ship at the age of seven, in 1761. She took her last name from her purchaser, who treated her with great tenderness, and had her educated. She began to write verses and the fame of the first of the negro poets of America spread to England, whence she received complimentary letters from the Countess of Huntingdon, the Earl of Dartmouth, and the preacher Whitefield.

At nineteen, that is to say, in 1773, a volume of her poems was published in England dedicated to the Countess. She married a Boston negro in 1778, with no great success, and died in 1784.

With a native love for big words, she had imbibed the pomposities and artificialities of the period so faithfully that on Oct. 26th, 1775, she sent a long poem to Washington from her refuge in Providence, with a letter in which she said:

"I have taken the freedom to address your Excellency in the enclosed poem, and entreat your acceptance, though I am not insensible of its inaccuracies. Your being appointed by the Grand Continental Congress to be Generalissimo of the armies of North America, together with the fame of your virtues, excite sensations not easy to suppress. Your generosity, therefore, I presume, will pardon the attempt." [8]

The verses are quite as good as many written by famous names of that century—which is after all no guaranty of their inspiration. She sings:

"Celestial choir! enthron'd in realms of light,
Columbia's scenes of glorious toils I write.
While freedom's cause her anxious breast alarms,
She flashes dreadful in refulgent arms. . . .
    The goddess comes, she moves divinely fair.
Olive and laurel binds her golden hair:
Wherever shines this native of the skies,
Unnumber'd charms and recent graces rise.
    Muse! how propitious while my pen relates
How pour her armies through a thousand gates;

As when Eolus heaven's fair face deforms,
Enwrapp'd in tempest and a night of storms;
Astonish'd ocean feels the wild uproar,
The refluent surges beat the sounding shore; . . .
Shall I to Washington their praise recite?
Enough thou know'st them in the field of fight,
Thee first in place and honours,—we demand
The grace and glory of thy martial land.
Fam'd for thy valour, for thy virtues more,
Hear every tongue thy guardian aid implore! . . .
Anon Britannia droops the pensive head,
While round increase the rising hills of dead. . . .
Proceed, great chief, with virtue on thy side,
Thy ev'ry action let the goddess guide.
A crown, a mansion, and a throne that shine,
With gold unfading, WASHINGTON! be thine."

For this sonorous pæan from Ethiopia, Washington wrote a charming acknowledgment to the young negress:

"MISS PHILLIS,

"Your favor of the 26th of October did not reach my hands, till the middle of December. Time enough, you will say, to have given an answer ere this. Granted. But a variety of important occurrences, continually interposing to distract the mind and withdraw the attention, I hope will apologize for the delay, and plead my excuse for the seeming but not real neglect. I thank you most sincerely for your polite notice of me, in the elegant lines you enclosed; and however undeserving I may be of such encomium and panegyric, the style and manner exhibit a striking proof of your poetical talents; in honor of which, and as a tribute justly due to you, I would have published the poem, had I not been apprehensive, that, while I only meant to give the world this new instance of your genius, I might have incurred the imputation of vanity. This, and nothing else, determined me not to give it place in the public prints.

"If you should ever come to Cambridge, or near head-quarters, I shall be happy to see a person so favored by the Muses, and to whom nature has been so liberal and beneficent in her dispensations. I am, with great respect, your obedient humble servant." [9]

Already he had begun to be selected as the namesake of that innumerable list of children, towns, counties, creeks, institutions, and articles of merchandise labelled George Washington, or just Washington.

Counting out certain Catholic saints, no human being has certainly ever had so many human beings of all colors and races named after him. One of the earliest children to lead the van was probably George Washington Robinson, son of Colonel Robinson of Dorchester, baptized on the first Sabbath in August, 1775. On the last Sabbath of October, George Washington Appleton was baptized at Andover.[10] There was no dearth of children coming along.

A diarist had computed in September, 1775, that during the early part of the siege of Boston, England had spent £3,000,000 and killed 150 Yankees at £20,000 a head to gain a mile of ground on Bunker Hill. "During the same time sixty thousand children have been born in America. From this data ———'s excellent mathematical head will easily calculate the time and expense requisite to kill us all, and conquer our whole territory."

And now that mile was lost, and Washington had sent Lord Howe literally to Halifax.

On April 3rd, 1776, he wrote to Benedict Arnold in Canada telling of the departure for Halifax, and warning him that Howe would probably attempt to penetrate Canada on the opening of the St. Lawrence River, and hoping that before that time Arnold would be in possession of Quebec. This must have been bitter reading to the wretched Arnold.

Washington sent him two companies of artillery and two mortars, and said that Arnold's conduct did him great honor.[11]

Then he wrote to Congress the familiar refrain that on account of lack of money, the New England militia "are gone home much dissatisfied." Nine of the regiments that had marched to New York had received only £500 each toward their pay, "and others not one farthing." [12]

He expressed a hope of finding money waiting for him in New York, and in that hope left Boston on April 4th.

Leaving Martha to follow with Jacky and Nelly in the carriage, Washington rode through Providence, Norwich and New London, interviewing Governor Trumbull on the way. He passed many of his plodding soldiers, most of whom were taken on board transports at New London and shipped to New York.

Washington arrived there on the 13th of April and began to inspect the fortifications laid out by General Lee, and he did his utmost to hasten reinforcements into Canada. He took over the home of William Smith as his headquarters.

He wrote to Reed still beseeching his company: "I fear I shall have a difficult card to play in this Government [New York], and could wish for your assistance and advice to manage it." [13]

The inhabitants of New York were soon complaining of the dirty habits of the soldiers quartered on them. Washington issued strict orders for cleanliness and the prevention of "Filth thrown out of the windows," etc.

The situation in New York was very delicate for him, since several British ships were in the harbor, and in communication with the loyalists, who were probably in the great majority in New York, a city then of about 20,000 people.

Washington was amazed at the strength of the Tories. Governor Tryon had been compelled to take refuge on one of the British ships, but he was still a menace and the Howes were so constantly expected that Washington arranged for a series of lookouts to signal their approach.

He wrote to the Committee of Safety of New York, appealing for its aid in crushing the activity of the loyalists, "so glaring, that even the enemy themselves must despise us for suffering it to be continued." [14]

New York had its own Civil War and, as in Boston, what would be called "the better element" was, with some striking exceptions, loyalist to the end and willing to suffer the loss of wealth, of power, even of life, for the King. A multitude of humble people showed the same resolution. Among the Tories were some of Washington's earliest friends in New York: Beverly Robinson, at whose home he had visited, Mary Philipse Morris, Dr. Myles Cooper of the College, and many more.

Another element floated from one allegiance to the other according to the army in power. To this group perjury was a mere convenience.

Those who were genuinely devoted to the cause of freedom toiled in the fortifications, and volunteered for hard duties, civil or military. They were disgraced by an ugly gang that displayed its patriotism in disgusting cruelties to helpless citizens. The Tory element, of course, had also its hoodlums.

Tarring and feathering was a favorite outdoor sport in New York as it was all about the country. At Kinderhook, New York, when a young loyalist at a "quilting frolic" where he was the only man cast aspersions on Congress, the girls, "exasperated at his impudence, laid hold of him, stripped him naked to the waist, and instead of tar, covered him with molasses, and for feathers took the downy tops of flags, which grow in the meadows, and coated him well and then let him go. . . . It is said Parson Buel's daughter is concerned in the affair." [15]

In Connecticut in April, 1776, when a mother had her baby baptized as Thomas Gage in honor of the British general, "a hundred and seventy young ladies formed themselves into a battalion." They marched "to pay their compliments to Thomas Gage, and present his mother with a suit of tar and feathers." But the father drove them off.[16]

With the women rampant, the men were not lacking in ardor. Sometimes there was a certain humor, cruel soever, in their actions, as when they punished a Tory by "taking off his breeches and giving him an absolution, by setting him on ice (to cool his loyalty)." [17]

The Tories caught a Connecticut parson with a parcel of Continental paper money in one of his moccasins and made him eat it and vow never again to "pray for Congress, or their doer of dirty work, Mr. Washington." [18]

On both sides a number of clergymen were killed.

On their way to join Washington's troops, a party of militia laid hold of a Connecticut farmer, made him carry one of his own geese for twenty miles, then tarred him, made him pluck the fowl and feathered him with its plumage.

But there was more cruelty than humor in much of this war of torture. Riding on a rail has always been a subject for hilarity, but when the rail was sharp, the result was often dreadful injury, occasionally amounting to castration.

Judge Jones, who was in New York at the time and endured much obloquy, testifies that Washington approved so much "this inhuman barbarous proceeding that he gave a very severe reprimand to General Putnam, who accidentally meeting one of the processions in the street, and shocked with its barbarity, attempted to put a stop to it, Washington declaring that to discourage such proceeding was to injure the cause of liberty." [19] This, of course, comes from an embittered enemy.

Pastor Shewkirk in his *Journal* writes:

"Here in town very unhappy and shocking scenes were exhibited. On Munday night some men called Tories were carried and hauled about through the streets, with candles forced to be held by them, or pushed in their faces, and their heads burned; but on Wednesday, in the open day, the scene was by far worse; several, and among them gentlemen, were carried on rails; some stripped naked and dreadfully abused. Some of the generals, and especially Pudnam and their forces, had enough to do to quell the riot, and make the mob disperse." [20]

A Dutchman, Peter Elting, wrote:

"We Had some Grand Toory Rides in this City this week, & in particular Yesterday, Several of them were handeld verry Roughly Being Caried trugh the Streets on Rails, there Cloaths Tore from there becks and there Bodies pritty well Mingled with the dust. Amongst them ware C—— Capt. Hardenbrook, Mr. Rapelje, Mr. Queen the Poticary & Lessly the barber. There is hardly a toory face to be seen this morning." [21]

The excesses grew so disgraceful that Congress forbade them and arranged that such Tories as would not take the oath of allegiance should be thrown into prison. Troops were sent to Long Island to disarm the loyalists, who made up almost the entire population there.

Everywhere the loyalists were treated with harshness. Millers refused to grind their corn; laborers would not work for them; fellow churchmen would not sit in church with them; merchants would neither buy from, nor sell to, them; they were denounced in the press; their property wrecked; their coaches burned; their effigies hung in front of their homes. Their very dignity unfitted many of them to compete with the radical rabble. [22]

The Rev. Charles Inglis of Trinity Church, afterwards Bishop of Nova Scotia, describes his own experiences:

"Soon after Washington's arrival, he attended our church; but on the Sunday morning, before divine service began, one of the rebel generals called at the rector's house (supposing the latter was in town,) and, not finding him, left word that he came to inform the rector that 'General Washington would be at church, and would be glad if the violent prayers for the king and royal family were omitted.' This message was brought to me, and as you may suppose I paid no regard to it. . . .

"One Sunday, when I was officiating, and proceeded some length in the service, a company of about one hundred armed rebels marched into the church, with drums beating and fifes playing, their guns loaded and bayonets fixed, as if going to battle. The congregation was thrown into the utmost terror, and several women fainted, expecting a massacre was intended . . .

"The rebels stood thus in the aisle for near fifteen minutes, till, being asked into pews by the sexton, they complied." [23]

Judge Jones describes General Charles Lee as a particularly severe Tory-chaser, saying that he came to New York in February "under orders from General Washington to fortify the city, swear the Tories, and take their property; which orders were as punctually as they were rigorously, wantonly, and cruelly carried into execution." [24]

The Tory picture of Washington is no more favorable as painted by Judge Jones, who, says he, "took possession of the city, converted it into a garrison, pulled down houses, dug up streets, built fortifications, and threatened, robbed, confined, imprisoned, and banished his Majesty's loyal subjects without mercy." [25]

Martha Washington and Jacky Custis and his wife shared the headquarters in New York, and Martha tried to make up her mind to be inoculated. Washington wrote to his brother, that she "talks of taking the smallpox: but I doubt her resolution." [26] In those days the inoculation was not with vaccine virus but with the human virus. They literally took smallpox, not cowpox. A little later Jacky and his wife returned to Virginia, where their first child, Elizabeth Parke Custis, was born. Washington turned over to Jacky the boy's entire estate with no charge for the hundreds of pounds his administration had cost him.

Washington was as much puzzled as ever over the intentions of the British, and he wrote to Congress about his uncertainties and his readiness to accept orders:

"The designs of the enemy are too much behind the curtain, for me to form any accurate opinion of their Plan of operations for the summer's Campaign; we are left to wander therefore in the field of Conjecture, and as no place (all its consequences considered) seemed of more importance in the execution of their grand Plan than possessing themselves of Hudson's River I thought it advisable to remove, with the Continental Army to this City so soon as the troops evacuated Boston, but if Congress from their knowledge, information, or believe, think it best for the General good of the Service that I should go to the Northward, or elsewhere, they are convinced I hope that they have nothing more to do than signify their commands." [27]

The same spirit of not merely willing but eager subordination is shown in his report of a mutiny that he quelled in New York. A regiment was so indignant at the assignment of a lieutenant-colonel that its members began to revolt and desert.

Washington ordered the regiment paraded between two others and harangued it until he "convinced them of their error and ill conduct and obtained a promise for their good behavior in future."

This was the foreshadowing of numberless similar outbursts of independence at its worst, pure Bolshevism that reached such a climax later as denied all authority and threatened the whole fabric of the government.

Through it all Washington was the meekest and the least jealous man in the army. Even in reporting instances of punishment inflicted on abusive and disobedient men and officers, or asking instructions as to filling vacancies, or exchanging prisoners, he could write, even to that Congress which was itself in an alarming and incessant state of mutiny:

"I would here take occasion to suggest to Congress (not

wishing or meaning of myself to assume the smallest degree of power in any instance) . . ." or "Before I have done,· with the utmost deference, and respect, I would beg leave to remind Congress of my former letters." [28]

He reported bad news from Canada, where the three Congressional Commissioners, Ben Franklin, Samuel Chase, and the Catholic Charles Carroll of Carrolton, and accompanied by John Carroll, later Archbishop of Baltimore, had no better luck than the generals. Franklin returned ill after a few days' experience of the coldness of the Canadian heart toward American promises, and the Commissioners advised the abandonment of Canada. But Congress would not yield.

For Canada to join the other colonies at that time would have looked to be the act of infatuation, of insanity. Howe was at Halifax and Burgoyne had brought over an army of fresh troops, including the terrible Hessians.

Outside Quebec the army of the wounded Arnold had rotted away with cold, famine and smallpox. Reinforcements arrived, but instead of entrusting them to the genius of Arnold, Congress sent General Wooster to fail for lack of inspiration. He was replaced by General Thomas of Dorchester Heights, who arrived in time to face the growing British power around Quebec, and see General Carleton come out at last and chase the Americans off in a panic so wild that they left behind cannon, muskets, baggage, sick and wounded. They left their kettles boiling and Lord Percy's men "ate their dinner from them." This must have been the pleasantest meal that Percy had eaten since the day before Lexington just thirteen months before.

Congress ordered a day of fasting, humiliation and prayer for Friday, May 17th, 1776, and the only apparent result of it was the capture by the British two days later of an outpost of Arnold's at The Cedars.

The collapse was so dire that General Schuyler was actually accused of planning it in order to destroy the country. He wrote to Washington that a hundred persons "have had a design to seize me as a Tory, and perhaps still have. There never was a man so infamously scandalized and ill-treated as I am." [29]

But Washington's trust in him was not diminished and he assured Schuyler that he regarded the charge "with an eye of disbelief, and sentiments of detestation and abhorrence." He sent to Schuyler other charges filed against him as an example of "the diabolical and Insidious Arts and Schemes carrying on by the Tories, and friends of government, to raise distrust, dissensions, and divisions among us." [30]

Disheartened by the situation, Congress called its obedient general to Philadelphia for a conference, President Hancock adding his hospitality to the summons:

"I request the favor, that you will please to honor me with your and your lady's company at my house, where I have a bed at your service."

When Hancock learned that Martha planned to take the inoculation in Philadelphia he did not shrink, but offered her the privilege of being "as retired as she pleases, and Mrs. Hancock will esteem it to have Mrs. Washington inoculated in her house." [31]

Mrs. Hancock was the delightful Dorothy Quincy, a bride of less than a year. The Washingtons declined, however, and stopped at an inn.

General Putnam was placed in command of New York with urgent orders to expedite the fortifications on Long Island, and in the Highlands of the Hudson, and to be ready to crush any uprisings of the restless Tories, many of whom were supposed to be in the ranks, stirring up a general mutiny. [32]

Martha went with her husband when he left New York, May 21, 1776. He examined the works on Staten Island,

and on the Jersey Shore. They slept at Perth Amboy and reached Philadelphia May 23. Washington went into sessions with a special committee day after day, while Martha (who had been vaccinated before she left New York by Dr. John Morgan, director general of the army hospitals) awaited the outcome. Two weeks later, Washington was able to write to his brother:

"Mrs. Washington is now under inoculation in this city; and will, I expect, have the smallpox favorably. This is the thirteenth day, and she has very few pustules. She would have written to my sister, but thought it prudent not to do so, notwithstanding there could be but little danger in conveying the infection in this manner. She joins me in love to you, her, and all the little ones. I am, with every sentiment of regard, dear Sir, your most affectionate brother."

In the meanwhile the question of independence was seething. Virginia took a definite stand on May 15th, when its convention unanimously resolved to instruct its delegates in Congress to propose "to that respectable body to declare the Colonies free and independent States, absolved from all allegiance to, or dependence upon, the Crown or Parliament of Great Britain."

Washington was delighted by "so noble a vote," but he wrote to his brother his anxiety lest Virginia compromise on another defective constitution. "Every man should consider that he is lending his aid to frame a constitution, which is to render millions happy or miserable, and that a matter of such moment cannot be the work of a day."[33]

His vision was gaining grandeur, but he could hardly have imagined that the United Colonies would not be able even to "patch up some kind of a constitution" until after seven years of war and five years of wrangling had passed over their unhappy heads.

The action of Virginia promptly aroused the violent hostility of several other colonies.

The committee of five appointed to confer with Washington, Gates and Mifflin included R. H. Lee and John Adams. It was promptly enlarged to fifteen. Its resolutions included a strong belief that Canada must be reconquered and that it was "expedient to engage the Indians in the service of the United Colonies."

Washington managed at last to secure the company of Joseph Reed by getting him the appointment of Adjutant General. He pleaded for a quartermaster general, but did not secure one for months. He set on foot also the formation of a Board of War and Ordnance, the foundation of the War Department. As he wrote June 20, 1776:

"The instituting a war-office is certainly an event of great importance, and, in all probability, will be recorded as such in the historic page." [34]

Washington persuaded Congress to offer a bounty of $10 for each three-year enlistment. And he must have strongly urged independence, for on June 7th, his fellow Virginian, R. H. Lee, as instructed by the Virginia convention, laid before Congress his immortal resolution that the Colonies "are, and of right ought to be, free and independent States."

On June 3rd, Congress had royally informed Washington that he might return to New York at his convenience, and on June 6th he was back.

He left Martha in Philadelphia to recuperate from the smallpox and return to Mount Vernon, but Lord Dunmore was still at large and she did not set out for two months.

Immediately on reaching New York, Washington wrote to General Schuyler that Congress planned to reinforce the Canadian Army and wanted Indians engaged, "though Congress have not particularized the mode for raising and engaging 'em." He thought that two thousand might be enough.[35]

Schuyler glumly answered that he wondered where the Indians were to be found, and doubted that they could be prevented from joining the British. Congress went so far as to offer the Indians not only good pay, but a hundred dollars for every British officer they captured and thirty for every private. American money, however, was even less acceptable to the Indians than to the Americans. The soldiers rarely got any at all.

Washington wrote to Congress that the troops left in Boston were "almost mutinous for want of pay (several months of which being now due)," and took the liberty to ask once more what was to be done about money.

It was a question that he kept repeating throughout the war, and Congress could never find any satisfactory answer, since the Colonies would give it no authority, and refused to permit taxation.

The phrase, "the news is alarming," also began to be reiterated in all his letters.

Canada was more than a thorn in the side. It was a Niagara of blood and treasure. Reinforcements were poured north by the thousand only to starve or turn black with smallpox, or run away at the sight of the enemy. General Thomas died of smallpox. General Sullivan, who succeeded him, hoped only to die or defeat overwhelming numbers. He did neither. He retreated with the rest.

Even the teamsters conspired to destroy all hope. Several hundred barrels of expensive pork arrived late and ruined because the wagoners lightened their weight by drawing off the brine.

At last the all but indomitable Benedict Arnold despaired, and on June 13th wrote to Sullivan:

"The junction of the Canadians with the Colonies . . . is now at an end. Let us quit them and secure our own country before it is too late." [36]

Sullivan retreated, Arnold gave up Montreal and fell back to St. Johns, closely pursued by Carleton, the brilliant and charming gentleman who "saved Canada"—from the rest of the colonies. Returning for a last survey of the advancing British, he galloped to the water's edge, stripped and shot his horse to save it from British use, and pushed his own boat from shore, "the last man to leave Canada." [37]

So Arnold returned to the scene of his first victory, Fort Ticonderoga, but put on so bold a face that Carleton returned to Canada. Thus Arnold in his very desperation saved the American cause from destruction. Van Tyne says: "But for this delay Burgoyne would have succeeded, there would have been no surrender at Saratoga, and there probably would have been no French alliance. This seemingly petty conflict set going vast forces which soon involved in war half the civilized nations of the world." [38]

No wonder Washington revered the soldier in Arnold, much as his honest soul must have bewailed the hero's inability to keep his books straight.

As an ironical reward for his flawless courage, his flawful financial affairs were soon under investigation and he felt himself outrageously mistreated. He was even ordered under arrest, but General Gates tactfully preferred to dismiss the court. The incident was another preparation of Arnold's heart for his most famous deed.

The northern armies wasted away, but feasting went on in Babylon, and even while the fleet of Howe was creeping toward the harbor of New York, the New York Provincial Congress gave "an elegant entertainment to his Excellency, General Washington, and his suite." [39]

At this affair, no less than thirty-one "toasts were drunk." The very list shows the confusion of mind and the truth of the fact that most of the patriots still believed that the English people were waging a civil war:

"1. The Congress. . . . 5. The protesting Lords. . . .
7. Mr. Burke. . . . 9. The friends of America in both
houses of Parliament. . . . 11. The Whig's throughout the
British Empire. . . . 14. May the strength of the British
Constitution expel the poison of corruption. . . . 23. May
the generous sons of St. Patrick expel all the venemous rep-
tiles of Britain. . . . 28. The memory of the late noble
Lord Howe."

Lord Howe, who was adored by the Americans that
fought under him, and whose death at Ticonderoga in 1758
was commemorated by a monument set up in Westminster
Abbey as a gift from the city of Boston, was the brother of
the new Lord Howe, who commanded the advancing British fleet, and of Sir William Howe, who commanded the
land troops.

Since it would have implied a dangerous Tory mind to
refuse to pledge any of those thirty-one toasts and since the
wine was Madeira, it may well be imagined that not all the
guests could stand up for the last time, and that many of
them must have found their thick tongues muffing the sonorous phrase, "Civil and religious liberty to all mankind."

Old General Putnam was certainly overcome, since Captain Gibbs of Washington's bodyguard, wrote to his "dear
Penelope":

"Our good General Putnam got sick and went to his quarters before dinner was over, and we missed him a marvel,
as there is not a chap in the camp who can lead him in the
Maggie Lauder song." [40]

Washington, however, was used to serial cups of Madeira,
and in all the records of him there is no insinuation that he
ever showed the effects of his countless potations.

Seven days later a soldier was executed for attempting
Washington's assassination—and the soldier was a member
of his own bodyguard.

XXVIII

THE PLOT TO ASSASSINATE HIM

"LAST night was discovered a most Infernal plott against the lives of Gen[l] Washington & Putnem &c—Some of the Villains concerned are in safe custody among them are Mr Matthews our Mayor Gilbert Forbes a Gunsmith, a fifer & Drum[r] of Gen[l] Washingtons Guard &c the particulars are not yet Transpiered, . . . whilst the Regulars made the attack some persons were to blow up the powder house & others were to destroy Kings brige to prevent reenforcements coming in from New England.

"In short the plott was a most damnable one & I hope that the Villains may receive a punishment equal to perpetual Itching without the benifit of scratching." [1]

So wrote the commissary general of the New York troops, Peter T. Curtenius, to Colonel Richard Varick on June 22, 1776. Another echo of the sensation is found in a letter written to his sister by Dr. Solomon Drowne, a surgeon in the American army:

"The whole was discovered (as I am informed) by a serg[t] of y[e] Guards, whom they wanted to take into the Plot, and who, having got what he cou'd from them, discovered all to the General.

"The Drummer of y[e] Guards was to have stabb'd y[e] General. The pretty Fellows are in safe Custody, and I hope I shall be able to give you a better account of them in my next."

Surgeon Eustis wrote:

"Their design was . . . to have murdered (with trembling I say it) the best man on earth: Gen[l] Washington was to have been the first subject of their unheard of SACRICIDE."

The plot against Washington was threefold. He was to be poisoned, stabbed, and turned over to the British to be hanged.

In addition to this, it was said that the city was to be burned, and a powder magazine blown up; a mutiny was to break out in the army, Tory troops were to rise, and a naval attack was to be made on the city up both rivers.

If such a plan had succeeded, the Revolution might have been ended in a night, seeing that the Howes were coming in across the horizon. Nothing, however, is more dangerous in an assassination plot than covering too much territory and enlisting too many participants. Simplicity is of the very essence of an artistic assassination.

In the punishment of such plots the same faults are usual. Too many people are included, and cooling judgment acquits many who may, or may not, be lucky enough to escape execution by excited judges.

There is no reason to believe now that Mayor David Matthews was concerned in the design against Washington. There was not even evidence enough to bring about a trial, and he was sent into Connecticut as a prisoner under suspicion of "treasonable practices." He strove in vain to secure a hearing, and wrote to an old friend, the secretary of the Provincial Congress:

"I have made so many fruitless applications lately that I am almost discouraged putting pen to paper again. Is it not very hard Mr. McKesson that the Convention will not furnish me with some resolve or certificate to enable me to contradict a most hellish report that has been propagated, and is verily believed throughout this Colony, that I was concerned in a Plot to assassinate General Washington and blow up the Magazine in New York? The Convention well know that such a report prevails. They also know it is as false as hell is false. . . . May God only spare my life to meet my enemies face to face." [2]

Washington wrote to Congress:

"The matter has been traced up to Governor Tryon; and the mayor appears to have been a principal agent or go-between him and the persons concerned in it." [3]

Yet there is probably no more justification for the accusation of Governor Tryon than for that of Mayor Matthews.

But cities are panicky things and Judge Daniel Horsmanden, who was still living, could remember the burning alive of twelve negroes and the hanging of eighteen other slaves in New York City in 1741 on a ridiculous charge that they had planned to burn the town. A frightened fifteen-year-old girl, an indentured servant, was the cause of that hola-caust. Her testimony caused also the hanging of a young man for being a Catholic priest, a capital offence in New York until after the Revolution.[4]

The Commander-in-Chief's guard had existed for only three months, having been constituted March 12th, 1776, at Cambridge in a general order, dated the day before:

"The General being desirous of selecting a particular number of men as a Guard for himself, and baggage, The Colonel, or Commanding Officer, of each of the established Regiments, (the Artillery and Riflemen excepted) will furnish him with four, . . . His Excellency depends upon the Colonels for good men, such as they can recommend for their sobriety, honesty, and good behavior; he wishes them to be from five feet, eight Inches high, to five feet, ten Inches; handsomely and well made, and as there is nothing in his eyes more desirable, than Cleanliness in a Soldier, he desires that particular attention may be made, in the choice of such men, as are neat, and spruce." [5]

He commissioned Caleb Gibbs of Massachusetts to be captain, and his own nephew, George Lewis, to be lieutenant.[6]

When Washington returned from Philadelphia in June, 1776, without his wife, he took up his quarters in the Mortier House, later famous as Richmond Hill, Aaron Burr's country place; and the Guard was established close by.

Near at hand was a tavern kept by one Corbie, and there Gilbert Forbes, a gunsmith, apparently corrupted at least three members of the guard with money. These three were Thomas Hickey, the drummer, Greene, and the fifer, Johnson.

Hickey was an Irishman who had deserted from the British army and settled in Wethersfield, Connecticut.

The affair began in the Serjeant's Arms Tavern, where a certain waiter, William Collier, had his suspicions aroused by the whispering and letter writing of some of the patrons. He concealed himself in a closet and overheard enough to lead him to report the matter to a friend of Washington, who reported it to the provincial congress, which ordered the seizure of Gilbert Forbes. In his possession was found the copy of an Association entered into May 13th, 1776, by a group of men "deeply sensible of the miseries brought on this devoted country, by the wicked artifices of an ambitious faction."

They agreed to do their best to restore the authority of the King, by inculcating loyalty, and exposing the machinations of the "illegal and arbitrary congress," and frustrating their operations.

A number of letters were found, describing the various steps taken and the injuries endured.

Congress appointed a secret committee of enquiry, of whom three did most of the work, Philip Livingston, John Jay, and Gouverneur Morris.

Livingston's son, a clergyman, visited Forbes, the gunsmith, in his cell and by talk of his approaching death and promises of mercy, frightened him into making a confession accusing Hickey and other members of the Guard.

Other testimony brought Mayor Matthews under suspicion, and the committee decided to arrest him.

Washington's authority was asked, and he gave it in an indorsement to General Greene, to send a detail out to Flatbush, where Matthews was arrested at his home at one A.M., and taken in irons to the city hall in New York.

Washington himself is said to have gone out with Captain Gibbs of his guard and other picked men in a midnight round-up, and to have arrested forty persons, including the drummer, the fifer, and Private Barnes of his own guard, also his housekeeper, who was the daughter of the famous tavern-keeper, Sam Fraunces.

Mayor Matthews admitted that he was in touch with Governor Tryon, but utterly denied any knowledge of a plot against Washington. Matthews supposed that the conspiracy concerned gun-running and the arming of the loyalists for self-defence, which was just as legitimate at that time of chaos as the arming of the Sons of Liberty for their own defence.

Mayor Matthews, however, had tried to keep out of the active plotting on either side, and when Thomas Hickey told him he was one of Washington's guards but was eager to serve the King, and was enlisting men for that service, Matthews, according to his own testimony, said he had nothing to do with such enlistments. He refused to look at a list of recruits and said he did not want to know their names. As for Hickey, he "advised him to return to his quarters, for that if he was discovered he would be brought to the gallows; on which he went away and examinant has neither seen nor heard of him since." He also denied all other knowledge.

Hickey, who was said to have been busily engaged with others in the great British industry of counterfeiting and passing Continental money in order to destroy its value, was arrested on that charge, together with Michael Lynch, also of the General's Guards. While in jail he talked with others whom he believed to be of the Tory opinion.

The woman in the case, Washington's housekeeper, was arrested as a blind, for she had given warning to Washington that Hickey had tried to cast her in the rôle of Lucrezia Borgia. She pretended to be sympathetic, and joined the conspiracy in order to learn more of it.

Since Washington was very fond of green peas, Miss Fraunces consented to prepare a dish of them for Hickey to poison. The blood-curdling preliminaries were carried out in the kitchen. Hickey stirred the venom into the dish and Miss Fraunces carried it to Washington, who was in the know.

He made a casual excuse for declining the peas, which must have given Hickey's heart a wrench, followed by another when the dish was thrown out to the chickens and those that gobbled promptly fell over, dead.

The sight must also have interested Washington if he watched it from the dining-room window. The incident does not appear in the court-martial proceedings. It was first described years after by that indefatigable gleaner of legends, Benson J. Lossing,[7] who says he had it from a man who had it from a close friend of Miss Fraunces.

Frail as this evidence is, the attempt to poison Washington may well have been made as Lossing recounts it, and Washington may well have preferred to keep it from the records. Certain it is that Miss Fraunces was arrested and released, and Washington was ever after a close friend of her father.

When the committee reported to the New York Provincial Congress, that body pleaded lack of competence and jurisdiction for such a trial, and turned the matter over to the army. The civil courts, of course, still derived their sole authority from the crown, and, since the authority of the crown was denied and at the moment impotent, there were no courts at all.

It is one of the striking phases of the Revolution that in many communities, life muddled along without law courts, and went so little worse than usual that many of the citizens, like John Adams' horse-jockey neighbor, might have exclaimed, "There are no courts of justice now and I hope there will never be another."

On receipt of the recommendations of the Provincial Congress, Washington appointed a general court-martial. Hickey and the others, however, were tried, not for attempting to kill Washington, but for "exciting & joining in a Mutiny & Sedition, & of treacherously corresponding with, inlisting among, and receiving Pay from the Enemies of the united American Colonies." [8]

At the trial held on June 26th, 1776, William Green testified that he and Hickey went into the plot solely to dupe the loyalists, especially Forbes, the gunsmith, whose "Pulse beat high in the Tory scheme." Green advised Hickey to report the matter, which was merely one of a loyalist revolt, but Hickey said that he would wait until they had made further discoveries.

Gilbert Forbes, however, tried to squirm out of responsibility by declaring that Green had sought to enlist him in the King's service, and urged so persistently that Forbes consented. He gave Hickey "a ½ a Dollar, & this was all the Money Hickey ever receiv'd from me."

William Welch testified that Hickey led him to a grog shop and told him "that this Country was sold, that the Enemy would soon arrive & that it was best for us old Countrymen to make our Peace before they came or they would kill Us all." Welch said he "did not relish the Project, & we parted."

Isaac Ketchum testified that he was already in jail when Hickey was brought in "on suspicion of counterfeiting." Hickey asked why Ketchum was there.

"I told him, because I was a Tory. On this a conversation ensued upon politicks. In different conversations he informed me that the Army was become damnably corrupted; that the fleet was soon expected; and that he and a number of others were in a band to turn against the American Army when the King's troops should arrive, and asked me to be one of them. The plan, he told me, was, some were to be sick, and others were to hire men in their room. That eight of the General's Guard were concerned, but mentioned only Green by name. He further told me that one Forbes, a tavern-keeper, was to be their Captain, but that the inferior officers were not yet appointed, lest the scheme should be discovered."

The rest of the report is blunt and brief:

"The prisoner being here called upon to make his defence, produces no evidence; but says, 'he engaged in the scheme at first for the sake of cheating the Tories, and getting some money from them, and afterwards consented to have his name sent on board the man-of-war, in order that if the enemy should arrive and defeat the Army here, and he should be taken prisoner, he might be safe.'

"The Court being cleared, after mature consideration, are unanimously of the opinion that the prisoner is guilty of the charge against him, and of a breach of the fifth and of the thirtieth articles of the Rules and Regulations for the government of the Continental Forces; and the court unanimously sentence and adjudge that the prisoner, *Thomas Hickey*, suffer death for said crimes by being hanged by the neck till he is dead.

"Samuel H. Parsons, *President*."

And that is all. This short and vague document is manifestly a record only of things for the public to know. It was shrewd policy to suppress any official recognition of the plan to assassinate Washington.

A good deal more is implied in Washington's grim order of June 27th, for the execution of one of his bodyguard, and rumor said that Hickey was a favorite of his:

"After Orders. Thomas Hickey belonging to the General's Guard having been convicted by General Court Martial whereof Col. Parsons was President of the crimes of 'Sedition and mutiny, and also of holding a treacherous correspondence with the enemy, for the most horrid and detestable purposes,' is sentenced to suffer *death.* The General approves the sentence, and orders that he be hanged tomorrow at Eleven o'clock.—

"All the officers and men off duty belonging to Gen'l Heath's, Spencer's, Lord Sterling's and Gen'l Scott's Brigades, to be under Arms, on their respective parades, at Ten o'clock to morrow morning, to march from thence to the Ground between Gen'l Spencer's and Lord Sterling's encampments to attend the execution of the above sentence.

"The Provost Marshal immediately to make the necessary preparations, and to attend on that duty tomorrow—

"Each of the Brigade Majors to furnish the Provost Marshal with twenty men, from each Brigade, with good arms and bayonets, as a guard on the prisoner to and at the place of execution." [9]

The next day, Washington issued a warrant to the Provost Marshal, and at ten o'clock the same morning there was enacted an American "Hanging of Danny Deever."

Besides the regiments "in 'ollow square," it was said that there were "over twenty thousand people present"—which would mean that nobody in New York could have been absent.

The prisoner was led out to a tree in a field belonging to Colonel Henry Rutger, near Bowery Lane at the intersection of the present Grand and Chrystie streets.

An eye witness, Surgeon William Eustis, described the last hour of the first Revolutionary soldier to die the dog's death:

"He appeared unaffected and obstinate to the last, except that when the Chaplains took him by the hand under the Gallows and bad him adieu, a torrent of tears flowed over his face; but with an indignant scornful air he wiped 'em with his hand from his face, and assumed the confident look . . . with his last breath the fellow told the spectators, that unless Gen¹ Greene was very cautious, the Design would as yet be executed on him." [10]

This was not the first of Washington's executions. He believed in the high moral influence of the gallows as well as the resounding lesson of the whip. As the twenty-five-year-old Commander-in-Chief of the Virginia forces nineteen years before, he had begged for months the forbidden privilege of hanging deserters. Before he got the authority he put up a gallows forty feet high and as soon as his prayer was granted, hanged two men.[11]

After the death of Hickey, the Guard was never again suspected of treachery, though various members were often in trouble and were tried for drunkenness, marauding, rioting, striking officers, foul and abusive language, burglary and other offences. Some were acquitted, some imprisoned, some whipped. In 1778, Washington sentenced three of his guard to be hanged, but two escaped.[12]

Following the execution of Hickey, Washington issued this order emphasizing the moral of it:

"The unhappy Fate of Thomas Hickey, executed this day for Mutiny, Sedition and Treachery; the General hopes will be a warning to every Soldier, in the Army, to avoid those crimes and all others, so disgraceful to the character of a Soldier, and pernicious to his country, whose pay he receives and Bread he eats.—And in order to avoid those Crimes, the most certain method is to keep out of temptation of them, and particularly to avoid lewd Women, who, by the dying Confession of this poor Criminal, first led him into practices which ended in an untimely and ignominious Death." [13]

That advice of his to "avoid lewd Women" may have suggested the curious aftermath of this trial, for the sensation did not end with the hanging of Hickey, or the uncertain disposal of the guardsmen, Green, Johnson, Barnes and Lynch, who may have been included in Surgeon Eustis' remark, "We are hanging them as fast as we find them out." There were executions also in Albany in connection with a similar conspiracy against the northern officers.

In England, however, where the propaganda factory was in full blast, the account of the trial seemed as tame as that intercepted letter of Harrison's, to which some unknown artist added the felicitous lines about his regretting that he had not "fitted" the washerwoman's pretty daughter for his General.

Perhaps it was the same impish soul that decided to point up the dull records of the Hickey trial, and inject a little feminine romance into the career of the dull husband Washington seemed.

To certain European minds of that day, a great warrior without a mistress or two was almost inconceivable, and certainly unacceptable. Washington's lack of anything of the sort was repaired by the invention of "Mary Gibbons," whom he "maintained genteely" and visited with his pockets full of state papers, which her other friend copied while the girl from Jersey entertained the general from Virginia.

As soon as possible after the trial, one J. Bew published in London a shilling shocker called *Minutes of a Conspiracy against the Liberties of America*. It claimed to be a reprint of the actual records of the Hickey case as found among the papers of the fugitive secretary of the committee, who left them behind when the British captured New York.

In his ignorance of the real names of the committeemen, the author selected such names as pleased his whim, and put them on the committee. To eke out his chosen number of fourteen, he made up four purely fictitious names. In no case did he hit upon the name of any of the real committeemen. The three men who did all the work were not even mentioned.

He invented also some witnesses, William Cooper, John Clayford and William Savage, and used them for the exceedingly convincing, though altogether imaginary, testimony. According to this, one Jacobus Lawrence, a tavern keeper, had a devoted housekeeper, Jemima, who had told him of the suspicious behavior of certain mysterious customers. So the landlord "made an excuse to go into the room for some gingerbread . . . upon this one of the men said to me, Landlord, we shall never have peace in America till somebody serves General Washington as he meant to serve the plover next season.

"*Court.* Did the others hear him say this?

"*Lawrence.* Yes; and seemed to wait for my answer, I told them by way of drawing out of them all I could, (by the holiness of my oath I meant nothing more) I told them, I wished things were as they used to be, but I did not see how any body dared to shoot so great a man as the General; upon this the man with a snuffy face, jumped up and said there was one who could do that easy enough; and then asked me if a good sum of the old New-York currency would not tempt me to be accessary *if I was sure no harm would happen to me?*

"I asked, where the New York currency was to come from; I was told Mr. Lott had reserved 7000£. which was to be distributed among those who would assist.

"I said, assist, to do what? they said, to murder General Washington and all the Livingstons.

"Upon this I said, that his Excellency was like a saint, and the Livingstons, apostles, who opened the eyes of the people in America, and that I should be afraid of being hanged if I was knowingly to hurt a hair of their heads; upon this the Scotchman shrugged up his shoulders, and all were silent. I was desired to step out, but they soon after called me in again, and one of them gave me ten dollars to swear secrecy, which I was then tempted to do, but am now sorry for it.

"This was the substance of the evidence given in by Mr. Lawrence." [14]

A very English touch, the reference to plover. There is better to come:

"William Cooper, soldier, sworn.

"*Court.* Inform us what conversation you heard at the Serjeant's Arms?

"*Cooper.* Being there the 21st of May, I heard John Clayford inform the company, that Mary Gibbons was thoroughly in their interest, and that the whole would be safe. I learnt from enquiry that Mary Gibbons was a girl from New Jersey, of whom General Washington was very fond, that he maintained her genteely at a house near Mr. Skinner's,—at the North River; that he came there very often late at night in disguise; he learnt also that this woman was very intimate with Clayford, and made him presents, and told him of what General Washington said.

"*Court.* Did you hear Mr. Clayford say any thing himself that night?

"*Cooper.* Yes; that he was the day before with Judith, so he called her, and that she told him, Washington had often said he wished his hands were clear of the dirty New-Englanders, and words to that effect.

"*Court.* Did you hear no mention made of any scheme to betray, or seize him?

"*Cooper.* Mr. Clayford said he could easily be seized and put on board a boat, and carried off, as his female friend had promised she would assist: but all present thought it would be hazardous.

"William Savage, sworn.

"*Court.* Was you at the Serjeant's Arms on the 21st of May? Did you hear any thing of this nature?

"*Savage.* I did, and nearly as the last evidence has declared; the society in general refused to be concerned in it, and thought it a mad scheme.

"*Mr. Abeel.* Pray, Mr. Savage, have not you heard nothing of an information that was to be given to Governor Tryon?

"*Savage.* Yes; papers and letters were at different times shewn to the society, which were taken out of General Washington's pockets by Mrs. Gibbons, and given (as she pretended some occasion of going out) to Mr. Clayford, who always copied them, and they were put into his pockets again."

After learning that these copies were sent to Governor Tryon on board the warship, "Duchess of Gordon," the Committee felt it high time to call on General Washington. As the Court remarked: "It would be but justice to the General, as he is in some way affected by the last witness."

The Committee "had many conferences on the subject with General Washington, and many other officers," but not a soul was tactless enough to express the slightest surprise at finding that Washington was keeping a mistress and not keeping his papers.

The testimony of "James Clayford" is given, but it consisted mainly in protestations of innocence. Other witnesses, however, testified "that he used frequently to boast of his amours with Mrs. Gibbons; that he proposed with this woman's assistance to seize General Washington's person, and carry him off."

Clayford's finish in the court is genuine Drury Lane melodrama:

"*Mr. Byvank.* Have you nothing farther to say in your defence?

"*Prisoner.* I have been treated cruelly, tried without judge or jury; it's nothing but a scheme to punish the innocent, and get clear of honest people.

"*Court.* It is our opinion that you are guilty, and you are to be re-manded to the gaol from whence you came, and we recommend to you to prepare for that death you deserve, and to which you are condemned by the authority of your country.

"The prisoner was then very abusive, calling the court tyrants and murderers, but the guard hurried him away."

In the scene where Mayor Matthews is haled before the cruel tribunal, the opportunity is not lost for some eloquent loyalist oratory, carrying out the second of the two purposes of the forgery, which were: to print spice for sale, and to stimulate dissension among the rebels.

The name of Mary Gibbons is to this day bandied about as evidence of Washington's profligacy. But she belongs among the fabulous heroines in the amazing realm of propaganda.

INDEPENDENCE DECLARED, FOR WASHINGTON TO
SECURE

THE evolution of Washington had gone far and fast.
Passing through New York a year before, he had
agreed with the provincial Congress in "that fondest
Wish of every American Soul, an accommodation with our
Mother Country," and pledged his "every Exertion . . . to
the Re-establishment of Peace and Harmony."

Nine months later, he had returned to New York in exactly the opposite mind, having re-pledged his every exertion to the prevention of reunion with Great Britain, and
despising his former faith. He could now write to his
brother with contempt for those "who are still feeding themselves upon the dainty food of reconciliation."

Once the mood of war possesses the heart, the mere suggestion of peace is an irritant, and Washington, having had
all too much experience of the lethargy of his countrymen,
dreaded the further let-down of peace parleys and appeals
to return to the dear old mother-country.

He was suspicious and resentful of the very approach of
commissioners from England bearing offers of peace. He
looked forward to "a very bloody summer of it" and protested:

"Things have come to that pass now, as to convince us,
that we have nothing more to expect from the justice of
Great Britain; also, that she is capable of the most delusive
arts; for I am satisfied, that no commissioners ever were designed, except Hessians and other foreigners; and that the
idea was only to deceive and throw us off our guard. . . .

no man, that entertains a hope of seeing this dispute speedily and equitably adjusted by commissioners, will go to the same expense and run the same hazards to prepare for the worst event, as he who believes that he must conquer, or submit to unconditional terms, and its concomitants, such as confiscation, hanging, &c., &c." [1]

He wrote thus to his brother during his brief visit to Philadelphia, where he upset completely his former contempt for what he had called "setting up for independency and what not" a year and a half before.

With the rest of the radicals, his hatred of parliament and his love of the amiable misguided George III had turned into a centered rage against the King.

The very moment of the transition is indicated in the letter he wrote to Joseph Reed, on April 1, 1776, in which he ridiculed the flight from Boston of "the king's (I think it idle to keep up the distinction of ministerial) troops." Exactly ten months before, he had written to George William Fairfax concerning the flight from Lexington of "the ministerial troops (for we do not, nor can we yet prevail upon ourselves to call them the King's troops)." [2]

In Williamsburg, Washington had toasted the King and the Queen with the others. In New York he requested the person not to pray so violently for the King. A little later, in Williamsburg, Nicholas Creswell would note a still further progress in the attitude toward royalty:

"Dined at Williamsburg with two Colonels, 5 Majors, 7 Captains, and a number of inferior Officers. The Grace: G—d D—m the King of England, by Colnl. Innis, for the Military dinner. I paid 27s. D—m the Military and the times together." [3]

Realizing the benumbing influence of reopening the reconciliation proposals, Adams, Jefferson and the other radicals felt that they must act at once, before it was too late.

It was, therefore, a fear of peace that forced through the Declaration of Independence.[4]

Still, the separation had to come, and the ancient regret nursed by Trevelyan and some American historians for the unnecessary split in the British Empire is fantastic in view of the subsequent development of the United States.

At any rate, the radicals felt that the hour had struck, and the cry, "We are forever free!" must be uttered now, though a year before John Adams had said, "that there are any that pant after independence is the greatest slander in the province," [5] and Ben Franklin had said he had "never heard the least expression of a wish for separation,"—not "from any person, drunk or sober." [6] Multitudes now were most solemnly drunk with the new wine.

Even as late as February, 1776, says Allan Nevins,[7] the introduction of the subject of independence into the Provincial Congress of South Carolina "caused such an outburst of indignation that if the radicals had pressed it, the Congress would have dissolved then and there."

There was still almost fifty percent of the Congress ready to revolt from the revolution, and yet not willing to surrender all grievances against England.

The radicals made an absolute tergiversation, then accused the Tories of treason. "Incomparably the strongest words then uttered against the new proposal of Independence," says Tyler,[8] "were uttered, not by American Tories, but by some of the American Whigs."

They pleaded that peace was at hand, everything that had been demanded about to be granted, and freedom forever established under the British constitution. But the radicals were organized. They had a political machine—what came to be known later as a steam roller—and they drove it home over whatsoever bodies blocked its way. The radicals were right in the long run, as often, though they dealt cruelly, as usual, with those who were of a less agile faith, and less contemptuous of consistency.

So, as everybody knows, the Declaration of Independence took its place among the great documents of time. It was not passed on the day of its celebration, and it was not many things that it is thought to be, but it was tremendous and immortal.

Nearly everybody who knows anything about the Liberty Bell knows now that it did not ring out the glad tidings, and was not cracked in that service. But it is still hallowed for what it might have done.

Other cold facts that will never alter the cherished legends are these: "The Declaration of Independence is not the official act by which the Continental Congress voted in favor of separation from Great Britain," says Carl Becker.º That act was the resolution voted on July 2, 1776, "and if we were a nation of antiquaries we should no doubt find an incongruity in celebrating the anniversary of our independence on the 4th of July."

The Declaration has been called "Mr. Jefferson's advertisement of Mr. Lee's resolution." July 4th was devoted to tearing the manuscript to pieces with criticisms and amendments (including the elision of five hundred words) and the final adoption, by all the colonies but New York, of the statement that on July 2nd the colonies had become free and independent States. The Declaration was ordered engrossed on July 19th, and the first signatures were affixed on August 2nd, the last, long after.

The signers' names were kept secret for six months for the better security of their necks.

Many hearts were wrung by the Declaration, for it meant to them exile from the old "home" in England. There were thousands who still hoped to chant, "God save our gracious King."

More important still in numbers and in immobility toward either side was the generally unmentioned and unconsidered, yet immensely weighty bulk of the populace, that did not care very much what was done so long as it was not called away from home to do it—the vague, enormous, eternal *tertium quid* that says, "A plague o' both your houses! give us peace and quiet!"

These people do not ordinarily even speak. Their taciturnity equals their inertia and is the despair of the passionate. Few of them are so amiably expressive as the Philadelphian Graydon [10] describes:

"Mr. John Ross, who loved ease and Madeira, . . . declared for neutrality, saying, that *let who would be King, he well knew that he should be subject.*"

Against such charming lethargy the rebels and the Tories alike were powerless.

On the very day the Declaration was passed, the province of New Jersey adopted a constitution containing a clause rendering its own instrument automatically null and void as soon as reconciliation was secured.

But reconciliation had gone glimmering. A door had slammed that would never be opened, though it seemed often enough in the next few years to be on the point of falling off its hinges.

The best of it was that the creators of American freedom had glimpses of their own greatness. They indulged nobly in what at its worst became famous as "Yankee brag," but at its best has been amply justified.

The classic importance of the Declaration was not lost upon the men who were closest to it. John Adams said that a greater question "perhaps, never was nor will be decided among men." [11]

Never dreaming that the Fourth of July would become

the sacred feast of freedom, he wrote to his wife on July
3rd:

"The second day of July, 1776, will be the most memorable epocha in the history of America. I am apt to believe
that it will be celebrated by succeeding generations as the
great anniversary festival."

Yet Adams could also say in 1822, "There is not an idea
but what had been hackneyed in Congress for two years before." [12] To which Jefferson witheringly replied that R. H.
Lee traced it still further back—to Locke's treatise on Government, indeed; and that though he "turned to neither
book nor pamphlet while writing it," he did not consider it
as any part of his charge "to invent new ideas altogether and
to offer no sentiment which had ever been expressed before." [13]

Hamilton said: "The sacred rights of man are not to be
rummaged for among old parchments or musty records.
They are written as with a sunbeam in the whole volume of
human nature." [14]

But Fitzpatrick designates the Declaration as peculiarly "a
Virginia product, for George Mason's Bill of Rights was
adopted June 12, 1776; Jefferson's Preamble was adopted
(with the Constitution) May 29th, and Lee's resolution of
independence closely approximates the language of Virginia's resolutions of independence which were passed by
the Convention May 15th, the authorship of which rests
jointly in Patrick Henry, Thomas Nelson, Edmund Pendleton and Meriwether Smith." [15]

Though that other Virginian, Washington, contributed to
it nothing of philosophy or literature, all of its authors depended on him to confirm it with his generalship.

In Virginia Doctor, now lieutenant, George Gilmer, had
put it vigorously: "A good soldier is now the most important
character in the state."

Piety as usual adapted itself to war, and many agreed with him in granting a vacation to the inconvenient portions of the creed: "Give thy cloak to him that took thy coat; Turn the other cheek, are proverbial expressions which are not applicable to the present contest. The Scriptures do not, in general, require any acts of kindness to our enemies which are confessedly prejudicial to our own interests."

The call now was: "Let us pray for Washingtons, Putnams, Schuylers, to spring up from the wilds of America."

He regretted that "Gold and wealth, in these degenerate days, may be of service to gain a Ruffian to a Villian's aid," but he called upon the people to face privation boldly, and the women to "animate your husbands to the field of battle. . . .

"Ye tender fair! ye Virgins, whose hearts are on the brink of yielding to the fond one's wish, boldly postpone the mingling Joys, and spurn the lover that would linger in this hour of danger." [16]

These were the Virginians who had sent Washington to Congress to restore England to her old motherliness. Now Thomas Jefferson's pen wrote new duties for his willing sword.

It occurred to no one that Washington was foredoomed to a vital duel with Jefferson. But Jefferson was what Van Tyne [17] calls him, "the life enemy of the tide-water aristocracy," to which Washington belonged. He could not know how literally Jefferson meant some of his grandiose phrases about freedom and equality; that the two would lock horns in later years on those very phrases; and that Washington would be overthrown, along with Adams and the whole school. They were radicals now, but would in due time be rated as hidebound Tories and the enemies of all that they subscribed to in 1776.

Washington's own spiritual biography is written in the history of the Declaration.

The signers of it had forgotten, or chose to seem to forget, what he also had already forgotten: the real causes of the Revolution. As Carl Becker notes: "These 'causes' which the Declaration sets forth are not quite the same as those which a careful student of history, seeking the antecedents of the Revolution, would set forth. The reason is that the framers of the Declaration were not writing history but making it." [18]

He comments on this amazing fact: "In all the controversy leading up to the Revolution the thing chiefly debated was the authority of the British Parliament. . . . Nevertheless, the Declaration does not mention the British Parliament. So striking an omission must have been intentional."

The King bears all the brunt of the war now, and almost the only allusion to Parliament is the word "others"—the King "has combined with others."

The sacred "rights of British subjects," which Washington rose to defend, were also things forgotten, and out of date.

The sacred rights of all American citizens were, in the eyes of many of them, similarly tossed into the dust bin. "The Declaration of Independence proclaimed," says Van Tyne,[19] "not only war with England but a civil war between the Whigs and Tories in America."

The loyalists, who still abhorred what Washington had recently abhorred, rushed to arms to defend from him the very principles that had called him to arms. There grew up a loyalist militia, which was as fickle as the rebel militia, and as apt in shifting its allegiance and changing its perjuries according to the changing fortunes of the British and the rebels. There were regiments of loyalist regulars who enlisted for the duration of the war as well as the Continentals.

Some authorities say that there were actually more American-born soldiers and officers in the loyalist troops than on the other side. It has been alleged that the colony of New York alone furnished more loyalist troops than all the other colonies furnished patriot troops.

Fortescue [20] says that the loyalists made better soldiers and officers than the patriots, and wisely comments that therefore "our admiration is increased for such men as Washington and Greene."

The Tories could honestly declare that they were generally what the rebels had boasted of being, Englishmen; and that "the non-English strains of the back country lent great propulsive force to the movement for independence and republican government." Quoting Joseph Galloway's statement that in the patriot army "there were scarcely one-fourth natives of America, about one-half Irish, the other fourth were English and Scotch," Schlesinger goes on to say: "This statement fails to do justice to the other foreign-born soldiers who fought in the War of Independence." [21]

On the other hand, many English-born officers fought for the patriots and the influence of the recent English immigrant, Thomas Paine, can never be overestimated as a persuasive force in convincing the multitude that anything except independence was an outrage on common-sense.

And now Independence had been declared. All that was necessary was for General Washington to secure it.

As if the Declaration of July 2nd had summoned the spirits, and only evil ones, from the vasty deep, on that same evening, Sir William Howe's transports, after gathering for days in the offing, drew up to Staten Island.

On July 2nd, while Congress was passing the Declaration unbeknownst to Washington, he had issued this order to his troops:

"The time is now near at hand which must probably determine, whether Americans are to be Freemen, or Slaves, whether they are to have any property they can call their own, whether their Houses, and Farms, are to be pillaged and destroyed, and they consigned to a state of wretchedness from which no human efforts will probably deliver them. The fate of unknown millions will now depend, under God, on the Courage and Conduct of this Army. Our cruel and unrelenting Enemy leaves us no choice but a brave resistance, or the most Abject Submission; this is all we can expect— We have therefore to resolve to conquer or die. . . .

"Evening Orders.—'Tis the General's desire that the men lay upon their Arms in their tents and quarters, ready to turn out at a moments warning, as there is the greatest likelihood of it." [22]

The next day he wrote to Congress:

"Several ships more arrived within the Hook making the number that came in then, 110, and there remains no doubt of the whole of the Fleet from Hallifax being now here. Yesterday Evening 50 of 'em came into the Bay and anchored on the Staten Island side. Their views I cannot precisely determine but am extremely apprehensive as a part of 'em only came, that they mean to surround the Island [Long Island] and secure the whole stock upon it. I had consulted with a Committee of the Provincial Congress on the subject, and a person was appointed to superintend the business and to drive the stock off. . . .

"Our reinforcements of militia are but small yet—their amount I can not ascertain, . . .

"I must entreat your Attention to an application I made some time agoe for Flints we are extremely deficient in this necessary article and shall be greatly distressed if we cannot obtain a supply— Of Lead we have a sufficient quantity for the whole Campaign, taken off the Houses here." [23]

Lord Howe, Sir William's brother, soon joined him with a battle squadron, convoying troops direct from England. And General Sir Henry Clinton, returning from his failure to break down Fort Moultrie and capture Charleston, contributed two thousand more men.

"It was an imposing array," says General F. V. Greene,[24] a descendant of General Nathanael Greene's, "more than 400 transports and 32,000 soldiers the largest expedition that England had ever sent abroad; convoyed by 10 line-of-battle ships and 20 frigates, manned by more than 10,000 seamen, and armed with about 1,200 guns, many of them 64-pounders and 74-pounders, which completely outclassed the guns which had been collected with so much difficulty by Knox."

The bungling of the British ministry under Lord George Germaine, the "Secretary-at-War," together with the accidents and weather-whims that no one could overcome, had brought this armada to New York after the best part of the year was gone.[25]

But Howe had been unable to leave Halifax earlier since he could not budge without provisions and the fleet of victuallers was so late that he wrote to Germaine, "I tremble when I think of our present State of Provisions, having now meat for no more than thirteen days." [26]

But now he was here and Washington, on his side had only a motley horde of some eighteen or twenty thousand men, four thousand of them scattered among the forts in New York and up the North river, and nine or ten thousand across the East river on Long Island. Of these, great numbers were unfit or unwilling.

The defence of the metropolis of New York, and the vital artery of the Hudson river was one of the most difficult problems ever faced by a general. Every possible position was easily flanked or taken in reverse by providentially or diabolically arranged waterways, of which the enemy with its vast naval superiority could take full advantage.

Whatever post Washington might occupy was strategically censurable. Whatever he might do would be wrong in advance and in retrospect.

To fight for New York at all was militarily fatuous and futile. To give it up without a fight would be politically fatal.

XXX

HE FACES THE BRITISH ARMADA

JUST twenty-two years before this strange July, the twenty-two-year-old Washington, then a British provincial colonel, had surrendered Fort Necessity in the Great Meadows to the French.

All that the Fourth of July had meant to him till now was the day after that rainy tragedy. On July ninth, a year later, he had turned back in flight from the French, with the dying Braddock in his arms.

On July third, 1775, he had become commander-in-chief of the tatterdemalion troops of all the colonies and was facing the British as a rebel and a traitor. July, 1776, found him just escaped from assassination in a thwarted general uprising of his own fellow-countrymen against him. His heart was bitter, but he remembered past bitternesses as present comforts and reassurances. His dismal old Julys came back to remind him that in spite of all his defeats, he had lived and climbed.

Receiving a letter of congratulation from his old friend, Adam Stephen (who had shared with him the woes of Great Meadows and Braddock's Field), he wrote in an unpublished answer:

"I thank you for y^r Kind Congratulations in the discovery of the vile machinations of still viler Ministerial Agents. I hope the untimely fruit of their Intentions will in the end recoil upon their own heads—all the measures heretofore projected, has done so I think, except in Canada, where an unaccountable kind of fatality seems to have attended all our movements since the death of poor Montgomery. . . .

"I did not let the anniversary of the 3ᵈ or 9ᵗʰ of this Instᵗ pass of without a grateful remembrance of the escape we had at the Meadows and on the Banks of Monongahela.—the same Provedence that protected us upon those occasions, will, I hope, continue his Mercies, & make us happy Instruments in restoring Peace & liberty to this once favour'd, but now distressed Country." [1]

It was not until July 10th, 1776, that Washington received the Declaration of Independence from Philadelphia. He immediately issued an order announcing that Congress had "dissolved the connexion which subsisted between this Country and Great Britain," and calling the several brigades to be drawn up on their respective parades at six o'clock to hear "the declaration of Congress, shewing the grounds & reasons of this Measure, to be read with an audible voice." [2]

He thus indicates his understanding that the Declaration was not the act of separation but the explanation of it.

Several copies were distributed to the higher officers. Washington wrote to Congress that "agreeably to the request," he had caused the reading, "the expressions and behavior, both of officers and men, testifying their warmest approbation." [3]

But the grandson of Joseph Reed says:

"No one can read the private correspondence of the times, without being struck with the slight impression made on either the army or the mass of the people by the Declaration. Mr. Reed in his letters does not allude to it. The truth was, that the Declaration in itself was a mere form. . . . An army of rebels with swords drawn against their King, cared little whether there was a proclamation of independence or not." [4]

The main celebration of the reading took place in a spirited attack on the equestrian statue of King George in Bowling Green. A joyous lynching bee was held. Ropes were thrown about the image of the divinely anointed and it was tumbled from its altar and beheaded by acclamation.

The leaden body of horse and man weighed four thousand pounds, and was run into bullets by the ladies of Litchfield, who made 42,000 cartridges out of it. The gilt head was hung on a pole at Fort Washington, recaptured there and taken to England.

The next day Washington issued an order rather mildly disapproving the destruction of the "statute":

"Though the General doubts not the persons who pulled down and mutilated the statute in the Broadway last night were actuated by zeal in the public cause, yet it has so much the appearance of a riot and want of order in the army, that he disapproves the manner, and directs that in future these things shall be avoided by the soldiery, and left to be executed by the proper authority." [5]

On July 12, 1776, he had to inform Congress that "about half after three o'clock this evening, two of the enemy's ships of war, one of forty and the other of twenty guns, with three tenders, weighed anchor in the bay opposite to Staten Island, and, availing themselves of a brisk and favorable breeze, with a flowing tide, ran past our batteries up the North River, without receiving any certain damage that I could perceive, notwithstanding a heavy and incessant cannonade was kept up from our several batteries here, as well as from that at Paulus Hook. They, on their part, returned and continued the fire as they ran by.

The island is so narrow at that point that some of the cannon balls from the ship passed clear across and fell into the opposite river.

Washington described the panic caused by the cannonade in a letter to the New York convention:

"When I consider, that the city of New York will in all human probability very soon be the scene of a bloody conflict, I cannot but view the great numbers of women, children, and infirm persons remaining in it, with the most melancholy concern.

"When the men-of-war passed up the river, the shrieks and cries of these poor creatures running every way with their children, were truly distressing, and I fear they will have an unhappy effect on the ears and minds of our young and inexperienced soldiery. Can no method be devised for their removal?"

A committee was appointed to remove the people, and numbers of patriots abandoned the city in the same misery that had marked the exodus of the loyalists from Boston. But New York was never the scene of that "bloody conflict" Washington expected.

And now Admiral Howe's great fleet of warships, convoying transports loaded with 10,000 Hessians, came up the Bay from England and joined Sir William Howe.

In spite of the enemy's immense superiority and command of the water, once more, as at Boston, Washington raged to attack and had to be held in leash by his unanimous council. He actually submitted a plan to make a general onslaught on Staten Island. It was only after he had been disciplined repeatedly by his inferiors and dreadfully whipped in the field that he learned to retreat and retreat till he earned the name of the American Fabius. At this time he was Percy Hotspur.

Lord Howe and Sir William were unquestionably devoted to the task of ending the war without imbruing their hands in American blood. And they were cordially welcomed in 1776 by perhaps a majority of the Americans, the loyalists; and thousands of indubitable Americans took up arms and fought with them against the rebels.

The meekness of Lord Howe's approach was dazing to the rebels. In the first place he brought a number of letters of introduction to various American citizens as if he were a visiting author expecting to be invited to tea. Among his letters was one to the new Adjutant-General Joseph Reed, who had been educated in England and had married there a merchant's daughter, Miss De Berdt. From her brother, Dennis, Lord Howe brought a fervent prayer for hospitality.[6]

It was sent into the lines and Reed in a quandary sent it to Congress. Next, Howe sent up a flag of truce to request a conference with Washington. Joseph Reed describes what followed:

"A flag came in from Lord Howe. The general officers advised the General not to receive any letter directed to him as a private gentleman. I was sent down to meet the flag. A gentleman, (an officer of the navy,) met us, and said he had a letter from Lord Howe to Mr. Washington.

"I told him we knew no such person in the army. He then took out a letter directed to George Washington, Esquire, and offered it to me. I told him I could not receive a letter to the General under such a direction.

"Upon which he expressed much concern, said the letter was rather of a civil than military nature; that Lord Howe regretted he had not come sooner, that he had great powers, and it was much to be wished the letter could be received. I told him I could not receive it consistently with my duty. Here we parted.

"After he had got some distance he put about, and we again met him. He then asked me under what title General—but catching himself, Mr. Washington chose to be addressed. I told him the General's station in the army was well known, that they could be at no loss, that this matter had been discussed last summer, of which I supposed the Admiral could not be ignorant. He then expressed his sorrow at the disappointment, and here we parted." [7]

In the allusion to what had been discussed last summer, Reed doubtless referred to Washington's reprisals against Gage who said he recognized no commissions but the King's, and was told that a commission from a free people was better. There was also a little give-and-take with Howe.

Washington wrote to Congress describing the rejection of the "Esquire" letter, and added:

"I would not upon any occasion sacrifice essentials to punctilio; but in this instance, the opinion of others concurring with my own,

I deemed it a duty to my country and my appointment, to insist upon that respect, which, in any other than a public view, I would willingly have waived. Nor do I doubt, but, from the supposed nature of the message, and the anxiety expressed, they will either repeat their flag, or fall upon some mode to communicate the import and consequence of it." [8]

Congress passed resolutions saying that he "acted with a dignity becoming his station." He had demanded respect for his epaulettes, not for himself.

On the 19th of July, 1775, an aide of Sir William Howe called to enquire if the Adjutant-General of the British army might interview "General Washington." This favor was granted at once, and Washington instructed Reed to make notes afterward of what occurred. According to these, the British adjutant, Colonel Patterson, tried to explain that the address, "George Washington, Esq. &c. &c.," was similar to one sent to General Howe by Washington the summer before, and that Howe meant no derogation from the respect due General Washington.

"Your Excellency," he said, " '&c. &c.' implies everything."

"So it does," said Washington, "and anything."

He added: "My letter last summer was in answer to one I received under a like inscription."

Colonel Patterson, who had in his pocket a letter addressed to "George Washington, Esq., &c. &c." took it out, but Washington absolutely declined it. So he delivered his message verbally.

It concerned the captured British General Prescott, who was old and ill and so rigorously treated that he might die. Washington said he always tried to make the lot of captives as easy as possible and retorted that Colonel Ethan Allen and other officers were badly treated.

Colonel Patterson said they were out of Sir William's

department. Then he took up Lord Howe's desire for reconciliation, and said that the brothers "had been specially nominated Commissioners by the King."

Washington answered: "From what has transpired, they have only the power to grant pardons. Those who have committed no fault, need no pardon. We are only defending what we deem our indisputable rights."

"That is a matter that would open a wide field," said Colonel Patterson. "In any case, it was kind of you not to blindfold me as is usually done."

He rose and Washington said:

"Won't you take part in a small collation?"

"Thank you, I had a late breakfast and I must hurry back to General Howe. I am sorry I have failed in my mission."

"Before you go, let me introduce the general officers."

After the presentations, he was led back to his whaleboat, confessing that he was awe-struck in Washington's presence.[9]

Lord Howe said later that, while he might address General Washington verbally, he could not use the expression in writing.[10] This must have been on orders from the King. Nevertheless he eventually took the step of writing to Washington under his proper title.

Howe complained that Congress had spoken in resolutions with great respect of his dead brother, "drawing by manifest inference a contrast between the survivors and the deceased." With "a tear standing in his eye," he sighed:

"I hope America will one day or other be convinced, that, in our affection for America, we also are Howes. My compliments to General Washington." [11]

A thousand pities it is that war and the rankling memories it leaves cast such false lights of hatred and suspicion on sincere gentlemen whom irreconcilable differences separate. The Howes honestly wanted to make peace. Washington and the radicals honestly did not want any such peace as the Howes could offer. They had already snubbed the well-meaning but officious Lord Drummond even more sharply when he had tried in January to effect a reconciliation.

Foiled on every side, the Howes waited only for re-inforcements to try the effect of a good drubbing. They were joined by Lord Dunmore, also by Clinton and Corn-wallis, slinking in from Charleston's nobly defended gates.

Also the Hessians were there.

The Americans had not objected to English employment of mercenaries when they had fought for the colonies against the French, but they were maddened at the atrocity of bring-ing in the Hessians now.

Atrocity it was, but it was first committed by the royal slave-dealer, who sold his own people, saw his peasants dragged from their farms, crowded into transports packed like slave-ships, and shipped across a gale-swept ocean to fight people they had hardly heard of. But they had to fight or be whipped to death, or shot.

The Hessians were told that the Americans would scalp and torture at the blazing-stake all who fell alive into their hands. The Americans were told that the Hessians were Huns from hell, who raped all the women they encountered and burned all the houses they saw.

Propaganda is no new thing, and the Americans did their best to encourage the Hessians to desert the British task-masters and become freemen in a paradise. They printed handbills in German and had them distributed among the Hessians by German spies, offering a thousand acres of land to a colonel, and fifty to a private, as an irresistible tempta-tion. They also offered religious freedom.

The forever clever Benjamin Franklin proposed that these papers be used as tobacco wrappers so that the soldiers could read them before their officers could seize them.

Washington did his part in the distribution, but none of the Hessians came over at this time, though there was that usual trickle back and forth of deserters which seemed never to cease during the war.

It was reported that the Scots Highlanders were in such mutinous humor that "Howe had one shot, hung five or six, and flogged many." They supposed America already conquered and had brought along their churns, their plows, and, of course, their women.

The Hessians at their worst did a good deal of plundering, but hardly more than the Americans.

Their innate savagery is seen in the fact that it was to them that Americans owe the idea of the hitherto unknown Christmas tree. The Hessians set up their first American Christmas tree at Trenton. And Washington hung a present on it.

Their first acquaintance with him roused the superstitious fear of the poor yokels, for in July, 1776, as a return of the compliment paid to the statue of their King by Washington's troops, the British soldiers on Staten Island decided to burn the rebel leaders in effigy. It pleased them to prepare figures of Washington, Lee, Putnam, and the president of Princeton University. Doctor Witherspoon was represented as reading a late address of his. The soldiers tarred and feathered all the other images well, and were just tarring Washington when a rainstorm drove them off.

At night the match was applied and the rest were consumed, but Washington was too wet to burn. The tar on him, however, boiled so furiously that the Hessian witnesses ran away in terror.[12]

All the while Washington was making every effort to build up an army to cope with the invaders. Congress did its best to give him what he asked, and resolved 50,000 men into the service, though Washington could hardly muster

8,000 effectives. It called out 13,000 militia from the northern colonies and originated what was called a "flying camp" of 10,000 to be enrolled from the middle colonies and established in New Jersey. It would have been a useful body, but it never was completed. The name, however, could have been applied to many a camp thereafter.

The militia came in so slowly that Congress created nine new battalions from Pennsylvania, New Jersey and Virginia—created them (in the words of Major Ganoe [13]), "as one would raise his bank account by merely adding figures in his check book."

An auction for men ensued. The colonies tried to raise their own quotas by outbidding the bounties offered for the Continental, or regular, troops. Connecticut and Massachusetts raised the offer by $33.33. New Jersey saw that offer and raised it to $53.33. Connecticut and New Hampshire boosted it to $86.66.

The soldier with a family to think of could choose between taking a $10 bounty for three years' enlistment with the Continentals and $86.66 extra for a few months' enlistment with the state militia. Besides, Congress paid with its own suspicious paper; the colonies with good money while it lasted.

Even a well-meaning patriot might find the colonial service more attractive than the Continental. The larger glory belongs to the few who accepted the longer service and took their chance in the fate of the nation and its money.

At Washington's request, Congress created four new major generals, Heath, Spencer, Sullivan and Greene, omitting the magnificent Arnold and others who lacked personal pull at Philadelphia.

The only riddles now were: where would the British strike, how would they be met there, and with what? Washington must be ready everywhere and he could not be ready anywhere. He and the British faced each other for weeks across the Bay of New York, wondering and waiting.

Francis Lightfoot Lee wrote to his brother, R. H. Lee, concerning the ease with which the two British ships had run up the Hudson River on July 12th:

"It always appear'd to me that our Generals placed more confidence in their batteries than they deserved. It seems probable that Howe will land his Army above King's bridge, & cut off all communications with N. York by land, while the fleet does the same by sea, in which case our Army must starve or attack the Enemy in their entrenchments. I fear such an event is not sufficiently attended to, the defence of N. York seems to engross all their tho'ts." [14]

The criticism is just, and two-edged. Washington had sent Lee to New York to supervise a vast amount of fortification that never was used. The real point at issue was Long Island.

Yet Washington has been harshly judged for fighting there at all, instead of sticking to the mainland. But New York was on an island, too.

Furthermore, the town of New York was so close to Brooklyn and so completely commanded by the bluff in Brooklyn called Columbia, or Brooklyn, Heights that if he had left it unoccupied, the British could have set up their guns there and shot the town to pieces.

Therefore, Washington was compelled to fortify Columbia Heights, and he did so. His cannon threatened any ships that might try to bombard New York or pass up the East River.

Columbia Heights was to New York exactly what Dorchester Heights and Bunker Hill were to Boston. It was, as Johnston [15] says, "the key to the entire situation. Lee considered its position and security of 'greater importance' than New York."

He had written to Washington this wise observation:

"Should the enemy take possession of New York, when Long Island is in our hands, they will find it almost impossible to subsist. . . . What to do with the city, I own, puzzles me; it is so encircled with deep navigable water, that whoever commands the sea must command the town. . . . God preserve you, my dear General, from all disorders, at least until we have trampled Satan under our feet. My love to Mrs. Washington and all the ladies. Adieu!" [16]

In spite of all the critics, Long Island was a logical and necessary point to hold if New York were to be held.

Of course, in an exclusively military sense, the town ought not to have been held. It ought to have been burned and left a waste, as Moscow was. Greene, Lee and others wanted to burn it. But it would still have made a pleasant camp for the British, and the first attempt at its destruction would probably have been met by a wild uprising of all the inhabitants, who were none too fond of the rebels anyway.

When the rumor spread that it was to be burned if lost, the Convention of New York very heroically wrote to Washington, "The Convention will cheerfully submit to the fatal necessity of destroying that valuable city whenever your Excellency shall deem it essential to the safety of this State or the general interest of America." But they hoped that the firing might not be left to "the wanton act of an individual." [17]

Washington answered: "I am so sensible of the value of such a city, and the consequences of its destruction to many worthy citizens, and their families, that nothing but the last necessity, and that such as should justify me to the whole world, would induce me to give orders for that purpose." [18]

Its destruction would have been a confession to the whole world and to money-lending France, that the Americans could not protect their most important town.

A military argument by itself is not necessarily a good

military argument, for waging successful war involves a hundred other considerations. Political strategy is essential, too.

Howe was an ingenious strategist and he ought to have attempted at once what he tried later, what Lightfoot Lee expected in his letter: he ought to have sailed up the Hudson and landed troops to the north of New York. He would have then had Washington and the bulk of the colonial forces tied up in a bag.

Washington had, indeed, been informed by his spies, that the Howes intended to do just that: "They mean to hem us in by getting above us and cutting off all communication with the country." [19]

Still he felt that he must fight. Wars are not won by being afraid of the rules of military grammar.

The Provincial Congress of New York had written to the Continental Congress more than a year before:

"If the Enemy persist in their Plan of subjugating these States to the Yoke of Great Britain, they must, in Proportion to their Knowledge of the Country, be more and more convinced of the Necessity of their becoming Masters of Hudson's River, which will give them the entire Command of the Water Communication with the Indian Nations, effectually prevent all Intercourse between the Eastern and Southern Confederates, divide our Strength and enfeeble every Effort for our common Preservation and Security. That this was their original Plan, and that Gen! Carleton and Gen! Howe flattered themselves with the delusive Hope of uniting their Forces at Albany, every Intelligence confirms, and it appears to the Committee that they will not give up this grand Object until they shall finally relinquish the Project of enslaving America." [20]

Against this crucial attempt the New York Congress had, on July 16, 1776, appointed a secret committee for "Obstructing the Channel of Hudson's River, or annoying the Enemy's Ships on their Passage up said River."

The measures chosen included fire-ships at Fort Wash-

ington, booms at Fort Montgomery, chains at Pollopels
Island, and *chevaux-de-frise* at West Point.

Captain Hazlewood was put in charge of the fire-ships
and he got ready ten rafts, twelve fire-grappling irons with
radiating hooks to be thrown from the yards and catch in
the enemy's rigging; a thousand fire-arrows to be shot into
the sails; slow fuses and combustibles including pine-knots,
cotton, drenched in turpentine, and alcohol.

On the night of August 16th, 1776, the fire-ships made
a descent on the two British warships and their tenders that
had loitered in the upper river since the 12th of July.

General Heath, who watched the spectacle with General
Clinton, described it thus:

"The Night was pretty dark; we soon found that the Gallies and
Fire Vessels were silently moving up with the Tide. After some
Time, and almost immediately after the Sentinels on Board the
English Ships had passed the Word, 'All is well,' two of the Fire
Vessels flashed into a Blaze; the One close on the side of the
Phoenix, and the Other grappling one of the Tenders. To Appearances, the Flames were against the side of the Phoenix; and there
was much Confusion on Board. A Number of Cannon were discharged into the Fire Vessel in order to sink her. A Number of
Seamen ascended and got out on the Yard-Arm, supposed to clear
away some of the Grapplings. The Fire Vessel was along side, as
was judged, near Ten Minutes, when the Phoenix either cut or
slipped her Cables, let fall her Fore Top Sail, wore round and
stood up the River, being immediately veiled from the Spectators
by the Darkness of the Night. The Rose and the other two
Tenders remained at their Moorings." [21]

Washington reported the event to Congress,[22] and more
fully to Governor Trumbull of Connecticut, adding the
words:

"It is agreed on all hands, that our people, engaged in this affair,
behaved with great resolution and intrepidity. One of the captains,
Thomas, it is to be feared, perished in the attempt or in making

his escape by swimming, as he has not been heard of.   His bravery entitled him to a better fate." [23]

In a vivid story written by a participant, Joseph Bass, who managed to escape, the death of Captain Thomas and of a number of women and children and British soldiers was gruesomely established:

"Bass and his Crew made their way to the Shore, while the Panic-struck Crew of the Ketch were seen pouring from their Quarters in the utmost Consternation.   Several of them perished in the Flames, others jumped into the Water, and were rescued by the other Vessels of the Fleet; and the Ketch soon burned so as to part from her Moorings, when she drifted on Shore, and was consumed to the Water's Edge.

"Capt. Thomas was not so fortunate.   He was far in the Rear, and the Light from Bass's Ship showed his Position to the Enemy; who opened a vigorous Cannonade and prepared themselves to meet the Attack.   But, nothing daunted by being discovered, he bore down on the Phoenix, and became grappled with her.   He then applied the Match to the Combustibles, but in such a way that his retreat to the Boat was cut off, and he was obliged to leap overboard to escape the Flames.   Five of his Men were compelled to follow his Example, and not being able to reach the Boat, all perished in the Water.

"Notwithstanding the Phoenix was on Fire in several Places, she was saved from Destruction by cutting away Portions of her Rigging, and slipping her Cables.   In the Attack, the Enemy lost nearly seventy Men, besides some Women and Children who were on board the Ketch." [24]

The work of these fire-ships was in its way as brilliant a feat as the venture of Decatur and his ketch into the harbor of Tripoli in 1804.   Perhaps the fate of those British sailors and their women, the first burnt offerings on the altar of American liberty, may have convinced Howe that the Hudson was too dangerous a road to travel.   At any rate he preferred to move across the narrow water between Staten and Long Islands and give Washington the first American battle in the open.

Unfortunately for Washington, General Greene, the most brilliant of his generals save Arnold, fell ill with swamp fever soon after he was promoted major-general and had to write to Washington that he could not command or even ride a horse. He wrote to his brother:

"Gracious God! to be confined at such a time!" [25]

To supply his place temporarily, Washington turned over the command to General Sullivan, and Sullivan's command to the Earl of Stirling (né William Alexander).

Lord Stirling's title was not recognized in England, but it was dearly cherished in America. Washington never omitted his "My Lord" at the beginning of his letters. Stirling was born in the city of New York, the son of James Alexander, a brilliant Scotch lawyer who had come over as a refugee in 1716. William became a surveyor, and in time surveyor general of New Jersey, so he and Washington must have found many congenial topics.

He was not such a snob as he seemed, for he was as much interested in land speculation as Washington was. Indeed, he revived the long-lapsed title he wore for the sake of certain old grants to an earlier Lord Stirling. The British refused to recognize his claim, and he became one of the ardent radicals of New Jersey. He was made colonel of the rebel militia, having gained his military experience as a commissary and later as aide-de-camp to General Shirley in the French and Indian Wars.

When his activities in 1775 were rebuked by the royal governor, William Franklin, he promptly took the governor prisoner, and had him sent to Connecticut for confinement during the rest of the war.

This Franklin was, of course, Benjamin's by-blow, whom the Rev. Dr. Stiles describes as Dr. Franklin's son "by his first Concubine." [26]

Lord Stirling was called "Drunkard Stirling" by General

Charles Lee, but that was after many things had happened. At this time Lee praised him as "a great acquisition, . . . a most zealous active and accurate officer." [27]

In the lull before the storm whose delayed crash kept Washington on tenterhooks, he took the time to write letters to his wife and to Lund. Of his letters to Martha we know only what she said when she wrote to her sister from Philadelphia, August 20, 1776:

"I am still in this town and no prospect of leaving it. The General is at New York he is very well and wrote to me yesterday . . . that another devision of Hessians is expected before they think the regulars will begin their attack on us. Some hear think there will be no battle after all . . . I thank god we shant want men. The Army at New York is very large . . . I doe, my dear sister, most religiously wish there was an end to the war." [28]

An unpublished letter to Lund Washington, August 19th, 1776, shows that Washington was still at heart only a farmer away from home, thinking of pleasanter things to plant than corpses:

"Dear Lund: Very unexpectedly to me another revolving Monday is arrived before an attack upon this City, or a movement of the Enemy—the reason of this is incomprehensible, to me. . . .

"There is something exceedingly misterious in the conduct of the Enemy.—Lord Howe takes pains to throw out, upon every occasion, that he is the Messenger of Peace—that he wants to accommodate matters—nay, has Insinuated, that he thinks himself authorized to do it upon the terms mentioned in the last Petition to the King of G. Britain— But has the Nation got to that, that the King, or his Ministers, will openly dispense with Acts of Parliament—and if they durst attempt it, how is it to be accounted for that after running the Nation to some Millions of Pounds Sterlg to hire and Transport Foreigners, and before a blow is struck, they are willing to give the terms proposed by Congress before they, or we, had encountered the enormous expence that both are now run to— I say, how is this to be accounted for but from their having received some disagreeable advices from Europe; or by having some Manouvre in view which is to be effected by procrastination.—

"What this can be the Lord knows—we are now passed the Middle of August and they are in possession of an Island only which it never was in our power, or Intention to dispute their Landing on.— this is but a small step towards the Conquest of this Continent. . . .

"There is no doubt but that the Honey locust if you could procure Seed enough, so that Seed would come up, will make (if sufficiently thick) a very good hedge, so with the Haw, or thorn, and if you cannot do better I wish you to try these—but Cedar or any kind of ever Green, would look better, &c. . . .

"As Lord Dunmore and his Squadron have joind the Fleet at Staten Island, you will, I should think, have a favourable oppertunity of sending of your Flour, midlings, ships stuff &c.— Corn will, more than probably, sell well sometime hence . . . remember that the New Chimneys are not to smoke."

He gives minute instructions for the planting of groves, including:

"All the clever kind of Trees (especially flowering ones) that can be got such as Crab apple, Poplar, Dogwood, Sasafras, Lawrel, Willow (especially yellow & weeping Willow, twigs of which may be got from Philadelphia)."

He speaks of "the Hollow by the wild Cherry tree by the old Barn," writes about the collection of certain bonds, and discusses horses, especially one that he will let Mr. Custis use on his payment of a fixed price to be returned if Washington should want the horse, "by this means he will (if it should not prove an absolute Sale) have the use of the Horse and I, the use of the money." [29]

On August 22nd Howe moved at last, and Washington issued this order to his soldiers:

"The Enemy have now landed on Long Island, and the hour is fast approaching, on which the Honor and Success of this Army, and the Safety of our Bleeding Country depend. Remember, officers and soldiers, that you are Freemen, fighting for the blessings of Liberty, that Slavery will be your portion, and that of your posterity, if you do not acquit yourselves like men. Remember how your Courage and Spirit have been dispised and traduced by your cruel invaders; though they have found by dear experience, at Boston, Charlestown, and other places, what a few brave men, contending in their own land, and in the best of causes can do, against base hirelings and mercenaries.— Be cool, but determined, do not fire at a distance, but wait for orders from your officers.

"It is the General's express orders, that if any man attempts to skulk, lay down or retreat without orders, he be instantly shot down as an example, he hopes no such Scoundrel be found in this Army, but on the contrary, every one for himself, resolving to conquer or die, and trusting to the smiles of Heaven upon so just a cause, will behave with Bravery and Resolution." [30]

On that same day, he went across the river to inspect the terrain, but the British contented themselves with occupying Flatbush and reconnoitring.

By a singular irony, the devastating battle did not break till August 27th, the very day appointed by the New York Convention, as

"A day of Fasting, Humiliation, and Prayer to Almighty God, for the imploring of His Divine assistance in the organization and establishment of a form of Government for the security and perpetuation of the Civil and Religious Rights and Liberties of Mankind, and to supplicate his further protection in the war which now rages throughout America." [31]

The Tory parson, Shewkirk, said that in New York, shaken by the thunder of distant battle, and deserted by the troublesome soldiers, this day of fast "was not and could not be observed. . . . As only a few of our people came, we kept only a little meeting in the forenoon. . . . The result of the battle was an agreeable disappointment for all honest men; for what could such a fast signify when men want to pursue measures against the Word and Will of God." [32]

He was a Tory, of course, and, as usual in war, each side solemnly advertised itself the exclusive agent of the deity.

XXXI

THE BATTLE OF LONG ISLAND

NOTHING could be simpler than the strategic story of the battle of Long Island:

The Americans chose to defend a wall of hills with three gates in it. They forgot to shut the third gate.

After having appointed Sullivan to command the troops on Long Island, Washington set Putnam over him and there was confusion as to their exact provinces. Sullivan was angry at the time, but after the battle he was eager enough to deny that he was in command.

Putnam moved the troops out of Lee's fortifications forward to a long wooded ridge extending from Gowanus Bay far to the northeast, and set them to work digging in and building obstacles. But he made no investigation of his outposts.

The outposts on sighting the approach of the British landing parties fell back, burning wheatfields and barns. It was on August 22nd that Sir William Howe declared his intentions and landed without opposition at Gravesend. He put ashore about fifteen thousand men, a regiment of cavalry and forty guns.

Washington sent over six regiments to reinforce Putnam, but withheld further help till he could be sure of Howe's plan.

"If they should attack General Sullivan this day, and should show no disposition to attack me likewise, at the making of the next flood, I shall send such further reinforcements to Long Island as I may judge expedient, not choosing to weaken this post too much, before I am certain that the enemy are not making a feint upon Long

Island to draw our force to that quarter, when their real design may perhaps be upon this." [1]

Three days later Howe brought over most of his Hessians, leaving only a few thousand on Staten Island to protect the place. With about twenty thousand men he now confronted less than half the number, who were, however, posted on high ground.

It would have seemed easy to send ships up the East River behind the American lines and compel the surrender of the whole force, and thus, perhaps have put an immediate end to the war with little bloodshed.

The British believed in the plan, but were hesitant about acting on it. They apparently supposed that the East River was well obstructed, and that the land batteries in New York, Brooklyn and on Governor's Island were dangerous.

An admiral of that time had to realize that he was three thousand miles away from home, and that the stormy Atlantic was a dangerous crossing for a shattered vessel.

Furthermore, he had only his sails to rely on, and the winds would not obey his needs. At this season they ordinarily blew from the southwest and would have given Lord Howe just the steam he wanted to run the batteries and provide the lower jaw of the nutcracker that was to crush Washington. To his disgust, the wind decided to pour down the East River for days with force enough to make his sailing up it almost impossible. The best he could do was to get five ships into New York harbor, where they threatened the town and the right flank of the Brooklyn position, and made Washington keep a large force in New York to repel a menaced bombardment and landing.

Having elected to fight the American army where he found it, Howe extended his line along the base of the American hill-positions and made a great show of preparing just such a frontal attack as the Americans hoped for. The rebels dreamed of another Bunker Hill with a difference, and never suspected that Howe was merely "amusing" them, as the strategists say.

Howe had studied his map and spent four days in reconnoitering, and he knew the lay of the land. There were three highways leading from the Gravesend plains across the hills to the hamlet of Brooklyn and the old Fulton ferry. One, called Gowanus road, followed the coast line at a short distance through a pass at the western end of the rampart ridge, and through the marshes to the river shore. This was defended by Lord Stirling's men.

The middle road, three miles to the East, left the town of Flatbush and climbed the center of the hills and down again on the other side. This road was straddled by General Sullivan's troops, whose left wing under Colonel Miles extended eastward indefinitely but not far enough to reach the leftmost road.

This third road struck northeast from Flatland, crossing the so-called New Lots to Jamaica Pass, where it met at right angles the highway that ran from Jamaica along the ridge and down to Bedford, behind the ridge.

There was still another highway further east, but too far off to count.

The American right flank rested on the water. The American left flank was in the air.

The Jamaica Pass was plainly the gateway to the left flank.

Howe assumed that it would naturally be guarded by a strong detachment, at least, but felt that it was well worth forcing. He decided to go through it in person, with Lieutenant-General Clinton in command of the advance, followed by Lord Percy, Lord Cornwallis bringing up the reserve.

Under cover of darkness, at nine o'clock on the evening

of August 26th, 1776, the British began a long all-night march. Clinton reached the Jamaica pass about two hours before daybreak and made elaborate preparations for an attack. He sent forward patrols to feel out the enemy's positions, and then advanced, as Howe's report states, "with such a disposition as must have insured success, had he found the enemy in force to oppose him." [2]

Prepared to make a grand assault on a little Gibraltar, Clinton could hardly believe his antennæ. His advance patrol reported that the vital pass was held by nobody at all except five sleepy officers who had surrendered in a daze.

Without so much as a gunshot, the left flank of the American position was turned and the way was open unopposed to the rear. And nobody even suspected that the British were marching blithely along behind the lines.

At the extreme right of the doomed rebels, Earl Stirling faced the Scotch Major-General Grant, the same man who had enraged Washington in 1758 on the Forbes expedition, when he took Washington's men with him to attack Fort Du Quesne, lost most of them, and got himself captured. [3] He had been only a Major, then, and was now a Major-General.

He had so far forgotten his own mishaps that when he became a member of Parliament, he had made a speech expressing his contempt for the American rebels, and declaring that with five thousand men he could march from one end of the continent to the other.

By an odd chance, Earl Stirling had been in England at the time and from the visitor's gallery had heard Grant deliver that boast. And now the two men faced each other, with Washington in the background.

Stirling made a speech to his men, told them of Grant's scorn, and said:

"He may have his five thousand men with him now—we

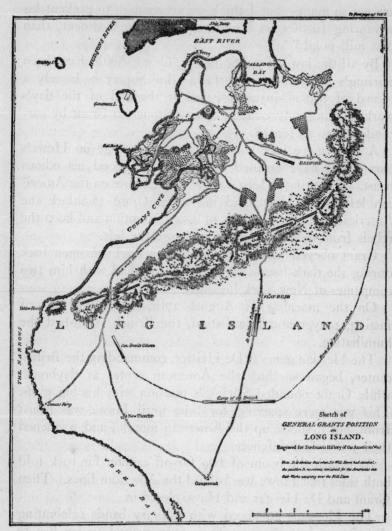

THE BATTLE OF LONG ISLAND.
(From Stedman's "American War.")

are not so many—but I think we are enough to prevent his advancing further on his march, over the continent, than that mill-pond." [4]

By all the laws of poetic justice, Grant should have been Stirling's prisoner by nightfall. But history is largely a record of prosaic injustices, and at the end of the day's work, Stirling only escaped being prisoner to Grant by surrendering to a Hessian.

A little more luck and a little more energy on Howe's part might have enabled Grant to make good his odious boast. Expecting at least a show of resistance on the American left flank, Howe had instructed Grant to attack the American right at midnight to divert attention and keep the rebels from sending reinforcements to the left.

Grant obeyed his orders and drove Stirling's men back during the dark hours. Incidentally he had with him two companies of New York loyalists.

On the morning of August 27th, 1776, the day of fasting, prayer and humiliation, the British furnished the humiliation.

The Hessian general De Heister, commanding the British center, began shelling the American center at daybreak, while Grant pounded Stirling's position with his big guns. This was mere sparring for time until Howe was heard from, but it shook up the American morale, and weakened their unfinished defences.

At length the boom of two far-off cannon far back told both sides that Howe was behind the American lines. Then Grant and De Heister and Howe closed in.

The Hessians advanced with military bands celebrating the victory in advance. They even paused under fire to form line with parade-ground precision. Sullivan's men, caught between two fires, were driven hither and yon like cattle in a blazing corral. Turning to face the British they were driven back upon the Hessians. The Hessians had been especially drilled in bush-fighting and when they had advanced bravely up the forested steep they took cover behind fallen logs or darted from tree to tree like Indians. They were accused of pinning many Americans to the trees with their bayonets and committing savage atrocities. Probably some of them did, but the most authoritative reports credit them with great courtesy to the prisoners, and their own accounts describe their wretched efforts to convince the terrified foreigners that they intended no murder. Otherwise General Sullivan and Lord Stirling might have been listed among the dead.

General Sullivan made desperate struggles to extricate his men from their doom for hours, then tried to hide himself in a field of corn; but the Hessians ransacked the battle-ground like children on a treasure hunt and three grenadiers dragged out General Sullivan.

While the Hessians were mopping up the center, Grant's men were crushing the right. Lord Stirling would have done better to retreat at once, but he made a stubborn resistance for several hours with a mixed force of cowards and heroes.

Colonel Smallwood and his Maryland men arrived late from New York and were sent to his rescue only to be rolled up in his disaster. The bravery of this band was very notable.

Between Stirling's hill position and the fortifications of the original lines stretched bogs and creeks, and ghastly scenes were enacted there among the panic-stricken soldiers floundering through smothering mud and drowning in the waters.

Lord Stirling wandered about among the wreckage of his division for hours trying to stem the tide. Finally, realizing that all was lost, he made an effort to escape by way of the mill dam in the bog, but was cut off by Grant's men. Rather than surrender to him, Stirling fled bravely through the British fire and made his way to the Hessians. He asked for General De Heister, and was politely welcomed.

The British turning movement was ludicrously successful. Colonel Miles, who commanded the left wing and was, theoretically at least, responsible for guarding Jamaica Pass, claimed that he suspected that the British would use that pass, had hired men to patrol it and wanted to march to it at once, but was overruled until too late to do anything.

As for Howe, his men were so impetuous in leaping upon the back of the American lines that he had to restrain them. They chased the fugitives into the fortifications around Columbia Heights, and wanted to go on and finish the job. But, with that obstinate indolence of his, though he was sure they could have succeeded, Howe forbade them to make the try "as it was apparent that the lines must have been ours at a very cheap rate by regular approaches." [5]

Howe has been invariably abused for his efforts at protecting his own men and the enemy from slaughter. In war all standards are topsy-turvied and what is divine in peace is despised in war.

Washington sent over reinforcements but did not arrive on the field till the battle was almost over. He had remained in New York to make sure that the British ships in the harbor were not going to attack the city, against which they made certain threatening movements. Then he had himself rowed over.

He took his post on a conical hill and watched the conclusion of the bloody burlesque, and he is described as wringing his hands in agony of heart and exclaiming, as he saw the annihilation of the Marylanders:

"Great God! what must my brave boys suffer today!" [6]

A soldier, Hezekiah Munsell, who was near him during the engagement, gives this picture of him:

"It has been said by some that General Washington never left his saddle during the day; but I saw him walk along the lines and give his orders in person to the colonels of each regiment. I heard him give orders to Col. Hart, which were much like the following:

" 'If the enemy come to attack us, let them approach within twenty yards before you fire.'

"It was thought to be a stratagem of the enemy to draw our fire, and then force us from the entrenchment; but Washington was too old for them. I also heard Washington say:

" 'If I see any man turn his back to-day I will shoot him through; I have two pistols loaded; but I will not ask any man to go further than I do; I will fight so long as I have a leg or an arm.'

"This is but a scrap of what the brave Washington said on that occasion. He said the time had come when Americans must be freemen or slaves: quit yourselves like men, like soldiers; for all that is worth living for is at stake.

"While Washington was giving his orders to our colonel, there was in the pond, where the mill stood, a man who was attempting to escape from the enemy, an inhabitant of the island probably, who was stuck in the mud. Some proposed to go and help him. Washington said no, knowing that they would be in the same predicament, and thus liable to be taken by the enemy. What became of the poor fellow I never knew." [7]

Another soldier gave this report:

"Gen. Washington rode slowly past the whole of our rear, encouraging the troops. When passing the place where I was posted, he said in an animating tone, (I recollect distinctly his words), 'Remember what you are contending for.' " [8]

The Battle of Long Island was a sad second chapter to his career as Commander-in-Chief. The first had been a story of siege, the brilliant organization of the Continental army and the driving of Howe out of the city of Boston. The second chapter was the return of Howe, Washington's first pitched battle in the open, and complete breakdown at every point.

A Rhode Island captain, Olney, wrote:

"Had it been left to the British Generals to make a disposition of our troops, it is a chance if they would have made it more advantageous to themselves." [9]

As for the behavior of the men, in a mad chaos of glorious individual bravery, valor's better part, discretion, and downright poltroonery, the Americans were killed, wounded, captured, or routed by Englishmen, Highlanders, Hessians, and loyalists.

One of the British generals alleged that the very camp women hilariously joined in the holiday and actually captured prisoners. [10]

The result of the day, according to Mrs. Loring's husband, the commissary of prisoners, was that the British captured 3 generals, 3 colonels, 4 lieutenant-colonels, 3 majors, 18 captains, 43 lieutenants, and 1006 privates. [11]

The British, according to Howe, lost 5 officers, and 56 men killed; 12 officers, 245 men wounded and missing. 1 officer and 20 grenadiers of the marines captured. To the Hessians he allotted 2 men killed, 3 officers and 23 men wounded. [12]

Washington set his loss first at from seven hundred to a thousand, and afterwards at eight hundred. [13] There was a great controversy over his veracity, and he was widely accused of "wilful misrepresentation."

Enough has previously been quoted to prove that Washington was always ready to put out false statements to conceal from the enemy the weaknesses of his army, and often confessed that he constantly had to deceive his own people and even his own officers.

Henry P. Johnston, [14] after a most painstaking analysis of all the returns, states that "Washington's original estimate at its largest limit—one thousand, killed, wounded, and prisoners—was almost precisely correct. Of this there can be no question whatever, the proof being a matter of record."

This is a respectful way of saying that Washington let slip the truth in his haste, and afterwards with great care repeated a falsehood and stuck to it.

But military men like physicians and some others are licensed to tell lies for benevolent reasons.

Johnston also sums up the question of the responsibility for the defeat with the words, "Upon Washington certainly the responsibility cannot rest." [15]

Since he did not arrive until the battle was nearly over, this is technically true. Since his army was outnumbered and in a woeful state of unpreparedness, the responsibility would involve no disgrace.

Brevet-Brigadier General Charles Francis Adams not only places the responsibility on his shoulders, but indulges in criticisms that are interesting for their analytic quality, not to say, their sacrilegious tone:

"When, some years ago, I had occasion to make a study of operations about New York in August, 1776, I was amazed at the mistakes, from a military point of view, of which Washington was then guilty. Even more amazing, however, was the partisanship of the American historians. In their unwillingness to see any blemish in the career of Washington, their narratives amounted to little less than a falsification of history—a literary misdemeanor, not to say crime, for which the only plea in justification possible for them to enter would be lack of technical knowledge. Suppressing incontrovertible facts, they gave credence to absurd stories. . . .

"Washington appears to have disregarded almost every known principle of strategy or rule of tactics, some of them in a way almost grotesque. For instance, while lying on Long and Manhattan Islands awaiting the sluggish movements of Howe, a body of Connecticut cavalry appeared, volunteering their services. Substantial, well-mounted men, they were some 400 in number. Washington declined to accept their services as mounted men, on the extraordinary ground that operations being then conducted on islands, there could be no occasion for cavalry. Men, however, were greatly needed, and he suggested that members of the troop should send back their horses and agree to serve as infantry. When they declined so to do, he roughly dismissed them.

"In reaching this decision it is not too much to say that Washington betrayed a truly singular ignorance of what can not be regarded otherwise than as the elementary principles of military movements . . . the disaster of the 27th of August on Long Island, involving, as it did, the needless destruction of the very flower of the American army, was wholly due to the lack of a small mounted force. . . .

"A British division, under the command of Clinton, made a night move on Brooklyn by the easternmost of the three roads. That road, under any known rules of warfare, even the most elementary, should have been picketed, and watched by a mounted patrol. Twenty-five men would have sufficed; fifty would have been ample. Four hundred men could have picketed the whole of Washington's front, and, holding the enemy in check, have given ample notice of his approach.

"To neglect such an obvious precaution was so unpardonable as not to admit of explanations. As a matter of fact, the road in question was left not only uncovered, but it was not even observed. The American army had no cavalry, its commander having sent the mounted men offered him home on the curiously suggestive ground that they could be of no possible service, as on islands 'horses can not be brought into action.' By this unconsciously innocent remark the trained military expert learns that, at the time it was made, Washington had no conception of the duties and functions of a mounted force in connection with any extended military operations; . . . The disaster was, as I have said, wholly due to the lack of cavalry on Long Island, and a consequent defective outpost service. Yet these facts, so pregnant with both inferences and consequences, are not even alluded to by any historian of the operations. . . .

"The disaster of August 27 on Long Island just failed to bring irretrievable ruin on the cause of American independence. Even as it was, gravely compromising Washington, its influence was perceptible on the whole course of military operations during the succeeding three years. To Washington it was a lesson from which he learned much. Thenceforth he adopted Fabian tactics." [16]

In another work, Adams [17] says the same things and others quite as ruthless. It is undoubtedly true that Washington was not learned enough in war to realize the need of cavalry, but there are other things to consider.

In the first place, there was cavalry from New York on the island, but the New York Congress had sent it away on a cattle drive, as there was a double anxiety: to gather in beef for American soldiers, and to prevent the British from getting fresh beef and milk.[18] There were hired patrols also that failed to do their duty. There were actually five mounted officers at the pass, who let themselves be surprised.

In the second place, Washington declined the cavalry two weeks before the enemy landed on Long Island, and gave as his imperative reason the absolute lack of forage:

"There is not more forage on hand or to be had than is absolutely necessary for the use of our working and artillery horses, and . . . the men can only be a moth and a check to the service, as they cannot act as horsemen in case of action, or if they could, forage could not be found to support them. . . . I would not be supposed by this to discourage the troops of horse from being in constant readiness in the different States . . . they will be much more useful than the militia to throw in succors to a place in an emergency." [19]

He wrote to Governor Trumbull the same things twice:

"Forage is not to be procured; and if it could be, it would only be at a great expense, without a single advantage arising from it." [20]

When the Connecticut men pastured their horses at Kingsbridge at their own charge for "half a dollar per week each," Washington asked Congress to repay the money.[21]

Perhaps there was another reason for Washington's dismissal of the Connecticut cavalry. We have a picture of that body in the memoirs of Alexander Graydon, who took part in the battle of Long Island and, some time before it, caught this glimpse of those horsemen to whose absence Adams charges the defeat:

"Among the military phenomena of this campaign, the Connecticut light horse ought not to be forgotten. These consisted of a considerable number of old fashioned men, probably farmers and heads of families. . . . Instead of carbines and sabres, they generally carried fowling pieces; some of them very long, and such as in Pennsylvania, are used for shooting ducks. Here and there, one, 'his youthful garments well saved,' appeared in a dingy regimental of scarlet, with a triangular, tarnished, laced hat . . . as the general had no use for cavaliers in his insular operations, they were forthwith dismissed. . . .

"An unlucky trooper of this school . . . was taken by the enemy. . . . The British officers made themselves very merry at his expense, and obliged him to amble about for their entertainment. On being asked, what had been his duty in the rebel army, he answered, that it was *to flank a little and carry tidings.*" [22]

Graydon seems to repeat the quaint theory that cavalry could not be used on an island, but it is not improbable that Washington was disgusted by the look of the men. If his snobbery lost him the battle, he never knew it.

One may share Charles Francis Adams' horror at the grovelling flattery of historians and at the strategy of the disaster of Long Island, yet understand why Washington should be rather pitied than scorned.

He had never had any experience in a large command, nor ever any command at all in an important pitched battle. At Braddock's Defeat he had been a messenger only. On Forbes' Expedition he had not encountered the enemy.

Nobody could have confessed more publicly than he did that he lacked experience. He protested it on his nomination, repeated it and repeated it. It was the truth and he could hardly have been counted on to overcome it on his first clash. If he had ever seen cavalry in use, he would not have ignored its value.

If he had inherited the command of a large and experienced body of troops, as did most of the great commanders of the past, he might have done far better, or he might have been legitimately blamed for failure.

Scathing criticism is as cruel to him as the sickening adulation that has been heaped on his military memory is cruel to other officers.

He had not expected to win the battle anyway, but had written to Congress:

"We shall attempt to harass them as much as possible, which will be all that we can do." [23]

As often happens in such outpost actions, the harasser was harassed.

Captain Colby says:

" 'The Battle of Long Island' was not a 'battle' at all in the military sense of the word. It was merely an affair of outposts. The Brooklyn troops met the enemy and were driven behind their fortified lines, with some losses, but not decisive losses. They managed to escape . . . the entire proceeding was but the beginning of that steady withdrawal before superior force that was to characterize the operations of the next few months." [24]

That escape was so perfectly managed and attended with such amazing luck that it has been acclaimed as a masterpiece of retreat. Even Adams [25] has this to say of it:

"That Washington, throughout these trying days, bore himself courageously and with great outward calmness in presence of imminent danger does not admit of question. On the other hand, divested of all gush, patriotism, hero worship and rhetoric generally, the cold historical truth would seem to be that, aided by a most happy fortuitous concurrence of circumstances and the extreme supineness of his opponents, he on this occasion, keeping his head under wearing conditions and taking advantage of all the resources at his command, extricated himself and his army, at a most critical juncture, from an inherently false position into which neither he nor they ever should have either put themselves, or allowed themselves to be put."

XXXII

HIS MASTERLY RETIREMENT

"NOTHING but a miracle of negligence, slowness, and stupidity could possibly have saved the forces—the half of his army—which Washington had exposed on Long Island, and, in point of generalship, nothing except the English letting them go when they *were there*, was so miserable as Washington's sending the Americans to that island." [1]

So writes a British historian, and his words echo faintly the rage of the British officers with Howe, and the frenzy of his soldiers whom he recalled from completing their pursuit and breaking into the fortifications with the probable result of capturing Washington, Putnam and all the jumbled rebels.

General U. S. Grant described how he ordered his men to charge the first line of the Confederates at Missionary Ridge in 1863, and how the troops, having done their stint, swept on without orders in an overwhelming fury and stormed the ridge, causing a "panic so great that Bragg and his officers lost all control over their men. . . . Thousands threw away their arms in flight." [2]

If Howe's men had been less obedient they might have crushed the rebellion then and there.

But Sir William sat down to a slow siege while Washington changed his mind. First he brought over three more regiments, including many Marblehead fishermen, who proved more useful with their oars than with their guns.

Then he went about the trenches encouraging the men, who had not only to buck up under the shame of defeat and its disorganization, but to endure a protracted rain that forced many of them to stand waist deep in water. The "continual rain," says Graydon, "though never very heavy, was never less than a searching drizzle . . . we had no tents to screen us from its pitiless pelting." [3]

The food was pickled pork but it could not be cooked. The weapons were in bad shape and bayonets were few. Nothing is more miserable than a drenched soldier.

Of course, the enemy were also wet and wretched. Furthermore, they could do little toward advancing their parallels. There was some skirmishing on the picket lines. Washington called it "pretty smart." [4]

The morning of the 29th showed that the British had thrown up a long breastwork uncomfortably close, and Washington began to realize that he must retreat. His problem kept him awake and he did not sleep until it was solved.

All this time he had been too restlessly busy to send Congress more than a brief message by his secretary, Robert H. Harrison, who crossed to New York and wrote it at night. All that Harrison vouchsafed to Congress concerning the defeat was this:

"Early this morning a smart engagement ensued between the enemy and our detachments, which, being unequal to the force they had to contend with, have sustained a considerable loss; at least many of our men are missing. Among those that have not returned, are General Sullivan and Lord Stirling." [5]

This was mild enough certainly.

At "half past four A.M." on the 29th, Washington wrote a little note to Congress. In dreary and unwitting irony he referred to the scheme of bribing the Hessians with offers of free land:

"As to the encouragement to the Hessian officers, I wish it may have the desired effect. Perhaps it might have been better had the offer been sooner made."

In view of the trouncing the Hessians had just given the Americans and the amount of land they had just taken without being asked, this sentence would be immensely funny if it were not so pathetic. He added:

"I am sorry to inform Congress that I have not yet heard either of General Sullivan or Lord Stirling . . . nor can I ascertain our loss. I am hopeful, part of our men will yet get in; several did yesterday morning."

He simply could not swallow the bitter medicine of his defeat. He wrote of the storm, "the weather of late has been extremely wet." The lack of tents "distresses us beyond measure . . . which has occasioned much sickness, and the men to be almost broke down." [6]

In his perplexity, he called a council of war and eight solid reasons were found for withdrawal, including a fear that the worn-out men could not be forced into action again; alarming evidence that the British ships in the Bay were trying to get up the river and a shift of wind would bring them across the line of retreat; and news that a number of British warships had sailed round the island, entered the Sound from above and reached Flushing Bay.[7]

Even if these ships could not get down through Hell Gate, they could make it easy for Howe to march away to the northern tip of the island, cross handily into Westchester county, and thus choke off all American supply and make retreat impossible.

This was what Howe should have done from the first, since he was so set upon a bloodless reconciliation. It was just what he did a little later, when the bird had flown.

Once the decision to retreat was made, Washington displayed great genius in his management. It was, of course, essential to keep the enemy from discovering his plan. It was almost more necessary to keep his own unreliable troops from finding it out.   He could not even depend on his sheep to let him extricate them from the mire.

His skill in deception was called into full play.   Instead of sending for boats to carry his men back to New York, he had Mifflin send word to General Heath at Kingsbridge:

"We have many battalions from New Jersey which are coming over to relieve others here.   You will please therefore to order every flat bottomed boat and other craft at your post, fit for transporting troops, down to New York as soon as possible." [8]

The same order was sent to New York to Assistant Quartermaster Hughes, who worked so hard to fulfil it that "for twenty-two hours he never dismounted from his horse." [9]

The canny Washington next issued a general order to his troops:

"As the sick are an encumbrance to the Army, & Troops are expected this afternoon from the flying Camp in Jersey . . . the commanding Officers of Regt's are immediately to have such sick removed . . .   As the above Forces under Gen¹ Mercer are expected this afternoon, the General proposes to relieve a proportionate Number of Regiments, & make a change in the situation of them.

"The Commanding Officers of Regiments are therefore to parade their men with their Arms, Accoutrements, and Knapsacks, at 7 ºClock, at the Head of their Encampments & there wait for Orders." [10]

What could be more eloquent of Washington's distrust of his men than all this pretence, this lullaby about relieving them with fresh troops, lest they stampede and commit wholesale hara-kiri.

All sorts of boats began to arrive at dusk, rowboats, sailboats of every canvas.   The regiments were shifted here and there and each supposed itself the lucky one to be relieved.

As the Marblehead men sat to their oars and the jaded

soldiers pressed forward in the black gloom, a dim figure on a great horse darkled in the light of the few lanterns. It was Washington seeming to be everywhere in spirit or flesh.

Then the tide turned adverse, and a wind-driven rain from the northeast threatened to smash the rowboats with the sailboats.

A little before midnight the gale died down and the men and horses piled in, sinking many of the craft till their edges were within three inches of the water.

Providence was certainly watchful, if not always amiable. Washington had told certain trustworthy troops under General Mifflin to man the works till the last moment and then cover the retreat.

As the successive regiments received their orders to withdraw and marched away into the dark, leaving gaps in the ranks, the adjoining regiments received whispered orders to extend their lines and fill the space so that the British would not suspect how thinly held they were.

Alexander Graydon, who was with one of the regiments appointed to remain till all the rest were gone, tells how, in his ignorance of the real meaning of all the agitation, he supposed a night attack was intended:

"There was a deep murmur in the camp which indicated some movement; and the direction of the decaying sounds, was evidently towards the river. About two o'clock, a cannon went off, apparently from one of our redoubts, 'piercing the night's dull ear,' with a tremendous roar. If the explosion was within our lines, the gun was probably discharged in the act of spiking it; and it could have been no less a matter of speculation to the enemy, than to ourselves. I never heard the cause of it; but whatever it was, the effect was at once alarming and sublime." [11]

A chilling incident was due to one of those confusions that make all night-movements of troops peculiarly dangerous and peculiarly terrifying. Washington's aide, Alexander Scammel, who later became adjutant-general, misunderstood the orders Washington gave him and rode from left to right of the line ordering the regiments to withdraw as he reached them.

When he gave the word to Mifflin, Mifflin was sure he was mistaken and said so, but Scammel insisted that the order was authentic, so Mifflin called in his pickets and sentinels and moved to the rear, forgetting one poor man, Major Leggett. Colonel Hand, who marched at the head of Mifflin's division, gives one of the most dramatic and convincing first-hand accounts of Washington that exists. It tends to confirm the other statements of the frequency with which Washington swore in battle, though his profanity was solemn enough:

"On arriving at the Church, I halted to take up my camp equipage, which in the night I had had carried there by a small party. Gen. Mifflin came up at that instant, and asked the reason of the halt. I told him, and he seemed very much displeased:

" 'Damn your pots and kettles, I wish the devil had them; march on.'

"I obeyed, but had not gone far before I perceived the front had halted, and hastening to inquire the cause, I met the Commander-in-chief, who perceived me and said:

" 'Is not that Col. Hand?'

"I answered in the affirmative. His Excellency said he was surprised at me, in particular; that he did not expect me to abandon my post. I answered, that I had not abandoned it; that I had marched by order of my immediate commanding officer.

"The General replied that it was impossible. I told him I hoped if I could satisfy him I had the orders of Gen. Mifflin, he would not think me particularly to blame. He said he undoubtedly would not. Gen. Mifflin just then coming up, and asking what the matter was, his Excellency said:

" 'Good God! Gen. Mifflin, I am afraid you have ruined us by unseasonably withdrawing the troops from the lines.'

"Gen. Mifflin replied with some warmth:

" 'I did it by your order.'

"His Excellency declared that 'it could not be.'

"Gen. Mifflin swore,

" 'By God, I did'; and asked: 'Did Scammel act as an aide-de-camp for the day, or did he not?' His Excellency acknowledged he did. 'Then,' said Mifflin, 'I had orders through him.' The General replied:

" 'It is a dreadful mistake'; and informed him that matters were in such confusion at the ferry, that unless we could resume our posts before the enemy discovered we had left them, in all probability the most disagreeable consequences would follow. We immediately returned, and had the good fortune to recover our former stations, and keep them for some hours longer, without the enemy perceiving what was going forward." [12]

Colonel Hand also describes "the frightful disorder into which affairs had fallen at the ferry, notwithstanding the efforts of Washington and his officers to control the troops.

"The panic, which had never relaxed its paralyzing hold on the minds of the more craven, had now infected even the bravest; and it was only the noble fellows who still held the entrenchments that preserved their self-control and native courage.

"Within the lines resided a lady, whose husband and brother were officers of the American army, and present with their commands. During the dreadful uproar which prevailed, while the mob of soldiers, maddened by fear, was crowding the declivity from Sands street to the water, these officers, despairing of restoring order, and apprehensive of an immediate attack, rushed into the house, and desired her to fly with her child, as they expected every moment to be cut to pieces. The only avenue of escape was by the ferry; but the fugitive lady found that an impassable barrier of men, rendered ungovernable by fright, cut off her access to it.

"With all her exertions and entreaties she could not approach nearer to it than a quarter of a mile; and so great were the trepidation and anxiety, that she saw the soldiers in the rear mounting on the shoulders of their comrades in front, and clambering over their heads, to be nearer the means of escape."

He tells of the feelings of the men who had to return to the trenches and wait "in the gloom of that sad morning, with an impassable River and a flying army in their rear, and the awakening hosts of a resistless and triumphant enemy in their front." He goes on:

"At length the imperative order came from Washington for the retreat; and, silent as they had stood through the long hours of that portentous night, they marched away. It was full time. The dawn was already struggling with the murky atmosphere which mercifully obstructed its rays. Already the enemy's scouts, and reconnoitering parties, warned by the unnatural silence, were stealing through the tangled *abatis*, and peering through the embrasures of the redoubts, or cautiously raising their heads above the parapets, to pierce the mystery of this ominous stillness. . . .

"Amid the gloom moved one majestic form, controlling the elements of discord, and struggling with inexhaustible energy, to master even the apparent decisions of fate. Unshaken by the terrors of that dreadful night, unmoved by the appalling dangers that threatened every instant to overwhelm that throng of despairing men, he sat on his gray battle horse, by the Brooklyn ferry, through those long hours of dismay, like the genius of destiny. On that stern, calm face, the conflicting emotions which swelled his heart, left no trace.

"All the tremendous possible disasters must have been clear to his apprehension. He saw how those thousands of unmanned and terror-stricken soldiers, would melt away before the awful storm of shot and shell that in another hour might rain upon them. He saw the enemy's batteries, of forty guns, wheel into position for close firing, on the hill at Concord and Prospect streets. Fifteen thousand bayonets gleamed on his vision as they sunk to the irresistible charge. And two thousand cavalry swept before his mental vision, in pursuit of the wretched fugitives who still survived.

"Thus, conscious of the dangers which impended, and unappalled by their imminence, he sat amid the tumult, whose genius was to mould these unpromising elements into a result that should vindicate, for all time, his unequalled power and endurance."

This reads perhaps perfervid now, but it was a feeble expression of the emotions of that forlorn hope of American liberty.

The retreat was not altogether unknown. A loyalist woman tried to carry the news to the British. Her windows had been wantonly fired into by soldierly ruffians because she had persisted in drinking the forbidden tea.

Her house was near the ferry and she was one of the first to understand what was going on. She had an opportunity to inflict an enormous revenge that might have changed all history.

Knowing that she would be recognized, she sent a negro slave to inform the first British officer he could find. And this poor black fell in with a Hessian officer who knew no English, and threw the babbling imbecile into the custody of the guard.[13]

Broad daylight illumined Washington as he found himself almost alone on the shore. His horse was compelled into one of the last boats, and he stepped in after it.

The British followed so close that they captured or killed a few stragglers who could not resist the chance to steal a little loot, and forced one boat to return.

Major Abraham Leggett of the rear-guard describes his narrow escape:

"We then was order'd to Choak up the Street with waggons and carts to Prevent the Light Horse from Rushing Down upon us— at this time no boats—I Prepar'd myself to Swim the River flood tide But Fortunately Two Battoes Struck the Shore—by this Time there was but a few of us left—we all Hurred on Board and Shoved off—the Enemy Rush'd Down on the Hill and Commenced a Brisk fire. Fortunately no one was Hurt in our Boat— the other Boat had four wounded." [14]

Other British troops reached Columbia Heights, withdrew the hastily driven spikes from the abandoned cannon, fired at the retreating boats, and watched the army crowded on the opposite shore.

The fog that had settled on the river and made it impossible for the oarsmen to see one another lifted in time to permit the British to witness the last of the great retreat.[15]

There has been a mighty pother about that fog. It was too fine a thing to be left as artless nature flung it. It had to be improved as a divine cloud thrown about the weary soldiers, Providence protecting her favorites.

The Rev. Dr. Gordon[16] in his history calls the fog a "heavenly messenger," and it apparently did shroud Mifflin's men and the breastworks long enough to cover their retreat. But, as Johnston[17] says:

"Nothing is more certain than that the fog did not rise until shortly before dawn of the 30th, full six hours after the retreat had begun. . . . More than half the army was over before the fog appeared; but it protected the covering party, and saved us the loss of considerable baggage and other material."

Foreigners and military critics praised and still praise the retreat as a masterpiece. But it bore no such look to the dejected Americans of the army or out of it. Vast numbers who were in went out at once. Nobody joined.

Pastor Shewkirk, who abhorred the rebels, described their return to town:

"*Friday 30th.*—In the morning, unexpectedly and to the surprize of the city, it was found that all that could come back was come back; and that they had abandoned Long Island; when many had thought to surround the king's troops, and make them prisoners with little trouble. The language was now otherwise; it was a surprising change, the merry tones on drums and fifes had ceased, and they were hardly heard for a couple of days.

"It seemed a general damp had spread; and the sight of the

scattered people up and down the streets was indeed moving. Many looked sickly, emaciated, cast down, &c.; the wet clothes, tents,— as many as they had brought away,—and other things, were lying about before the houses and in the streets to-day; in general everything seemed to be in confusion. Many, as it is reported for certain, went away to their respective homes. . . . At night, the few that came or would come, had a meeting on the texts; and the next day we ended this troublesome month with the watch-word, 'He that believeth shall not make haste.' 'Grant me to lean unshaken, &c.' " [18]

Poor Washington, who had just finished the first of an endless series of retreats, was so exhausted, and his secretaries so fagged, that he did not write to Congress till the next day, August 31st, 1776, and then he confessed his weariness:

"Inclination as well as duty would have induced me to give Congress the earliest information of my removal, and that of the troops, from Long Island and its dependencies, to this city the night before last; but the extreme fatigue, which myself and family have undergone, as much from the weather since, as the engagement on the 27th, rendered me and them entirely unfit to take pen in hand.

"Since Monday, scarce any of us have been out of the lines till our passage across the East River was effected yesterday morning; and, for forty-eight hours preceding that, I had hardly been off my horse, and never closed my eyes; so that I was quite unfit to write or dictate till this morning.

"Our retreat was made without any loss of men or ammunition, and in better order than I expected from troops in the situation ours were. We brought off all our cannon and stores, except a few heavy pieces, which, in the condition the earth was, by a long continued rain, we found upon trial impracticable; the wheels of the carriages sinking up to the hobs rendered it impossible for our whole force to drag them. We left but little provisions on the island, except some cattle, which had been driven within our lines, and which after many attempts to force across the water, we found it impossible to effect, circumstanced as we were."

He gave a few lines to the battle and the loss:

"We suppose it from seven hundred to a thousand killed and taken."

He added the startling fact that General Sullivan, captured on the 27th, was already back in town, released on parole by the amiable Howe to carry proposals of peace to Congress.

Washington evidently did not want to let Sullivan convey any such message, but he says:

"I have consented to his going to Philadelphia, as I do not mean, or conceive it right, to withhold or prevent him from giving such information as he possesses in this instance."

Almost curtly he concludes:

"I am much hurried and engaged in arranging and making new dispositions of our forces; the movements of the enemy requiring them to be immediately had; and therefore I have only time to add, that I am, with my best regards to Congress, &c." [19]

He may have sent his "best regards to Congress," but, he had no kind regards for the militia. On the day before, for all his busy weariness, he had taken time to write to the President of the New York Convention to explain his sudden reappearance in town, and add:

"It is the most difficult thing in the world, Sir, to know in what manner to conduct one's self with respect to the militia. If you do not begin, many days before they are wanted, to raise them, you cannot have them in time; if you do, they get tired and return, besides being under but very little order or government whilst in service. However, if the enemy have a design of serving us at this place, as we apprehend they meant to do on Long Island, it might not be improper to have a body in readiness to prevent or retard a landing of them on the east of Haerlem River, if need be. In haste, and not a little fatigued, I am." [20]

He would not tell his disconsolate army, however, how he distrusted it. He issued an order on August 31, of the usual bravado:

"Now, our whole Army is collected together, without water intervening, while the Enemy can receive little assistance from their ships; their Army is and must be divided into many bodies, and fatigued with keeping up a communication with their ships; whereas ours is connected and can act together; they must effect a landing, under so many disadvantages, that if officers and soldiers are vigilant, and alert, to prevent surprise, and add spirit when they approach, there is no doubt of our success.

"The General hopes the several officers, both superior and inferior, will now exert, themselves, and gloriously determine to conquer, or die— From the justice of our cause—the situation of the harbor, and the bravery of her sons, America can only expect success. Now is the time for every man to exert himself, and make our Country glorious, or it will become contemptable." [21]

Two days later he poured out his bitter heart to Congress in a long letter of profound importance:

"As my intelligence of late has been rather unfavorable, and would be received with anxiety and concern, peculiarly happy should I esteem myself, were it in my power at this time to transmit such information to Congress, as would be more pleasing and agreeable to their wishes; but, unfortunately for me, unfortunately for them, it is not. Our situation is truly distressing. The check our detachment sustained on the 27th ultimo has dispirited too great a proportion of our troops, and filled their minds with apprehension and despair.

"The militia, instead of calling forth their utmost efforts to a brave and manly opposition in order to repair our losses, are dismayed, intractable, and impatient to return.

"Great numbers of them have gone off; in some instances, almost by whole regiments, by half ones, and by companies at a time. This circumstance, of itself, independent of others, when fronted by a well-appointed enemy superior in number to our whole collected force, would be sufficiently disagreeable; but, . . . with the deepest concern, I am obliged to confess my want of confidence in the generality of the troops."

Now he broached in his strongest language words of wisdom then and now and forever—words that his country seems never to take to heart; a lesson it always forgets and has to see written out again and again in the precious wasted blood of its first ardent but untrained volunteers:

"I am persuaded, and as fully convinced as I am of any one fact that has happened, that our liberties must of necessity be greatly hazarded, if not entirely lost, if their defence is left to any but a permanent standing army; I mean, one to exist during the war. Nor would the expense, incident to the support of such a body of troops, as would be competent to almost every exigency, far exceed that, which is daily incurred by calling in succor, and new enlistments, which, when effected, are not attended with any good consequences.

"Men, who have been free and subject to no control, cannot be reduced to order in an instant; and the privileges and exemptions, they claim and will have, influence the conduct of others; and the aid derived from them is nearly counter-balanced by the disorder, irregularity, and confusion they occasion."

Then he gave the worst of his bad news: he felt that he ought to abandon New York. Should he burn it as well?

"Till of late, I had no doubt in my own mind of defending this place; nor should I have yet, if the men would do their duty; but this I despair of. It is painful, and extremely grating to me, to give such unfavorable accounts; but it would be criminal to conceal the truth at so critical a juncture. . . .

"If we should be obliged to abandon the town, ought it to stand as winter-quarters for the enemy? They would derive great conveniences from it on the one hand; and much property would be destroyed on the other. It is an important question, but will admit of but little time for deliberation. At present, I dare say the enemy mean to preserve it, if they can. If Congress, therefore, should resolve upon the destruction of it, the resolution should be a profound secret, as the knowledge of it will make a change in their plans." [22]

Congress hastily answered that New York must not only be preserved from fire, but from Washington's own marauding soldiers as well.

On the same day, ignorant of the action of Congress, Washington let his smoldering wrath blaze up against his troops. He told them what he thought of them, promised to kill the evil ones himself. He told them they were thieves as well as poltroons:

"Some instance of infamous Cowardice, and some of scandalous plunder, and Riot, having lately appeared, the General is resolved, to bring the offenders to exemplary punishment, the notion which seems too much to prevail, of laying hold of property, not under immediate care, or guard, is utterly destructive of all Honesty, or good Order, and will prove the ruin of any Army, when it prevails. It is therefore hoped the Officers will exert themselves to put a stop to it on all future occasions. If they do not, e'er long Death will be the portion of some of the offenders." [23]

The next day he had to write to Congress:

"Our affairs have not undergone a change for the better . . . The militia under various pretences are daily diminishing. . . . On Monday night a forty-gun ship passed up the Sound."

He had her bombarded to shelter behind an island, but the Admiral with the main fleet was in the bay, and other ships were in the upper river. They had come round Long Island.

"Communication is entirely cut off. . . . I have sent away and am removing above Kingsbridge, all our stores that . . . will not be immediately wanted." [24]

If he had thought ill of his troops before, he would now behold superlatives of panic that led him to imitate old Braddock, and beat his officers and men across the backs they turned to the enemy.

Braddock had been slain in his rage, and Washington wanted to die. He stood out alone in front of his fleeing troops and invited the bullets to end his agony of shame and helplessness.

XXXIII

"THE CROWNING DISGRACE"

THE Hessians had been encouraged to hope that they could add to their pay by taking plunder from the sacrilegious savages who denied their divine King. By similar reasoning the Americans had justified the pillage of a continent from the Indians.

But Washington's soldiers, if he himself can be believed among a multitude of witnesses, rivalled the Hessians in cruelty and viciousness, not only toward the loyalists whom Congress and soldiers alike robbed of their every right as Americans, but toward their fellow-patriots.

The soldiers were not entirely without excuse. Most of them had not had a cent of pay for two months. And New York even then was uncomfortable for visitors without money.

As Washington wrote:

"I must take the liberty of mentioning to Congress the great distress we are in for want of money. Two months' pay (and more to some battalions) is now due to the troops here, without any thing in the military chest to satisfy it. . . . As it may . . . produce consequences of the most fatal tendency, I entreat the attention of Congress to this subject." [1]

Besides, many of the soldiers were farmers who wanted to take home with them trophies of their visit to the great city of almost twenty thousand inhabitants.

Graydon [2] tells that when the guards at Kingsbridge stopped one of them "with a number of *notions* in a bag, there was found among them, a cannon ball, which, he said, he was taking home to his mother for the purpose of pounding mustard."

The rank and file were so loose in their attendance at camp that Washington ordered three roll calls a day to keep them in hand and prevent such "diabolical practices" as robbing houses, apple orchards and gardens.[3]

He was particularly distressed by the Connecticut militia which was already "reduced from six thousand to less than two thousand and in a few days will be merely nominal." [4]

He tried to write politely to the Governor of the State that the Connecticut militia were really not feeling well, or had left home too soon, or something.

"I fear, that the militia, by leaving their homes so suddenly, and in a manner unprepared for a long absence, have sustained some injury."

But his disgust got the better of him, and he went on:

"Their want of discipline, the indulgences they claim and have been allowed, their unwillingness, I may add, refusal to submit to that regularity and order essential to every army infecting the rest of our troops more or less, have been of pernicious tendency, and occasioned a good deal of confusion and disorder." [5]

He praised the zealous governor for his "strenuous exertions and prudent forecast," and Connecticut tried to redeem herself by ordering heavy levies, while Massachusetts, as usual, responded swiftly to the need by drafting a fifth of her population.[6]

Congress ordered to the North still more troops from the South. But this only increased the fires of ancient prejudice between the two sections. As usual after a defeat, acrid consolation was found in tossing the blame from one side to the other. The Southern troops had in general behaved as well as possible, and they lumped the Northern heroes and cowards in one contemptible bundle.

Doctor Gordon quotes a letter from an unnamed brigadier concerning the hostility between the different sections:

"It has already risen to such a height, that the Pennsylvania and New-England troops would as soon fight each other as the enemy. Officers of all ranks are indiscriminately treated in a most contemptible manner, and whole colonies traduced and vilified as cheats, knaves, cowards, paltroons, hypocrites, and every term of reproach, for no other reason, but because they are situated east of New-York. Every honor is paid to the merit of good men from the south; the merit, if such be possible, from the north is not acknowledged; but if too apparent to be blasted with falshood, is carefully buried in oblivion. The cowardice or misbehaviour of the south is carefully covered over, the least misconduct in the gentlemen of the north is published with large comments and aggravations."

Going about collecting material for his history from all sources, interviewing toillessly—and tiresomely, and plagiarizing freely, Dr. Gordon may be believed when he cites this statement of some eminent man to a member of Congress:

" 'Almost every villany and rascality that can disgrace the man, the soldier or the citizen, is daily practised without meeting the punishment they merit. So many of our officers want honor, and so many of our soldiers want virtue, civil, social, and military, that nothing but the severest punishments will keep both from practices which must ruin us. The infamous and cruel ravages, which have been made on the wretched distressed inhabitants of this unfortunate island (New-York) by many of our soldiers, must disgrace and expose our army to detestation. I have heard some tales of woe, occasioned by the robberies of our army, which would extort sighs from the hearts of tygers. Our men are at present only robbers; that they will soon be murderers unless some are hanged, I have little doubt.' "

He tells of a surgeon who was drummed out of camp for selling certificates of disability "at sixpence sterling, and any one was welcome to a certificate for that sum." Others did the same. He says that some of the surgeons had never seen an operation, and "were unlettered and ignorant to a degree scarcely to be imagined." [7]

The diminution of Washington's army, now numbering about 20,000, was not altogether due to desertion. Washington said that "the fourth part of our whole army" was incapacitated by illness. [8]

There were thousands of sick and wounded lying about the town in ghastly misery without proper care. The condition of the hospitals of that day, even in time of peace, was frightful; in war it was unbelievable. Washington had gone so far as to break up the regimental hospitals, because of their evils. Now he pleaded with Congress for nurses, even if their pay had to be increased to "a dollar a week . . . for less they cannot be had."

There were no women nurses, of course; for the example of a Florence Nightingale was nearly half a century away. The day of anæsthetics and asepsis was still farther off.

Washington's unfortunate invalids had to be tended mainly by soldiers assigned to the task "whose service by that means is entirely lost and but little benefit rendered to the sick." He was trying to get them out of town against the day of evacuation, and he could not find fit "places for their reception. I fear their sufferings will be great and many." [9]

The efforts at reconciliation made Washington as sick as anything else, realizing as he did that every time the nation paused to argue peace its war morale was lessened. But he had no meddlesomeness in his nature and offered no protest against the commission sent by Congress to debate with Howe. John Adams and Franklin were on it and they had a parley that achieved everything polite and nothing political.

Lord Howe was authorized to grant pardons even to Washington. John Adams, however, was expressly excepted from forgiveness. But, says Trevelyan,[10] "he was not aware that, to the mind's eye of the British admiral, he would appear at the conference with a halter round his neck."

Lord Howe said that, on his dead brother's account, he felt such love for America, that if it were overwhelmed, he would lament its ruin like a brother's love. To which Franklin answered that the Americans would do their utmost to save him from that grief.

Much claret and cold ham and time and etiquette were consumed, but the conference was mainly repartee, more or less solemn, except for Franklin, who was in his element. The delegates positively refused to give up independence.

So the British crept closer and closer to New York; but they never bombarded it. It looked like a pleasant place for Sir William's gambling and Loring, and he was as eager to keep it from harm as Congress was.

But he realized that he needed far more troops than he had, if he were to garrison the continent, and he begged England to send him large reinforcements.

Congress bestirred itself to strengthen Washington and generously voted him eighty-five regiments to be enlisted for five years. To enlist them was all but impossible. To hold them for five years was hardly to be dreamed of. The vote, however, showed that Congress was persuaded of the inevitably long duration of the war. Washington was more than ever convinced that he could do nothing but act on the defensive.

He began to refer to the Long Island collapse as the engagement of a "detachment,"[11] and to feel that he had done the right thing in fighting the battle, in spite of "an expense of labor, which now seems useless, and is regretted by those, who form a judgment from after-knowledge."

He explained the enemy's plan as an effort at "taking post in our rear while the shipping effectually protects the front," in order to "oblige us to fight them on our own terms, or surrender at discretion, or by a brilliant stroke endeavor to cut this army in pieces." He continues:

"History, our own experience, the advice of our ablest friends in Europe, the fears of the enemy, and even the declarations of Congress, demonstrate, that on our side the war should be defensive (it has even been called a war of posts), that we should on all occasions avoid a general action, nor put any thing to risk, unless compelled by a necessity into which we ought never to be drawn. . . .

"With these views, and being fully persuaded, that it would be presumption to draw out our young troops into open ground against their superiors both in number and discipline, I have never spared the spade and pickaxe. I confess I have not found that readiness to defend even strong posts at all hazards, which is necessary to derive the greatest benefits from them." [12]

He thought that though New York was "considered as the key to the northern country," he could do without it and still hold the river by establishing strong posts at Mount Washington and on the Jersey side opposite, and with improved obstructions in the stream.

General Lee had advocated the city's destruction in case it could not be held, as early as December, 1775.[13] John Jay had cherished a still more startling plan which he later described: Had he been vested with absolute power, he would have "desolated" all Long Island, Staten Island, the city and county of New York,—everything below the mountains before the British reached New York. He would then have stationed the main body of the army in the mountains on the East, and eight or ten thousand men in the Highlands on the west side of the river, and he would have set the soldiers to toppling over and shoveling the mountains into the river until it was so shallowed as to afford only depth sufficient for "an Albany sloop." Thus by destroying the river as a channel, and by fortifying every mountain pass, the state would find itself "absolutely impregnable against all the world on the sea side, and would have nothing to fear except from the way of the Lake."

This was magnificent as a dream and a military vision in those days of no dynamite, and as excellent strategy as the inundation of Holland, but such ruthless intellectualisms are vain in a republic, and though Jay was a New Yorker, the other wavering citizens would have been sure to protect the fabric of New York at every hazard.

The same situation confronted military men in 1861-65. All the management of the Civil War on the Northern side was founded on the salvation of the city of Washington, and even the devotion of the Confederates would not release Robert E. Lee from the shackles of defending Richmond at all costs.

Lee was as willing to sacrifice Richmond if necessary as George Washington now was to destroy New York, but neither could defy public opinion and his political masters. Lee's masterly strategy, however, led him to defend Richmond by keeping the Federal army busy at a distance. But Washington (who was incidentally Lee's step-grandfather-in-law, Lee having married the granddaughter of Jacky Custis) had neither the training nor the obedient troops for any such policy of military pugilism.[14]

Still hunting consolation for the crumpling of his plans on Long Island, Washington flattered himself that "we have not only delayed the operations of the campaign, till it is too late to effect any capital incursion into the country, but have drawn the enemy's forces to one point, and obliged them to decline their plan, so as to enable us to form our defence on some certainty." [15]

After being convinced that he must abandon New York, his council overruled the advocates of evacuation and decided that a part of the army should "attempt to maintain the city a little longer."

It was this shilly-shallying that brought upon its army its supreme disgrace and almost its destruction.

In preparing for the defensive war ahead of him, Washington had, on Sept. 2nd, already completed a plan of reorganization, forming his army into three grand divisions, or corps: one he assigned to Putnam, with the command of the city; one to Spencer (who was to replace Greene until he recovered from his fever), for the defence of Harlem from a British landing; and one to Heath, who was stationed at Kingsbridge.[16]

At Washington's request, Howe had exchanged General Sullivan's parole for General Prescott's freedom, and Lord Stirling for General MacDonald, who had been captured in North Carolina six months before.

Greene came out of his fever in a new fever of impatience to be gone from New York before it was too late. He wrote to Washington a letter keenly foretelling what the British might and surely would do, and giving the gravest warnings. Its frankness was the best evidence of Greene's superior military abilities and his intense devotion to Washington. It is worth quoting at some length as proof that there was a military genius in America, a Quaker who loved to read books on tactics:

"Dear Sir: The critical situation which the army is in, will, I hope, sufficiently apologize for my troubling your Excellency with this letter. The sentiments are dictated, I am sure, by an honest mind—a mind which feels deeply interested in the salvation of this country, and for the honour and reputation of the General under whom he serves. . . .

"Suppose the enemy should run up the North River several ships of force and a number of transports at the same time, and effect a landing between the town and middle division of the army; another party from Long-Island should land right opposite; these two parties form a line across the Island, and entrench themselves. The two flanks of this line could be easily supported by the shipping;

the centre fortified with the redoubts, would render it very difficult if not impossible to cut our way through. . . .

"It has been agreed that the city of New-York would not be tenable if the enemy got possession of Long-Island and Governour's Island. They are now in possession of both these places. . . .

"The City and Island of New-York are no objects for us; we are not to bring them into competition with the general interests of America. Part of the army already has met with a defeat; the country is struck with a panick; any capital loss at this time may ruin the cause. 'Tis our business to study to avoid any considerable misfortune, and to take post where the enemy will be obliged to fight us, and not we them.

"The sacrifice of the vast property of New-York and the suburbs, I hope has no influence upon your Excellency's measures. Remember the King of France. When Charles the Fifth, Emperor of Germany, invaded his Kingdom, he laid whole Provinces waste; and by that policy he starved and ruined Charles's army, and defeated him without fighting a battle. Two-thirds of the property of the city of New-York and the suburbs belongs to the Tories. We have no very great reason to run any considerable risk for its defence. . . .

"I give it as my opinion, that a general and speedy retreat is absolutely necessary, and that the honour and interest of America require it.

"I would burn the city and suburbs, and that for the following reasons: If the enemy gets possession of the city, we never can recover the possession without a superiour naval force to theirs; it will deprive the enemy of an opportunity of barracking their whole army together, which, if they could do, would be a very great security. It will deprive them of a general market; the price of things would prove a temptation to our people to supply them for the sake of the gain, in direct violation of the laws of their country.

"All these advantages would result from the destruction of the city, and not one benefit can arise to us from its preservation, that I can conceive of. . . .

"I have said nothing at all about the temper and disposition of the troops, and their apprehensions about being sold. This is a strong intimation that it will be difficult to get such troops to behave with proper spirit in time of action, if we should be attacked." [17]

The brilliant and devoted Greene was writing history in advance. He asked for a council of war and it met on the 7th and voted him down. He won over enough officers to call for a new meeting on the 12th, and of the thirteen officers, ten voted to abandon the town. The orders of Congress forbade its destruction. The three officers who wanted to hold on were afterwards described by General McDougall as "a fool, a knave, and an obstinate, honest man,"—meaning Generals Spencer, James Clinton, and Heath.

Now Washington began to make ready to leave. He ordered Heath to ruin the roads from the landing points towards Kingsbridge, fell trees and dig pits, "have them broke up, and destroyed in such a manner as to render them utterly impassable." [18] He called on Mercer to detach troops to him and on Clinton to hurry the defences of the Highlands of the Hudson.

The New York Convention, which had referred to "the arts of the Tories in construing into a defeat the late prudent retreat from Long Island," requested his Excellency, General Washington, to

"cause all the Bells in the different Churches and publick edifices in the City of *New-York* to be taken down and removed to *New-Ark* in *New-Jersey*, with all possible despatch, that the fortune of war may not throw the same into the hands of our enemy, and deprive this State, at this critical period, of that necessary though unfortunate resource for supplying our want of cannon. . . .

"And the Convention of this State pledge the publick faith that the respective Churches shall be furnished with Bells of equal goodness and value whenever their constituents, free from the apprehension of having their civil and religious rights violated by any earthly Power, shall be enabled to return their publick thanks to the Supreme Ruler of the universe for graciously rescuing them from the gulf of tyranny." [19]

The Convention apologized to Washington for giving him so much trouble. He answered, "The measure I highly approve of," asked for more militia, and for "four large

Albany sloops" to "remove our sick to Orange-Town." [20]
The bells were removed and pealed thereafter from cannon-
mouths. Later when New York burned, Governor Tryon
accused Washington of stealing the bells to prevent an
alarm.[21]

On the eleventh of September, Washington wrote to
Congress that the enemy had occupied Montresor's (now
Randall's) Island in the mouth of the Harlem River, and
landed troops, and he expected several attacks.
"How the Event will be, God only knows." [22]
On Friday the 13th, Washington had a lucky escape from
death. A visitor, Colonel Joshua Babcock from Rhode
Island, describes the scene:

"Just after dinner three frigates and a forty-gun ship (as if they
meant to attack the city) sailed up the East River, under a gentle
breeze, towards Hell-Gate, and kept up an incessant fire, assisted
with the cannon at Governour's Island. The batteries from the
city returned the ships the like salutation. Three men agape, idle
spectators, had the misfortune of being killed by one cannon
ball. . . . One shot struck within six foot of General Washington,
as he was on horseback riding into the Fort." [23]

Overworked and overworried, it was strange that Washington kept alive at all. His only assistants were a few
young men, "beardless boys" to help him in his "vast hurry
of business." [24] He was so busy packing up to move that he
had no headquarters in town and breakfasted with Colonel
Babcock at Putnam's headquarters the next morning at six
o'clock. They met again in the same place an hour before
dinner to discuss the defence of Rhode Island and the building of a fortification to protect the few friendly people on
Tory Long Island. The question was, "If so, where at?"
That evening at dusk he set out for Harlem and his
headquarters. W. H. Shelton [25] paints the scene:

"It was eight miles to Harlem. We can imagine Washington
'proceeding,' at the head of his staff and bodyguard of light horse,

along the fragrant country road in the early September evening, now strung out at a brisk gallop and now bunched up as the head of the column reins in to pick its way over doubtful ground. . . . As to just how or where General Washington passed the night we have no reliable information. He may have been in the saddle the better part of the night, but he evidently arrived at the Morris house before morning."

This was the home built for Mary Philipse by her husband, Captain Roger Morris. That former fellow aide to Braddock was now in England waiting for the storm to blow over. His wife was a Tory in exile—at Yonkers. This historic house was later bought for the little Providence trollop, Betty Bowen, by her wealthy French husband, Jumel. Still standing in beauty it is better known as the Jumel Mansion, than as Washington's headquarters.

So many places have been his headquarters, but we have only one Betty Jumel.

While Washington was riding to the Morris house, six enemy ships went up the East River to join the others. Soon he received two expresses, one telling him that three or four thousand British had marched to the Long Island shore and were being moved across to Montresor's Island; the other that "uncommon and formidable movements were discovered among the enemy."

He rode to his main body at Harlem to meet the expected British landing, but "nothing remarkable happened that night."

So he began another chapter on a Sunday, the busiest and most perilous day in his whole life. Here is his own unfinished account of the Sabbath of September 15th, 1776, as his secretary sent it to Congress. That Sabbath was even worse than the Fast Day on Long Island:

"Three ships of war came up the North River as high as Bloomingdale, which put a total stop to the removal, by water, of any more of our provision; and about eleven o'clock those in the East

River began a most severe and heavy cannonade, to scour the grounds, and cover the landing of their troops between Turtle Bay and the city, where breastworks had been thrown up to oppose them.

"As soon as I heard the firing, I rode with all possible despatch towards the place of landing, when, to my great surprise and mortification, I found the troops that had been posted in the lines retreating with the utmost precipitation, and those ordered to support them (Parsons's and Fellows's brigades) flying in every direction, and in the greatest confusion, notwithstanding the exertions of their generals to form them.

"I used every means in my power to rally and get them into some order; but my attempts were fruitless and ineffectual; and on an appearance of a small party of the enemy, not more than sixty or seventy, their disorder increased, and they ran away in the greatest confusion, without firing a single shot.

"Finding that no confidence was to be placed in these brigades, and apprehending that another party of the enemy might pass over to Haerlem Plains and cut off the retreat to this place, I sent orders to secure the heights in the best manner with the troops that were stationed on and near them; which being done, the retreat was effected with but little or no loss of men, though of a considerable part of our baggage, occasioned by this disgraceful and dastardly conduct.

"Most of our heavy cannon, and a part of our stores and provisions, which we were about removing, were unavoidably left in the city, though every means, after it had been determined in council to evacuate the post, had been used to prevent it.

"We are now encamped with the main body of the army on the Heights of Haerlem, where I should hope the enemy would meet with a defeat in case of an attack, if the generality of our troops would behave with tolerable bravery. But experience, to my extreme affliction, has convinced me that this is rather to be wished for than expected. . . .

"Sir, The above Letter is merely a copy of a rough one sketched out by his Excellency this morning, and who intended to sign it; but having rode out and his return or where to find him uncertain, I have sent it away without and have the honor, &c.,

"ROBERT H. HARRISON." [26]

Washington's story is dramatic enough, yet it needs the supplement of others who saw not only the disgrace, but Washington in a most volcanic fury.

The American troops were entrenched at vantage points on both river shores. Their spirit is shown in the story written by Private James S. Martin of the Connecticut troops, stationed at Kip's Bay, now the foot of East Thirty-fourth Street:

"Half of our regiment was sent off under the command of our Major, to man something that were called 'lines,' although they were nothing more than a ditch dug along on the bank of the river, with the dirt thrown out towards the water. . . . We arrived at the lines about dark, and were ordered to leave our packs in a copse wood, under a guard, and go into the lines without them; what was the cause of this piece of *wise* policy I never knew; but I knew the effects of it, which was, that I never saw my knapsack from that day to this; nor did any of the rest of our party, unless they came across them by accident in our retreat. We 'manned the lines' and lay quite unmolested during the whole night. We had a chain of sentinels quite up the river for four or five miles in length.

"At an interval of every half hour, they passed the watch-word to each other—

" 'All is well.'

"I heard the British on board their shipping answer,

" 'We will alter your tune before tomorrow night'—and they were as good as their word for once.

"It was quite a dark night, and at daybreak, the first thing that saluted our eyes, was all the four ships at anchor, with springs upon their cables, and within musket shot of us. . . .

"As soon as it was fairly light, we saw their boats coming out of a creek or cove, on the Long Island side of the water, filled with British soldiers. When they came to the edge of the tide, they formed their boats in line. They continued to augment these forces from the Island until they appeared like a large clover field in full bloom . . . all of a sudden, there came such a peal of thunder from the British shipping, that I thought my head would go with the sound. I made a frog's leap for the ditch, and lay as still as I possibly could, and began to consider which part of my carcass was to go first.

"The British played their parts well; indeed, they had nothing to hinder them. We kept the lines till they were almost levelled upon us, when our officers seeing we could make no resistance, and no orders coming from any superior officer, and that we must soon be entirely exposed to the rake of the guns, gave the order to leave the lines. In retreating we had to cross a level clear spot of ground, forty or fifty rods wide, exposed to the whole of the enemy's fire; and they gave it to us in prime order; the grape shot and langrage flew merrily, which served to quicken our motions. . . .

"We had not gone far (in the highway) before we saw a party of men, apparently hurrying on in the same direction with ourselves; we endeavored hard to overtake them, but on approaching them we found that they were not of our way of thinking; they were Hessians. We immediately altered our course." [27]

The best troops in the world might have been shaken up by that first salvo of five broadsides at once. Crouching in their trenches they were picked off by sharpshooters in the fighting tops. When they peered over the edges of the crumbling earthworks, they saw the battleships as furnaces of rolling, fire-streaked smoke, and looming through the murk, eighty-four barges packed with soldiers.

These were disturbing enough as they came on under the barrage of grape shot, but when the boats turned and aimed a little north of the trenches to cut off the retreat, the militia broke. Their supports and reserves broke with them in a grand Marathon to Harlem, with every man for himself and the Hessians take the hindmost.

Five thousand troops had been left in the city under General Putnam, to carry off the stores and the cannon. They saw that the trap was closing, and made a wild scramble for Harlem. Colonel Knox, who was trying to salvage the remaining artillery, had to leave it behind. He was so convinced of the hopelessness of escape that he took refuge on a height called then Bunker's Hill or Bayard's

Hill Fort. General Silliman joined him there with many men, and they prepared to die hard.

Old Israel Putnam was galloping madly in all directions on a foaming horse, trying to save as much as he could of his command. For some time he had for his aide, young Aaron Burr, a valiant blade who had returned from the disasters in Canada in time to share the disasters of Long Island and Kip's Bay.

Burr rode through the panic to Bunker's Hill and ordered Knox and Silliman to retreat. Knox vowed he would defend the fort to the last.

Burr, who could rival anybody in heroism and nobody in heroics, mocked this answer, and said that with a single howitzer he could shoot the fort to pieces himself. Knox was stubborn and Burr, acting under the authority of his general, turned from the officers to the private soldiers, told them that if they stayed they would be killed, crippled, or hung like dogs before night, and promised to lead them to safety. They promptly abandoned their officers and followed Burr.[28]

He kept his word, though by this time the British had landed and spread a thin line clear across the Island.

Burr was doing the sort of work that Washington must have done at Braddock's Field when he also was only an aide.

While the New Englanders were fleeing from the ships in the East River, the New Jersey and Pennsylvania militia were fleeing in equal disorder from British ships that sailed up the Hudson as high as Bloomingdale and sprayed the defenders of the shore with grapeshot and shell.

The mad rush north from the city was joined and confused by the westward movement of the East River troops and the eastward retreat of those from the Hudson.

The whole island was one panic of scattered soldiers,

running, sprawling, creeping, hiding, stabbing with bayonets, biting cartridges, firing them, throwing away muskets, packs, everything. Americans, British and Hessians were all intermingled.

The day was "insupportably hot and few or none had canteens." [29] But thirst was their least torment. An anguish of fear made a Judgment Day of the whole American force, while the Hessian peasants ran after them laughing and wondering that they should have been fetched so far to defend England from such cattle.

Washington was in Harlem, four miles from Kip's Bay when he heard the first roar of the British cannon. He rode to the guns like mad, sending aides with orders to officers to form up their troops and hurry to the rescue of the fugitives. He sent another back to order Harlem Heights well garrisoned.

He reached at last the farm of Robert Murray on what has since been known as Murray Hill. There was a great cornfield where Forty-second Street now runs and the Grand Central Terminal stands.

A panting mob of fugitives swirled about him, but he saw, to his partial comfort, that Generals Putnam, Fellows and Parsons were coming up with their troops to make a stand.

He shouted to them:

"Take the walls! Take the cornfield."

The troops ran to cover and braced themselves for the shock of the British pursuit. But, as Private Martin wrote, "the demons of fear and disorder seemed to take full possession of all and everything on that day." [30]

The militia's frenzy of fear swept off the men who had been brave enough to march thus far against the enemy, and they whirled away with the rest, men and officers and all.

Now another sort of demon took full possession of Washington. "Throwing his hat upon the ground in a transport of rage and indignation," [31] he cried: "Are these the men I am to defend America with?"

He drew his pistols and snapped them at his men—he always thought a coward better dead. But his pistols would not fire.

It was said that he drew his sword and threatened to run the cowards through.[32] It is known that he used the cane-whip he carried, and he beat his people over the shoulders in an insane hatred of their shameless cowardice. He flogged not only private soldiers, but officers as well.

He lashed colonels across the shoulder blades, swinging his plunging horse this way and that in the torrent of men gone rat. He flailed a brigadier-general.

What he was saying all this while is not recorded, but it could not have been his prayers.

The other generals followed his example, but in vain. The brave Colonel Smallwood wrote home to the Maryland Convention:

"I have often read and heard of instances of cowardice, but hitherto have had but a faint idea of it till now. I never could have thought human nature subject to such baseness. I could wish the transactions of this day blotted out of the annals of America. Nothing appeared but fright, disgrace, and confusion. Let it suffice to say, that sixty Light Infantry, upon the first fire, put to flight two brigades of the Connecticut troops—wretches who, however strange it may appear, from the Brigadier-General down to the private sentinel, were caned and whipped by the Generals Washington, Putnam, and Mifflin, but even this indignity had no weight, they could not be brought to stand one shot." [33]

From such wrath officers and army fled and Washington was left alone—his staff keeping aloof in awe.

The advance party of fifty or sixty British who had frightened off ten times their number, approached the spot where a brigade had stood. They were within a hundred yards of the lonely Washington. He would be shot or captured in a moment.

But he did not care. He was so blind and hopeless that he preferred death. His own devoted General Greene describes his mood:

"Fellows's and Parsons's whole brigade ran away from about fifty men, and left his Excellency on the ground within eighty yards of the enemy, so vexed at the infamous conduct of the troops, that he sought death rather than life." [34]

It was then that it was left to his staff to save him from his paralysis of ire. One of them rode up, caught his bridle, and led his horse away while Washington sat in the saddle, a dead man breathing.

Meanwhile the leaderless mob straggled north, with the enemy embarrassed by the ease of its conquest. Colonel Donop's Hessians worked southward as far as the present Twenty-third Street, taking prisoners by the score. A little faster work and they might have bagged thousands.

Along what is now the western edge of Central Park, Putnam's army hurried unobserved, while across the screen of trees a British column paralleled it along what has since become Fifth Avenue.

"Colonel Grayson has repeatedly said, speaking humorously,

" 'Mrs. Murray saved the American army.' "

Dr. Gordon is the authority for this and he felt it necessary to add that Colonel Grayson was "speaking humorously." Doubt has been cast upon the story, but it was generally believed at the time as Gordon tells it:

"When the Americans were withdrawn, and no prospect of action remained, the British generals repaired to the house of Mr. Robert Murray, a gentleman of the quaker persuasion. The lady of the house being at home, entertained them most civilly, with what served for, or was cakes and wine. They were well pleased with the entertainment and tarried there near two hours or more; gov. Tryon seasoning the repast, at times, by joking Mrs. Murray about her American friends, for she was known to be a steady advocate for the liberties of the country. Meanwhile, the Hessians and the British, except a strong corps which marched down the road to take possession of the city, remained upon their arms inactive. . . . A good body of troops with two field pieces, in about 20 minutes or less, could have taken such a position as would have necessarily cut off Putnam's retreat." [35]

With nightfall, pursuers and pursued were exhausted with running and the day ended with the Americans sheltered in the lines Washington had prepared for them on Harlem Heights. But their misery was not over, for as Colonel Humphrey tells:

"That night our soldiers, excessively fatigued by the sultry march of the day, their clothes wet by a severe shower of rain that succeeded towards the evening, their blood chilled by the cold wind that produced a sudden change in the temperature of the air, and their hearts sunk within them by the loss of baggage, artillery, and works in which they had been taught to put great confidence, lay upon their arms, covered only by the clouds of an uncomfortable sky." [36]

The next morning the British were up and at the chase again, and so contemptuous of the Americans that when they drove in a patrol they inflicted on the fugitives the ultimate shame of the whole appalling rout. A cry of ironic bugles followed at the heels of the patriots, sounding the fox-hunt call, the "View, halloo!" that means: "Fox in sight and on the run."

Joseph Reed wrote to his wife, "I never felt such a sensation before—it seemed to crown our disgrace." [37]

Washington had followed too many a slinking fox not to know that fox-chase signal. It must have been the final torment. In any case, it woke him again to resolution.

He would save that rabble in spite of itself, and make it repay that foreign insolence.

XXXIV

A MONTH IN HARLEM

THE peculiar cruelty of those derisive bugles was that they satirized the wrong men.

For it is the business of a patrol to fall back as soon as it develops the lines it is feeling out. Furthermore that patrol was under the command of Colonel Thomas Knowlton, as brave a man as ever was, and it had not retreated without giving proof of fearlessness.

A full half-hour its hundred and twenty remained holding off four hundred of the enemy, until its commander saw that it was about to be flanked and ordered it to return. It had already lost ten of its number, and was literally almost decimated.

It was in the pursuit of this tactically correct retreat that some British officer laughingly told the buglers to give them the "View halloo!" He may have been one of the officers that died in the British retreat across that same fox-hunt field.

Washington had prepared a stronghold on Harlem Heights for his army before it moved out of New York just a day too late, with the loss of what was left of its good name, along with 17 officers, 350 men, few of them killed or wounded; also many of its heavy cannon and most of its "Tents, Baggage and Camp-equipage." [1]

The Harlem Heights have since been known as Washington Heights from their distinguished tenant of a month. They lie north of the sudden valley that cuts through the high wall of the Hudson, a little to the north of the point on

487

Riverside Drive called Claremont, where Grant's Tomb now stands.

This valley, known then as the Hollow Way, slants now as then from the present 125th street and Eighth avenue to the river at 130th street. The Americans were camped along its northern edge and on back to Washington's headquarters at 161st street. The position was so strong, having the Hudson on its right, lowlands on its left and the Hollow Way in its front, that the British could not have attacked it without great loss, held as it was by about 9,000 men under Washington, with Heath and about 5,000 at Kingsbridge.

The British established themselves a mile and a half to the south of the Hollow Way, at about 98th street, with pickets thrown forward to 105th street, where the Jones house then stood.

Having no cavalry, Washington entrusted his advance patrol work and scouting to Colonel Knowlton, a six-footer, an Indian fighter, and one of the first to join on after the battle of Lexington. He had opposed the seizure of Bunker Hill as unmilitary, but he went along and came back famous. He was the man that Washington had planned to send in to the attack on Staten Island as soon as the British landed there.

Following the battle of Long Island, Knowlton had organized his "Rangers" from select sharpshooters and picked officers. One of his captains was the schoolmaster, Nathan Hale, who had reluctantly consented to risk his life as a spy, had vanished after a conference with Washington, and was now somewhere within the British lines.

He was eccentric enough to have grown weary of taking the country's pay for a year without having "rendered any material service," and he felt that "every kind of service, necessary to the public good, becomes honorable by being necessary." [2]

On the morning after the Kip's Bay panic, Knowlton was out with his Rangers before the dawn to find out just where the British were. He dropped down the Hollow Way, climbed the opposite hill, and scouted along the plateau to what would now be 104th street and Riverside Drive, before he struck Howe's picket line and, after a half-hour's exchange of sharpshooting, turned homeward to give in his information. He was followed to the rim of the Hollow Way by the British, who stopped there and taunted him with the fox-hunt calls.

Washington arrived in time to be greeted by the insulting tantara. It stung him, yet how dared he rebuke it? He had lost all faith in the quality of his men. But Adjutant-General Reed, who had been out with Knowlton, wrote, "I came off to the General & after some little Hesitation prevailed on him to let a Party go up." He wanted merely to reinforce Knowlton, but Washington decided to try a foxy little trick of his own. He gave Reed Knowlton's men and Major Leitch and the third Virginia regiment of the tavern-keeper, Weedon, freshly come from the Fredericksburg region.

Washington told Reed to try to steal round to the rear of the British, while he sent Lieutenant-Colonel Crary with a body of troops down to the right of the Hollow Way in pretence of formal attack. He hoped to lure the British off the opposite hilltop.

The ruse succeeded, and the British descended while Reed's men filed off unseen. They were led astray, however, by a misguided officer, and began to climb the rocks of the present-day Morningside Park. They had hoped to come in behind their prey, but unfortunately struck it on the flank. A hot skirmish ensued and Leitch fell mortally wounded with "two balls in his Belly and one in his hip." [3]

A moment later, Knowlton, as he breasted the ledge, was

also mortally wounded. Reed brought him off on his own horse, "& when gasping in the Agonies of Death all his Inquiry was if we had drove the enemy." [4]

Though Washington had not intended a real action, and merely hoped to bag the British advance party, he was so amazed to see his men really holding their ground that he kept throwing in reinforcements under Putnam, Greene, and Clinton, until he had eighteen hundred men at work.

He could hardly believe his eyes. His men were actually fighting!—and in the open! They were driving the British back!

On the other side Highlanders and Hessian reinforcements came up and there was a long dispute in a field of buckwheat probably on a site partly included in the present grounds of Columbia University, which has moved a long way since it was the King's College where Washington established his stepson, Jacky Custis.

More amazement for Washington. His troops stood fast for two hours. It was the British that broke and retreated from the buckwheat field into an orchard, only to be driven through it and back to their original lines.

In modern language, the rebels had driven the British from 130th street to 105th street—a mile and a quarter—in an action lasting from 11 A.M. to 3 P.M.

This was startling enough to bring up Howe and Cornwallis and more Hessians with such overpowering numbers that Washington sent an aide to call his men in. Yet, as Reed wrote to his wife:

"The pursuit of a flying Enemy was so new a Scene that it was with Difficulty our Men could be brought to retreat—which they did in very good Order—We buried the Dead & brought off the wounded on both sides as far as our troops had pursued. . . . You can hardly conceive the Change it made in our Army." [5]

They were men again. The foxes had run the dogs home. The New Englanders, who had furnished most of the troops in the war and taken even more than their share of the blame, had redeemed their tarnished honor, and had tasted glory. "The New England men have gained the first Lawrells," wrote Captain Gooch.[6]

The percentage of loss was very high. The British had 14 men killed and two officers mortally wounded, 11 officers and 146 men wounded. The American loss, variously given, may be set at four officers and 30 men killed, and about 100 wounded and missing.[7]

Of course the British called it a victory since they held the field, but the Hessian Donop boasted that if it had not been for his Yägers, the Highlanders and the English would have been captured. Howe, while praising "the few troops that yesterday beat back a verry superior Body of the Rebels," rebuked their impetuosity.[8]

But Washington issued an order giving his "most hearty thanks" to his men, though he gently reproved inferior officers who had changed his orders:

"The Behaviour Yesterday is such a Contrast to that of some Troops the day before, as must shew what may be done when Officers and Soldiers will exert themselves. Once more therefore the General calls upon Officers and Men to act up to the Noble Cause." [9]

In his next letter to Congress he could indulge in the rare luxury of good news: "The troops charged the enemy with great intrepidity, and drove them." [10]

But the battle of Harlem Heights, hardly a battle nor yet fought on Harlem Heights, was the last pleasant message to Congress for a long while. A profound lull followed. Howe was afraid and unwilling to attack and it took him a month to perfect his next plan.

Washington was forced to resume the old begging note.

His lost tents and equipment must be replaced. Reinforcements from New England were coming in, but with "not a single Tent nor a necessary of any kind . . . not a pan or a kettle." [11]

He returned to his familiar tone with the men. He felt that he had the makings of an army and he determined to build it. In an order for Sept. 20th, he gave warning:

"Any officer or soldier therefore, who . . . presumes to turn his back and flee, shall be instantly shot down, and all good officers are hereby authorized and required to see this done, that the brave and gallant part of the Army may not fall a sacrifice, to the base and cowardly part, or share their disgrace in a cowardly or unmanly Retreat." [12]

Thievery still went on to such a shameful degree that he wrote to Congress asking for authority to check the crime wave:

"Such a Spirit has gone forth in our Army that neither publick or private Property is secure—Every Hour brings the most distressing complaints of the Ravages of our own Troops who are become infinitely more formidable to the poor Farmers and Inhabitants than the common Enemy. Horses are taken out off the Continental Teams; the Baggage of Officers and the Hospital Stores, even the Quarters of General Officers are not exempt from Rapine. Some severe and exemplary Punishment to be inflicted in a summary Way must be immediately administered, or the Army will be totally ruined." [13]

His relations with his soldiers were so intense that it is interesting to pay some heed to the courts-martial that followed thick and fast. They furnish also a remarkable cross-section of the state of mind of the troops.

Of course, all armies steal, often with no more malice than college students raiding a town for the fun of it. But the unpaid, unclothed patriots seem to have been unusually active.

Independence was indigestibly rich fare for the illiterate poor, and, like the suddenly uprisen peasants of Russia, they mistook it for communism. All property was theirs. They felt themselves as good as their officers—they could not have been worse than some of them. But a battlefield is a poor place for arguments and assertions of equality.

Among the prisoners tried at Harlem Heights were two ensigns charged with damning their officers, saying that they would not obey, claiming they could turn out as good a company, and threatening to bring up the rest of their comrades to fight it out.

They even went so far as to utter the remarkable statement that "there was no one more than another who had the command of the detachment." [14]

As the proud utterance of free citizens in a republic where all are on the level, this was magnificent. In the temporary, but necessary, despotism of an army, it had proved fatal. Yet the court-martial sentenced the two ensigns to a mere reprimand, which was tantamount to encouragement.

A lieutenant was tried for the two-way offence of striking and cursing an inferior and cursing and threatening his superior. The testimony is picturesque, especially as it shows the usual, the inevitable, flat contradiction of witnesses:

"Captain Hubbel. Last Wednesday morning Lieutenant Stewart came to my hut and inquired for Ensign Phelps, calling him a damned coward. I sent for the man, who is a Sergeant in my company; he came up, and Lieutenant Stewart told him he wanted to know his name to report him for a coward, for he had behaved like a damned coward the day before, and told him he was not fit for an Ensign; on which Phelps replied, he was as fit for an Ensign as he (Stewart) was for a Lieutenant. Upon which Lieutenant Stewart immediately struck him in the face with the flat of his hand.

"I went off and complained to Colonel Silliman, and Lieutenant Stewart came up with the Adjutant of our regiment, when Colonel Silliman very mildly talked with Lieutenant Stewart, and told him he ought to have taken another course; Lieutenant Stewart grew warm, when Colonel Silliman ordered him under an arrest.

"On this, Lieutenant Stewart took his hat and flung it on the ground, and said, 'I'll go to my tent—all you can do is to take my commission, but I am a gentleman, and will put it out of your power, for I will resign it, and in less than two hours will be revenged on you, God damn you.' He soon went off. He damned Colonel Silliman several times. . . .

"Captain Smith. I went up with Lieutenant Stewart to Colonel Silliman, and Lieutenant Stewart showed the utmost complaisance to the Colonel, and begged to be heard; the Colonel refused to hear him, and ordered him under an arrest. Lieutenant Stewart grew warm, and made use of some hasty expressions.

"The Court after mature consideration, are of opinion, that Lieutenant Stewart is guilty of striking Sergeant Phelps, but the Court are of opinion that Lieutenant Stewart was provoked to do so; and the Court are of opinion, that Lieutenant Stewart is not guilty of threatening the life of Colonel Silliman.

"Robert Magaw, President." [15]

An Ensign Macumber was accused of plundering and mutiny. Major Box had found him with a party of twenty, "all loaded with plunder such as house furniture, table linen, and kitchen utensils, China and delf ware." They also had some women's clothing among their effects. Major Box stopped them and they refused to be arrested. When he cocked his pistol, several of the party said they would blow out Major Box's brains. So Major Box went away for help and, returning, took Macumber into custody.

The court-martial heard Macumber's accusers and his friends, and acquitted the prisoner of everything but disrespect, for which they sentenced him to be reprimanded.

Washington, in disgust at such pampering, ordered a new trial and made the sagaciously cynical note:

"It is to be observed that the men who were to share the plunder, became the evidence for the prisoner. G. W."

On a second trial the Ensign was sentenced to be cashiered. This was so gentle a rebuke for threatening to shoot an officer, that it almost amounted to a mutiny of the court-martial against the Commander-in-Chief.[16]

On the day of Knowlton's death, not all the men had been heroes. Adjutant-General Reed had an experience with one fugitive who was scared enough to try to kill the officer who tried to make a man of him. His name was Ebenezer Leffingwell and he was brought to trial. Reed described the affair in a letter to his wife. It followed the killing of his horse under him:

"But the greatest was from one of our own Rascals who was running away, upon my driving him back a second Time he presented his Piece & snapp'd at me at about a Rod Distance—I seized a Piece from another Soldier & snapp'd at him—but he had the same good Luck. He has been since tried & is now under Sentence of Death—but I believe I must beg him off as after I found I could not get the Gun off, I wounded him in the Head & cut off his thumb with my Hanger." [17]

In his testimony, Reed added this detail to the picture of the wretch's utter collapse:

"I found him after this lying in a ditch; on his seeing me he fell to bellowing out, and I should have shot him could I have got my gun off." [18]

In those days the flintlocks missed fire as often as a modern cigar-lighter.

At the trials it was noteworthy that no matter what the prisoner was charged with, his own officer usually testified in his favor. This was partly because it is an officer's duty and impulse to protect his men, but more because of company politics: the officer's commission depended on the continued favor of his men and Washington felt that this spirit was fatal to discipline.

So Leffingwell's lieutenant testified that he had seen nothing but bravery in the man's conduct at first, though he admitted that he had lost sight of him later. Macumber was sentenced to death.

Washington cordially approved the sentence and ordered him "shot at the head of the army on the grand parade."

This entry on the 23rd, is Ebenezer Leffingwell's epitaph in history, written by Washington himself, with deep regret:

"The General, from his former good character, and upon the intercession of the Adjutant-General, against whom he presented his firelock, is pleased to pardon him; but declares that the next offender shall suffer death, without mercy."

The next prisoner, a lieutenant, pleaded guilty to being A.W.O.L. and was "mulcted of one month's pay." Inasmuch as he would probably never have got it anyway, the loss was slight.

The sergeant, Phelps, whom Lieutenant Stewart had charged with being a damned coward, was defended by his captain, and acquitted.

On the 26th the court-martial tried Private McCormick for "mutiny, attempting to desert, and firing on his own party." He was accused of threatening a pursuer with his tomahawk, and swearing that he would not be prevented from going to see his wife if he had to be the death of some of his regiment.

It was testified that he had no wife. He was sentenced to die. Washington approved the sentence, yet even that was not carried out, for his captain set him free, was tried—and acquitted!

Private William Bowen made an unfortunate defence. Charged with robbery, he gave drunkenness as his excuse. He was thereupon found guilty of that also, and sentenced to receive thirty-nine lashes for the robbery and twenty lashes for the drunkenness. Washington's comment is brief: "(Approved)."

Another who said he was going for clean clothes was

sentenced, not only to thirty-nine lashes, but to be discharged the service. The arresting officer testified that the man had no clean clothes.

Washington protested that the floggings were of no effect:

"For the most atrocious offences, one or two instances only excepted, a man receives no more than thirty-nine lashes; and these, perhaps, through the collusion of the officer, who is to see it inflicted, are given in such a manner as to become rather a matter of sport than punishment; but, when inflicted as they ought, many hardened fellows, who have been the subjects, have declared that, for a bottle of rum, they would undergo a second operation." [19]

William Higgins was found breaking open a chest and "tucking a gown and cloak into his bosom."—Thirty-nine on the bare back.

Two deserters—"39"—"(Approved)."

Two others named Wadder and Vanvreedenburgh—the same.

Three lieutenants, for being absent without leave. Both cashiered.

A captain was accused of cowardice in a rowboat attack on Montresor's island. He was charged with lying down in the bottom of the boat and howling:

"For God's sake, retreat! We shall all be cut off," and "Clap to your oars, my boys; we are safer there than here."

But his men said he said:

"For God's sake, let us go back where the Colonel and Major are fighting, and die with them!"

This was a trifle over-heroic, yet the court found such a contradiction of testimony that the captain was sentenced merely to dismissal.

Washington was furious. He charged the court with "compassion," and ordered a new trial, adding:

"To convict an officer of the crime of cowardice, and in a case where the enterprise failed on that account, where several brave men fell because they were unsupported, and to impose a less punishment than death, . . . will . . . render it, hereafter, difficult, if not impossible, to make an exemplary punishment, and especially in the case of a common soldier, who will suppose distinctions are made by officers in the case of an officer."

The court stoutly answered that the General had not seen the witnesses, nor realized the contradictions and the incredibility of some of them. The court stuck to its verdict.

On September 30: Two deserters—39 lashes. Two who intended to return—20 lashes.

Washington was brought into it on October 7th. A Sergeant Douglass was accused of exciting mutiny and saying "that the Generals had sold the troops upon Long Island, and had brought the army up to Haerlem, to sell them there."

A captain heard him shouting, "God save the King," and saying he would have no other king.

General Greene, in his letter of Sept. 5, had spoken of the talk among the soldiers that they might be "sold." Here was one who declared it. He was ordered to receive 39 lashes and Washington approved the sentence.

A lieutenant was tried for saying that his colonel had been a coward and hidden twice, once in a ditch and "again among some potatoes in a yard."

It was ordered that he beg the colonel's pardon at the head of the regiment, and that his confession be "inserted in the publick paper." He was also dismissed.

Washington was baffled on every hand. His men stole, deserted, defied their officers; the officers protected them in their iniquities and were more iniquitous.

For a whole year he had been trying to persuade Congress to give him a regular army recruited for the year, well-officered, well-paid, well-clothed and permanent enough to profit from training. He had been respectful to the point of servility, and he was just where he started, with two disasters on his hands and more on the way.

General Charles Lee, who had spoken and written of and to the Congressmen with his usual bluntness, wrote to General Gates about this time:

"Congress seem to stumble every step—I do not mean one or two of the Cattle, but the whole Stable—I have been very free in delivering my opinion to 'em—in my opinion General Washington is much to blame in not menacing 'em with resignation unless they refrain from unhinging the army by their absurd interference."

A little later he wrote to Benjamin Rush in Philadelphia:

"For God's sake get some military men into your Senate, for *inter nos* all the resolves of Congress relating to Military affairs are absurd, ridiculous and ruinous. They raise the laughter and provoke the indignation of every Man of Common Sense. Where is the Cloathing so long promis'd for the Army? Why do you not make an handsome establishment for Engineers? We have three very able Foreigners in my family, and you put New-England Carpenters at the head of this important Department. Why have you not Magazines establish'd in various Provinces?" [20]

But Lee wanted to see a Dictator, and he would rather be than see one. Washington could not be openly disrespectful to the supreme authority. The best he could do was a long, long letter which should be a Bible of military policy. A few sentences from it must be cited:

"From the hours allotted to sleep, I will borrow a few moments to convey my thoughts on sundry important matters to Congress. . . .

"We are now, as it were, upon the eve of another dissolution of our army. . . . It is in vain to expect, that any more than a trifling part of this army will again engage in the service on the encouragement offered by Congress. . . . When men are irritated, and their passions inflamed, they fly hastily and cheerfully to arms; but, after the first emotions are over, to expect among such people as compose the bulk of an army, that they are influenced by any other principles than those of interest, is to look for what never did, and I fear never will happen; the Congress will deceive themselves, therefore, if they expect it."

He gives a very keen analysis of the feelings of military men, explaining why they will not make sacrifices that ruin them while the stay-at-homes prosper. He pleads for the officers:

"They ought to have such allowances, as will enable them to live like and support the character of gentlemen, and not be driven by a scanty pittance to the low and dirty arts, which many of them practise, to filch from the public more than the difference of pay would amount to, upon an ample allowance. Besides, something is due to the man, who puts his life in your hands, hazards his health, and forsakes the sweets of domestic enjoyment."

He asks why a captain in the Continental service should receive only five shillings per day when a British captain receives ten. He begs for a bounty to encourage enlistment, including the proffer of at least a hundred acres of land, a suit of clothes and a blanket. If officers and men are suitably rewarded, good officers and good men will volunteer.

Now that the only merit an officer has is his ability to find recruits, the men treat him as an equal, and "regard him no more than a broomstick."

He points out the false economy of the militia idea:

"Certain I am, that it would be cheaper to keep fifty or a hundred thousand in constant pay, than to depend upon half the number and supply the other half occasionally by militia. . . . The jealousy of a standing army, and the evils to be apprehended from one, are remote, and, in my judgment, situated and circumstanced as we are, not at all to be dreaded; but the consequences of wanting one, according to my ideas formed from the present view of things, is certain and inevitable ruin. For, if I was called upon to declare upon oath, whether the militia have been most serviceable or hurtful upon the whole, I should subscribe to the latter."

And now he rises to what Lee called "menacing 'em with his resignation." He meekly yet adroitly masks a threat under a surprise that Congress has not asked for his resignation:

"In a word, the difficulties, which have for ever surrounded me since I have been in the service, and kept my mind constantly upon the stretch, the wounds, which my feelings as an officer have received by a thousand things, which have happened contrary to my expectation and wishes; the effect of my own conduct, and present appearance of things, so little pleasing to myself, as to render it a matter of no surprise to me if I should stand capitally censured by Congress; added to a consciousness of my inability to govern an army composed of such discordant parts, and under such a variety of intricate and perplexing circumstances;—induces not only a belief, but a thorough conviction in my mind, that it will be impossible, unless there is a thorough change in our military system, for me to conduct matters in such a manner as to give satisfaction to the public, which is all the recompense I aim at, or ever wished for."

Having compiled "in a word" this 165-word threat, he turned shy again, apologized "for the liberties taken in this letter, and for the blots and scratchings therein, not having time to give it more correctly." [21]

His letter threw Congress into a whirlpool of debate and certain steps were taken with the usual compromises between the mutually jealous colonies and their mutually jealous representatives. But things were not bettered, and instead of actions that would make possible a good army, Congress passed resolutions making good strategy impossible.

It was only to his few intimate friends and his relations at home that Washington let himself go. He could write to his brother the desolating story of the Kip's Bay disgrace and his present helplessness, and groan:

"Fifty thousand pounds should not induce me again to undergo what I have done." [22]

He could cry out to his cousin Lund:

"If I were to wish the bitterest curse to an enemy on this side of the grave, I should put him in my stead with my feelings." [23]

What must he not have written to Martha, who waited so eagerly for the good news that did not come?

The more one studies Washington's passionate life and tempestuous letters, the more amazing it is that he should have become a legend of marble serenity, of unmoved and undespairing confidence, the great "silent, unwavering" man of godlike calm.

His references to impending ruin are numberless. His language is as strong as the English vocabulary affords. According to the syntax of his time, his letters always have a certain formality when compared with the colloquialism at which present-day writing generally aims; but compared with most of the letters of his contemporaries, they are fervid to the point sometimes of frenzy, as when he describes to Lund the vanishing of his army almost as fast as he builds it:

"I discharged a regiment the other day that had in it fourteen rank and file for duty only, and several that had less than fifty. . . . I see the impossibility of serving with reputation, or doing any essential service to the cause by continuing in command, and yet I am told that if I quit the command inevitable ruin will follow from the distraction that will ensue.

"In confidence I tell you that I never was in such an unhappy, divided state since I was born."

He is haunted by the possibility of his death and asks to be justified in his grave for his inevitable failure:

"If I fall, it may not be amiss that these circumstances be known, and declaration made in credit to the justice of my character. And if the men will stand by me (which by the by I despair of), I am resolved not to be forced from this ground while I have life."

He turns again on the militia, that poor home-made sword of splintered lath that he was expected to fight all England with. Then, with an amazing abruptness, a surge of home-sickness for his Mount Vernon softens his exhausted ire:

"With respect to the chimney, I would not have you for the sake of a little work spoil the look of the fireplaces, tho' that in the parlor must, I should think, stand as it does; not so much on account of the wainscotting, which I think must be altered (on account of the door leading into the new building,) as on account of the chimney piece and the manner of its fronting into the room."

He tells of "the chimney in the room above, and the chimney in the new room" which is to be "exactly in the middle of it—the doors and every thing else to be exactly answerable and uniform—in short I would have the whole executed in a masterly manner." He orders a window in the new cellar, and tells Lund:

"Let Mr. Herbert know that I shall be very happy in getting his brother exchanged as soon as possible, but as the enemy have more of our officers than we of theirs, and some of ours have been long confined (and claim ye right of being first exchanged,) I do not know how far it may be in my power at this time, to comply with his desires.

"Remember me to all our neighbors and friends, particularly to Colo. Mason, to whom I would write if I had time to do it fully and satisfactorily. Without this, I think the correspondence on my part would be unavailing—

I am with truth and sincerity,
Dr Lund yr Affect'e friend."

A very human heart, that. Having relieved itself of his resentments; having cried out against his masters, the Congress; having abused his servants, the soldiers, he remembers pleasant homely things, and ends serenely with messages to the neighbors and apologies for not writing oftener.

Truly known, he is seen to be almost volatile in his quick recoveries from gloom at the first thrust of sunshine through the clouds, and his prompt return to gloom when they close in again.

From a little before midnight of the 20th of September to the next noon, Washington and his army watched from Harlem Heights what promised to be the burning of New York that had been so much debated. General Greene seemed about to get his wish. The English had expected the attempt and told stories of New York rebels fighting New England and New Jersey rebels because the outsiders wanted to fire the town. It was said that the New York soldiers refused to march out until after the others were gone.

On the night of the Great Fire, the British stated that they caught a New England Captain with a match in his hand and more in his pocket and that he was "sacrificed on the spot to the fury of the soldiers." [24]

A Pennsylvania lieutenant met a similar fate. A letter of September 28, 1776, states:

"According to the report of a flag of truce who came to our lines soon after, those that were found in or near the spot were pitched into the conflagration, some hanged by the heels, others by their necks with their throats cut. Inhuman barbarity! One Hale in New York, on suspicion of being a spy, was taken up and dragged without ceremony to the execution post and hung up." [25]

Tench Tilghman wrote to his father that some of the rebels "were executed next day upon good grounds."

Colonel Silliman wrote to his wife:

"I believe it was not the regulars, but some of our own people in the city that set it on fire, for they executed several of our friends there for it the next day." [26]

Washington was accused of sending Nathan Hale and other spies into the town to destroy it, but there is no shred of evidence to prove it, and it is impossible to believe, since he had promised Congress that he would do all in his power to prevent its destruction. Nearly five hundred houses were burned and nearly a quarter of the city destroyed before the flames were checked.

Nathan Hale was captured in New York on the day of the fire, and not previously on Long Island, as so often stated. He was executed on the 22nd of September at a spot in the neighborhood of what is now First avenue and Fifty-fifth street.[27] He is one of the nation's sacred figures now, but his name rested in oblivion until it was rescued in 1799.

While Washington was the target of execration as a second Nero, he was also the butt of much more or less sprightly ridicule.

Soon after he lost Long Island and New York, he appeared as the unheroic hero of a farce called "The Battle of Brooklyn," published by the Tory printer, Rivington.[28] This farce was a retort to the American play published at Philadelphia and called, "The Fall of British Tyranny." In that work the British leaders were caricatured as "Lord Mocklaw, Lord Hypocrite, Lord Religion, Judas Hutchinson, Admiral Tombstone," and the like, and the Americans were lauded as demigods of virtue.

The play included a generous tribute to the British dead at Bunker Hill. They were called "powdered beaux—fops—fribbles—skip jackets—jack puddings—noblemen's bastards and whores' sons."

The ending was an apotheosis of Washington and his generals, with a final allusion to Paine's "Common Sense," which by a noble effort was made to rhyme with "Independence."

The "Battle of Brooklyn" reversed the procedure with equal ribaldry. It has been called "unutterably coarse—a triumphant exhibition of vigor in the flinging back of filth at the enemy—in these respects, therefore, an authentic memorial of the very spirit and procedure of the time." [29]

The characters are four generals: Washington, Putnam, Sullivan, Stirling; three Colonels: Lasher, a Shoemaker, Clark, a Retailer of Rum, and Remsen, a Farmer. Also there is a New England Parson, Chaplain to General Putnam, and his name is "Ebenezer Snuffle." Joe King and Noah are two servants, and Skinner is "a Thief employed by Putnam." There are only two women, "Lady Gates" and her servant, Betty.

The first scene lies "within the rebel lines, an Apartment at Brooklyn." Here Lord Stirling, who was famous for his intoxications, comes forth howling for his valet, who has grown so democratic that when Milord says, "Devil Damme Sir," he answers, "Pray who do you damn so?" He tells his master:

"You drank *stinkabus* enough last night to split the head of an Indian."

He twits Stirling on his paper manufactory as a source of counterfeit money, but at length takes mercy on him and fetches him some peach brandy—"it so admirably fits a man for the cabinet and the field." The sectional feuds and the cowardice of the Americans are ridiculed.

The second scene of this shapeless concoction is "a Room at Brooklyn Ferry," where Lady Gates, a woman of evident frivolity, is told by her maid that General Washington will wait on her after the Council.

Washington's moral character is now traduced. That famous and infamous interpolated paragraph in Harrison's letter concerning the imaginary washerwoman's daughter whom Harrison was going to "fit" for his general had evidently already begun its long career; for in this somewhat unquotable scene, Betty tells how the infirm and stingy "General Harrison" tried to prepare her for General Washington, whom she describes as "the sweetest, meekest, melancholy fighting Gentleman."

He was generous too, for he gave her a thirty dollar bill.

The very frank conversation is interrupted by a noise outside; but it is only some New England colonels in a mutiny, refusing to fight.

The scene changes to Brooklyn Church where there is a council of the four generals and much Yankee bombast about destroying the British. Washington appears and the farce makes him say what he had often said, tragically:

"My apprehensions from the King's troops, believe me, are trifling compared with the risque we run, from the people of America at large."

Remorse overcomes him:

"O Sullivan! my heart never consented to this ruin of my native country."

Later, in soliloquy, he exclaims:

"O! cursed ambition! What have I sacrificed to thee?"

His bombast ends in a yawn:

"Heigh! ho! Bless me, so late, and my engagements to a lady not complied with."

The British often asserted that Washington kept safely away from the battle, and in the second act of the farce, at "Gwanas," *i.e.*, Gowanus, he arrives late, having evidently been detained by the lady, to find everything in a general panic, his troops in retreat and most of them stuck in the mud. The play ends in this confusion.

With such burlesques of humor and pathos, the people amused themselves while waiting for news from the fronts. There had been a protracted lull for weeks.

Howe gave Washington a respite while he made ready to do what he might have done from the first. But he had his own difficulties. After the Battle of Long Island it had taken him two weeks to get boats enough to cross the East River.[30]

He was still a pauper in horses and wagons. He had bought a hundred horses from the Tories on Long Island, and hired eighty two-horse wagons with drivers, but he still had less than a fifth of the number necessary to the movement of his troops.[31]

Washington had been enlarging his army, but slowly and with little improvement in quality. The new nation had now a paper strength of 40,000 men and 2,400 officers, but less than half the number were both present and fit for duty, and they were scattered at various posts.[32]

Much time and money had been spent in perfecting Fort Washington which, with Fort Lee opposite and a string of booms, chains and submerged hulks, was supposed to prevent the British from going up the Hudson.

On October 8th, three British ships of war with two or three tenders ran the two forts and sailed blandly across the obstructions, to the acute dejection of the beholders.

Fort Washington's twin, Fort Lee, had been named after General Charles Lee as a tribute of a respect and a confidence that had rivalled the trust in Washington and now surpassed it. Lee was watched for anxiously on his return from South Carolina, where, under his command, the British had been driven off from Charleston. Washington had written him with an informality and an affection he rarely displayed in his letters, signing himself, "Your most affectionate, G. Washington," and addressing him as "My Dear Lee."

"Notwithstanding I shall probably feel the effect, I do most cordially and sincerely congratulate you on your victory over Clinton and the British squadron at Sullivan's Island. A victory undoubtedly it is, when an enemy are drubbed, and driven from a country they were sent to conquer." [33]

It was Washington who underlined the word "your."

On October 7th, Lee had reached Philadelphia in response to orders from Congress, from whom he received new orders to go to Harlem.[34]

There was a general feeling that he was much needed there. Colonel William Malcolm had written:

"General Lee is hourly expected, as if from heaven, with a legion of flaming swordsmen." [35]

Doctor Gordon says that when Lee reached Harlem, "the troops were mightily elated with his presence, and felt themselves stronger by 1,000 men." [36]

He shocked everybody on his arrival at Harlem Heights by urging the immediate abandonment of the whole region, including the precious Fort Washington.

Greene could not endure the thought and he persuaded Washington to his opinion. Greene had been so right about abandoning New York that his ideas properly had great weight. But even a genius has his lapses, and this was Greene's worst.

The posthumously discovered indications of Lee's subsequent dealings with the enemy and his clash with Washington at Monmouth have blackened everything he ever did, but the charge that he was a British hireling from the start is ridiculous. Every letter and act of his shows his eagerness to defeat the British and his great strategical wisdom.

He pleaded for cavalry at a time when nobody else in America seemed to realize its value. Even Washington had to learn it by defeat. Lee wrote, "For God's sake, send me some cavalry." On his way to Charleston he had personally appealed to the Virginians to form volunteer companies of light dragoons.[37]

Johnston says that if the lines laid out by Lee on Long Island had been retained, the battle would have gone otherwise.[38] Now Lee besought Washington to flee from Harlem without delay.

And if Washington had taken his advice he would have relieved his record of a disaster that was almost fatal to his reputation at home and set the prospective foreign allies of America to looking for a general more reliable as an investment.

XXXV

A MONTH IN WESTCHESTER

WHILE he was being misrepresented in the ribald farce, "The Battle of Brooklyn," Washington was playing a somewhat farcical rôle of his own on Harlem Heights.

Eighteen years before, when he was on his march to Fort Du Quesne with Forbes, he had written to Sally Fairfax from camp that he would rather be at home "playing a part in Cato . . . doubly happy in being the Juba to such a Marcia as you must make." [1]

Now he played to an audience of two Indians with his whole army as the supporting cast. The performance was at the request of General Schuyler, who was having trouble persuading the northern Indians to collect British scalps instead of American. He had been called upon at Albany by two skeptical redskins, who wanted to see for themselves. So he wrote to Washington and suggested that they be shown round, and "some presents made them." [2]

Ten days later Washington answered describing the visit of the Cayugas, whom he called "Caughnugas," the little drama he played for them, and how he had all his troops drawn out to impress them:

"I showed them every civility in my power, and presented them with such necessaries as our barren stores afford and they were pleased to take. I also had them shown all our works upon this island, which I had manned to give 'em an idea of our force, and to do away the false notions they might have imbibed, from the tales which had been propagated among 'em. They seemed to think we were amazingly strong, and said they had seen enough without going to our posts in Jersey, or to the other side of Harlem river." [3]

Six days later, Schuyler replied:

"I am very confident the manner in which you have treated the Cayuga sachems will be attended with very salutary consequences." [4]

On that same day Washington's council of war decided to abandon Harlem Heights immediately as untenable. Delay might be fatal since Howe had begun his next move.

As usual he botched it, fortunately for Washington.

On the morning of October twelfth, Howe turned over the City of New York to Lord Percy with sufficient troops for a garrison, put the rest of his men into boats, passed safely through the perils of Hell Gate and landed in Westchester County, at Throgg's Neck (originally Throckmorton's and sometimes known then as Frog's Neck—or Point). He had a fog to hide his movements and Washington, whose headquarters looked across the Harlem river to the East river, could not see and did not learn of his movements for five hours.

If Howe had landed at Pell's Point he could probably have captured most of the American army. But misinformation, bad maps and over-cautiousness led him to pick out what was practically an island with a narrow causeway and bridge, and two fords to the mainland. And the Americans under Colonel Hand had already pulled up the planks of the bridge and put up breastworks, behind which they kept up a strong enough fire to prevent Howe from crossing. Reinforced, they held him for five days. This Achilles is said to have had his Briseïs, Mrs. Loring, with him. Congress had time to pass a resolution forbidding the abandonment of Fort Washington. Which settled that question for Washington and his staff.

But the flank of Washington's army had been turned and he seems to have been in some bewilderment. He thought Howe might be feinting to conceal some other move. He rode about reconnoitering and conferring. He was too busy to report to Congress for nearly two weeks, and hardly a line of his exists for this fretful period, which he spent largely in the saddle.

First he thrust out his left wing to overlap the British line and keep up his own communications with the country and his source of supplies.[5]

On the 16th a Council of War was held at Kingsbridge and it was agreed that Harlem Heights must be abandoned. The Hudson river obstructions were insufficient to keep the enemy fleet from moving up that stream, and the enemy was already in the rear to the east, cutting at the communications.[6]

On the same day Washington inspected Pell's Point near the present Pelham and ordered an outpost established.

Two days later, Howe picked up his army and cleverly set it down there at daybreak, unopposed and even unobserved.

But Colonel Glover of Marblehead was on hand with his fishermen and sailors, and other Massachusetts regiments, a force of about 750 men, with three field pieces.

The stone walls of that region made parapets everywhere and Glover put up such a superb fight that he held Howe fastened to the shore for a whole day, with a loss to the Americans of only six men killed and twelve wounded. Some American historians set Howe's loss at from eight hundred to a thousand. But Howe's figures are not available and so bloody a defeat makes no appearance on the British records, where it would surely have been conspicuous if actual.

Yet the battle of Pell's Point on October 18th, 1776, has been too much ignored, for, as William Abbatt[7] claims, it gave Washington vitally necessary time to complete his evacuation of Harlem Heights and his dreadfully slow progress across Howe's front to the North.

Washington certainly appreciated the fight, for he expressed his gratitude to Colonel Glover with an apology for the delay:

"The hurried situation of the General for the two last days, having prevented him from paying that attention to Col. Glover, and the Officers and Soldiers who were with him in the skirmish on Friday last, that their Merit and good behavior deserved—He flatters himself that his thanks, tho' delayed, will nevertheless be acceptable to them, as they are offered with great sincerity and cordiality." [8]

Howe lingered at New Rochelle where he was reinforced by Knyphausen's Hessians.

Through his aides and other helpers, Washington kept sending out appeals for cartridges, horses, oxen, and provisions. He was afraid of his soldiers when hungry, and he wrote to the Commissary-General to hasten subsistence.

"If this is not done, I fear, I am certain that the fatal consequences attending on mutiny and plunder must ensue." [9]

He stated his military attitude toward the enemy, simply:

"They must never be allowed, if it is possible to avoid it, to get above us, and possess themselves of the upper country. As soon as I heard that they had landed at Frog's point, and that they had digested a plan of getting into our rear, I gave orders that the provisions and other stores should be removed from Norwalk, &c., into the country, to the White-Plains, as the first and most convenient stage: whether they have, I have no certain information. In short, sir, I beg that you will have supplies immediately in our rear, to be drawn or moved back, as circumstances may be, or the most fatal and alarming consequences to this army and the liberties of America may, and will in all probability, follow. You must not stop on account of expense, nor to collect large quantities before they are sent off."

In the midst of his own feeling that his hour was about to strike, he received from the North the news of the complete ruin of Arnold's fleet on Lake Champlain, a defeat so dire that Arnold was glad to be alive and able to report his disaster to Washington:

"I think we have had a very fortunate escape, and have great reason to return our humble and hearty thanks to Almighty God for preserving and delivering so many of us." [10]

There was bad news from nearer home in the report of Colonel (not General) Putnam who went out on a personal reconnaisance and brought back word that the British were closing in on White Plains and the stores ought to be withdrawn to a safer place.

Washington was creeping toward it as fast as he could, keeping the Bronx river between him and Howe, who must have been surprised when he saw that tiny silver thread coiling through the meadows. For it is said that the British War Office, studying the map, had ordered the navy to proceed up the Bronx and attack what American ships it found there. [11]

The only ships that have ever sailed those waters have been children's toy yachts, though there are a few reaches where a flat-bottomed boat or a canoe may find support. To one familiar with that most exquisite of brooks, which now runs through a park all its distance, there is something excruciatingly amusing in the thought of the British navy supporting Howe's march on White Plains by forcing its way up the Bronx.

In Howe's time, however, it was wooded and thicketed and its banks in places were so steep that a commander is said to have reported home:

"We have crossed the Bronx without the loss of a single man!" [12]

He must have begun the tradition of its greatness, for the modern English historian Fortescue speaks thus of Washington's gradual drawing out of his line toward White Plains:

"Leaving two thousand men in Fort Washington, he changed front from south to east, extending his army in detached camps, each of them strongly entrenched, for some eighteen miles along a line of hills that runs northward from Kingsbridge to White Plains; his front being everywhere covered by a deep river called the Bronx, of which every ford was defended by powerful works." [13]

Westchester county had its own civil war and Washington was not in altogether friendly country. In fact he had to send Lord Stirling to disperse a loyalist band known as the Queen's Rangers and led by Robert Rogers.

There was a dearth of horses and oxen in both armies, and Washington's men had to drag some of their wagons and cannon for a short distance, then unhitch, turn back and bring up the others to the same point, and so on alternately.

On October 22nd, 1776, Washington reached White Plains and began to dig in with his entire army (save for about 1,400 at Fort Washington, 600 at Kingsbridge and 4,500 across the Hudson at Fort Lee, under General Greene.) By the 25th Washington had about 13,000 men camped on high ground behind a double line of trenches forming a squat U.

His left flank was folded back at a swamp near a lake, his right at the Bronx river. On the other side of the stream was a height called Chatterton's Hill, which he entrusted to General McDougall. The artillery included two guns from the battery of young Captain Alexander Hamilton.

Howe came up on October 28th with about the same number of men as Washington had. He also had some recently arrived cavalry, which caused such terror in the eyes of the Americans and scattered them so quickly, that Washington issued a special order on October 27th:

"The General, observing that the army seems unacquainted with the enemy's Horse, and that when any parties meet with them,

they do not oppose them with the same alacrity which they show in
other cases, thinks it necessary to inform the officers and soldiers
that in such a broken country, full of stone walls, there is no enemy
more to be despised, as they cannot leave the road; so that any party
attacking them may be always sure of doing it to advantage, by
taking post in the woods by the roads, or along the stone walls,
where they will not venture to follow them. And as an encouragement to any brave parties who will endeavour to surprise some
of them, the General offers one hundred dollars for every Trooper,
with his horse and accoutrements, which shall be brought in, and
so in proportion for any part, to be divided according to the rank
and pay of the party." [14]

Nevertheless the advance posts in front of his lines at
White Plains took no advantage of the offer when the British
advance cavalry appeared, but preferred the safety of the
rear to the dubious value of a Continental hundred-dollar
bill.

Howe recognized at once the strategic value of Chatterton's Hill and attacked it first. The Hessian Colonel Rall
discovered still another hill commanding the flank of Chatterton's and crossed the river to seize it.

Colonel Haslet of Delaware, who was on Chatterton's
Hill, stated that when the second shot of Howe's preliminary
cannonade wounded a militiaman in the thigh, the whole
regiment broke and fled.[15] The men evidently believed
that the best use for thighs was for their own preservation.

After one costly frontal attack Rall worked round to the
rear and drove the Americans off in a serial capture of stone
wall after stone wall.

On one occasion, after delivering a volley that scattered
the Hessian Grenadiers "like leaves in a whirlwind" the
Americans leaped over the wall and stripped the fallen of
their arms and accoutrements—and rum, "Which we had
time to drink round with before they came on again."

Washington's secretary, Harrison, explaining to Congress

that "the situation of our affairs not permitting his Excellency to write himself, I have it in charge," said that the battle for the hill was over in "about a quarter of an hour," which does not allow for a very stubborn defence. He put the American loss at "between four and five hundred in killed, wounded and missing." [16]

This would have been a frightful carnage for fifteen minutes, but it was afterwards learned that at least two hundred of the missing were militia who were missing after the first volley of the enemy.

The American actual loss is therefore put at about two hundred. The British report shows that the hill cost Howe five officers and twenty-three men killed and one hundred and twenty-six wounded, besides a loss of seventy-seven Hessians.[17] Howe had meant to attack the main position simultaneously, but something prevented, which he later declined to explain "for political reasons." [18]

At the time of the attack on Chatterton's Hill Washington seems to have been absent on a reconnaisance in the wrong direction. When the news of the battle reached him, he said with the greatest calm to his companions:

"Gentlemen, we have other business now than reconnoitering. You will repair to your posts and do the best you can." [19]

The histories all say that the capture of Chatterton's Hill ended the "affair" known as the Battle of White Plains, and that Howe, though reinforced, lingered inactive for four days without attack. According to General Heath's *Memoirs*, however, on November 1st Howe made certain shifts of position indicating an attack on a detached hill at the left, the opposite end of the line from Chatterton's. Heath had sent Colonel Malcolm to entrench himself there when the British threatened it.

A deep hollow cut it off from the main position and Heath

took pains to guard that with a regiment posted behind a wall. This maneuver was of no particular importance except that Heath gives a glimpse of Washington under fire, for as soon as a very severe artillery duel began between Howe and Malcolm, he rode up to the hill.

"His first question to General Heath was:

" 'How is your division?' He was answered:

" 'They are all in order.'

" 'Have you,' said the Commander-in-Chief, 'any troops on the hill, over the hollow?' He was answered:

" 'Malcolm's regiment is there.'

" 'If you do not call them off immediately,' says the General, 'you may lose them, if the enemy push a column up the hollow.'

"He was answered that, even in that case, their retreat should be made safe; that a strong regiment was posted at the head of the hollow, behind the wall; that this regiment, with the oblique fire of the division, would so check the enemy as to allow Malcolm to make a safe retreat. The Commander-in-Chief concluded by saying:

" 'Take care that you do not lose them.'

"The artillery of the division was so well directed as to throw the British artillerymen several times into confusion; and, finding that they could not here make any impression, drew back their pieces, the column not advancing.

"The British made no other attempt on the Americans while they remained at White-Plains. The two armies lay looking at each other, and within long cannon-shot. In the night time the British lighted up a vast number of fires, the weather growing pretty cold. These fires, some on the level ground, some at the foot of the hills, and at all distances to their brows, some of which were lofty, seemed to the eye to mix with the stars, and to be of different magnitudes." [20]

The retirement of Howe's artillery was vigorously described by the Maryland colonel, Gist, successor to the valorous Colonel Smallwood who had been wounded in the Chatterton's Hill engagement:

"The General ordered us to abandon our back lines, which, in our present situation, was rendered useless to us. The enemy immediately took possession of them; and judging that we were making a precipitate retreat, formed the line, and advanced upon us with a large column to bring on the attack, the artillery on each side keeping up a smart fire; and they soon found their situation disagreeable, and as if ashamed of the attempt, they sneakingly skulked behind a wood, and retired unseen to the lines." [21]

As a matter of fact Washington was withdrawing his whole army to Northcastle Heights. His chief purpose in holding White Plains as long as he did was to gain time for removing his accumulated stores.

As Tench Tilghman wrote:

"This we did effectually, and then gave them possession of a piece of ground which they dare not occupy, because it is secured by our cannon from the heights. All matters are as quiet as if the enemy were one hundred miles distant from us; and his Excellency is just going to ride. I must therefore to horse, and bid you adieu." [22]

One must rely on Washington's aides and others for word of him during this period. But things went along as usual. There was desertion before, during, and after the battle; and a series of courts-martial in which the guilty were generally acquitted or only scolded.

Harrison wrote to Congress for Washington:

"Our situation . . . is altered in no instance, unless in the number of our troops, which is every day decreasing by their most scandalous desertion and return home." [23]

If it is monotonous to read even a few of the numberless reports of this sort, it can be imagined what a monotony of despondency it meant to Washington to write or to dictate them. But the very watchword of his campaigns might have been: "Cheer up, the worst is yet to come."

Howe now had Washington in a most dreadful position, having split his army in two. By driving Washington into the hills, he had isolated him from Fort Washington and Fort Lee, twenty-five miles away.

But Washington might well have been amazed at the very existence of his army. Quick movements would have encircled and captured it.

And Howe could move quickly. There was at times a feline quality in his strategy. He had the "pounce instinct." As long as his mouse lay quiet he was indolent. Suddenly he would fasten it down—and let it run.

The mystery of Howe's action and inaction is deepened here at White Plains. His eternal repetition of Whip-Washington-and-let-him-go infuriated the Tories in America and in England. When at last he went home, he was investigated.

Among the riddles asked him were: Why in the name of either place, he did not attack Washington's weak line? and why he stopped at taking a hill outside it? He answered:

"An assault upon the enemy's right which was opposed to the Hessian troops, was intended. The committee must give me credit when I assure them that I have political reasons, and no other for declining to explain why that assault was not made. . . . By forcing the lines we should, undoubtedly, have gained a more brilliant advantage, some baggage, and some prisoners; but we had no reason to suppose that the rebel army could have been destroyed." [24]

Cornwallis made the same evasive reply when quizzed:

"From political motives it is impossible for either the General or myself to explain these reasons." [25]

Perhaps the mystery of Howe's behavior is no mystery at all, or rather a mystery of human nature, a political, not a military, mystery.

The United States has had reasons enough to know how often a political passion will stretch patriotism to bursting. In the Civil War there were fanatic party hatreds that looked treasonable and kept the Northern cause on the verge of ruin.

In the Continental Congress there were men calling themselves ardent patriots who let Washington plead in vain while they wrangled with their personal or partisan enemies.

So England was the scene of a desperate political war between Whigs and Conservatives. The Whigs hated the King before the Americans learned to abuse him. They rejoiced at everything that embarrassed the ministry. They opposed every form of military or naval supply, until France entered the war, when the fear of invasion and defeat by an historic foe unified them to an extent.

But at this time, in 1776, the Whigs were so fierce that when Howe won the Battle of Long Island, Charles James Fox wrote of it as "the terrible news from Long Island." [26] It was said that the Whigs chose "buff and blue" as their colors, because Washington wore them.

When Edmund Burke learned of the Great Fire in New York he lauded it as a glorious achievement of the rebels, who were, incidentally, entirely unwilling to accept the credit for it.[27]

As Lecky [28] says, the Opposition to the King spoke in Parliament "in a strain which would have been perfectly becoming in the American Congress and the American cause was spoken of as the cause of liberty."

The Howes were Whigs who had vowed not to fight America. They came pleading for peace. They treated the Tories with great contempt.

To the professional soldier, as Channing [29] points out, the war brought double the peace-time pay. Why should he hurry to finish his task and return to poverty and boredom in a garrison town? Howe needed money. His seat in Parliament had cost him too much. He loved luxury.

With his political animosity toward the King and the Conservatives, with his tenderness for the Americans, and his financial profit involved, why should he be expected to fight a war of extermination?

He has been occasionally accused of cowardice, which is a ridiculous charge against one of such proved courage. He has been accused of licentiousness and love of gambling, but many ruthless warriors have been guilty of both.

Indolence has been the chief charge against him, and it may be a sufficient explanation. It is amazing to find how small a percentage of humanity has the ability to follow anything through to the end, whether a sonnet, a hundred-yard dash, a painting, a political campaign, or what not? Perhaps Howe was merely one of the majority.

Howe loved, perhaps, to box with Washington, and had not the heart or the will-power to put him out when he had him against the ropes.

But at times he would strike and show what he could do. So now, having shoved Washington out among the wooded rocks, he turned and took some pleasure and pride in attacking a really strong fort. That was interesting.

When he suddenly withdrew from Washington's front he left a puzzled group behind him. Where was he going?

The Hudson was of the greatest importance. What was to prevent him from cutting across to the Highlands and taking West Point with the aid of the ships that could not be stopped from going up the river? If he took those posts, the troops to the north would be crushed between him and Carleton.

If he crossed the river, what was to stop him from going on to Philadelphia and driving Congress out into the wilderness?

On his way over he might gather in Forts Washington and Lee.

With this perplexity in his mind, Washington, on November 6th, 1776, resumed his letters to Congress, referring to the "sudden and unexpected movement." The design "is a matter of much conjecture and speculation." The enemy might still try to flank him "by a sudden wheel."

He speaks of a council of war which unanimously agreed to throw troops into New Jersey in expectation of Howe's movement thither. He adds:

"Nor shall I be disappointed if he sends a detachment to the southward for the purpose of making a winter campaign." [30]

But he was in such despair of receiving replacements of the deserters, or reinforcements that he wrote to the several States for aid.

He wrote to Greene that he was "inclined to think, that it will not be prudent to hazard the Men and Stores at Mount Washington; but, as you are on the spot, leave it to you to give such orders, . . . as you may judge best, and so far revoking the order given to Colonel Magaw to defend it to the last."

He had been away from Greene for some time and under the influence of Charles Lee, yet he followed his rule of giving advice, not orders, to distant commanders.

Greene answered on November 9th, with a confidence that he never afterward had, that he wanted to hold on to Fort Washington:

"I cannot conceive it to be in any great danger. The men can be brought off at any time. . . . I was over there last evening. The enemy seem to be disposing matters to besiege the place; but Colonel Magaw thinks it will take them till December expires." [31]

Just exactly one week later, Colonel Magaw surrendered the fort after a few hours' fighting—and to a Hessian!—with a loss of 59 killed, 2,818 prisoners, 146 pieces of artillery, 12,000 shot, shell and case, 2,800 muskets and 400,000 cartridges. If Knyphausen had closed in half an hour earlier he would have included among his prisoners Generals Mercer, Putnam, Greene and—George Washington.

XXXVI

THE RETREAT ACROSS THE JERSEYS

THE little garrison of Fort Washington had been simply swamped. Howe had ordered Knyphausen to march west from New Rochelle to the south of the Harlem river; Cornwallis to camp to the north of that stream; Lord Percy to come up from New York to the Hollow Way; thirty flatboats to be fetched up the Hudson and round into the Harlem to carry Cornwallis over the Harlem—the batteries could not even stop the barges. And then Howe marched across to Dobbs Ferry on the Hudson, moved south and clamped the lid on.

A dozen British and fifteen Hessian regiments, totaling 13,000 men, surrounded less than 3,000 men.

Washington was in such grave doubt as to the possibility of saving the fort that he left White Plains with Putnam and Mercer and a few troops, crossed the Hudson at King's Ferry, and rode down to Fort Lee on the New Jersey side.

He was shocked to find that no progress had been made in perfecting the obstruction of the river, which was so important to the success of the war. Yet he remembered the orders from Congress to hold the fort at all costs.

He remembered that he had resigned himself to a war of retreats and obstacles. But, as Alexander Graydon, who was one of the Fort Washington garrison, wrote:

"The idea, about this time, seems to have been taken up of making our resistance, a war of posts; or of disputing, inch by inch, our ground. This sort of war, however . . . appears to be scarcely practicable, unless it should have the good fortune to be protected by a succession of Thermopyles." [1]

Fort Washington was no Thermopylae.

Graydon quotes Lee's question: supposing it tenable, what purpose did it answer to keep it? He blames Washington for the disaster, in terms that were gentle considering the torment Graydon endured as a captive.

In spite of Greene's eagerness to hold the fort, Washington was dubious. He wanted to go over and see it with his own eyes. It was a "risque," but he braved it. He crossed the Hudson with the other generals in a rowboat. He walked right into the assault, for the first cannonade began and the first line of outposts was forced in before Washington had finished the steep climb from the shore.

Under fire he studied the ground and interviewed Magaw, who assured him that he could hold out for months. In any case it was too late now to remove either men or stores. As Greene wrote to Knox:

"There we all stood in a very awkward situation. As the disposition was made, and the enemy advancing, we durst not attempt to make any new disposition; indeed, we saw nothing amiss. We all urged his Excellency to come off. I offered to stay. General Putnam did the same, and so did General Mercer; but his Excellency thought it best for us all to come off together, which we did, about half an hour before the enemy surrounded the fort." [2]

Graydon says:

"It is a fact, not generally known that the British troops took possession of the very spot on which the commander in chief, and the general officers with him, had stood, in fifteen minutes after they left it." [3]

By the time Washington's boat had left the shore the fort was surrounded, and there must have been great sorrow in his eyes and in his heart as he stared back at the futile resistance of the men whose loss he owed to the meekness of his soul and his reluctance to discard the counsel of other patriots.

By the time he reached Fort Lee there was terrible slaughter going on across the river, and from his eyrie, he could doubtless see the flash of bayonets quenched in the bodies of his people. A soldier suffers few things more keenly than watching a fight that he cannot join, especially when it is destroying his men. Washington must have observed the surrender and the march-out of the garrison.

But he did not see what he might have seen if he had lingered but a few minutes more in the fort that was his namesake, for Graydon tells of the rumor having spread to New York that Washington was among the prisoners, and the greetings that met the sorry troop:

"On the road as we approached the city, we were beset by a parcel of soldiers trulls and others, who came out to meet us. It was obvious, that in the calculation of this assemblage of female loyalty, the war was at an end; and that the whole of the rebel army, Washington and all, were safe in durance.

" 'Which is Washington? Which is Washington?' proceeded from half a dozen mouths at once; and the guard was obliged to exert itself to keep them off. Some of them assailed us with vollies of Billingsgate; and colonel Maxwell, who rode along side of us, and whom I immediately recognized for a captain Maxwell, who had once lodged at my mother's, had enough to do to silence one of them, calling out repeatedly:

" 'Away with that woman! Take her away! Knock her down, the bitch! Knock her down!' " [4]

Poor Greene was a brave and a wise man whom the event had turned for the moment into a destructive fool. He was heartbroken. He wrote to Knox in incoherent misery:

"I feel mad, vexed, sick, and sorry. Never did I need the consoling voice of a friend more than now. Happy should I be to see you. This is a most terrible event: its consequences are justly to be dreaded. Pray, what is said upon the occasion? A line from you will be very acceptable." [5]

But Washington took all the blame. And there was an abundance of it.

One of the signers of the Declaration of Independence, Benjamin Harrison, wrote to Robert Morris that three other signers were rumored to be conspiring against Washington, including R. H. Lee already:

"We have a story circulating here that there has been a motion made in Congress to divide the command of the army and that R. H. L. was at the bottom of it. it makes much noise, and if true, will effectually do his business, we are also informed that Genl. Washington's character has been attack'd publicly by S. & J. Adams, and that the Genl. has been so inform'd Your being sent to Camp gives me some reason to fear that these reports may be true, and that my worthy Friend resents such treatment, I know his value & would not loose him, if we do, America will repent it by the loss of her Liberty." [6]

The failure, of course, turned many a violent Son of Liberty into a silent Tory. William Hooper wrote to Joseph Hewes:

"It flows from me like my heart's blood (but this is not a term to palliate) the growth of Tories exceeds all comprehension, it is a weed that lately discovers itself in soils where I the least expected it—but the least success on our part will instantly extinguish it." [7]

General Charles Lee wrote to Washington with a gloatingly sympathetic I-told-you-so:

"Oh General, Why would you be overpersuaded by men of inferiour judgment to your own? It was a cursed affair." [8]

When the news reached Europe, Fort Washington was added to the long list of Washington's other defeats and the opinion spread that he was a very good man, but a mediocre soldier, and fatally unlucky. The decision abroad was that some foreigner of distinction should be sent over.[9] But the story of foreign activities must wait until the next volume.

Washington realized his unpopularity and it cut him to the quick, for he was no soldier of fortune like Lee; no seeker after military laurels in the sport of war, like many another. He was a farmer who had left his home to toil without pay of any sort and he wanted the kind feelings of his neighbors. He was a trustee of the infant nation and he asked nothing but his good name. Losing that was a suffering even amid all his other trials.

What army he possessed had the hideous incohesion of sand. And it was running away like sand through his vainly clutching fingers.

He had to write home another woeful letter explaining his new failures. He told his brother how the fort in whose name the family had taken such pride had been held "contrary to my wishes and opinion," but "I did not care to give an absolute order for withdrawing the garrison, till I could get round and see the situation of things, and then it became too late."

He told again of his year-long appeals for a regular army, and of what he was getting—a politician's army:

"But the measure was not commenced till it was too late to be effected, and then in such a manner, as to bid adieu to every hope of getting an army, from which any services are to be expected; the different States, without regard to the qualifications of an officer, quarelling about the appointments, and nominating such as are not fit to be shoeblacks, from the local attachments of this or that member of Assembly.

"I am wearied almost to death with the retrograde motion of things, and I solemnly protest, that a pecuniary reward of twenty thousand pounds a year would not induce me to undergo what I do; and after all, perhaps, to lose my character, . . .

"God grant you all health and happiness. Nothing in this world would contribute so much to mine, as to be once more fixed among you in the peaceable enjoyment of my own vine and fig-tree." [10]

Realizing that Fort Lee was now useless and helpless, Washington, then at Hackensack, ordered Greene to strip it for evacuation, but a deserter from the British brought him word of the approach of Lord Cornwallis, who crossed the Hudson suddenly with 4,500 men with such secrecy and speed that Greene could only escape with his men, leaving his tents standing as well as his provisions and artillery. He had barely time to join Washington at Hackensack and watch Cornwallis hurry by to seize the last stronghold on the lower Hudson.

Washington had started to write a letter to Congress on November 19th, 1776, and had not found time to finish it. He was telling them that the army was about gone, and that the terms of enlistment of many troops were expiring immediately. He added this postscript:

"21st—The unhappy affair of the 16th has been succeeded by further misfortunes. Yesterday morning a large body of the Enemy landed between Dobb's Ferry and Fort Lee. Their object was evidently to inclose the whole of our troops and stores that lay between the North and Heckenseck Rivers, which form a very narrow neck of land. . . . We lost the whole of the cannon that was at the Fort, except two twelve pounders, and a great deal of baggage—between two and three hundred tents, about a thousand barrells of flour and other stores in the Quarter Master's department. This loss was inevitable. As many of the Stores had been removed as circumstances and time would admit of; the Ammunition had been happily got away." [11]

To Lee, whom he had left at Northcastle with troops to guard the Highlands and who had written to him for instructions, he had to confess the loss of "the Fort called by your Name," and to admit:

"With respect to your situation, I am very much at a loss what now to determine."

But one thing he was sure of: "That the enemy are evidently changing the seat of war to this side of the North River."

The Jerseys would now ask protection and, not receiving it, would turn against the army and infect Pennsylvania, which was even more Tory than usual, seeing that Congress was shaking in its boots. So he suggested that Lee join him. He did not order him to come, or ask him to; he expressed an opinion:

"I am of opinion, and the gentlemen about me concur in it, that the public interest requires your coming over to this side of the Hudson, with the Continental troops." [12]

Lee decided that he was needed where he was, and ordered Heath to send 2,000 men. Heath declined, saying that he had Washington's orders to stay. Lee chose to read Washington's phrases literally as a suggestion, not an order. He began to feel that he must be the savior of the country and he must save it in his own way. It was perhaps a sincere belief in Washington's unfitness to command; and his ambition to rescue the colonies from the tyrant he hated was a legitimate ambition. But he lost his head, and in some delusion of grandeur, apparently resolved to let Washington crash alone.

He wrote to the President of the Massachusetts Council on November 21st, saying that there was grave danger of an invasion of New England, which Washington could not oppose. And again the next day:

"Indecision bids fair for tumbling down the goodly fabrick of American freedom, and, with it, the rights of mankind. 'Twas indecision of Congress prevented our having a noble army, and on an excellent footing. 'Twas indecision in our military counsils which cost us the garrison of Fort Washington, the consequence of which must be fatal, unless remedied in time by a contrary spirit."

He called on Massachusetts to raise an army of its own contrary to Congress' orders:

"We must save the community in spite of the ordinances of the Legislature. There are times when we must commit treason against the laws of the State for the salvation of the State. The present crisis demands this brave, virtuous kind of treason. For my part . . . I will stake my head and reputation on the propriety of the measure. . . . In the meantime send up a formidable body of Militia to supply the place of the Continental troops, which I am ordered to convey over the river. Let your people be well supplied with blankets and warm clothes as I am determined by the help of God to unnest 'em even in the dead of winter. Let me hear from you soon." [13]

He probably planned to wait till Howe reached the Delaware and then by a swift march, recapture New York. In any case he declined to follow Washington who had spoken of the concurrence of the "gentlemen of his family" in the opinion that Lee should come to New Jersey.

There was one gentleman of Washington's "family" who believed that Lee should come over into the Jerseys not only to help them—but to command them.

A more cruel defection than that of his jealous and ambitious buffoon rival, Lee, was the desertion of Joseph Reed, the man Washington preferred to all others, the one who had been his best secretary, but would not remain, would not return in spite of Washington's repeated beseeching. Reed liked Washington, who loved him.

But on the day after the fall of Fort Lee and the confusion that followed it, Reed wrote to Charles Lee, the Englishman (the italics are added):

"I do not mean to flatter, nor praise you at the Expence of any other, but I confess I do think that *it is entirely owing to you that this Army & the Liberties of America so far as they are dependant on it are not totally cut off.*

"*You have Decision, a Quality often wanting in Minds otherwise valuable* & I ascribe to this our Escape from York Island—from Kingsbridge & the Plains—& I have no Doubt *had you been here the Garrison at Mount Washington would now have composed a Part of this Army.* Under all these Circumstances I confess I ardently wish to see you removed from a Place where I think there will be little Call for your Judgment & Experience to the Place where they are like to be so necessary. Nor am I singular in my Opinions—*every Gentleman of the Family the Officers & soldiers generally have a Confidence in you*—the Enemy constantly inquire where you are, & seem to me to be less confident when you are present. . . .

"They hold us very cheap in Consequence of the late Affair at Mount Washington where *both the Plan of Defence & Execution were contemptible*—if a real Defence of the Lines was intended the Number was too few, if the Fort only, the Garrison was too numerous by half. . . . *Oh! General—an indecisive Mind is one of the greatest Misfortunes that can befall an Army*—how often have I lamented it this Campaign.

"All Circumstances considered we are in a very awful & alarming State one that requires the utmost Wisdom & Firmness of Mind." [14]

To this Lee answered three days later:

"I receiv'd your most obliging flattering letter—lament with you that fatal indecision of mind which in war is a much greater disqualification than stupidity or even want of personal courage—accident may put a decisive Blunderer in the right—but eternal defeat and miscarriage must attend the man of the best parts if curs'd with indecision." [15]

As chance managed it, Washington had sent General Reed to Burlington to implore help from the New Jersey Assembly. When Lee's letter arrived in camp, Washington, opening it naturally, read it, and understood.

To learn that Reed, of all men, was writing to Lee the things Washington could easily glean from Lee's answer, was a dagger in Washington's heart.

But, being Washington, he forwarded Lee's letter to Reed with this magnificent apology:

"The enclosed (Lee's letter) was put into my hands by an express from White Plains. Having no idea of its being a private letter, much less suspecting the tendency of the correspondence, I opened it, as I had done all other letters to you from the same place and Peek's Hill, upon the business of your office, as I conceived and found them to be. This, as it is the truth, must be my excuse for seeing the contents of a letter which neither inclination nor intention would have prompted me to. I thank you for the trouble and fatigue you have undergone in your journey to Burlington, and sincerely wish your labours may be crowned with the desired success. With best respects to Mrs. Reed, I am, dear Sir, &c.

"GEORGE WASHINGTON." [16]

The magnanimity, the unreproachful majesty, of that letter must have crushed Reed. No rage, no accusation of treachery, no scorn, could have been so unbearable.

Before leaving for Burlington, Reed had told Washington that he wished to resign as Adjutant-General, but would serve as a volunteer on the staff. From Burlington he sent his resignation to Congress, and notified Washington, to whom, he was sure, he must be offensive.

Washington sent a message of earnest appeal to recall his resignation, and Reed, despatching a second messenger after the first, recaptured the document and rejoined Washington.

It was more than three months before Reed could mention the letter to Washington, who had gone on as if it had never been written. Then Reed referred to it in a letter of complete embarrassment.

He recurred to it again three months later, after Washington had made him a general of cavalry. On receiving a letter of profound regret at the difficulty of regaining lost friendship, Washington wrote an answer that belongs here because it depicts the pain he had received at a time of supreme wretchedness:

"Your favour of the 4th was given me by Joseph Arrowsmith just as Mr. Peters informed me that he was about to set out for Philadelphia. I could not resist the inclination, however, of detaining him long enough to write you a short letter, to thank you as I do most sincerely, for the friendly and affectionate sentiments contained in yours of the above date toward me, and to assure you that I am perfectly convinced of the sincerity of them.

"True it is, I felt myself hurt by a certain letter, which appeared at that time to be the echo of one from you. I was hurt, not because I thought my judgment wronged by the expressions contained in it, but because the same sentiments were not communicated immediately to myself. The favourable manner in which your opinions, upon all occasions, had been received, the impression they made, and the unreserved manner in which I wished and required them to be given, entitled me, I thought, to your advice upon any point in which I appeared to be wanting. To meet with any thing, then, that carried with it a complexion of withholding that advice from me, and censuring my conduct to another, was such an argument of disingenuity, that I was not a little mortified at it. However, I am perfectly satisfied that matters were not as they appeared from the letter alluded to.

"I sincerely wish that you may accept the appointment of Congress, and the post I am desirous of placing you in, . . . Mr. Peters waiting obliges me to conclude, and I do it with great truth, Dear Sir, Your obedient, and affectionate servant,

"GEORGE WASHINGTON." [17]

The friendship was renewed, but the time was to come when the rusty arrow would be twisted and plunged deeper into the old wound by the restless hand of Charles Lee.

After he had forwarded to Reed the letter of Charles Lee in which Lee revealed not only Reed's low opinion of Washington, but also his own, Washington let Lee know that he had read it, but made no comment on its contents.

It had taught him, however, that his most experienced general and the second in command was convinced of his "disqualification" and angling to succeed him.

With his own staff turning against him, with Congress paying him little heed, driven out of Westchester and New York where the Tory majority was now persecuting the patriots; with New Jersey even more strongly loyalist, back of him, Washington was lone and forlorn. Seeing the shifting loyalties of the turn-coats, the greed of the officers, the bounty-loving, home-loving soldiers, the wrangles and trades in Congress, with what a sardonic smile he would have read, if he could have read, the sonorous exordium of Bancroft's *The American Revolution*, which sounded the keynote for all good American historians to chant:

"The hour of the American Revolution was come. The people of the continent with irresistible energy obeyed one general impulse, as the earth in spring listens to the command of nature, and without the appearance of effort bursts forth to life in perfect harmony. The change which Divine wisdom ordained, and which no human policy or force could hold back, proceeded as uniformly and as majestically as the laws of being, and was as certain as the decrees of eternity. . . . And why should man organize resistance to the grand design of Providence?" [18]

Bancroft knew better. He was aware of what he was writing. He had read the truth. But with a tranquil conscience and the loftiest motives, he discarded all that did not fit into his laurel wreath and played up all that did. And he left Washington little to be but a striding god followed by a throng of angels in a battle against devils whom they threw over the alabaster walls of America.

Washington would never have recognized the picture of himself or of his times.

For the next month Washington was like a shepherd trying to carry a mob of terrified sheep out of the reach of ravening wolves toward a fold of uncertain strength. He could not trust his flock to fight and now he knew that they did not trust him.

Cornwallis' first move against Washington was to draw a line that would shut him in between the Hudson and the Hackensack rivers. He began to back away. As he wrote to the Governor of New Jersey:

"Finding we were in the same danger of being pent up between Hackinsac and Passaic Rivers, that we had been between the North and Hackinsac; and finding the country, from its levelness and openness, unfit for making a stand, it was determined to draw the whole of our force over to this side of the river, where we can watch the operations of the enemy, without danger of their surrounding us or making a lodgment in our rear.

"But, as our numbers are still very inadequate to that of the enemy, I imagine I shall be obliged to fall down towards Brunswic, and form a junction with the troops, already in that quarter, under the command of Lord Stirling.

"As the term of the enlistment of the Flying Camp, belonging to Jersey, Pennsylvania, and Maryland, is near expiring, it will occasion so great a diminution of my army, that I submit it to your judgment, whether it would not be proper for you to call together such a number of militia, as, in conjunction with the troops I shall have left, will serve to cover the country and stop the progress of the enemy, if they should attempt to penetrate. If the weather continues favorable, I am apprehensive that they will attempt to make amends for the slowness of their operations at the beginning of the campaign." [19]

He had sent General Mifflin to Philadelphia to stir up Congress. Mifflin was a very eloquent man. Washington also called on Schuyler to send him all the troops he could spare from the north, where things were frozen up. They could not reach him in time.

He called again and again to Lee to come to his aid.

There is one pathetic instance of his eagerness to delude Howe, who learned to call Washington "the old fox."

A fox with the hounds right on its heels in open country has little chance to exploit its skill in anything except speed, and Washington reeling backward across New Jersey could exercise no more strategy than a battered prizefighter sliding along the ropes from corner to corner. But he made one effort that was not disclosed for a hundred years or more.

He had written to General Lee that a letter of his had fallen into the enemy's hands "by the negligent and infamous conduct of the post rider." [20]

This may have given him a suggestion, for six days later he wrote to Lee a letter of such contrast to his others that it must have been composed for its effect and carefully planted for capture.

It turned up in 1877 among the Hessian papers in Germany, when General Stryker went abroad to search the archives.

Keeping in mind Washington's frantic reiterations to Lee that if he did not make haste to join him, the army would be destroyed and Philadelphia's fall end the hopes of liberty, there is something tragi-ludicrous in the complacent letter, which Washington manifestly wrote for foreign consumption:

"MY DEAR GENERAL:

"The movements of the enemy are, since I wrote you from Newark, of such a nature as things stand at present, sincerely to be wished for. I have feared that they would take Newark, Elizabeth Town and Amboy for their winter quarters in order to undertake from these places early in the spring an attack on Philadelphia and at the same time having a favourable season ahead that they would make a diversion on the Delaware river with their fleet. The advantages they have gained over us in the past have made them so proud and sure of success that they are determined to go to Philadelphia this winter. I have positive information that this is a fact and because the term of service of the light troops of Jersey and Maryland are ended they anticipate the weakness of our army. Should they now really risk this undertaking then there is a great probability that they will pay dearly for it for I shall continue to retreat before them so as to lull them into security." [21]

Even Washington's quiescent sense of the ridiculous must have been strained when he wrote as he staggered from town to town, from despair to despair:

"The movements of the enemy are . . . sincerely to be wished for . . . they will pay dearly for it for I shall continue to retreat before them so as to lull them into security."

Perhaps the letter had some influence, for something certainly lulled Howe.

A cold rain gave Washington's half-naked troops a poor relief from British pursuit, but on November 27th, he wrote to Lee:

"They are now pushing this way—part of 'em have passed the Pasaick. . . . The distress of the troops for want of cloathes I feel much; but what can I do?"

What could he do? He had "Scouts and detachments out to harrass them and watch their motions and to gain, if possible, intelligence of their designs."

He left Newark just in time to escape the enemy "whose advanced guards were entering the town by the time our rear got out."

There were indications that more British troops were about to land at Perth Amboy and pursue him from there. The British were "collecting and impressing all the wagons they could find"—which were fortunately few.

He fell back to Brunswick.

The time of that great Flying Camp expired on November 30th and away it flew. Almost nobody would reenlist.

"But what is still worse, altho' most of the Pennsylvanian's are enlisted till the first of January, I am informed that they are deserting in great numbers." [22]

The Board of War was so desperate that it proposed enlisting British prisoners. Washington opposed it. Such soldiers were "most backward, for fear, I suppose, of falling into the hands of their former masters, from whom they expect no mercy." The Hessians preferred victory and pillage to American bribes, though Washington advocated letting prisoners escape provided they carried back and distributed the little leaflets offering free land to deserters.

As he fled, he was afraid to carry stores because "we know

not today where we shall be obliged to remove tomorrow."

That meant hunger and discontented soldiers and more excuses for desertion.

And yet in all this frantic wonder as to the fate of his dwindling band, he found time to write to the mother of Alex Graydon. She had evidently appealed to him to forward a letter to her son in captivity:

"Madam, Your letter to your son (enclosed to me) went in the day after it came to my hands, by a flag which happened to be going to New-York.

"I am very sorry for the misfortune of your son's captivity, but these are accidents which must be experienced and felt in war. Colonel Cadwalader, who has been suffered to return to Philadelphia, would be able to inform you of your son's health. Any hard money, which you may be able to forward to me, or Mr. Tilghman, (who is of my family) shall be contrived to him by some means or other." [23]

By the first of December he had no more than four thousand men, including a thousand militia.

The New Jersey provincial legislature was in flight from town to town and on the second of December it dissolved, "leaving each member to look to his own safety." [24]

Already on November 30th the Philadelphia Council of Safety had published a warning to the citizens to be ready to leave any moment.

To the fugitive Governor, Washington had written the day before that Howe would reach the Delaware in a week or ten days, unless he could be "opposed by more than my present numbers."

"General Lee is on his march down to join me; but, if the enemy should throw in a body of men between us, he will be obliged to make a considerable circuit to avoid them. The boats and craft, all along the Delaware side, should be secured; particularly the Durham boats used for the transportation of produce down the river. Parties should be sent to all the landings, to have them removed to the other side, hauled up, and put under proper guards." [25]

At last Lee had decided to yield to Washington's repeated messages. He had been unable to secure enough militia to attack New York. But he came at a snail's pace.

Yet, curiously, he may have saved Washington from immediate destruction after all, for his movements fretted Howe and when at last Lee crossed the Hudson, Howe feared that he might strike Cornwallis in the rear. So the British moved with more caution. [26]

They moved slowly for another reason. They, too, were famished. Cornwallis reported that they had no flour supply and lived from day to day on what they could pick up in the distracted country. They had to stop now and then to bake bread, or starve. [27]

And, of course, the roads were atrocious, the horses and wagons weak and few.

Still they had their King back of them and Washington had only a maelstrom.

His one means of making a stand in New Jersey was to add Lee's men to his. But Lee was hard to budge and Washington dared not crack the whip. It was not his nature to crack the whip over a general, though he had beaten a brigadier across the back for cowardice.

Assuming that Lee would eventually come into New Jersey, Washington feared that the British would keep him off as they had kept his own troops from Fort Washington. His last hope was to reach the Delaware.

He wrote to Lee on the same day that the enemy undoubtedly meant "to push for Philadelphia. The force I have with me is infinitely inferior in numbers. . . . I must entreat you to hasten your march." [28]

That evening the enemy appeared on the heights opposite Brunswick, and there was "a smart cannonade." Washington fled at once out of Brunswick, and Greene wrote bitterly to Governor Cooke of further desertion.

"Two brigades left us at Brunswick, notwithstanding the enemy were within two hour's march and coming on. The loss of these troops at this critical time reduced his Excellency to the necessity to order a retreat again. . . . When we left Brunswick, we had not 3000 men." [29]

On the 2nd of December Washington was in Princeton. He left Greene and Stirling there and hurried to Trenton on the 3rd, where he ordered all stores hastily transported across the Delaware. He hoped that "being disencumbered of my baggage and stores," he might do something worth doing, and urged that the Pennsylvania militia should come to him there and give a little encouragement to the New Jersey men.

He was humiliated and amazed at Lee's silence. No word had come from him in nine days, though Washington had sent a daily express. When the first letter came he must have winced to read it:

"I could wish you would bind me as little as possible, not from any opinion, I do assure you, of my own parts, but from a persuasion that detached Generals cannot have too great latitude, unless they are very incompetent indeed." [30]

General Howe was on his way faster than Lee, not only with reinforcements but with promises of amnesty to all who would return to allegiance within sixty days. There was a stampede to exchange an old oath for a new one.

Dr. John Morgan wrote to Lee that "the precipitate Retreat of our Troops from Hackensack has made thousands of Tories." [31]

Lee came drifting along, out-Howeing Howe, refusing to be hurried and substituting for obedience to orders a patronizing promise to do Washington more good by hang-

ing on to the British rear. He promised to attack at what
he should decide to be the proper moment. He reported
five thousand men—nearly twice as large an army as Washington's and in good spirits.

He wrote: "I cannot persuade myself that Philadelphia
is their object at present." [32]

And Philadelphia was not Howe's object at first. He had
ordered Cornwallis to stop at Brunswick. To hold all of
New York and half of the Jerseys would have satisfied
Howe, who hoped to see a general rush for the pardons he
offered.

But Washington was so weak that he was an irresistible
temptation to Cornwallis, who also pointed out that Howe
must protect the loyalists throughout the state. Howe saw
the point.

Suddenly on December 6th, Howe arrived at Brunswick
and pressed forward with Cornwallis to Princeton, driving
Greene and Stirling away as fast as they could run.

Washington had intended to return and fight, and was on
his way to Princeton when he met his men on the retreat.

Warned that the enemy were advancing by different
routes and trying to get in back of him, he fell away to
Trenton in all haste and loaded his troops on the boats that
his providence had provided. In spite of Howe's mysterious
delay at Princeton, Washington barely escaped him.

"Their van entered, just as our rear guard quitted." [33]

He had removed all the boats there were on the river, but
he feared that they were bringing their own.

"If so, it will be impossible for our small force to give them any
considerable opposition in the passage of the river; indeed they
[may] make a feint at one place, and, by a sudden removal, carry
their boats higher or lower before we can bring our cannon to play
upon them."

Cornwallis marched thirteen miles along the river in a vain search for boats.[34] But it was still easy to build rafts and pole across.

Washington wrote to Lund:

"I tremble for Philadelphia. Nothing, in my opinion, but Gen. Lee's speedy arrival . . . can save it. . . . We have prevented them from crossing; but how long we shall be able to do it God only knows as they are still hovering about the river. And if everything else fails, will wait till the 1st of January, when there will be no other men to oppose them but militia . . . except the Virginia regiments and the shattered remains of Smallwood's, which, by fatigue, want of clothes, &c., are reduced to nothing."

And then the thunderbolt:

"Our cause has also received a severe blow in the captivity of Gen. Lee. Unhappy man! Taken by his own imprudence, going three or four miles from his own camp, and within twenty of the enemy, notice of which by a rascally Tory was given a party of light horse seized him in the morning after travelling all night, and carried him off in high triumph and with every mark of indignity, not even suffering him to get his hat or surtout coat. The troops that were under his command are not yet come up with us, though they, I think, may be expected to-morrow.

"A large part of the Jerseys have given every proof of disaffection that they can do, and this part of Pennsylvania are equally inimical. In short, your imagination can scarce extend to a situation more distressing than mine. Our only dependence now is upon the speedy enlistment of a new army.

"If this fails, I think the game will be pretty well up, as, from disaffection and want of spirit and fortitude, the inhabitants, instead of resistance, are offering submission and taking protection from Gen. Howe in Jersey." [35]

In front of Washington was the British lion ramping up and down the stream looking for a crossing. Back of him was Philadelphia in a mad stampede. Congress juggled resolutions, told Washington just what to do, appointed a day of fasting and humiliation, "as soon as possible." They had not even time to fast. But they went so far as to call on all the "officers civil and military" to repent and reform. They issued a particular law against swearing and immorality.

They called on Washington to contradict a scandalous report that they were going to adjourn.

He wisely suppressed the resolution. And they adjourned.

They who had been so afraid of a military man that they ruined all his possibilities, now turned over to Washington "full power to order and direct all things relative to the department and to the operations of war."

It was on December 12th that they made him Dictator.[36]

He had implored them for a year and a half to give him a regular army. Instead they made him Dictator of a reversion to chaos.

The country was shaken with stories of horrible atrocities. Whether they were true or not, exaggerated, multiplied or manufactured, the fear of them was there. New Jersey was another Belgium, and a Committee of Safety published this "extract of a letter from an officer of distinction in the American army."

"Since I wrote you this morning, I have had an opportunity of hearing a number of the particulars of the horrid depredations committed by that part of the British Army which was stationed at and near Pennytown, under the command of Lord Cornwallis. Besides the sixteen young women who had fled to the woods to avoid their brutality, and were there seized and carried off, one man had the cruel mortification to have his wife and only daughter (a child of ten years of age) ravished; this he himself, almost choked with grief, uttered in lamentations to his friend, who told me of it, and also informed me that another girl of thirteen years of age, was taken from her father's house, carried to a barn about a mile, there ravished, and afterwards made use of by five more of these brutes.

"Numbers of instances of the same kind of behaviour I am assured to have happened; here their brutish lust were their stimulas; but wanton mischief was seen in every part of the country; every thing portable they plunder and carry off, neither age nor sex, Whig or Tory, is spared; an indiscriminate ruin attends every person they meet with; infants, children, old men, and women, are left in their shirts, without a blanket to cover them in this inclement season; furniture of every kind destroyed or burnt; windows and doors broke to pieces; in short, the houses left unhabitable, and the people left without provisions, for every horse, cow, ox, hogs, and poultry, carried off; . . .

"Another instance of brutality happened near Woodbridge. One of the most respectable gentlemen in that part of the country was alarmed by the cries and shrieks of a most lovely daughter; he found an officer—a British officer—in the act of ravishing her; he instantly put him to death; two other officers rushed in with fusees, and fired two balls into the father, who is now languishing under his wounds. I am tired of this horrid scene; Almighty Justice cannot suffer it to go unpunished; he will inspirit his people (who only claim that liberty which he has entitled them to) to do themselves justice, to rise universally in arms, and drive these invading tyrants out of our country.

"Published by order of the Council of Safety. Geo. Bickham, Secretary pro tem." [37]

Galloway [38] (who did not love the rebels any more) says that Congress had affidavits taken of cases of rape to shame the enemy.

To rule such a pandemonium and redeem it they had made Washington Dictator—a brave word. They looked to him to save them. But he must have felt less like Julius Cæsar than like the poor outlaw the *New York Mercury* described two days before Christmas:

"The Rebels are everywhere mouldering away like a rope of sand. With the most impotent bravadoes, they have not yet had the spirit to make any thing like a stand in a single encounter. The New-England people have neither money nor recruits; and the rest of the Colonies are nearly drained of their resources. Ruin, therefore, and destruction must be the consequence of continuing the war any longer.

"Mr. Washington, with about two thousand poor wretches, who can get no subsistence but by following him, has fled to Lancaster, in Pennsylvania. Many people of Philadelphia are retired, with their goods and effects, into the back country, with but little provision for the winter.

"The chain of posts formed by the British troops reach within seventeen miles of Philadelphia, upon the banks of the Delaware, and the first strong frost will afford them a natural bridge over it." [39]

Thousands of Americans were turning against the cause. Even Joseph Galloway, native-born and a member of the First Continental Congress, went over to the British and devoted his pen to scarifying the patriots and scarifying even the British generals because of their sloth in destruction.

Yet an Englishman, that little Thomas Paine, who had made Independence rhyme with Common Sense, was with Washington. He had carried a musket on the muddy trudges through New Jersey.

But at night by a lantern, he wrote things on a drumhead, and showed them to Washington. They stirred Washington as "Common Sense" had stirred him and he had them read aloud to his shivering soldiers.

These writings were published and reprinted in such quantities that they seemed to cover the land like autumn leaves. They were published serially as various numbers of *The American Crisis*.[40]

Because they are old and familiar it is easy to condescend to them. A platitude is a dead thing that was once alive. And Thomas Paine's works have the fault once found with *Hamlet:* they are "too full of quotations."

But they flamed then, and warmed cold souls, rekindled faint hearts, started a blaze that would not be trodden under.

That was a night of nights when Paine, crouching over a drum, wrote the first words. They beat like a drum. And that was indeed a morning when the ragged, blue-nosed, bare-footed, sniffling, blear-eyed, unpaid regulars and militia heard in the air like another reveille this cry for the first time:

"These are the times that try men's souls. The summer soldier and the sunshine patriot will, in this crisis, shrink from the service of their country; but he that stands it *now*, deserves the love and thanks of man and woman. Tyranny, like hell, is not easily conquered; yet we have this consolation with us, that the harder the conflict, the more glorious the triumph. . . . Heaven knows how to put a proper price upon its goods; and it would be strange indeed if so celestial an article as FREEDOM should not be highly rated."

These phrases, these arguments, and appeals are so pat to their occasion that they revive the scene of their birth. One can feel the thrill of pride they gave those shabby forefathers who were such glorious fools, and gave their descendants such cause for pride and gratitude.

Paine's line of argument would hit the farmer and the villager as common sense. His music would beautify their day. His eloquence would make them stand up straight and feel that they were fighting for something worth famine, nakedness and shame, and death.

Paine knew that those men understood religious talk, and he was a very religious, God-loving man, though antipathetic to the Christian dogma. For the sake of his message he even called himself a Christian.

But he was sincere when he wrote:

"I have as little superstition in me as any man living, but my secret opinion has ever been, and still is, that God Almighty will not give up a people to military destruction, or leave them unsupportedly to perish, who have so earnestly and so repeatedly sought to avoid the calamities of war, by every decent method which wisdom could invent."

He admitted there was a panic, but great folk had known panics times enough:

"Britain has trembled like an ague at the report of a French fleet of flat-bottomed boats; and in the fourteenth century the whole English army, after ravaging the kingdom of France, was driven back like men petrified with fear; and this brave exploit was performed by a few broken forces collected and headed by a woman, Joan of Arc. Would that heaven might inspire some Jersey maid to spirit up her countrymen, and save her fair fellow sufferers from ravage and ravishment!"

With poignant directness he brought duty home and made it a privilege. Nobody was too stupid or too wise to feel the greatness of the thought back of his anecdote of the Tory tavern-keeper, the man he had met who clung to his child's hand and used "this unfatherly expression:

" 'Well! give me peace in my day.'

"Not a man lives on the continent but fully believes that a separation must some time or other finally take place, and a generous parent should have said,

" 'If there must be trouble, let it be in my day, that my child may have peace.' "

This is as noble an epitaph for the founders of a nation as ever was written. Paine could be sentimental, and he could shock:

"Let them call me rebel and welcome, I feel no concern from it; but I should suffer the misery of devils, were I to make a whore of my soul by swearing allegiance to one whose character is that of a sottish, stupid, stubborn, worthless, brutish man. I conceive likewise a horrid idea in receiving mercy from a being, who at the last day shall be shrieking to the rocks and mountains to cover him, and fleeing with terror from the orphan, the widow, and the slain of America. . . .

"By perseverance and fortitude we have the prospect of a glorious issue; by cowardice and submission, the sad choice of a variety of evils—a ravaged country—a depopulated city—habitations without safety, and slavery without hope—our homes turned into barracks and bawdy-houses for Hessians, and a future race to provide for, whose fathers we shall doubt of.

"Look on this picture and weep over it! and if there yet remains one thoughtless wretch who believes it not, let him suffer it unlamented."

This was the sort of thing that Washington could love well enough to feed his soldiers for breakfast. The Reverend Ezra Stiles [41] says that these "publications & exertions excited the public Spirit" and increased Washington's army.

They increased his soul as well and he meditated a great thing.

XXXVII

DICTATOR

"MY neck does not feel as though it was made for a halter," said Washington, passing his big hand over his long throat.

He had been asking Reed if Pennsylvania would support the rebels in case they were driven from the Delaware river and on past Philadelphia into the western mountains.

Reed answered dismally that if the eastern counties were subdued, the back counties would surrender. Washington sighed:

"We must retire to Augusta County in Virginia. Numbers will be obliged to repair to us for safety; and we must try what we can do in carrying on a predatory war; and if overpowered we must cross the Alleghany Mountains."

This conversation was reported by the Reverend Dr. Gordon,[1] who had it on good enough authority to make it credible. It is confirmed by everything in Washington's character. Rather than submit and accept whatever punishment or mercy might be vouchsafed, he was ready to retreat into that Ohio country he had explored, willing to become an outlaw, a Robin Hood, keeping up a guerilla war on tyranny. He would turn Indian rather than return English.

The all but incredible thing is, not that he should have pondered such a scheme, but that he escaped having to carry it out.

The Congress that had made him Dictator had lacked the legal authority to create such an extra-legal office.[2] It had simply invented its own authority to exist, and now it was seeking a new hiding place for its frail being.

Congress had loaded its effects into wagons, especially the printing press from which it issued its edicts, and also its money, which General Putnam could not persuade the Philadelphians to accept at face value in spite of his threats of death and destruction. Nobody has ever succeeded in forcing money to be worth more than it actually is worth. People are eager to believe in everything mythical except money.

The government of the United States was on wheels in December, 1776, and the Congress was driven out of its capital, as it would be again thirty-six years later, when the English came again. Fifty years after that, President Lincoln's government would be packed "in a valise" against the invasion of the Virginians under Robert E. Lee.

Though Washington caught from the drooping hand of that Congress the awful torch of power, he did not apply it to the destruction of liberty.

Julius Cæsar accepted from the Roman Senate the name of dictator and used the army for his own aggrandizement. He would have perverted the ancient republic into a kingdom if his own friends had not stabbed him; and even then his avengers turned it into an empire.

The noble William of Orange, made Stadtholder to save the Netherlands from Spain, established himself as king under a name that smelt no sweeter after it had become hereditary.

The Protector Cromwell consolidated his own power and left it to his son.

During Washington's lifetime a young Corsican soldier was on the way up from poverty to dazzling tyranny. Called to honors in the French republic, he would begin to clutch at power on power until he had not only crowned

himself an emperor but seated his relatives and favorites
on such thrones as he could empty.

Even now over in France in 1776, there were several
aspirants for Washington's command, encouraged to expect it, too, by the slowly arriving news of his rapidly accu-
mulating defeats.

One of them, the Comte de Broglie, who had on his staff
the young Lafayette and the German adventurer, Johannes
Kalb, known as the Baron de Kalb, was especially keen to
lead the colonials. He had his agents working with the
American representatives in France, and he was so hopeful
of being called that he had his stipulations all ready when
his envoy, Kalb, actually came to America.

De Broglie decided to revive the title of Stadtholder.
He would command all the troops and control the foreign
negotiations. He must have a great deal of money. The
Americans must see to it that their ally, the King of France,
made the Comte a Duc. He must have his own officers
about him. He must be brought over in state at sufficient
expense. He must have abundant pay. He must not be
asked to stay longer than three years, and he refused in
advance to be King.[3]

The danger was very real at the moment that some such
man should be put in command of the American hopes by
the French, whose aid was vital, for supplies, munitions,
money, credit, and moral support.

In desperation Congress made Washington dictator.
And what did he do with the sceptre? Did he brandish it
from a throne? Did he design himself a new uniform and
new insignia as Napoleon did? Did he mock and ignore the
senate that appealed to him to save it? No, he manifested
not one whit less of deference to Congress because of its
humiliation. He consulted it still, apologized for taking
the least action when an emergency prevented the delay of

asking its permission. He asked for no title. He demanded
nobody's banishment, nobody's head. He asked for not
one cent of money, having taken none at all up to now.

In fact he joined with other officers in borrowing money
on his personal credit in order to put up cash for bounties to
bribe his soldiers to remain a few weeks longer for the redemption of the cause.

As soon as Congress found it safe to return temporarily
to its capital he relinquished his power. When he found
that other officers were combining to take his command
away, he made no outcry of conspiracy. He modestly
passed along his accidental discovery to Congress for its
action. He made no effort to revenge himself by having
his rivals thrown out of their offices. He treated them with
sympathy in their defeat.

He conducted himself always as merely one among the
soldiers of liberty, their leader only because, and while,
they asked him to lead. He conceived leadership as merely
the distinction of carrying the heaviest burdens with the
most cruel responsibilities and the least repose.

When at last an adoring soldier wrote to him that he
ought to be king, he did not indulge in any dramatics like
Cæsar, or any hypocrisies, or even in any florid disclaim-
ers. He simply wrote the man that his suggestion was an
insult and must not be repeated.

He was sublime in his meekness. He was something new
in the history of mankind. He dealt with power in an
original way and he saved his country not only from military subjection but from eternal warfare with its own ambitious citizens. He established a tradition that no American has since presumed to combat, a tradition like a vast invisible barrier to self-aggrandizement upon the trampled
liberties of the people.

He had not even the encouragement of imagination or

prophecy. There were times when he foresaw the future of the continent and spoke of the duty of his generation to millionfold posterity.

But at present, as usual, his clear eyes were on the next thing. The enemy was across a little river, able to build boats, force one of the fords, or come up in ships. Behind him Congress had fled to the woods. About him was a little body of soldiers whose enlistments were about to expire. Washington called the expiration of their enlistments their "political deaths." [4] More and more of them were unwilling to wait a few weeks and were deserting—what he might have called committing political suicide.

Whatever was to be done must be done quickly. But his men were in such a state of poverty that they could not move. There were hundreds of them that had not even a pair of shoes to their feet and were naturally unwilling to leave their tents. A few of them were sturdy enough to march barefooted on the icy snow, but the rest could not be persuaded to cripple themselves for life before they could even reach the perils of battle.

His men had been ragged always, often immodestly exposed. Now he wrote: "Their distresses are extremely great, many of 'em being entirely naked and most so thinly clad as to be unfit for service." [5]

One result of England's old refusal to permit woolen manufactories in America was that many of such uniforms as the soldiers had were of linen only.

The very dregs of humiliation were reached when the American army had to accept the charity usually reserved for paupers, beggars and tramps. The women and the kindly men of Philadelphia scurried about, gathered up such cast-off garments as could be secured for nothing, and sent them to Washington's shivering vagabonds.

And he, the exquisite, the aristocrat, the fop who imported

his raiment from England, demanding the finest fabric cut to
the latest mode, and who proclaimed that cleanliness and
neatness were the most important attributes of a good soldier, was so reduced in pride that he was grateful for second-
handed shabbiness to cover the raw hides of his pitiful
rabble.

And the Dictator actually wrote, three days before
Christmas:

"Your collection of old cloathes for the use of our army deserves my warmest thanks; they are of the greatest use, and shall
be distributed where they are most wanted." [6]

He was encouraged by this gratuity to ask for further
alms:

"I think if the Committee, or some proper persons, were appointed to go through the County of Bucks and make a collection
of blankets, &c., in the manner you have done in Philadelphia, it
would be better than doing it in a military way by me, for many
people, who would be willing to contribute or sell, if asked to do
so by their neighbors or acquaintances, feel themselves hurt when
the demand is made, backed by an armed force. But I would at
the same time remark that if any, who can spare without inconvenience, refuse to do it, I would immediately give proper assistance
to take from them."

Five days later, having received a number of long coats
lined with red flannel, he was inspired to propose that the
linings should be ripped out and made into waistcoats and
drawers. [7]

Nothing so saps the courage of a soldier as a cold belly
and goose-pimpled thighs.

The need for money was unusually dire, and he wrote an
unpublished letter on the same day to somebody in Philadelphia, probably to Robert Morris, the Philadelphia banker
and speculator.

"For godsake hurry Mr Mease with the Cloathing as nothing will contribute more to facilitate the Recruiting Service than warm comfortable Cloathing to those who engage:—Muskets are not wanted at this place, nor should they, or any other valuable stores in my judgment be kept in Philadelphia, for Sorry I am to inform you, my dear Sir, that unless the Militia repair to the City for defence of it, I see no Earthly prospect of saving of it after the last of this Instant, as that fatal vote of Congress respecting the appointment of new Officers has put the Recruiting business upon such a footing, and introduced so much confusion into the old Regiments, that I see no chance of raising men out of them; by the first of next month then, we shall be left with five Regiments of Virginia, one of Maryland—Colo Hands and the Remains of Miles; Reduced so much by sickness, fatigue &ca as in the whole not to exceed, but fall short of, 1200 Men—Upon these and the Militia, is all our dependance, for you may as well attempt to stop the Winds from blowing, or the Sun in its diurnal, as the Regiments from going when their term is expired.

"I think with you Sir (that however missed you may be in Congress) your presence in the City cannot be dispensed with—I will give you the earliest information in my power of immediate danger; in the meantime, I advise for the Reasons before mentiond that you detain no Papers you can possibly do without for I am satisfied the Enemy wait for two events only to begin their operations upon Philadelphia—Ice for a Passage, and the dissolution of the poor remains of our debilitated army. . . .

"The Commissary (Mr. Wharton) informs me that he cannot prevail on the Millers to grind, & that the Troops in consequence, are like to suffer for want of Flour—this if I understand him proceeds either from disaffection, or an unwillingness to take Continental Money in pay, which in fact is the same thing—this must be remedied by fair, or other means.—" 8

This is presumably the traditional letter that came to Morris when the Treasury was empty, and he had no recourse but to appeal to the Quaker, John Martin:

"I have a letter from General Washington & require a certain sum in specie, and you must let me have it. Your security shall be my note and my honor."

The Quaker, whose creed forbade war and all aid to war, compromised with his conscience by answering:

"Thee knows, Robert, I am a man of peace but if thee wants it thyself, thee shall have it."

And he turned over the money that made the Battle of Trenton possible.

The capture of Charles Lee was a staggering shock to Washington, who needed both wisdom and men. Before he knew of what must have been a galling experience to the proud Lee, Washington had sent not only letters but messengers in search of him. He had finally despatched Lord Stirling on the hunt with these unpublished instructions dated December 14th, the day after Lee's mishap:

"My Lord, Repair with all possible expedition to Genl. Lee's Camp.—Know his Situation, Numbers, &ca.—Send Officers you can confide into Genl. Gates, & Heath, to be informd of their numbers, condition, and when they may be expected at Pitts Town.

"Use every possible means without regard to expense, to come with certainty, at the Enemys strength, situation and movements— without this we wander in a wilderness of uncertainties & difficulty, & no plan can be formd upon a Rational plan.—When you see Genl. Lee & converse with him as also (Gates & Heath if possible) what probable mode of attack can be attempted & give me the earliest advice of it—. . .

"Weigh every circumstance of attack, & retreat properly, that nothing that can be guarded against, may be unprovided for.—Give me the earliest and best advice of every matter.—and do all in your power to inspirit the Militia, & bring them into use to the best advantage." [9]

The nausea that Lee experienced when he looked out of his window and saw himself netted—and by men of his old English regiment—must have been rendered even more loathsome to his high stomach by the fact that he had just been writing a letter denouncing Washington to General

Gates, also English born, also contemptuous of the Virginian, and also ambitious to supplant him:

"Entre nous, a certain great man is most damnably deficient—He has thrown me into a situation where I have my choice of difficulties—if I stay in this Province I risk myself and Army and if I do not stay the Province is lost for ever—I have neither guides, Cavalry Medicines Money Shoes or Stockings—I must act with the greatest circumspection—Tories are in my front rear and on my flanks—the Mass of the People is strangly contaminated—in short unless some thing which I do not expect turns up We are lost—our Counsels have been weak to the last degree." [10]

Fortunately Lee had been captured by a patrol at a distance from his troops. His leaderless army was brought up at last to Washington by General Sullivan, its five thousand "in good spirits" having dwindled to a wretchedly ill-equipped two thousand.

Washington was too big to permit another man's ambition to seem a treason to the nation and there was no insincerity in his expressions of regret at the loss of Lee: "I feel much for the loss of my Country in his Captivity." [11] "Our country has lost a warm friend and an able officer." [12]

He proved how he valued Lee by offering to exchange six field officers for him. [13] But Howe would not consent. He had some hope of hanging the man for open treason, but Lee had taken the precaution to resign his royal half-pay commission before he entered the service of the rebels. He was eventually exchanged and died in America, after causing Washington much further trouble.

Long years after, the grave of his reputation was opened and he was branded a traitor.

The good name of his admirer, Adjutant-General Reed, also came under suspicion and his fame was subjected to ferocious attack. He was accused of being so frightened in December, 1776, after the flight across the Delaware as to turn Tory and apply to the Hessian commander, Von Donop, for a protection. There was talk of a duel over it with Colonel Cadwalader in 1782. Reed lost an election, and the accusations seemed to be established by a letter from Von Donop, offering a protection to Colonel Reed. This was taken as such proof of his duplicity that the historian, Bancroft, wrote a pamphlet against him, following a vitriolic anonymous publication called *Nuts for Historians to Crack*.[14]

Then it was discovered that the Colonel who received Von Donop's "protection" was a Colonel Read of New Jersey.

Reed's grandson came to the rescue of his good name and Bancroft withdrew his charge.

To complicate the coincidence further, General Stryker found in Germany a letter sent by Reed to Von Donop asking for a conference in the name of Washington to see if an agreement could not be made to spare the town of Burlington from bombardment.

Reed was so far indeed from being a traitor that he redeemed himself perfectly by his energy and his fearless scouting within the enemy lines.

He did splendid work also as Washington's envoy to Philadelphia, where he went to plead for troops, as did the valiant Smallwood, too badly wounded to fight. They succeeded in persuading the Philadelphia city militia to join Washington, but the rest of Pennsylvania was almost immoveable, being rather inclined to favor the British than the rebels. The Quakers, with certain distinguished exceptions, were distinctly hostile and Washington wrote that the Pennsylvania militia not only refused to obey the summons but "exult at the approach of the enemy, and on our late misfortunes."[15]

He doubted that they were "to be trusted with arms in

their hands," and asked that they be secretly seized and stripped of their weapons before they could hide them.

Never was a people in such a curdle of confusion. It must be remembered that the majority of the Americans were poor, and subdued to the harsh necessities of their trades. The need of money and the cries of hungry children warred with patriotic ideals even where they were cherished.

The spirit of independence was new. The radicals were not always impressive or trustworthy. The neighbors looked at one another and saw uncertainty on every side. The soldiers could not fight. The General could not win. The Congress could not agree. The army was unpaid and indecent, hungry and timid. And the national money was a painful joke.

Clever speculators were growing rich. Grafters were cheating everybody. Soldiers were demanding bigger and bigger bounties. The farmers and the small merchants got the worst of it on all sides. And the British were apparently on the crest of the wave, and a tidal wave at that.

The lack of heroism was not beautiful, but it was natural, and the struggle for bare existence was difficult.

The situation was altogether so obscenely ugly that many historians have felt it their duty to conceal it entirely. To John Adams, however, in the midst of it, the scene lacked all the enchantment of distance, and he wrote a tribute to his times that no Tory could have surpassed:

"The spirit of venality is the most dreadful and alarming enemy America has to oppose. . . . If God Almighty does not interfere by his grace to control this universal idolatry to the mammon of unrighteousness, we shall be given up to the chastisement of his judgments. I am ashamed of the age I live in." [16]

His language is no stronger than Washington's was on many occasions, and their authority is not to be questioned.

In contrast to his testimony as to the facts there is something sickening in the pious treacle that historians like Bancroft pour over the scene, blandly extracting sweetness and providential grace from the agonies that Washington had to wallow through:

"The sharp tribulation which assayed his fortitude carried with it a divine and an animating virtue. Hope and zeal illuminated his grief. His emotions come to us across the century like strains from an eternity which repairs all losses and rights all wrongs; in his untold sorrows his trust in Providence kept up in his heart an under-song of wonderful sweetness. The spirit of the Most High dwells among the afflicted, rather than the prosperous; and he who has never broken his bread in tears knows not the heavenly powers. The trials of Washington are the dark, solemn ground on which the beautiful work of the country's salvation was embroidered." [17]

There is nothing in this offertory to explain the miseries of the Tories or of the Hessians, who were quite as religious and quite as helpless and quite as sincere in their miserable bewilderments.

Deaf to that heavenly "under-song of wonderful sweetness," which Bancroft heard so plainly at a distance of nearly a century, Washington sought only to get enough men together to shoot down enough British and Hessians to keep them at a safe distance.

He wrote to his brother:

"In a word, my dear Sir, . . . I think the game is pretty near up." [18]

He wrote to Congress:

"I rather think the design of General Howe is to possess himself of Philadelphia this winter, if possible; and in truth I do not see what is to prevent him, as ten days more will put an end to the existence of our army."

Washington had been both picking up and letting fall regiments and parcels of regiments. On December 22nd,

1776, his adjutant's return showed 679 officers and 10,804 men, of which practically half, 5,399, were sick, detached, or on furlough, leaving 6,164 present for duty, plus about 500 men from the North, under the command of General Arthur St. Clair; about 1,000 Philadelphians, and 400 New Jersey militia—a total of 8,064, of which about 6,000 were available for action.[19]

Even before Howe left Trenton Washington, realizing that the war was over, unless he could do something startling, had been aching to throw himself across the river and either catch Howe unawares or smash his own army before it evaporated.

The problem would have been somewhat the same as at Boston with three great differences: Howe had no ships to protect him; he had no fortifications, and Washington was at bay, besieged, driven to a sally of some kind.

On December 14th, before he knew that Howe was gone or that Lee was captured, he wrote to General Gates, who was on his way south:

"I expect General Lee will be there this evening or to-morrow, who will be followed by General Heath and his division. If we can draw our forces together, I trust, under the smiles of Providence, we may yet effect an important stroke, or at least prevent General Howe from executing his plans." [20]

On the same day he wrote to the Governor of Connecticut (whose situation was so alarming that Washington countermanded his order to General Heath to join him, ordered him back to Peekskill and sent Arnold to New London) that with the aid of Gates' troops he might try something:

"They may, in conjunction with my present force, and that under General Lee, enable us to attempt a stroke upon the forces of the enemy, who lie a good deal scattered, and to all appearances in a state of security. A lucky blow in this quarter would be fatal to them, and would most certainly rouse the spirits of the people, which are quite sunk by our late misfortunes." [21]

Gates came down from the North with Benedict Arnold but they brought only 500 frostbitten men through a freezing snowstorm. Washington welcomed Gates as an old friend and asked him to stay and help, but Gates made an excuse of sickness and pushed on to Congress. He had a scheme of his own for saving the nation, and it did not include Washington.

Left alone with his problem, the Dictator was desperate enough to make an attempt at building up a little artillery, and he took the liberty of bribing recruits by increasing their pay by twenty-five percent, which was still far below that of the English and French artillery service.

Even for this unavoidable act, the Dictator apologized to Congress, and asked permission to make certain essential decisions without referring them to Congress "at the distance of a hundred and thirty or forty miles. . . .

"It may be said, that this is an application for powers that are too dangerous to be entrusted. I can only add, that desperate diseases require desperate remedies; and I with truth declare, that I have no lust after power, but I wish with as much fervency as any man upon this wide-extended continent for an opportunity of turning the sword into the ploughshare. But my feelings, as an officer and a man, have been such as to force me to say, that no person ever had a greater choice of difficulties to contend with than I have." [22]

In the midst of his catalogue of difficulties, he gave voice to one great word, for it seems to have suddenly occurred to him that it might be possible to turn the destructive jealousies of the colonies into a constructive rivalry for honors. And he revealed that his ideal was national. He had a country at last, a poor thing, but his own:

"I have labored, ever since I have been in the service, to discourage all kinds of local attachments and distinctions of country, denominating the whole by the greater name of AMERICAN, but I have found it impossible to overcome prejudices; and, under the new establishment, I conceive it best to stir up an emulation." [23]

Five days later he began to do things that made the word "American" clang in the ear of the world. He gave it its first real acquaintance with Victory.

XXXVIII

THE RETURN TO TRENTON

HIS early training in Indian warfare and bush-fighting had taught Washington the importance of deceiving while not being deceived, and of quick recovery from defeat by an unexpected recoil.

In his larger command he enlarged his grasp to an unusual realization of the value of military intelligence in both its forms of espionage and counter-espionage.

The Revolution was a civil war at least in the sense that the combatants on both sides spoke the same language; the dialects were equally confused among loyalists and rebels. This made it easy to send spies, but almost impossible to keep them off.

Washington had a private fund for employing secret agents: he had several cipher codes and he kept himself informed as to the chemicals of espionage, invisible writing and other devices.

His constant cry was, "Give me spies! Buy me spies!"

One of a general's duties is to supply the enemy with misinformation and Washington did his best in that direction. For example, he wrote to Colonel Cadwalader:

"Keep a good look-out for spies, and endeavor to magnify your number as much as possible." [1]

And to Putnam:

"You will give out your strength to be twice as great as it is. . . . You will keep as many spies out as you will see proper. A number of horsemen, in the dress of the country, must be constantly kept going backwards and forwards." [2]

Another part of Washington's bluff was the stiff tone he kept up in his correspondence with Howe concerning the exchange of prisoners. He never admitted for a moment that there was a large possibility that his own whole army would soon be a prisoner.[3]

Saved temporarily by the interposition of the icy Delaware, he guarded every ford and crossing-place with troops under the strictest orders to build redoubts and park their wagons at such a distance that in case of unavailing opposition they could retire on the next unit without loss of precious equipment.

He neglected no means to keep eager eyes inside the hostile lines.

"Let me entreat you to find out some person, who can be engaged to cross the river as a spy," he wrote to his four brigadier-generals, Lord Stirling, Hugh Mercer, Adam Stephen, and the recently commissioned French engineer, Roche de Fermoy:

"Expense must not be spared . . . and it will readily be paid by me. We are in a neighborhood of very disaffected people. Equal care therefore should be taken, that one of these persons does not undertake the business in order to betray us." [4]

One of his most trusted spies was John Honeyman, who led a life of infernal disgrace for the sake of the cause. It has always been the peculiar curse of the spy's most essential duty that he must be abhorred by the people he is saving, disowned by the officers who employ him, and left to extricate himself as best he can from a degrading death.

Washington found Honeyman, a Scotch-Irishman, a former member of the bodyguard of General Wolfe, at Hackensack. And Honeyman agreed to pretend to be a butcher and cattle drover.

There was no protection for him except an intervention of Washington once or twice when he was about to meet his

WASHINGTON'S PRIVATE CIPHER CODES.

fate. Honeyman's wife was provided with a letter from Washington asking mercy for "the wife and children of John Honeyman of Griggstown, the notorious Tory," but it was stated that this order was to furnish "no protection to Honeyman himself." [5]

Honeyman, desiring to bring in information, allowed himself to be captured by Washington's scouts on December 22nd, and was taken across the river where he gave information of priceless use in the Battle of Trenton.

He was allowed to escape again and tell the Hessians of his maltreatment. So well did he play his part that a year later he was thrown into the Trenton jail for high treason. He was found guilty, too, but released again by secret influence, for future trouble.

The loyalists maintained that the rebels were mainly foreigners, and the names of the second jury that voted Honeyman guilty are striking evidence of the charge:

"Hendrack Probasco, Hendrick Stryker, Reyneir Veghte, Van Lieu, Van Cleef, Voorhees, Jost Kesciu, Martinis Nevyus." [6]

A splendid monument glorifies Nathan Hale and his name is a household word in America, though he failed in his short mission; but for John Honeyman, who made the first great victory possible, there is oblivion.

Among Washington's other spies was an uncannily intelligent idiot boy who did invaluable work. He died of starvation and his name perished with him.

When Howe decided to call the campaign a campaign and on December 13th marched off to New York with Cornwallis, leaving his Hessians marooned in bleakest New Jersey, Washington's spies brought him word as soon as they could cross the river.

The news was so inconceivably good and so contrary to common sense that Washington believed it must be a feint. [7]

His bewilderment is still shared by all historians, for Howe's conduct is so inexplicable on all grounds of human intelligence and on all military, patriotic, merciful or mercenary grounds that perhaps Bancroft's line of thought was the correct one:

God made him do it, so as to save Washington from annihilation.

This would be more satisfactory, however, if Washington had been allowed to enter into something approaching comfort, but the joy was as brief as it was brilliant. He was always just about to be what he never quite was, destroyed entirely.

Though he was constantly thanking heaven for sparing him at the last moment, he did not fail to give equal credit to the more merciful Howe.

Years afterward he confessed that he owed his escape to "Nothing but the infatuation of the enemy." [8]

The loyalist Galloway [9] with furious irony spoke of Howe as "calculating with great accuracy the exact time necessary for his enemy to escape," and of avoiding his destruction because "he despised a conduct so unfair and ungenerous against a defeated army."

Howe's departure from Trenton for New York was to Galloway "an unparalleled absurdity," as was his disposition of the troops in cantonments "made stronger, and stronger, as their distance from the enemy, and consequently their danger, decreased." The "most censurable part of his conduct" was this:

"The frontier posts, or those nearest to the enemy, were committed to the command of foreigners, who could not understand the language of the country. One of them left at Trentown, the most important post in his whole line of cantonments, was brave, but totally unfit for his station. He was obstinate, passionate, and incessantly intoxicated with strong liquors."

Of course, Howe had his reasons, such as they were. One was this:

"The campaign having closed with the Pursuit of the Enemies Army near ninety Miles by Lieut. Gen. Cornwallis's Corps, much to the honor of his Lordship and the Officers and Soldiers under his Command, The Approach of Winter putting a Stop to any further Progress." [10]

Another was: "The weather having become too severe to keep the field, and the winter cantonments having been arranged." [11]

The word "arranged" solves all. Your average professional soldier becomes so paralyzed by the sanctity of what has been arranged that he will see the destruction of the world rather than upset the schedule.

The military and naval provinces, like the scientific, the artistic, the political and others, tend to develop priestcrafts, orthodoxies, and rituals so rigid that it is sacrilege to disturb them and no decent respectable officer would presume even to question them.

So Howe, having taken great pains to figure out the distribution of his troops into cantonments for the winter, felt that he had already postponed their occupation too long. He nobly put behind him the temptation to hunt down the rebels in the closed season and turned his back on such easy prey.

When asked why under heaven he put Hessians next to Washington, he answered that the Hessians had been previously assigned to the left of the line. Trenton was the left of the line. What more could be asked?

His reason for going into winter quarters and scattering his New Jersey garrison in groups so far apart and so small was that he could not otherwise provide his horses with sufficient forage. To which Galloway retorted:

"He either did not, or would not consider that the country was full of grain, hay, and dry forage, and that this was much to be preferred to green, which would rather scour and weaken his horses, than add to their strength; and this kind of forage he had, or might have had in his magazines, or might have procured in his march through the country." [12]

Howe sent Clinton with five thousand men in transports to seize Newport and they succeeded. He wanted a harbor and he found it. If Clinton had been sent up the Delaware river, says Abbé Raynal,[13] "the new republic had been stifled in that important and celebrated city which gave it birth."

But Howe thought that the occupation of Newport meant an early end to "the unhappy contest maintained by the deluded people." [14]

He was a peace commissioner for his King as well as a soldier, and hence he was "fighting with one arm behind his back." [15]

In any case, though the undenied and undeniable fact is almost beyond belief, Howe went back to New York and his Bostonienne, and Cornwallis had his luggage put aboard a homebound ship for a voyage that he did not take. Most of the army of thirty thousand, outnumbering the total population of New York by one-third, returned and settled down like a cloud of locusts upon the city.

The command of New Jersey was entrusted to Major-General Grant, who was by way of progressing nobly with his boast in Parliament. He had already travelled from Long Island halfway across New Jersey. Having said that with five thousand men he could march from one end of the continent to the other, he now said:

"I will undertake to keep the peace in New Jersey with a corporal's guard."

He sent his Hessians orders that they could not read; and Colonel Rall, who was in command at Trenton, would not obey the ones he understood. He refused to put up any fortifications whatever.

This may not have been the blind folly that some maintain. Perhaps he was challenging the Americans to a combat, and felt that nothing could bring them to the field except a pretence of his unpreparedness to meet them.

With a little better luck and a less resolute opponent than Washington, Howe might have gained immortality as the gentle redeemer of the prodigals of the British Empire. With a little better luck of a different sort, Rall might have won that glory by wheedling the last of the rebels into his trap and springing it.

But they outrageously chose to accept his invitation on the one day of the year when no honest Hessian would be in a mood of anything but brotherly love and Yuletide stupor.

Rall's poor soldiers had their sorrows in plenty. It was just as cold on their side of the Delaware as on the other. They had no beds and had to lie on straw in rickety buildings. They also were ill provided with shoes, and their uniforms were not appropriate for an American winter. They also lacked underwear, yet Rall would not approve the requisitions of his subordinate officers.[16] He seemingly planned, as soon as the river froze, to make a dash for Philadelphia and luxury.

This was the brilliant Rall who had taken Chatterton's Hill from Washington in fifteen minutes by an unforeseen flanking movement. Washington was plotting to return the compliment with usury.

Rall's name has been spelled in almost every imaginable way. He wrote it "Rall." Washington wrote it "Rohl." Howe wrote it "Raille." Other variants were Raile, Rawle, Ralle, Rahl, Rhal, Rhalle and Roll.[17]

He had under his command about 1,400 Hessians. He

himself was under the command of Colonel Von Donop, who was stationed down the river about six miles at Bordentown. Both forces were constantly harassed, ambushed, spied on. Messengers were shot dead as they cantered along the road. Outpost duty was a fearsome thing in this strange land among people who were as savage to them as they were to the natives.

They could not understand why they were here; but that did not matter for they belonged body and soul to the Prince of Hesse and they were here earning money for him whom even the officers addressed in their formal reports as "Merciful Father of the Country" and "Most gracious Prince and Lord," "in deepest reverence." [18]

The moment Washington and his officers learned that Howe and Cornwallis had marched away with the outnumbering army of British, leaving on guard an outnumbered post of foreigners, there came first a sigh of relief at being spared, and then a gasp of excitement at an opportunity suddenly revealed.

Probably everybody, Washington and all the generals simultaneously, thought of attacking Trenton immediately. Washington certainly did. Then the hope faded for a week on account of the problems of holding the army together at all, the loss of Lee and the poor state and small number of Gates' reinforcements. Then the project was abruptly revived.

After the event there was a great contest for the glory of suggesting the attack on Trenton.

Lord Mahon [19] in his *History of England* gives Benedict Arnold the credit. But Arnold did not reach the camp until December 20th and was despatched to New England the next day.

Charles Lee is said to have claimed that he sent the formulated plan from New York. But he was captured on the day that Howe abandoned Trenton, and there is no reason to give him any sprig of the laurels, though he gets them all in an old German broadside that turned up in 1898. Written partly in French and devoted to American heroes, it presents Washington as supported by Mars and Minerva and next to him General Lee, *"Tantot Vainqueur Tantot Vaincu."* Underneath a scene of the battle of Trenton is this statement giving him the glory: "La Bataille de TRENTVICE, où les Hessois furent défaits par le Général Leé." [20]

General Hugh Mercer has been acclaimed as the originator of the attack on Trenton. Also General Greene is often mentioned as the father of the thought, but there is no proof of it. He did write on December 21 to the Governor of Rhode Island:

"Our force is small . . . but small as it is, I hope we shall give the enemy a stroke in a few days. Should fortune favor the attack, perhaps it may put a stop to General Howe's progress." [21]

But on the same day, Robert Morris wrote to Washington from Philadelphia:

"I have been told today that you are preparing to cross into the Jerseys. I hope it may be true." [22]

Three days before that, Christopher Marshall had written in his diary:

"News that our army intended to cross at Trenton into the Jerseys."

But even this was four days after Washington wrote to Gates announcing the "stroke" he planned.

Everybody in Pennsylvania seemed to have heard about the new plan, except the Hessians, who could not understand even what their own British officers were telling them. Von Donop claimed that Washington's officers were coming over and talking of surrendering in order to spy on his situation. The Hessians were a quaint combination of Babes in the Woods and Wolves in the Fold.

Adjutant-General Reed has been urged as the inventor of the Trenton assault. On the 22nd of December he wrote from Bristol, where he had been receiving the reports of scouts scattered through New Jersey:

"We are all of opinion, my dear General, that something must be attempted to revive our expiring credit, give our cause some degree of reputation, and prevent a total depreciation of the Continental money, which is coming on very fast; that even a failure cannot be more fatal, than to remain in our present situation . . . the scattered, divided state of the enemy affords us a fair opportunity of trying what our men will do, when called to an offensive attack.

"Will it not be possible, my dear General, for your troops, or such part of them as can act with advantage, to make a diversion, or something more, at or about Trenton?

"Allow me to hope that you will consult your own good judgment and spirit, and not let the goodness of your heart subject you to the influence of opinions from men in every respect your inferiors." [23]

But, as soon as he received this, Washington sent for Reed and told him that the plan had already been perfected, then sent him back to Bristol with orders to accompany Colonel Griffin and a party of 450 militia, largely Philadelphia boys, on a raid through New Jersey to beat up the Hessian camps. They did splendid work and managed to decoy Von Donop twelve miles away from Bordentown and eighteen miles from Trenton, with his whole force, except 80 men left there on guard.

When Reed returned to Bristol he received this word from Washington, dated Dec. 23, 1776:

"Christmas-day at night, one hour before day, is the time fixed upon for our attempt on Trenton. For Heaven's sake, keep this to yourself, as the discovery of it may prove fatal to us; our numbers, sorry I am to say, being less than I had any conception of; but necessity, dire necessity, will, nay must, justify *any* attempt." [24]

Reed marched the men down to the river, but the drifting ice was discouraging. He and another officer crossed to reconnoiter and could not get back. They went to Bordentown and hid there.

On the 24th Washington wrote to Congress one of his most despondent letters concerning the failure of soldiers to reenlist. He was about to be left with five regiments only, "comprising in the whole at this time from fourteen to fifteen hundred effective men. This handful, and such militia as may choose to join me, will then compose our army." [25]

He had been further distressed by Gates' thin excuse for hastening away to Congress. [26]

On Christmas day Washington received "discouraging Accounts" from Colonel Reed, but he would not be put off again as he had so often been. He wrote to Colonel Cadwalader:

"I am determined, as the Night is favourable, to cross the River and make the attack upon Trenton in the Morning. If you can do nothing real at least create as great a diversion as possible." [27]

Washington's original plan was very ambitious. His army would make three attacks at once. He would cross with 2,400 men at McKonkey's Ferry about nine miles to the north of Trenton, and march down on the town from above.

General Ewing (also called Irvin, Irwin, and Erwing, who had been at Braddock's Field with him) would cross at Trenton Ferry right opposite the village and endeavor both to cut off Rall's retreat and to prevent Von Donop from

sending up reinforcements from Bordentown. Ewing had
92 officers and about 1,000 men.[28]

Cadwalader, who had about 1,800 men, was to cross the
river a mile or two further south, attack Mount Holly,
Black Horse and Bordentown, and close in on Trenton from
below. If the battle had gone as Washington laid it out,
his triumph would have been dazzling, and he might have
reversed the situation so rapidly that he would have ended
the war in the very opposite manner from the opportunity
ignored by Howe.

But he had so much abominably bad luck mingled with
the good that the theory of providential management is an
insult to Providence, deifying an inferior Howe.

Washington had to be his own providence with a small
"p." He provided in advance that all the boats available
on the Delaware should be gathered secretly at convenient
rendezvous. The barges for his own troops he had drawn
up behind a little island north of McKonkey's ferry and
put them in charge of the Marblehead men who had made
the retreat from Long Island such a work of art.

On Christmas Eve Washington took supper at General
Greene's headquarters. Christmas night was selected for
the attack because of the Hessians' well known fondness for
the sacred festival and their custom of drinking even more
heartily on that day than on secular occasions.

Washington sent an express to bring up Doctor Shippen
and as many assistants as possible to take care of the casual-
ties, which he expected to be heavy. Never were surgeons
less needed.

At two o'clock Christmas afternoon the first regiment
began to move. An hour later all were on their way to
McKonkey's ferry. Many of them were barefoot in spite
of a last moment raid on the supplies in Philadelphia, and
this path of glory like so many others of that day could have

been traced across the white snow by the footprints of frozen blood.

A modern note is struck in the order that all the officers should set their watches by Washington's. It was literally a zero hour.

Each soldier carried forty rounds of ammunition, which was double the entire supply at Boston. But there were not half so many soldiers.

The hope was to put the eighteen cannon with their horses and the horses of the small cavalry attachment across the river as well as the infantry before midnight so as to beat the dawn to Trenton in a bitter parody of the hero of Gray's "Elegy,"

> "Brushing the dew with hasty steps away
> To meet the sun upon the upland lawn."

Everything now began to conspire to thwart Washington's high hopes and tease him with despair. At noon on Christmas day the ice began to break up in the creeks above and fill the hitherto clear river with floating obstacles, not very thick but sharp and menacing in the eddies of the rough current.

At sunset just as he was about to ride to the ferry and was poised with foot in the stirrup and reins and whip in hand, Major Wilkinson offered him a letter of regrets from General Gates, pleading an indisposition and unavoidable absence. Washington snapped:

"What a time to hand me letters!" [29]

Then he swung his long leg across the saddle of the chestnut sorrel he had chosen for the signal honor of that battle, and galloped to the water's edge, where the Marblehead men were doing their best with the restless hippopotami of the big Durham boats thirty or forty feet long, and such other "gondolas" as they had collected.

The cavalry and artillery horses danced in the cold,

bucked, kicked and stamped the ice, snorting white smoke from their nostrils. The cannoneers grunted and heaved at the job of hoisting the cannon into the reeling barges, and burly Colonel Knox, whose voice was famous, bawled like a bull in language quite unlike that he had used in his Boston bookshop.

The infantrymen standing by for hours and hours as spectators wrapped their arms about themselves for lack of better clothing, listened to the castanets of their teeth and bent now and then to chafe their protruding marble toes and refasten the old rags about their cracked and chilblained soles.

They did not much resemble a conquering host and Washington himself looked as little as possible like his statuary and portraiture.

He was in a mood of fierce anxiety and his grey eyes must have looked like points of ice. A man who saw him there brings him back to earth from the Olympic ideals by recording that he had a very red nose, which was "apt to turn scarlet in the wind. . . . He was not what ladies would call a pretty man." [30]

He was not engaged in a pretty business. It was something better than that, and it was well for America and the world that he was no "sunshine patriot," and was willing to implore his Falstaff's host to stand by him for one farewell attempt to take something home with them besides stories of how fast they could run.

His officers were none too handsome either, and it must be remembered in looking at their innumerable portraits that their handsome uniforms were largely contributed by the painters. They themselves wore almost anything and doubtless their noses were as red as Washington's.

There were red noses in Trenton, too—the noses of the pickets and sentinels compelled to spend the Christmas night sober and cold and on the alert while their comrades drank and sang old German Lieder.

Colonel Rall's nose was encarnadined also with drink. He was making a night of it, trying to drown his memories of wassail in Hesse with draughts of Jersey applejack or rum or whatever there was to drink at the house of Stacey Post, where he dropped in for a game of checkers after making the rounds in response to a message from General Grant that Lord Stirling was planning an attack.

Rall had found everything in good shape except that he had put up no earthworks and had scorned to provide a rallying point in case of a major attack. His comment had been whatever the Hessian was for:

"Fudge! these country clowns can't whip us!" [31]

At seven or eight o'clock a picket was attacked. There was a general uproar—and the troops fell in. Colonel Rall put himself at their head and learned that the assailants had been driven off. They were that pack of Philadelphian boys scouting about and they fled at the first alarm.

Major von Dechow wanted to send patrols to all the ferries, and he would certainly have seen Washington's army gathered about its boats across the river, if Rall had not pooh-poohed the idea and told him that the morning would be time enough.

Von Dechow was indignant, but the troops were dismissed to the resumption of their revels, and Rall went to the house of Abraham Hunt, the rich man of the town, rather uncertainly a Tory, who did a deathless service to the rebels by entertaining Rall all night at cards and getting him thoroughly drenched with liquor.

The storm that assailed the windows later made it all the pleasanter within doors.

While Rall was making merry in Trenton, Washington was as miserable as possible at McKonkey's Ferry. He had based his plans on having his whole army in Jersey by mid-night, but had succeeded only in transferring a small guard for the landing place, when at eleven o'clock, writes Captain Hull of Connecticut, "as violent a Storm ensued of Hail & Snow as I ever felt." [32]

Captain Thomas Rodney of Delaware described it:

"It was as severe a night as I ever saw. The frost was sharp, the current difficult to stem, the ice increasing, the wind high, and at eleven it began to snow. It was only with the greatest care and labor that the horses and the artillery could be ferried over the river." [33]

To his fat enough wife the too-too fat Colonel Knox wrote, calling her "My Dearly Beloved Friend":

"A part of the army, consisting of about 2,500 or 3,000 passed the river on Christmas night, with almost infinite difficulty, with eighteen field pieces. The floating ice in the river made the labor almost incredible."

As an example of what a change it makes in a man to turn from the sword to the pen, it is picturesque to note in passing that Knox ended this vivid letter of his concerning the unsurpassed magnificence of his work that night with these words:

"His Excellency the General has done me the unmerited great honour of thanking me in public orders in terms strong and polite. This I would blush to mention to any other than to you, my dear Lucy; and I am fearful that even my Lucy may think her Harry possesses a species of little vanity in doing [it] at all." [34]

But then he was only twenty-six years old, though he must have felt a hundred by the time Washington called him to cross the river with him and superintend the arrange-ment of the troops for the march.

It is probably useless to attempt to efface from popular memory the infinitely ubiquitous picture of "Washington

Crossing the Delaware," though it is as false in every detail as might be expected from the fact that it was made in Germany by Herr Emanuel Leutze, who first exhibited it in Munich, where they did not know that the boat in which Washington rode was not at all the sort of skiff depicted. The premature Star Spangled Banner that twitches away from its staff had not yet been designed by Francis Hopkinson, and Washington knew too much to pose for his picture standing upright in a flatboat bunted by chunks of ice and floundering through the rushing swirl of a swift river.

If he had attempted it he would have sat violently upon that part of the anatomy to which he referred in his remark to Colonel Knox, who was extremely broad of beam and sat in the stern of Washington's boat.

There is an unusually credible tradition among the many often-spoken but never-printed anecdotes of Washington, that he provoked a big much-needed laugh in his dreary audience by turning to Knox, whose weight was tilting the barge lopsided, and saying:

"Shift your weight, Knox, and trim the boat."

Only, "weight" was not the exact term he used; for the real Washington was man among men enough to prefer a venerable Anglo-Saxon word when it said what he meant.[35]

Ferrying any army across any stream at noon is task enough, and always prolific in delays, but that dark embarkment was harrowing.

When Washington reached the other side and while he waited for his horse to be brought over he sat on an empty bee-hive with his brain undoubtedly buzzing.[36]

He never had a strong voice and Colonel Knox played Stentor for him, his "deep bass heard above the crash of ice." But it was not loud enough to be heard in Trenton or to interrupt the reiterated *"Noch einmal!"* of Colonel Rall calling for more liquor.

Rall did not even hear the knock on the door or the parley with the negro servant of the loyalist Wall, or Mahl, who stole across from Pennsylvania to warn the soldiers of his King that the rebels were coming. The slave was afraid to disturb the roisterers with any more false alarms and he refused to let the Tory in.

So Wall wrote on a paper a note telling of what grim freight was crossing the river, and persuaded the negro to hand it to the Colonel.

Rall glanced at it with bleary eyes. He saw that it was in English and was in no mood to call for a translation. He stuffed it unread into his waistcoat pocket while the negro dismissed the Tory with the word that the Colonel had received his message.

Perhaps officers should not be permitted to have pockets in their uniforms.

Though the Delaware is less than a fifth of a mile wide at the crossing place, the difficulties and obstacles caused such delays that the last man over did not reach the shore until after three o'clock.

It took another hour to form the march according to the orders which Washington had drawn up with great care and issued Christmas morning, providing for guides, scouts dressed as farmers, and "spikes and hammers to spike up the enemies' cannon in case of necessity, or to bring them off if it can be effected, the party to be provided with drag-ropes for the purpose." [37]

To his old comrade, Adam Stephen, he gave the advance party, to be supported by Mercer and Stirling under Greene. These were to march by the Pennington road, the farther highway from the river, and Washington chose to accompany "this, the 2d division or left wing."

The right wing he gave to Sullivan, with Glover and Sargent, and St. Clair as the reserve. This was to march by the nearly parallel road along the river. "A profound silence to be enjoined, and no man to quit his ranks on the pain of death."

The password was to be "Victory or Death."

The two highways into Trenton parted at the Bear Tavern, about a mile from the ferry, and ran at a widening interval for about four miles when the upper road united with the highway to Pennington and closed in on the river road, meeting it at the outskirts of Trenton, thus forming a tall letter O.

About daybreak Colonel Rall came to feel that sleep was even sweeter than more liquor. He rose and meandered to his headquarters, twisted out of his clothes, flung off the waistcoat with the mute note in its pocket, and passed into a profound slumber, dreaming perhaps of future Christmases in better palaces than Trenton could afford.

Among the confused shreds of good and bad luck that complicated that day's work was the activity of the patrol sent out at about five o'clock. If it had been lazier and had waited for an hour and a half, or less lazy and had gone a mile or two further, it would have discovered the rebels and given the alarm.

Washington would then have had to fight the clever Rall in the open. Rall was a genius in attack with a poor talent for defence and Washington might have been killed. He might have seen his men driven back to the river and in among the ice cakes. And history might have been changed in quite another way.

Even if his two thousand and more had defeated Rall, the Hessians could have retreated in good order, and Washington would have had only a heavy list of killed and wounded and a village to hold for a few days. Among the dead might have been Alexander Hamilton and James

Monroe, which would have made another difference in history as we know it.

And it all depended on the work of a patrol. If Bancroft's theory is true and the game was all conducted by Providence, there must be a great interest in patrols up above.

XXXIX

THE DAY AFTER CHRISTMAS

AT four o'clock in the tardy winter morning of December 26, 1776, Washington was ready to leave the Delaware shore. He had seven miles to go on slippery roads. His troops numbered, he said, "about Three or four & twenty hundred." [1]

He was in a most cheerless mood. The delays, he wrote, "made me despair of surprising the town, as I well knew we could not reach it before the day was fairly broke. But as I was certain there was no making a retreat without being discovered and harassed on repassing the river, I determined to push on at all events." [2]

If he had known what was happening to his other two divisions, he would have been even more hopeless. General Ewing had been able to make no headway at all across the ice. He could not even get a boat started.

Colonel Cadwalader, after failing at Bristol Ferry, marched to Dunk's with his exceedingly naked troops, lacking shoes, stockings, and coats.

He succeeded in landing six hundred men on the other side when the tide turned and piled up a three-hundred-foot glacier in the river. Just before dawn he called back the six hundred and gave up, assuming that Washington must have failed also.

Such a wilderness of happy mishaps was surely never known. If Ewing had landed any men at all, he would have alarmed the whole garrison and foiled Washington's last chance.

588

Washington, once more in the depths of gloom, took a last look about at his gloomy army huddled in a grove of hickory and black oak, then gave the order:

"Shoulder firelocks!"

The muskets went up and slanted to the rear. Forty-eight hundred feet began to pound the snow on the mile march to the Bear Tavern at the crossroads. Three miles further on they reached the village of Birmingham.

Since he was so late and the men so fagged with their night's exposure and toil, Washington let them halt for a taste of breakfast from the three days' cooked rations they had brought along.

He himself, as Stryker says, "without dismounting . . . partook of the hospitality of Benjamin Moore." [3]

This one may assume to be a manner of saying that he had a mug of rum, a beaker of Madeira, or perhaps a tumbler of hot toddy. However preferable, it would be an anachronism to assume that he took a glass of orange juice and a cup of coffee, or even a dish of tea.

Word came back to Washington from General Sullivan up the line that the rain was ruining the muskets and soaking the powder. According to one of his staff, Washington sent back the answer:

"Tell General Sullivan to use the bayonet. I am resolved to take Trenton." [4]

When the next command to march was given, many of the soldiers had to be wakened from heavy sleep into which they had fallen, half-dead from exhaustion.

The force had divided, hoping to meet again in Trenton, but with every assurance of a warm welcome.

The sun rose like a half-frozen farmer not yet able to warm himself and Washington, seeing it with dismay, called:

"Press on, press on, boys!"

The storm of rain and sleet and hail and snow made

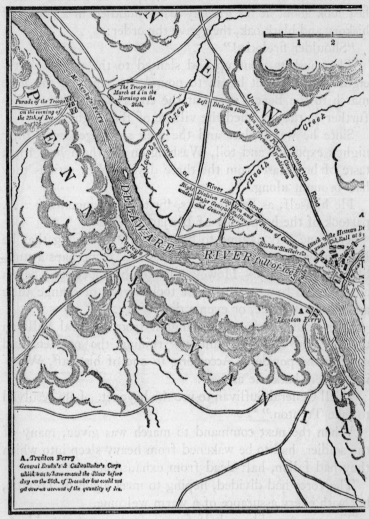

A. Trenton Ferry
General Erwin's & Cadwallader's Corps
which was to have crossed the River before
day on the 26th. of December but could not
get over on account of the quantity of Ice.

THE BATTLE OF
(From the map by

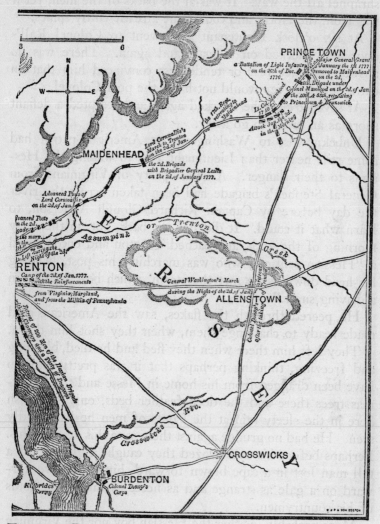

TRENTON, DECEMBER 26, 1776.
William Faden, London, 1777.)

shrapnel all the way. It was at the backs of the men, yet it was from the North and cooled the already chilly spines.

At six o'clock Lieutenant Piel went to Colonel Rall's door and knocked on it again and again. There was no answer. Either fear or tenderness convinced him that an extra hour of sleep would not harm the poor Colonel.

At seven o'clock he knocked again and accepted a defiant snore as an order to go away.

Unbeknownst to Washington, an American patrol had come still nearer than Lieutenant Piel to waking the Hessians to their danger. A small party of Virginians from General Stephen's brigade had been taken across the river the day before by Captain Richard Clough Anderson, to learn what it could. It did not get back, but, in the early morning of the 26th, approached Trenton and encountered a "Hessian sentinel, who was marching his post, bending his head down as he met the storm, which beat heavily in a driving snow."

He peered through the flakes, saw the Americans and made ready to challenge them, when they shot him down.

They left him there when they fled and he died, bleeding and freezing, thinking perhaps that it was pretty hard to have been dragged from his home in Hesse and the Christmas trees there and the deep feather beds, only to perish here in the sleety rain at the hands of men he had hardly seen. He had no grudge against them save this death of his. Perhaps before his eyes glazed they caught a glimpse of a tall man lost in a cape blown forward, himself blown forward on a gale as strange and as fierce as this in the souls of his countrymen.

More probably, neither the Hessian boy nor the Virginian farmer knew of each other's existence.

As for the patrol that killed the Hessian sentinel, it fled toward McKonkey's ferry, where its members were dazed to behold the American army advancing like ghosts formed out of snowflakes.

The patrol drew out into a field and was recognized as American before the advance guard fired into it. Captain Anderson's son described what followed:

"General Washington approached and asked who was in command and where he had been. I have frequently heard my father remark that he never saw Gen¹ Washington exhibit so much anger as he did when he told him where he had been and what he had done. He turned to Gen¹ S[tephen] and asked how he dared to send a patrol from camp without his authority, remarking:

" 'You, sir, may have ruined all my plans, by having put them on their guard.'

"He then addressed my father in a very calm and considerate manner and told him that as he and his men must be very much fatigued after such hard service, he should march in the van guard, where he would be less harrassed by the fatigue of the march." ⁵

Washington was afterwards glad that Anderson had unwittingly duped the Hessians into the belief that but a small American patrol was about, and he said so.

It was all of eight o'clock when Washington came to a house where a farmer chopping wood gaped at the sight of the troops. He was scared dumb when a huge officer galloped across to him to enquire:

"Can you tell me where the Hessian picket is? You need not be frightened, it is General Washington who asks the question."

His face brightened and he pointed to the distant house of a Mr. Howell, where the Hessians could be seen running out, shouting and firing. Their bullets passed over Washington's head. Two of the sentinels were captured. The others reached Captain Altenbockum's picket.

He drew his sword, formed his men and retreated firing to the village, where the drums and bugles were heard in fury, just before the boom of a cannon announced that General Sullivan had reached Trenton a little ahead of Greene and Washington.

What Washington saw is described by one of his staff:

"General Washington's face lighted up instantly, for he knew that it was one of Sullivan's guns. We could see a great commotion down toward the meeting-house, men running here and there, officers swinging their swords, artillery-men harnessing their horses. Captain Forrest unlimbered his guns.

"Washington gave the order to advance, and we rushed on to the junction of King and Queen streets. Forrest wheeled six of his cannon into position to sweep both streets. The riflemen under Colonel Hand and Scott's and Lawson's battalions went upon the run through the fields on the left to gain possession of the Princeton road. . . .

"While this was taking place on the Pennington road Colonel John Stark, from New Hampshire, in the advance on the river road was driving Knyphausen's men pell mell through the town. Sullivan sent a portion of his troops under St. Clair to seize the bridge and cut off the retreat of the Hessians toward Bordentown." [6]

This staff officer says nothing of one reported exclamation of Washington as he drew his sword:

"There, my brave fellows, are the enemies of your country. Remember now what you are about to fight for." [7]

It is to be hoped that he did not say it, for it sounds more like the old-school historian who took lessons in elocution and had a quenchless thirst for resounding platform pieces to speak.

Such oratory would have been as useless as it was un-Washingtonian, for it could not have been heard in the

storm and his men were not gathered about him in an audi-
torium. They were coming up in a long and straggling
column and doubtless their immediate officers were running
and howling orders for deployment and bayonet work.

All the dialects of New England, New York, Pennsylvania, Maryland and Virginia were crackling, mingled with
Irish, Scotch, English, and French. There was a war of
languages, for the Hessians were exchanging remarks in
German.

Lieutenant von Wiederhold's diary writes the guard's cry
of "The Enemy! Turn out!" as:

"Der Feind! der Feind! heraus! heraus!"

His picket bravely waited till the Americans had fired
three times before his men gave a volley and retreated. But
they hit nobody for all their deliberation.

Some of the Hessians might almost have made a breastworks of their names, for Captain von Altenbockum vied
with Captain von Schimmelpfennig and Lieutenant von
Grothausen, while the eighteen-year-old Lieutenant Kimm
was killed almost at once.

Captain Samuel Morris of the Philadelphia light horse
was so touched by the lad's collapse that he was dismounting
to aid him when General Greene ordered him to his duty.[8]

The Americans, sweeping on, charged up to the mouths of
the cannon the Hessians were trying to swing into play.
They shot down the horses at guns whose officers were trying to save them by flight.[9]

About six hundred Hessians and twenty English horsemen
fled along the Bordentown road and escaped to Von Donop.

Another mob of Hessians was cut off by De Fermoy and
Stephen, who took their assigned positions on Assunpink
Creek. Stirling ordered a charge and Captain William
Washington and Lieutenant James Monroe were wounded.
They and two privates were the only ones to be hurt unless

there is truth in the tradition that two soldiers were frozen to death.

According to Galloway [10] great numbers of the Hessians made no attempt to fight but began to load their accumulated plunder on wagons in the hope of making off with these perquisites. He says they paid no heed to the orders of their commander. But it would have made little difference what they did or he commanded. They were doomed from the first.

As for Rall, never could man have been more befuddled. He was so steeped in liquor and sleep that even when the firing began and Piel beat on his door again he looked from an upper window in his nightshirt, and yawned:

"*Was ist's? Was ist los?*"

The astounded Piel asked if he had not heard the firing. He said he would be down at once.

He was awake enough now and fairly leapt into his clothes. He appeared in the street as the cannonballs began to shoot through it. He was not struck but mounted his horse and began to give orders to form his men back of the poplar trees in the graveyard of the English church.

To one officer who was seeing that horses were hitched to a battery, he cried the German for:

"My God! the picket is coming in. Push your cannon ahead!"

The streets were being stitched with cannon fire and Alexander Hamilton's men did conspicuously well with his battery, scattering the Hessians as fast as they formed.

Washington and his staff and his escort of Philadelphia Light Horse took post on high ground where Princeton avenue now runs. It was said that a bullet disabled his chestnut sorrel and he had to take another.

While he watched his long awaited triumph with deep calm, Colonel Rall grew so confused that he could not even reply to his officers asking for orders. He mumbled in despair, and then in hope, and then cried:

"*Vorwärts! vorwärts!*"

But nobody obeyed the dreamer. The Americans were firing and charging from every side, from cover in cellars and windows, from fences and trees. It is said that some of them made a laughing watchword of Thomas Paine's recent phrase:

"These are the times that try men's souls!"

Rall's mind faded and cleared; he consented now to a retreat, now to a charge.

The Hessian band that had played so gaily at Long Island while the Yankees fled now struck up and tried to cheer the defenders of Trenton, but they fell too fast.

Colonel Rall was pierced by a bullet that seemed merely to annoy him, but he grew weaker and weaker from the loss of blood yet continued to try to summon his own Rall regiment men to a counter-assault, crying:

"*Alles was meine Grenadiere sind, vorwärts!*"

But his men felt no confidence in him or in anyone. They fought or surrendered or fell. The rain wet the powder of foe and friend alike, and the Hessians knew not which way to turn. The Americans at last were relying on that most convincing of arguments, the bayonet. A few whose powder was sheltered, hid, chuckling, and took their pick of the Hessian officers.

Suddenly Rall received two bullets in his side and was knocked off his horse. He lay on the ground for a moment, then had himself lifted and supported into the Methodist church.

As he passed a wounded lieutenant, Rall murmured a word of sympathy. The lieutenant recovered.

Some of the troops began to put up handkerchiefs on spontoons to signify that they had had enough.

One group made its way to a creek where women and musicians were standing in dismay, fearing the icy water as much as the random bullets. A few soldiers tried to cross and were drowned. Others escaped. Others surrendered. Everything was everywhichway.

But at last the rabbit-drive ended. Washington rode into town. Young Major Wilkinson came up to him and reported, with General St. Clair's and General Sullivan's compliments, that the Von Knyphausen regiment had surrendered.

Washington shook hands with the boy and said:

"This is a glorious day for our country, Major Wilkinson."

Rall was carried on a church bench to his own headquarters and undressed. The last blow of fate was the falling from his pocket of the Tory's warning note. It was read to him and he groaned, "If I had read that at Mr. Hunt's, I'd not be here—"

"*Hätte ich dies zu Herrn Hunt gelesen, so wäre ich jetzt nicht hier.*"

When his wounds were dressed, he received two callers, Washington and Greene. He doubtless remembered his frequent wish that he might capture Washington. It was only one more taste of wormwood to stare up at him now in an infancy of helplessness.

Through an interpreter Washington expressed his sympathy with all the grace of his gentle soul. Rall asked that his men be treated kindly. Washington promised that, said a few words, and retired.

Like the mortally wounded Braddock, Rall lived on long enough to drain the last dregs of regret. He died the following night, and the place of his burial in Trenton is unknown.

The pain in his thrice-riddled body must have been

nothing to the torture in his soul. Drugged with wine and sleep, he had been hardly able to shake off his slumber and go down into the street where the despised rebels were shattering his troops and his pride.

Confusion had confounded confusion as he fought the fumes in his brain and babbled at his men, seeking an escape where there was none. There followed the ultimate shame of limping to the empty church and lying there on his back in a pew while his people were shot into submission.

He must have wandered a deep hell of remorse for betraying his prince and his men and his own soul. So his long soldiering ended in an immortal failure in a bleak village. The only kindness his fate could begrudge him was to let him die at last.

The least risks soldiers take are the hazards of the bullet. Their own mistakes and the lotteries of military luck are their deadliest hazards.

Everything had promised Washington as great a disgrace as Rall's. He had come late, with a third of his men, in broad daylight. Nothing had happened as he planned.

If he had been wounded and captured he might well have been strung up as the traitor the King called him. His only safety was to absolve himself by victory over his King from the laws of the King.

What he had done now was merely to dash across a narrow river and capture an outpost of mercenary soldiers disorganized by a Christmas revel, an intoxicated commander and a driving storm of rain and snow.

His troops slew 22 of them, wounded 28 too badly to move, and 56 others who were taken across the river among the 868 prisoners.[11]

His own army had four wounded and none killed at all.

His triumph was so precariously snatched from an overpowering enemy that, instead of pushing on as he had hoped, he was glad to be able to return across the river and stand on guard against the revenge of insulted pursuers.

But he had tasted victory and so had his men. For once they had followed where he led, had marched up to the attack, had charged on cannon, had taken an enemy army prisoner.

They limped home to their boats and the icy river, but their shoulderblades were not turned to the foe in terror. They had made an orderly attack and an orderly retreat, the two first lessons in good soldiery.

Washington had at last an army, a little one but a good one. The moment he had a weapon he wielded it well.

He had known that immediate victory was vital. A week's delay would have been as fatal as a disastrous defeat.

But even he could not have dreamed of the shock that brief incursion gave to the British Empire. He could not have foreseen how it would stir the doubtful Americans to the belief that success and hope lay with him; how they would come flocking to him who had been abused for indecision, yet lashed out so ferociously at so dark an hour.

They would flock away again after the dazzling successes that immediately followed Trenton. He would have Valley Forge to weather and treasons and panics for years on years.

But he planted one foot on eternal glory when he made the raid on Trenton.

Washington-like, he took no credit to himself. He uttered no Cæsarian, "I have come, I have seen, I have conquered."

He wrote to Congress, his masters for all of his dictatorship:

"I have the pleasure of congratulating you upon the success of an enterprise, which I had formed against a detachment of the enemy lying at Trenton, and which was executed yesterday morning. . . .

"In justice to the officers and men, I must add, that their behavior upon this occasion reflects the highest honor upon them. . . .

"When they came to the charge, each seemed to vie with the other in pressing forward; and were I to give a preference to any particular corps, I should do great injustice to the others." [12]

He had earned and his men had earned this respite from the old reports of "dastardly cowardice." He never had to whip them over their backs again.

On the first of January he wrote to Congress that he had crossed the Delaware again to face the furious Cornwallis, called back from his ship, and the indignant Howe, recalled from his divertisements. He was going out to meet the enemy on their own ground.

Incidentally he apologized for having pledged his personal credit as other officers did theirs, and borrowed gold enough to hire an army for six weeks longer.

He paid even those reluctant soldiers a compliment: "The troops felt their importance, and would have their price."

He had proved himself a general. He had taught his soldiers to fight. He was now resolved to teach them to persevere in the war for a country, even if he had to pay for their education himself. It was just dawning upon them that they had a country to fight for.

AFTERWORD

This volume carries Washington no farther for the very simple and stubborn reason that it was impossible to go beyond this point without leaving still untold a multitude of facts important or picturesque or both.

Many of them have lain undisclosed (or at least uncollated with reference to Washington) in countless manuscripts, in scattered archives, in pamphlets, monographs or in ponderous collections of documents.

Washington, like every other animal, vegetable and mineral, was an evolution in body and character. With him as with all other earthly beings, environment played a vital part and changed him while he changed it. It is no sacrilege to represent him as a boy before he became a man, and a man before, and while, he became a god.

And there is no kindness to him in suppressing the facts, for the more fully the truth about him is told, the greater his achievement becomes.

The actual Washington has been long enough dispossessed of his character and even of his name. He has been left to wander like that other pilot, the unburied Palinurus, through oblivion for more than a hundred years, his words censored, his deeds miswritten and his humanity concealed. It is hard to imagine what comfort or pride George Washington could find in paradise, looking down to see incense burned and hymns chanted before a pompous caricature of himself.

There is no glory in that for him, since his last name came from his father and his mother selected his first in honor of a kindly friend.

The pity of all this falsehood was that it defeated its own object, and made a lie out of a man peculiarly devoted to the truth. Washington was a supreme realist with an intense interest in the facts about everything from manure to patriotism.

He was an unusually truthful man and never tried to deceive himself. He rarely tried to deceive anybody else, except, of course, in the usual ways sanctified by ancient custom to dealers in real estate, horse-traders, and military people.

He seems to have destroyed none of his records and accumulated everything. He piled up an enormous pyramid of documents and was pathetically eager not to be misunderstood. He made a beginning at correcting the spelling and grammar of some of his writings, but he made no attempt to falsify their meaning.

What would be his amazement if he could return and read what Sparks, Bancroft and others made out of the writings, the activities and the character of himself and his contemporaries?

Like the poor woman who had her skirts cut off while she slept, he would gasp:

"Can this be I?"

It may be remembered that in the old poem, the distracted woman felt that her little dog would be able to decide: if he barked at her, she was not herself. And he did! And she moaned, "This is not I!"

Could the Washington we know have gone home to his pack of hounds, what a howl they would have set up!

The cruelty of this misguided perversion of history is the injustice it does to Washington, for there is nothing more precious to a man than sympathy and the sweet privileges of pitying affection.

Pathos is the most endearing of all qualities, and it has

been impossible to love or feel sorry for the Washington of the text books.

Yet he himself was an infinitely pathetic, lonely figure. He was in no sense a god struck from the brow of Providence in full uniform. He was a poor struggler with infinite difficulties at a time when chaos groaned in a swoon of torment, from whose travail a nation was born and shaped amid cries of pain and writhings of uncertainty.

Nobody knew just what was the right or the helpful thing to do or what the outcome would be and Washington was as profoundly bewildered as anybody.

Everybody who knew him spoke of his shyness, his embarrassment. He inspired awe and reverence also, but for the purity of his patriotism and the loftiness of his ideals. Yet he was wretchedly afraid of himself, and he had no ambitions except to grow rich, be free, cultivate his farm and his friends, his charities and the other charms of this world, and leave behind him an honorable name.

He was forever being appealed to to save friends, relatives, regiments, colonies, or the nation from their own mistakes and jealousies, and he did his best for them, going into debt to lend money, taking on trusteeships to the neglect of his own affairs, forever writing letters and keeping books, though he loved to dance and follow the hounds and shuffle the cards and let the theater display before him the woes and entanglements of people who would not ask him to arrange their lives for them.

To take such a man, suppress his outbursts of impatience, his mistakes, his foibles, his ignorances, his unwisdoms; to correct his spelling, his grammar, his whole life into a text book of rhetoric and a copybook of conduct for children is not only a hypocritical outrage on truth, but also a heartless disservice to Washington.

To go farther and make of selected contemporaries a

pediment group of similar temple-statuary is to multiply the crime.

Strange to say, the people who are so particular about suppressing every flaw of reality in the characters they have selected for deification, have no scruples whatsoever in dealing out the most merciless injustices and slanders to everybody who ran counter to their coterie of manufactured gods.

A vast amount of so-called American history is infamous in its dishonesty, unfairness and distortion. The fanatics who would burn the honest books and lynch the living delvers into fact, are willing even to lynch the dead and defile the very graves of Americans as well as foreigners who merely guessed wrong or in all sincerity and honesty opposed what has since appeared to be the more fortunate, more desirable or at least the more successful plan. In many instances, their whole sin was their consistency, their loyalty and their fidelity to their oaths.

I yield to nobody in love of my country and gratitude to its builders, but I consider it no part of decent patriotism to be a traitor to the truth, or to filch from my country's enemies or its misguided citizens their honest dues.

The important thing, in the long run, is what actually happened or was said or written and what were the real motives of the participants in, and the victims of, the great turmoil from which the United States emerged.

I am as eager to be fair to the loyalists, the Tories, the neutrals, the British, the Hessians, and the opponents of Washington, as to the radicals, the heroes, cowards, and philosophers on the winning side.

I have a passionate eagerness to learn and to tell without timidity or manipulation just what the facts were. If that be treason, then treason is a duty. Or, perhaps, some of those who shout the word loudest are themselves the traitors.

Very few errors of fact were pointed out in my first volume and none of them of much moment, though one prominent historian was widely quoted in the press as saying that the first volume contained "exactly 297 absolutely false statements." He was good enough to write to me, however: "On two careful readings of the book I have not found one statement that I could call absolutely false."

What he had really said was that he had found 297 "disparaging statements." In totting up his "disparagements" he said that he had included every allusion to Washington's dancing, drinking, swearing, dressing well, or falling in love.

But I could not honestly excise these statements since Washington himself was the authority for them. Furthermore I did not and do not consider it in the least "disparaging" to say that Washington did any or all of these things. I am glad he did them, and still consider it a biographer's duty to record them.

The period covered by the present volume is far more complex and is so pervaded by disputes in all the documents that I cannot hope to have escaped blunders. When the eyewitnesses conflict hopelessly and the great historians are at war, it is impossible to escape controversy. But none of my blunders have been intentional and I shall be grateful for any corrections of them.

I have endeavored to cling to Washington's own text as far as possible in the welter of contradictions, and to remain with him in the story of the Revolution.

Again as in the first volume my incessant endeavor has been to let Washington tell his own story in his own words, and to try to see his world and his times as they must have looked to him, not as they appear to a backward gaze across a landscape filled with tall oaks that were once acorns, and monuments that were once men.

I have read, I think, all of his published writings and as

many of his manuscripts as I could obtain access to, within the scope of this volume. I have read also as much of the published matter concerning him and this period as I found available.

Encountering everywhere the most complicated contradiction, I have tried to choose the most probable account, and to indicate the uncertainty.

While I have sought to base my allegations of fact on the original sources, I have tried to take advantage of the wisdom of the great historians who have recently made a revolution in the history of the Revolution, and I have tried to give full credit for borrowed ideas or materials.

It surprised even me, who thought I had been somewhat familiar with his writings, to find how exceedingly emotional Washington was, how bewildered, how sensitive, and how frank in his criticisms.

It is very touching to note his concern about the public opinion of his efforts, and the pain it gave him to be harshly criticized for inactivity that he could not help and dared not justify even to his own friends and fellow-officers.

He made no pretensions whatever to unusual wisdom or ability, and protested incessantly that he was ignorant, inexperienced and incompetent to his problems, but that his motives were honorable, unselfish, and unmercenary.

The man himself is infinitely more appealing, pitiful, heartbroken, tragic, gay, witty, tender, gracious, tactful, fearless, ferocious, heroic and, at his loftiest, sublime than the dull gray bore manufactured by stupid dullards, stodgy politicians and mongers of untruisms.

All that I have tried to do is to "restore" an old masterpiece by mopping off the daubs and accretions and letting the original colors shine forth in their variety and brilliance, shadow and radiance.

For access to the manuscripts I am deeply indebted to the

courtesy of the curators of all the treasuries in which Washingtoniana are stored, the Library of Congress, the Huntington Library, the Pierpont Morgan Library, the New York Public Library, the Virginia State Library and the Rosenbach Collection.

Mr. William L. Clements, who brought the Clinton papers to this country, and their curator, Professor Randolph Greenfield Adams, have been exceedingly kind in furnishing numerous photostats, but I have been unable to take advantage of their generosity in this volume, owing to the necessity for concluding it at the end of 1776.

To the Huntington Library and the Pennsylvania State Normal School I am grateful for permission to reproduce the two portraits of Washington, both by C. W. Peale. The frontispiece is particularly interesting since it was done under such difficulties at Valley Forge that a piece of bed ticking was used as a substitute for canvas. Its authenticity was verified by Charles Henry Hart in an article published in *McClure's Magazine* for December, 1896.

Most of the copy and proofs have enjoyed the careful reading of Mr. Willard O. Waters of the Huntington Library. The index was prepared by Mr. O. S. Wadleigh. Mr. J. Dale Eunson and Mr. Geoffrey Shurlock were of great help in countless details, and I cannot omit a word of profound gratitude for the indefatigable toil and unflagging encouragement of my wife.

APPENDIX I

NOTES AND REFERENCES

CHAPTER I

1. Sam. Briggs, *The Essays, Humor, and Poems of Nathaniel Ames, Father and Son, . . . from their Almanacks,* pp. 269, 270, 339.

2. Capt. B. H. Liddell Hart, *A Greater than Napoleon, Scipio Africanus.*

CHAPTER II

1. Robert Benchley, *The Early Worm,* p. 61.

2. From the original in the Huntington Library, dated at Alexandria, Nov. 13, 1757.

3. S. M. Hamilton, *Letters to Washington,* II, p. 231. Capt. Stewart's letter is quoted in volume I of this work, p. 342.

4. Thomas Jefferson, *Notes on the State of Virginia,* 3rd ed., p. 50.

5. Ferdinand Marie Bayard, *Voyage dans l'Intérieur des Etats-Unis, à Bath, Winchester, dans la Vallée de Shenandoha,* etc. (Paris, 1797), p. 76. See also A. J. Morrison's *Travels in Virginia in Revolutionary Times,* p. 83.

6. Ford, *Writings of Washington,* II, p. 180.

7. Ford, *Writings,* II, p. 183.

8. As the published versions differ widely, an exact transcription is here made from the original in the Library of Congress.

9. *Letters and Recollections of George Washington, Being Letters to Tobias Lear,* etc., p. 137.

10. Quoted by Lodge, *Life of Washington,* II, p. 387, from a letter in Toner's collection.

11. G. W. P. Custis, *Recollections,* p. 481.

12. J. M. Toner, *George Washington as an Inventor and Promoter of the Useful Arts,* cited in W. S. Baker's *Early Sketches of George Washington,* p. 13.

13. Ford, *Writings,* II, p. 189. This letter was quoted at length in Vol. I, p. 460.

14. Ford, *Writings,* II, p. 175 n.

15. Ford, *Writings,* II, p. 184 n.

16. Ford, *Writings,* II, p. 185 n.

17. Ford, *Writings,* II, p. 170.

18. Ford, *Writings,* II, p. 179.

19. Wilson Miles Cary, *Sally Cary, a Long Hidden Romance of Washington's Life.* See Vol. I of this work, p. 183.

20. Ford, *Writings,* II, p. 186.

21. Ford, *Writings*, II, p. 187 n.   The indenture agreement made with John Askew is published in W. C. Ford's *Washington as an Employer and Importer of Labor* (privately printed, 1889), p. 25.   In this Askew agrees to "work duely from sunrise to sunset allowing proper times only for eating and if he shall loose any time at his said work either by negligence sickness or private business of his own the days and hours so lost is to be made up by him the said John Askew at the year's end."

CHAPTER III

1. Ford, *Writings*, II, p. 171.   Letter to Richard Washington.
2. Dr. Louis K. Koontz, *The Virginia Frontier*, 1754-1763 (Johns Hopkins Univ. Studies), p. 131.
3. *Dinwiddie Papers* (Virginia Hist. Coll.), II, p. 389.
4. Archer B. Hulbert, *Historic Highways*, V, p. 117.   Also Vol. I of this work, p. 382-3.
5. Ford, *Writings*, II, p. 101.   See also Vol. I of this work, p. 414.
6. Ford, *Writings*, II, p. 183 n.
7. Koontz, op. cit., p. 96.
8. Avery, *History of the U. S.*, V, p. 183.
9. Ford, *Writings*, II, p. 171.
10. Ford, *Writings*, II, p. 179.
11. Ford, *Writings*, II, p. 183.
12. Ford, *Writings*, II, p. 185 n.
13. Ford, *Writings*, II, p. 188 n.
14. E. S. Corwin, *French Policy and the American Alliance of 1778*, p. 37.   "We must be on our guard against exaggerating the merely material aspect of the losses wrought France by the Seven Years' War.   On the map, no doubt, Canada and Louisiana comprised an impressive domain, but regarded from the point of view of commerce and trade-balances they were essentially worthless, Louisiana being practically uninhabited and Canada hardly returning the cost of administration.   On the other hand Guadeloupe and Martinique, in place of which England had finally and somewhat reluctantly consented to take Canada, were commercially of great value.   France's real loss, apart from the enormous outlay of the war, was in prestige.   Her armies had been defeated, her fleets annihilated, her allies disappointed and disgruntled."
15. Corwin, op. cit., p. 40.
16. B. Franklin, *The Interest of Great Britain Considered with Regard to Her Colonies*, London, 1760, p. 39.
17. Sparks, *Life of James Otis* (Library of American Biography, 1844, 2nd series), II, p. 92.
18. Ford, *Writings*, II, p. 191 n.

CHAPTER IV

1. J. M. Leake, *The Virginia Committee System and the American Revolution* (Johns Hopkins University Studies), p. 47.

2. Paul Leicester Ford, *The True George Washington*, p. 298.

3. Fitzpatrick, *Diaries of Washington*, I, p. 155. The other citations can be found under their several dates. The Ledger citations are from the manuscript.

4. Rev. Andrew Burnaby, *Travels Through the Middle Settlements in North-America in the Years 1759 and 1760*, London, 1775, pp. 47, 35. For the early theatre, see G. C. D. Odell, *Annals of the New York Stage*, I, p. 3, and especially L. G. Tyler, *Williamsburg, the Old Colonial Capital*. Many of the descriptions of Williamsburg are taken from this book.

5. Tyler, op. cit., p. 226.

6. J. A. C. Chandler and T. B. Thames, *Colonial Virginia*, p. 292.

7. Chandler and Thames, op. cit., p. 294.

8. Chandler and Thames, op. cit., p. 293.

9. John Ferdinand D. Smyth, *A Tour in the United States of America*, London, 1784, Vol. I, p. 21.

10. Fitzpatrick, *Diaries*, I, 160.

11. See his letters in the *Calendar of Virginia State Papers*, I, pp. 456, 502.

12. His home was recently rescued from destruction and beautifully restored by the Kenmore Association.

13. Mrs. Roger A. Pryor, *The Mother of Washington and Her Times*, p. 178.

14. R. C. Winthrop, *Life and Letters of John Winthrop*, I, p. 255.

15. M. D. Conway, *George Washington and Mount Vernon* (Memoirs Long Island Hist. Soc.), p. xliii.

16. Washington's answer to Congressional resolutions of sympathy for his mother's death.

17. Gen. Dabney Herndon Maury, *Recollections of a Virginian in the Mexican, Indian, and Civil Wars*, p. 2.

18. John T. Goolrick, *The Life of General Hugh Mercer*, p. 99.

19. John T. Goolrick, *Historic Fredericksburg*, p. 72.

20. Edward Lewis Goodwin, *The Colonial Church in Virginia*, p. 37 n.

21. Julius F. Sachse, *Washington's Masonic Correspondence* describes the wave of anti-Masonic feeling that swept the country and the fervid denials of Washington's membership. He says that Jared Sparks, Boston, Feb. 18, 1833, wrote denying that he had ever seen any of Washington's letters indicating that he was a Mason.

CHAPTER V

1. Of Ledger A, fourteen photographic copies were made under the direction of Worthington C. Ford, and distributed among as many libraries. Of B, also in the Library of Congress, no copy has been made.

2. Paul L. Haworth, *George Washington, Country Gentleman*, p. 193.

CHAPTER VI

1. Norman Hapgood, *George Washington*, p. 98.

2. Paul L. Haworth, *George Washington, Country Gentleman*, p. 87.

"All told, according to Mr. Gaillard Hunt, who has them in charge, the Washington manuscripts in the Library of Congress is the largest collection of papers of one person in the world."

3. J. B. McMaster, *A History of the People of the United States*, II, p. 452. "The outlines of his biography are known to every schoolboy in the land. Yet his true biography is still to be prepared. General Washington is known to us, and President Washington. But George Washington is an unknown man. When at last he is set before us in his habit as he lived, we shall read less of the cherry-tree and more of the man. Naught surely that is heroic will be omitted, but side by side with what is heroic will appear much that is commonplace. . . . We shall see him refusing to be paid for his services by Congress, yet exacting from the family of the poor mason the shilling that was his due. We shall know him as the cold and forbidding character with whom no fellow-man ever ventured to live on close and familiar terms. We shall respect and honor him for being, not the greatest of generals, not the wisest of statesmen, not the most saintly of his race, but a man with many human frailties and much common sense, who rose in the fullness of time to be the political deliverer of our country."

Against this view, Lodge protested in his biography, II, pp. 305, 332, 333, 352, 353: "Men who are loudly proclaimed to be faultless always excite a certain kind of resentment. It is a dangerous eminence for any one to occupy. . . . Then again, Washington's fame has been so overshadowing, and his greatness so immutable, that he has been very inconvenient to the admirers and the biographers of other distinguished men. . . .

"This false attitude both of praise and criticism has been so persisted in that if we accept the premises we are forced to the conclusion that Washington was actually dull, while with much more openness it is asserted that he was cold and at times even harsh. 'In the mean time,' says Mr. McMaster, 'Washington was deprived of the services of the only two men his cold heart ever really loved.' 'A Cromwell with the juice squeezed out,' says Carlyle somewhere, in his rough and summary fashion. Are these judgments correct? Was Washington really, with all his greatness, dull and cold? . . .

"He never talked or acted with an eye to dramatic effect, and this is one reason for the notion that he was dull and dry; for the world dearly loves a little charlatanism, and is never happier than in being brilliantly duped. . . .

"He would take no salary from Congress, says Mr. McMaster, in fine antithesis, but he exacted his due from the family of the poor mason. . . . He did not extort the debt from the family of the poor mason, but collected it from the second husband of the widow, in response to a voluntary advertisement. It was very careful and even close dealing, but it was neither harsh nor unjust."

4. Joseph Dillaway Sawyer, *Washington*, I, p. 237 n. "One purchase by the Department of State totalled over two hundred folio volumes."

5. See Vol. I of this work, p. 407.

6. See William L. Clements, *The William L. Clements Library of Americana*; and Randolph G. Adams, *The Headquarters Papers of the British Army in North America*.

7. W. E. Woodward, *George Washington, the Man and the Image*, p. 109.

8. Eugene E. Prussing, *Washington's Legal Education,* an unpublished address delivered to the Chicago Law Club, Oct. 2, 1925.

CHAPTER VII

1. Ford, *Writings,* XII, p. 360.
2. Paul L. Haworth, *George Washington, Country Gentleman,* p. 68.
3. Haworth, op. cit., p. 90.
4. Fitzpatrick, *Diaries,* I, p. 153, April 14, 1760; p. 158, May 1, 1760.
5. Fitzpatrick, *Diaries,* III, p. 161, Jan. 15, 1787.
6. Haworth, op. cit., p. 111.
7. Ms. Letter to Thos. Newton, Dec. 14, 1773, in Library of Congress, *George Washington Papers,* XVII, p. 113.
8. W. C. Ford, *Washington as an Employer and Importer of Labor* (Privately Printed, 1889), p. 33.
9. Quoted in Ulrich B. Phillips' *Plantation and Frontier Documents, 1649-1863,* p. 319.
10. Ford, *Writings,* XII, p. 359.
11. J. F. Jameson, *The American Revolution Considered as a Social Movement,* p. 78.
12. A. O. Craven, *Soil Exhaustion as a Factor in the Agricultural History of Virginia and Maryland* (University of Illinois Press).
13. Moncure D. Conway, *Barons of the Patomack and the Rapahannock,* p. 2.
14. Daniel Grinnan, *Virginia Magazine of History,* July, 1927, p. 313.
15. Letter to Robert Cary, Esqr., & Co., August, 1770. MS. in Library of Congress, *George Washington Papers,* XVII, p. 49.

CHAPTER VIII

1. Mrs. Anne H. Wharton, *Through Colonial Doorways,* p. 8.
2. Dreer Collection. See Vol. I of this work, p. 459.
3. G. W. P. Custis, *Recollections,* p. 503.
4. Fitzpatrick, *Diaries,* II, p. 442 n.
5. Frances Wills, *Why the Fair Sex was Fair in Mrs. Washington's Day,* New York *World,* Nov. 28th, 1926. The manuscript is in the Pennsylvania Historical Society Collection.
6. S. M. Hamilton, *Letters to Washington,* III, p. 361.
7. Mrs. Roger A. Pryor, *The Mother of Washington and Her Times,* p. 64.
8. Paul Wilstach, *Mount Vernon,* p. 102.
9. William Nelson, *The American Newspapers of the 18th Century as Sources of History.* (Report of the Am. Hist. Assn, 1908), I, p. 216.
10. Jonathan Boucher, *Reminiscences of an American Loyalist,* p. 64.
11. Boucher, op. cit., p. 50.
12. Ford, *Writings,* II, p. 258.
13. S. M. Hamilton, op. cit., III, pp. 317, 318, 320, 324.

14. Ford, *Writings*, II, p. 276.
15. Ford, *Writings*, II, pp. 277, 332, 316.
16. S. M. Hamilton, op. cit., IV, p. 42.
17. George C. D. Odell, *Annals of the New York Stage*, I, p. 171.
18. S. M. Hamilton, op. cit., IV, p. 44.
19. Ford, *Writings*, II, pp. 323, 330.
20. Fitzpatrick, *Diaries*, II, p. 34 n.
21. Ford, *Writings*, II, p. 376.
22. Custis, *Recollections*, p. 33.
There is an authentic portrait of her in riding habit, but a frequently published picture is said by Charles Henry Hart to be a well-known portrait of Mrs. Siddons by Lawrence. "Frauds in Historical Portraiture" (Reports Am. Hist. Assn., 1913), I, p. 97. It is credited to Nellie by P. L. Ford and G. W. P. Custis, who say it was painted by Gilbert Stuart. J. D. Sawyer, II, 332, gives it as the portrait of Nelly's daughter.
23. Ford, *Writings*, II, p. 262.
24. Ford, *Writings*, II, p. 455.

CHAPTER IX

1. Ford, *Writings*, II, p. 129.
2. J. Franklin Jameson, *The American Revolution Considered as a Social Movement*, p. 100.
3. Haworth, *George Washington, Country Gentleman*, p. 16.
4. Ford, *Writings*, II, p. 200.
5. Ford, *Writings*, II, p. 207 n.
6. Fitzpatrick, *Diaries*, I, p. 139.
7. Ford, *Writings*, II, p. 259.
8. Ford, *Writings*, II, p. 285 n.
9. A. R. Spofford, *Lotteries in American History* (Report of American Historical Association, 1892), p. 186.
10. Quoted in Charles Frederick Stansbury's, *The Lake of the Great Dismal*, p. 148. John Spencer Bassett has edited the works of Col. Byrd, and finds his descriptions of the swamp "too unfavorable." The description and the proposal to drain the swamp have been privately printed in an edition by Earl Gregg Swem.
11. Fitzpatrick, *Diaries*, I, p. 189 and note.
12. Fitzpatrick, *Diaries*, I, p. 227.
13. Fitzpatrick, *Diaries*, I, p. 363 n.
14. A. B. Hulbert, *Washington and the West*, p. 193 n.
15. Haworth, op. cit., p. 286.

CHAPTER X

1. These phrases were used in an eloquent address delivered by Dr. John H. Finley before the University of Pennsylvania in February, 1927 (published in the *Pennsylvania Gazette*, Feb. 25, 1927). They are employed in

the excellent but over-enthusiastic *Historic Highways* of Archer Butler Hulbert. In Vol. III, p. 26, he says, "Washington was the original expansionist—not for expansion's sake, truly, but for country's sake and duty's. If Washington was the father of his country, he was in a stronger and more genuine sense the father of the West." He even sees a glorious act of God in the shooting of Jumonville,—which the French called the "assassination"; "if ever a finger was lifted by order of Providence it was the finger which fired the first gun of the French and Indian War in the Alleghany vale."

In his *Washington and the West* (1905), p. 4, he repeats his own words: "Washington was our first expansionist, not for expansion's sake, truly, but for country's sake and duty's." He ends his volume (p. 199) with the statement that Washington was "the greatest man in America had there been no Revolutionary War." Lodge in his *Life*, II, pp. 7-16, gives Washington so much credit that he suspects his own enthusiasm, and writes: "Ah, says some critic in critic's fashion, you are carried away by your subject; you see in a simple business enterprise, intended merely to open western lands, the far-reaching ideas of a statesman. Perhaps our critic is right." J. D. Sawyer in his biography, says, I, p. 151: "Washington was, indeed, the Father of the Great West. It was his foresight that enabled the United States, at a time far in the future from his day, to anchor the Golden West within her boundaries."

2. Albert T. Volwiler, *George Croghan and the Westward Movement*, p. 66.

3. C. W. Alvord, *The Mississippi Valley in British Politics*, I, p. 79.

4. Alvord, op. cit., I, p. 90.

5. Willard G. Bleyer, *Main Currents in the History of American Journalism*, p. 76.

6. Franklin, *Writings* (Smyth Ed.), III, p. 358.

7. Franklin, *Works* (Bigelow Ed.), IV, p. 141, quoted by F. J. Turner, *The Frontier in American History*, p. 182.

8. Alvord, op. cit., I, p. 348.

9. Alvord, op. cit., I, p. 314 n.

10. Sparks, *Writings*, II, p. 481. See also Vol. I of this work, pp. 78, 310.

11. Volwiler, op. cit., p. 164. Croghan's early career has been discussed in Vol. I of this work.

12. Volwiler, op. cit., pp. 182, 189, 191, 198, 234.

13. Volwiler, op. cit., p. 13.

14. Alvord, op. cit., II, p. 131.

15. The royal proclamation is given entire in Morison's *Sources and Documents Illustrating the American Revolution*, p. 1.

16. Alvord, op. cit., II, p. 112.

17. Alvord, op. cit., II, p. 110, citing Washington's letter of Jan. 31, 1770, in the *Mississippi Valley Historical Review*, I, p. 99.

CHAPTER XI

1. Ford, *Writings*, II, p. 218.

2. S. M. Hamilton, *Letters to Washington*, III, p. 295.

3. S. M. Hamilton, op. cit., III, pp. 302, 330.

4. A. B. Hulbert has devoted a whole volume to the journey of 1784 in his *Washington and the West,* and both accounts are reproduced entire in Ford's edition of the *Writings,* and Fitzpatrick's of the *Diaries.*

5. Fitzpatrick, *Diaries,* II, p. 288 (1784).

6. Haworth, *George Washington, Country Gentleman,* p. 22.

7. Volwiler, *George Croghan and the Western Movement,* p. 249.

8. Volwiler, op. cit., p. 274.

9. Volwiler, op. cit., p. 279.

10. S. M. Hamilton, op. cit., IV, pp. 118, 121.

11. S. M. Hamilton, op. cit., IV, p. 294.

12. Volwiler, op. cit., p. 297.

13. Alvord, *The Mississippi Valley in British Politics,* II, pp. 162, 164.

CHAPTER XII

1. Ford, *Writings,* II, p. 325.

2. Ford, *Writings,* II, p. 346 n.

3. Ford, *Writings,* II, p. 341.

4. Ford, *Writings,* II, p. 343 n.

5. Ford, *Writings,* II, pp. 371, 372, 374, 375, 376.

6. Ford, *Writings,* II, pp. 386, 391, 410, 392.

7. Bennett Allen, quoted in W. S. Baker's *Early Sketches of George Washington,* p. 31.

8. Charles A. Beard and Mary R. Beard, *The Rise of American Civilization,* I, p. 115.

9. Ford, *Writings,* II, p. 404. A more exact version is given in S. M. Hamilton's *Letters to Washington,* IV, p. 337 n. Robert Adam's letter is on p. 325.

10. S. M. Hamilton, op. cit., p. 356. In the Revolutionary War, Washington procured for Woelper a commission to command a company of the German Battalion.

11. Ford, *Writings,* II, pp. 408 n, 412.

12. Alvord, *The Mississippi Valley in British Politics,* II, p. 187.

13. G. A. Ward, *Journals and Letters of Samuel Curwen,* p. 92.

14. Burke's *History of Virginia,* III, p. 375, cited in Ford's *Writings,* II, p. 352 n.

15. Avery, *History of the United States,* V, p. 181.

16. Alvord, op. cit., II, p. 187.

17. Avery, op. cit., V, p. 183.

18. Theodore Roosevelt, *The Winning of the West,* I, pp. 233, 240.

19. Ford, *Writings,* II, pp. 462, 454.

20. Ford, *Writings,* II, p. 459.

21. Ford, *Writings,* II, p. 465.

22. Alvord, op. cit., II, p. 112.

23. F. A. Ogg, *The Old Northwest* (Chronicles of America), p. 39. On April 25 Washington wrote to Edward Graham a long letter quoted by Fitzpatrick in the *Diaries,* I, p. 391 n., describing his prolonged and harrow-

ing trials and his reasons for doing what he did. "Rather than be at the trouble and expense of dividing with others I bought and exchanged until I got entire tracts to myself. After the Patents were granted and the Land thereby secured, I concerned myself no further with any part thereof excepting my own." He was still bitter at the fact that the "expence" had been largely thrown on him, "nor has the latter been reimbursed to this day."

24. Ford, *Writings*, II, p. 448.

CHAPTER XIII

1. Ford, *Writings*, II, p. 380.
2. Ford, *Writings*, II, p. 383 n.
3. G. C. D. Odell, *Annals of the New York Stage*, I, p. 165.

CHAPTER XIV

1. Fitzpatrick, *Diaries*, I, p. 336 n.
2. G. W. P. Custis, *Recollections*, p. 496, contains a reproduction of this list of expenses.
3. W. S. Baker, *The Engraved Portraits of Washington*, p. 11.
4. Ford, *Writings*, II, p. 349.
5. Ford, *Writings*, II, p. 380.
6. Ford, *Writings*, II, p. 384.
7. S. M. Hamilton, *Letters to Washington*, IV, p. 234.
8. S. M. Hamilton, op. cit., IV, pp. 262, 324.
9. S. M. Hamilton, op. cit., p. 369 n. Letter to James Tilghman, Feb., 1774.
10. B. J. Lossing, *Mary and Martha*, p. 126. Lossing says he copied the letter from the original "preserved by the family of her grandson, at Arlington House, so late as 1860."
11. Custis, op. cit., p. 85.
12. Custis, op. cit., pp. 89, 91.

CHAPTER XV

1. Sparks, *Life of Washington*, p. 105. The names of the hounds are taken from Washington's *Diaries*, *passim*.
2. Ford, *Writings*, II, p. 191 n. Sparks, II, p. 338: see Ch. III of this volume.
3. Ford, *Writings*, II, p. 193.
4. G. E. Howard, *Preliminaries of the Revolution*, p. 41.
5. Beer, *British Colonial Policy*, 1754-1765, p. 269.
6. Cited by F. A. Mumby, *George III and the American Revolution*, p. 126.
7. G. E. Howard, op. cit., pp. 119, 106-7.
8. James Truslow Adams, *Revolutionary New England*, pp. vii, 292.

9. J. M. Leake, *The Virginia Committee System and the American Revolution* (Johns Hopkins University Studies, 1917), p. 109.

10. Schlesinger, *Colonial Merchants*, p. 98.

11. Beer, op. cit., p. 282.

12. Lecky, *England in the Eighteenth Century*, III, p. 351. Woodburn, *The Causes of the American Revolution* (Johns Hopkins University Studies), p. 28. Lord Brougham, *Political Philosophy*, III, p. 329.

13. G. E. Howard, op. cit., p. 7.

14. J. T. Adams, op. cit., p. 7.

15. Charles L. Lingley, *The Transition in Virginia*, p. 114. Van Tyne, *Causes of the War of Independence*, p. 148.

16. See Volume I of this work, p. 314.

17. Van Tyne, op. cit., p. 155. A French spy who was present wrote an account of it as follows:

"One of the members stood up and said he had read that in former times tarquin and Julus had their Brutus, Charles had his Cromwell, and he Did not Doubt that some good American would stand up in favor of his Country, but (says he) in a more moderate manner. And was going to continue, when the Speaker of the house rose and said, he, the last that stood up, had spoke traison and was sorey to see that not one of the members of the house was loyal Enough to Stop him, before he had gone so far. Upon which, the Same member stood up again, (his name is henery) and said that if he had affronted the Speaker, or the house, he was ready to ask pardon, and he would show his loyalty to his majesty, King G the third, at the Expense of the last Drop of his blood, but what he had Said must be atributed to the Interest of his Country's Dying liberty which he had at heart, and the heat of passion might have lead him to have said something more than he intended, but again, if he had Said anything wrong, he beged the Speaker and the houses pardon; some other members Stood up and backed him on which that afaire was droped."

18. Leake, op. cit., p. 116. The growth of the story is given in Morison, *Sources and Documents*, p. 15.

19. Ford, *Writings*, II, p. 200 n.

20. Lingley, op. cit., p. 44 n.

21. Ford, *Writings*, II, p. 207.

22. G. E. Howard, op. cit., p. 79.

23. John Adams, *Works*, X, p. 2471.

24. F. J. Hinkhouse, *The Preliminaries of the American Revolution as Seen in the English Press*, p. 75.

25. Ford, *Writings*, II, p. 211 n. Sparks, II, p. 345.

26. Ford, *Writings*, II, 210 n. Sparks, II, p. 344.

27. Van Tyne, op. cit., pp. 246, 248.

28. Schlesinger, op. cit., p. 135.

CHAPTER XVI

1. Ford, *Writings*, II, p. 263.

2. Ford, *Writings*, II, p. 267 n.

3. Fitzpatrick, *Diaries*, I, p. 324.

4. Among those who mistake Hays' Raleigh Tavern for a private house are Schlesinger, *Colonial Merchants*, p. 136; Van Tyne, *Causes of the War of Independence*, p. 264; Howard, *Preliminaries of the Revolution*, p. 200.

5. Fitzpatrick, *Diaries*, I, p. 325 n.

6. G. E. Howard, *Preliminaries of the Revolution*, p. 200.

7. Ford, *Writings*, II, p. 269.

8. Schlesinger, *Colonial Merchants*, pp. 170, 180.

9. Schlesinger, op. cit., pp. 64, 110, 237 n., 506.

10. Van Tyne, op. cit., p. 266.

11. Schlesinger, op. cit., p. 197 n.

12. Ford, *Writings*, II, p. 270 n., p. 284 n. (Library of Congress, *George Washington Papers*, XVII, p. 48).

13. Fitzpatrick, *Diaries*, I, p. 344.

14. Schlesinger, op. cit., p. 236. Ford, *Writings*, II, p. 338.

15. Schlesinger, op. cit., p. 249.

16. Ford, *Writings*, II, p. 335.

17. Mellen Chamberlain, *John Adams*, p. 13, cited by G. E. Howard, op. cit., p. 206.

18. Adams, *Works*, X, pp. 185, 288.

19. Van Tyne, op. cit., p. 367.

CHAPTER XVII

1. John C. Fitzpatrick, *The Spirit of the Revolution*, p. 106.

2. Samuel Adams, *Writings* (Cushing Ed.), II, pp. 334-337.

3. Letter of March 27, 1772, to Lord Hillsborough, cited by Schlesinger, *Colonial Merchants*, p. 256.

4. Dr. Edward C. Collins, *Committees of Correspondence of the American Revolution* (Report of American Historical Association, 1901), I, p. 245. Sparks, *Life of Gouverneur Morris*, I, p. 30, thus describes their purpose: "The primary movement was to bring the people to understand their interests and act in concert, and the first means used to attain this end was the establishment of Committees of Correspondence in different parts of the country. These committees were chosen by the people in towns, counties, parishes, districts, or smaller neighborhoods. They were intrusted with certain powers, which enabled them to correspond with each other and to represent in some sort the political views and objects of constituents. So necessary was this system in itself, and so well adapted to promote the general welfare, that it was acceded to everywhere, and in a short time committees were so universally appointed throughout the colonies, that the friends of liberty had speedy and direct channels opened with each other in every part of the continent. This increased their mutual intelligence, gave them confidence and encouragement, harmonized their sentiments, and sowed the seeds of union." John C. Fitzpatrick (*The Spirit of the Revolution*, p. 100) has much the same spirit toward them: "The development of the mechanics of a civil government to meet the necessities created by the struggle for political liberty is the most interesting of all the interesting phases of the American

Revolution. In this development the Committees of Correspondence, of Observation, of Inspection, of Intelligence, and of Safety were most important organisms. They formed the bridge by which the colonists passed over the morass of political destruction from the ruins of a repudiated, paternalistic tyranny to the firm ground of self-administered government beyond. . . .

"To establish a political machine of this character, extraneous to and unrecognized by any legal sanction, was difficult and dangerous as well. So dangerous was this that the Boston committee felt it wise to bind its members by oath not to divulge its proceedings. . . .

"The Virginia resolves of March 12, 1773, were the signal for an intercolonial unity of action never before obtained. Before a year had passed, every Colony, except Pennsylvania, responded with a committee organization. . . .

"It was this group organization that controlled at the outbreak of the hostilities of the Revolutionary War, and it held steady the reins of governmental power and authority until the royalist machinery was shaken loose and democratic governments set up and set in motion. In the rosters of these committeemen of 1773 are to be found the names of nearly every Revolutionary patriot most familiar to us."

5. Schlesinger, *Colonial Merchants*, p. 261, citing Frothingham, *Rise of Republic*.

6. Van Tyne, *Causes of the War of Independence*, p. 375.

7. It was Hutchinson who called Adams "the Grand Incendiary." The "eggs of sedition" phrase was used by Daniel Leonard (who wrote under the name of "Massachusettensis") in the *Mass. Gazette & Post-Boy*, Jan. 2, 1775.

8. G. E. Howard, *Preliminaries of the Revolution*, p. 266.

9. M. L. Weems, *Life*, p. 67.

10. Franklin, *Writings* (Smyth), VI, p. 178.

11. Sparks, *Life and Writings of Gouverneur Morris*, I, p. 23.

12. Van Tyne, op. cit., p. 394.

13. Hon. J. W. Fortescue, *History of the British Army*, III, p. 34. Their treatment is thus described by Fortescue, p. 36:

"The soldiers were daily accosted by such endearing names as 'lobster scoundrel,' 'red herring,' and 'bloody back,' this last term alluding of course to the results, soon to be experienced by American soldiers under Washington, of a flogging at the halberts. The troops, having strict orders never to strike an inhabitant, whatever the provocation, endured these insults with a forbearance which speaks volumes for their discipline; but this did not save them from most violent and barbarous assaults. . . . Officers and men were frequently arrested upon frivolous charges and required either to find heavy bail, which when produced was generally refused for no reason whatever, or to go to gaol; then, when the case came up for trial, the prosecution disappeared and the accused was instantly acquitted. . . . Matters reached at length such a pitch that, on the application of two privates to General Mackay for redress after a murderous assault upon them, the General was fain to give them half a guinea apiece, and advise them to abandon the prosecution of their assailants, since, however good their cause, there was no redress for soldiers in Boston."

At the end of a long account, he says:

"I have been careful to give these details, since Mr. Fiske, generally an impartial writer, has written that 'any manifestation of brute force in the course of a political dispute was exceedingly disgusting and shocking' to the Americans (*American Revolution*, I, p. 71)."

Fortescue finds numerous serious errors in Fiske's history.

14. Van Tyne, op. cit., p. 289.

15. G. E. Howard, op. cit., p. 205.

16. S. G. Fisher, *The Struggle for American Independence*, I, p. 148.

17. M. L. Weems, *Life*, p. 73.

18. Boucher, *Reminiscences of an American Loyalist*, pp. 96, 116. Moses Coit Tyler, in his *Literary History of the Revolution*, devotes Ch. XIV to a eulogy of Boucher's fine qualities as a brave and sincere man.

CHAPTER XVIII

1. Letter of an unnamed member of the Assembly to a friend in London, Williamsburg, May 20, 1774. Force's *American Archives*, 4th Series, I, p. 340.

2. J. M. Leake, *The Virginia Committee System and the American Revolution* (Johns Hopkins University Studies), p. 144.

3. M. D. Conway, *Edmund Randolph*, p. 15. James Otis' statement is cited by Lecky, *American Revolution*, p. 173.

Schlesinger (Discussion in Report of American Historical Association, 1921, p. 183) said that in giving the three main causes of the colonial revolt as economic unrest, the American people, and propaganda, an equal cause has been omitted, religious influence. "The stool should have four legs instead of three." He cites John Adams, and adds, "the opinion of Tories like Joseph Galloway and Judge Thomas Jones, who regarded the terms Congregationalist and Presbyterian as virtually synonymous with rebel and disloyalist." He went on to say, "Careful study should be made of the part played by holy days and anniversary celebrations in promoting colonial disaffection. When the radicals wished to focus public attention upon some measure they had in view they were likely to prepare the minds of the people by announcing a day of 'prayer and humiliation.' Closely akin to this practice was the one of commemorating the anniversaries of such events as the repeal of the stamp act and the occurrence of the Boston Massacre."

General Gage in Boston saw through the fast day device, but lacked the discretion to pretend solemnity. He agreed with one of his officers who wrote that the New Englanders were "the most arrant cheats and hypocrites in America" (Trevelyan, *The American Revolution*, I, p. 206), and actually issued a proclamation against Hypocrisy. And thus, says Trevelyan, he "paralysed forever and a day, his power of acting as an intercessor between the Crown and the colony."

4. The confusion as to the date, which is variously given, seems to be settled by J. M. Garnett, *Early Revolutionary History of Va.* (Va. Hist. Soc. Coll., 1891), p. 18.

5. Jefferson, *Writings*, IV, pp. 201, 348, 357.

6. Isaac S. Harrell, *Loyalism in Virginia*, p. 27.
7. Harrell, op. cit., p. 26.
8. Bishop Meade, *Old Churches, Ministers and Families of Va.*, I, p. 174.
9. Conway, op. cit., p. 16. (On leaf 287 of the typewritten copy of Randolph's History in the Huntington Library.)
10. Conway, op. cit., p. 379 (do., leaves 262, 266).
11. John Adams, *Works*, II, p. 62, cited in Van Tyne's *Causes of the War of Independence*, p. 325.
12. Ford, *Writings*, II, pp. 422 n., 432 n.
13. Ford, *Writings*, II, pp. 417, 420.
14. "At a General Meeting of the Freeholders and other Inhabitants of the County of *Fairfax*, at the Court House in the Town of *Alexandria*, on *Monday*, the 18th day of *July*, 1774:

> GEORGE WASHINGTON, Esquire, *Chairman*, and
> ROBERT HARRISON, Gentleman, *Clerk*.

"*Resolved*, That this Colony and Dominion of *Virginia* cannot be considered as a conquered country, and, if it was, that the present inhabitants are the descendants, not of the conquered, but of the conquerors. That the same was not settled at the national expense of *England*, but at the private expense of the adventurers, our ancestors, by solemn compact with, and under the auspices and protection of, the *British* Crown, upon which we are, in every respect, as dependent as the people of *Great Britain*, and in the same manner subject to all his Majesty's just, legal, and constitutional prerogatives; that our ancestors, when they left their native land, and settled in *America*, brought with them, even if the same had not been confirmed by Charters, the civil Constitution and form of Government of the country they came from, and were by the laws of nature and Nations entitled to all its privileges, immunities, and advantages, which have descended to us, their posterity, and ought of right to be as fully enjoyed as if we had still continued within the Realm of *England*.

"*Resolved*, That the most important and valuable part of the *British* Constitution, upon which its very existence depends, is the fundamental principle of the people's being governed by no laws to which they have not given their consent by Representatives freely chosen by themselves, who are affected by the laws they enact equally with their constituents, to whom they are accountable, and whose burthens they share, in which consists the safety and happiness of the community; for if this part of the Constitution was taken away, or materially altered, the Government must degenerate either into an absolute and despotick monarchy, or a tyrannical aristocracy, and the freedom of the people be annihilated.

"*Resolved*, Therefore, as the inhabitants of the *American* Colonies are not, and from their situation, cannot be represented in the *British* Parliament, that the Legislative power here can, of right, be exercised only by our Provincial Assemblies, or Parliaments, subject to the assent or negative of the *British* Crown, to be declared within some proper limited time, . . .

"That while we are treated upon an equal footing with our fellow-subjects, the motives of self-interest and preservation will be a sufficient obligation, as was evident through the course of the last war; . . .

"*Resolved*, That the powers over the people of *America*, now claimed by the *British* House of Commons, in whose election we have no share; in whose determinations we have no influence; whose information must be always defective, and often false; who in many instances may have a separate, and in some an opposite interest to ours; and who are removed from those impressions of tenderness and compassion, arising from personal intercourse and connection, which soften the rigours of the most despotick Governments, must, if continued, establish the most grievous and intolerable species of tyranny and oppression that ever was inflicted upon mankind.

"*Resolved,* That it is our greatest wish and inclination, as well as interest, to continue our connection with, and dependence upon, the *British* Government; but though we are its subjects, we will use every means which Heaven hath given us to prevent our becoming its slaves. . . .

"*Resolved,* That every little jarring interest and dispute which hath ever happened between these Colonies, should be buried in eternal oblivion; that all manner of luxury and extravagance ought immediately to be laid aside, as totally inconsistent with the threatening and gloomy prospect before us; that it is the indispensable duty of all the gentlemen and men of fortunes to set examples of temperance, fortitude, frugality, and industry, and give every encouragement in their power, particularly by subscriptions and premiums, to the improvement of arts and manufactures in *America;* that great care and attention should be had to the cultivation of flax, cotton, and other materials for manufactures; and we recommend it to such of the inhabitants as have large stocks of sheep, to sell to their neighbours at a moderate price, as the most certain means of speedily increasing our breed of sheep and quantity of wool. . . .

"*Resolved,* That *George Washington,* Esquire, and *Charles Broadwater,* Gentleman, lately elected our Representatives to serve in the General Assembly, attend the Convention at *Williamsburg,* on the first day of *August* next, and present these Resolves as the sense of the people of this county upon the measures proper to be taken in the present alarming and dangerous situation of *America.*" (Force's *American Archives,* 4th Series, I, pp. 597-600.)

15. Nicholas Creswell, *Journal,* 1774-1777, pp. 26, 253.
16. John Adams, *Works,* II, p. 360.

CHAPTER XIX

1. Quoted by Norman Hapgood, *Washington,* p. 109. These words are included in a letter from Gage to Washington, Aug. 13, 1775. See Ford, *Writings,* III, p. 79 n. The letter was signed by Gage, but written for him by Burgoyne, except the last paragraph.
2. Ford, *Writings,* II, p. 427 n.
3. W. W. Henry, *Patrick Henry,* I, p. 213.
4. Watson, *Annals of Philadelphia,* I, p. 419.
5. S. G. Fisher, *The Struggle for American Independence,* I, p. 221.
6. Avery, *History of the United States,* V, p. 214.
7. M. D. Conway, *Edmund Randolph,* p. 9.
8. Watson, op. cit., I, p. 421.
9. *Memoir of Bishop White,* p. 189. Many historians say that it was

John Adams who proposed that an Episcopalian lead in prayer, but John Adams in a letter to his wife (*Familiar Letters*, p. 37) on Sept. 16, 1774, says: "Mr. Samuel Adams arose and said he was no bigot, and could hear a prayer from a gentleman of piety and virtue, who was at the same time a friend to his country." In this same letter John Adams says that there was opposition to any kind of worship on account of the divergence of belief until Sam Adams made his plea.

10. G. E. Howard, *Preliminaries of the Revolution*, p. 295.

11. S. G. Fisher, op. cit., I, p. 238.

12. John Adams, *Works*, X, p. 277.

13. Ford, *Writings*, II, p. 440 n.

14. W. W. Henry, op. cit., I, p. 247.

15. Adams, op. cit., II, p. 370.

16. Quoted from the *Pennsylvania Gazette*, in Fitzpatrick's *Diaries*, II, p. 164.

17. Watson, op. cit., I, p. 286.

18. Channing, *History of the U. S.*, III, p. 149.

19. S. M. Hamilton, *Letters to Washington*, V, p. 49.

20. Ford, *Writings*, II, p. 441.

21. Ford, *Writings*, II, p. 445 n.

22. *Letters of R. H. Lee*, I, p. 130.

23. Ford, *Writings*, II, p. 445 n.

24. *Letters of R. H. Lee*, I, p. 110.

25. Thomas Jones, *History of New York During the Revolutionary War*, II, p. 346.

26. Ford, *Writings*, II, pp. 463-4, 463 n.

27. Ford, *Writings*, II, p. 472.

28. Ford, *Writings*, II, p. 473.

29. S. M. Hamilton, *Letters to Washington*, V, p. 121.

CHAPTER XX

1. John Adams, *Works*, II, pp. 415-8. Ford, *Writings*, III, p. 479.

2. Capt. John Stuart's Narrative, *Magazine of American History*, 1877, p. 743.

3. *Lee Papers* (Collection of New York Historical Society, 1871), I, p. 5.

4. G. H. Moore, *The Treason of Charles Lee*, p. 33.

5. F. B. Dexter, *The Literary Diary of Ezra Stiles*, I, p. 454.

6. Force, *American Archives*, 5th Series, I, p. 116.

7. *Familiar Letters of John Adams to His Wife*, p. 59.

8. C. F. Adams in *Proceedings of Massachusetts Historical Society*, IV, p. 70.

9. Warren-Adams *Letters* in *Proc. Mass. Hist. Soc.*, I, p. 47.

10. Force, *American Archives*, 4th Series, II, p. 1281.

11. Austin, *Life of Gerry*, I, p. 79. Force, op. cit., II, p. 906.

12. Adams, *Life and Works*, II, pp. 415, 418.

13. Force, op. cit., II, pp. 1848, 1850.

14. *Familiar Letters of Adams*, p. 65.

15. F. B. Dexter, op. cit., I, p. 618.

16. Force, op. cit., II, pp. 1849, 1847.

17. Force, op. cit., II, p. 1019. For the Hancock letter, see Ford, *Writings*, III, p. 39 n. John Adams, *Works*, IX, pp. 357, 359.

18. Ford, *Writings*, II, p. 483.

19. Ford, *Writings*, II, p. 486.

20. Ford, *Writings*, II, p. 487.

21. Force, op. cit., II, p. 1031.

22. Mrs. Roger A. Pryor, *The Mother of Washington and Her Times*, p. 246.

23. G. H. Moore, op. cit., p. 32.

24. *George Washington's Accounts of Expenses, etc.*, with annotations by John C. Fitzpatrick, p. 7.

25. *Familiar Letters*, p. 303.

CHAPTER XXI

1. Jonathan Boucher, *Reminiscences of an American Loyalist*, p. 109, gives an interesting evidence of Washington's antipathy to independence at this time, in his account of a meeting that took place when Washington crossed the Potomac to attend the second Congress:

"There had been a great meeting of people, and great doings, in Alexandria on the occasion; and everybody seemed to be on fire, either with rum, or patriotism, or both. Some patriots in our boat huzzaed, and gave three cheers to the General as he passed us; whilst Mr. Addison and myself contented ourselves with pulling off our hats. The General (then only Colonel) Washington beckoned us to stop, as we did, just, as he said, to shake us by the hand. His behaviour to me was now, as it had always been, polite and respectful, and I shall for ever remember what passed in the few disturbed moments of conversation we then had.

"From his going on the errand he was, I foresaw and apprised him of much that has since happened; in particular that there would certainly then be a civil war, and that the Americans would soon declare for independency.

"With more earnestness than was usual with his great reserve he scouted my apprehensions, adding (and I believe with perfect sincerity) that if ever I heard of his joining in any such measures I had his leave to set him down for everything wicked. Like Hazael, he might have said, Is thy servant a dog that he should do this great thing? So little do men know of themselves, and so dangerous is it to make one false step. . . .

"This was the last time I ever saw this gentleman, who, contrary to all reasonable expectation, has since so distinguished himself as that he will probably be handed down to posterity as one of the first characters of the age."

In the same work, p. 133, Boucher expressed his horror at the thought of Episcopalians joining with Puritans. He pleaded with the southern delegates not to combine with the New Englanders:

"Now, have you no suspicions that your fellow-patriots from the North meditate a Reformation, as they call it, in Church as well as in State? . . .

It should not be thought necessary to inform you that Republicanism will but ill accord with the genius of the people whom ye say ye represent. . . . O 'tis a monstrous and an unnatural coalition; and we should as soon expect to see the greatest contrarieties in Nature to meet in harmony, and the wolf and the lamb to feed together, as Virginians to form a cordial union with the saints of New England.

"We charge you then, as ye will answer it to your own conscience, and to Him who is the discerner of Consciences, to be on your guard how ye countenance any measures which may eventually lead, first to a separation from Great Britain, and afterwards to the subjugating these Southern colonies to those of the North."

2. Boucher (op. cit., p. 136) on August 6th, 1775, wrote to Washington this bitter denunciation:

"If I am still in the wrong, I am about to suffer such punishment as might satisfy the malice of even the most vindictive enemy . . . all those who with you are promoting the present apparently popular measures are the true enemies of their country . . . Your party to serve an obvious party purpose exceedingly magnify the numbers of those whom they suppose to take part with you . . . a Tory at all in the power of a Whig never escapes ill treatment merely because of his being a Tory. . . .

"You have borne to look on, at least as an unconcerned spectator, if not an abettor, whilst like the poor frogs in the fable, I have in a manner been petted to death. I do not ask if such conduct in you was friendly: was it either just, manly, or generous? It was not: no, it was acting with all the base malignity of a virulent Whig. As such, Sir, I resent it: and oppressed and overborne as I may seem to be by popular obloquy, I will not be so wanting in justice to myself as not to tell you, as I now do with honest boldness, that I despise the man who, for any motives, could be induced to act so mean a part.

"You are no longer worthy of my friendship; a man of honour can no longer without dishonour be connected with you. With your Cause I renounce you; and now, for the last time, subscribe myself, Sir, Your humble servant, JONATHAN BOUCHER."

By that time Washington was in such deep water, so bitterly denouncing, and denounced by, his own partisans, that Boucher's abuse was but one more drop in the shower.

3. *Familiar Letters of John Adams to His Wife,* p. 70.

4. Channing, *History of the United States,* III, p. 169 n. The statistics of the losses at Bunker Hill are in some confusion. Fortescue, *History of the British Army,* III, p. 162, says that the results of Bunker Hill encouraged the Americans "to a blind and fatal confidence in undisciplined troops, which went near to bring ruin to their cause. Notwithstanding the mistakes of generals and the deplorable waste of excellent troops, Bunker's Hill was probably a greater misfortune, taken altogether, to the Americans than to the British."

5. Charles Martyn in his *Life of Artemas Ward,* p. 140 *et passim,* defends Ward from the traditional charges against him with much documentary evidence; and states that though he did not leave his house, it was the headquarters where he belonged—he was also suffering from an attack of calculus.

He praises Ward for fighting the battle of Bunker Hill since it prevented "the enemy from moving out of Boston onto the mainland, and it resulted in driving them out of Boston into the sea."

6. Charles Francis Adams, *Studies Military and Diplomatic*, pp. 9, 13, 14.

7. Thomas Jones, *History of New York During the Revolutionary War*, I, p. 55.

8. *Celebration of the 139th Anniversary of the Journey of Washington from Philadelphia to Cambridge*, p. 13. This work describes the whole journey in careful detail.

9. These addresses were published in the New York *Gazette* for July 3, 1775. See also *Addresses of the City of New York to George Washington with His Replies*, privately printed, N. Y., 1867. His letter to Congress is in Ford, *Writings*, II, p. 496.

10. Henri Doniol, *Histoire de la participation de la France à l'établissement des États-Unis d'Amérique*, IV, p. 634; V, p. 720.

11. Ford, *Writings*, III, pp. 11, 2. Force, *American Archives*, 4th series, II, p. 1472. See also the description of the camp in a letter by the Rev. William Emerson, Sparks, *Writings*, III, p. 491.

12. Amory, *Old Cambridge and New*, p. 23; S. A. Drake, *Historic Fields and Mansions of Middlesex*, p. 262; cited by Martyn, *Artemas Ward*, p. 152 n.

13. *Familiar Letters of John Adams to His Wife*, p. 276. (Four A.M., May 22, 1777.)

14. Martyn, op. cit., p. 150.

15. Ford, *Writings*, III, p. 15.

16. *Lee Papers*, II, p. 146.

17. *Lee Papers*, I, p. 197. Washington's letter to Gen. Thomas is in Ford, *Writings*, III, p. 39.

18. *Lee Papers*, I, p. 196.

19. Martyn, op. cit., p. 159 n.

20. Justin Winsor, in *Narrative and Critical History of America*, VI, p. 142 n., says: "The assumption of command by Washington under this tree rests, so far as the writer knows, on traditions only, and he knows of no detail of the ceremonies given by contemporary evidence, though writers have much exercised their ingenuity in giving various attendant circumstances."

21. Martyn, op. cit., p. 153 n.

22. In Winsor's *Memorial History of Boston*, III, pp. 100, 89.

CHAPTER XXII

1. Fortescue in his *History of the British Army*, III, devotes Chapters XXII-XXV to the war in India and the attention given to it in Parliament.

2. Belcher, Henry, *The First American Civil War*, I, p. 259. Prof. Edward E. Curtis in his *The Organization of the British Army in the American Revolution*, has only to mention to ridicule the common American assumption concerning the British army that "it was a smooth-running fighting machine which failed because badly directed . . . We are asked to picture

Washington's men as ragged and half-starved while Howe's are to be imagined as warmly clothed and well-fed."

The average strength of a British regiment was 477, organized into one battalion of 10 companies, of which one was grenadiers who no longer carried hand-grenades, and one of light infantry. Cavalry regiments usually numbered 288 men in six troops. The weapon was the "Brown Bess," a flintlock weighing 14 pounds and carrying 300 yards, though ineffective beyond a hundred yards. A high wind blew the powder out of the pan. A rain ruined it so that not one shot in four would go off. The British flints were notoriously poor.

The soldiers carried an equipment weighing, at Bunker Hill, 125 pounds. In 1927 the pack of the United States soldiers was reduced from 79 to 57 pounds.

Infantry officers carried spontoons or half-pikes instead of swords, and often took flintlocks into action. The pay was 8 pence a day for privates, mostly used up for subsistence, uniform, etc. Women were carried along and whipped for offences as readily as the men. It is said that Burgoyne had 2,000 women with him.

So successful was British recruiting that the paper strength of 48,000 in 1775 was increased to 110,000 by 1781, of which 56,000 were in America and the West Indies.

The great difficulty was securing horses for the artillery. Supply and transport services were in a very crude state. There was no medical corps in the modern sense, the surgeons not being required even to have a diploma, wearing no uniforms and being socially inferior.

When Howe was locked up in Boston he might have cut his way through Massachusetts to New York if he had had land transport, and even the evacuation of Boston was almost prevented by lack of water transport. Wagons in America were few and weak as even Braddock found when Americans were friendly to him.

Professor Curtis sums up the British difficulties as follows:

"The failure of British arms in the American Revolution cannot be ascribed to want of courage on the part of officers and men. No braver troops ever shed their blood for the flag of England than those who thrice charged up Bunker Hill or attacked the American lines at Saratoga. The failure was due partly to inept generalship, partly to natural difficulties, and partly to maladministration. . . . Efficiency, in the sence of the word to-day, was practically unknown throughout British officialdom at the time of Germain and North. With the business of military administration distributed among a half-dozen jealous departments, it is sometimes remarkable that the troops received any food and clothing at all. The absence of centralized authority, the want of departmental harmony, the clashing of various boards, the jealousies of high officials, all combined to reduce the chances of military success to the lowest terms."

3. Fortescue, op. cit., III, pp. 169, 171.

4. The poet, Rogers, put on a black suit and wore it to the time of his death. The Constitutional Society of London met June 7, 1775, and subscribed £100 for "the relief of the widows, orphans and aged parents of our beloved American fellow-subjects, who, faithful to the character of

Englishmen, preferring death to slavery, were for that reason only, inhumanly murdered by the King's troops." This sum was sent to Benjamin Franklin. See *Proc. Mass. Hist. Soc.*, 1858-60, IV, p. 24.

Incidentally, it may be noted that the English press was almost always open to the defence of the American rebels, while the rebel press of America never admitted a word for the English. See Hinkhouse, *Preliminaries of the American Revolution as Seen in the English Press*, pp. 23, 161, 186, &c.

5. Belcher, op. cit., I, p. 255.

6. C. A. and M. R. Beard, *The Rise of American Civilization*, I, pp. 255-7.

7. J. T. Adams, *New England in the Republic*, p. 9.

8. Fortescue, op. cit., III, p. 169.

9. S. G. Fisher, *The Struggle for American Independence*, I, pp. 251-3.

10. J. Franklin Jameson, *The American Revolution Considered as a Social Movement*, pp. 73-75, 103.

11. S. G. Fisher, op. cit., I, p. 252. He cites Washington's own statements in 1777, "We are only about four thousand strong," and in 1780 that "our whole operating force amounts to only 10,400 rank and file." Ford, *Writings*, V, p. 242; VIII, p. 235. Knox's figures are given by Major General Emory Upton, *The Military Policy of the United States*, pp. 9, 20; F. L. Huidekoper, *The Military Unpreparedness of the United States*, pp. 13, 19. There is a great conflict in the accounts of the numbers. A writer in the *American Historical Review*, 1896, I, p. 81, says that more than 250,000 were enlisted during the war, 67,907 from Massachusetts, 31,939 from Connecticut, and 26,678 from Virginia.

12. Jameson, op. cit., pp. 73-5.

13. Lorenzo Sabine, *Loyalists of the American Revolution*, I, pp. 145, 150. Sabine, who tried to do justice to the loyalists, was not trying to justify his own ancestors, for he says, p. 139: "My father's father received his death-wound under Washington at Trenton; my mother's father fought under Stark, at Bennington." Yet he could not treat the forefathers "as little short of divinities . . . something I own, is due to the dignity of history; but something, too, is due to the dignity of truth." The matter of bounties is discussed by J. T. Adams, *New England in the Republic*, p. 19, where he tells how the towns were fined for not keeping up their quotas; and since the draft was unpopular, some of the towns resorted to taxation and raised money to hire men either at home or outside. Towns began to bid against each other, and there was a boom in bounties. One man, Fostwick, hired boys at £60 each to enlist and desert. He finally disappeared when his trick was discovered. The drafted men hired substitutes where possible, as was done on both sides during the Civil War, and the cry arose that the rich escaped the duty while the poor carried the burden. Adams shows that the support of indigent families and the meeting of requisitions was a genuine hardship to some of the small towns. See also C. K. Bolton's *The Private Soldier Under Washington*, p. 46, where he quotes evidence that in some communities there were not enough men left to get in the necessary harvests. Washington in 1779 (Ford, *Writings*, VII, p. 505) says that recruits were "hired at about 1500 dollars each for 9 months service."

14. Herbert Friedenwald, *The Continental Congress*, Am. Hist. Rev., 1895, pp. 233-4.

15. C. A. and M. R. Beard, op. cit., I, p. 253.

16. James H. Stark, *The Loyalists of Massachusetts*, p. 75.

17. W. B. Reed, *Life and Correspondence of Joseph Reed*, I, p. 243. General Orders, Oct. 3, 1776. Force's *Archives*, 4th series, I, p. 5; II, p. 1082.

18. John Whiting, *Revolutionary Orders of General Washington*, selected from the MSS., pp. 39, 93.

19. The account of Washington's attack on his own Virginia riflemen is taken from T. C. Amory's *Life of Maj. Gen. Sullivan*, I, p. 69.

20. John Whiting, op. cit., pp. 39, 64.

21. Frank Moore, *Diary of the American Revolution*, I, p. 110.

22. *Diary of Richard Smith*, Am. Hist. Rev., 1896, p. 289.

23. William Jay, *Life of John Jay*, VI, p. 31. The whole question of the negroes in the army is fully handled in C. K. Bolton's *The Private Soldier Under Washington*, pp. 20-24.

24. Force, op. cit., 4th series, I, pp. 1349-50.

25. Richard Frothingham, *The Siege of Boston*, p. 212.

26. Ford, *Writings*, IV, pp. 31, 31 n.

27. Stark, op. cit., p. 89.

28. *Wm. Barton's Journal* (Proc. New Jersey Historical Society), II, p. 31.

29. W. L. Stone, *Life of Joseph Brant*, I, p. 426.

30. This letter is in the Huntington Library, addressed to Col. John St. Clair, May 11, 1758.

31. Ford, *Writings*, III, p. 16.

32. John C. Fitzpatrick, *The Washington Scandals*, *Scribner's Magazine*, April, 1927.

33. Lodge, *Life of George Washington*, II, p. 391.
"Vigorous animal passions were inevitable, of course, in a man of such a physical make-up as his. How far he gave way to them in his youth no one knows, but the scandals which many persons now desire to have printed, ostensibly for the sake of truth, are, so far as I have been able to learn, with one or two dubious exceptions, of entirely modern parentage. I have run many of them to earth; nearly all are destitute of contemporary authority, and they may be relegated to the dust-heaps. If he gave way to these propensities in his youth, the only conclusion that I have been able to come to is that he mastered them when he reached man's estate."

CHAPTER XXIII

1. Ford, *Writings*, III, p. 21. The horrible and incurable state of disorganization is shown in Kapp's *Life of F. W. Von Steuben*, p. 115.

2. Ford, *Writings*, III, p. 13.

3. *Dinwiddie Papers* (Va. Hist. Soc. Coll.), I, p. 92. Ford, *Writings*, I, p. 42. See Vol. I of this work, p. 100.

4. *Orderly Book*, July 22, 1775. Ford, *Writings*, III, p. 32 n. See also L. C. Hatch, *The Administration of the American Revolutionary Army* (Harvard Historical Studies), X, p. 13. Frothingham, *Siege of Boston*, p. 218.

5. Ford, *Writings*, III, pp. 58, 209, 62. W. B. Reed, *Life of Joseph Reed*, p. 216.

6. Force, *American Archives*, 4, III, p. 1667.
7. Ford, *Writings*, III, p. 31 n.
8. E. E. Hale, in Winsor's *Memorial History of Boston*, III, p. 86.
9. Ford, *Writings*, III, p. 67.
10. Ford, *Writings*, III, p. 73, and note.
11. Ford, *Writings*, III, p. 75 n.
12. This letter is in the Pierpont Morgan Library from which the citation is made. It differs in a few unimportant points only from the version in Ford's *Writings*, III, p. 96.

Ford thinks that the suppressed passages were deleted by R. H. Lee, for reasons legitimate enough at the time, and not by Dr. Sparks.

The difficulty of persuading volunteers to come forward from other colonies in view of the greed of the New Englanders for office was also sarcastically referred to in an unpublished letter in the New York Public Library. It is addressed to George Clinton, dated August 25, 1775, and promises civility to a young Mr. White whom Clinton recommended. Washington planned to give him the post of aide "if an acquaintance of mine, for whom I have wrote to Virginia . . . should not come, . . . I propose to take Mr White into my Family." But Edmund Randolph came and took the post.

13. Ford, *Writings*, III, p. 92, omitted by Sparks. Also the letter to Josiah Quincy, Ford, *Writings*, III, p. 196.
14. Ford, *Writings*, III, p. 137.
15. Ford, *Writings*, III, pp. 25 n., 53 n. Force, *American Archives*, 4th Series, II, p. 1738. The matter of uniform is discussed by Charles H. Warren, *The Buff and Blue Uniform*, Proc. Mass. Hist. Soc., IV, p. 149. He noted that when Washington's portrait with his blue ribbon was seen abroad, the fable was started that he was a Marshal of France. But he said himself that he was never one, and, besides, a Marshal does not wear a blue ribbon. John C. Fitzpatrick has a valuable chapter on the uniform in his *The Spirit of the Revolution*, pp. 117-138. He notes that the first uniform was brown; the second blue; the final, blue with red facings. See also S. G. Fisher, *The Struggle for American Independence*, I, p. 359. Schuyler's letter to Washington, July 1, 1775, is given in Sparks, *Correspondence of the American Revolution*, I, p. 252.
16. Ford, *Writings*, III, pp. 146, 191, 195, 214.
17. Ford, *Writings*, III, pp. 231, 262. For the history of Washington's dealings with the sea, note Gardner W. Allen's *A Naval History of the American Revolution*.
18. Ford, *Writings*, III, p. 238.
19. Ford, *Writings*, III, p. 246. Sparks, *Writings*, III, p. 179, changes "I pray God" to "I pray God's mercy," and "flea bite" to "totally inadequate."
20. Ford, *Writings*, III, pp. 242-244.
21. Ford, *Writings*, III, p. 247. Sparks, *Writings*, III, p. 178, omits "dirty."
22. Ford, *Writings*, III, p. 254.
23. *The Lee Papers*, I, p. 226.
24. Ford, *Writings*, III, pp. 263, 272.
25. Ford, *Writings*, III, p. 293.

26. Ford, *Writings*, III, pp. 64-99 (Aug. 4, 1775).

27. Ford, *Writings*, III, p. 171 (to Robert Carter Nicholas, Oct. 4, 1775).

28. Ford, *Writings*, III, p. 145. Washington's circular letter and the minutes of the council are given in Force's *American Archives*, 4, III, p. 767.

29. Ford, *Writings*, III, p. 398 (to Joseph Reed, Feb. 1, 1776).

30. Ford, *Writings*, III, p. 222 (to Major-General Ward, Nov. 17, 1776).

31. From the Firle Papers at Gage's home, Firle Place, quoted by Belcher, *The First American Civil War*, I, p. 207.

32. The instructions to the congressional committee are given in Force's *American Archives*, fourth series, III, p. 847. The fascinating subjects discussed are given on pp. 1156-1163. The vote of Congress on p. 1958.

33. The correspondence with Gage is given in Ford, *Writings*, III, pp. 77, 79 n. and 90, as well as in Force's *American Archives*, 4, III, p. 246.

34. *Life of Reed*, I, p. 115. Washington's order of reprisal, issued through his then secretary, Joseph Reed, is in Force's *Archives*, 4, III, p. 328 n.

35. Dartmouth had the same idea and proposed it to Gage while Gage was forwarding Burgoyne's similar report to Dartmouth. Both documents are in the Firle papers. See Belcher, op. cit., I, p. 199.

36. The references to Mrs. Loring are in Henry Belcher, *The First American Civil War*, I, pp. 120, 195; II, pp. 101, 145; Thomas Jones, *History of New York During the Revolution*, I, p. 351; II, p. 86 n. Stark's *Loyalists of Massachusetts* has a biography of the Lorings, p. 424. See Sabine, *Loyalists of the American Revolution*, II, p. 27.

37. George E. Hastings, *Life and Works of Francis Hopkinson*, p. 293.

38. Moore, *Diary of the American Revolution*, II, p. 142.

CHAPTER XXIV

1. M. D. Conway, *George Washington and Mount Vernon* (Memoirs L. I. Hist. Soc.), IV, pp. 314, 316.

2. W. W. Henry, *Patrick Henry*, I, Ch. XI-XIV, tells of Henry's activities and Dunmore's War. Ford, *Writings*, III, p. 463.

3. Dunmore is defended by the British historian, Stedman, *The American War* (1794), I, Ch. III. He shows that the loyalists of Virginia suffered much from the Whigs and blames the rebels for part of the Norfolk fire.

4. This letter was published in full in S. B. Webb's *Correspondence and Journals*, I, p. 92, and reproduced in Tyler's Quarterly Historical and Genealogical Magazine, April, 1926, p. 245. It is evidently the correct version of a garbled form of which Ford wrote (in a note to another letter to Lund, dated Sept. 31, 1776): "This letter has not a little puzzled me." The version Ford saw included part of the 1776 letter, but this version is entirely different.

5. Ford, *Writings*, III, p. 43 n.

6. This letter, in neither Ford's nor Spark's collections, is quoted by M. D. Conway, op. cit., p. liv; it is dated May 5, 1780, and written to Col. Fielding Lewis.

7. Ford, *Writings*, III, p. 128.

8. The letter from V. Crawford is in W. H. Smith's *The St. Clair Papers*, I, p. 356. Crawford's charmingly individual spelling has plainly been standardized by the editor. Sparks, *Writings*, III, pp. 211, 212 n., discusses Dunmore's agent, Connolly, and their plans concerning Western lands. In Sparks, *Correspondence of the American Revolution*, I, p. 88, is a letter from R. H. Lee to Washington concerning the Western lands.

9. Ford, *Writings*, III, p. 236.

10. Ford, *Writings*, III, p. 300. Mason's letter to Washington is cited by B. J. Lossing, *Mary and Martha Washington*, p. 137.

11. Ford, *Writings*, III, p. 180.

12. Ford, *Writings*, III, p. 232.

13. Ford, *Writings*, III, p. 229. Reed, *Life and Correspondence of President Reed*, I, p. 128. The letter is dated Nov. 20, 1775.

14. *Extracts from the Diary of Charles Marshall*, p. 51.

15. *Lee Papers*, I, p. 207.

16. Reed, op. cit., I, p. 134. Ford, *Writings*, III, p. 277. Sparks wrote W. B. Reed (see I, p. 125 n.) that Washington's letters to Reed's grandfather, Joseph Reed, "seemed to me the most imperfect I had ever seen from his pen. . . . I used more caution in selecting from these letters than from any others." Reed printed them as Washington wrote them to Joseph Reed, of whom he was more fond than Reed was of him—just as Alexander Hamilton later came to inspire an affection he could not requite.

17. Martha's letter, now in the Pierpont Morgan Collection, is quoted in Mrs. A. H. Wharton's *Martha Washington*, p. 135.

18. Frank Moore, *Diary of the Revolution*, I, p. 201. Jan. 30, 1776.

19. Reed, op. cit., I, pp. 134, 137. Ford, *Writings*, III, p. 277.

20. John Adams, *Works*, IX, 270. This Mercy Warren, daughter of James Otis and wife of James Warren, was then a poetess and later the author of a history of the Revolution in which she irritated John Adams. At the present time, however, she wrote for Mrs. Adams the following description of Martha:

"I took a Ride to Cambridge and waited on Mrs Washington at 11 o clock where I was received with the politeness & Respect shown in a first interview among the well bred & with the Ease & Cordiallity of friendship of a much Earlier date. If you wish to hear more of this Ladys Character I will tell you I think the Complacency of her Manners speaks at once the Benevolence of her Heart & her affability Candor & Gentleness quallify her to soften the hours of private Life or to sweeten the Cares of the Hero & smooth the Rugged scenes of War. I did not dine with her though much urg'd but Engaged to spend the ensuing day at headquarters. She desired me to Name an early hour in the Morning when she would send her Chariot and Accompany me to see the Deserted Lines of the enemy and the Ruins of Charleston. A Melancholy sight the Last which Evinces the Barbaraty of the foe & leaves a Deep impression of the suffering of that unhappy town. Mr Custice is the only son of the Lady (I) Have Discribed, a sensible Modest agreeable young Man. His Lady a Daughter of Coll Calvert of Mariland, appears to be of an Engaging Disposition but of so Extremely Delicate a Constitution, that it Deprives her as well as her friends of part of the pleasure which I am persuaded would Result from her Conversation did she enjoy a greater

Share of Health. She is pretty, genteel Easy & Agreable, yet it is evident it is not owing to that want of Vivacity which renders youth agreable, but to a want of Health which a Little Clouds her spirits." (*Mercy Warren* by Alice Brown, p. 126.)

21. Reed, op. cit., I, pp. 142, 157. Ford, *Writings*, III, pp. 340, 411. (Feb. 10, 1776.)

22. Reed, op. cit., I, p. 144. Ford, *Writings*, III, p. 344. (Jan. 14, 1776.)

CHAPTER XXV

1. Isaac N. Arnold, *Life of Benedict Arnold*, p. 37.
2. C. Stedman, *History of the American War* (1794), I, p. 131. He quotes Ethan Allen's famous words and tells the story of his duping the trusting Captain De la Place; see also Fortescue, *History of the British Army*, III, p. 155.
3. Force's *American Archives*, 4, II, p. 1833.
4. Henry Belcher, *The First American Civil War*, I, p. 167.
5. Stedman, op. cit., I, p. 132.
6. Fortescue, op. cit., III, p. 155. All the accounts of the Canadian campaign differ widely in their figures and even in their dates. This is characteristic of military history, but unusually so of these events.
7. Ford, *Writings*, III, p. 76.
8. Ford, *Writings*, III, p. 121.
9. Ford, *Writings*, III, p. 125.
10. Ford, *Writings*, III, p. 268 n.
11. Sparks, *Correspondence of the American Revolution*, I, p. 114.
12. Sparks, op. cit., I, p. 116.
13. Ford, *Writings*, III, p. 360.

CHAPTER XXVI

1. Ford, *Writings*, III, p. 344.
2. E. E. Curtis, *The Organization of the British Army in the American Revolution*, p. 143.
3. H. Belcher, *The First American Civil War*, I, p. 202.
4. Letter from Col. Moylan to Joseph Reed, Dec. 5, 1775. W. B. Reed, *Life of Reed*, I, p. 133.
5. Ford, *Writings*, III, pp. 282, 295, 285, 307, 313 n.
6. D. Ramsay, *History of the American Revolution*, I, p. 261.
7. L. C. Hatch, *The Administration of the American Revolutionary Army*, p. 17.
8. Ford, *Writings*, III, p. 311 n.
9. Ford, *Writings*, III, p. 313.
10. Ford, *Writings*, III, p. 320. To Governor Cooke.
11. Ford, *Writings*, III, p. 317.
12. Ford, *Writings*, III, p. 396. Jan. 31, 1776.
13. Ford, *Writings*, III, p. 318.

14. Ford, *Writings*, III, pp. 325, 328.

15. Ford, *Writings*, III, p. 332.

16. Ford, *Writings*, III, p. 340.

17. Letter of Mrs. Adams, March 1, 1776, cited by Charles Martyn, *Artemas Ward*, p. 189.

18. Ford, *Writings*, III, p. 417.

19. Ford, *Writings*, III, p. 425. Charles Martyn, op. cit., p. 199 n., points out the "curious error" of Sir George Trevelyan, who represents Washington as being too prudent to wish to attack, I, p. 369.

20. Ford, *Writings*, III, p. 428. To Governor Trumbull, Feb. 19, 1776.

21. *Letters on the American Revolution*, 1774-1776, edited by Margaret Wheeler Willard, p. 190.

22. Willard, op. cit., p. 255.

23. Willard, op. cit., p. 276-9.

24. Charles Martyn, op. cit., p. 124-5. C. F. Adams, *Studies Military and Diplomatic*, p. 13, says that the original plan of occupying both Prospect and Bunker Hills was "bold, well-conceived, calculated to produce the results desired," but the force that was to occupy Prospect Hill mysteriously failed to do so.

25. Martyn, op. cit., pp. 195, 198, 199 and notes.

26. Daniel McCustin in *Papers Relating Chiefly to the Maryland Line*, p. 33. Cited by Martyn, op. cit., p. 203 n.

27. Martyn, op. cit., pp. 104, 119.

28. Martyn, op. cit., p. 205 n.

29. Stedman, *History of the American War*, I, p. 167.

30. Ford, *Writings*, III, p. 450. Martyn, op. cit., p. 212, quotes Howe's order of Saturday: "the whole Garrison to be under Arms at 4 o'clock" Sunday morning "to be in readiness to embark." He was not therefore driven out by seeing the enemy on Dorchester Heights.

31. Lieutenant Bangs, *Journal*, p. 15, cited by Martyn, op. cit., p. 210.

32. Ford, *Writings*, III, p. 457 n.

33. Ford, *Writings*, III, p. 460.

34. Ford, *Writings*, III, pp. 459, 472 n.

35. James Wilkinson, *Memoirs of My Own Times*, I, p. 33.

36. Martyn, op. cit., p. 216. *The Lee Papers*, II, p. 13.

37. Martyn, op. cit., p. 215. Reed, *Joseph Reed*, I, p. 177.

38. Ford, *Writings*, III, p. 475.

39. J. H. Stark, *The Loyalists of Massachusetts*, p. 348. On pages 133-136 he gives a list of 927 refugees. Trevelyan, *The American Revolution*, I, p. 373.

40. Belcher, *The First American Civil War*, I, p. 192.

41. Lorenzo Sabine, *Loyalists of the American Revolution*, I, p. 91.

42. J. H. Stark, op. cit., p. 57. For a full story of the Simsbury Mines, see R. H. Phelps, *Newgate of Connecticut*, p. 32. See also McMaster, *History of the People of the United States*, I, p. 99.

43. Ford, *Writings*, III, p. 506. Sparks, *Writings*, III, p. 343. March 31, 1776, to John Augustine Washington. In quoting the letter to Reed, Sparks omits the repetition with no indication. The letter to Reed is given in full in Ford, *Writings*, IV, p. 1.

CHAPTER XXVII

1. This letter of March 17, 1776, included in neither Sparks nor Ford, is quoted by Martyn, *Artemas Ward*, p. 214.

2. Ford, *Writings*, III, p. 485.

3. Ford, *Writings*, III, p. 493; cf. III, p. 97.

4. Stedman, *The American War*, I, p. 167.

5. Sparks, *Life of Washington*, p. 163 n. Ford, *Writings*, IV, p. 26 n. The diploma of Harvard is given in full by Ford, *Writings*, IV, p. 6 n.

6. Ford, *Writings*, III, p. 397, to Joseph Reed, Jan. 31, 1776.

7. Ford, *Writings*, III, p. 417, to Joseph Reed, Feb. 10, 1776.

8. Quoted from the *Pennsylvania Magazine*, April, 1776, by Ford, *Writings*, III, 442 n.

9. Ford, *Writings*, III, p. 440.

10. Frank Moore, *Diary of the American Revolution*, I, pp. 121, 159, 133. *Letters Written at the Time of the Occupation of Boston* (Hist. Coll. Essex Inst.), XIII, p. 198.

11. Ford, *Writings*, IV, p. 7.

12. Ford, *Writings*, IV, p. 9.

13. Ford, *Writings*, IV, p. 20.

14. Ford, *Writings*, IV, p. 21.

15. Moore, op. cit., I, p. 141.

16. Moore, op. cit., I, p. 219.

17. Moore, op. cit., I, p. 358.

18. Moore, op. cit., I, p. 414.

19. Thomas Jones, *History of New York*, I, p. 102.

20. Cited by H. P. Johnson, *The Campaign of 1776* (Memoirs of Long Island Historical Society), p. 92 n. He reproduces the entire diary in Part II, p. 101.

21. *New York City During the American Revolution* (privately printed for the Mercantile Library Association), p. 98.

22. Claude H. Van Tyne, *The American Revolution*, pp. 28-34. In his book, *The Loyalists of the American Revolution*, Professor Van Tyne gives full treatment to the subject. There is a fine statement of the Tory side of the case in Moses Coit Tyler's article, "Loyalists in the American Revolution" (Proc. N. Y. Hist. Assn.), XIII, p. 267, 275, 279, 280:

"For the Tory side so much was to be said in the way of solid fact and of valid reasoning, that an intelligent and a noble-minded American might have taken that side, and might have stuck to it, and might have gone into battle for it, and might have imperilled all the interests of his life in defence of it, without any just impeachment of his reason or of his integrity—without deserving to be called, then or since then, either a weak man or a bad one. . . .

"Finally, the whole strength and dignity of their historic claim is not appreciated until we recall the fact that, for the first ten or twelve years of the Revolution,—from 1764 to 1776,—the entire Whig agitation was conducted on a perpetual disavowal of the purpose or the desire for independence. In every form in which a solemn affirmation could be made and reiterated, it was affirmed by the Whigs during all those years that the only object of their agitation was to obstruct and to defeat a bad ministerial policy, thereby to secure a redress of grievances; that, as for independence, it was the thing they abhorred, and it was mere calumny to accuse them of designing or of desiring it. . . .

"First, it is an error to represent the Tories of the American Revolution as a party of mere negation and obstruction. . . .

"Secondly, it is an error to represent the Tories of the American Revolution as a party opposed either to any reform in the relations of the colonists with the mother-country, or to the extension of human rights and liberties here or elsewhere. From the beginning of the agitation, they clearly saw, they strongly felt, they frankly declared, that the constitutional relations of the colonies with the mother-country were in a crude state, were unsatisfactory, were in need of being carefully revised and reconstructed. This admission of theirs, they never recalled. . . .

"Thirdly, it is an error to represent the Tories of our Revolution as composed of Americans lacking in love for their native country, or in zeal for its liberty, or in willingness to labor, or fight, or even to die, for what they conceived to be its interests."

23. Rev. Charles Inglis, "State of the Anglo-American Church in 1776," *Documentary History of New York*, III, p. 1056.

24. Jones, op. cit., I, p. 82.

25. Jones, op. cit., I, p. 83.

26. Ford, *Writings*, IV, p. 57, to John Augustine Washington.

27. Ford, *Writings*, IV, p. 66.

28. Ford, *Writings*, IV, pp. 74-76, May 11, 1776.

29. Ford, *Writings*, IV, p. 93 n.

30. Ford, *Writings*, IV, p. 90.

31. Ford, *Writings*, IV, p. 89 n.

32. The fortifications of New York are described in great detail in Johnson's *The Campaign of 1776*.

33. Ford, *Writings*, IV, p. 107, letter to John Augustine Washington, Philadelphia, May 31, 1776.

34. Ford, *Writings*, IV, p. 164.

35. Ford, *Writings*, IV, pp. 112, 154 n.

36. Force, *American Archives*, 4th Series, VI, p. 1104.

37. Isaac N. Arnold, *The Life of Benedict Arnold*, pp. 95-101.

38. C. H. Van Tyne, *The American Revolution*, p. 118.

39. Ford, *Writings*, IV, p. 163 n.

40. Frank Moore, *Diary of the American Revolution*, I, p. 254.

CHAPTER XXVIII

1. *New York City During the American Revolution. The Hickey Plot*, pp. 66, 76. Eustis' letter is given in H. P. Johnston's, *The Campaign of 1776* (Memoirs Long Island Historical Society), Part II, p. 129.

2. Edward Floyd de Lancey's notes to Thomas Jones' *History of New York*, II, p. 416. To John McKesson, Aug. 21, 1776.

3. Ford, *Writings*, IV, p. 188.

4. Daniel Horsmanden, *The New York Conspiracy or a History of the Negro Plot.*

5. Ford, *Writings*, III, p. 466 n.

6. A full history of the Guard is given in Dr. Carlos E. Godfrey's *The Commander-in-Chief's Guard.* He gives a brief account of the plot.

7. B. J. Lossing, *Life of Washington*, II, p. 177 n.: "These facts were related to a friend of the writer (Mr. W. J. Davis), by the late Peter Embury, of New York, who resided in the city at the time, was well acquainted with the general's housekeeper, and was present at the execution of Hickey." On the other hand, Joseph Reed wrote: "The plot you mention, though romantic in some of its parts, had a real foundation. It originated with Governor Tryon, and was to be executed by the mayor and inferior agents, whom he had corrupted for that purpose. . . . I cannot think assassinating the Generals had any share in it." (See W. B. Reed, *Life of Reed*, I, p. 191.)

8. The Proceedings are given in full in Force's *American Archives*, 4, VI, pp. 1084-6.

9. From Washington's Orderly Book. Ford, *Writings*, IV, p. 188 n.

10. Letter to Dr. David Townsend of Boston, June 28, 1776, in the N. E. Hist. and Gen. Register, XXIII, p. 208, cited by Godfrey, op. cit., p. 32. H. P. Johnson, op. cit., p. 129. See also a newspaper account quoted in Frank Moore's *Diary of the American Revolution*, I, p. 256 n.

11. See Vol. I of this work, pp. 309, 329.

12. Godfrey, op. cit., pp. 63-66.

13. Ford, *Writings*, IV, p. 188 n.

14. *Minutes of a Conspiracy Against the Liberties of America*, published by John Campbell, Philadelphia, 1865, pp. 15, 20, 25. This is a limited reprint (with introduction, copious notes and an appendix containing extracts from the actual committee proceedings) of the edition of J. Bew. In his article, "The George Washington Scandals," *Scribner's Magazine*, April, 1927, p. 390, John C. Fitzpatrick gives at some length the history of the Bew publication and riddles its pretensions to serious acceptance.

CHAPTER XXIX

1. Ford, *Writings*, IV, p. 106, to John Augustine Washington, Philadelphia, May 31, 1776.

2. Ford, *Writings*, IV, p. 5; II, p. 474.

3. Nicholas Creswell, *Journal*, p. 209.

4. Van Tyne, *The American Revolution*, p. 104.

5. John Adams, March, 1775.

6. Franklin, *Works*, V, p. 7.

7. Allan Nevins, *The American States*, p. 110.

8. Moses Coit Tyler, *The Literary History of the American Revolution*, I, p. 481.

9. Carl Becker, *The Declaration of Independence*, p. 3.

10. (Alexander Graydon), *Memoirs of a Life Chiefly Passed in Pennsylvania*, p. 105.

11. Cited by Van Tyne, op. cit., p. 82. The letter to his wife is in *Familiar Letters of John Adams and His Wife*, p. 193.

12. Adams, *Works*, II, p. 512.

13. Jefferson, *Writings* (Memorial edition, 1905), XV, p. 462—to James Madison, Aug. 30, 1823.

14. Hamilton, *Works* (Lodge), I, p. 70. Cited by Fisher, *The Struggle for American Independence*, I, p. 34. Fisher (I, p. 25) is unique in assigning particular credit for the theory of human rights to Burlamaqui, and to Beccaria, as well as Grotius, Puffendorf, Locke, and Montesquieu.

15. John C. Fitzpatrick, *The Spirit of the Revolution*, p. 3.

16. *Gilmer Papers*, Va. Hist. Soc. Collections, VI, pp. 123, 121, 120, 88, 128.

17. Van Tyne, op. cit., p. 83.

18. Carl Becker, op. cit., pp. 6, 18.

19. Van Tyne, op. cit., p. 87.

20. J. W. Fortescue, *A History of the British Army*, III, p. 200. Charles M. Andrews in *The Colonial Background of the American Revolution* (p. 180) makes some exceedingly suggestive remarks on the cleavage caused by the Declaration: "I am never quite sure that those who are loudest in their approval of the Declaration of Independence would be among the revolutionists were they to face a similar issue to-day, or that those who talk most insistently about patriotism would have been among those whom they love to call the 'patriots of '76.' Are we consistent in glorifying revolution in the past and abhorring it in the present or in ennobling many of those who committed acts that to-day we would execrate as offenses against law and order? 'Dead radicals,' says a recent writer, 'are eulogized because the issues for which they fought are as dead as the men who advocated them. Belief in them has become traditional and therefore eminently respectable.' To this truism may be added the further one, that a revolutionist who is unsuccessful is likely to be condemned as a criminal, whereas he who succeeds is sure to be dubbed a patriot, a statesman, a hero, or a saint. It is always too much for human nature to glorify the losing side."

21. A. M. Schlesinger, *New Viewpoints in American History*, pp. 5-7.

22. Ford, *Writings*, IV, pp. 200, 202 n.

23. Ford, *Writings*, IV, p. 201.

24. F. V. Greene, *The Revolutionary War*, p. 33. He gives Washington at the end of August, 20,328 men fit for duty, with a paper strength of 33,363. Fortescue, op. cit., p. 184, gives Howe 25,000 and Washington 18,000. Ganoe, *The History of the United States Army*, p. 29, gives Howe 35,000 and Washington 8,000 fit for duty. Very careful computations of the strength of the two armies and their composition are given in H. P. Johnston's *The Campaign of 1776* (Memoirs of the Long Island Historical Society), Ch. III.

25. Stedman, *The American War*, I, pp. 191, 192, points out that if Howe had arrived two months earlier he would have found Washington with only "nine thousand men fit for duty, two thousand of whom were entirely destitute of arms." Howe, having "nearly thirty thousand men" the Americans "must then have been inevitably overwhelmed."

26. E. E. Curtis, *The Organization of the British Army in the American Revolution*, p. 101.

CHAPTER XXX

1. This letter is in the New York Public Library, the Emmett Collection, EM 1144, July 20, 1776, to Gen. Adam Stephen.

2. *Orderly Book*, July 10, 1776. Ford, *Writings*, IV, p. 226 n.

3. Ford, *Writings*, IV, p. 225.

4. Wm. B. Reed, *Life and Correspondence of Joseph Reed*, I, p. 195.

5. Ford, *Writings*, IV, pp. 226, 236 n., 242, 347. See Bolton, *The Private Soldier Under Washington*, p. 115. H. P. Johnston, *Campaign of 1776*, p. 93 n. S. G. Fisher, *The Struggle for American Independence*, I, p. 491.

6. Reed, op. cit., I, p. 197, gives the letter in full and the replies of Robert Morris, who incidentally had voted against the Declaration of Independence though he later signed it.

7. Reed, op. cit., I, p. 204, letter to Chas. Pettit, July 15, 1776.

8. Ford, *Writings*, IV, p. 250. The resolution of Congress is given on p. 250 n., from the *Journals* of July 17, 1775.

9. Reed, op. cit., I, p. 205. The dialogue is reproduced from Reed's notes with practically no change save from the third to the first person.

10. Reed, op. cit., p. 210.

11. Sparks, *Life of Washington*, p. 173 n., quoting a letter to Congress from Colonel Palfrey, paymaster general. See Van Tyne, *American Revolution*, p. 104. The mission of Lord Drummond is described in Ford, *Writings*, III, p. 420 n.; IV, p. 350, where Washington's letter to him of August 17, 1776, is given with illuminating notes.

12. Washington's and Franklin's letters concerning the Hessians are in Ford, *Writings*, IV, p. 370; Force, *American Archives*, 5th Series, I, pp. 1066, 1193. The Resolutions of Congress are on pp. 1602, 1607. The account of the Scotch efforts at desertion is in Frank Moore's *Diary of the Revolution*, I, p. 293, and the story of burning the effigies in the same work, I, p. 277.

13. Major W. A. Ganoe, *The History of the United States Army*, p. 28.

14. MS. Letter in the Emmett Collection, New York Public Library, EM 1099.

15. Henry P. Johnston, *The Campaign of 1776* (Memoirs of Long Island Hist. Soc.), III, p. 55.

16. *Lee Papers*, I, p. 310.

17. Force, *American Archives*, 5th Series, I, p. 1531.

18. Ford, *Writings*, IV, p. 361.

19. Ford, *Writings*, IV, p. 335.

20. E. M. Ruttenber, *Obstruction to the Navigation of Hudson's River*, pp. 5-23.

21. Quoted in Ruttenber, op. cit., p. 25, from Heath's *Memoirs*.

22. Ford, *Writings*, IV, p. 348 n.

23. Ford, *Writings*, IV, p. 353.

24. Ruttenber, op. cit., pp. 27-30, quotes the detailed account of Joseph Bass, as published in the *Worcester Magazine* in 1826.

25. F. V. Greene, *General Greene*, p. 41.

26. F. B. Dexter, *The Literary Diary of Ezra Stiles*, II, p. 159. See also

The Life of William Alexander, Earl of Stirling, by his grandson, W. A. Duer, LL.D. (N. J. Historical Society).

27. *Lee Papers,* III, p. 393 (Nov. 29, 1779), I, p. 309 (Feb. 19, 1776).
28. This letter is in the Pierpont Morgan Library.
29. This letter is in the Huntington Library.
30. Ford, *Writings,* IV, p. 362 n.
31. Force, op. cit., I, p. 1470.
32. H. P. Johnston, op. cit., Appendix, p. 114. Washington's exclamation is, of course, only a tradition, but it is a contemporary one. See Moore, op. cit., I, p. 297. Extract from a letter from New York, Sept 1, published in the *Freeman's Journal,* Sept. 28, 1776. See Thomas W. Field, *The Battle of Long Island,* pp. 489, 52. This exclamation is inscribed on the monument in Prospect Park, Brooklyn, erected "In Honor of Maryland's Four Hundred, Who, on this Battlefield, August 27th, 1776, saved the American Army." Rev. Ezra Stiles included it in his collection.

CHAPTER XXXI

1. Ford, *Writings,* IV, p. 362.
This account of the battle is taken mainly from the following works in addition to the general and familiar histories:
Washington's letters in Ford's *Writings.*
Force's *American Archives,* 5th Series, Vol. II.
Alexander Graydon's *Memoirs of a Life.*
Howe's report of the battle, sent to Lord Germaine and included in Thomas W. Field's *The Battle of Long Island* (Memoirs of L. I. Hist. Soc.), Vol. II, p. 378.
Stedman's *The American War.* (Stedman was an officer with Howe.)
Field's work is a large volume filled with documents.
An even more accurate study of the battle is contained in Henry P. Johnston's *The Campaign of 1776* (Memoirs of L. I. Hist. Soc.), Vol. III, with war documents.
Fortescue's *History of the British Army,* III, p. 183.
G. W. Greene's *Life of Maj.-Gen. Nathanael Greene,* and his *Historical View of the American Revolution.*
F. V. Greene's *General Greene,* and his *The Revolutionary War.*
Gen. B. F. Johnson's *General Washington.*
Gen. H. B. Carrington's *Battles of the American Revolution,* and *Washington the Soldier.*
A study of the battle by Captain Elbridge Colby, aided by a manuscript account by Lt. Col. Oliver F. Spaulding, published in Moss's *Manual of Military Training,* II, Chapter XXI.
Charles Francis Adams' *Studies Military and Diplomatic,* pp. 22 to 59, a most scathing criticism of Washington's management of the battle, and his "Plea for Military History," in Report of the American Historical Association, 1900, I, p. 195.
2. T. W. Fields, *The Battle of Long Island,* p. 379.
3. See Volume I of this work, p. 394.
4. W. A. Duer, *Life of Lord Stirling,* p. 162 n.

5. T. W. Fields, op. cit., p. 380.

6. T. W. Fields, op. cit., p. 202.

7. T. W. Fields, op. cit., pp. 502-3.

8. T. W. Fields, op. cit., p. 506.

9. T. W. Fields, op. cit., p. 518.

10. C. F. Adams, *Studies Military and Diplomatic*, p. 34.

11. Force's *American Archives*, 5th series, I, p. 1258. T. W. Fields, op. cit., p. 415. H. P. Johnston, *The Campaign of 1776*, p. 176. Loring included as the third general, General "Udell," referring to "Woodhull," also two lieutenants who were not in the army.

12. Howe's report in Force, op. cit., I, p. 1256. T. W. Fields, op. cit., p. 382.

13. Ford, *Writings*, IV, p. 376 (to the President of Congress, Aug. 31, 1776—"we suppose it from seven hundred to a thousand killed and taken"); p. 388 (to Governor Trumbull, Sept. 6, 1776—"we lost, in killed, wounded, and prisoners, from seven hundred to one thousand men"); p. 389 n. (to the Massachusetts Assembly, Sept. 19, 1776—"we lost about eight hundred men, more than three-fourths of which were taken prisoners"); p. 426 (to John Augustine Washington, Sept. 22, 1776—"we lost about eight hundred men, more than three-fourths of which were taken prisoners").

14. H. P. Johnston, op. cit., p. 202. He gives a very full account of the controversy over Washington's accuracy, with the figures given by the various historians, American and British.

15. H. P. Johnston, op. cit., p. 192.

16. C. F. Adams, "A Plea for Military History" (Report of Am. Hist. Assn., 1900), I, p. 206.

17. C. F. Adams, *Studies Military and Diplomatic*, pp. 21-113, wherein he not only criticizes Washington severely, but denounces the falsity of all American history up to that time.

18. Capt. Elbridge Colby, Moss' *Manual of Military Training*, II, Ch. XXI, pp. 3, 4.

19. Ford, *Writings*, IV, p. 217 n.

20. Ford, *Writings*, IV, p. 217 n.

21. Ford, *Writings*, IV, p. 238.

22. Alex. Graydon, *Memoirs of a Life*, p. 136.

23. Ford, *Writings*, IV, p. 359.

24. Capt. E. Colby, op. cit., p. 6.

25. C. F. Adams, *Studies Military and Diplomatic*, p. 47.

CHAPTER XXXII

1. Knight's *Pictorial History of England*, I, p. 271.

2. U. S. Grant, *Personal Memoirs*, II, Ch. 42.

3. Alexander Graydon, *Memoirs of a Life*, p. 145.

4. Ford, *Writings*, IV, p. 372.

5. Sparks, *Writings*, IV, p. 513.

6. Ford, *Writings*, IV, p. 371.

7. Ford, *Writings*, IV, p. 374 n.

8. H. P. Johnston, *The Campaign of 1776*, p. 218.

9. H. P. Johnston, op. cit., p. 219.

10. H. P. Johnston, op. cit., Part II, p. 30.

11. Graydon, op. cit., p. 147-8.

12. T. W. Field, *Battle of Long Island*, pp. 281, 282, 284, 287. Col. Hand's narrative was first published in W. B. Reed's *Life of Reed*, I, p. 227.

13. T. W. Field, op. cit., p. 276.

14. T. W. Field, op. cit., p. 500.

15. Graydon, op. cit., p. 148: "Taking the helm myself, I so luckily directed the prow, no object being discernible in the fog, that we touched near the centre of the city . . . in less than an hour after, the fog having dispersed, the enemy was visible on the shore we had left. . . . I had not slept for two nights."

16. Wm. Gordon, D.D., *The History of the . . . Independence*, II, p. 103.

17. H. P. Johnston, op. cit., pp. 223-4 n.

18. H. P. Johnston, op. cit., Part II, p. 115.

19. Ford, *Writings*, IV, pp. 373-6, August 31, 1776.

20. Ford, *Writings*, IV, p. 373 n., Aug. 30, 1776.

21. Ford, *Writings*, IV, p. 376 n.

22. Ford, *Writings*, IV, p. 378.

23. Ford, *Writings*, IV, p. 382 n.

24. Ford, *Writings*, p. 383 n.

CHAPTER XXXIII

1. Ford, *Writings*, IV, p. 387.

2. Alex Graydon, *Memoirs of a Life*, pp. 152, 153.

3. Ford, *Writings*, IV, p. 383.

4. Ford, *Writings*, IV, p. 397.

5. Ford, *Writings*, IV, p. 399.

6. Gen. H. G. Carrington, *Washington the Soldier*, p. 116.

7. Wm. Gordon, D.D., *History of the . . . Independence*, II, pp. 113-115. Dr. Gordon, for example, quotes on p. 109 the exact words of Washington without giving credit to their source, and has been accused of stealing the major part of his history from Dodsley's *Annual Register*. It is known, however, that he took some trouble to gain information at first hand, and corresponded with Washington to that end.

8. Ford, *Writings*, IV, p. 427.

9. Ford, *Writings*, IV, p. 405.

10. Sir George O. T. Trevelyan, *The American Revolution*, II, p. 261. He gives an excellent account of the conference, which is also described in the formal report to Congress, Force, *American Archives*, 5th Series, II, p. 1342, in Adams' letters and Howe's secretary's account.

11. Ford, *Writings*, IV, p. 389.

12. Ford, *Writings*, IV, p. 391.

13. *Lee Papers*, I, p. 229. John Jay's plan is given in W. B. Reed's *Life of Reed*, I, p. 235 n.

14. The fatal influence of the determination to save Richmond from capture is well shown in the papers of Col. Charles Marshall as recently edited by Major General Sir Frederick Maurice under the title *An Aide-de-Camp of Lee*, particularly p. 182 ff. A singularly lucid account of the internal dissensions of the Confederacy, resistances of its states to centralization and their withholding of troops from the main army is given in Nathaniel W. Stephenson's *The Day of the Confederacy* (Chronicles of America, Yale University Press, V.), p. 30.

15. Ford, *Writings*, IV, pp. 391, 396.

16. Carrington, op. cit., p. 115.

17. Force, *American Archives*, 5th Series, II, p. 182. See also Sparks, *Writings*, IV, p. 85.

18. Force, op. cit., pp. 239, 240.

19. Force, op. cit., pp. 662, 665.

20. Force, op. cit., pp. 240, 241.

21. Ford, *Writings*, IV, p. 398 n.

22. Ford, *Writings*, IV, p. 398 n.

23. Force, op. cit., p. 442. Colonel Joshua Babcock to Gov. Cooke, Sept. 21, 1776.

24. H. P. Johnston, *Campaign of 1776*, pp. 227-8.

25. W. H. Shelton, *The Jumel Mansion*, p. 27. In this work by the curator of the historic museum now restored and kept in perfect beauty by the Daughters of the Revolution, there is a very full and well-documented account of the Morrises, of Washington's timid courtship of Mary Philippse, of his stay in the house as a general, and of the great fire in New York.

26. Ford, *Writings*, IV, p. 406. Sept. 16, 1776. He wrote almost exactly the same words to Governor Cooke the next day, Ford, IV, p. 410. Ford omits the duplicate account. The complete letter is in Force, p. 367.

27. Document No. 27 in H. P. Johnston, op. cit., Part II, p. 8.

28. H. P. Johnston, op. cit., p. 238; M. L. Davis, *Memoirs of Aaron Burr*, I, p. 100.

29. Colonel David Humphrey, Document 31, H. P. Johnston, op. cit., Part II, p. 90.

30. H. P. Johnston, op. cit., Part II, p. 93.

31. Alex. Graydon, op. cit., p. 153. General Heath says in his *Memoirs* under date of Sept. 15, "and here it was, as fame hath said, that General Washington threw his hat on the ground, and exclaimed: 'Are these the men with which I am to defend America?'" Since Washington so often ended his written sentences with the preposition, it is safe to say that he did not speak a "with which."

32. Gordon, op. cit., II, p. 111.

33. Force, op. cit., II, p. 1013. So Tilghman says: "He laid his Cane over many of the officers who shewed their men the example of running" (H. P. Johnston, op. cit., Part II, p. 86).

34. Force, op. cit., II, p. 370.

35. Gordon, op. cit., p. 111.

36. H. P. Johnston, op. cit., Part II, p. 90.

37. Reed, op. cit., p. 237. H. P. Johnston, *The Battle of Harlem Heights*, p. 135, gives a more exact version.

CHAPTER XXXIV

1. H. P. Johnston, *The Campaign of 1776*, p. 244 n. Ford, *Writings*, IV, p. 428.

2. H. P. Johnston, *The Battle of Harlem Heights*, pp. 29-30. This monograph corrects many old errors as to positions and other details, covers every phase of the situation and includes all the documents. Reed's letters are also found in W. B. Reed's *Life of Reed*, I, pp. 237-8. The same author's earlier *Campaign of 1776* is also a valuable work. In spite of the painstaking work of Johnston, the accuracy of his geography of the battle was attacked by Dr. Thomas Addis Emmett, who maintained, in *The Magazine of History*, Sept., 1906, and in other controversies, that his boyhood recollections, coupled with an old map published in Lamb's *History of New York*, II, p. 120, and other arguments proved that the buckwheat field was not near the present grounds of Columbia University but in the Harlem Flats to the direct east, and not to the south, of the American front line position on Harlem Heights.

3. Col. David Griffiths, Johnston, *Battle of Harlem Heights*, p. 172.

4. Johnston, op. cit., pp. 135, 155. Captain Brown of the Rangers, at whose side Knowlton fell, says, "the Ball entered the small of his Back.— I took hold of him, asked him if he was badly wounded? he told me he was; but, says he, I do not value my Life if we do but get the Day. . . . He desired me by all Means to keep up this Flank. He seemed as unconcern'd and calm as tho' nothing had happened to him."

5. Johnston, op. cit., p. 137.

6. Johnston, op. cit., p. 154.

7. Johnston, op. cit., pp. 87-8.

8. Johnston, op. cit., pp. 225, 200.

9. Johnston, op. cit., p. 162. Ford, *Writings*, IV, p. 415 n.

10. Ford, *Writings*, IV, p. 417.

11. Ford, *Writings*, IV, p. 422.

12. Ford, *Writings*, IV, p. 423 n.

13. Ford, *Writings*, IV, p. 425.

14. Force, *American Archives*, 5th series, II, p. 589.

15. These court-martial proceedings are found in Force, op. cit., pp. 467-8, 499, 500, 501, 551, 568, 590, 610, 613.

16. Washington wrote to Congress about this "exceedingly extraordinary" verdict, and gave it as an instance of the difficulty of enforcing discipline and the low quality of the "general run of officers." Ford, IV, p. 449.

17. H. P. Johnston, op. cit., p. 138.

18. Force, op. cit., p. 500.

19. Ford, *Writings*, IV, p. 448.

20. *Lee Papers*, II, pp. 261, 263.

21. Ford, *Writings*, IV, pp. 438-451. Sept. 24, 1776. See also pp. 466-470, Oct. 4, 1776, and many other letters of the same nature.

22. Ford, *Writings*, IV, p. 429, to John Augustine Washington, Sept. 22, 1776.

23. Ford, *Writings*, IV, p. 458, to Lund Washington, Sept. 30, 1776.

24. An excellent account of the New York fire is in W. H. Shelton's

The Jumel Mansion, Chapters IV and V, where the possibility that Nathan Hale went to New York for the purpose of burning it and was caught in the act is discussed. Trevelyan, *American Revolution,* II, p. 310 n., quotes an exact compilation of the houses burned, making the exact total 493 instead of the thousand or more often mentioned.

25. Shelton, op. cit., p. 55.

26. Shelton, op. cit., p. 51.

27. H. P. Johnston, op. cit., p. 30, says 3rd Avenue and 65th Street, but his later investigations while preparing a privately printed biography of Nathan Hale led him to fix on the spot mentioned in the text.

28. *The Battle of Brooklyn,* A Farce in Two Acts. Printed for J. Rivington in the Year of the Rebellion, 1776. New York.

29. Moses Coit Tyler, *The Literary History of the American Revolution,* II, p. 208.

30. H. P. Johnston, op. cit., p. 32.

31. E. E. Curtis, *The Organization of the British Army in the American Revolution,* p. 7. See also H. P. Johnston, op. cit., p. 221, a letter from Howe's assistant secretary.

32. Force, *American Archives,* 5th series, III, pp. 499, 663, 702.

33. *Lee Papers,* II, pp. 15, 208.

34. G. H. Moore, *The Treason of Charles Lee* (Lee Papers, IV), p. 369.

35. Moore, op. cit., p. 371.

36. Gordon, *History of the . . . Independence,* II, p. 117.

37. Sir Henry Bunbury, *Memoirs of Charles Lee* (Lee Papers), IV, p. 273. See also II, p. 435.

38. Johnston, op. cit., p. 14.

CHAPTER XXXV

1. Ford, *Writings,* II, p. 101. This letter to Sally Fairfax from the Forbes Expedition, Sept. 25th, is discussed in Vol. I of this work, p. 413.

2. Force, *American Archives,* 5th series, II, p. 832, Oct. 1, 1776.

3. Force, op. cit., II, p. 973, Ford, IV, p. 494 n.

4. Force, op. cit., II, p. 1079. Oct. 16th, 1776.

5. Force, op. cit., II, p. 1077. Gen. Greene to Gov. Cooke, Oct. 15, 1776.

6. Force, op. cit., II, p. 1117.

7. Wm. Abbatt, "The Battle of Pell's Point or Pelham" (Proc. N. Y. State Hist. Assn., 1910), IX, p. 267. In Force, op. cit., III, p. 471, is an account of the battle of Pell's Point setting the British loss at "not less than 500." See also J. H. Brandow's *Washington's Retreat Through Westchester County* in the same volume, p. 113, and Stephen Jenkins, *The Story of the Bronx,* p. 143.

8. Ford, *Writings,* IV, p. 501 n.

9. Force, op. cit., pp. 1138, 1137, 1136.

10. Force, op. cit., p. 1117.

11. Randall Comfort, *History of Bronx Borough,* p. 42.

12. Randall Comfort, op. cit., p. 42.

13. J. W. Fortescue, *History of the British Army,* III, p. 191.

14. Force, op. cit., III, p. 1283.

15. Force, op. cit., III, pp. 653, 473.

16. Force, op. cit., II, p. 1282.

17. F. V. Greene, *The Revolutionary War*, p. 53. Fortescue, op. cit., gives the British loss as 214 killed and wounded, 99 Hessians killed and wounded.

18. Fortescue, op. cit., p. 192, referring to the investigation of Howe later by the House of Commons.

19. Heath's *Memoirs*, p. 77, cited by W. B. Reed, *Life of Reed*, I, p. 246.

20. Heath's *Memoirs* for Nov. 1, cited by Force, op. cit., III, p. 485.

21. Force, op. cit., III, p. 487.

22. Force, op. cit., III, p. 486.

23. Force, op. cit., III, p. 494.

24. *The Narrative of Lt. Gen. Sir Wm. Howe* (London, 1780), p. 6, cited by Fisher, *The Struggle for American Independence*, I, p. 527. See also Trevelyan, *American Revolution*, III, p. 84.

25. See Fisher, op. cit., pp. 528 n., 145.

26. Fox, *Correspondence*, I, pp. 169-171.

27. See Fortescue, op. cit., III, p. 198.

28. W. E. H. Lecky, *American Revolution*, pp. 334-6.

29. Edward Channing, *History of the United States*, III, p. 232.

30. Ford, *Writings*, V, p. 1. The Council of War is given in Force, op. cit., III, p. 543.

31. Ford, *Writings*, V, p. 11 n.

CHAPTER XXXVI

1. Alex. Graydon, *Memoirs of a Life*, p. 154.

2. H. P. Johnston, *The Campaign of 1776*, Part II, p. 100.

3. Graydon, op. cit., p. 178.

4. Graydon, op. cit., p. 201.

5. H. P. Johnston, op. cit., Part II, p. 101.

6. This letter is in the Rosenbach Company's collection. The date is Dec. 18, 1777.

7. This letter is also in the Rosenbach collection. The date is Nov. 1, 1776.

8. *Lee Papers*, II, p. 288.

9. Chas. J. Stillé, *Comte de Broglie, the Proposed Stadtholder of America*. Penn. Mag. of History, Jan., 1888. See also Doniol's *La Participation*, etc.

10. Ford, *Writings*, V, p. 39. To John Augustine Washington. Nov. 19, 1776.

11. Ford, *Writings*, V, p. 43.

12. Ford, *Writings*, V, p. 45.

13. *Lee Papers*, II, pp. 291, 303.

14. *Lee Papers*, II, p. 293. W. B. Reed, *Life of Reed*, I, p. 255.

15. *Lee Papers*, II, p. 305. Reed, op. cit., I, p. 257.

16. Reed, op. cit., p. 258.

17. Reed, op. cit., p. 260. Ford, *Writings*, V, p. 432.

18. George Bancroft, *The American Revolution*, I, pp. 21, 23.

19. Ford, *Writings*, V, pp. 50, 54, 54 n., 55, 56.

20. Ford, *Writings*, V. p. 52, Nov. 24, 1776.

21. Stryker, *The Battles of Trenton and Princeton*, p. 326.

22. Ford, *Writings*, V, pp. 57 n., 59, 58.

23. Alex. Graydon, op. cit., p. 208.

24. Ford, *Writings*, V, pp. 60, 60 n., 61 n.

25. Ford, *Writings*, V, p. 61.

26. *Sir W. Howe's Observations*, p. 66, cited by Reed, I, op. cit., p. 269.

27. E. E. Curtis, *The Organization of the British Army*, p. 102.

28. Ford, *Writings*, V, p. 62.

29. Ford, *Writings*, V, p. 62 n.

30. *Lee Papers*, II, p. 322.

31. *Lee Papers*, II, p. 327.

32. *Lee Papers*, II, p. 338.

33. Ford, *Writings*, V, p. 72.

34. Fortescue, *History of the British Army*, III, p. 196.

35. Ford, *Writings*, p. 77.

36. Force, *American Archives*, 5th series, III, p. 1606.

37. Force, op. cit., p. 1376.

38. J. Galloway, *Letters to a Nobleman on the Conduct of the War* (2nd Ed.), p. 43. The affidavits were published in the Pennsylvania Evening Post, April 24th, 29th, May 1st, 3rd, and 10th, 1777.

39. Force, op. cit., p. 1377.

40. Thomas Paine, *The American Crisis*, No. I, 1925, pp. 263, 278.

41. F. B. Dexter, *The Literary Diary of Ezra Stiles*, II, p. 111.

CHAPTER XXXVII

1. Wm. Gordon, *History of the . . . Independence*, II, p. 127.

2. Van Tyne, *The American Revolution*, p. 134.

3. Charles J. Stillé, *Comte de Broglie, the Proposed Stadtholder of America*. (Penn. Mag. of Hist., Jan., 1888), p. 12. See also Charlemagne Tower, *The Marquis de La Fayette*, I, 23 ff. Friedrich Kapp, *Leben des Amerikanischen Generals Johann Kalb*, gives Broglie's letter outlining his plan and demands, p. 88.

4. Ford, *Writings*, V, p. 77.

5. Ford, *Writings*, V, p. 103.

6. Ford, *Writings*, V, p. 104 n., to the Pennsylvania Council of Safety, Dec. 22, 1776.

7. John C. Fitzpatrick, *The Spirit of the Revolution*, p. 125.

8. This letter is in the Huntington Library; the name of the addressee is missing. Appended to it is the anecdote quoted.

9. This letter, reproduced by permission, is in the Rosenbach Collection.

10. *Lee Papers*, II, p. 348. Ford, *Writings*, V, p. 97 n. Stryker, op. cit., p. 57.

11. Ford, *Writings*, V, p. 100.

12. Ford, *Writings*, V, p. 109 n.

13. Stedman, *The American War*, I, p. 227.
14. George Bancroft, *Joseph Reed, a Historical Essay. Nuts for Historians to Crack.* W. B. Stryker, *The Reed Controversy*, and *The Battles of Trenton and Princeton*, pp. 75-78.
15. Ford, *Writings*, V, p. 98.
16. John Adams, *Familiar Letters*, p. 232.
17. Cited by Stryker, op. cit., p. 66.
18. Ford, *Writings*, V, p. 111. Dec. 18, 1776.
19. These are General Stryker's figures, op. cit., p. 85. They confirm Lord Stirling's estimate, and contradict Force's Archives and Ford's note (V, p. 130), largely because they added Lee's 2000 men, who were already included in the main muster.
20. Ford, *Writings*, V, p. 92.
21. Ford, *Writings*, V, p. 95.
22. Ford, *Writings*, V, p. 114.
23. Ford, *Writings*, V, p. 117.

CHAPTER XXXVIII

1. W. S. Stryker, *The Battles of Trenton and Princeton*, p. 311.
2. Ford, *Writings*, V, p. 152.
3. See Ford, *Writings*, V, p. 105.
4. Ford, *Writings*, V, p. 93.
5. Stryker, op. cit., p. 88.
6. Stryker, op. cit., p. 358, document No. 35.
7. Ford, *Writings*, V, p. 100 n.
8. Ford, *Writings*, VIII, p. 394.
9. Joseph Galloway, *Letters to a Nobleman*, pp. 49-52.
10. Order of December 14, 1776. Cited by Stryker, op. cit., p. 48 n.
11. Ford, *Writings*, V, p. 100 n.
12. Galloway, op. cit., p. 61.
13. Abbé Raynal, *History of the Revolution*, cited by Stryker, op. cit., p. 37.
14. Capt. W. M. James, *The British Navy in Adversity*, p. 58.
15. James, op. cit., p. 51.
16. Stryker, op. cit., p. 99.
17. Stryker, op. cit., p. 41 n.
18. Stryker, op. cit., pp. 401-423.
19. Cited by Stryker, op. cit., p. 90.
20. Julius F. Sachse, *An Old Broadside* (Proc. Am. Philosophical Society, xxxvii, no. 15), pp. 47-48.
21. J. T. Goolrick, *Hugh Mercer*, p. 49: "Historians with one accord give credit and glory to Mercer. Major Armstrong . . . who was present at the council of officers . . . is authority for the statement that Mercer suggested the expedition." Greene's letter is in Force, *American Archives*, 5th series, III, p. 1342.
22. Stryker, op. cit., p. 65 n.
23. W. B. Reed, *Life and Correspondence of Joseph Reed*, I, p. 272.
24. Ford, *Writings*, V, p. 126.

25. Ford, *Writings*, V, p. 130.
26. *St. Clair Papers*, I, p. 30.
27. Quoted by Stryker, op. cit., p. 132.
28. The figures of strength were carefully compiled by Stryker.
29. *St. Clair Papers*, I, p. 30.
30. David Ackerson, quoted by Lodge, *Life of Washington*, II, p. 387.
31. Report of Hessian War Commission to the Prince. Stryker, op. cit., p. 420.
32. Letter of Captain William Hull, Document 51 in Stryker, op. cit., p. 375.
33. Stryker, op. cit., p. 133.
34. Document 46, Stryker, op. cit., p. 371.
35. Stryker, op. cit., p. 137, says that Washington "for once indulged in a little pleasantry at the expense of Colonel Knox, which greatly amused that officer, and put the rest of the officers in the best of humor when the story was told them." But he does not allay the curiosity he aroused. Owen Wister in his *Seven Ages of Washington* devotes a page or two of high praise for the vigor of Washington's expression but only increases the torment. This is another instance of the sort alluded to in the chapter on the Diaries. Washington is upheld as our purest ideal, but it would be a penal offence to quote everything he said.
36. Stryker, op. cit., p. 137, and note.
37. The order is given in full in Stryker, op. cit., p. 113.

CHAPTER XXXIX

1. Stryker, *The Battles of Trenton and Princeton*, p. 428. Letter to Colonel Cadwalader, Dec. 27, 1776.
2. Ford, *Writings*, V, p. 132.
3. Stryker, op. cit., p. 141.
4. Diary of an Officer on Washington's Staff, Document 37, Stryker, op. cit., p. 362. He tells also the anecdote of the woodchopper.
5. Memorandum by General Robert Anderson, Stryker, op. cit., p. 373. See also Reed's *Life and Correspondence of Joseph Reed*, I, p. 277, concerning the good effect of this patrol attack in lulling the Hessians.
6. Stryker, op. cit., p. 363. Stryker says, p. 150, that Greene began the fighting the first but refers to the attack on the outpost as does Tench Tilghman, p. 366.
7. Stryker, op. cit., p. 144.
8. Stryker, op. cit., p. 150.
9. Tench Tilghman's letter to his father, Document 41, Stryker, op. cit., p. 366.
10. Joseph Galloway, *Letters to a Nobleman*, p. 54.
11. This is Stryker's careful estimate. Washington wrote to Congress: "The number that submitted was twenty-three officers and eight hundred eighty-six men."
12. Ford, *Writings*, V, p. 132.

APPENDIX II

THE POSEYS

Washington's relations with old Captain John Posey and his family are so picturesque, stirred him to such agitation, and subjected him to such scandal that they deserve an interlude to themselves.

Though Posey served under him as a captain in the Forbes campaign of 1758,[1] Washington long referred to him as "Mr. Possey."

He owned a plantation lying below the mouth of Dogue Run on the Potomac, and lived just below Mount Vernon. In 1753 a profitable ferry from his farm to a plantation in Maryland had been authorized. Washington often crossed it and paid toll. Posey's plantation had also a good fishing landing for seine hauling, and the necessary buildings for curing fish.[2]

At all this adjoining land and water Washington gazed with such longing eyes as King Ahab fastened on Naboth's Vineyard. But he could not stoop to acquire it by Ahabian methods, and Martha was not in the least like Queen Jezebel. What Posey's wife was like seems not to have been recorded beyond the fact that she had a hot temper, and was the mother of Thomas Posey (as well as of Hanson and Milly); but a strange story still goes about concerning her. She was born Lucy Frances Thornton, daughter of George Thornton of Orange County, Virginia.[3]

Captain Posey makes his first appearance in Washington's Diary on January 1st, 1760, in this company:

"Tueday, 1. Visited my Plantations and receivd an Instance of Mr. French's great love of Money in disappointing me of some Pork, because the price had risen to 22/6 after he had engaged to let me have it at 20/.

"Calld at Mr. Possey's in my way home and desird him to engage me 100 Bar'ls of Corn upon the best terms he could in Maryland.

"And found Mrs. Washington upon my arrival broke out with the Meazles."[4]

In February we learn that Posey secured the corn from "Mr Hunter the Priest," a Catholic living in Maryland—a Catholic might not live in Virginia. In the same month on a Sunday, "Captn. Possey, and Mrs. Possey dind here, He obliqu'ly hinted a design of selling his 145 acres of Wood Land on Muddy hole." In 1761 Washington's indentured carpenters built for Posey a barn at a cost of £97.[5] In March Washington used Posey to

[1] R. A. Brock, *Dinwiddie Papers* (Va. Historical Society Collection), I, p. xix.

[2] J. M. Toner, *Diary of Col. George Washington*, 1774 (Report of Am. Hist. Assn.), 1892, p. 122.

[3] S. M. Hamilton, *Letters to Washington*, III, p. 341 n.

[4] Fitzpatrick, *Diaries*, I, p. 107.

[5] Fitzpatrick, *Diaries*, I, p. 178 n.

buy 210 acres of land from two orphan children. He and Posey were fellow vestrymen.

In 1763 Posey, already in debt to others, turned to Washington for money, and began to appear in that formidable Ledger A.

Having given a mortgage for £700 and received only £254. 17, Posey was soon in the bog again, and reappears in Ledger A:

"1765. Oct 24 To Cash lent him upon a Security of
his Land & Slaves £750."

Daniel Webster had a plan of paying off one creditor by borrowing from another. Posey improved upon it by getting his creditors to double their own loans. The next year saw him indebted further for interest:

"1766 To a Years Interest &ca &ca £37."

By the year 1769, he owed Washington £1,047 on this second loan. When Washington asked for his money, Posey reverted to form and requested a further loan of £500.

This naturally threw Washington into a state of unusual emotion and, instead of telling it verbally to Posey, he poured out his thought in one of the longest and most eloquent letters he ever wrote. His words are almost vocal still in their tangled syntax. They preach a gospel of good business wisdom, and include a startling confession of Washington's own financial embarrassment. A few phrases have been italicized as beacon lights:

"SIR, It is difficult for me to tell which was greatest; my surprise or concern at finding by your letter of the 20th that instead of being able with the money I agreed to lie somewhat longer out of to discharge your debts, that you wanted to borrow a further sum of £500 to answer this purpose. I was in hopes, and you gave me the strongest assurance to believe, that when I lent you (and very inconvenient it was for me to do it) the first sum of £700, you could therewith not only discharge all your creditors, but in two years time sink the principal, which was lent to effect that end.

"How it comes to pass then, that instead of being prepared in twice two years to discharge my claim, you should require £500 more to satisfy others, is, as I at first said, entirely beyond my comprehension, . . .

"Even the interest thereof is a pretty little income, and would be such a moth in your estate as would inevitably destroy it, be your notions of saving and industry extended to never so high a degree. . . .

"That *it is entirely out of my power, without selling part of my own estate,* to contribute further thereto, you may easily be convinced of when I tell you, and affirm it, that I find it next to impossible to extract any part of the money which is due to me; that *I have struggled to the utmost of my power for two years past unsuccessfully, to raise four or five hundred pounds to lend a very particular friend of mine,* who I know must sell part of his estate without it; and that *I have not yet discharged the sums you involved me in the payment of* before, having my bond out to Mr. Green's estate for the £260 you borrowed of him. *I cannot raise money to discharge it,* altho' I have used my true endeavors for that purpose. Add to these some engagements of my own which there is a necessity of complying with, or doing acts of injustice. . . .

"There is a large field before you, an opening prospect in the back country for adventurers, where numbers resort to, and where an enterprising man with very little money may lay the foundation of a noble estate in the new settlements upon Monongahela for himself and posterity. The surplus money which you might save after discharging your debts would possibly secure you as much land as in the course of twenty years would sell for five times your present estate. . . .

"I would only ask whether it would be better to labor under a load of debt where you are, . . . or to pluck up resolution at once and disengage yourself of those incumbrances and vexations . . ." [6]

This cascade of splendid advice seemed to give Posey not the least bit of help. Three days later he evidently tried again to borrow from Washington, offering now to pawn some of his purchased lands and such of his negroes as he had not already put up as collateral for his earlier debts to Washington and others.

This inspired another scorching letter:

"You are not only reduced to the last shifts yourself, but are determined to involve me in a great deal of perplexity and distress on your account also. Why else will you press so hard upon me to do more than I have already done, and consented to do, in waiting two years longer for my money, when it is not only inconvenient, but very disadvantageous also for me to do so, and when I have informed you as every body else I suppose may also do, that the security I have upon your lands and slaves is only answerable for the £750 lent and interest. . . .

"And while I am mentioning this matter, it is highly necessary to inquire what is become of Henley, Jacob, Winney, Sylvia, Lett, Sarah, Nan and Henrietta Farthing, Negroes contained in your bill of sale to me, but which I see nothing of in the estimate above mentioned.

"Thus much I have said on a supposition that I was acting as a money lender only, and was looking for clear and indisputable surety; but in truth the prospect of gain and advantage to myself was not the motive that led me to advance you this money. 'Twas done to serve your family, and if possible to save your estate from dispersion, while there remained a probability of doing it. . . . To stave off the dreadful hour of resigning part of your possessions into the hands of your creditors, engrosses too much of your thoughts."

After a further excoriation of the hapless wretch, whom one can almost see standing fat and shivering before his judge, Washington's kind heart relented a little:

"However, . . . I will become your security to Colo. Mason for three hundred pounds, on condition that you do at the same time add other things to my present security that are under no incumbrance to any person what so ever, and allow me the absolute right and privilege (as you yourself proposed) of disposing of them for ready money. . . . But I once more caution you against a measure of this kind, as it may be destructive of your estate. . . .

"P.S. I have this instant been informed that you have declared you paid

[6] Ford, *Writings*, II, pp. 213, 226.

me all you owed me except about £20. Does such disingenuity as this deserve any favour at my hands? I think any body might readily answer for you, no."

In spite of this final thrust, Washington continued friends with Posey. We have no record of his activities in 1767, but in 1768 he records eleven fox hunts on which Posey accompanied him. Even their dogs were on excellent terms, for in June, 1768, Washington gravely immortalizes the fact that "About this time Captn. Posey's Bitch Countess was discovered lind to Dabster, and was immediately shut up and none but Sterling sufferd to go to her."

The more one studies the Diaries the more one marvels at the events that Washington wanted to remember and those he was willing to forget.

Having no other way to make money, Posey decided to run for the House of Burgesses. As an old soldier he had a claim to military lands and he may have thought that he could pick up a fortune in Williamsburg. But though there were only three candidates for the two seats, he ran third.[7]

The next year saw Posey's complete ruin. As his security, Washington was involved in the legal proceedings against him, and he closed out Posey for the time being:

Washington bought up the claims of the other creditors, and acquired all of Posey's plantation except twelve acres, adding them to his Dogue Run plantation. Three years afterward he bought in the last of Posey's ground, took over the ferry rights and ran that business henceforth.[8]

Posey lost even his religious dignity, for in 1770 he was replaced as vestryman in Truro parish by Martin Cockburn, a Scotchman who married a Virginia girl and, finding that she would not leave home, settled down beside her.[9]

The degeneration of Captain Posey followed rapidly. One of his sons became a bartender in a tavern. The Captain's wife died and he cast about, as other Virginians had done before, and not only Virginians, to see if he could mend his purse by marriage. But the only "fortune" available was not enticing, as he describes her in a lively portrait which should be added for contrast to the well-filled gallery of Virginian dames. Evidently his first wife had been none too amiable:

"I could been able to Satisfied all my old Arrears, Some months AGoe, by marrying old widow woman in this County, She has Large soms cash by her, and Prittey good Est.—She is as thick, as she is high—And gits drunk at Least three or foure a weak—which is Disagreable to me—has Viliant Sperrit when Drunk—its been Great Dispute in my mind what to Doe,—I beleave I shu'd Run all Resk's—if my Last wife, had been Even temper'd woman, but her Sperrit, has Given me such Shock—that I am afraid to Run the Resk Again." [10]

A little later he was in jail, and in October, 1773, Washington wrote in his cashbook:

"By Charity—given Captn. Posey. £4."

[7] Fitzpatrick, *Diaries*, I, p. 301 n.
[8] J. M. Toner, op. cit., p. 123.
[9] Fitzpatrick, *Diaries*, I, p. 301 n.
[10] S. M. Hamilton, *Letters to Washington*, IV, p. 66.

This might be the last of Posey except for a tradition that will not down. Captain John had a son, Thomas, who is described as having been six feet, two inches high, with light brown hair and blue eyes, and so powerfully built that he killed several men with his own sword in battles.[11]

This striking resemblance to Washington and the closeness of the families are doubtless to blame for the persistent fable that he was the natural son of Washington, who would have been only eighteen at the time of the child's birth.

A discussion of such a story seems to be justified by the fact that it is whispered everywhere. The truth has this virtue, that, though it sometimes strips a man of fictitious glories, it also protects him from ugly libels.

John C. Fitzpatrick[12] has frankly discussed this fable along with a number of other scandals that hiss about Washington's fame the more vigorously the effort is made to canonize him. Like all other mouth-to-ear gossip it bolsters itself with verbal documents that do not exist. Thus, the writer of this book was told by an eastern librarian that a certain Chicago genealogist had found absolute proofs of Washington's relation to the boy. When the Chicago genealogist was consulted he said he had not an iota of evidence, and did not believe the story.

Mr. Fitzpatrick quotes the alleged evidences, including a statement that the reason the eighteen-year-old Washington went to the Barbados with his dying brother Lawrence was to escape the consequences of this "unwelcomed paternity." He disposes of an alleged miniature of the boy bearing an alleged likeness to Washington; and proves by photography of the manuscript that a letter addressed to Thomas Posey by Washington does not begin "My dear Son," as stated, but "My dear Sir." Furthermore, it ends with "Your most obdt. & humbl. Servt."

The Diaries offer further ammunition against the slander. If the boy was Washington's it is hardly probable that his mother would be welcomed in Martha's home and his sister almost adopted as a ward and the constant companion of Patsy Custis.

Thus in the Diaries, one notes that on Saturday, February 2nd, 1760, "Mrs. Possey and 2 of her children came and stayd the night here. . . . Sunday, 3d. Mrs. Possey went home and we to Church at Alexandria." On the following Sunday, "Captn. Possey, and Mrs. Possey dind here." March 25th, "Mrs. Possey and some young woman whose name was unknown to anybody in this family dind here." In April, 1768, again "Mrs. Posey dined here."

The daughter, Amelia or Milly, was frequently at Mount Vernon. In 1769 he "rid round to my Harvest field in the Neck with Mrs. Washington, Patcy, and Mill Posey." In April, 1770, "Patcy Custis and Milly Posey went to Colo. Mason's to the Dancing School." Ledger A shows that Washington paid the fee for both girls.

In July, 1772, he says: "Went up in the afternoon with Mrs. Washington, J. P. Custis, Miss Custis, and Milly Posey to a Ball in Alexandria."

[11] George Wilson, letter to the *William and Mary Quarterly*, VI, p. 65.

[12] John C. Fitzpatrick, "The George Washington Scandals," *Scribner's Magazine*, April, 1927, p. 393.

In 1774 Hanson Posey came to call on Jacky Custis.

Thomas Posey seems not to be mentioned in any of Captain John's letters nor is he alluded to in the Diaries, but it is known that Washington helped to pay for his education.[13] But then he was always contributing to the education of boys, his stepchildren, three nephews, Doctor Craik's son, and an unknown boy named John V. Weylie. Furthermore, he saw to the education of Posey's other boys.

Hence Mr. Fitzpatrick exclaims: "If every child whose education was assisted by Washington were to be stigmatized, in consequence, as his natural offspring, the distinction of being the Father of His Country might take on a new meaning."

Rejecting utterly the blight on his name and Washington's, it may be noted that Thomas Posey had a brilliant life and atoned for his father's shiftlessness. He was so good a colonel in the Revolution that Washington put him at the head of the troops nearest the enemy in the lines about Valley Forge, and in 1792, when war with France was brewing, recommended him to Gen. Knox as an adjutant-general with the rank of Colonel, saying:

"Colonel Posey, who wants to be employed, might, if ready at his pen, make a good one; for, in other respects, (and I do not know that he is deficient in this,) he is said to be an excellent officer." [14]

That does not sound like the language any man, particularly a Washington, would use concerning his own son to one of his oldest and closest friends.

Thomas Posey's tomb at Shawneetown, Illinois, carries this legend:

"In the American Republic he was Colonel in the Revolution of '76: Gen'l in the Legion of the U. S. Army; Lieut. Governor of Kentucky, Senator in Congress, and Governor of Indiana. He died as he lived, a pious Christian, on the 18th of March, 1818."

It is curious to note that his son, General Alexander Posey, "by a movement of his troops, ended the battle of Bad Axe and with it the Black Hawk War." His grandson, Gen. Carnot Posey, of Louisiana, was a brigadier general in Pickett's division at Gettysburg, and was killed soon after in Virginia. He left two sons, John and Carnot, who were murdered by negroes in Mississippi, and avenged by a mob that killed four of them.[15]

[13] Fitzpatrick, *Diaries*, II, p. 410 n.
[14] Ford, *Writings*, XII, p. 154.
[15] George Wilson, op. cit., VI, p. 66.

APPENDIX III

THE GREAT LAND COMPANIES

It is possible to mention only a few of the once eminent figures in the mad scramble for the new world of the then West.

Pownall's and Hazard's Scheme

Some Connecticut people had planned to establish colonies in western Pennsylvania, and for the Pennsylvanians Franklin wrote a plea, inviting them to move on further west, and recommending the Ohio Valley.

Governor Thomas Pownall of Massachusetts had been an advocate of western Expansion, too, and Pownall's Proposition for a great colony in the West dates from 1754, when he discussed it with Franklin at the Albany conference.

Franklin's plea to the Connecticut colonists fell into the hands of a Philadelphia merchant, Samuel Hazard, and inspired him to request a grant from the King and make himself a lord-proprietor. Business men had their dreams in those days.

Hazard's modest request was for a slice of the world beginning a hundred miles west of Pennsylvania, extending a hundred miles west of the Mississippi, and running along back of the mountains of Virginia and the Carolinas.

As early as 1755 he obtained from Connecticut a release of its claim on the region. He recruited several thousand followers. He explored the country and was about to sail for England to see the King when he died.

Thereupon the officers of his company allied themselves with the "Military Adventurers," the first company definitely to make application for the vast territory opened by the peace of 1763.

Lyman's Mississippi Adventurers

To the Americans of later generations the name of Major-General Phinehas Lyman means nothing. Yet at that time he had a resounding renown. He was a brave man, a Yale graduate and Commander-in-Chief of the Connecticut troops from 1755 on. While Washington was going along as an uncommissioned extra aide to Braddock, Lyman was marching to Albany with twelve hundred of his own men, within a hundred of Braddock's entire force. He joined William Johnson in the advance against the French under their commander-in-chief, Dieskau.

When Johnson was wounded, Lyman actually took command and, under the fiercest fire for four hours directed the army to a complete victory and the capture of the wounded Dieskau.

In 1762 when Washington was a farmer, Lyman was Commander-in-Chief of the American troops sent to join the British in the successful siege and capture of Havana.[1]

On his return he organized the "Military Adventurers," all of them officers of the late war. As their agent "he drew up a petition for the region bounded by the Ohio and Great Kanawha Rivers, the Allegheny Mountains, and the colony of Pennsylvania." He is said to have gone to England in 1763; he was certainly there in 1766, and his petition was sent to the Board of Trade in London in 1768, but not taken up until after Sir William Johnson had begun his tremendous scheme to buy from the Iroquois a vast part of their country.[2]

General Lyman went to England, where he spent eleven years in futile efforts.

At last, "strained in mind, and broken-hearted, he resolved never again to look his friends at home in the face," says his biographer. But in 1774 he received a grant of land on the Mississippi in the present state of Mississippi, as well as an annuity of £200 for his military services.

He sailed for home, and in 1776 took his family and a few friends with him to the Southwest.

They settled on the river and took no part in the Revolution—he was sixty years old at the outbreak of it, and was of Tory sympathy. His wife died there, and in 1781 the Spaniards invaded his realm. He moved near Natchez, where he died. Now his followers were driven out, and crossed the Indian-infested wilderness to Savannah, thirteen hundred miles in a hundred and forty-nine days. Two of Lyman's daughters perished on the way, and the journey has been likened to Whitman's march to Oregon.[3]

The conquest of the West is packed with such stories of foresight, brave ambition and hardships, and it is unjust to forget these heroes, doubly unjust to lump all their identities under one man who never even claimed their glory.

The Walpole Company and Vandalia

One of the largest corporations trying to corner western lands was known as the Walpole.

"Franklin was the really moving spirit in the enterprise," said Herbert B. Adams, "but he persuaded Thomas Walpole, a London banker of eminence, to serve as the figure-head." [4]

They worked together at first under the corporate name of "The Walpole Company," planning to buy 2½ million acres on the Ohio and establish a colony to be called "Vandalia."

The name "Vandalia," like the names of other speculative corporations, had been a matter of much thought. For a while a compliment to William Pitt (to whom the victory over the French was largely credited) was planned

---

[1] Rev. Wm. O. Stearns, *Proceedings*, New York State Hist. Assn., 1901, p. 58.

[2] Alvord, *The Mississippi Valley in British Politics*, II, p. 92.

[3] Rev. Wm. O. Stearns, op. cit., p. 61.

[4] Herbert B. Adams, *Maryland's Influence in Founding a National Commonwealth* (Maryland Historical Society, 1877).

and the ghastly name of "Pittsylvania" almost adopted. The Queen looked more valuable and "Charlotta" was considered.

Just then a popular book appeared, tracing the Queen's lineage clear back to the Vandals, and "Vandalia" seemed an inspiration.[5]

The Vandalia grant was hotly opposed by the Earl of Hillsborough, who succeeded Lord Shelburne as President of the Board of Trade in 1763, and as colonial Secretary of State in 1768. Hillsborough was the enemy of western expansion, and feared that it would result in the depopulation of Ireland, where he had large estates, and even of Great Britain.

This is in itself a comment on the fable of Washington's being the father of the West, for a British minister was already dreading the depopulation of the empire by the movement of his people into the West, at a time when Washington had not even established his claim to the soldiers' lands.

Hillsborough fought the Vandalia scheme with violence, but Franklin and his colleagues worsted him, the King was brought over and Hillsborough resigned. Still the grant was delayed. Year followed year and the "government of Vandalia" was not authorized.

The Virginia Grants

The colony of Virginia, which claimed nearly all the land in America not already settled, also made separate grants that conflicted with her own Ohio Company's claims. She deeded away about two million acres thus, including one parcel of a hundred thousand acres to John Robinson, Washington's partner in the Dismal Swamp business.

The French and Indian War had postponed the Ohio Company's plans naturally, since the only tenants of the land were the enemy.

When peace came, the Ohio Company had a petition before the King and the Board of Trade by March 2, 1763, and sped a representative across to London. This was Washington's close friend, Lieutenant Colonel George Mercer, who sailed July 8, 1763.

But all the other corporations had agents there, too, using their influence with warm friends, or warming up cold ones.

The Ohio Company had been a harsh disappointment to Washington, and he was sick with the deferment of possessing his share of those 200,000 acres promised him and his men so long ago for their military toil. He knew that most of his soldiers and brother officers were in no position to make use of their acres when (and if) they got them, and he planned to buy up all the claims he could. But first the British must renew their assent to the claims.

In the meanwhile, he was eager to gather in other square miles of that mysterious land inhabited only by Indians who had neither rights nor title deeds.

The Mississippi river had an attractive sound. He never learned to spell it, but he loved it.

The Mississippi Company

A "Mississippi Company" would have an even braver sound than the "Ohio Company," so nineteen Virginia gentlemen hastened to form one. Wash-

[5] Alvord, op. cit., II, pp. 119, 187.

ington's name was the last on the list simply because his name began with a "W." In spirit he was an Abou ben Adhem.

Among other charter members were his half-brother, John Augustine Washington, Richard Henry Lee, Thomas Ludwell Lee, William Lee, Henry and William Fitzhugh.

These distinguished gentlemen planned to enlarge their group to fifty, and ask the King for no less than two and a half million acres along the river. Each of the associates was to receive fifty thousand acres as soon as the crown granted the petition. While they were at it they begged the King to forego quitrents, fees and taxes for twelve years as a compensation for their "great expense, dangers, hardships and risques," in return for which they would try to plant two hundred families of the King's subjects on the land. Dr. Arthur Lee was selected as their agent.[6]

Kentucky was the land this company wanted to exploit, and Kentucky was the land that General Lyman's Military Adventurers wanted to exploit.

Thirty-one-year-young Washington glowed with the thought of adding these 50,000 acres to the 5,000 he would garner from the Ohio Company, and at least 45,000 more that he could doubtless buy up cheap from old soldiers in needy circumstances. These 100,000 acres added to what he had inherited, gained by surveying, purchase, trade, and marriage, would make him a landlord indeed. With loving interest he copied out the rules and regulations of the Mississippi Company, and his manuscript is in the Library of Congress still.

Washington paid in his initiation fee of £25. 13. 9., and an assessment in 1768 of £16. 18. 9.

But postponement sickened the company and it gradually died out as sick corporations do. The shareholders received not a square inch of land, and on January 1, 1772, Washington finally wrote it off his books as a loss of £27. 13. 5. It was not much to spend for a chance at fifty thousand acres of what is now Illinois and Kentucky.

Other Schemes

In the meanwhile New Yorkers were conspiring in the same direction, flattering the Prince of Wales by promising to call their new empire New Wales. An English soldier of fortune, Charles Lee, who would clash with Washington later, had another magnificent scheme.

British officers, among them Colonel Bouquet, had another plan.

A writer in Edinburgh proposed to form a province taking in everything from the Ohio to the Mississippi. He thought he could win the King by naming it after his wife and calling it hideously "Charlotina"! [7]

To sum up the claims and clarify a little the chaos, which is no more confusing to the reader than it must have been to the distracted British

[6] Alvord, op. cit., II, p. 93.

[7] F. L. Paxson, *History of the American Frontier*, p. 22, and G. E. Howard in *Preliminaries of the Revolution*, p. 229, spell it "Charlotiana."

ministry and the hopeful pioneers, the following principal schemes may be listed: [8]

The Ohio Company; petitions of 1748 and 1752.	Illinois Scheme, 1766.
Franklin's Plan, 1754-56.	Amherst's Detroit Plan, 1767.
Pownall's Proposition, 1754-1756.	Indiana Company, 1768.
Hazard's Scheme, 1755.	Vandalia, 1769-1776.
Mississippi Co., petitions of 1763 and 1768.	Transylvania, 1775.
	Georgiana.
New Wales Colony, 1763.	Lyman's Mississippi Colony.
Charlotina, 1763.	Illinois Purchases.
Phinehas Lyman's Plan, 1766.	Wabash Purchases.
	The Grand Ohio Company.

In view of this catalogue it is manifest that Washington was only one of a multitude. This is said in no derogation of his honorable ambitions, but to disprove the fantastic tendency to rob everybody else of honors and lay them all at his feet. Nobody would be more surprised than Washington to learn what posterity has done with him, for his own impression of himself must have been that he was so far from being a gigantic power that he could hardly attract any attention at all to his modest and ancient petitions.

Everybody in America was clutching at the new West, and the English little knew what magnificent longings they would turn into magnificent rebellion when they decided to grant none of the petitions, but make a ridiculous pretence of respecting the rights of the Indians, and an insane promise to keep the whites out.

Of all the competing companies, Washington and the other Virginians feared most the Walpole Vandalia Company, which Franklin wrought for. Its encroachments on their claims and grants were alarming.

In 1770 Washington, who saw his own soldiers' lands smothered under the Vandalian claims, wrote a protest to Governor Botetourt, the new royal representative, who had arrived in Virginia the year before.

He reviewed the history of the Ohio Company's grant to his soldiers as an "absolute compact," no less good for having lain "in a dormant state for some time." He asked for one change in the tract allotted, and ended:

"This favor, my Lord, would be conferring a singular obligation on men, most of whom, either in their persons or fortunes, have suffered in the cause of their country; few of them benefited by the service; and it cannot fail to receive the thanks of a grateful body of men, but of none more warmly than of your Lordship's most obedient and humble servant." [9]

The Grand Ohio Company

In a futile effort to satisfy the Virginians and everybody else, the Vandalia or Walpole Company was finally reorganized as the Grand Ohio Company. This huge corporation simply absorbed the Virginia Ohio Company, though

[8] The list is taken from Alvord's maps based on John Mitchell's map.

[9] Ford, *Writings*, II, p. 272.

it made provision for the 200,000 acres of land bounties promised by Dinwiddie to Washington and his men.

For securing this guarantee, Col. George Mercer claimed the credit. He wrote Washington that he had "agreed with, or I may rather say prevailed with, the great Land Company." [10]

Croghan wrote of the Grand Ohio Company that its grant would contain over thirty million acres—as he put it "thirty od millians of ac^{rs} and the offise will open att £10 Sterling per hundred and a half penny for a^r quit-rent which will make a handsome division to the 72." The seventy-two shareholders were mostly Englishmen except Croghan, Benjamin and William Franklin, the four Whartons and William Trent.

Croghan and Trent were accused by Baynton and Morgan, two of the former partners in the Indiana Company, of ditching their interests, and Morgan wrote Croghan that Trent was "not worth giving a Kick in the Breech to, or a Pull by the Nose." He challenged Trent to a duel.[11]

This was the same Trent whom Washington had accused of a cowardice in 1754; but he had been acquitted by a court.

Croghan's personal claim of 200,000 acres was gathered in by the Grand Ohio octopus, but Washington's personal claim, though protected in the grant, was still to be fought for.

[10] Ford, *Writings*, II, p. 340 n.
[11] Volwiler, *George Croghan and the Westward Movement*, p. 271.

APPENDIX IV

THE ORIGINS OF THE REVOLUTION

Just when and how and why the Revolution started are subjects upon which no two historians agree. The old school emphasized, as the revolutionists did, the nobler phases of the love of liberty and the hatred of oppression. The new school emphasizes the economic and social conditions that drove the Americans into a revolt, and the political developments in the whole empire that impelled the British to turn their kingdom into a vast commercial corporation while Parliament carried on a life and death struggle with a King and a Junta [1] determined to restore the long-lost absolutism of earlier monarchs.

The revolutionists themselves called the breach a "civil war" until the idea of independence was gradually and reluctantly accepted. Even Parson Weems called it a civil war more than once.[2] But some of the later historians, and many of the professional patriots of today, have found in the mere suggestion of a civil war something belittling to the glory of a war for independence. Yet Washington himself called it "civil discord." [3]

Washington and his fellows at first absolved George III of all blame, and said that they fought only his corrupt and misleading ministers. Gradually they came to abhor the monarch and to believe that he was really a despot, though they did not therefore absolve his subjects at home, who were fighting the same King with such vigor as to make them allies of the Americans, and to cripple the attack on the colonies. Such tolerance was hardly to be expected of them since Parliament upheld the war, and, as Lecky says, "All the measures of American coercion that preceded the Declaration of Independence were carried by enormous majorities in Parliament."

To the middle age of historians, as to the demagogues, George III was an archfiend of iniquity and George Washington an archangel of purity. Neither was either.

The Beards [4] say that the concept of the American Revolution as a quarrel caused by a stubborn King and obsequious ministers shrinks into "a trifling joke," a "myth that must be dismissed as puerile." The English Whig historians (who have the same desire to celebrate the Whigs of 1770 as the Americans to glorify their heroes), after having "raked over every word of the King's correspondence have found no passage showing that George III

[1] The people of that time usually called a *junta* a Junto.
[2] M. L. Weems, *Life*, p. 65.
[3] Ford, *Writings*, II, p. 444.
[4] Charles A. and Mary R. Beard, *The Rise of American Civilization*, I, pp. 201, 210.

used his authority to force the enactment of a single coercive law directed against the American Colonies." [5]

Most of the principles on which Parliament waged the war preceded the accession of George III. He was actually insane and in confinement at the time the Stamp Acts were passed. According to the pleasant medical systems of the day, his own butler was horsewhipping him daily to cure his mental illness and drive the devils out.

George III was famous for his chaste devotion to his queen, who bore him nine sons and six daughters. Gardiner [6] says that his "example of domestic propriety" strengthened his ministry, and that his home life was in fact so pure as to be "insufferably dull. . . . The sons of the household were driven by the sheer weariness of such an existence into the coarsest profligacy."

Morality was in fact actually fashionable in certain circles that aped royalty.

Unfortunately, it is all too often found that highly moral people, like George III, who have conquered their own fleshly temptations, if any, are equally determined to conquer other people's spiritual ambitions; and George III undeniably tried to be a godlike autocrat to his own people for their own good, while incidentally cherishing a pious hope that the erring Americans might be restored to the fold of the divinely anointed and appointed King.

For their hatred of the third George, as for so many other false beliefs, the later Americans are indebted to Parson Weems, of whom Sydney G. Fisher [7] says: "He is inimitable. He will live forever. He captured the American people. . . . He said exactly what they wanted to hear. He has been read a hundred times more than all the other historians and biographers of the Revolution put together."

Parson Weems explained the Revolution easily. It was because the King wanted money for his "hungry relations" and the ministers "stakes for their gaming tables, or diamond necklaces for their mistresses." [8]

The recent historians have gone to the sources, the original manuscripts and the actual utterances of the heroes, and have come back with explanations that are probably nearer the truth than could be realized either by the participants themselves, who were too near, or by the next generations, who were too reverent.

To turn history into a revivalist's sermon, as Bancroft [9] and others did, and insist that the Americans of 1776 were a holy people raised up and "chosen to keep guard over the liberties of mankind," and to find in every victory a clear manifestation of God's intervention and in every defeat a proof of his chastising love—is to imply that God did not know what He was about, blundered on all occasions, and came incessantly so close to losing

[5] C. A. and M. R. Beard, op. cit., p. 281.

[6] S. R. Gardiner, article on George III, *Encyclopædia Britannica*, 11th ed., XI, p. 742.

[7] S. G. Fisher, *The Legendary and Myth-making Process in Histories of the American Revolution*, p. 66.

[8] M. L. Weems, op. cit., p. 62.

[9] Bancroft, *History of the United States*, VII, p. 21.

the war to the British that if the wicked French had not come to the rescue, the devil would have carried off the palm.

The sense of sportsmanship, fair play and common honesty also turns the modern historian away from the old school of exalting forefathers by lying about their foes, of proving men demigods by concealing their intense humanity, and of juggling the figures in a manner that would send a poor bookkeeper to the penitentiary.

Some of the most scholarly of recent historians have had to show almost as much heroism as the forefathers revealed, for every effort to lay the plain facts before the public has been met by ferocious accusations of treason and even to the ludicrous charge that they were bought with British gold. It is a sad commentary if Americans have to be bribed by foreigners to tell the truth.

So profound a scholar as Professor C. H. McIlwain [10] suggests that the Revolution actually took place in England as early as 1649, when Parliament dethroned and decapitated King Charles I, and established the Commonwealth.

This Revolution was followed by the Revolution of 1688, which changed the constitution without asking the consent of the dominions belonging to the English Kingdom.

According to this refreshing and well-argued view, instead of the Americans rebelling against the British Constitution in 1775, it was the British who violated it in 1688, while the Americans adhered to it until the separation was brought about.

Something like this was, indeed, the thought of Otis, the Adamses, George Mason and other creators of the American Revolution. They maintained that the new Parliament, the throttling English merchant monopolists, and the autocratic King were overthrowing ancient and sacred constitutional privileges inalienable from the colonists both as human beings and as English subjects.

Yet the Colonists had also been incessantly grasping at more and more power, more and more freedom, violating laws they found inconvenient, overthrowing charters, and overpowering royal governors by withholding their salaries and perquisites. By the year 1765, they were managing their own lives fairly well, and resented the efforts of the new English ministries to restore old laws and restrictions as if they were inflicting new and unheard-of tyrannies.

That is why the Beards [11] say: "The American ruling classes . . . had already wrested the government from the royal authorities by 1765; their uprising was designed to preserve what they had, rather than to gain something new and untried."

The Americans were renewing in 1770 the wrath they had felt as Englishmen at the Puritan Revolution of 1640.

It was the Puritan Parliament that took over all the lands belonging to the King. It was Cromwell's Parliament that forbade foreign ships to trade with the colonies and passed the first of the Navigation Acts ordering only

[10] C. H. McIlwain, *The American Revolution.*
[11] Charles A. and Mary R. Beard, op. cit., p. 187.

English ships to be used for colonial cargoes—an act that was more honored in the breach than the observance.

It was Cromwell's Puritans who persecuted Washington's ancestor, Rev. Lawrence Washington, and drove his sons to America. Indeed, the Puritans drove to America the ancestors of nearly all the Virginians who took the lead in the Revolution.[12]

The Revolutionists themselves were not sure when the Revolution began, and were still more confused as to why. John Adams wrote in 1815:

" 'A history of the first war of the United States is a very different thing from a history of the American Revolution. . . . The Revolution was in the minds of the people, and in the union of the colonies, both of which were accomplished before hostilities commenced. This revolution and union were gradually forming from the years 1760 to 1776.' And to another correspondent he wrote: 'But what do we mean by the American Revolution? Do we mean the American war? The Revolution was effected before the war commenced. The Revolution was in the minds and hearts of the people.' " [13]

It is possible and not unreasonable to see some truth in all the different schools. The Revolutionists undoubtedly were fighting for their bread and butter, their incomes, and their hopes of prosperity. They inevitably "rationalized" their behavior by giving it noble explanations.

And after all there is as much dignity in fighting for wages or lands and

[12] John Esten Cooke, *Virginia*, p. 229, says:

"Washington was the great-grandson of a royalist who took refuge in Virginia during the Commonwealth. George Mason was the descendant of a colonel who fought for Charles II. Edmund Pendleton was of royalist origin, and lived and died the most uncompromising of Churchmen. Richard Henry Lee, who moved the Declaration, was of the family of Richard Lee, who had gone to invite Charles II to Virginia. Peyton, and Edmund Randolph, President of the First Congress, and Attorney-General, were of an old royalist family. Archibald Cary, who threatened to stab Patrick Henry if he was made dictator, was a relative of Lord Falkland, and heir apparent at his death to the barony of Hunsdon. Madison and Monroe were descended from royalist families,—the first from a refugee of 1653, the last from a captain in the army of Charles I. And Patrick Henry and Thomas Jefferson, afterwards the great leaders of democratic opinion, were of Church and King blood, since the father of Henry was a loyal officer who 'drank the King's health at the head of his regiment'; and the mothers of both were Church of England women, descended from royalist families.

"The point may seem unduly elaborated. But it is well to establish the disputed questions of history, and this one has been disputed. One of the highest authorities in American history has described the Cavalier element in Virginia as only 'perceptible.' It was really so strong as to control all things—the forms of society, of religion, and the direction of public affairs."

[13] Adams, *Works*, X, p. 180.

against unjust taxes as in anything else, since wages, lands, and taxes are vital factors in human dignity. "Their altars and their fires" is only a pretty phrase for men's right to live their lives and to keep themselves warm.

The American colonies were like Spartan children exposed on a wintry hillside. They survived and grew. They found themselves in a fruitful paradise. As manhood came, awe and subordination fell from them. They would go their own ways. The old-fashioned parent tried to keep them children and lost the battle.

To the economic and social explanations should be added the biological, the ecological.

Thomas Paine said it all when he wrote:

"To know whether it be the interest of their continent to be Independent, we need only ask this easy, simple question: "Is it the interest of a man to be a boy all his life?" [14]

All other explanations and accusations are in a sense mere details in the presence of the great fact that the colonies grew up. They had a right to their independence, and they had a right, a duty, to destroy all obstacles to it. Money, as usual, played its part. Overgrown children inevitably hate to turn their earnings over to their parents. Concerning his purse, everybody is always tetchy. But that also is right—or, at least, it is natural.

Trouble with England was no new thing. No system of managing the colonists had ever succeeded. The colonies had been planted as "commercial speculation started in the interests of private traders," [15] yet the English idea that the colonies existed for the good of the mother country and owed her support and veneration provoked rude laughter among the colonists. They claimed all the rights of Englishmen under the vague Constitution, and denied all the obligations.

They paid His Majesty a little lip-reverence, but they had no reverence for the merchants who now ruled England, except as creditors easy to swindle and bulldoze. The royal governors who came out were speedily made servants by the simple device of withholding their pay unless they toed the mark.

"It was in fact a principle with the Provincial Assembles," says the British historian, Fortescue, "to thwart their Governor, whether he were right or wrong, on every possible occasion; for, as is so common in representative bodies, they were more anxious to assert their power and independence than to prove their utility and good sense." [16]

That also is honorable enough.

For the British soldiers who fought in their behalf, the colonists had even less respect, since their gorgeous uniforms excited ridicule, and their frequent bad behavior in battle served as a good excuse for forgetting the frequently worse behavior of the colonists.

Already the English in America were a foreign race with ideas radically

[14] Thomas Paine, *The American Crisis*, III, 1777. *Works* (Patriots' Ed.), II, p. 321.

[15] H. E. Egerton, *The Causes and Character of the American Revolution*, p. 4.

[16] J. B. Fortescue, *History of the British Army*, II, p. 271.

different from those of the English in England. As early as 1748 a Swedish traveller, Peter Kalm, had foreseen the split between the two peoples. Others had foreseen it even earlier. John Wesley, in a sermon published in 1778, says that his brother in the year 1737 heard the Bostonians saying, "We must be independent; we will be independent." [17]

To the English, the American colonies were only colonies, and not the most important ones. Both the East and the West Indies offered more profit, and Americans can never realize how small a part of the empire their thirteen were; how many other interests and necessities filled the mind of the British ruling classes, how many other rival powers hampered their power to repress the American uprising.

For one thing they were rather contemptuous of the American colonies, as the colonies were of one another. The Americans had besought protection from the French and the Indians, yet had failed to do their share in the war and had been not only mutually jealous, but insolent and truculent to the mother country.

Worse yet, while dragging both money and soldiers from England to fight their battles, they had gone on outrageously making illicit fortunes by smuggling supplies to the enemy and prolonging the war that enriched them. They had always been irrepressible smugglers, but their wartime smuggling seemed to the English unpardonable.[18] Lecky [19] says: "The smuggling was even defended by a wonderful cynicism that it was good policy to make as much money as possible out of the enemy."

Colonel Byrd of Westover had written: "The Saints of New England . . . have a great dexterity at palliating a perjury . . . nor can any people like them slip through a penal statute." [20]

The northern colonies, the mercantile and seafaring provinces, did most of the smuggling. Even in England as in all countries smugglers were active, but the laws of trade imposed on the colonies were so rigid that evasion was inevitable. One rule required that practically every product of Europe or Asia must go through England and pay a duty there on its way to America; another required that practically all American exports should go through England and pay a duty there on their way to other nations.

The colonists' ships carrying permitted cargoes to other ports than English would pick up drygoods, tea, wines, gunpowder, and return straight home with them. Fish might be shipped direct to Mediterranean ports, and the English could not easily prevent a straight return with forbidden cargoes. But most of the illicit trade was with the French West Indies, which the British tried in vain to monopolize. Hence the importance of molasses, sugar, and rum in the Revolution.[21]

The extent of this contraband trade is astounding. England had been collecting from customs only one or two thousand pounds a year, and at an expense of seven or eight thousand pounds. Yet John Adams admitted that

[17] John Wesley, *Sermons* (Emory Ed.), I, p. 502.
[18] Schlesinger, *Colonial Merchants*, p. 45.
[19] Lecky, *American Revolution*, p. 47.
[20] Cited by Schlesinger, op. cit., p. 40.
[21] Schlesinger, op. cit., p. 41.

if the customs had been efficiently managed, the duties on molasses alone should have amounted to twenty-five thousand pounds a year.[22]

The corruption was enormous and universal, and some of the Governors took their share of the bribery.

Now that the colonies had grown rich from the conflict that left England loaded with war debts, it seemed only fair to England that they should assume their share of the burdens, pay their quota of the taxes, and put a stop to illegal trade. Beer[23] notes that Governor Dinwiddie as far back as 1755 had proposed a general tax as a punishment of the colonies for their outrageous failure to support Braddock's expedition. He prophesied that they would be "inflamed if they hear of my making this Proposal, as they are averse to all Taxes." He knew his Virginians.

In the same year "writs of assistance" had been invoked to authorize royal officers to break into ships, warehouses and packages to verify their suspicions. This innovation was naturally resisted as a sacrilege.

From the start, the mother country had been at odds with her froward children. This, too, was to be expected; for the colonies had been peopled by hardly any but those who would naturally be resentful of direction from home.

First, there were the freedom-loving pioneers, who fled from Europe because they felt shackled there. Next, there were the religious and political malcontents, who had either been exiled or had exiled themselves. Finally, there were great numbers who had been carried thither against their wills as kidnapped or indentured servants, convicts, and ne'er-do-wells who had been shipped out of England for England's good. Probably half of the immigrants were servants or slaves. There were half a million negro slaves in America by 1775, and in each of Washington's battalions there was an average of 54 slaves, especially freed for enlisting.[24]

Add to these an enormous and increasing number of Irish, Scotch-Irish (making up a sixth of the population), 200,000 Germans, Swedes, French, Dutch, Jews and other un-English, anti-English immigrants, and the opposition is complete.

In the new world the pioneers had had to learn self-sufficiency or perish. Having learned it they would practice it.

As the commerce of America developed, ship-building and seafaring prospered mightily. Rum, molasses, tobacco, offered more wealth than gold mines. Competing manufactures could be easily repressed for a time, but that was because they were of slow growth. The American continent was self-sustaining and its ambitions mounting. The colonies were even issuing paper money for their own convenience. No one can say indisputably just when, how, or why the Revolution began.

But since a beginning must be made somewhere, the year 1763 is as convenient a date as any for the start of the Revolution.

[22] Adams, *Works*, X, pp. 246, 348.
[23] G. L. Beer, *British Colonial Policy*, 1754-1765, pp. 45, 47.
[24] C. A. & M. R. Beard, op. cit., pp. 84, 103, 107, 274.

APPENDIX V

RELIGIOUS CAUSES OF THE REVOLUTION

It is well known (perhaps too well and too extravagantly known) that much of the immigration to America was due to flight from religious oppression. The New Englanders hated the Episcopalians next to the Catholics. In 1638 they had spoken of bishops as "Knobs and wens and bunchy popish flesh." [1]

The Puritans, believing marriage to be a civil contract, forbade ministers to officiate. The Anglicans wanted to put it altogether in the hands of Episcopalian clergymen. England still has a shadow of Anglican state-church domination. The shadow was substance then.

As early as 1638, Archbishop Laud tried to compel Episcopalianism in America and to send over a bishop backed with force. The Puritan Parliament cut off Laud's head and ended the authority of the bishops.

When the King came back the church and the bishops came back with him. From then on there was a constantly recurring effort to force the Anglican church power on America. It was constantly fought off or evaded by the colonists. [2]

In the infatuation that came upon the British after the victory of 1763, the Anglicans joined with the merchants, whose opinion of the colonists was that of a newspaper writer in England who said:

"I have always considered the Colonies as the great farms of the public, and the Colonists as our tenants, whom I wish to have treated kindly whilst they act as such." [3]

This, in the opinion of another letter-writer, was equivalent to saying that they "looked upon the American Colonists as little more than a Set of Slaves, at work for us, in distant Plantations, one Degree only above the Negroes, that, we carry to them."

Along with the restrictions on American trade came the project to set up an Episcopal throne. The colonists asked if they must add "ecclesiastical bondage" and "Episcopal palaces" to their burdens. When the merchants and laborers of England squealed with terror at the ruin facing them from the American boycott and begged for the withdrawal of the Stamp Act, five bishops joined the Lords in opposing the repeal.

[1] Van Tyne, *Causes of the War of Independence*, p. 350.
[2] The details of this long history are found in A. L. Cross, *The Anglican Episcopate and the American Colonies, Harvard Historical Studies*, IX, Ch. IV.
[3] Hinkhouse, *The Preliminaries of the American Revolution as Seen in the English Press, 1763-1775*, p. 102.

An American contributed to a London newspaper a letter in which he said: "The Sight of Lawn Sleeves here would be more terrible to us than ten thousand Mohawks, or the most savage Indians in this Quarter of the Globe."

A pro-American wrote that "when the late Tory ministry had decided upon the humiliation of America, they had thought it would not be decent to exclude the churchmen from a share of despotism over the Americans." [4]

There was almost as much opposition in Old England as in New, where John Adams, in the Boston *Gazette* in 1765, spoke with "utter contempt of all that dark ribaldry of hereditary, indefeasible right,—the Lord's annointed,— and the divine, miraculous, original of government, with which priesthood had enveloped the Feudal monarch in clouds and mysteries, and from whence they had deduced the most mischievous of all doctrines, that of passive obedience, and non-resistance."

This was called Treason in Virginia, but in New England it was only good stiff talk. When the Boston "Massacre" took place, the Rev. John Lothrop preached about "Innocent Blood Crying to God from the Streets of Boston," referring to the dead rioters; and Doctor Chauncey protested against sparing the lives of the soldiers and declared that if Governor Hutchinson pardoned them he would "make himself a partaker in the guilt of their murder, by putting a stop to the shedding of blood of those who have murderously spilt the blood of others."

They were great encouragers of blood letting, those preachers of the Prince of Peace!

The Presbyterians and the Congregationalists carried their religious doctrines over into the political field and furthered Locke's fashionable theory that government was a civil compact and the people had a right to choose their own rulers and limit their power. This doctrine proclaimed from the pulpits reached multitudes who could not or did not read the few papers and the many pamphlets. Patrick Henry was brought up on the sermons of Rev. Samuel Davies, who preached that the British Constitution was "but the voluntary compact of sovereign and subject." [5]

But the Anglicans taught that disobedience to the Lord's anointed was rebellion, and incurred eternal damnation.

In a book that Boucher wrote later on the causes of the Revolution, he traced the divine right of governments straight from Adam, insisted that the duty of obedience to the worst government was an ordinance of God, and said that he could not find "the word liberty, as meaning civil liberty, in all the Scriptures." He urged that Kings and princes, "so far from deriving their authority from any supposed consent or suffrage of men . . . receive it from God, the source and original of all power." [6]

John Wesley, who abhorred the whole spirit of the American rebels, called independency "this evil disease," and preached that Satan hoped by "adding to all those other vices, the spirit of independency, to have overturned the

[4] Hinkhouse, op. cit., pp. 132, 134.

[5] Van Tyne, op. cit., pp. 359, 362, 356.

[6] Jonathan Boucher, *View of the American Revolution*, pp. 511, 525.

whole work of God, as well as the British Government in North America." [7]

Patrick Henry had had both his eyes and his eloquent lips opened by the knowledge of the insatiable greed of the Anglican clergy when they refused to accept their salaries in tobacco at the commutation price established by the Assembly.

Since the established church at home palmed off on America its poorest clergymen, the Americans palmed off on the clergymen their poorest tobacco. Washington himself speaks of "the common transfer Tobo. a large proportion of which we pay towards the support of a Minister in York County," and of Mr. Valentine's poorest quality of tobacco as "worse than that which he himself has applied to the payment of the Minister's Salery." [8]

But when the parsons appealed to England, Patrick Henry had leapt from obscurity to fame in so scathing an attack on the mercenary churchmen that the jury, partially composed of Presbyterians, had awarded the rector one penny.

"The Anglican clergy, in appealing to the power of the king against the colonial will, had awakened an embittered sentiment," says Eckenrode.[9] "They were unfortunate, too, in invoking royal assistance at the time when the controversy over taxation was rising into importance, and they consequently incurred a double measure of odium. It was in these years, when the civil and ecclesiastical powers were opposed, that dissent flourished all through the colony and began to be formidable."

The Anglican church had never made good its authority in the northern colonies, but in the southern it held such power that American clergymen could only be ordained by sailing 6,000 miles. One of the reasons offered for sending a bishop to America was in order to save all that trouble.

Originally the Anglicans had imposed upon Virginia laws bluer than New England's best indigo, such laws, for instance, as the death penalty for staying away from church, a whipping for failure to be catechised, death to deny the divinity of Christ. The laws were modified or ignored, and Thomas Jefferson was enabled to be a vestryman, a Burgess and a governor, though, if there had been shown that high reverence for the law which is so often demanded, "he would have been deprived of the custody of his children, publicly whipped every day until he acknowledged the Trinity, and imprisoned until he asked forgiveness of the church." [10]

It was just because the clergy in America were so lax in enforcing doctrines and suppressing dissenters that the fervent members demanded the presence of a bishop in America.

Dr. Samuel Johnson was one of the most ardent agitators for such an Episcopate that it might put down "faction and delusion." But then he loathed Americans so violently that even Boswell defended them from his ferocity.

[7] John Wesley, *Sermons* (Emory Ed.), I, pp. 505, 504.
[8] MS. in Library of Congress, *George Washington Papers*, XVII, p. 48.
[9] Eckenrode, *The Separation of Church and State in Virginia* (Va. State Library, 1910), p. 26.
[10] W. E. Curtis, *The True Thomas Jefferson*, p. 308.

As usual there were rich men who subscribed funds or left bequests for the church's benefit, and thousands of pounds were thus provided to push the bishops overseas.[11]

A war of pamphlets, sermons, letters to the papers, and coffee-house argument followed. In Parker's New York *Gazette*, March 14, and April 18, 1768, one who signed himself "Timothy Tickle" snapped what he called a "Whip for the American Whig":

"Depend upon it, when the *apostolical monarchs* are come over, and well established in their American dominions, you, and such as you, will be chastised with *scorpions*. . . . Then, O dreadful! The torrent of episcopal vengeance! Then all who will not be so senseless as to adore the *mitre* and *surplice*, and dedicate both their consciences and their purses to his *episcopal Majesty*, may lay their account with—with what? with something I will not yet particularly name, but what one may easily discover, by turning over a Church history or two. This may be the fate of many, unless indulgent heaven interpose, by not suffering the *right reverend and holy tyrants* to plunge their spiritual swords in the souls of their fellow creatures; . . .

"Let my lords the bishops be once landed and fortified in their palaces, guarded by their dependents, and supported by their courts, and instead of this coaxing and trimming we shall soon hear the thunder of excommunication uttered with all the confidence and pride of security. The soft bleatings of the lamb will be changed into the terrible howling of the wolf; and every poor parson whose head never felt the weight of a bishop's hand will soon know the power of his pastoral staff, and the arm of the magistrate into the bargain."

The "Centinel" cried: "Every attempt upon American liberty has always been accompanied with endeavours to settle bishops among us." [12]

That very Dr. Myles Cooper, president of King's College in New York, to whom Washington entrusted Jacky Custis, and whom he invited to visit him at Mount Vernon, came down to Virginia in 1771 to secure "the cooperation of their brethren in that region in procuring an American Episcopate." [13]

But when a small convention of Virginia clergymen asked for a bishop, four ministers protested that "the establishment . . . would tend greatly to . . . infuse Jealousies and Fears into the Minds of the Protestant Dissenters, and . . . to endanger the very Existence of the British Empire in America."

Thereupon the House of Burgesses on July 12, 1771, unanimously passed a resolution thanking the four clergymen for their "wise and well-timed Opposition . . . to the pernicious Project." Washington was not present, for, according to his Diaries, he did not reach Williamsburg till the 15th, but he would probably have voted with the rest. One cannot imagine him voting alone for an English bishop to rule the awakening American soul.

In 1769 the Burgesses had appointed a standing committee on religion.[14]

[11] A. L. Cross, op. cit., p. 111.

[12] A. L. Cross, op. cit., pp. 197, 205.

[13] A. L. Cross, op. cit., pp. 231-5.

[14] J. M. Leake, *The Virginia Committee System and the American Revolution*, p. 53 n.

Having put itself on record as opposed to an Episcopate, the House of Burgesses tried to organize a church court, but it came to nothing. In a letter to Boucher, who was one of the clergymen who petitioned for a bishop and thus gave great offence, Washington describes the failure of the Burgesses to settle on anything:

"After a tiresome, and in my opinion, a very unimportant Session, I returned home about the middle of last Month. . . . The expediency of an American Episcopate was long & warmly debated, and at length rejected. As a substitute, the House attempted to frame an Ecclesiastical Jurisdiction, to be composed of a President and four other clergymen, who were to have full power and authority to hear and determine all matters and causes relative to the clergy, and to be vested with the (power) of Suspension, deprivation, & visitation. From this Jurisdiction an Appeal was to be had to a Court of Delegates, to consist of an equal number of Clergymen and Laymen; but this Bill, after much canvassing, was put to Sleep, from an opinion that the subject was of too much Importance to be hastily entered into at the end of a Session." [15]

Here again Washington, as always, in religious matters, shows no emotion whatever. He found the session "tiresome and unimportant." But Boucher later fell into such violent controversies with his parishioners that they tried to lock him out, and he preached with a loaded pistol on either side of his Bible. Afterward he wrote that the dispute over the American Episcopacy was "clearly one great cause" of the Revolution.

Another blow to the establishment was passed in 1772, giving dissenters some relief from the persecutions and imprisonment visited upon Baptist and other preachers.

The toleration was illiberal, but it was something. Greater demands from Baptists and Presbyterians were pouring in, but the outbreak of war threw the Anglican church into the dust along with the English crown.

[15] Ford, *Writings*, II, p. 347.

BOOKS CONSULTED AND QUOTED

Adams, Charles Francis, Plea for Military History (Report of the American Historical Association), Washington, 1901.

Adams, Charles Francis, Studies, Military and Diplomatic, New York, 1911.

Adams, Herbert B., Maryland's Influence in Founding a National Commonwealth (Maryland Historical Society), Baltimore, 1877.

Adams, James Truslow, New England in the Republic, Boston, 1926.

Adams, J. T., Revolutionary New England 1691-1776, Boston, 1923.

Adams, John, Familiar Letters to His Wife, New York, 1876.

Adams, John, Works, with a Life of the Author, 10 volumes (edited by Charles Francis Adams), Boston, 1850-56.

Adams, Randolph Greenfield, Headquarters Papers of the British Army in North America, Ann Arbor, 1926.

Adams, Randolph Greenfield, A History of the Foreign Policy of the United States, New York, 1926.

Addresses of the City of New York to George Washington with his replies (privately printed), New York, 1867.

Allen, Gardner W., Naval History of the American Revolution, 2 volumes, Boston, 1913.

Alvord, Clarence Walworth, The Mississippi Valley in British Politics, 2 volumes, Cleveland, 1917.

American Historical Association, Annual Reports, Washington, 1889 et seq.

American Historical Review.

American Irish Historical Society, Journal, New York.

Ames, Nathaniel, Almanack. See Briggs.

Amory, T. C., Memoir of Major-General Sullivan, Philadelphia, 1879.

Andrews, Charles M., The Colonial Background of the American Revolution, Yale University Press, 1924.

Annual Register, London, 1777 et seq.

Anonymous, Nuts for Historians to Crack, Philadelphia, 1856.

Armstrong, William C., The Battles in the Jerseys (New Jersey Society of the Sons of the American Revolution), 1916.

Arnold, Isaac N., The Life of Benedict Arnold, Chicago, 1880.

Austin, James T., Life of Elbridge Gerry, 2 volumes, Boston, 1829.

Avery, Elroy M., History of the United States, 7 volumes, Cleveland, 1908.

Baker, William S., Bibliotheca Washingtoniana, A Descriptive List of the Biographers and Biographical Sketches of George Washington, Philadelphia, 1889.

Baker, William S., Early Sketches of George Washington, Philadelphia, 1894.

Baker, William S., The Engraved Portraits of Washington, Phila., 1880.

Bancroft, George, A History of the United States, 10 volumes, Boston, 1834-74.

Bancroft, George, The American Revolution, 3rd ed., 4 volumes, 1859.

Bancroft, George, Joseph Reed, A Historical Essay, New York, 1866.

Bassett, John Spencer. See Byrd.

Battle of Brooklyn, A Farce of Two Acts: As it was performed in Long-Island on Tuesday the 27th Day of August, 1776, N. Y., in the Year of the Rebellion, 1776.

Bayard, Ferdinand Marie, Voyage dans l'Intérieur des Etats-Unis, à Bath, Winchester, dans la Vallée de Shenandoa, etc., Paris, 1797.

Beard, C. A. and M. R., The Rise of American Civilization, N. Y., 1927.

Becker, Carl, The Declaration of Independence, New York, 1922.

Beer, George Louis, British Colonial Policy, 1754-1765, New York, 1922.

Belcher, Henry, The First American Civil War, 1755-1778, 2 volumes, London, 1911.

Benchley, Robert, The Early Worm, New York, 1927.

Bleyer, Willard S., Main Currents in American Journalism, New York, 1927.

Bolton, C. K., The Private Soldier Under Washington, New York, 1902.

Bolton, Rev. Robert, History of Westchester County, 2 volumes, N. Y., 1881.

Boucher, Jonathan, Reminiscences of an American Loyalist, 1738-1789, Boston, 1925.

Boucher, Jonathan, A View of the Causes and Consequences of the American Revolution, London, 1797.

Briggs, Sam, The Essays, Humor and Poems of Nathaniel Ames, Father and Son, . . . from Their Almanack, Cleveland, 1891.

Brock, R. A. See Dinwiddie Papers (Virginia Historical Society Collection), Richmond, 1883.

Brown, Alice, Mercy Warren, New York, 1896.

Burnaby, Rev. Andrew, Travels Through the Middle Settlements in North America in the Years 1759-1760. London, 1775.

Byrd, Colonel William, The Writings of, Ed. by J. S. Bassett, N. Y., 1901.

Calendar of the Correspondence of George Washington with the Continental Congress. Prepared from the original Mss. in the Library of Congress by John C. Fitzgerald.

Calendar of the Correspondence of George Washington with the Officers, 4 volumes, Library of Congress, Washington, 1915.

Calendar of the Washington Manuscripts in the Library of Congress. Compiled under the direction of Herbert Friedenwald, Ph.D., Wash., 1901.

Calendar of Virginia State Papers, Richmond, 1890.

Campbell, John, Minutes of a Conspiracy against the Liberties of America, Philadelphia, 1865.

Carrington, General H. B., Battles of the American Revolution, N. Y., 1877.

Carrington, General Henry B., Washington the Soldier, New York, 1899.

Cary, Wilson Miles, Sally Cary, a Long Hidden Romance of Washington's Life, with Notes by Another Hand (privately printed), New York, 1916.

Celebration of the 139th Anniversary of the Journey of Washington from Philadelphia to Cambridge.

Chamberlain, Mellen, John Adams, Boston, 1898.

Chandler, J. A. C., and Thames, T. B., Colonial Virginia, Richmond, 1907.

Channing, Edward, A History of the United States, 6 vols., N. Y., 1909-1926.

Channing, Edward, and Albert Bushnell Hart, Guide to the Study of American History, Boston, 1897.

Clements, William L., The William L. Clements Library of Americana at the University of Michigan, Ann Arbor, 1923.

Colby, Elbridge, Account of the Battle of Long Island, in Moss' Manual of Military Training, 2 volumes, Menasha, Wis., 1925.

Collins, Edward C., Committees of Correspondence of the American Revolution (Report of American Historical Association), Washington, 1901.

Comfort, Randall, History of Bronx Borough, New York, 1906.

Conway, Moncure D., Barons of the Potomack and the Rapahannock, New York, 1892.

Conway, Moncure D., George Washington and Mount Vernon (Long Island Historical Society), Brooklyn, 1889.

Conway, Moncure D., Edmund Randolph, New York and London, 1888.

Cooke, John Esten, Virginia, A History of the People, Boston, 1903.

Corwin, Edward S., French Policy and the American Alliance of 1778, Princeton University Press, 1916.

Craven, Avery O., Soil Exhaustion as a Factor in the Agricultural History of Virginia and Maryland (University of Illinois Press), Chicago, 1927.

Cresswell, Nicholas, Journal, 1774-1777, New York, 1924.

Cross, A. L., The Anglican Episcopate and the American Colonies (Harvard Historical Studies), New York, 1902.

Curtis, Edward E., The Organization of the British Army in the American Revolution, Yale University Press, 1926.

Curwen, S., Journals and Letters, 1775-1784 (S. A. Ward, ed.), N. Y., 1842.

Custis, G. W. P., Recollections and Private Memoirs of Washington, New York, 1860.

Custis, William Elroy, The True Thomas Jefferson, Philadelphia, 1901.

Dexter, F. B. See Stiles.

Dinwiddie Papers, 2 volumes, edited by R. A. Brock (Virginia Historical Collections), Richmond, 1883.

Doniol, Henri, Histoire de la participation de la France à l'établissement des Etats-Unis d'Amérique, 5 volumes, Paris, 1890.

Duer, William A., Life of William Alexander, Earl of Sterling (New Jersey Historical Society), New York, 1847.

Eckenrode, H. J., The Separation of Church and State in Virginia (Virginia State Library), Richmond, 1910.

Egerton, H. E., The Causes and Character of the American Revolution, Oxford Clarendon Press, 1923.

Emmett, Thomas Addis, The Battle of Harlem Heights, reprinted from The Magazine of History, 1906.

Field, Thomas W., The Battle of Long Island (Memoirs of the Long Island Historical Society), Brooklyn, 1869.

Finley, Dr. John H., Address before the University of Pennsylvania (Pennsylvania Gazette, Feb. 25, 1927).

Fisher, Sydney George, The Legendary and Myth-Making Process in Histories of the American Revolution, Am. Phil. Society, Phila., 1912.

Fisher, Sydney George, The Struggle for American Independence, 2 volumes, Philadelphia and London, 1908.

Fiske, John, The American Revolution, 2 volumes, Boston, 1896.

Fitzpatrick, John C., Diaries of George Washington, Published for the Mount Vernon Ladies' Association of the Union, 4 vols., Boston and N. Y., 1925.

Fitzpatrick, John C., George Washington's Accounts of Expenses, etc., Boston and New York, 1917.

Fitzpatrick, John C., The George Washington Scandals, in *Scribner's Magazine*, April, 1927.

Fitzpatrick, John C., The Spirit of the Revolution, New Light from some of the Original Sources of American History, Boston, 1924.

Force, Peter, American Archives, 4th and 5th series, Washington, 1837-1853.

Ford, Paul Leicester, The True George Washington, Philadelphia, 1896.

Ford, Worthington C., Life of George Washington, 2 volumes, Boston, 1899.

Ford, Worthington C., Washington as an Employer and Importer of Labor, Brooklyn, 1889 (privately printed).

Ford, Worthington C., The Writings of George Washington, 14 volumes, New York, 1889-93.

Fortescue, the Hon. J. W., A History of the British Army, 11 volumes, London, 1910-1923.

Franklin, Benjamin, The Interest of Great Britain Considered with Regard to Her Colonies, London, 1760.

Franklin, Benjamin, Works (Bigelow Ed.), 10 volumes, New York, 1887-88.

Franklin, Benjamin, Writings (Smyth Ed.), 10 volumes, New York, 1905-7.

French, Allen, The Day of Concord and Lexington, Boston, 1927.

Friedenwald, Herbert, The Declaration of Independence, New York, 1904.

Frothingham, Richard, The Siege of Boston, Boston, 1849.

(Galloway, J.), Letters to a Nobleman on the Conduct of the War in the Middle Colonies, London, 1779.

Ganoe, Major W. A., History of the United States Army, New York, 1924.

Garnett, J. M., Early Revolutionary History of Virginia (Virginia Historical Society Collections), Richmond, 1891.

Gilmer, George, The Gilmer Papers (Virginia Historical Society Collections), Richmond, 1887.

Godfrey, Dr. Carlos E., The Commander-in-Chief's Guard, Washington, 1904.

Goodwin, Edward Lewis, The Colonial Church in Virginia, Milwaukee, 1927.

Goolrick, John T., Historic Fredericksburg, Richmond, 1922.

Goolrick, John T., The Life of General Hugh Mercer, New York, 1906.

Gordon, William, History of the Rise, Progress and Establishment of the Independence, 3 volumes, New York, 1794.

(Graydon, Alexander), Memoirs of a Life Chiefly Passed in Pennsylvania, Harrisburg, 1811.

Greene, Francis Vinton, The Revolutionary War and the Military Policy of the United States, New York, 1911.

Greene, Francis Vinton, General Greene, New York, 1898.

Greene, George Washington, Life of Maj.-Gen. Nathanael Greene, 3 volumes, New York, 1878.

Greene, George Washington, Historical View of the American Revolution, Boston, 1865.

Halliday, Carl, Woman's Life in Colonial Days, Boston, 1922.

Hamilton, Stanislaus Murray, Letters to Washington and Accompanying Papers (Society Colonial Dames of America), 5 volumes, Boston, 1898.

Hapgood, Norman, George Washington, New York, 1901.

Harland, Marion, The Story of Mary Washington, Boston, 1892.

Harlow, Ralph Volney, Samuel Adams, New York, 1923.

Harrell, Isaac S., Loyalism in Virginia (Duke Univ. Press), Durham, 1926.

Hart, Capt. B. H. Liddell, A Greater than Napoleon, Scipio Africanus, Boston, 1927.

Hastings, George E., Life and Works of Francis Hopkinson (Univ. of Chicago Press), Chicago, 1926.

Hatch, Louis Clinton, The Administration of the American Revolutionary Army, New York, 1904.

Haworth, Paul Leland, George Washington, Country Gentleman, Indianapolis, 1925.

Heath, William, Memoirs of Major-General William Heath, Boston, 1798.

Henry, William Wirt, Life, Correspondence and Speeches of Patrick Henry, 3 volumes, New York, 1891.

Hinkhouse, Fred J., Preliminaries of the American Revolution as seen in the English Press, New York, 1926.

Horsmanden, Daniel, The New York Conspiracy, or a History of the Negro Plot, New York, 1810.

Howard, George Elliott, Preliminaries of the Revolution, New York and London, 1905.

Huidekoper, Frederic Louis, The Military Unpreparedness of the United States, New York, 1915.

Hulbert, Archer Butler, Historic Highways of America, 16 volumes, Cleveland, 1902-5.

Hulbert, Archer Butler, Washington and the West, Cleveland, 1911.

Inglis, Rev. Charles, State of the Anglo-American Church in 1776, in Documentary History of New York, 4 volumes, Albany, 1850.

James, Capt. W. M., The British Navy in Adversity, London, 1926.

Jameson, J. Franklin, The American Revolution Considered as a Social Movement, Princeton University Press, 1926.

Jay, William, Life of John Jay, New York, 1833.

Jefferson, Thomas, Notes on the State of Virginia, Newark, 1801.

Jefferson, Thomas, Writings, 20 volumes (Memorial ed.), Washington, 1905.

Jenkins, Stephen, The Story of the Bronx, New York, 1912.

Johns Hopkins University Studies, Baltimore.

Johnston, General Bradley T., General Washington, New York, 1897.

Johnston, H. P., The Battle of Harlem Heights, New York, 1897.

Johnston, H. P., The Campaign of 1776 (Memoirs of the Long Island Historical Society), Brooklyn, 1878.

Jones, Thomas, History of New York during the Revolutionary War, 2 volumes, New York, 1879.

Kapp, Friedrich, Leben des Amerikanischen Generals Johann Kalb, Stuttgart, 1862.

Kapp, Friedrich, Friedrich der Grosse und die Vereinigten Staaten von Amerika, Leipzig, 1871.

Kapp, Friedrich, Life of Frederick William von Steuben, New York, 1859.

Koontz, Dr. Louis K., The Virginia Frontier, 1754-1763 (Johns Hopkins University Studies), Baltimore, 1925.

Leake, Dr. James Miller, The Virginia Committee System and the American Revolution (Johns Hopkins University Studies), Baltimore, 1917.

Lear, Tobias, Letters from George Washington to Tobias Lear, N. Y., 1906.

Lecky, W. E. H., The American Revolution, 1763-83, being the chapters and passages relating to America from the author's History of England in the Eighteenth Century (edited by James Albert Woodburn), New York, 1926.

Lecky, W. E. H., A History of England in the Eighteenth Century, 8 volumes, London, 1878-90.

Lee, Richard Henry, Letters, 2 vols. (James Curtis Ballagh, ed.), N. Y., 1911.

Lee Papers, 4 vols., Coll. of the New York Historical Society, N. Y., 1872-5.

Letters and Recollections of George Washington, Being letters to Tobias Lear and others between 1790-99, New York, 1906.

Letters Written at the Time of the Occupation of Boston, in Historical Collection of the Essex Institute, Salem, 1876.

Lingley, Charles R., The Transition in Virginia from Colony to Commonwealth, Baltimore, 1910.

Lodge, Henry Cabot, Life of George Washington, 2 volumes, Boston and New York, 1920.

Lossing, Benson J., Life of George Washington, 3 volumes, New York, 1860.

Lossing, Benson J., Mary and Martha, the Mother and Wife of George Washington, New York, 1886.

Lossing, Benson J., The Pictorial Field-Book of the Revolution, 2 volumes, New York, 1851-2.

Marshall, Charles, Extracts from the Diary of, Albany, 1877.

Marshall, John, The Life of George Washington, 5 volumes, Philadelphia, 1804-7. Reprinted Fredericksburg, 1926.

Martyn, Charles, Artemas Ward, The First Commander-in-Chief of the American Revolution, New York, 1921.

Massachusetts Historical Society, Proceedings.

Maurice, Maj.-Gen. Sir Frederick, An Aide-de-Camp of Lee, Boston, 1927.

Maury, Gen. Dabney Herndon, Recollections of a Virginian in the Mexican, Indian and Civil Wars, New York, 1875.

McCustin, Daniel, Papers relating chiefly to the Maryland Line. Cited by Charles Martyn, Artemas Ward, New York, 1921.

McIlwain, Charles Howard, The American Revolution; a Constitutional Interpretation, New York, 1923.

McMaster, John B., A History of the People of the United States, 8 volumes, New York and London, 1915.

Meade, Bishop, Old Churches, Ministers and Families of Virginia, 2 volumes, Philadelphia, 1897.

Moore, Charles, The Family Life of George Washington, Boston, 1926.

Moore, Frank, Diary of the American Revolution, 2 volumes, N. Y., 1860.

Moore, G. H., The Treason of Charles Lee, New York, 1860.

Morison, S. E., Sources and Documents illustrating the American Revolution, 1764-1788, Oxford, 1923.

Morrison, A. J., Travels in Virginia in Revolutionary Times, Lynchburg, Va., 1922.

Moss and Lang (Col. Jas. A. and Major John W.), Manual of Military Arms, 2 volumes, Menasha, Wis., 1925.

Mumby, Frank Arthur, George III and the American Revolution, Boston, 1925.

Nelson, William, The American Newspapers of the Eighteenth Century as Sources of History (American Historical Association Annual Reports, 1908).

Nevins, Allan. The American States during and after the Revolution. New York, 1924.

New England Historical and Genealogical Register.

New Jersey Historical Society, Collections, New York.

New York during the American Revolution (privately printed for the Mercantile Library Association), New York, 1861.

New York Historical Society, Collections, New York, 1869 et seq.

New York State Historical Association, Proceedings, New York, 1901 et seq.

New York State Historical Association, Quarterly Journal, Albany.

Odell, George C. D., Annals of the New York Stage (Columbia University Press), New York, 1927.

Ogg, F. A., The Old Northwest (Chronicles of America, 50 volumes), Yale University Press, 1921.

Paine, Thomas, Life and Works (The Patriots' Edition, 10 volumes), New Rochelle, 1925.

Parkman, Francis, Montcalm and Wolfe, 2 volumes, Boston, 1925.

Paxson, Frederic L., History of the American Frontier, 1763-1893, Boston, 1924.

Pennsylvania Magazine of History and Biography.

Phelps, R. H., Newgate of Connecticut, Hartford, 1892.

Phillips, Ulrich B., Plantation and Frontier Documents, 1649-1863, Cleveland, 1909.

Prussing, Eugene E., The Estate of George Washington, Deceased, N. Y., 1927.

Prussing, Eugene E., Washington's Legal Education, an unpublished address delivered to the Chicago Law Club, October 2, 1925.

Pryor, Mrs. Roger A., The Mother of Washington, New York, 1903.

Ramsay, David, History of the American Revolution, London, 1793.

Reed, W. B., Life and Correspondence of Joseph Reed, 2 volumes, Philadelphia, 1847.

Roosevelt, Theodore, The Winning of the West, 3 volumes, N. Y., 1900.

Ruttenber, E. M., Obstructions to the Navigation of Hudson's River, Albany, 1860.

Sabine, Lorenzo, Loyalists of the American Revolution, 2 volumes, Boston, 1864.

Sachse, Julius F., Washington's Masonic Correspondence as found among the Washington Papers in the Library of Congress, Philadelphia, 1915.

Saint Clair Papers, Edited by W. H. Smith, 2 volumes, Cincinnati, 1882.

Sawyer, Joseph Dillaway, Washington, 2 volumes, New York, 1927.

Schlesinger, Arthur Meier, The Colonial Merchants and the American Revolution, 1763-1776, New York, 1918.

Schlesinger, Arthur Meier, New Viewpoints in American History, N. Y., 1925.

Schumacher, Ludwig, Life of Major-General Lord Sterling, New York, 1897.

Shelton, William H., The Jumel Mansion, Boston, 1916.

Smith, Richard, Diary (American Historical Review), 1896.

Smith, William H., The St. Clair Papers, 2 volumes, Cincinnati, 1882.

Smyth, John F. D., A Tour in the United States, London, 1784.

Sparks, Jared, Correspondence of the American Revolution, 4 volumes, Boston, 1853.

Sparks, Jared, Life and Writings of Gouverneur Morris, 3 volumes, Boston, 1832.

Sparks, Jared, The Life of George Washington, Boston, 1844.

Sparks, Jared, The Life of James Otis (Library of American Biography, 2nd series), Boston, 1834.

Sparks, Jared, The Writings of George Washington, 12 volumes, Boston, 1834.

Spofford, A. R., Lotteries in American History (Report of the American Historical Association), Washington, 1892.

Stansbury, Charles F., The Lake of the Great Dismal, New York, 1925.

Stark, James H., The Loyalists of Massachusetts and the Other Side of the American Revolution, Boston, 1910.

Stedman, C., History of the American War, 2 volumes, London, 1794.

Steiner, Bernard C., The Life and Correspondence of James McHenry, Cleveland, 1907.

Stephenson, Nathaniel W., The Day of the Confederacy (Chronicles of America, 50 volumes), Yale University Press, 1921.

Stiles, Ezra, The Literary Diary of (Edited by F. B. Dexter), 3 volumes, New York, 1901.

Stillé, Charles J., Comte de Broglie, the Proposed Stadtholder of America, Pennsylvania Magazine of History and Biography, January, 1888.

Stone, William L., Life of Joseph Brant, 2 volumes, Albany, 1865.

Stryker, William S., The Battles of Trenton and Princeton, Boston and New York, 1898.

Stryker, William S., The Reed Controversy, Trenton, 1885.

Stuart, Capt. John, Narrative, in the Magazine of American History, 1877.

Thayer, William Roscoe, George Washington, Boston, 1922.

Toner, Dr. J. M., Diary of Col. George Washington, 1774 (Report of the American Historical Association), Washington, 1892.

Toner, Dr. J. M., George Washington as an Inventor and Promoter of the Useful Arts, Washington, 1892.

Tower, Charlemagne, The Marquis de La Fayette in the American Revolution, 2 volumes, Philadelphia, 1926.

Trevelyan, George Macaulay, History of England, New York, 1926.

Trevelyan, Sir George Otto, The American Revolution, 3 volumes, New York, 1908.

Turner, Frederick Jackson, The Frontier in American History, New York, 1921.

Tyler, Lyon Gardiner, Williamsburg, the Old Colonial Capital, Richmond, 1907.

Tyler's Quarterly Historical and Genealogical Magazine, Edited by Lyon G. Tyler, Richmond.

Tyler, Moses Coit, Literary History of the Revolution, 1763-1783, 2 volumes, New York and London, 1897.

Upton, Maj.-Gen. Emory, The Military Policy of the United States, Washington, 1904.

Van Tyne, Claude H., The Causes of the War of Independence, being the first volume of a History of the Founding of the American Republic, Boston, 1922.

Van Tyne, Claude H., The American Revolution, 1776-1783, New York and London, 1905.

Van Tyne, Claude H., The Loyalists in the American Revolution, N. Y., 1902.

Virginia Historical Society Collections, Richmond.

Virginia Magazine of History and Biography, Richmond.

Virginia State Papers, Calendar, Richmond.

Volwiler, Albert T., George Croghan and the Westward Movement, 1741-1782, Cleveland, 1926.

Walpole, Horace, Memoirs of the Last Ten Years of the Reign of George II, Edited by Lord Holland, London, 1847.

Ward, S. A., Journals and Letters of Samuel Curwen, 1775-1784, New York, 1842.

Warren, Charles H., The Buff and Blue Uniform (Massachusetts Historical Society Proceedings), Boston, 1859-1894.

Washington and Lee University, Historical Papers, Lexington, Va.

Washington, George, Writings. See Conway, Ford, Hulbert, Lear, Sparks, Toner.

Watson, John F., Annals of Philadelphia and Pennsylvania in the Olden Time, 2 volumes, Philadelphia, 1857.

Webb, S. B., Correspondence and Journals, reproduced in Tyler's Quarterly Historical and Genealogical Magazine, April, 1926.

Weems, Mason L., The Life of George Washington, Philadelphia, 1837.

Wesley, John, Works (John Emory, ed.), 7 volumes. Third American Edition, New York.

Wharton, Anne H., Through Colonial Doorways. Quoted by Carl Halliday, Woman's Life in Colonial Days, Boston, 1922.

White, William, Memoir of the Life of (Bird Wilson, ed.), Phila., 1839.

Whiting, John, Revolutionary Orders of General Washington, N. Y., 1844.

Wilkinson, James, Memoirs of My Own Times, 3 volumes, Phila., 1816.

Willard, Margaret Wheeler, Letters on the American Revolution, 1774-76, Boston, 1925.

William and Mary Quarterly, Williamsburg.

Wills, Frances, Why the Fair Sex Was Fair in Mrs. Washington's Day, article in the New York World, Nov. 28, 1926.

Wilson, Bird, Memoir of the Life of the Right Reverend William White, D.D., Philadelphia, 1839.

Wilson, James Grant, Memorial History of the City of New York, 4 volumes, New York, 1892.

Wilstach, Paul, Mount Vernon, New York, 1916.

Winsor, Justin, Memorial History of Boston, 4 volumes, Boston, 1880.

Winsor, Justin, Narrative and Critical History of America, 8 volumes, Boston, 1889.

Wister, Owen, The Seven Ages of Washington, New York, 1922.

Woodburn, James Albert. See Lecky.

Woodburn, James Albert, The Causes of the American Revolution (Johns Hopkins University Studies), Baltimore, December, 1892.

Woodward, W. E., George Washington, the Man and the Image, N. Y., 1926.

INDEX

GEORGE WASHINGTON

The Rebel and the Patriot

1762-1777